DATE DUE			

An Unsettled People

Social Order and Disorder in American History

ROWLAND BERTHOFF

HARPER & ROW, PUBLISHERS
New York, Evanston, San Francisco, and London
1817

To TIRZAH

Is àillidh thu, a bhean mo ghaoil, mar Thirsah,
maiseach mar Ierusalem, uamhasach mar
shluagh le'm brataichibh.

—Canticles, vi, 4.

AN UNSETTLED PEOPLE: SOCIAL ORDER AND DISORDER IN AMERICAN HISTORY.
Copyright © 1971 by Rowland Berthoff. All rights reserved. Printed in the
United States of America. No part of this book may be used or reproduced in
any manner whatsoever without written permission except in the case of brief
quotations embodied in critical articles and reviews. For information address
Harper & Row, Publishers, Inc., 49 East 33rd Street, New York, N.Y. 10016.
Published simultaneously in Canada by Fitzhenry & Whiteside Limited,
Toronto.

STANDARD BOOK NUMBER: 06-040654-2

LIBRARY OF CONGRESS CATALOG CARD NUMBER: 79-123915

Contents

An Unsettled People

Maps

Figures

Foreword

The writing of a piece of history is apt to stretch on into a rather different epoch from that in which it was conceived. The long gestation may endow it, however, with an unanticipated relevance to its changed surroundings.

A decade ago, during an era of "new conservatism" in political thought, neoorthodoxy in religion, and a fashionably apathetic manner among the young, I thought it timely to look into the history of American society from a neoconservative perspective, that is, with a certain "postmodern" detachment from the liberal individualism that pervades most of the American past and the writing about it. The essential character of that past had already been summed up by Richard Hofstadter:

Above and beyond temporary and local conflicts there has been a common ground, a unity of cultural and political tradition, upon which American civilization has stood. That culture has been intensely nationalistic and for the most part isolationist; it has been fiercely individualistic and capitalistic.

But American life no longer was confined to such simplicities. "In a corporate and consolidated society demanding international responsibility, cohesion, centralization, and planning," Hofstadter warned, "the traditional ground is shifting under our feet. It is imperative in a time of cultural crisis to gain fresh perspectives on the past."[1]

New imperatives sometimes enable scholars to rise above their own old preconceptions and to see them in a new context. A number of young historians of the 1940s and 1950s were arriving, from various directions, at much the same insight: that in many of the classic struggles of American history the combatants had shared, after all, a fairly narrow common ground. Louis Hartz and Daniel J. Boorstin pointed out the long continuity of the liberal, pragmatic tradition and the absence of the "feudal" patterns of Europe. David M. Potter attributed the distinctiveness of the American character to the freedom which general affluence assured to a "people of plenty." Oscar Handlin's view of the peasant immigrants of the nineteenth century was surprisingly like John Higham's interpretation of the American nativists who had sought to exclude them from the country; both types had been caught in a modern web of rapid economic growth, social individualism and instability, and anxious reaction. David Donald detected a similar set of circumstances behind the abolitionists of the 1830s, and Hofstadter found that another version of it had impelled the Populist and Progressive movements at the turn of the next century. Most of these historians on the whole admired the common American tradition they had discovered even while deprecating its evident deficiencies. Altogether their fresh perspective on the American past suggested that a basic revision of American historiography was just around the corner.[2]

Unfortunately this embryonic school of interpretation was prematurely given the misleading name of "consensus," which led even some of its progenitors to repudiate it. The term seemed quite belied by the obvious American record of conflict—between geographical sections, economic classes, political parties, religious sects, ethnic groups, and individuals. Since the moral sympathies of scholars had usually been enlisted in these conflicts, they resisted the idea that the opposing sides, whatever common ground they had occupied, were more alike than different. At the annual meeting of the American Historical Association in 1960 a panel that had been invited to sharpen the issue between "conflict" and "consensus" instead signaled the general rout of the latter.[3] How could a national history full of nonconformists and revolutionaries, practical frontiersmen and moral reformers, a history whose central event was a Civil War, be reduced to the bland amiability that consensus implied? My own suggestion that many of the conflicts had been engendered by causes common to both sets of antagonists—not by any agreed-upon *consensus* among them, to be sure, but by similar social dislocations that had affected both in ways that were only superficially different—was not followed up in the turbulent 1960s, when "consensus" became a byword for the shabbiest sort of political chicanery.[4]

Since 1960, however, historians have explained a wide variety of political movements in terms of a common social theme—the peculiar disorganization, or pluralism, to give it its favorable name, of American life from the earliest settlements to the present. That theme has been somewhat obscured by the usual concentration of these studies on political phenomena to which the social circumstances were contributory. The historian has typically been content to label the politically relevant social categories. When he had demonstrated, for instance, that certain voters had affiliated with the Jacksonian Democrats because of their social identity as Catholic Irishmen, or that both reformers and conservatives in the progressive era came from the middle classes, he seldom went on to inquire what it meant to be an Irish Catholic or a middle-class American and how such religious, ethnic, and status categories fit into a larger social structure. Although that halfway approach leaves the political question itself half unanswered, it has helped give American social history a more intelligible shape than anything achieved by the merely eclectic scholars of the 1920s and 1930s who first took up the subject.

What then should social history consist of? To some the term still suggests one of two old approaches: either a general history that includes as many kinds of human affairs as possible, or simply the "pots and pans" story of "how the people lived" which political historians used to ignore. The first of these, although commendably ambitious, seldom gets beyond a disjointed series of chapters on various topics. The second, when it has not simply fallen into antiquarian irrelevance, has typically produced a trivial variety of economic history, or home economics history. It is a third, less diffuse concept that has been emerging recently: the history of the social *structure*.

The present danger is that this definition may suffer as much from narrowness as the older ones did from indiscriminate inclusiveness. Recent students, following their egalitarian predilections as Americans, have tended to equate social structure with its most readily measurable part, the ladder of socioeconomic classes. To the degree, furthermore, that the society of a midwestern frontier county or an eastern industrial city assured its individual members easy "social mobility" from one class to another—or, to be more exact, from one economic level of occupation, income, and property to another—the historian has usually concluded, as contemporaries did, that it was a *good* society. But precisely because of this economic mobility and the popular attachment to it, social classes have been about the least substantial components of the modern American social structure. Differences between *economic* classes at any given time were real enough and can indeed be measured with some accuracy. But they did not readily coalesce into well-defined, stable social-status groups, and even when they did they were generally regarded as anomalous in a professedly classless society. A *social* history organized around such *economic* classes is bound to suffer from the limitation.

It should be doubly instructive to historians dissatisfied with old lines of interpretation, moreover, that for all the popularity of economic individualism, or "social mobility," its practical consequences were often unhappy. The anxieties which historians have recently detected at the root of various political movements after 1820 evidently had something to do with the uncertainties of a society which lacked an accepted pattern of reciprocal rights and duties among well-founded classes. They also had something to do with the dissolution of other old social patterns—the functionally integrated family, community, and parish church of an earlier day—which Americans had not specifically intended to discard along with the old class distinctions. In a new country where the rapid advance of physical settlement entailed a progressively *unsettled* structure of social institutions of all kinds, the sources of uncertainty, anxiety, and half-irrational reaction were deep and wide. But American historians are only now beginning, on one hand, to follow the lead of French and English demographers and measure birthrates and marriage rates and the communal patterns of slums and suburbs as well as the rate of individual economic mobility and, on the other, to assess how well the family, the community, and other social institutions functioned.

We may define social history, in short, in terms of the development of the social structure and of the functional relationships—or lack of them—among all its parts. Although American society has always belonged to the larger Western society, it deserves separate study, furthermore, because of the peculiarly rapid breakdown of all its old primary institutions and the slowness with which a new, more satisfactory structure has developed. At present, any attempt to make American social history as precise and as broad as this is hampered by the enormous gaps in the story left by past historians' concentration on economic growth and mobility. Certain sections of this book, as the seasoned reader of history will observe, are drawn from very well-worked fields—the westward movement, immigration, industrialization, urbanization, and "social mobility" —in all of which the importance of individualistic, anti-institutional movement and material change has long been recognized. The almost total lack of historical study of the family, the social community, or the no less ubiquitous voluntary associations has required the author, in his inability to write all the missing monographs himself, to hammer other sections together out of whatever evidence comes to hand, though not without a growing assurance that the conventional and speculative parts of the book reinforce each other and point to the same general conclusions. But even if this book accomplishes nothing more than to convince more deliberate scholars of the need to find more solid evidence, it will perhaps have served for its time.

To call for intensive work on neglected areas of American social history is by no means to claim primacy for social values in human affairs, nor is it to push social history forward as the master key to history in general. (Neither is it to discourage current efforts to explain political, intellectual, or cultural phenomena in social terms.) Rather, both the successes and the failures in the American social experience strengthen the classically conservative belief— the orthodox medieval belief, indeed—that all human concerns are properly linked according to a hierarchy of values. Some aspects of life exist, that is, for the sake of others, and these latter are more important. At the base of the hierarchy lie the economic values, necessary but subservient, of adequate production and equitable distribution of material goods. Upon that system rest the specifically social values of satisfactory relationships among men in a reasonably stable, secure institutional structure, the system with which social history is primarily concerned. But a stable social structure is less important in itself than as the foundation, in turn, for other, loftier values of mind and spirit—esthetic and intellectual achievement of some excellence and perhaps even what is variously called self-fulfillment, redemption from sin, or salvation of the soul. The history of these chief cultural and spiritual ends of man in America would require another book vastly longer than this, and one much harder to write.

In limiting ourselves for the time to the institutional structure that incorporates specifically social values, we should not lose sight of its place in this larger scheme of things. Americans have often done so, especially in the nineteenth and early twentieth centuries, when they virtually denied the existence of any hierarchy among values—that economic values were in any practical way inferior to social values or that, indeed, economic relationships were not the most important social relationships as well. And except for increasingly perfunctory genuflections toward a rapidly receding God, the pragmatism and pluralism of popular attitudes and liberal thought abandoned the dominant position once held by cultural or spiritual values. In the mid-nineteenth century the conduct of economic affairs was substantially freed from the old social, cultural, and spiritual imperatives of "feudal" times.

In a negative way, the practical consequences demonstrate the ethical imperative of a ruling hierarchy of values. Abandoning it resulted, at too many points, in an unsatisfactory social structure (and, for that matter, a defective economic system). It was precisely at junctures when the social order was coming unhinged that a pervasive sense of insecurity threw up those half-irrational phenomena that have recently interested political historians, from the Salem witch trials of 1692 to the despairing cry of the 1960s for "law and order." Evidently some more organic, integrated system was desperately needed—some adequately functioning set of relationships among the organized institutions of a well-founded social structure. Exactly what the latter *ought* to have been is not the business of a historian to say. There have been many adequately organic societies here and there in the course of history, and men have conceived of more perfect models yet. A historian is reluctant to prescribe any one model for all future times and places. But the history of American society strongly suggests that if men subvert or abandon the values embodied in a well-ordered institutional structure, and so dismantle the social foundations for cultural achievement and spiritual serenity, they proceed at their own grave peril.

In recent years the general sense has been growing, at both ends of the political spectrum, of a need for an orderly, equitable social community—and for a more satisfying cultural and spiritual life. If this inherently conservative tendency can be disengaged more explicitly than hitherto from the remnants of nineteenth-century economic individualism—a process to which the historian can contribute—American society may eventually complete the cycle of development which this book describes, from adequate order through a period of excessive disorder and back again toward some satisfactory order. That cycle resembles, though it has lagged behind, the cycle of economic development—from the mercantilist controls of the eighteenth century through the liberal individualism of the nineteenth and latterly once again to a kind of neomercantilist system—which historians of the past generation have delineated. What the cultural and spiritual effects of the new economic system and a more organic social order may prove to be is impossible to foresee. A historian of the structure of American society can only hope that better understanding of that neglected aspect of the past may provide a better base for the history of more important matters, of the American mind and spirit as well as of American politics, and ultimately for a better understanding of the history of the country in all its aspects. He may be excused for further hoping that his perennially present-minded countrymen may be able, partly through an enhanced sense of that history, to rise above its peculiar limitations.

It is more than a gracious custom that requires a historian to thank the colleagues, editors, and institutions upon whom he has called for advice and aid in writing a book. Although historians usually work alone, the old saw about their repeating each other contains an inevitable truth. No one can know enough of the history of any sizable subject to be able to say that he has never levied on the work of others. To list all the influences on a book which represents a dozen years of one's reading and teaching would, however, almost double the length of the book itself. Instead I have limited the endnotes almost entirely to direct quotations, though where possible the reference is to a relevant secondary study rather than the contemporary source. The bibliographical essay is intended to single out the most substantial published work.

Certain individuals and institutions have contributed directly to the writing of this book. Now that I have to supervise a later generation of graduate students, I am more mindful than ever that it was the "GI Bill" which twenty years ago enabled me to become a historian. The Fulbright Act in turn permitted me to spend a year in Wales, among people not far removed from a traditional peasant society, and a later year at Edinburgh, where the sixteenth, eighteenth, and twentieth centuries still sort comfortably together. Summer research grants from Princeton University and a grant from the American Council of Learned Societies supported a specific piece of research in the Pennsylvania anthracite region and so got me into the heart of the industrial nineteenth century that is the rather dolorous heart of this book.

The twin themes of social mobility and social order were first introduced to me by Oscar Handlin in a way that seemed to give the most satisfactory meaning to the graduate work at Harvard that was deflecting an instinctive medievalist into American history. I was also particularly fortunate to go on to teach at Princeton, where Woodrow Wilson's preceptorial system made me consider week by week the sense that my colleagues—especially Wesley Frank

Craven, Eric Goldman, Robert A. Lively, and Charles G. Sellers—
were making of American history, and subjected me in turn to
their friendly criticism. Professor Craven is so much the virtual
coauthor of the first third of this book that I hasten to absolve him
of any responsibility for the use to which I have put his ideas. My
colleagues, seminar students, and the unfailingly sceptical under-
graduates over the last half dozen years at Washington University
have never hesitated to question and refine my cruder hypotheses
in the fashion that makes history, after all, a cooperative enterprise.

I am especially grateful to Sam B. Warner, Jr., John Higham,
and James M. Smith for their detailed criticism of the manuscript
from points of view that are no less useful for being inherently
irreconcilable with my own. Early encouragement by Edwin Barber,
then at Harper & Row, and alert monitoring of successive drafts
by Georgiana Remer, Mary Lou Mosher, and Jere Grant have helped
immeasurably. If my brother Warner Berthoff, whom I can always
rely upon as at once my severest and most sympathetic critic, has
not read every word of the final version, it is because I have had
to rewrite so much of it in response to his marginal notations,
admonitions that English must be "kept up," and explosions of
dismay, as well as hearty rejoicing when a phrase or idea hit the
mark.

My wife, who would be as much at home among the old handloom weavers of Lanarkshire as she is in a midwestern suburb,
has been my most constant source of insight into American society
as well as encouragement in getting on with a book about it. The
dedication is the only part of the book that is not subject to revision.

Saint Louis   R.B.
January 1970

PART ONE

The First American Society, 1607–1775

I. Origins

American society began in a long series of business failures. Of the dozen English colonial ventures in North America in the seventeenth century, none that survived into the eighteenth—to say nothing of those that did not—managed to fulfill the original economic purposes of its promoters. The portent was a curious one for a society which one day would value economic success above all else.

The fruits of colonization were sweeter for many of the early emigrants to America and for the economy of the mother country than for the promoters—or for the native Indians to whom the benefits of trade and the gospel were piously extended. But the greatest colonial achievement was of a sort at which the official prospectuses, charters, and instructions hardly hinted: the establishment of a viable branch of the familiar English social order. Success in so commonplace a sphere, due more to habit and the practical circumstances in which the colonists found themselves than to the economic, religious, or political calculations of the promoters, seemed quite unremarkable. How else would Englishmen live, once any considerable number of them had settled in the New World, but in a version of the old English society? The measure of the social achievement of the American colonists would come later, when their nineteenth-century successors, having at last found keys to wealth beyond the wildest dreams of colonial avarice, heedlessly abandoned the old order at the risk of social failure more sweeping than any of their economic successes.

1. FOUNDATIONS OF SETTLEMENT

The North American colonial enterprises of the seventeenth century were designed to carry out the broad economic policy that historians call mercantilism. In the course of the previous hundred years the medieval spiritual ideal of universal Christendom had broken down into a Europe of nation-states and virtually national churches, some Catholic and others Protestant. By the end of the Thirty Years' War in 1648 most of the principal states had turned away from fighting for religious creeds and toward the simpler economic goal of national power through self-sufficiency in trade and manufactures. Although the first English and Dutch colonial ventures in North America, between 1607 and 1624, were still aimed at breaking the imperial monopoly of the Catholic powers of Spain and Portugal, they also sought to free their national economies from dependence on foreign countries for raw materials and to provide markets for the mother country's manufactures. Colonization on such terms was far removed from the spiritual mission of the past, and yet Englishmen and Dutchmen did not value material progress merely for its own sake. The social ideal to which the mercantilist age aspired, hardly less than the Middle Ages had done, was an integrated social organism, all of whose parts should contribute to the spiritual as well as material well-being of the whole. Expansion of trade and manufactures was expected to advance the general welfare of this well-balanced "commonwealth."

In each of the English colonies in North America, as in England itself, more than a vestige survived of the transcendently spiritual purpose which medieval society had professed. But rather than being the dominant force in most colonies, the church was little more than a customary English institution, brought over as a matter of course along with other institutions. When the Virginia Company, promoter of the first permanent English colony in North America, required its colonists to attend church in the difficult early years, it was making the church an agency for the support of an economic enterprise that needed all the prayer it could get. Of course certain other colonies had a more old-fashioned concern with upholding true religion for its own sake. The planting of the New England provinces between 1620 and 1640 and of Pennsylvania in the 1680s was aimed at something more exalted than enrichment of the English commonwealth, at nothing less than a heightened, purified version of the spiritual ideal of the Middle Ages. But the Puritans and Quakers were the only promoters of new colonies who valued a prosperous, stable social order chiefly as the necessary foundation for the church's otherworldly role of salvation of souls. Elsewhere the overriding aim was the enrichment of the colonizers and the commonwealth.

Even these differences proved less important than the common character of Anglicans, Puritans, and Quakers as Englishmen of their time. Although their disputes were bitter enough in the seventeenth century, they were all members of the troubled society that had engendered them. Their various creeds and theologies did not lead the colonists to very different concepts of the proper social order. Puritans, logically deducing their mores from the divine revelation of the Bible, found no bar therein to most of the practices of English society to which they were accustomed. The arrangements that seemed to accord with the covenant theology, their version of Calvinism, conformed quite well to the actual structure of English society which others accepted with less disputation. It was a social structure in which a considerable amount of mobility and change was contained and channeled within a fairly stable structure of such traditional institutions as social classes, communities, and families as well as churches. The Puritan theology considerably fortified the founders of New England in perpetuating English ways in the wilderness, but the essential result was only marginally and temporarily different from that in other regions down the coast.

The concept of social class—rank or "degree"—was the best articulated in that age. Although hereditary nobility had never been as rigidly established by law in England as in most of Europe, social rank was real and as a rule the individual was expected to cleave to that to which he was born. In actual practice, by the seventeenth century English society had left far behind it the medieval idea of fixed status. But neither did men accept, for another two hundred years, the modern notion that individuals should be free to make any economic or social contracts they pleased. The early seventeenth century being in fact a time of rapid economic and social change, the old ideas of right and proper behavior did not quite keep abreast of current practice. Many an actual case of successful upward striving was looked upon askance, both from above and below, when measured against the divinely established standard whereby "the heavens themselves, the planets, and this center," as Shakespeare had Ulysses say,

> Observe degree, priority, and place,
> Insisture, course, proportion, season, form,
> Office, and custom, in all line of order.
>
>   . . . How could communities,
> Degrees in schools, and brotherhoods in cities,
> Peaceful commerce from dividable shores,
> The primogenity and due of birth,
> Prerogative of age, crowns, scepters, laurels,
> But by degree, stand in authentic place?[1]

Although a good many merchants, lawyers, placeholders, and other middle-class men were acquiring wealth, investing it in country manors, and turning themselves or at least their children into authentic gentlemen between 1540 and 1640, the opinion prevailed that in any orderly society the gentry, and even more so the nobility, should be distinguished less by mere property than by a fitting education, public service, and concern for the welfare of tenants and other dependents. Any landed gentleman, by the same token, was free to invest in the commercial ventures of the time—in overseas colonies, among others—without fear that such business interests would degrade him; quite the contrary, indeed, if commercial profits flowed in to bolster his estate. And so too with other classes: although some small yeoman freeholders and tenant farmers were losing ground, others managed to pass up and over the imperceptible line dividing their class from the lesser gentry. Of course there was bound to be headshaking over the pretensions of men not yet accustomed to their new position in life, but it was not seriously supposed—nor would it be for another two centuries in England—that they endangered the principle of rank or degree. The early seventeenth century was a time, in short, of great economic mobility and social climbing and also of precise calculation of the niceties of rank and precedence. The more solid the rungs of the social ladder, the easier it was to climb them.

Although historians, like Englishmen of that age, have been mainly interested in the class structure, ancient institutions of quite other sorts were no less fundamental to English society. The local community was seemingly as solid and timeless as any. Underlying the complex of judicial and administrative divisions—shires, hundreds, civil parishes, and manors—which centuries of feudal and royal authority had imposed upon the countryside, the village community of yeoman freeholders and peasant cottagers and laborers maintained an organic integrity of its own. At its center stood the church. As fellow communicants of the Church of England, all inhabitants were held to belong to the local parish. Although a few covertly persisted in holding to the old Roman allegiance and a few groups of Separatists openly withdrew, the usual wrangles between Puritan reformers and traditionalists in the early seventeenth century concerned control of the single, undivided parish church. Catholics, Separatists, Puritans, and conformists all assumed that the spiritual community would ultimately continue to be identical to the territorial community. The communal diversions—the May dances and games, the feasts or "church ales"—took place as a matter of course in the churchyard, and the church itself was the only edifice large enough to serve as the meetinghouse for secular as well as religious purposes.

The practical identity between neighbors, parishioners, and farmers was clearest when they, or the more substantial of them, met in the church to set forth the bylaws for the conduct of agriculture in the coming year and to elect the petty officers who would enforce them. Practical self-government by the community in its own affairs was the general rule, although the economic pattern of English villages varied greatly from one part of the country to another. Most of those in a broad central belt, from Dorset and Hampshire in the south through the Midlands north into Yorkshire and County Durham, still grew their crops on the medieval open-field plan. The arable land of the village was divided into two or three great common fields, and each landholder's "farm" consisted of narrow strips of land scattered among them. The system was a highly communal one, requiring constant cooperation. Immemorial custom usually dictated when wheat or barley should be sown in one field, peas and beans in another, and the third left fallow to restore the soil; it also regulated the pattern for grazing by the village herds on the common pastures and in the fields after harvest. All the same, the consent of the community of farmers lay behind the village bylaws and the authority of reeves, woodwards, haywards, and other petty functionaries.

Although the only authority to enforce village bylaws was the court of the lord of the manor, manorial jurisdictions ran along lines that often were quite separate from those of the village. In

Boundaries of open-field system

SCOTLAND

DURHAM

YORKSHIRE

WALES

EAST

ANGLIA

Yarmouth

Bristol

London

KENT

Southampton

WEST COUNTRY

CORNWALL

Plymouth

ENGLAND:

BOUNDS OF
THE OPEN-FIELD SYSTEM

many villages the jurisdictions of the courts of two or more land-lords, where petty criminal cases and civil suits were also tried, cut squarely across the boundaries of the working agricultural community. But to a remarkable extent the peasant community kept the essential tasks of sowing and harvesting, grazing and haymaking, in its own hands, where presumably they had been since long before the imposition of Norman feudal government in the eleventh century. In any event the integrity of the social community of an English village did not rest upon economic co-operation alone. Few villages in East Anglia, the West Country, or the Northwest had ever known the open-field system; the usual landholding there was a detached farm, a farm in the modern sense, enclosed within its own hedges or dikes. The farmer nevertheless was likely to follow local custom in his operations, and village society seems to have been as stable there as elsewhere.

The strength of the immemorial social order of the English vil-lage is indicated by the amount of actual movement and change that it was able to contain. It was not always so; many villages that had been thriving in the eleventh century, when their taxable property had been set down in Domesday Book, dwindled away during the vicissitudes of the next five hundred years and perhaps disappeared altogether, recalled only by the names of local fields and lanes. And in any village or town the high birthrate and death rate, and now and then some catastrophe, the worst of which was the Black Death which depopulated the countryside in the four-teenth century, caused a fairly rapid rate of replacement among the inhabitants. There was also considerable migration in and out. Recent investigation of two quite ordinary English villages in the seventeenth century indicates that the turnover of popula-tion ran as high as 5 percent a year, so that in the course of a decade as many as half the individual inhabitants died or moved away and were supplanted by others. Most of the turnover came from natural causes. The birthrate of one of these villages between 1676 and 1688 appears to have been as high as 37 per thousand people, and the corresponding mortality rate of 41 per thousand made the average life-span dismayingly short.

Those who lived did not normally expect to migrate elsewhere for very long. Of the many people who came and went year by year, most were young persons of local families who worked else-where for a time, probably in a very similar place nearby, eventually to return, marry, and settle down as householders like their parents and grandparents before them. Although from decade to decade this or that member of a family dropped from the scene, the parish records indicate that the family itself usually remained, "inhabiting the same buildings, working the same fields, . . . maintaining permanence in spite of the shortness of life, the fluctuations of prosperity, the falling in of leases, the wayward habits of young folk in service, and the fickleness of their employers."[2] Generations of intermarriage among local families created, moreover, a "blood brotherhood [in which] lay another of the great hidden strengths of the peasant community."[3] As principal components of the English social order the interrelated families and the village community that they composed illustrate the seeming paradox that Peter Laslett has neatly resolved: "an unchanging, unchangeable social structure may well be essential to a swiftly changing population."[4]

The local traders and craftsmen of the half-urban, still partly rural market towns were probably a good deal more mobile than the villagers. As far as they could, like greater men in the cities they looked forward to the modern bourgeois world rather than backward to antique custom. The forms of borough self-government which they had been granted sometime in the past by royal charter made their economic activities—guilds, weekly markets, annual fairs—coincide more exactly with their legal jurisdiction than was the case in most villages. But all these distinctions were differences in detail. Whether the English emigrant to the American colonies had been a citizen of a bustling town or a tradition-bound peasant villager, he had known what it was to belong to a community of fixed forms and fairly predictable patterns of behavior.

Economic change nevertheless disturbed a good many villages and boroughs in the late sixteenth and early seventeenth centuries. A long cycle of rising prices for grain and wool encouraged landowners—some of whom were urban merchants who surveyed their newly acquired estates with a capitalistic eye—to convert inefficient open-field villages to a new pattern of detached, enclosed farms. When the process of enclosure went to the length of obliterating the old arable fields and common pastures and turning the whole estate into a sheepwalk, the customary foundations of village society were destroyed as well. Since the new farming and grazing usually required fewer plowmen and harvesters, many of the small tenants and cottagers, if they could prove no title to their holdings beyond the customary acquiescence of the landlord, were evicted and cast adrift into the world.

The long series of local agrarian revolutions, together with industrial depression in the woolen-weaving trade of East Anglia, the West Country, and Yorkshire in the 1620s and 1630s, seemed to be tearing English society up by the roots. From the number of idle vagrants or "sturdy beggars," England appeared to have become grossly overpopulated. The population of 4 or 5 million in 1660 was perhaps twice as large as in 1500, but England of course had resources to employ a much greater number eventually; meanwhile it did not take unduly long to redistribute the excess in a settled economic pattern once again. By 1660 the fear had arisen, indeed, that there were too few Englishmen to maintain and advance the national interest. Such economic imbalances were not, however, the most crucial problems for many people in that age of religious and social unrest. After everyone displaced by enclosures and industrial crises found work again and settled down— perhaps in another village much like their old one—the links with the past of their own community and kindred nevertheless had been sundered. The social impact of economic dislocation could be particularly severe for peasants and artisans, since such people had expected a customary sort of stability in which all the ordinary hazards of life would be bearable.

From the mid-seventeenth century to the mid-eighteenth the pace of economic change and mobility slackened in England, and the prescriptive institutions of English society gained a new stability. The wave of village upheavals was over for the time. The enclosure movement virtually ceased, leaving most of the old open-field villages untouched. Innovation of other kinds also proceeded very slowly. The state gradually perfected a system of mercantile regulation adequate to protect the existing level of commerce, agriculture, and industry, and the English population, no longer considered excessive, grew at a moderate rate until about 1750. Stability rather than progress and change remained the normal expectation for most people. Even the rebels of the Glorious Revolution of 1688 could quite credibly proclaim, in the usual English way, that they were conservatively defending a customary, prescriptive constitution against radical innovation by an arbitrary monarch. Englishmen never ceased to promote economic expansion, both at home and across the seas, but for some time to come their successes were not so great as to endanger greatly the even balance of their society.

Certainly the English colonial ventures of any part of the seventeenth century, though they were aimed at economic expansion, were not intended to produce social or cultural novelties. In the course of time, as the society of the New World diverged from that of the mother country, it often seemed that the original colonists must have been as steeped in the dissidence of dissent as their successors were. But most of them, like most immigrants to America at any later time, emigrated mainly for economic ends. Neither they nor the sizable minority who put spiritual purposes foremost were discontented with the basic social structure of the old country as much as with their place in it or with some other temporary condition. They had no plans to alter it fundamentally in the New World.

The first English colonies, between 1607 and 1630, were established not by the state but by trading companies which the state chartered in order to lure investors into contributing to the mercantile prosperity of the entire commonwealth. The companies that looked to North America for dividends were not the first; Englishmen had already opened trade with Russia, West Africa, and the Levant, and in 1600 the East India Company, which proved the most successful of the overseas ventures, set the precedent of joint-stock organization which was shortly adopted by the American companies. At the outset the purpose of the latter was not to plant new societies, nor even to settle extensive tracts of land with any great number of colonists, but rather, as the other companies had done in Africa and in the East, to establish trading posts or "factories" at convenient points on the coast, with the consent of the local rulers, for commerce with the native population. In India such a purely commercial plan was practicable with neither military conquest, political domination, nor displacement of the Indian people; why not carry on the same sort of business with the "Indians" of North America?

In spite of the maritime exploits of English seamen since John Cabot's voyages of a hundred years before, in 1600 the coastline between Newfoundland and Spanish Florida was largely unexplored and its native inhabitants unknown. In the eyes of the first English colonists, the American Indians sufficiently resembled the Indians of India to warrant calling their clusters of wigwams "towns" and their tribal chiefs "kings" and "emperors"—with "princesses" like Pocahontas for daughters—and to encourage the hope of a large and profitable exchange of English manufactures for furs and other valuable native products. Far from plotting against the aborigines, the English promoters and investors expected to conduct trade to the mutual profit of both peoples and, among other fringe benefits, to convert the Indians to Christianity.

Furthermore, if goods such as glass, wine, silk, iron, and gold, which England was procuring from abroad to the detriment of its mercantile balance of trade, were not obtainable from the natives, they might be worked up from American materials by English artisans. The factories then would be manufactories as well as trading posts. Most important, perhaps, they would also serve as bases from which to search for a water route around or through the North American continent to the Orient, a passage connecting the oceans in the way that the rivers of Russia, as the English Muscovy Company had discovered, connected the Baltic with the Black and Caspian seas. If such a "northwest passage" were found, a company's trading posts in America would become supply stations for shipping. Whatever combination of these purposes proved practicable, the outlying agricultural settlement around the posts would presumably be only large enough to provision the ships and the garrison.

The first permanent settlement was begun along all these hopeful lines in 1607 by the Virginia Company of London, chartered the year before. The "adventurers" or investors in the company included city merchants, country gentry, and some two dozen peers —a typical group of propertied Englishmen seeking larger opportunity to multiply their capital than either their English estates or trade with the European continent could provide. The expedition, commanded by Captain Christopher Newport, a veteran of the Muscovy Company, carried instructions to seek out a waterway to the South Sea or Pacific Ocean. The first post, Jamestown, among the swamps of the peninsula north of the lower James River, was chosen for its defensibility against the Indians by land or the French and Spaniards by sea; the obvious defects of the site for farming or for a large population were unimportant in terms of the company's primary goals of exploration, trade, and manufacturing.

Unfortunately the magnificent estuaries of Chesapeake Bay narrowed into rapid-choked upland streams, and the scattered Indian bands, though helpful enough during Jamestown's desperate "starving time," were no great source of furs, to say nothing of the other hoped-for goods. Expert artisans, some of them Germans and Poles, were brought over from time to time in the next dozen years to make glass, silk, iron, tar, pitch, potash, and other promising manufactures, but nothing came of their efforts. Lumber provided the only important return cargoes in the first few years; although it was in demand in England, it was too bulky to make very profitable voyages. Quite unexpectedly, however, by 1615 a West Indian variety of tobacco was found to be the most likely staple crop. In spite of moral and economic objections, in which King James himself joined, that it was a useless and harmful luxury, an insatiable English demand for tobacco was quickly excited. From that time on, contrary to the intentions both of the company and of the English government, Virginia was almost entirely an agricultural settlement.

The Virginia Company, whose repeated failures led it through a long series of reorganizations and attempts to raise new capital, could respond to the success of tobacco growing only indirectly, by turning itself virtually into a land company. In 1618 it began to allot land in the colony in dividends of a hundred acres per share among the stockholders and settlers. To attract new immigrants, the company devised the "headright" system, later adopted by most of the other English colonies, permitting anyone who paid an immigrant's passage, whether his own or another's, to claim fifty acres for himself. Land was also granted to company officers in reward for service and also, for the military security of the colony, to persons who would engage to settle on the Indian frontier. About the same time the company inaugurated a plan for "particular plantations," each of several thousand acres, which would be undertaken within the colony by separate groups of investors. Although the few plantations that were started on that scale, such as Southampton Hundred and Berkeley Hundred up the James, were no more successful than the company itself, smaller individual ventures in tobacco growing proved so workable that the word "plantation"—originally synonymous with "colony" —soon came to denote simply a large private farm. Henceforth the society around Chesapeake Bay would rest upon a base of individual tobacco planters, large and small, rather than on a unified organization like the Virginia Company.

The company, still trying to promote towns and manufactures as well as the tobacco trade, prospered no better than before. After a series of financial crises, political squabbles in England, and in 1622 a devastating Indian attack, the company's charter was withdrawn by the crown in 1624. For the next century and a half Virginia was a royal colony, supervised by London as directly as circumstances permitted through an appointed governor and council. Royal government did not alter, however, the economic and social pattern, based on widely dispersed tobacco plantations and a permissive system for granting new land, to which the company had had to resort during its brief eighteen years.

The closest parallel to the Virginia Company was the Dutch West India Company, chartered in Amsterdam in 1621, which founded its first North American settlement on the Hudson River in 1624, just as the Virginia Company was being dissolved. The Dutch counted New Netherland on the Hudson as only a minor interest compared to their other ventures in West Africa, South America, and the Caribbean. Although they held the colony for forty years, their multipurpose venture was almost as unrewarding as that of the Virginia Company.

The Dutch West India Company established a string of small forts and trading posts up the Hudson, from Governor's Island and New Amsterdam on Manhattan Island to Fort Orange at the mouth of the Mohawk River, as well as isolated outposts on the Delaware and Connecticut rivers, which the colony claimed as its southern and eastern boundaries. Since New Netherland lay athwart the Hudson-Mohawk river system, the longest waterway, south of the St. Lawrence, leading into the interior of the continent, the company enjoyed unmatched access to the fur trade—the most lucrative trade that the Indians could offer. European goods, including liquor and muskets, were exchanged for beaver and other furs trapped by the local Indian bands along the Hudson as well as by the distant tribes about the Great Lakes for whom the Iroquois, on the colony's northwestern frontier, acted as middlemen. It was not the company which profited most from the fur trade, however, but individuals trading on their own account, some of whom were company officers acting contrary to their instructions.

The Dutch company had as little interest as the Virginia Company in colonizing an extensive farming society, but presently farms and villages, some Dutch and some English in population, scattered themselves across Long Island, Staten Island, Manhattan, and along both sides of the Hudson. In spite of recurrent trouble with the Indians, New Netherland survived as a society mainly of small merchants and smaller farmers, differing from most other colonies in only one respect. Although the company's plan of 1629 for large private "patroonships," reminiscent of the Virginia scheme for particular plantations, succeeded in only one instance —Rensselaerswyck, near Fort Orange—a series of great land grants to favored individuals fastened on the colony a unique pattern of landlords and tenant farmers which persisted as late as the nineteenth century. But growth was slow. In 1664, after forty years of company rule, New Netherland had fewer than ten thousand white inhabitants, of highly mixed European origins, strung out from the Mohawk to the Delaware, and in that year an English fleet easily seized the colony. Some of the colonists on the Delaware were Swedes and Finns, the remnants of an even less successful trading company, a Swedish venture begun in 1638 and taken over by the Dutch in 1655; their only mark on American society was the introduction of the Scandinavian log cabin.

In New England the great majority of the first settlers between 1620 and 1640 were Puritans—Calvinists dissatisfied with the limited reformation of the Church of England—who went to America to establish a church entirely purified of Romish corruptions as an object lesson to the established church at home. But because even an exemplary "city upon a hill" cost money to establish and maintain, each of the several New England ventures relied originally on the support of merchants and other investors organized in some form of trading company. The Plymouth Company, chartered like the Virginia Company in 1606, failed to develop the hoped-for trade with the Indians at its post at Sagadahoc on the Kennebec River and never established anything more than a few small fishing stations along the coast of Maine. In the 1620s the grandiose plans of a chartered group called the Council for New England, for subsidiary trading companies, came to nothing. Several other groups of merchants, either under royal charter or a patent from one of the chartered companies, supported settlements along the coast at Plymouth, Dorchester, Salem, and points in Maine; the colonists were expected to fish and acquire furs and other valuable products of the country for shipment to England. In each case the story was much the same: "the expected profits did not materialize, and the merchants . . . withdrew their support and attempted to recover as much as they could of their investments."[5] The "Pilgrims" of Plymouth Colony, the best remembered and least practical of these enterprisers, spent the better part of a generation paying off their debt to their English backers.

The Massachusetts Bay Company, which in 1629 undertook the largest of the New England colonial ventures, began like its predecessors. The main objective of the Puritan gentlemen, merchants, and clergymen of the company was not profit, however, so much as a refuge from the persecution imminently threatening nonconformists in England. The company accordingly contrived to ship itself—both its charter and its officers—to New England with the first fleet in 1630. The initial expenses of colonization were assumed by a separate group of merchants in England and

America in exchange for seven years' privilege in trading in certain exports and imports. The original commercial company was thereby fully transformed into a self-supporting society and quasi-independent state, isolated by the width of the North Atlantic from effective interference by king or archbishop.

Among the nearly twenty thousand emigrants to New England during the great Puritan migration of the 1630s there were ambitious individuals who set about to supply the newcomers, organize overseas commerce, and make their own fortunes. The great majority of people were content to take up farming in the townships they quickly settled around Massachusetts Bay and also, within a few years, along Narrangansett Bay, Long Island Sound, and the lower Connecticut Valley. From the earliest years, society in the colonies of Plymouth, Massachusetts Bay, Rhode Island, Connecticut, and New Haven, no less than in Virginia and New Netherland, consisted of a few merchants and a great many practical farmers. Because of their transcendently spiritual purpose as Puritans, their social communities were much more close-knit than those of any of the other American colonies. But, being seventeenth-century Englishmen rather than medieval ascetics or cloistered monks, the New Englanders managed, like colonists elsewhere, to reconcile pursuit of their earthly, material vocations with their spiritual calling.

After 1630 the day of the colonizing joint-stock company was over. For the next fifty years, from the chartering of Maryland in 1632 and Carolina in 1663, through the reconstituting of New Netherland as New York and New Jersey in 1664, down to the beginning of Pennsylvania in 1682, the English government employed another indirect device, the proprietary colony, to extend its mercantile empire. Under a form of landholding that had been obsolete in England for nearly four hundred years, the crown granted political jurisdiction over a province, as well as ownership of the land, to a private individual or group. These proprietors were to rule their domains on the frontier of empire in America just as the English palatine lords had done on the marches of Wales or Scotland in the thirteenth century; usually the medieval bishopric of Durham in northern England was specified as the model. Within such a colony writs ran in the name of the lord proprietor rather than the king; the proprietor appointed governor, council, and judges to rule it for him; and his agent granted or sold land in the colony in his name.

The fact that certain proprietors, notably in Maryland and Carolina, laid out quixotic schemes for completely feudal societies, to be ruled by such archaic figures as landgraves, barons, and lords of manors, each authorized to hold a court for his tenants, has somewhat obscured the actual nature of the societies which took root in the proprietary colonies. The feudal trappings no doubt were attractive to members of the English gentry and lesser nobility who considered becoming, or sending their younger sons to become, provincial proprietors or tenants-in-chief, and the promise of rents from an American peasantry may well have whetted a hope of bolstering their English estates. Perhaps such features of the provincial constitutions were actually set forth to entice investors into the project, just as the king himself from time to time had padded the exchequer by selling honorific but otherwise empty titles, including Nova Scotian baronetcies. Similarly, in all the proprietary colonies the promise of religious toleration proved useful as a special inducement to certain kinds of potential settlers: Catholics and Puritans in Maryland, French Calvinists or Huguenots in Carolina, and Quakers, German sectarians, and Irish Presbyterians in Pennsylvania and New Jersey.

No colonial proprietor managed to turn his feudal blueprint into a set of viable social institutions, except in one small but important respect. When a proprietor sold land, gave it away as bonuses to his officers, or granted headrights (after the Virginia example) to importers of immigrants, he retained the right to collect an annual quitrent, the most lasting practical relic of feudalism.* If collected with any efficiency by the proprietary government, quitrents of a modest two to four shillings a year for a hundred acres could bring the proprietor a sizable income—in Maryland as much as £8000 in 1767. The prospect of such revenue partly explains the willingness of colonial proprietors to give away headrights and other land grants, and thereby settle the colony quickly with quitrent-payers, rather than wait to sell land at the highest possible price.

In the end, because of inefficient or negligent collection and the

* Not rent in the modern colloquial sense, quitrents were originally payments in commutation of the personal services owed by English tenants to their feudal lords; by paying a sum of money they were quit of other obligations for the year. Colonial quitrents could legally be claimed not only by the proprietors in their colonies but by the earlier joint-stock companies. The Virginia Company in fact did not attempt to collect quitrents down to the time of its dissolution in 1624; quitrents were not part of the Dutch land system in New Netherland; and the Puritan colonies of New England from the start replaced feudal tenures with simple freehold. In the royal colonies, Virginia after 1624 and New York after 1685, quitrents were owed to the crown, but only in Virginia were they systematically collected (yielding £3000 to £4000 a year) and then not until the eighteenth century.

evasions of settlers in Pennsylvania, the Carolinas, New York, and New Jersey, most of the proprietors' dreams of fat rent-rolls never materialized. In all these colonies, much as in Virginia and New England, society consisted not of feudal tenants, in anything but the narrowest, vestigial sense, but of virtual freeholders, whether small farmers or great planters and land speculators. But the existence of the quitrent in some form in all the proprietorships, and also in the "royal" colonies, which were directly under the crown, suggests that their founders' economic motives were much like those of investors in joint-stock companies. After the grandiose schemes for manors and baronies, like those for manufacturing silk or glass, mining gold, or trading with the Orient, had all dissolved into the thin American air, the governing authority of every colony, whether company, proprietor, or the crown, found in land its one great asset and in the establishment of a society of landholders the real colonial future.

In view of the early and continuing importance of land in the settlement of all the English colonies in North America, ordinary immigrants were likely to be persons who set a high value on landownership and could reasonably aspire to it—potentially, any yeoman freeholder or tenant farmer who was dissatisfied with his prospects in England and yet not so depressed as to lack all hope of getting ahead. The great majority of emigrants to colonial America, at whatever point their origins can be analyzed, consisted of a middling sort of Englishmen, neither gentlemen in comfortable circumstances nor impoverished peasants but small farmers and artisans, and now and then certain younger sons of gentlemen who saw in the New World a chance to improve their fortunes and maintain their social standing. For such men, cheap land in the colonies—or land given freely in headrights of fifty acres—was a powerful magnet.

Being less discontented with the structure of English society than with what it held for them, such immigrants carried to America the quite conventional social ideas of their age and country. At the same time that they grasped the opportunity to better themselves, they accepted English ideas of rank or degree, of deference on the part of inferiors and responsible exercise of authority by superiors, and of an organic community extending outward from the family and the village, borough, and county to the national commonwealth. Those social ideals were hardy enough to dominate American society for nearly two centuries, despite all the changes in its practical circumstances.

II. The Limits of Colonial Progress

Colonial society rested upon an odd combination of archaic ideas and practical change. Its working structure, derived from an English society which was not literally either unchangeable or unchanging, proved considerably more mutable in the strange environment of the New World. The failure of the elaborate plans of the trading companies, the futility of the feudal schemes of provincial proprietors, and the feebleness of royal control all were aspects of the same thing: a lack of any central authority strong enough to maintain a customary English order against the general drift toward individual enterprise among the material opportunities of a remote new country. Only in New England, where religion and communal organization were dedicated to sustaining each other, did the original purposes of colonization seriously check the pace of practical change. Even there, the same tendency was apparent from the beginning among farmers and planters, shopkeepers and overseas merchants, artisans and millowners, frontiersmen and land speculators.

And yet by later standards the progress of the American economy in its first two hundred years was glacially slow. In part it was held back by the difficulties of the natural environment, potentially rich though the New World was. In part the brake was the colonists' own lingering attachment to the old organic, interdependent commonwealth. The conservative social ideal and the low pressure of practical change went well together. In that preindustrial age economic progress gathered headway without tipping the balance against a viable form of the old social order.

2. THE LAND

"A vast deal o' land for a verra few people," was the dour retort of Thomas Carlyle to the nineteenth-century American boast of national prosperity and individual success.[1] The high ratio of acres to men since the beginning of settlement of the continent has often been cited to explain the high wages, successful fortune-hunting, and general upward leveling toward a society of comfortably middle-class people. And indeed Americans have been a "people of plenty" almost from the first, a few thousands or millions of mankind peculiarly blessed with boundless resources and general affluence.[2] But the material bounty of America has never been uniformly distributed, nor has economic progress gone forward at a constantly rising rate throughout American history. During the first two hundred years, before the massive expansion of the nineteenth century, economic progress was limited in a variety of ways. Until the obstacles could be breached, the flood-waters of change would not sweep away the customary, organic social order that the English colonists brought to America.

The land itself, challenging in its continental vastness, limited the forward movement of the very settlement that it invited. Since exploration and settlement had to proceed almost entirely by water, the extent of each of the settled regions of colonial America was determined as much by the coastline and the navigable rivers as by the provincial boundaries marked off by royal charter on the uncertain maps of the seventeenth century. Although no northwest passage through or around the continent was ever found, settlement of the interior flowed up and along more than a dozen systems of waterways, several of them of truly continental grandeur. The course of settlement left traces in the names of the navigable rivers. Most of those that first opened a way inland from the sea were given European names before settlement began—Charles, Hudson, Delaware, York, and James rivers, Albemarle Sound, Ashley, Cooper, Savannah. Those that became known in the course of settlement generally retained Indian names—Merrimac, Connecticut (first settled overland), Susquehanna, Shenandoah, Rappahannock, Pee Dee, Santee, Edisto. Each of the regional societies that spread back from the coastal bays and up the river valleys was united around such waterways and separated from other regions by the intervening land. Although that pattern has since been reversed and then virtually obliterated by the railway, superhighway, and airline, it was an economic, social, and cultural reality during the greater part of American history.

The Chesapeake region, grandest of all these water systems, was the earliest settled. The prime requisite for the trading post of the Virginia Company in 1607 was security from foreign attack, doubly assured by the James estuary and, as the French naval blockade of Yorktown would decisively confirm in 1781, by the capes encircling the mouth of Chesapeake Bay itself. Saint Marys, the first settlement in Maryland, had similar advantages. The situation of Virginia and Maryland, and later of neighboring North Carolina behind the nearly landlocked Albemarle Sound, permitted from the outset the characteristically loose arrangement of tobacco plantations scattered along the "necks" or peninsulas between the rivers, a pattern which was also the most profitable for the individual planter. His plantation enjoyed the easiest conceivable connections with the European market. The lower, Tidewater area was directly open to ocean shipping, and during the eighteenth century tobacco from the headwaters in the rolling upland or Piedmont district could be taken down on smaller craft and transshipped at the fall line of river rapids. Consequently the society of the Chesapeake region, including both the Tidewater and Piedmont in all three colonies, consisted of detached, independent planters and farmers, large and small, with hardly a town worth the name. Although such a society already foreshadowed the disorganized frontier of the later West, its dependence on river communications helped to hold it within traditional bounds as each new county was organized contiguous to the older ones. Thomas Jefferson, living within sight of the Blue Ridge at the western limit of this society, was as much and as little of a "frontiersman" as the great planters of the lower James.

The settled parts of New England, comparable in area to the Chesapeake region, took shape around another distinctive system of waterways, more favorable than those of the Chesapeake for some enterprises, less so for others. By the late seventeenth century the nine original colonial ventures in New England had coalesced into the four provinces of Massachusetts Bay, Connecticut, Rhode Island, and New Hampshire. In spite of official bound-

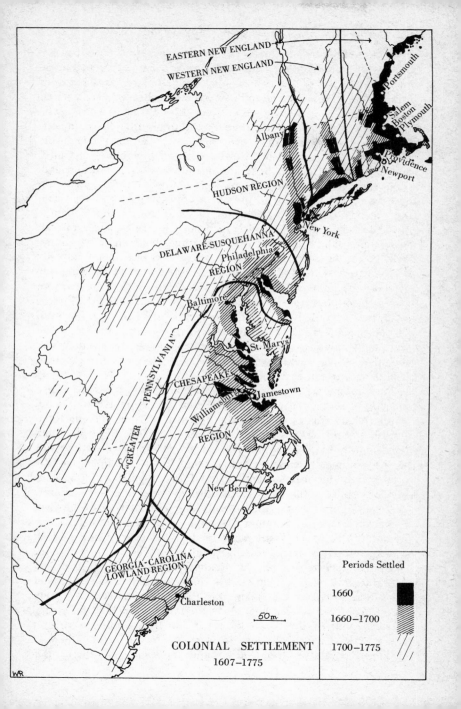

EASTERN NEW ENGLAND
WESTERN NEW ENGLAND

Portsmouth
Salem
Boston
Plymouth
Albany
Providence
Newport

HUDSON REGION

New York

DELAWARE-SUSQUEHANNA
REGION

Philadelphia

Baltimore

St. Marys

CHESAPEAKE

Williamsburg
Jamestown

REGION

"GREATER

"PENNSYLVANIA"

New Bern

GEORGIA-CAROLINA
LOWLAND REGION

Charleston

50 m

COLONIAL SETTLEMENT
1607–1775

Periods Settled

1660
1660–1700
1700–1775

WR

aries, New England was more broadly divided into two distinctive regions of settlement, eastern and western. Between the alluvial lowlands of each of these regions lay the belt of rough upland terrain of eastern Connecticut and central Massachusetts. The eastern region spread like two overlapping fans inland from Massachusetts Bay on the east and Narragansett Bay to the south. The many natural harbors fostered the growth of ports—thriving mercantile towns like Boston, Salem, Newburyport, Portsmouth, Newport, and Providence, and such notable fishing havens as Marblehead, Gloucester, and the Maine villages. The sandy coast south of Boston and the rockbound coast to the north afforded little soil for farming except inland along the rivers, all of them but the Merrimac unfortunately short. The Narragansett country, a strip of salt marsh and sandy or rocky soil extending about eight by twenty miles along the western shore of Narragansett Bay, having already been cleared by the Indians and lying convenient to shipping, became a prosperous grazing district in the eighteenth century. From Narragansett Bay the Blackstone River opened a further line of settlement into the backcountry of eastern New England. But even Yankee perseverance at scratching a living from thin, stony soil was daunted by the barren uplands beyond the coastal rivers, where the sparsely populated townships continued to mark the practical boundary between east and west.

The settlements of western New England were arranged like a reversed L along the Connecticut River and Long Island Sound. (Long Island was attached to the province of New York in 1664, but all except the western end around New York Bay was populated mainly by New Englanders.) Although the Connecticut was almost completely closed to ocean shipping by sandbars, it was bordered by the broadest and richest farming valley in New England. In spite of the two provincial boundaries that cut squarely across the Connecticut Valley—and though in later years the river itself was made the boundary between New Hampshire and Vermont—the course of settlement made the valley a single social region. Its first settlers came overland from the east in the 1630s —from Dorchester, Cambridge, Watertown, and Roxbury to Windsor, Hartford, Wethersfield, and Springfield—but most of the later migration flowed up the valley from the places first settled farther down. After the 1660s, when New Englanders reached the virtual western limit of their colonial expansion by founding a ring of towns west of New York Bay in New Jersey and a few others at detached points on the Hudson and the Delaware, their main frontier thrust was thus channeled northward into Vermont. Not until after the Revolution, when they crossed the Green Mountains to the valley of Lake Champlain, were the Yankees ready to move on westward out of the New England regions where five or six generations of their ancestors had lived.

The Hudson Valley, no more than 40 miles broad but extending 150 miles from the sea to the mouth of its northwestern branch, the Mohawk, was so self-contained a region of settlement in the seventeenth and eighteenth centuries as to force eventual realignment of several provincial charter boundaries to accord with social realities. By the terms of both its Dutch and English charters the province of New Netherland or New York extended east to the Connecticut River, but in fact the Berkshire and Taconic hills between the Hudson and Connecticut valleys formed the practical boundary between Yankees and Yorkers which New York formalized with Connecticut in 1731 and with Massachusetts in 1773. To the southwest another *de facto* social boundary of the Hudson region, falling considerably short of the old Dutch claim to the Delaware, took in only the nearer half of New Jersey. (New Jersey, after being formally detached in 1664 as a separate province, until 1702 was subdivided, aptly enough, into the separate proprietorships of East and West New Jersey.) Long after that time the old "province line" across New Jersey marked the approximate limit of the regional society of New York; in other directions both the society and the province coincided almost exactly with the narrow valley of the Hudson.

West Jersey faced southwest toward Pennsylvania, both provinces being part of the region of the Delaware and Susquehanna valleys. Although the Susquehanna River ultimately joins the headwaters of Chesapeake Bay, for seventy-five miles south of the Blue Mountain both the Susquehanna and the Delaware traverse the same level region of rich limestone soil. That inviting region also included the "three lower counties" (the later state of Delaware) on the west bank of Delaware River and Bay, a circumstance still marked by their inland boundary with Maryland. Delaware's peculiar official status, neither wholly a royal colony nor yet an integral part of proprietary Pennsylvania, reflected its place in a region defined by the rivers and the course of settlement.

By about 1730, when this fertile quadrant had been occupied, settlers were beginning to penetrate north and west through the "water gaps" and "wind gaps" into the narrow Appalachian valleys, but a far larger number moved southwest where the Delaware-

Susquehanna region merges imperceptibly into western Maryland and, west of the Blue Ridge, into the Shenandoah or Great Valley of Virginia. There they were politically bound to the society of the Chesapeake but socially and geographically somewhat distinct from it. When they pushed this new "Greater Pennsylvania," as it has been aptly called, on into the backcountry of the Carolina Piedmont after 1750, they finally left the waterways and opened the "Great Wagon Road," the first major overland route in colonial America.[3] Only then, and shortly afterward on the northwestern frontier of New England, did the course of settlement at last break out of the regions defined by the bays, sounds, and river valleys of the Atlantic coast.

The lowland settlements of South Carolina and Georgia were shaped most singularly of all by waterways: the hundred-mile coastline of tidal creeks and "sea islands" upon which the eighteenth-century society of rice and indigo planters distinguished themselves for a West Indian kind of opulence and near-insular detachment from the other mainland colonies. The tidewater district was uniquely cut off from the Piedmont of South Carolina by a broad belt of sandy pine barrens some sixty miles back from the coast. As frontiersmen coming down from Pennsylvania occupied the remote backcountry in the 1750s, South Carolina formed two regional societies far more sharply divided than those of any other province.

Modern communications one day would overrun the natural boundaries between the colonial regions of settlement. Recent study of eastern American dialects suggests, however, the strength of regional distinctions in colonial society. On the twentieth-century dialect map the lines between the three major speech areas— northern, "midland," and southern—run along the outer limits of the old Greater Pennsylvania: on the north the "province line" between East and West New Jersey; on the south the Blue Ridge and pine-barren border between the coastal regions and the backcountry. Within each section the outlines of the colonial regions of settlement can be discerned: eastern and western New England; the Hudson Valley and its outliers; the Delaware-Susquehanna region and its southwesterly extension; the Chesapeake region; and lowland South Carolina and Georgia. In colonial times probably none of these dialects was as distinct as it later became, but clearly the regional groupings into which colonial society fell have left their mark on modern American speech. It was within the natural limits of those regions, each of them united by waterways

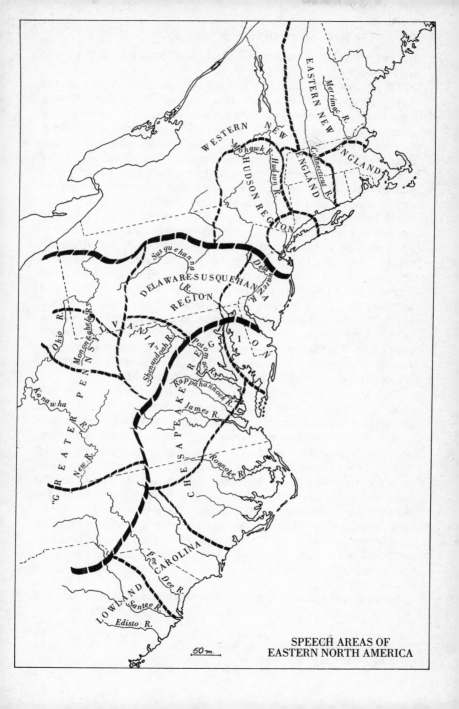

SPEECH AREAS OF
EASTERN NORTH AMERICA

but set off from the others by land, that American society first took shape.

The American Indian, like the land he occupied, figures in the history of white society mainly as an environmental phenomenon, open to certain kinds of exploitation but posing at the same time a barrier to settlement and economic progress at certain points. Since at first the Indians saw the whites as useful, within limits, to their own purposes, they did not oppose colonization. Having known no other humankind than themselves, they attached far greater importance to their own intertribal relationships than to any common identity of red men against whites. The Algonquin tribes of New England, the lower Hudson, Delaware, and Susquehanna valleys, and the Chesapeake region had common traditions of their remote origins which, in addition to language, set them off from the Iroquoian tribes in the backcountry of both New York and the Carolinas. When Europeans first appeared, they found a confusing pattern, in shifting flux for centuries past, of alliances and fixed hostility among various tribes and their local bands. To the Indians the newcomers appeared simply as a congeries of groupings of the same sort, useful as allies, dangerous if unfriendly. Except for such "empires" as the Iroquois Five (later Six) Nations in New York and Powhatan's confederacy in Virginia, no steady Indian alliance confronted the white intruders.

The initial relationship between whites and Indians was not military or political but commercial, somewhat on the lines that the original trading ventures of the English and Dutch companies had expected: the Indians trapped furs for the European market, and the Europeans provided manufactured goods of use to the Indians. Even when white men were allied with one tribe against another, they were more esteemed as suppliers of cloth, metals, firearms, and liquor than as fighting men. Indians had little use for other features of white society, neither for the ill-adapted European agriculture from whose failures in the early years they so often had to rescue the struggling settlements nor for the latter's incomprehensible religion. "When we pray," a Dutch clergyman said of the Mohawks, "they laugh at us."

Some of them despise it entirely; and some . . . stand astonished. . . . I tell them that I am admonishing the Christians, that they must not steal, nor commit lewdness, nor get drunk, nor commit murder, and that they too ought not to do these things. . . . Then they say I do well to teach the Christians; but immediately add, . . . "Why do so many Christians do these things?"[4]

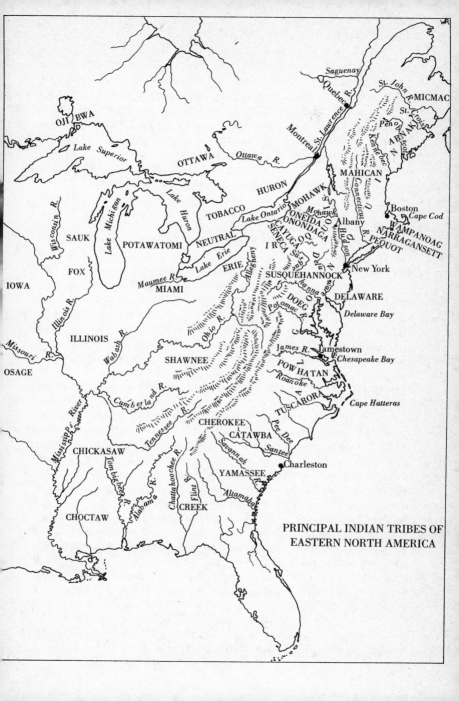

PRINCIPAL INDIAN TRIBES OF
EASTERN NORTH AMERICA

Nor did white society ever borrow much from Indian culture beyond a few native foods and innumerable place names.

Commercial relations between white colonists and Indian tribesmen were disturbed in two ways. From the beginning the pattern of trade was incompatible with the pattern of settlement which quickly developed. As each colony grew into an agricultural society instead of a mere scattering of trading posts, it pressed ever deeper into the Indians' tribal lands. Fraud and force were not normally involved, although from time to time war gave an opening for conquest. Usually the colonial governments took care to purchase land in due form soon after, if not before, settlers began to occupy it. Even the most regular land purchases, however, caused trouble. To the Indian mind the land of the tribe (or rather of the local bands into which tribes were subdivided) was a communal resource to the use of which, whether for hunting or agriculture, others might be admitted. To Europeans the purchase of land meant its permanent appropriation, sooner or later as the private and exclusive property of individual farmers. And one land purchase inevitably led to another; there was to be no end to the expansion of white society. Almost any use of land by white men, for that matter, undermined the Indian economy by exterminating the game which they hunted for food and for pelts to trade. For the Indian tribe the choice ultimately lay between becoming indigent dependents of white society or resisting further encroachment.

Trade in itself hastened Indian dependence, crippled Indian resistance, and disorganized tribal and commercial relationships alike. It was profitable for those tribes who happened to be strategically situated between the sources of beaver pelts or deerskins and the posts where European firearms could be secured. Other tribes whom they could then subjugate or decimate were not so fortunate. The power of the Iroquois against their neighbors on all sides was less the result of their famous confederacy than of their position astride the Mohawk River route from the fur country around the Great Lakes and of the superior armament of muskets which the thriving peltry trade enabled them to buy. Unlike firearms, the "firewater" which Indians also prized was an unmitigated disaster for those Indians who obtained it in trade, by demoralizing, disorganizing, and, when added to epidemics of smallpox, measles, and other European diseases, destroying whole tribes. Eventually, as the supply of furs was "trapped out" in the tribal areas adjacent to the white settlements and the trade was pushed farther west, almost all the eastern Indians sank into economic dependence, cultural demoralization, and social dissolution.

Before this process of destruction had run its usual course over several decades, however, the two races usually coexisted to what seemed their mutual advantage. During the first dozen years of the Virginia Colony the "emperor" Powhatan, finding white aid useful to his confederacy against his up-country enemies, tolerated the Englishmen and indeed helped them to survive their early "starving time." But the rapid transformation of the colony into a swarm of land-hungry tobacco planters inevitably provoked conflict, climaxed in 1622 when the Indians massacred several hundred of the outlying planters and, in retaliation, the survivors carried fire and sword through the Indian villages. Between 1622 and 1644 a form of the old relationship was restored. The colony fixed and fortified its Indian frontier on a line above Jamestown—"Middle Plantation," the later Williamsburg, was one of the frontier posts—and averted trouble by deflecting settlement southward. In 1644 a second great Indian attack provoked new reprisals that finally crippled the confederacy. Although the frontier line was redrawn by treaty and guaranteed by colonial law against further white incursions, the confederation tribes had entered the final stage of physical and social debilitation and faded away thereafter, even before the land-engrossing planters appeared. By the 1670s the Virginia frontier lay open to white fur traders as far as the Shenandoah Valley and the southeastern headwaters of the Ohio.

New Netherland went through a similar cycle during its forty-year history. The Dutch fur traders dealt both with the local Algonquin bands along the Hudson and, to the northwest, with the Iroquois in their strategic role of middlemen to the tribes trapping beaver about the Great Lakes. Although the Dutch farmers were too few to spread far inland on either side of the Hudson, they were soon embroiled in petty but perennial Indian troubles—trespass, pilfering, and occasionally murder, followed by harsh reprisals. It was the gross mismanagement of Indian affairs by the government of the colony, however, that precipitated the general border warfare of 1643–1645 and, in 1655, an Indian attack on New Amsterdam just when the Dutch garrison was off conquering the Swedish colony on the Delaware. After 1664, when New Netherland became New York, the colony was relieved of the local Indian problem by the steady degeneration of its Algonquin neighbors. The Iroquois were not so easily removed. Strong in men and muskets and controlling English access to the inexhaustible hinterland of beaver, they were a military power which Great Britain found indispensable in the eighteenth century as an ally against the French in Canada. Until the American Revolution the Six Nations remained an impenetrable barrier athwart the Mohawk Valley, the natural route for westward expansion from New York and from New England as well.

The first New Englanders accounted themselves divinely favored by the circumstance that smallpox—in fact, a European disease which the maritime explorers of a few years before had probably introduced—had already swept most of the Indians from around Massachusetts Bay, "so as," Governor John Winthrop rejoiced, "God hathe hereby cleered our title to this place."[5] Among the red imps of Satan who remained, however, the Wampanoags had proved helpful to the Plymouth Colony in its hungry first years. The Puritan commonwealth also managed to coexist for several decades with most of its Indian neighbors. The ruthless war of 1637, in which the combined New England colonists, with the aid of the Narragansetts, extirpated the Pequots from the Connecticut frontier, fortunately was an isolated occurrence during the first two generations of settlement. Villages of other local tribes—including a few of Christian converts or "praying Indians"—continued to live interspersed among the Puritan towns.

In the end the tribes of New England, like those of the Hudson Valley and Virginia, were pressed in front by the land-hungry white farmers and from the rear by the powerful Iroquois. In 1675–1676 both ends of that frontier exploded. In New England the Wampanoags, still in the backcountry of Plymouth, rose at last in desperation under their chief Metacomet, known as King Philip, and raised a general Algonquin coalition against their long-time white neighbors. Indian devastation of outlying towns set back the advance of settlement by some twenty-five years; not until 1700 were all of them reoccupied. But after two years of implacable campaigning by the united colonists, aided by the benign neutrality of the Iroquois, the Algonquin tribes of New England were shattered. Confined thereafter to a few reservations, their remnants had no further influence on the contemptuous white society that had displaced them.

The Chesapeake frontier—still on the Tidewater peninsulas—erupted at almost the same time. From the north the Iroquois pressed down upon the Susquehannocks, the Susquehannocks upon the nearby Doegs, and they in turn on the up-country tobacco planters. The latter, led by the young English gentleman Nathaniel

Bacon, lashed out at Governor William Berkeley's policy of defending a frontier line fixed thirty years before. "Bacon's Rebellion" was soon deflected into a general onslaught against the neighboring Indians—not only the offending Doegs and Susquehannocks but the debilitated local tribes as well. Although the province reverted after 1678 to a form of its old defensive policy, for the next century the Virginians faced no impenetrable Indian barrier but that lying far north of the Chesapeake—and west of New England —in the formidable persons of the Iroquois, the valued allies of the British crown, and their dependents the Delawares.

Another imperial alliance with tribal power hemmed in the far southwestern frontier. The tribes just beyond the settled lowlands of South Carolina were broken in the Yamassee War of 1715–1716, but the Cherokees, Creeks, and other powerful tribes of the interior, with whom the Carolinians conducted a profitable trade in deerskins, remained firmly in place throughout the colonial period. On one hand, they were useful allies against Spanish Florida; on the other, they were as impervious a barrier to Anglo-American settlement on the southern flank of the Appalachians as the Iroquois were on the northern. Since neither barrier was broken through until after 1775, colonial society was interdicted from expansion into either the Northwest or the Southwest, the lands of brightest promise for a later generation of Americans.

In spite of an often difficult terrain and spasmodic Indian troubles, a new society which numbered only a quarter of a million persons in 1700 and some two million by 1775 did not lack opportunity. Between the sea and the mountains there was fertile soil enough in the Delaware-Susquehanna plain, along the rivers and estuaries of the southern Tidewater and Piedmont, and even among the granite hills of New England, overlain as at first they were with the forest mold of centuries. But the ability of the colonists to make use of all this land was limited, partly by the difficulty of clearing the forests that blanketed the eastern part of the continent and partly by the inefficiency of their own agriculture.

Here and there the first settlers found land already clear: the old "Indian fields" of New England and the Chesapeake region, the still wider tracts everywhere from which the Indians had burned off the underbrush each year in order to hunt game more easily, the natural meadows of the southern Piedmont and Great Valley, and in the Carolinas the grassy savannas and canebrakes which provided an open range for cattle from the earliest years of settlement. Cattle and swine could roam in the woods too, but to turn hardwood forests into cultivated fields meant hacking out the trees one by one over the years. The "Yankee system" of land clearing, practiced by the careful farmers of Pennsylvania as well as the New Englanders, was to fell the trees with the ax, clear the undergrowth, and plow around the stumps until after several years they rotted away. Elsewhere the easier method of girdling, or killing a tree by cutting through its sap layer and leaving it to dry out for burning in a year or two, was more commonly used. Even though a farmer contrived to save labor by this slatternly procedure, he could clear hardly two or three acres a year. It might take five years to achieve comfortable subsistence and shelter and a dozen or more to put fifty acres under cultivation.

In spite of the difficulty of clearing, land was carelessly and wastefully farmed in all but one or two regions of colonial America. European agriculture would not furnish a greatly improved example until late in the eighteenth century, and many Old World farming practices, whether traditional or modern, have never been adaptable to American crops and climate. It is likely also that a considerable number of the English settlers of the seventeenth century had not been agriculturists in the old country and had to improvise for better or worse. Colonial farmers typically lacked capital for the tools and improvements necessary for efficient farming; the inventory of many a New England farmer's estate listed only a plow and harrow, a cart, and a few axes, spades, hoes, a scythe, and other small tools. Plows were clumsy wooden affairs, and only the woodsman's ax was well adapted to its New World uses. If American settlers knew the use of fertilizer in the old country, they soon forgot it; with plenty of fresh acres at hand, they could let their livestock unproductively manure the nearby woods where they roamed. From the American farmer's point of view a manure pile accumulating in the barnyard was merely a nuisance that ultimately might make it necessary, and easiest, to move the barn.

Above all, the abundance of cheap land—and the lack of labor and capital, especially at the beginning of settlement—fostered a wasteful, exploitive, "extensive" agriculture. The habit of mining the soil by planting the same crop year after year and then abandoning it for newly cleared fields meant that as the population grew, there would be a smaller area available for use. In the Chesapeake region, where successive crops of tobacco wore out the soil within a few years, planters grew accustomed to acquiring far more land than they could cultivate at one time. As early as the mid-seventeenth century the desolate "old fields" gave an odd impression of antiquity and decay in the New World. Whole districts like the Eastern Shore of Chesapeake Bay had to give up tobacco planting by 1700; within another fifty years even the new land of the Piedmont was well on the way toward the same devastation. In New England, although good soil was scarcer and the land more closely settled, the usual methods were only slightly better. On the typical eighteenth-century farm of over a hundred acres, as few as five might be cultivated, twenty used as meadows for hay, and the rest left to woodland and pasture, the latter comprising both "clear pasture" and old fields that had reverted to "brush pasture." In the rougher and poorer areas of New England that may have been an appropriate division, but in other parts as well, the wasteful farming methods, together with infestation by wheat rust and other crop diseases, led to an early and continuing pressure for migration to new lands. In the eighteenth century New England could no longer feed itself; the coastal towns had to import foodstuffs from the Delaware-Susquehanna region.

In Pennsylvania in the eighteenth century a more careful agriculture was practiced by the "Dutch" settlers, accustomed in Germany to good soil, crop rotation, deep plowing, and intensive use of the labor of all members of the family, including women and children. They sought out the best of the limestone soil, hard to clear though it was, and were reputed to put up barns for their livestock before they built permanent houses for themselves. The result could soon be seen in their prosperity and the export of their surplus wheat, cattle, and horses to other colonies. On the other hand, their Scotch-Irish neighbors from Ulster, a poorer country, were satisfied with inferior kinds of soil on which small patches could be cleared, by the Celtic "outfield" system of dispersed corn and livestock farms, and abandoned for new clearings when "the good" had been taken out of the land.[6] The use to which land was put in any colony thus owed something to old-country custom as well as to its cheapness and to the scarcity of labor and capital.

Except in German Pennsylvania, improvident farming practices impeded the process of capital accumulation that was vital in a new land. After years of labor a farm and its "improvements" all too often had to be abandoned almost as soon as the farmer's sons were grown, so that instead of plowing the profits back into their farm, the family had to start over again elsewhere. Although mining cheap soil gave an illusion of prosperity, in reality it constricted the use that could be made of the available land, the material base on which colonial society had mainly to be built.

3. LABOR

The supply of labor in colonial America was never sufficient to realize anything like the full economic potential of the land, but the colonists themselves were not to blame for that. Although the birthrate before the first federal census in 1790 cannot be even approximately calculated, it was undoubtedly high. As Benjamin Franklin observed in the eighteenth century, the population was doubling every twenty-five years, partly through immigration but probably more through natural increase. As late as 1800, a recent authority remarks, the annual rate—55 births per thousand people—was "markedly higher than that ever recorded for any European country and is equalled . . . only by such unusually fertile populations as the Hutterites and the inhabitants of the Cocos-Keeling Islands."[1] Even so, natural increase never supplied an adequate working force, except perhaps in New England, where the initial impetus of the great Puritan immigration of some twenty thousand people in the 1630s, set against the region's poverty of natural resources for their descendants to exploit, made further immigration from abroad superfluous. But in every other region of the country there was always more work to be done than hands to do it.

The European societies from which the needed labor would have to come, although they had always known a certain amount of change and mobility, had no experience of migration to the other side of the world; only emigration itself, in the course of time, could make such a venture seem normal. Until about 1760 it required very special circumstances in particular parts of the Old World, together with special inducements in the New, to pry loose any great number of people from their customary place and way of life. No great wave of emigration would have flowed from England to New England in the 1630s—those who came constituted the first and nearly the last mass movement of free, self-supporting immigrants in the colonial period—had England not suffered from an unusual coincidence of disturbances: on one hand, agrarian change and industrial depression, with the consequent notion that the country was overcrowded, and on the other, so much Puritan discontent with the Church of England that even gentlemen of good estate were willing to risk the voyage. Most men, whether they were merchants, gentry, farmers and tradesmen with some capital, or only poor peasants, had better or less risky prospects at home.

The Atlantic crossing was enough to deter all but the most desperate, determined, or helpless. Even for them there was little America-bound shipping to be found except in the ports of southern England and, in the eighteenth century, those of Ireland and Scotland. Ordinary emigrants from the interior of the European continent had to make an expensive journey of several weeks down the Rhine to a Dutch port, where they transshipped for England to seek a vessel for America. In sailing ships of fifty to two hundred tons the voyage took two to three months or longer, at the mercy not only of wind and water but, during half of the colonial years, of hostile men-of-war and pirates and, at any time, the horrors of the nameless "ship fevers" among passengers and crew.

America could offer only two surpassing inducements to immigrants: landownership for those who could pay their way, and special labor contracts for those who could not. Every colony south of New England, whether ruled by trading company, proprietor, or royal governor, operated a thriving land-office business, more for the sake of getting the province settled, putting the land into production, and collecting quitrents from the inhabitants than for immediate profit from land sales. Most new land was cheap enough —from £2 to £10 a hundred acres—but, particularly in the seventeenth century, it was more often given away in fifty-acre headrights. The headright system, devised by the Virginia Company in 1617, was continued by the royal government in Virginia after 1624 and adopted everywhere else but New England. To encourage persons with capital to subsidize immigration, land warrants for fifty acres were offered for each "head" they brought in. About the end of the seventeenth century, when such warrants began to be sold outright and thus lost their connection with immigration, the headright system merged into the land sale system.

Whether land warrants were granted or sold, it was left to the new owner to pick out the actual tract of land and register it at the provincial land office. If no other claimant protested, he was issued a patent of title. Some colonies stipulated "seating" requirements: in eighteenth-century Virginia, the cultivation of three acres in every fifty within three years or, later on, simply making improvements worth £10. But such restrictions were difficult to enforce and were generally ignored by the authorities as well as by the landowners. If the land system was to keep on attracting immigrants, it had to be almost completely permissive. Such a casual policy did not always turn out to serve the land seeker's interests, since the vague descriptions of the boundaries of overlapping claims could embroil him in endless litigation. But the goal of economic expansion, never easy to attain in spite of the efforts of the colonial land offices, took precedence over considerations of good order and social harmony.

The easygoing land policy even tended to perpetuate the shortage of labor which it was designed to remedy. Potential immigrants who were too poor to acquire cheap land in America were also likely to be too poor to emigrate there in the first place. Although those who managed to get to America could earn wages two or three times higher than in England, as soon as they accumulated a little capital they were tempted to buy farms of their own and perhaps seek to hire laborers themselves, leaving wage labor in shorter supply than ever. The colonial economy obviously needed a class of immigrant laborers who could not achieve independent landownership, at least for a period of years. There appeared very early, therefore, the seemingly paradoxical institutions, in the midst of abundant cheap land, of white indentured servitude and Negro slavery. Actually there was no paradox: servitude and slavery for some persons were direct consequences of the excessive opportunity for landownership which most others enjoyed. Slavery, and with it the perpetual American dilemma of an unfree caste in a free country, came into existence precisely because from the outset America was as free a country as it was.

Until about 1700 most of the bond laborers in the colonies were indentured servants—English men, women, and children who by a legal contract or indenture drawn up in the old country had agreed to serve a colonial master for a term of years, usually four or five, in return for passage to America, food, clothing, and shelter while in service, and "freedom dues" at the end. The arrangement was modeled on the indentures whereby English boys were apprenticed to master artisans, although the usual colonial servant was an adult and was not seeking, except incidentally, to learn a trade. The system was devised about 1619 by the Virginia Company, which shipped out cargoes of "servants" to be sold to individual planters for the cost of transportation. By 1624 servants comprised about 40 percent of the 1250 white people in the colony. Throughout the seventeenth century English shipping agents carried on a lively trade in cargoes of indentured laborers for

America. These white bond servants may have been as many as half or even two-thirds of all immigrants to the colonies south of New England in the seventeenth century.

The indentured servant was a kind of temporary slave rather than a free wage laborer; in fact, since there was no chattel slavery in English law, the colloquial terms "servant" and "slave" at first were interchangeable. The labor of the servant was the private property of his master, limited only by the terms of the indenture and the law of the colony. A servant could be sold or bequeathed as part of his master's estate; the master could farm out part of his service to pay a debt; there were masters who wagered and lost a servant in a game of cards. The servant could not marry or earn money on his own account without the master's consent, and for running away or other breaches of contract a year or two might be added to his term of service. He could be set to any work the master thought appropriate, typically as a plantation field hand in the Chesapeake tobacco region, as a farm laborer, or, if he happened to be one of the few who had the requisite education, as a bookkeeper or as Latin tutor to the master's children. When his term was up, he was free to make his own way in the world with the gift of such modest freedom dues as the law of the province specified the "custom of the country" to be, typically a suit of clothes, a few bushels of corn, and perhaps an ax, hoe, or musket—but seldom any land. Any experience of American farming or business the servant had happened to gain might also be useful.

The origins of most such persons are as obscure as their later fate. Only people too poor to pay their own way to America or in too desperate a plight to stay in England would be likely to sell themselves into temporary slavery in this way. Presumably they were uprooted individuals of the sort not uncommon in England at the time; certainly they included a large proportion of convicts, though many of the latter were no worse than thieves and vagabonds who accepted exile and servitude as better than the gallows or an English jail of the time. Such future Americans were often enough like one group described, in London about 1700, as "Ragamuffinly Fellows, showing Poverty in their Rags, and Despair in their Faces, mixt with a parcel of Young Wild Striplings like Runaway Prentices."[2] Recruiting of servants for the colonies was a regular business in seventeenth-century England and Ireland. The agents, some of whom probably deserved their reputation as crimps or kidnapers, brought groups of servants before a magistrate to be indentured and then sold both servant and indenture to a merchant or ship captain for resale to a master in the colonies.

Such recruits were unlikely to establish themselves securely in colonial society. According to the best recent estimate as many as eight out of ten indentured servants either died before the end of their terms, served them out and returned to England, or remained but never succeeded in acquiring property along with their legal freedom. Even in those colonies which included a land warrant among the freedom dues, it was a rare freedman who turned it into a farm of his own. Only one servant in ten seems to have become a landowner and perhaps one more an independent artisan. A few individuals managed, particularly in the early years, to become planters, merchants, and magistrates; seven members of the Virginia assembly of 1629 had been servants as recently as 1624, and even in later times an occasional well-educated immigrant, such as Daniel Dulany in Maryland in 1703, entered a term under indenture as a useful introduction to the country and to ultimate fortune. Like more recent instances of rags to riches, theirs were the memorable stories. But the broader significance of indentured servitude for American society lay in the fact that a large part of the original white population came from a lower social level in the old country than has been typical of immigrants at most periods in American history. For the purely economic purpose of recruiting some sort of labor force, most of the colonies were willing to overlook the potential social consequences.

Importation of Negroes from the West Indies or, especially in the eighteenth century, directly from Africa was a much starker case of economic urgency overriding social and moral misgivings. It was not that Africans were on a particularly lower stage of civilization. When the depredations of the slave traders began, in the sixteenth century, the commerce and craftsmanship, social structure, and cultural ingenuity of West Africa had been as complex as those of Europe. African experience as agricultural peoples, indeed, made Negroes as adaptable to plantation labor as the Indian was not. Those individuals who fell into slavery were quite likely, as prisoners of war or captives of raiding parties, to be superior members of their own tribal societies; not a few men of rank, skill, and formal learning survived the horrors of the "middle passage" to America. But they were markedly different in culture and appearance from the white colonists into whose society they were unwillingly and forcibly thrust to do the work the whites were too few to do cheaply for themselves.

Most of the cultural differences were too fragile to persist. Because of the mixture of African tribal origins and languages among the slaves and the degrading circumstances that were imposed upon them, their African culture was shriveled up within a generation or two by a casual but implacable sort of forced Americanization. The stages in the process remain obscure, but well before the end of the eighteenth century white and black Americans were inextricably bound together in only marginally variant forms of speech, religion, and other aspects of a common culture. Blackness, however, was ineradicable. The prejudice attached to it perpetuated the social inferiority of Negroes in America long after the original economic demand for their labor was forgotten.

Anglo-American color prejudice and the practical inferiority of blacks in America are virtually impossible for historians to disentangle as causes of the kind of slavery that came to exist in North America. In English law slavery did not exist in 1619, when the first cargo of Negroes was landed in Virginia, nor was the form it took in the English colonies in the seventeenth century derived from the existing varieties of slavery in Latin America or West Africa. It was an Anglo-American institution, indigenous to the West Indies and the North American continent. At first no legal distinction was drawn between white and black servants, but by the 1660s, when there were still far more white bondsmen than Negroes in the colonies, the color line had been clearly defined in law. It has been suggested that in order to encourage white servants to emigrate, colonial law gradually improved the terms of their service, while the Negroes, being involuntary immigrants for whom such inducements would be meaningless—and individually much more easily identifiable as servants should they try to run away—remained in a depressed status which white men soon convinced themselves was what the black race naturally deserved. The subsequently troubled history of race relations in America and England, on the other hand, tends to confirm the conventional supposition that the racial distinction between white servants and black slaves must have existed from the start, racial prejudice thus accounting for legal slavery rather than slavery for racial prejudice.

Conclusive evidence for either thesis may be unrecoverable. All that is certain is that between 1619 and 1670 any initial uncertainty about the Negro's status was inexorably resolved. The reference in a Virginia statute of 1661 to runaway "negroes who are incapable of making satisfaction by addition of time" implies that their enslavement had already been made perpetual. In 1670 Virginia specified "that all servants not being christians imported into this colony by shipping"—meaning Negroes rather than Indians—"shall be slaves for their lives," and in 1671 Maryland cleared up the last lingering doubt by deciding that conversion of a Negro to Christianity did not require that he be set free.[3] By the end of the century, when the southern planters, unable to obtain enough cheap white labor, resorted to massive importation of blacks, the law was ready for them.*

White indentured labor was almost completely replaced by Negro slave labor between 1680 and 1720 in the Chesapeake tobacco region; the South Carolina rice plantations, established at just that time by men from Barbados, always relied on the slave labor that was already familiar to them.† The reasons for the change were all economic, none social. The tobacco planters, after a period of depression in the 1660s and 1670s, enjoyed an expanded European market for their staple product, but the price they could get was so low as to require the cheapest possible production. A white field hand cost £2 to £4 for each year of service, and when he gained his freedom, after four or five years, a new servant had to be bought and trained. A Negro slave already "seasoned" to plantation labor in the West Indies, as most of the first ones were, cost £18 to £30, or only about £1 a year during his working life. Furthermore, he was at least as adaptable to the routine tasks of tobacco growing as the kind of Englishman who could usually be secured, and slaves produced not only tobacco but a crop of children who, for the minimal expense of rearing, were likewise the master's property for life. In any case, the late seventeenth century was not a period of great English emigration, and the people who came, including the first of the Scotch-Irish Presbyterians and German sectarians, were now diverted away from the southern plantation colonies by the good soil and the warm welcome extended by the tolerant

* Indians were also enslaved, though only for twelve years, by the Virginia Act of 1670. It was more usual, especially in New England after the Indian wars, to sell Indian captives in the West Indies than to keep them so close to their own country. By another Virginia statute of 1662 the English law that a child followed its father's status was changed so that the child of a Negro woman servant would also be a slave. If the purpose was to compensate the master of the mother of a bastard child for her loss of working time, the lasting effect was to declare the mulatto offspring of white men to be slaves and Negroes. The two interpretations of the origins of North American slavery are argued by Oscar Handlin, *Race and Nationality in American Life* (Boston, 1957), pp. 3–28, and Carl Degler, *Out of Our Past: The Forces That Shaped Modern America* (New York, 1959), pp. 26–39.

† The early appearance of slavery in New England, for the relatively small number of Negroes who were brought there, may be accounted for by the Yankee merchants' familiarity with the West Indies.

Quaker founders of New Jersey and Pennsylvania. (Thus the Quakers, later known for virtually the only antislavery movement of the eighteenth century, inadvertently helped fasten Negro slavery on the neighboring Chesapeake region.)

The southern planters had finally discovered a cheap, self-generating labor force with which to make the most of the earlier discovery of a profitable staple crop. Farmers who could afford to invest in a few slaves soon had an economic advantage over those who could not, an advantage which multiplied as the self-made planter reinvested the profits from cheap tobacco in more land and slaves. Ordinary white indentured servants, if they could still find a master to buy their labor, could look forward to even less opportunity in tobacco farming than formerly. As the large slaveholders of the tobacco region consolidated their position at the expense of the small farmers (the latter were never numerous among the rice plantations of the South Carolina low country), a new southern social structure took shape, as well as a new labor system.

"There could be no manner of doubt," the leading modern student of the subject concludes, "as to the desirability of the slaves from an economic standpoint, apparently the only standpoint that received serious consideration."[4] Certainly it was the only standpoint that prevailed in the eighteenth century. When occasionally certain colonies sought to stem the influx of Negroes—either out of concern for their social stability or merely in the hope of raising the price of tobacco or rice by restricting production—the imperial authorities refused to consider the proposal. As the English attorney-general of 1693 retorted, in another connection, to a plea for the welfare of the colonists' souls: "Souls! Damn your souls; make tobacco."[5] Usually the slaveowning planter followed the same economic standard of values, and the number of Negroes multiplied as tobacco and rice production expanded. In Virginia, where in 1670 there had been perhaps 2000 Negroes in a population of 40,000, by 1715 there were some 23,000 blacks and 72,000 whites; after another generation the 120,000 Negroes were over two-thirds as numerous as the 173,000 whites. In South Carolina as early as 1708 the 4000 Negroes already formed half the population; by 1765, in spite of a provincial bounty to encourage white immigration and a customs duty to restrict the mass importation of Negroes, the blacks numbered some 90,000, more than twice the 40,000 whites.

The day-by-day strains of wringing forced labor out of men of another race—"a Nation within a Nation"—were quite real for the master, besides the lurking popular fear of a mass uprising of blacks: New York City was as subject as the plantation colonies to recurrent frights that came to nothing.[6] The southern colonies devised the most elaborate slave codes in the eighteenth century. Slaves were confined to the plantation except with the master's written permission; the harshest corporal or capital punishment was imposed for breaches of discipline; the militia was turned into a slave patrol. Whether such precautions and penalties were required by the actual behavior of the slaves, in an era when many of them had not yet lost the warlike demeanor of African tribesmen, is uncertain. At the least the codes evince the social disadvantages of a merely economic solution to economic problems, in this case the problem of maintaining a large labor force. The Negro was, so to speak, the first effective labor-saving device that American ingenuity hit upon, but the social price for using men as machines or work animals was the racial crevasse that has divided America ever since. For three hundred years the moral dilemma of compulsory unfreedom for one ethnic group has vexed a society which has increasingly valued freedom for everyone else.

White immigrants of the eighteenth century, discouraged from going to the plantation regions and not needed in New England, found better opportunity both for contract labor and for land-ownership in the "Greater Pennsylvania" of the Delaware-Susquehanna region and its extension into the backcountry of the southern colonies. Many came as "redemptioners," a variant form of indentured servitude. Instead of entering into a labor contract before leaving the old country, the redemptioner simply struck a bargain with an agent or ship captain for passage to America and paid what he could; after landing he was given two weeks in which to find someone to make up the balance, either by seeking an employer himself or by letting the captain sell him for an appropriate term of service. The system was suited to immigrants who, unlike most of the earlier indentured servants, brought their families with them; the service of wife and children as well as the husband could be applied to their passage, sometimes at the risk of having the family broken up for sale "like so many cattle."[7] It represented a transitional stage between indentured or contract immigration, which was the special expedient of the seventeenth century for recruiting labor, and the "free," mainly self-supporting immigration of the nineteenth. The redemptioner was simply a poor immigrant who came to America without having been specially recruited and who, lacking capital to invest in the venture, devoted his family's labor to it instead.

Many of the Germans and Scotch-Irishmen who came to Pennsylvania in the eighteenth century were of this sort. The Germans, mostly from Switzerland, Baden, the Rhenish Palatinate, and other states on the upper Rhine, were ordinary peasants who had suffered the economic and social upheavals of the Thirty Years' War and were now uprooted by the wars of Louis XIV. They had sought refuge from the turbulence of the age in Anabaptism and other forms of pietism, but this nonconformity now drew down upon them a systematic persecution that further loosened their customary place in the homeland. Hounded by the authorities in both the Catholic and the Lutheran states, conscripted into military service contrary to their pacifistic faith, the sectarians, together with many ordinary Lutherans and Catholics who shared their economic difficulties, accepted the welcome which the Quaker proprietor of the new province of Pennsylvania held out to all comers. In religion a German Mennonite was much the same as an English Quaker, and there were Mennonites at Germantown in 1683, only a year or two after the first Quakers at Philadelphia.

Mass emigration of Germans began after 1710, when the British government settled some three thousand "poor Palatines" in the Hudson Valley, some of whom shortly made their way to Pennsylvania. Between 1710 and 1740 a medley of Mennonites, Amish, Dunkards or Baptists, Schwenkfelders, and a dozen other kinds of German sectarians took up land, perhaps after a few years of service, in the fertile Pennsylvania counties of Lancaster and Berks. Toward the middle of the century more Lutherans, Catholics, and Moravians emigrated than sectarians, though the latter never ceased to come until, in the nineteenth century, hardly any of them remained in Germany. In all, more than two hundred thousand Germans came to colonial America, the great majority forming that unusually persistent ethnic group the "Pennsylvania Dutch" (*Pennsylvanische Deitsch*).

A similar number of Scotch-Irish or Ulster Scots—or simply "Irish," as Americans called them in the eighteenth century before there were many Catholic Irish immigrants from whom to distinguish them—sought out America for another set of economic and religious reasons. They were already of tested immigrant stock, mostly Lowland Scottish, whom the English government had employed two or three generations before to dislodge the native "mere Irish" from the northern province of Ulster. The experience had made them a somewhat rough-honed people whose lack of other civilized graces was filled by a single-minded Presbyterian detestation of papists and popery. In the end they were ill-rewarded for their services.

The government that had "planted" their forebears in Ireland withdrew its favor in 1699 by discriminating against such Irish (largely Ulster) manufactures as woolens, linens, and glass and by excluding Irish shipping from the English imperial trade. As the long leases on farms in Ulster expired early in the eighteenth century and came up for renewal, the new terms seemed to the farmers, plagued as they were by recurrent cycles of bad harvests, to amount to extortionate "rackrenting." When Catholic Irishmen were willing to pay such rents and subsist on a smaller margin of income in order to recover their old place on the land, many of the Protestants were ready to emigrate to another "plantation" farther on. Furthermore, the Test Act of 1704, which barred non-Anglicans from various civil rights in Ireland as in England, discriminated against Presbyterians almost as much as against Roman Catholics. All these economic and religious grievances could be resolved in the colonies, Pennsylvania in particular, tolerant as it was of nonconformity and safely within the English trading system. From the 1720s onward the Scotch-Irish poured into the Quaker province, where they found the rough backcountry, beyond the fat German settlements, suitable for their kind of farming.

Although the last redemptioners arrived as late as 1820, already in the 1760s America had entered the nineteenth-century era of self-supporting immigration. There had always been free immigrants alongside the indentured servants and redemptioners, but after the peace of 1763 their numbers promised to answer the American demand for artisans and laborers as well as for land purchasers. In 1775 the Revolutionary War pinched off this new migration, which never fully resumed until after the end of the Napoleonic Wars in 1815. Nevertheless, well before the end of the colonial epoch American society had begun to emerge from the chronic dearth of labor that had made white servitude and Negro slavery seem necessary. Although those economic expedients had enabled Americans to make the most of the opportunities of a new country, the "drilling in" of ill-matched European laborers and African slaves seriously compromised the commonweal of American society for many years to come.[8]

4. WEALTH

The natural obstacles in the path of the American colonists, as they sought to turn the available land and labor to good account, held back both their economic progress and any inclination they may have felt to disavow old English social values. Among the latter, whatever the colonists' immediate purposes had been in coming to the New World, as good Englishmen of their time they accepted distinctions of rank or degree as eminently right and proper. They recognized, in particular, the fitness of having an aristocracy or gentry at the head of affairs, and among their own number there were always gentlemen ready to assume the burden of political and military command as well as economic and social leadership. Although the material foundations for such an upper class were far less ample than in England, the slow pace of economic development had a certain conservative effect. The near impossibility of accumulating a truly huge fortune, by English standards, virtually prevented most colonial gentlemen from lapsing into the irresponsibility of overmighty plutocrats.

At the other end of the social spectrum, colonial America was even more exceptional in lacking either a peasantry or a proletariat, except for the peculiar caste of Negro slaves, the white temporary bond servants, and perhaps the casual laborers of a few major port cities. The economy that permitted few men to grow overbearingly rich enabled most men to become comfortably middle-class freeholders and proprietors of farms or shops. The broad base of colonial white society was not sunk below the level of decent subsistence and social respectability. The degree of practical equality which ordinary men enjoyed seems to have moderated envy and anxiety in colonial times. Members of a lower class which was not too low were fairly content to defer, in the customary English way, to a gentry which, although newly rich, was not too haughty. Had the opportunities for exploiting land and labor and amassing wealth been greater in colonial America, the nineteenth-century collapse of old social norms might have occurred much sooner.

The way to wealth in the colonies was seldom simple or direct. Few fortunes were made out of a single enterprise or even a single kind of enterprise. This was particularly true in agriculture, the business of the great majority—perhaps 95 percent—of the people. Although farming was the commonest basis for the widespread economic self-reliance and social respectability, few farmers gained much more from it than that. Of course no district lacked its country gentlemen. Since landownership retained something of the social prestige that it had in England, men who were successful in more lucrative pursuits customarily invested in land. But their holdings seldom made them true English squires. Since most small farmers, in every colony but New York, were also freeholders, the landed gentleman was not a landlord who lived on his rents but simply a working farmer on a larger scale. Even the "planter" whose only business was farming was likely to find, furthermore, that his claim to gentility considerably overtaxed the income that his hundreds or thousands of acres could provide. In every region the upper class was a landed class, but agriculture was not its surest prop.

Mediocre soil made rural New England almost entirely a land of small farmers. Their farms usually ran from 75 to 150 acres, worth perhaps £300 to £1200, far enough above the mere subsistence level of an old-country cottage holding to allow the ordinary Yankee freeholder to claim the social standing of the old English yeoman. As a recent statistical study says of Northampton, Massachusetts, in the mid-eighteenth century:

The tax lists show that almost all the people were property owners, that the spread in the amount of property owned was not wide, and that the vast majority of men were farmers. Furthermore, . . . practically all men increased their holdings over a period of years.[1]

Although the Yankee farmer made what he could of such opportunity as his stony or sandy acres offered, the result of his labor seldom exceeded a comfortable competence. However assiduous his pursuit of the Puritan's earthly calling, he never struck upon natural riches such as men like him would one day find in the farther West. As the historian of the town of Kent, in the Connecticut Berkshire hills, observes, there were "Comstocks at Kent [who] did not discover the Comstock Lode, but they were looking for it."[2]

Two districts of New England provided somewhat greater chances. In the eighteenth century the Narragansett country of western Rhode Island supported the only class of "planters" in the northern colonies, a few score gentlemen livestock breeders and slaveowners. The largest estates ran to two or three thousand acres, divided into several farms, with perhaps forty Negro slaves, 60 horses, 50 to 150 head of dairy cattle, and 600 sheep. By 1750 the Narragansett planters owned some three thousand slaves. Besides breeding draft horses for the sugar mills of the West Indies and the saddle horse known as the Narragansett Pacer, their plantations produced wool, made a well-known variety of Cheshire cheese, and grew Indian corn for the white cornmeal that distinguished Rhode Island "jonny [journey] cake" from the corn bread of other regions. These prosperous gentry were further set off from the ordinary Yankee yeomanry by their adherence to the Church of England and by the provincial brilliance of Newport, their social as well as mercantile center, a place sufficiently fashionable for the much wealthier planters of South Carolina to resort to each summer.

The lower Connecticut Valley, the most propitious farming district in New England, fostered not only the respectable yeomanry noted at Northampton but also a local aristocracy known in the eighteenth century as the "river gods." As a landed gentry, however, these personages were hardly more than ordinary farmers: the wealth and influence of Israel Williams of Hatfield, with his modest inheritance of 109 acres and grazing rights on the town common, or John Worthington of Springfield, who had two farms with sixty-three head of cattle at his death in 1800, came, as we shall see, from enterprises other than agriculture.

Because of the Dutch pattern of large land grants, continued after 1664 by the English authorities, New York most closely resembled the English rural society of great landlords and small tenant farmers. Estates like the Van Cortlandt tract of 86,000 acres, the Philipse "manors" of 156,000 and 205,000, the Livingston estate of 160,000, and the million-acre patroonship of Rensselaerswyck fastened a system of tenancy on the Hudson Valley until well into the nineteenth century. The New York tenantry complained from time to time of their legal and political disadvantages, by comparison with the freeholders of other regions. The insecurity of their tenure was aggravated by the vaguely defined land grants, which tempted the great landlords to dispute the claims of such small landowners as there were. The New York tenant farmer seems, however, to have lived no less comfortably than the small freeholders of the regions to the east and south. Rent collecting was not the prime support of the New York aristocrat, who, like many an English or Dutch gentleman, relied on commerce and manufacturing (here primarily the fur trade and production of naval stores) to support his high estate.

If there was any part of colonial America where a farmer could thrive, it was the rolling plain of rich limestone soil in the Delaware-Susquehanna region, which became the commercial breadbasket of North America early in the eighteenth century. Although a kind of country gentry flourished, especially in the environs of Philadelphia, their fortunes were usually commercial, derived from shipping abroad the surplus grain, flour, flaxseed, pork, and beef of the small farmers. There as elsewhere a landed estate was a fitting investment and mark of gentility for the successful merchant. As in rural New England, the leading men of each locality had to be something more than mere farmers if their wealth were to justify their social pretensions. But this broad and fertile region is more noteworthy as the classic locus of what would later spread across the West as the typical American society of independent freeholding farmers.

From among the offspring of the Scotch-Irish and German peasants and farmers came the backcountry settlers who shortly moved north and west into the Appalachian Plateau and southwest along the valleys of the southern interior. Perhaps beginning as illegal squatters, a family might accumulate, through diligence, frugality, and good crops, a competence of a few hundred pounds, enough to make the parents secure in their old age and provide each son a small inheritance. But even in that felicitous region a successful farm produced a comfortable margin of security rather than great wealth. Since few more lucrative kinds of enterprise than farming were open to most men, the distribution of wealth among them was equal enough to inspire the ideal vision of a happy agrarian, pastoral society that was to seem the picture of perfection to later generations of Americans.

The classic aristocrats of colonial America, the planters of the Chesapeake region and the Carolina and Georgia coast, had the surest title to a traditionally English social preeminence. Since Chesapeake tobacco and Carolina rice and indigo were commercial staples, grown almost entirely to be shipped abroad, the southern planter became a commercial farmer within a few years of the first settlements. Tobacco growing could be highly profitable, especially in the early years. In Virginia in 1619 a certain planter, it was said, "by his owne labour hath in one year raised himselfe to the value of £200 sterling, and another by the meanes of sixe Servants hath cleared at one crop a thousand pound English."[3] In the mid-seventeenth century it was estimated that an investment of £50 would grow, in only two years, into an estate worth £600. Enormous tracts could be amassed through investing in the fifty-acre headright warrants of immigrants or by invoking official influence, both procedures often helped along by collusion and fraud. In the 1670s there were more than four hundred Virginia estates larger than a thousand acres, each of the dozen largest containing between ten and twenty thousand acres. As the critical English commissioner Edward Randolph observed in his report of 1696, so much land had been engrossed in a few hands that many former indentured servants and other poor men had to become tenants of the great planters or else move to "the utmost bounds of the colony for land."[4] Rents consequently made up a substantial part of certain planters' income, particularly in the Northern Neck between the Rappahannock and Potomac rivers. By no means, however, was the small yeoman farmer eliminated from the tobacco region. As late as 1750, when the average holding in Virginia ran to some 750 acres and some of the greatest estates took in more than 100,000 acres, only 10 to 15 percent of the Virginians were tenants.

In view of the limited transatlantic market for tobacco, farms and plantations frequently proved only too productive. In certain cycles of years and even whole decades in the late seventeenth and eighteenth centuries, an overstocked foreign market severely depressed the price the grower received. The planters blamed the British Acts of Trade for denying them direct access to continental Europe and sought, through provincial regulations of their own, to hold production down to the effective demand, but their ability to control prices three thousand miles away was necessarily limited. Such boom profits as from time to time they did enjoy were largely due to their wasteful practice of mining the soil in one new district after another as they spread across the Tidewater and Piedmont of Virginia and Maryland and up to the Blue Ridge.

By the middle of the eighteenth century a great many tobacco planters, whose grandfathers and great-grandfathers had established themselves as county oligarchs, were clinging to estates heavily encumbered by debt to English and Scottish creditors. The proportion of tenants and of landowners with less than one hundred acres, furthermore, was rapidly increasing, especially in the older Tidewater counties. In spite of certain planters' efforts to diversify agriculture after the pattern of the prosperous Delaware-Susquehanna region to the north, the easier alternative of moving on to new land encouraged most men to grind along on the old lines. In either case, this region of the classic "Old South," on the eve of the Revolution, rested upon a far flimsier economic base than that suggested by later generations' idealized recollection of a society of leisurely gentlemen planters and sturdily independent yeoman farmers.

The legendary picture had a degree of reality, which perhaps owed more to the persistence of traditional English social values than to American circumstances. Although over the years tobacco growing enabled many small farmers—even some who had immigrated under indenture—to turn themselves into a species of English gentry, there were other members of the Virginia elite who had a closer relationship to English society. "Most of Virginia's great eighteenth-century names, such as Bland, Burwell, Byrd, Carter, Digges, Ludwell, and Mason," a recent study points out, stemmed not only from successful tobacco growing but also from the immigration, about the middle of the previous century, of a number of members of "substantial families well connected in London business and governmental circles, . . . ambitious younger sons of middle-class families who knew well enough what gentility was and sought it as a specific objective."[5] Like other planters they and most of their descendants had to be active managers of their estates—businessmen-farmers rather than simply landlords—but they made their county society conform to the English model as closely as practical circumstances allowed. Their nineteenth-century successors who exalted the First Families of Virginia into so many royalist "cavaliers" no doubt exaggerated the blueness of their blood by English standards of gentility, but the great families of the Chesapeake region succeeded, whatever their origins, in screening the unleisurely life of a tobacco planter behind a convincing provincial version of English aristocracy. The inherited social ideal, reinforced by the sometimes ample, sometimes pinched opportunities of the tobacco trade, held even the most ambitious would-be plutocrats of the Chesapeake within a gentler way of life.

The brilliance of the Carolina plantation aristocracy perhaps drew less on English social ideals than on their flourishing exports of rice and indigo. Wealth flowed in so briskly upon them in the mid-eighteenth century as to make them seem more like the industrial plutocrats of the next century than the struggling tobacco gentry up the coast. Rice growing in the coastal swamps began about 1700 and enjoyed its greatest boom after 1730; indigo, as a complementary crop on drier ground, reached its peak in the quarter century between 1750 and the Revolution. As a Charlestonian observed in 1765,

the Planters here all get rich, which you need not wonder at when you see this small province export about 120,000 barrels of Rice worth 35 shillings Sterling on average, and upwards of 500,000 wt. of Indigo worth 3 shillings sterling round, besides many other articles as Corn, Lumber, Naval stores, Pork, Hemp, &c.[6]

A planter's investment in land and slaves could be recovered within a mere three or four years, and the most successful, whose estates ran to as many as fifty thousand acres and eight hundred slaves, were reputed to be worth £1500 or even £5000 a year. The enterprising rice and indigo planter has been aptly called a "bourgeois grown rich and seeking gentility," a self-made businessman not yet fully metamorphosed into a self-assured aristocrat.[7] "Their whole lives," a Charleston editor said of the planters in 1773,

are one continued Race: in which everyone is endeavoring to distance all behind him; and to overtake or pass by, all before him; everyone is flying from his inferiors in Pursuit of his Superiors, who fly from him, with equal Alacrity. . . . Every Tradesman is a Merchant, every Merchant is a Gentleman, and every Gentleman one of the Noblesse.[8]

Since the larger estates usually included a number of separate and perhaps widely scattered plantations of a few hundred acres, each of them worked by a hired overseer and several dozen slaves, the Carolina planter aspired to be an absentee owner, more concerned with a good return on his investment than on responsible leadership of the local community, whether of neighbors or slaves. He fled from the "country fevers" to Charleston—the one real town of the plantation regions—and if possible would "escape to the Northern Colonies" from May to November.[9] Like the West Indian sugar nabobs whose ostentation aroused conservative resentment when they returned to England, the Carolinians, some of whose ancestors had been planters in Barbados before 1670, displayed more interest in the perquisites and privileges of wealth than in its duty toward society. To a Bostonian like Josiah Quincy in 1773 South Carolina appeared to consist of nothing but "opulent and lordly planters, poor and spiritless peasants, and vile slaves," with no middle class of respectable freeholders such as formed the majority in nearly every other colony.[10] The Carolina low country was distinguished from other regions by a precociously overriding materialism; its headlong economic development and the rapid rise of its parvenu gentlemen—in 1710 the word "gentry" was there said to connote nothing more than "our most considerable men"—contrasted sharply with every other colonial region of North America.[11]

Elsewhere the most profitable use of land was not in farming or planting but in buying and selling real estate as a purely specula-tive commodity. The large acreage of a colonial farm or plantation is apt to be misleading, since the records do not systematically dis-tinguish between land intended for cultivation or grazing and land held only for profitable resale. "Acquisition of new lands," it has been observed, "was always the quickest and surest way to affluence in an expanding agricultural economy, making virtually every gentleman a land speculator."[12] As far as the ordinary farmer could, he too speculated in land; the wealth that his fields yielded so grudgingly might flow in effortlessly upon him as a trafficker in real estate. "Land was easy to buy, easy to sell," a historian of frontier New England observes, "and, best of all, prices were steadily rising."[13]

In New England, although the system of settlement in the seventeenth century kept land dealing under a social checkrein, as early as the middle of the century the business was so well developed that some of the leading men with reputations as over-seas merchants have been called "primarily real estate agents, not merchants at all."[14] The "river gods" of the eighteenth-century Connecticut Valley, who were quite undistinguished as agricultur-ists, derived the bulk of their fortunes from a land business done in tracts of thousands of acres. The Quaker merchants of Philadel-phia likewise looked inland for profits as well as across the sea. "Every great fortune made here within these 50 years," it was said in the 1760s, "has been by land."[15] The "manors" and "baronies," as the great land grants of Pennsylvania were ambitiously called in the proprietor's original plan, in fact were little more than real-estate investments practically devoid of any political or social function.

Land speculation took various forms. The great landlords of the Hudson Valley were more interested in collecting rents from their tenants than in selling parcels of land to freeholders. In the plantation colonies of the Chesapeake and Carolina coastal regions, whose economies were based on the hope, at least, of profitable staple crops, planters acquired vast reserves of land, some to sell on credit or to lease to tenants at a handsome eventual profit, but most of it for their own future use or that of their sons. Land engrossing in South Carolina and Georgia was necessary if the ambitious planter were to get control of enough swampland of the sort that could be adapted to rice fields. What the Carolinians did during boom times in the market for rice and indigo in the mid-eighteenth century, the gentlemen of the Chesapeake took up when a failing market plunged tobacco growing into depression. Land considered as a commodity of trade revived their hopes of fortune. As settlement moved into the backcountry beyond the Blue Ridge after 1730, they turned to buying and selling frontier tracts, the most conspicuous of which was the half-million acres granted to the Ohio Company in 1748. But speculative entrepreneurs of that magnitude were on the ground too early. Not until after the Revolution did they have the freedom to salvage the debt-ridden plantation economy through western ventures.

Although speculation in frontier land contributed to some of the largest colonial fortunes, that business, which repeatedly liquidated itself as each tract was sold off, could be only temporarily important in shaping the economy and society of any locality. The procurors of virgin land might of course carry their lucrative business on and on ahead of advancing settlement, and did so down through the nineteenth century, but a speculator's "estate" produced mere wealth rather than the complex social relationship of an English landlord to his domain. In fact, since land speculation was a business in which the common man could also dabble, it helped keep the middle class of small farmers free from economic domination by any sort of gentry. Nearly all the settlers of Kent in western Connecticut in the 1730s and 1740s were avid speculators as well as farmers, some of whom acquired from ten to forty times the hundred-odd acres needed for a single farm. A brisk trade continued long after the original sale of a tract; one farm lot in Kent changed hands ten times in the first ten years, and the average turnover in the first twenty-five years was four sales per lot.

In a small way the ordinary farmer-speculators could be as "resourceful opportunists and, at worst, conniving dissemblers" as the capitalistic entrepreneurs of that or any later age. Among the settlers of Kent one student has discerned the lineaments not simply of "the contented yeoman" but rather of "the embryo John D. Rockefeller."[16] When the ordinary settlers of the place indignantly petitioned against land engrossment by certain large absentee owners, it was perhaps less a matter of class conflict between farmers and capitalists than of competition between rival sets of land dealers. The land business, more than any other colonial enterprise, involved nearly everyone in the neglect of communal values for the sake of private gain. At the same time, perhaps because of the superficial connection of land speculation with more traditional uses of land—the great planter, the landlord-patroon, and the speculator were all masters of "estates"—Americans who plunged into that universal enterprise did not also explicitly disavow the old-fashioned values of harmony and mutual responsibility between social classes.

Those quasi-medieval social values may explain not only why certain influential individuals were favored with enormous land grants but also why their inferiors bore patiently with such favoritism. Although it is true that "in an aristocracy wealth guarantees status; status conveys privilege; privilege ensures power," the opposite sequence also applies; in colonial America those who had privilege and power could maintain their inherited status and secure opportunities for themselves—land grants in particular—to augment whatever fortune they had begun with.[17] Indeed, great wealth, high status, privilege, and power, and a certain responsibility in using them, were inextricably bound together in the aristocratic ideal which the society still recognized. To the egalitarian modern mind the process whereby "the great families were able to exploit their position for the benefit of their own class" seems an unacceptable conflict of interest.[18] Colonial Americans assumed that, except in cases of gross fraud and collusion, a quite proper *identity* of interest was involved. Since the magnate's ordinary economic, social, and political interests were expected to support each other, they were not normally considered to be incongruous.

The practice of granting broad tracts of the American wilderness to highly placed favorites began as early as the first royal charters to joint-stock companies and lords proprietor. Those grants were assumed to further the general welfare of the English commonwealth, to the upper and middling ranks of which the colonial proprietors or shareholders belonged. So too when they and their successors in turn regranted smaller but still princely parcels of land to favored individuals. When about 1620 the Virginia Company awarded several thousand acres to Sir Thomas Dale, "the first man of his Rank and Degree" to serve as governor, for meritorious service to the colony, the identity of interest between colony and individual leader was clear enough.[19] A New England town in the early years might do the same thing on a much smaller scale for its officers, "to gratulate them for services rendered."[20] A generation later, however, when the foundations of the great Virginia families of the next century were being laid by well-connected young Englishmen who happened to have inherited land claims or stock in the long-defunct company, the public interest had become alloyed with a stronger element of private advantage.

In the eighteenth century this change proceeded much further. Robert Carter—"King" Carter of Corotoman—amassed a great part of his three hundred thousand acres by issuing patents nominally to his sons, grandsons, son-in-law, and other dependents during his twenty years of diligent service as the land agent of the proprietors of the Northern Neck of Virginia. In Lord Baltimore's province of Maryland the onetime indentured servant Daniel Dulany turned his appointment to several influential offices to good account through wholesale speculation in land, much of which he acquired on credit contrary to the regulations expressly laid down by his patron, the lord proprietor. Royal governors like Alexander Spotswood of Virginia and Richard Everard of North Carolina in the 1720s and Benning Wentworth of New Hampshire in the 1760s took full advantage of their position, with the agreeable compliance of the land-hungry gentlemen of their provincial councils, to validate their own irregular claim to scores of thousands of acres of speculative frontier land. Seats on the governor's council, graced in almost every colony by members of the leading families, enabled the councilors themselves to augment the wealth and social standing that had put them there. A few at least were tempted to the most blatant fraud. Colonel Philip Ludwell, councilor and deputy auditor of Virginia, holding a headright warrant for two thousand acres for having brought in a party of forty immigrants, inserted a zero in the official documents and claimed twenty thousand.

The aristocratic influence that permitted such abuses of aristocratic position were, however, abuses of the ancient hierarchical principle that "riches, dignity, and power . . . pertained to the same individuals."[21] Although the cases of avarice and fraud were real enough, they occurred within a social and political system which still accepted an ethos of aristocratic responsibility. It is difficult to assess motives, especially from a *lack* of evidence, but conceivably there were many gentlemen whom a sense of the fitness of things restrained from excessive self-seeking in the offices of land agent, councilor, or governor. The pecuniary motives of the colonial land speculator, great or small, already resembled those of the economic man of the coming nineteenth century, but as a gentleman he also had to pay lip service at least to the old-fashioned obligations of gentility.

The social credentials of colonial merchants were easy enough for the landed gentleman to accept when he himself was so completely a businessman. Something more practical than gentility, however, blunted the keen edge of commercial profit-seeking. The overseas trade in which mercantile fortunes were made had to operate within geographical limits as narrow in their way as those that hedged in the planter and the land speculator. Colonial merchants dealt in three main categories of goods. First, there were the incomparable furs from the Indian country, chiefly beaver pelts from the Northwest and deerskins from the Southwest, trades increasingly concentrated at New York, Philadelphia, and Charleston until they began to decline after 1763. Second, the merchants exported the staple products of colonial agriculture and industry: Chesapeake tobacco, Carolina rice and indigo, Delaware-Susquehanna grain and cattle, New England horses, salt fish, and rum, and ship timber and naval stores from all regions. Third, they handled a great variety of foreign goods, especially English manufactures, West Indian molasses, Portuguese wine, and African slaves. From all these commodities the merchants wove, in the course of the seventeenth and eighteenth centuries, a complex pattern of trade with the Caribbean, West Africa, Southern Europe, and the British Isles, some of it direct, some made up of triangular and even more involuted voyages among a number of far-flung ports. When they could, American ships also intruded into the carrying trade between one foreign country and another.

A considerable part of the colonial trade was kept firmly in the hands of the merchants of London, Bristol, and other English ports and, after 1707, of Glasgow as well. Southern staple exports to Great Britain were handled mainly by factors or agents of English and Scottish firms. In Charleston such an agent might be a native Carolinian, perhaps a part-time planter or a planter's son, who traded on his own account as well, in rice, indigo, deerskins, naval stores, and slaves. But for the most part he dealt on commission for the British merchants who controlled the trade and took the lion's share of the profit. Although during the seventeenth century many Chesapeake planters had a similar share in the tobacco trade, in the eighteenth it fell so completely into the hands of

Glasgow merchants that the young Scotsmen whom they sent out as factors provoked a proverbial enmity among the Virginians. To miscall anyone a "lubber," a "thickskull," a "buckskin," or a "Scotchman" was to place him beneath contempt.[22] In Virginia the tobacco planter was seldom an overseas merchant or agent himself; the resident "sot-weed" factor represented a British businessman to whom the typical planter was deep in debt. Unable to compensate for low tobacco prices by dabbling in foreign trade, the Virginian suffered a double economic disadvantage from which the Charlestonian was happily free.

In the northern colonies, except for the direct importation of English manufactures the overseas trade was generally in the hands of Americans. Their position was only partly due to their ingenuity and enterprise in putting together a mercantile business from the rather unpromising materials at hand. They managed to make a virtue out of the hard fact that their hinterland produced little but timber and naval stores to interest British merchants. Unlike the tobacco, rice, and indigo of warmer parts, the grain, flour, livestock, fish, and rum of the northern provinces were not in demand in England and Northern Europe, which produced enough of their own. A potential demand existed, however, in Madeira, the Azores, and the West Indian sugar islands, which New Englanders began to supply as early as the 1640s. In the eighteenth century Philadelphia and New York as well as Boston, Salem, Newport, Providence, and many smaller Yankee ports battened on this exchange of foodstuffs for the wine of the Atlantic islands and the sugar and molasses of the Caribbean. Colonial merchants also shared in the English trade in slaves between West Africa and the West Indian and North American plantation colonies, paying for the Negroes with New England rum and then trading the human cargo for West Indian molasses from which to distill more rum.

The great diversity of these dealings, however impressive they appear on the conventional map of colonial "triangular trades," in fact indicates the limitations of colonial commerce. Particularly for the New England merchants, undersupplied by the unproductive backcountry of their region, every cargo had to be made up of small consignments of articles of many kinds; to dispose of these and assemble a return cargo might involve dozens of peddling transactions at several foreign ports. The master of the sloop *Rainbow* sailed from Providence in 1758 with the owners' instructions to "make the best of your way to Barbadoes. . . . If you think best Sell there, but if not goe Else where." The brig *George* of Providence cleared for Surinam in July 1768 with 72½ bushels of salt, 2600 feet of pine and 9867 feet of oak boards, 2911 feet of barrel heading, 5600 barrel staves, 46 "shaken hogsheads," 8 barrels of pork and 12 of "beef new and 3½ old," 80 barrels of flour, 94 barrels of alewives and 13 hogsheads of cod, 27 hogsheads and 4 barrels of tobacco, a hogshead of loaf sugar, 400 bricks, 200 boxes of candles, "31 dozen & 7 axes," 8 sheep, and a horse. Four months later the captain reported that he was taking on his return cargo of molasses, "very uncertain when I shall sail as I have my affairs in upward of 80 different hands, and none bad as I know of yet."[23]

A triangular slaving voyage could be particularly arduous. The brig *Sally* left Newport for West Africa in September 1764 with a cargo of rum, rice, candles, tobacco, tar, flour, sugar, coffee, and onions and an armament of seven swivel guns, powder, "40 Hand Cufs" and "40 Shakels," chains, pistols, "Cutleshes," and "Blunder Bursses," altogether worth $14,000. *Sally* arrived on the Guinea coast in November, but until the next August the captain was busy with petty trading both with the local chieftain and with other ship captains, buying and reselling small quantities of other goods as well as bartering parcels of his own cargo for slaves. By the time he weighed anchor on August 20, 1765, he had bought 196 slaves, sold 9, and lost 20 by death. Of his cargo of 167 Negroes, 4 more died before August 28, when, he wrote, the "Slaves Rose on us was obliged to fire on them and Destroyed 8 and Several more wounded badly." The survivors were "so disperited" that "some drowned themselves, some starved and others sickened and died"—88 dead, half the cargo, before *Sally* put into Antigua to sell them. The owners stoically reassured the captain that despite this financial disaster "your Self Continuing in Helth is so Grate Satisfaction to us, . . . we Remain Cheirful under the heavy Loss of our Interests."[24]

In the petty, difficult, and risky business of the colonial merchant the occasional huge return was often enough wiped out by unavoidable miscalculation if not by shipwreck. The only insurance for a prudent man was to spread his investments over a large number of ships and cargoes. Partly for that reason, and partly because of the general shortage of capital, the system of investing in ships and voyages was made remarkably easy, especially in the early years. Commercial ventures were divided into shares small enough for ordinary men to put their money into. In Boston in 1714 there were 544 persons, nearly a third of all the men of the town, who owned shares in the 1621 merchantmen and coasting vessels registered there, and fully 207 of them saw fit to write the honorific title of "merchant" after their names. At Charlestown, Salem, Gloucester, and Newbury the proportion of investors to population was only a little lower.

Within this very miscellaneous class of traders at least a few reached the eminence of English overseas merchants. Andrew Belcher, the leading merchant of Boston in the early eighteenth century, owned shares in 137 ships between 1699 and 1714, and sixty-eight other individuals bought into from 10 to 108 ships each. Samuel Lillie, who owned 52 ships outright, learned the folly of concentrating one's interests in 1707 when he went bankrupt and had to flee to London to escape arrest for debt.[25] Later in the eighteenth century, when vessels were larger and trade more complex, the business was gathered into the hands of a more distinctive class of merchants. Their economic interests were never far removed, however, from those of the ordinary townsman. Although the largest mercantile fortune in Boston at the end of the colonial period was said to approach £100,000, other ranking families had estates of less than £10,000; one of £30,000 was considered very large. Like most planters, farmers, or land speculators, the merchant found that the general limitations on economic progress held in check the growth of his own fortune.

Manufacturing, the last of the colonial ways to wealth, still awaited the industrial revolution of the nineteenth century. Many household needs were supplied by the farm or plantation household itself. Most production for customers or market was done in the shops of master artisans. Like farmers, planters, and many merchants, the master shoemaker, cabinetmaker, or silversmith was a very small proprietor, a capitalist whose hired journeymen and indentured apprentices, aspiring to become masters themselves, shared his economic interests and social outlook. A few craftsmen, like certain planters and merchants, acquired sufficient wealth and standing in the society of Philadelphia, Newport, or Boston to remove them from the run of "leather-apron men." But in spite of the weakness of the English craft-guild tradition in the half-formed occupational structure of the New World, these preindustrial craftsmen still "constituted a vertical, not a horizontal, section of colonial population."[26] The lower ranks of the carpenters or printers did not form an industrial working class or proletariat alienated from their employers.

The one relatively modern industry was iron smelting and forging. Because of the shortage of charcoal in eighteenth-century England, ironmasters in every colony, with inexhaustible forests near at hand and here and there surface deposits of bog iron and limestone, were able to produce pig and bar iron profitably for export as well as for the home market. By 1775 there were more blast furnaces and forges in North America than in England, and they turned out nearly a seventh of the world's supply. Usually remote from towns, even in southeastern Pennsylvania where the industry was most heavily concentrated, the "iron plantation" had to be a well-organized, nearly self-sufficient community of furnaces and forges, iron mines, charcoal house, grist and saw-mills, smithy, common bake oven, general store, workmen's houses, mansion house, and office, fields, orchards, and barns, all surrounded by thousands of acres of woodland for fuel. Such an enterprise required far greater capital than a printing or weaving shop or even a shipyard, ropewalk, or distillery, and the investors could hope for commensurately handsome returns. When five wealthy gentlemen organized the Baltimore ironworks in 1732, their capital investment of £3500 was "larger than anyone in Maryland had ever put into an industrial undertaking."[27] Within thirty years each of the five was making some £400 a year out of it, and the value of each share had risen from the initial £700 to about £10,000. Had there been opportunity for comparable profits in other manufactures, the colonial upper class would have been far richer than it was. But even the charcoal-fired blast furnaces of the eighteenth century were tiny enterprises measured against the steel or textile mills of a hundred years later. In colonial America the most ambitious manufacturing venture was only a little better way to wealth than agriculture, land speculation, commerce, or political influence.

Several of these enterprises had to be combined, in fact, to amass the leading colonial fortunes. The magnate of Charleston, New York, Philadelphia, Newport, Boston, or the Connecticut Valley was likely to be simultaneously a landed gentleman, a merchant, a land speculator, and a provincial official. Henry Laurens, the leading merchant of Charleston in the 1760s, dealt in deerskins, indentured servants, and slaves; as a planter of rice and indigo he owned or controlled some twenty thousand acres; he acted as banker or moneylender to lesser planters and country merchants or storekeepers; and he served nearly continuously in the Commons House of Assembly. The Brown brothers of Providence, commencing as ship captains, added to their mercantile business with the West Indies an ironworks and a spermaceti candle factory. From indentured servitude in a Maryland lawyer's office in 1703 Daniel Dulany rose to an estate of about £30,000 at his death, fifty years later, by means of his law practice, several tobacco plantations operated by overseers, the provincial offices of agent, attorney-general, judge of Vice-Admiralty, commissary-general, and delegate to the Assembly, the sale of tens of thousands of acres in the backcountry, a loan business, the Baltimore ironworks, and one venture in the slave trade.

Like a ship's cargo of a dozen commodities peddled through the West Indies for the accounts of some two dozen owners, the accumulation of such fortunes demonstrates both the variety of economic opportunity open to the enterprising and its limitations. Preoccupied from the beginning of settlement with seizing whatever chance presented, planters, merchants, farmers, and tradesmen were all drawn steadily away from the old social, cultural, and spiritual values of life toward a merely economic ethic of self-aggrandizement. Society, once dominated by, or at least deferential toward, the holy city of Puritan New England, the Quaker inner light of the founders of Pennsylvania, or the Anglican establishment of the southern colonies, slid into the hands of the merely successful.

This "gradual, subtle, but fundamental transformation" of colonial society remained incomplete, however, after a full century and a half of life in America.[28] Although within the first generation or two the new class of Yankee merchants practically displaced ministers and Puritan gentlemen as the ruling elite of New England, still the old English idea that society ought to be ruled by some sort of aristocracy, however constituted, continued to be generally accepted. This conservatism was due not only to the splendid example set by gentlemen worth £10,000 or £30,000, but perhaps equally to the fact that success in several quite different enterprises was required in order to accumulate such a substantial but not overwhelming fortune. Some ten thousand gentlemen in England had estates of more than £30,000, a figure which was a mere fraction of the inheritance of a great nobleman of the eighteenth century—or of the millions of a captain of industry in the America that was yet to be.

A few plantations, a countinghouse, influence at the provincial land office, perhaps shares in ships and ironworks—these would support a new family's pretensions to traditional gentility without tempting them to overweening arrogance or exciting undue envy among lesser men. Since the common man, furthermore, usually had free enough access to land and even to a share in commerce and land speculation to satisfy the petty ambitions of any ordinary Englishman, on the whole he remained unreflectingly content to behave with a measure of old-fashioned deference toward the great planter or merchant. The curious mixture in the colonial economy of widespread opportunity and limited upward mobility enabled Americans to emulate the traditional English pattern of a society based on rank or degree while inching their way toward the economic revolution that one day would quite overwhelm that old social order.

5. COMMONWEALTH

The contemporary English ideal of the commonwealth, in which the interest of every part would be harmoniously subordinated to the larger interest of the whole society, acted more explicitly as a brake, both on the acquisitive drive of individuals and on the general economic progress of colonial America, than the already somewhat archaic expectations of upper-class responsibility. In the conventional view, in any case, self-restraint had never been sufficient, on any level of society, to ensure the general welfare. Public regulation was always required to make men of every class accept their social responsibilities.

The special form which public economic policy took in the seventeenth and eighteenth centuries is usually described in terms of mercantilism, the theory and practice of the competing commercial systems of the maritime European empires of that time. Their immediate objective was a favorable balance of trade, and a strong naval defense, against the rest of the world. But state regulation of the economy still sought, at least tacitly, something far broader: a stable, harmonious social order. Beyond that it still looked, a little perfunctorily now, to the supremely moral goal of Christian salvation of souls. Although plain economic purposes were almost everywhere on the ascendant, the American colonists still acknowledged the spiritual and social values inherited from the Middle Ages. But whatever ends their public measures sought, the colonists believed that government had the right and duty, in the name of their particular provincial commonwealth or that of the larger commonwealth of the empire, to direct and to restrict their economic development as well as to promote it.

Theory and practice coincided most closely in New England. Although Calvinism had cast off the authority of pope and bishops, the economic ordinances of the Puritan provinces followed an ethical code inherited from the medieval scholastics. As good men of the Reformation, New Englanders pursued their earthly callings or businesses as intently as they sought their spiritual calling, having been divinely predestined for both vocations alike. But economic activity, which held peculiar temptations to the mortal sin of avarice, could not safely be left to free enterprise or individual conscience. The manner in which a man pursued wealth, and his use of it when he had won it, had to be governed for the sake of his own spiritual welfare and of the good order of the community. Human society was no less necessary to him than food, clothing, and shelter. Lest excessive delight in the acquisition and enjoyment of wealth usurp, above all, his affection for heaven, he was to seek it, in Roger Williams's words, "with dead and weaned, and mortified affections."[1]

Some of the absolute prohibitions of the medieval church and state had already been relaxed in England long before the era of colonization. Usury, in the old sense of the taking of any interest whatsoever on loans, was forbidden only when pushed to a "biting extremity," defined by Massachusetts law as more than a modest 8 percent.[2] Puritan moralists from John Winthrop in 1630 to Cotton Mather in 1695 agreed, however, that no one ought to lend at interest unless he could reasonably expect that the borrower would be able to repay. If a necessitous person could not make restitution, even after the money had been lent him in good faith, he was to be forgiven both principal and interest. A poor man was a proper object of charity, not of moneylending.

The notion of moneylending as a species of Christian charity was already a practical anachronism even in New England in the seventeenth century, but the medieval concept of public regulation of market prices was accepted in principle everywhere and enforced at least in the Puritan colonies. When men of that age spoke of every article's having its "just price," they referred, like later economists, not so much to an intrinsic value as to one calculated according to scarcity of supply and degree of demand. What they insisted upon, however, was that the scarcity not be artificially rigged by speculators. By provincial law one might not contrive to profit by "forestalling" the flow of goods to market, "engrossing" or cornering the supply, or "regrating," the ancient term for buying cheap and selling dear. Just price also meant a just wage, since "price" in the preindustrial economy was the colloquial term both for the wages of the journeyman cordwainer or blacksmith and for the sum his master charged for boots or horseshoes.

But public regulation extended beyond determining the natural ratio between supply and demand. It was especially necessary in a newly settled colony, when both goods and labor were in desperately short supply, to keep merchants and workingmen alike from the temptation to overcharge. In the 1630s the General Court of Massachusetts Bay attempted first to set the price of grain at no more than six shillings a bushel and artisans' wages at no more than two shillings for the twelve-hour working day; it soon substituted a blanket prohibition of "unreasonable prices" and "excessive wages"; and within a few years, such ceilings proving difficult to enforce, the court empowered the various towns to set prices and wages for themselves.[3]

The duty of civil authority, whether provincial or local, to punish "oppression" or "extortion" was never abrogated either in New England or elsewhere. Edward Palmer, convicted in 1639 of overcharging the town of Boston for a set of stocks, was fittingly sentenced by the town magistrates to be the first to sit in them. To buy a pair of boots at ten shillings and sell them again for fifteen, as Thomas Clark did at Plymouth in 1639, was condemned as extortion; for John Barnes to pay four shillings a bushel for rye and then, "without adventure or long forbearance in one and the same place"—that is, without the risk of transport or even the cost of storage—to resell it for five shillings was held to be illegal regrating.[4] Governor Winthrop recorded the case of a certain laborer who "took great wages above others, and would not work but for ready money, . . . scraped together about 25 pounds, and then returned with his prey into England, speaking evil of the country by the way."[5] But as the governor noted with satisfaction in his journal, the ungrateful profiteer was robbed of his riches in England and soon had to return to start over; divine justice pursued where Puritan magistrates could not. God's displeasure was no less plain against a Mr. Taylor, who had charged too much for milk and, "being after at a sermon wherein oppression was complained of . . . fell distracted."[6]

Not every case was so clear-cut. For overcharging for nails, buttons, and other articles Robert Keayne, a prosperous and respectable merchant of Boston, was punished by state and church alike in 1639. Fined £200 by the court, he was admonished "in the Name of the Church for selling his wares at excessive Rates, to the Dishonor of God's name, the offense of the Generall Cort, and the Publique scandall of the Cuntry."[7] Keayne, who was as devout a Puritan as Winthrop himself, never ceased to maintain his innocence. Even the most conscientious soul-searchers could differ on the precise line between just and oppressive prices. The appeal of

Mistress Anne Hutchinson's heresy of "antinomianism" (antiau-
thoritarianism) to many Bostonians in the mid-1630s, it has been
suggested, lay not only in her theological doctrine but also in a
certain restiveness against the commercial regulations laid down
by the magistrates. But although in later years the commercial
viewpoint steadily undermined the rigor of the original Puritan
ethic, not even colonial merchants ever wholly rejected the principle that economic self-interest ought to be governed according to
higher considerations. Whenever an emergency, from King Philip's
War in the 1670s to the Revolution a hundred years later, caused
the inflationary stringency of the early years to recur, government
was called upon to fix a just scale of prices and wages.

The concept of the just price was bound up with the broader
idea that persons of every social class or "degree" should have their
appropriate duties and rewards. The "middling" and "inferior"
sorts ought not to strive for the means with which to ape the
style of living of their betters. The Massachusetts General Court
in 1651 forbade persons "of mean condition [to] take upon them
the garb of Gentlemen, by wearing Gold or Silver lace, or Buttons,
or Points at their knees, or to walk in great Boots; or Women of
the same rank to wear Silk or Tiffiny hoods, or Scarfes"; such dress
was permissible only for the families of persons with estates over
£200, magistrates, military officers, and others "whose education
and imployment have been above the ordinary degree, or whose
estate have been considerable, though now decayed."[8] Again in
1672 a committee of the General Court censured "the excess of
pride of meane people that will weare no other shoes generally
but of the newest fashion and highest price" and who therefore
refused to work "but for Such wages what will mayntaine them in
this profuse expensive manner."[9] Regulation of the sale and use
of wine and tobacco or the wearing of silks, lace, and furs was intended not only to curb pride and vanity in all classes but particularly, as Cotton Mather preached in 1679, to prevent "Servants
and the poorer sort of People" from rising "above their estates
and degrees."[10] That such laws and sermons did not prevent a
considerable number of individuals from edging upward is suggested by the fact that magistrates and preachers saw a need to
enunciate them. Although the trend of the times lay in the direction
of individual mobility, private ambition was still expected to hew
fairly close to the social pattern sanctioned by tradition and authority.

In no phase of life did Puritan moral and social values more fully direct the course of economic progress than in the system the New Englanders devised for organizing new settlements. Most of them had originally been attracted to America for their souls' sake rather than simply to acquire wealth, and as they spread inland they spurned the permissiveness of other provinces seeking to lure immigration and promote economic development. Placing foremost the higher ends of the church and of the social order that supported it, they carried their tightly regulated system substantially unchanged onto the eighteenth-century frontier.

The original settlements of Plymouth, Massachusetts Bay, and Connecticut were shortly organized as townships or "towns," each one identical in membership with a single congregation. Each province supervised the laying out of later towns in the same way. Whenever migration from one of the older towns was required by the pressure of the prolific and long-lived population, together with "the strong bent of their spirits," as at Cambridge in 1635, the General Court of the colony granted a suitable tract of land to the migrating group, who were organized in one capacity as a board of proprietors of the common holding and in another as a new church and congregation.[11] The land proprietors, who in the seventeenth century were simply the original settlers, divided a portion of their new domain among themselves and held the rest in common for second and third distributions in which later arrivals and the rising generation might share. Apart from a small payment to extinguish any remaining Indian "title," the land was not sold; as the common property of society it passed into individual ownership for the common good. Whether their English background led the proprietors to lay out the allotments on the house-lot and open-field system of the Midlands or on the East Anglian and West Country pattern of enclosed farms, each town clustered about a central village and meetinghouse or perhaps, in the course of time, two or three such centers. This pattern ensured proper supervision of society by the town authorities, who, although they were democratically elected by the body of freemen, were regarded as answerable to God for faithful performance of the implicit covenant of the community with Him. (See Figures 1 and 2.)

Since rank or degree was the main prop of the social order prescribed both by scripture and by English custom, the proprietors paid due heed to the social standing of gentleman, yeoman, artisan, and laborer in allotting sufficient land to maintain each one at his proper station in life. The acreage which men received considerably exceeded whatever their estates had been before, either in England

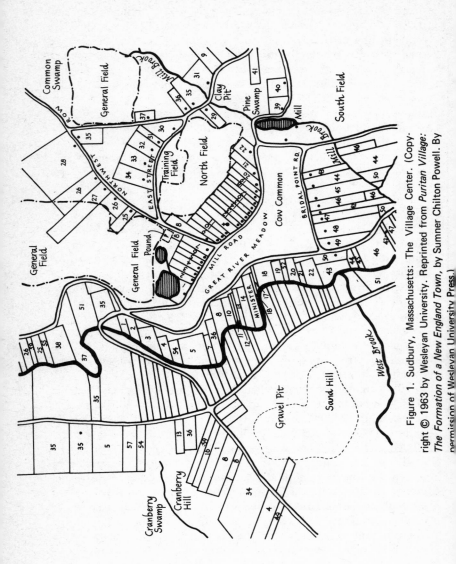

Figure 1. Sudbury, Massachusetts: The Village Center. (Copyright © 1963 by Wesleyan University. Reprinted from *Puritan Village: The Formation of a New England Town*, by Sumner Chilton Powell. By permission of Wesleyan University Press.)

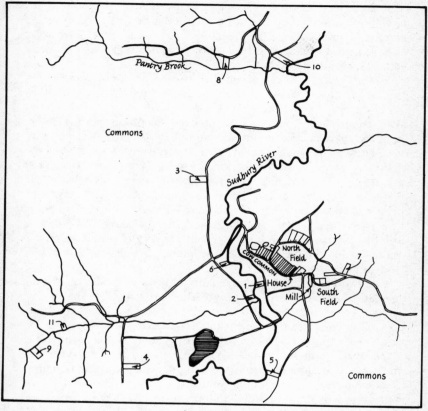

Figure 2. Grants of Land to John Goodnow, Sudbury. (Copyright © 1963 by Wesleyan University. Adapted from *Puritan Village: The Formation of a New England Town,* by Sumner Chilton Powell. By permission of Wesleyan University Press.)

or in their former town in New England, but the order of precedence among them was followed, perhaps modified by a shrewd guess at the future weightiness of certain promising individuals in town affairs. The hierarchy of property thus set up at the first land division might be rearranged when later divisions were made, as reputations rose or fell for reasons now obscure but once well enough known to the townsfolk. No one doubted that a well-defined social order was necessary.

As with other kinds of economic regulation, the principle of public control of settlement in New England survived long after a looser mode of practical operation had made it a hollow shell. Well before 1716, when the New England colonies began the practice of frankly auctioning off the land of newly projected western townships to the highest bidders, it was already the case that a proprietor of a new settlement was far more a land speculator than a custodian of a fledgling society. Merely economic considerations —revenue for the provincial treasury and personal profit for the investors—displaced the old religious and social ends. By that time New England had come to much the same stage of secularization as that which Virginia, Maryland, New York, the Carolinas, and most of the other colonies had already reached within their first few years.

Everywhere south of New England all sorts of public economic regulation tended to wither away early, partly because they were difficult to enforce but also because, in the absence of Puritan social compulsions, they seemed less necessary as the supply of goods and of labor increased. Only during the anxious early years of colonization or for some urgent purpose—such as the Virginia project of 1662 to build a town at James City by drafting building tradesmen from the counties to work at fixed wages—did the various provincial authorities attempt to fix prices and wages or to regulate consumption according to rank. Usually they were uncertain how to apply the conventional regulatory devices in the New World. Since cheap land was readily available to the ordinary man, for instance, rigorous wage controls would only drive artisans out of their own trades into farming, further reducing the supply of skilled labor and thereby forcing wages still higher. Far from abandoning the principle of social control, however, town or county authorities readily invoked it whenever it seemed useful. Charleston inveighed against forestalling, engrossing, and regrating in the local market as late as 1786. The medieval assize of bread—the official fixing of the price and weight of the standard loaf—persisted in many places throughout the eighteenth century, and the fees of men with some scarce professional skill—lawyers, surgeons, and apothecaries—were systematically regulated, even if laborers' wages were not.

Everywhere in eighteenth-century America, however, governmental regulation of the economy quite lost sight of such old spiritual and social ends as maintaining hierarchy in society and keeping greedy profiteers from being led into temptation. The goal of the official mercantilist policy of the age was still the welfare of the entire society or commonwealth, but this was now narrowly defined in the purely material terms of fostering trade and industry, from which everyone presumably would benefit. To promote economic progress in the eighteenth-century terms of a balanced trade, however, entailed a great deal of public regulation that was expressly calculated to have as restrictive, even regressive an effect on certain kinds of economic enterprise as the old ethical code.

According to mercantilist theory, the economy of the commonwealth ought to be sufficiently diversified to supply most of its own needs and a surplus for export more valuable than the things which it still had to import from abroad. Each of the American colonies, having no political ties to the others except through London and regarding itself as a detached economic entity, hoped to attain its own self-sufficiency and favorable balance of trade with its neighbors and the mother country as well as with the rest of the world. At the same time, the colonies accepted the role of members of the greater commonwealth of the British empire, each contributing to the imperial economy not through diversification and self-sufficiency but by specialization in those things that it could most usefully and efficiently produce. Since staple production and export of rice and indigo and importation of English manufactures were profitable to the South Carolinians, they were generally content with the imperial system. Since a similar concentration on tobacco seemed to bring the Virginia planters nothing but debt, they grumbled at the imperial economy and experimented with other crops to make their own commonwealth more self-sufficient. New England merchants, who were favored by certain imperial regulations and felt oppressed by others, battened on the former and evaded the latter by smuggling. But for all the complaints against specific applications of mercantilist principles, the open smuggling of goods, and the bribing of customs officers, it did not occur to Americans that government ought not to regulate trade whenever it might seem necessary and useful.

The Chesapeake colonies, frequently burdened with an over-abundant and unprofitable tobacco crop, were as active in devising means for self-regulation as in petitioning against imperial regulation. As early as 1640 Virginia destroyed half its crop and ordered further production cut back for the next two years; unfortunately the Maryland planters set about growing more and depressed the price again. Since no colony, as it happened, produced the entire supply of any crop or manufacture, restrictions of that sort were uncommon. Promoting the export trade was easier than attempting to limit production. A province could improve the reputation of its staples in foreign markets by keeping the local producers up to a decent standard of quality. In 1731 Virginia inaugurated the most elaborate and effective program, a system of official warehouses where all export tobacco was inspected and whole hogsheads of defective leaf were destroyed without compensation. Within a year the price of tobacco rose about five times. Massachusetts had undertaken to "gauge" the proper packing of beef and pork for export as early as 1641, and New York did so by 1665. Sooner or later every colony regulated the quality of its chief export commodities: fish in New England and New York, flour and bread in Maryland and the Middle Colonies, the rum of the Middle Colonies and New England, timber and naval stores almost everywhere, and, at various times and places, hemp, flax, grain, butter, rice, malt, indigo, horses, leather, and even commodities in general. All the colonies likewise offered bounties, particularly during the eighteenth century, to stimulate production or export of hemp, flax, silk, cloth, wheat (especially in the southern colonies), ships, and other goods. Few of these governmental attempts to diversify production actually succeeded in overcoming unfavorable natural conditions and the inertia of farmers and planters toward unfamiliar crops and the risk of endangering such profits as they were getting from the customary ones. The hope that bounties and inspection systems would stimulate a substantially higher rate of economic progress generally went unfulfilled. The principle, however, survived unbroken into the nineteenth century.

The imperial mercantile system of course did not. Less a system in fact than an untidy accretion of various Parliamentary Acts of Trade and Navigation between 1660 and 1760, the British imperial arrangements are the best remembered of the public economic regulations of that age because of the currency, until recent years, of an economic interpretation of the causes of the American Revolution. In fact, most historians of the period have now concluded, the imperial trading system had little importance in provoking the Revolution or even in shaping the internal economies of most of the colonies. The colonists themselves tolerated the system the more readily because only a few of the British regulations bore heavily on them, and most of those could be evaded without undue trouble.

The requirement, dating from 1660, that trade within the empire should move in English ships manned by English crews (or British after the Act of Union with Scotland in 1707) worked to the advantage of the colonies, since American-built ships and American seamen, and for that matter American merchants, were considered to be English. Although American vessels were reputed to be less well built as well as cheaper than those from British yards, a large part of the imperial merchant fleet came from America, especially in wartime when many English-built ships were pressed into naval service. A second category of regulations discouraged trade from northern Europe to the colonies by requiring transshipment and payment of duties at a British port. It is likely, however, that because of the commercial and personal connections between American and British merchants and the fashionableness of English styles and manufactures in the colonies, England would have held the lion's share of colonial business even without the Acts of Trade. Anyway, the Acts left the rest of Europe south of Cape Finisterre, including the Azores and Madeira, quite open to a direct and profitable trade in American rice, salt fish, and other foodstuffs and timber in exchange for salt—to preserve more fish—and Portuguese wines.

The most burdensome regulation was the Parliamentary "enumeration" of certain colonial commodities which could be sent only to Great Britain or to other British colonies. Although they could then be transshipped elsewhere, the additional cost of this procedure reduced the foreign market for such goods while enriching merchants in British ports. The enumerated list, beginning with tobacco, indigo, and cotton in the early 1660s, was extended in the eighteenth century, at least for certain periods of years, to such other commodities as rice, naval stores, furs, and British West Indian molasses. Some of these restrictions were practically meaningless. Enumeration of naval stores did not limit the market for them, since Britain needed all the masts, ship timbers, and pitch that the colonies could send and indeed offered bounties in the hope of getting more. As for furs, the French, who down to 1763 had their own much richer source of supply in Canada, supplied the continental European market.

Only two important items in the North American trade were onerously restricted by the Acts: molasses and tobacco. Molasses and sugar might be quite freely imported from the British West Indies for the northern distilleries, a transaction entirely within the imperial system. To compensate the West Indian planters for loss of a wider market, however, the Molasses Act of 1733 laid prohibitive duties on imports from the Spanish, French, and Dutch islands in the Caribbean. But since colonial thirst for rum easily absorbed the legal supply of duty-free molasses, North American merchants found that smuggling the forbidden varieties was well worth the risk—especially since the foreign trade also brought in hard cash to reduce their unfavorable balance of accounts with the mother country. Like the moderate revenue duties on Portuguese wines which they also generally evaded, the Molasses Act made business somewhat awkward but had little economic effect either on commerce or on distilling.

Tobacco, on the other hand, was the one enumerated staple export of North America that usually glutted the British market, even though the law sought to compensate the Chesapeake planters by forbidding tobacco growing in England—it had been successfully begun in the West Country in the seventeenth century. The great continental European market, which the Virginians briefly penetrated through Holland in the anarchic 1650s, was thus denied them after 1660, unless the tobacco was transshipped in England at prices that discouraged foreign demand. The complaints of the Chesapeake planters in the eighteenth century against the Acts of Trade, the supposed cause of their perennial insolvency, were the louder for the fact that they were the only Americans who were totally unable—since they were not shippers as well as growers of tobacco—to evade a restriction they regarded as unwise or oppressive.

Three kinds of colonial manufacturing were also regulated by laws which did not in fact significantly restrict them. According to mercantilist theory, it was the duty of a colony to supply suitable raw materials and of the mother country to send back whatever manufactures the colony could not make for itself. By acts of 1699 and 1732 the export of woolens and hats from any colony was forbidden, but in fact there was little intercolonial trade in those domestic manufactures. The Iron Act of 1750 reserved to the mother country a monopoly of the advanced processes of iron-rolling and slitting, but it was fairly easy for colonial ironmasters to escape official notice at their remote works, and for that matter the pig iron and bar iron that the act admitted duty-free into England gave them plenty of scope. It is true that certain other British regulations, such as the Privy Council's recurrent suppression of paper currency, with which various colonies tried to remedy their chronic lack of specie, hampered economic development more directly and annoyingly. The mercantile system held out solid advantages too: the favored position in the British market and the Royal Navy's protection of colonial shipping at purely British expense. But in general the imperial system had far less effect on the colonial economy, either as stimulus or restraint, than the natural environment and economic and social self-regulation by the Americans themselves.

The spiritual, social, and economic ideas that Americans inherited from their European past, varying in relative emphasis from region to region over the course of a century and a half, were perhaps less effective in holding back change than the practical circumstances of the New World. The barely tractable wilderness —waterways, forest, soil, aborigines—and the chronic shortage of labor for its exploitation or reduction were the most stubborn obstacles in the way of private enrichment and the general affluence of the commonwealth. Even while tempting men to shelve the spiritual and social ethic of the past in a rush of individualistic free enterprise, the North American continent bound them down under iron laws of its own. Although circumstances did not precisely reinforce the old ideas of what was socially fitting, neither were those traditions swept away overnight—in fact not until long after the end of the colonial era. The hemming in of economic progress kept the old European social values remarkably safe from radical upheaval. That would come later.

III. The First American Society

In view of the novelty of its circumstances, American society enjoyed remarkable stability and order during its first century and a half. Perched on the rim of a continental wilderness, forced to improvise an economic base out of unfamiliar climate, soil, crops, and distant markets, and arbitrarily ruled off into a dozen detached political jurisdictions, the first few generations of Americans nevertheless established a social order that seemed, in 1775, as likely to endure as any. Although the civilization of the Old World could not be transplanted across the ocean intact, neither the sea change nor the new environment radically deranged or dissipated that older order of things. In many respects the New World acted instead as a preservative of old ways. At a time when Western Europe itself was progressively falling away from the medieval ideal of an organic, status-bound community toward the modern liberal society theoretically composed of freely contracting individuals, the fledgling provinces of British North America held back from the brink of the social revolution that would shortly engulf the whole Atlantic world. The economic progress of colonial America was solid and substantial, but its gradual pace enabled the colonists to cling, as habit or inertia usually makes men prefer to do, to the values of the old familiar social order in which the traditional institutions of class, family, community, and church were still interlocked.

6. RANK AND DEGREE

At no point did the colonial American's received ideas about the structure of his society diverge more sharply from the way a statistician might objectively measure it than in the existence of a hierarchy of classes amid relative equality of wealth. Colonial classes reproduced one distinctive characteristic of the English class structure in being "separated by no marked lines," as Thomas Jefferson observed, "but shading off imperceptibly from top to bottom."[1] The colonial spectrum extended through little more, however, than the middle bands of English society. The half-developed, hand-to-mouth American economy provided, at one end, a decent subsistence for the majority but, at the other, only modest wealth for even the most fortunate. Nevertheless the colonists deferred to rank, or accepted its privileges and responsibilities, as though they still belonged to the society of London, East Anglia, or the West Country, where the pattern of social classes had been maturing for a thousand years.

The upper range, occupied in England by the nobility, the lesser gentry, and the great merchants, was represented in colonial society by a single almost undifferentiated elite. This varied from region to region according to the means available for gaining wealth. Perhaps because there were few practical occasions—economic, social, or political—for the wealthy merchants of one region to set themselves off against the great planters of another, it was not questioned that the status of one kind of gentleman was equivalent to that of the other. In any one province, indeed, the planters, merchants, land speculators, and such industrial entrepreneurs as there might be were very likely the selfsame persons. Still close to the sources of their fortunes in field or countinghouse, they were all working proprietors and capitalists on a modest scale.

Except for a few of the royal governors, who came and went, and an odd resident landlord like Lord Fairfax in the Northern Neck of Virginia, there were no noblemen—no dukes, marquises, earls, viscounts, or barons, and hardly any knights—to grace colonial society. The gentlemen of the governor's council, when they presumed to act as the provincial equivalent to the House of Lords, risked being told, as they were by the assembly in New York in 1693, that "the most opulent families, in our own memory, have risen from the lowest ranks of people." In no colony were they "another distinct state or rank of people in the constitution" like the House of Lords; as was well understood in the eighteenth century, they were "all commons," appointed to office and "hold[ing] their places during pleasure" of the governor, who was himself a mere appointee of crown or proprietor.² Ordinary members of the General Court, House of Burgesses, or Commons House of Assembly, since custom or law usually required them to be residents of the town or county for which they sat, sometimes seemed, to better-educated contemporaries, no better than "plain, illiterate husbandmen, whose views seldom extended farther than to the regulation of highways, the destruction of wolves, wild cats, and foxes, and the advancement of the other little interests of the particular counties which they were chosen to represent."³ They were not even figuratively knights of the shire.

At best the colonial gentleman resembled no one more closely than the upper-middle-class English townsman, the merchant-capitalist who had his country seat or manor as well as his townhouse and countinghouse. The title of "burgess" was adopted in Virginia for the assemblyman before it became apparent that boroughs were not going to spring up all across the plantation region, but as an equivalent for *bourgeois* in the sense of middle class it could well have been used everywhere. In agrarian Virginia as in mercantile New England, many of the leaders of society had remote connections with English merchant families, and like successful English merchants they regarded their landed estates as the most visible and practical patent of gentility. In the absence of anyone more exalted, these men of recently minted fortunes, few of which were as great as £30,000, played the role of provincial magnates quite credibly.

If "none of us grow very rich," the second William Byrd of Westover wrote of his Virginia neighbors in 1731, "the felicity of the climate hinders us from being very poor."⁴ Even in less temperate regions than the Chesapeake the broad mass of colonial Americans were quite well-off—"the middling sort"—by English standards. The small planters and farmers of the tobacco region, working a dozen or half-dozen slaves or none, the freeholding farmers of New England and the Delaware-Susquehanna region who dabbled in buying and selling real estate, even the tenant farmers of the Hudson Valley, together with shopkeepers and master artisans throughout the colonies, differed from the great planters, merchants, and land speculators of the colonial elite not so much in kind as in degree of material success. The ordinary farmer calculated his worth in land, livestock, and sometimes slaves by the hundreds of pounds against the magnate's thousands, but a poor New England hill farm that yielded a bare subsistence might be valued at £300, at least one hundredth the order of magnitude of the greatest colonial estates. Compared to the economic and social gulf between an English cottager and his noble landlord or, in nineteenth-century America, between a captain of industry and his laborers and clerks—or the small farmer of his time—the colonial gap was narrow enough. To an English observer in 1772 all rural New Englanders appeared much alike:

Nobody in these parts has the idea of a Superior, or of a Gentleman, other than themselves. They seem to be a good substantial Kind of farmers, but there is no break in their Society; their Government, Religeon, and Manners all tend to support an equality.[5]

The bottom ranks of colonial society were even less set apart as a definable class than were the gentry. Poor, landless individuals there were in considerable variety: longshoremen, ropewalkworkers, sailors, and other casual laborers about the docks of the port cities; freed servants just "out of their time"; the "lubbers," squatters, and poor whites who appeared at an early date in the South; the unfortunate old and indigent, the debilitated or insane, widows and paupers; and, perhaps most numerous, ordinary men's sons who were not yet established on their own as farmers or artisans. It has been demonstrated that nearly a third of the white men of Virginia at the end of the colonial era neither owned nor rented land. But it is also true that no such statistical or occupational category constituted a colonial working *class* in either their own or others' estimation. How many of these obscure persons hoped or expected to acquire land and reputable standing it is impossible to guess, but the possibility was real enough to prevent their thinking of themselves as members of a fixed class of peasants or paupers like men of their economic level in the old country.

Indentured servants and Negro slaves undeniably were laborers, but they formed no single laboring class within colonial society. Indeed, the oddity of their position was caused by the lack of any such class. Brought into the colonies by unusual, even violent, means in order to ease the chronic dearth of labor, both of these servile groups were beneath society rather than institutional components of it. White servants earned their freedom by a few years of bond labor and melted away into ordinary society. Negro slaves, at the other extreme, endured from one generation to the next the obloquy of caste. As the mere chattel property of individual masters, isolated like so many draft animals on detached farms and plantations, they were outcasts or helots rather than members of a class within society. The "place" allotted to the Negro was certainly not among other laboring men and women in a common working class.

An upper class of no great wealth or antiquity, a miscellaneous lower class whose disparate elements added up to considerably less than a majority of society, a broad middle class of various kinds of independent proprietors: by any objective measurement colonial Americans belonged to a fairly level structure with relatively great opportunity for the propertyless young man to improve his condition and status. But in their own estimation their society, although obviously simpler than the older European society of which it was a branch, was properly ordered by "Ranks and Degrees." Even Quakers, for all their humble origins and doctrine of spiritual equality, could extol, as the Philadelphia Yearly Meeting did in 1722, "the true honour and obedience due from Subjects to their Prince, inferiors to superiors, from Children to Parents, and servants to Masters."[6] If the circumstances of life in the New World sometimes gave a disturbingly loose rein to change and disorder, those were defects that time would remedy; stability and hierarchy were the old-fashioned social values which they sought to maintain despite the challenge of the ocean on one side and the wilderness on the other.

In the almost complete absence of lords, knights, bishops, deans, generals and admirals, or, in the entire course of 170 years, so much as a single peregrination by any royal personage, the less honorific English titles had to serve as precisely as possible to denote social rank. It was well enough to call a servant or slave simply by his Christian name of Tom or Pompey without a distinguishing prefix, except for such special locutions as "Negro Sam" or "Negro Suckey."[7] For the common man—the freeholding farmer or master artisan with servants—the old English "goodman" sufficed, at least in the seventeenth century, and "goodwife" for his spouse. "Master" or "Mr." and "Mistress" were still titles of distinction in the seventeenth century, reserved for the small minority who prided themselves on being on a par with the lesser gentry of England—the clergymen, lawyers, physicians, magistrates, large farmers or planters, the wealthier merchants and other businessmen, and of course masters of arts. (As late as the 1770s a degree put one on a level in polite society with men of estates of £10,000, so a graduate of Nassau Hall discovered in Virginia.) "Esquire," although accorded to very few in New England in the first generation, later was assumed there and elsewhere by such local and provincial dignitaries as justices of the county courts and members of the governors' councils, as a perquisite of office. As in contemporary England, the title was claimed by others of wealth and influence as a merely social distinction. On both sides of the Atlantic the word "gentleman," while retaining a suggestion of hereditary rank and freedom from manual labor, was now loosely used to connote a more generalized sort of social superiority, though not yet simply personal virtue wherever found. Although the self-made merchant or landowner was still a hardworking businessman, he reached a significant plateau in public esteem when he could write "Gent." after his name. Among the three generations of New Englanders in the seventeenth century hardly two hundred persons were formally recognized in public documents as gentlemen.

The fact that different legal papers ascribed "Gent.," "Esq.," and "Mr." to the same individual, or left his name quite unadorned by titles, indicates that social mobility made the accepted principle of hierarchy rather awkward to apply. Four-fifths of the men who were accorded those titles in Maryland in the mid-seventeenth century had not been called by them in England; a sort of "shipboard mobility" seems to have set in even while crossing the ocean.[8] In the eighteenth century, when colonial society was somewhat more settled, one might still presume to dub himself a personage of some sort of rank. Thus the word "merchant," which in England suggested a certain commercial eminence well above the general run of small traders, shopkeepers, and peddlers, was appended to their names by quite ordinary Americans on the strength of a few shares in a ship or cargo. The militia likewise provided titles, of rather uncertain social precedence, for many an otherwise undistinguished farmer, tradesman, or innkeeper whose neighbors elected him a company officer. For a man of the middling sort to be addressed as captain or colonel must have been immensely gratifying, especially in the eighteenth century, when commissioned rank in England was the preserve of persons of decidedly greater wealth and loftier social connections. A plethora of military titles perhaps helped, in an aristocratically minded society, to compensate for the actual dearth of distinctive social ranks; it continued to do so, oddly enough, well into the avowedly egalitarian nineteenth century.

The privileges of rank, especially of the highly mutable ranks of an immature society, required a good deal of calculation. The proprietors of new towns in seventeenth-century New England had to assess their own relative social worth in deciding how much land to allot to each, and from time to time the lawmakers and magistrates tried to restrain lesser men and women from affecting fashions in clothing that were overly sumptuous for their class. Overweening presumption had to be put down. For a tradesman to race his horse against a gentleman's, as a Virginia tailor did in 1674, might cost him a fine; for a planter's daughter to marry an overseer, "a dirty plebeian, without any kind of merit," as William Byrd remarked in 1732, was "the lowest prostitution."[9] Although all Christians—certainly all Puritan church members—were no doubt equal in God's sight, the allocation of their pews in church or meetinghouse was a matter of social protocol and had to be most carefully weighed "according to age, dignity, and [property-tax] list," as a Connecticut town meeting voted in 1744.[10] (See Figure 3.) At Harvard College the members of each freshman class were "placed" in an order of seniority, based originally upon some calculus of social and academic merit, by 1750 simply upon their fathers' conventional precedence as colonial governors, councilors, justices of the peace, plain Harvard graduates, or something less. Once ranked, an undergraduate kept his seniority through graduation, unless perhaps degraded a few places for misbehavior. When the system was given up, with the Harvard class of 1773, for an uninvidiously alphabetical order, no egalitarian reform was intended. Quite the contrary: the faculty was weary of the frequent "inconveniences" in trying to disentangle "the supposed Dignities of the Families" of county justices punctilious over whose commission bore the earlier date.[11]

As wealth accumulated among the families of fortunate planters, merchants, and other enterprisers, it supported a style of living grand enough to render unnecessary, by the end of the seventeenth century, the sumptuary laws that had once helped to distinguish greater from lesser folk. Americans of the better sort were never in doubt as to the most fitting way to display their good fortune. The constant flow of imperial trade, the example set by royal

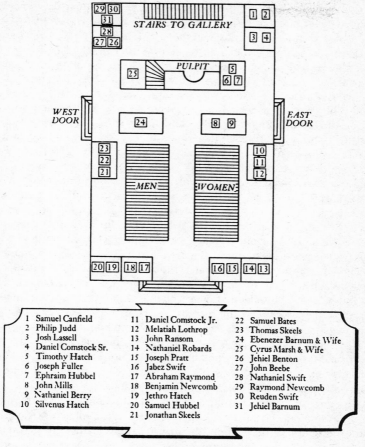

1	Samuel Canfield	11	Daniel Comstock Jr.
2	Philip Judd	12	Melatiah Lothrop
3	Josh Lassell	13	John Ransom
4	Daniel Comstock Sr.	14	Nathaniel Robards
5	Timothy Hatch	15	Joseph Pratt
6	Joseph Fuller	16	Jabez Swift
7	Ephraim Hubbel	17	Abraham Raymond
8	John Mills	18	Benjamin Newcomb
9	Nathaniel Berry	19	Jethro Hatch
10	Silvenus Hatch	20	Samuel Hubbel
		21	Jonathan Skeels

22	Samuel Bates
23	Thomas Skeels
24	Ebenezer Barnum & Wife
25	Cyrus Marsh & Wife
26	Jehiel Benton
27	John Beebe
28	Nathaniel Swift
29	Raymond Newcomb
30	Reuden Swift
31	Jehiel Barnum

Figure 3. Kent Meetinghouse, 1743-1744. The front seats, especially those around the pulpit, were most desirable and honorific. (Adapted from Charles S. Grant, *Democracy in the Connecticut Frontier Town of Kent,* p. 163. New York: Columbia University Press, 1961.)

governors and other English placemen, and their own occasional sojourns in London kept them abreast of current metropolitan fashion. The townhouse of the merchant of Boston, Newport, New York, or Philadelphia, the country seat of the Chesapeake or Carolina planter or Hudson Valley landlord, and the rambling mansion of many a weighty villager displayed the comfortable signs of English gentility: Georgian brick and stonework, furnishings after Chippendale, sideboards heavy with plate, walls lined with imported "Stampt Paper in rolls" and hung with family portraits, and a library of hundreds, sometimes thousands, of classical and reputable modern volumes. From periwigs, Nassau silks, "scarlet coats and waistcoats, laced and fringed," to coaches, calashes, chaises, and carriages emblazoned with the family arms and attended by footmen in livery, these provincial social distinctions were copied, if not actually imported, from England. They were not the artifacts of an indigenous American culture, though American silversmiths, cabinetmakers, and house carpenters devised their own graceful simplifications of English models. Too much perhaps has been made of what a tutor in Virginia in 1773 called the "overgrown" library of the gentleman planter or merchant as an index of their intellectual concerns, but that they knew the fashion in books as well as "the breeding of courts," as Governor Lovelace of New York observed in 1668, there is no doubt. In the course of the eighteenth century, as such things increasingly set them off from the plain-living small freeholders and artisans, there appears to have been a "growth of aristocracy and a general hardening of class distinctions," even of arrogance.[12]

The outward show of American wealth and English fashion was brilliant enough, given the absence of truly ducal splendor, to validate the claim of the colonial gentry to public leadership of their towns, counties, and provinces. The men "of good estates and abilities" whom the crown or the lord proprietor appointed to the governor's council—the provincial senate and supreme court combined—represented, in every colony except perhaps Rhode Island, a little group of leading families. After two or three generations, indeed, they coalesced into an oligarchy of cousins. "They are all incorporated either in blood or marriages," the governor of Virginia observed in 1732; nearly two-thirds of the Virginia councilors from 1680 to 1776 came from twenty-three interrelated families of the tobacco aristocracy.[13] Even in Connecticut, where the councilors were fairly democratically elected, the freemen gave their votes to almost as narrow a group of families. Deputies to the provincial assemblies, though more popularly elected than members of the British House of Commons, came, quite as often as did M.P.'s, from among what passed for the "better sort" of their towns or counties. Although the qualified property-owning voters, unlike the forty-shilling freeholders of England, were a majority in every province long before the Revolution, they were content to choose among two or three candidates whose substance and rank would fittingly support the dignity of office. The local electors responded to the patronage or "influence" of the local magnates, which usually took the form of liberal largess of food and drink at the polls, as heartily in Virginia as at elections for the unreformed Parliament, and it was as usual for men of education, political understanding, and probity, as well as wealth, to be returned to Williamsburg as to Westminster.

The forms of local government varied considerably, from the southern county courts and parish vestrymen to the town meetings and selectmen of New England. In Virginia the county justices, commissioned by the governor from a list nominated by the court itself, and the vestries, which perpetuated themselves entirely by co-optation, were tight little oligarchies serving virtually for life. Their members also shared among themselves and their kind such important places as county sheriff and commissions in the militia. In New England, partly because of the direct democracy of annual elections and town meetings, the moderator and selectmen—and also the appointed justices of the peace—came from a broader spectrum of local society. But there too the more substantial townsmen usually held these leading offices. No doubt the gentry of a backcountry Yankee town lacked the elegance of the southern planter of "long-tailed family," but the lesser neighbors of both kinds of gentlemen looked up to them as the fittest leaders in local affairs.[14]

An English gentleman's duty toward society also required open-handed liberality to his peers and ungrudging generosity to the unfortunate. In America the scattered pattern of settlement in most regions made hospitality both necessary and pleasant. When the tobacco planter traveled about the countryside, he could count on a warm welcome at isolated plantations, since towns and decent inns were rare and his host was always eager for news and company. The great houses of the Chesapeake region took in a steady stream of casual visitors, perhaps uninvited but nonetheless welcome to stay for a month or more. Charity was a still clearer obligation of the Christian gentleman as steward of the wealth with which God had favored him. Beyond maintaining one's family and heirs in fitting style and contributing to government and the church, the amassing of riches could only be justified, as Anglicans, Puritans, and Quakers alike were used to hearing, by "Giving of what may supply the necessities, and Relieve the Calamities of the indigent."[15]

Systematic charity, based on the sixteenth-century English poor laws, varied from province to province according to the degree to which the state had taken over the ancient role of the church in dispensing alms. Where the Anglican church was established, responsibility for paupers and orphans might be retained by the parish vestry, as in Virginia, or, as in Maryland and New York in the eighteenth century, be left to the civil authorities of county or town. In New England, where civil and ecclesiastical functions were thoroughly mixed together in practice, if not in theory, the town selectmen provided for the local poor. Among the Quakers of Philadelphia their own meetings cared for the poor, Friends and others alike, even after a public almshouse was built in 1732. Whether the poor were relieved by the agency of church or state, out of money raised by tithes, taxes, or free bequests, almsgiving was at only one remove a practical obligation of men of substance.

Demands upon the charitable were less pressing in America than in England. To newly settled communities that were only beginning to accumulate capital, the care of "poor, decayed, and impotent persons"—feeble old people, men disabled by disease, accident, or war wounds, the blind, insane, and "idiotic," widows and orphans, the bastards and even the legitimate children of servants (particularly the mulatto offspring of white women servants)— seemed an exceedingly heavy burden.[16] But expedients could be devised to whittle it down. The incompetent could be boarded with private families at little expense to the taxpayer; children and others who could be turned into useful citizens were indentured as servants or apprentices. The colonies were also afflicted from an early date with "vagrant, idle, and dissolute persons," nimble enough to wander about, cadge a living, and keep one jump ahead of the town or county magistrates—a career which some of them may have followed in England before being bound over for labor in America in order to cure them of such habits.[17] Unable to deport them further, American overseers of the poor usually followed Cotton Mather's prescription for discriminating charity: "Find 'em work; set 'em to work; keep 'em to work. Then, as much of your bounty to them as you please."[18] Indolence, believed to be the great cause of poverty, was a dereliction of duty to the common-wealth as well as a mortal sin which preachers of every church denounced. Except in seaports like Boston, New York, Philadelphia, or Charleston at times when an inconveniently large number of poor immigrants, perhaps Scotch-Irishmen or Germans, were landed, there was seldom any lack of work to be done in colonial America. Fortunately for a new country, the need of the colonial poor for charity was as limited as the modest fortunes of the colonial rich.

For similar reasons other traditional social obligations of rank did not much trouble the colonial gentry. Except on the great estates of the Hudson Valley, the Northern Neck of Virginia, and a few other districts, the usual English relationship of landlord to tenant was not the American pattern. Although planters and land speculators might fondly think of themselves as lords of manors, few of them resembled the old-fashioned English squire whose park and mansion dominated a village of tenant farmers' houses and peasant cottages. The great planter of the tobacco and rice colonies was only a grander version of the freeholding farmers of his county; even the poor "lubber" who squatted on a patch of land that he neither owned nor rented was no one's economic dependent. The leading villagers of New England towns, such as the "river gods" of the Connecticut Valley, were superior to the run of their neighbors mainly in the greater scale of their enterprises and their fortunes. In the cities neither the merchant gentry nor the principal master artisans ruled over any great number of dependent employees, and if the nascent urban proletariat of sailors, longshoremen, and casual laborers in eighteenth-century Boston, New York, or Philadelphia were occasionally as turbulent as those of London or Bristol, they rioted not so much against their betters as among themselves. The "Pope Day" or Guy Fawkes set-to between the North End and South End gangs of Boston every Fifth of November posed no threat to the respectable classes. Even indentured servants, who, like ordinary apprentices, were bound by law to a master, were dependent upon his benevolence for only a few years.

Slavery was the one plausible equivalent to the ancient dependence of the English peasantry on their manorial landlords. To the slaveowner, his tobacco or rice plantation with its cluster of slave cabins near the great house seemed a kind of English village, the white overseer was his manorial steward or bailiff, and the Negro field hands, artisans, and domestic servants were his "people," to be ruled according to a version of the English ideal of paternal firmness tempered with compassion. And indeed the complete dependence of the chattel bondsman on his master's will, except when the county justices—who themselves were slaveowners—chose to intervene in cases of flagrant brutality or outright murder, made slavery seem simply an archaic kind of unfreedom.

The plantation was not, however, an English village, nor was the slave a cottager, a medieval serf, or even the kind of slave that had been known in England seven or eight hundred years before. He was of a different race and color from his master, and although after two or three generations in America he no longer had a distinctively African language and culture, neither did he have the traditional share of the English peasant in the folk-culture of the master's country. A slave was not a vassal or a henchman or a retainer; as the mere property of his master he was more accurately regarded as a beast of burden in the shape of a man. No doubt many masters were duly compassionate, just as more than a few were brutal, but all of them had acquired Negro slaves for their labor rather than for their society.

Not only the training, work, food, and shelter of the slave but also his movements off the plantation, his right to work on his own account, his trial and punishment for minor infractions, the integrity of his family, even any right to formal marriage, rested on nothing more solid than his master's sense of what was fitting and profitable. Only the slaveowner who managed to keep solvent as well as conscientious could ensure that husbands, wives, and children would not be separated and sold far away after his death. Slaves who could not work had of course to be cared for, but the cost of keeping those who lived to old age was lightened for the planter by the regular crop of black infants. As soon as the slave child was ten years old, he was valued at half the price of a prime field hand. Negroes who belonged to one of the great slaveowners of the Chesapeake or Carolina coastal regions had less contact with the master in any event than with the hired overseer of a particular plantation. However solicitous of their welfare the planter might be, the overseer's success was more assuredly measured by the profits he could wring from land and slaves than by his magnanimity. And yet, since even the most degraded slaves were human beings as well as black field hands, their masters did assume something of the air of feudal lords in the assurance that the ancient right of an aristocracy to rule society properly rested in their hands.

The gentry of the northern provinces who had few slaves and

not many white dependents were no less assured of the rightness of old distinctions. Although the "middling sort" of farmers and artisans were not economically subservient to them, except among the tenantry of the great estates of New York, they generally remained within the customary English social pattern of deference by the vulgar and of liberal condescension by the "better sort."[19] Everywhere the practical conditions that would ultimately upset these received attitudes were already present. But in spite of the relatively equal distribution of wealth in colonial America and the constant upward movement of successful individuals, it was not until after the Revolution that Americans began to reflect upon the implications for rank or degree in their society.

7. WELL-GOVERNED FAMILIES

The fundamental institution of colonial society was not rank or class—even the gentry did not consistently act together as an organized group—nor was it the detached individual; it was the family household. In practice as well as theory the family in seventeenth-century Europe was still an integral component of the system of economic production, the community, the church, and the political commonwealth. Its internal structure was already quite modern. Only in remote, unprogressive regions like the Scottish Highlands could the primitive clan any longer be found, a "family" of hundreds or thousands of persons claiming common descent with their chief from some half-mythical ancestor. The largest family was now a much smaller group, a household or perhaps a number of households immediately related by blood or marriage, and such other dependents as lived with them. It could be as "extended" (to use the sociologist's word) as the numerous connections of an English nobleman whose house was the center of cousinly influence; usually it was as "nuclear" as the two or three generations—parents, young children, and perhaps grandparents if they survived—who shared the two or three rooms of a peasant cottage. Particularly among peasants and artisans, whose wives and children could work together in a common set of occupations under the father's direction, this conjugal family was an economic entity and an organic part of local society.

Neither the families nor the detached individuals who emigrated to the colonies had any reason to suppose that American families would be different. The old ideal pattern, like many of their other social values, indeed survived substantially intact in spite of the abrasions of a hundred years or more of American life. Although the circumstances of the New World and the oncoming modern age ignited a process of individualistic fission in the structure of the nuclear family, the corresponding change in men's ideas of proper familial relationships burned with a much slower fuse.

Customary patterns of work and the chronic shortage of labor in America still required almost everyone who lived under one roof to work together. The family of the farmer, small planter, or artisan might include not only husband and wife, their minor children—perhaps seven or eight living out of eight or nine born—and such aged grandparents and spinster aunts as there might be, but also journeymen, servants and apprentices working out the term of their indentures, and other "help"—often boys and girls in their teens hired out by the year. Negro slaves might be treated like other servants, especially on a farm where there were only one or two of them. As a fastidious lady traveler observed in Connecticut in 1704, slaves ate at the master's table, and "into the dish goes the black hoof as freely as the white hand."[1] It was also quite common in all parts of the country for a family to take in a child or two from some other family; whether legally indentured as a servant or not, such a boy or girl was as much a member of the master's household as of his own parents'. It has been suggested that the New England Puritans, who thought first of salvation, accepted this practice as most likely to ensure the discipline which the child's own parents might be too lenient to enforce. Too many parents, the complaint ran in the 1650s, permitted their children to act "as if hail-fellow well met (as they say) and no difference twixt parent and child," so that children were tempted to "carry it proudly, disdainfully and scornfully towards parents."[2] In any part of the country a more pressing reason for the farming out of children to others was the large number of mouths to feed in families that had little to spare for them. (Perhaps twice as many survived to the age of twenty as in the ordinary English family of the time.) Whatever explanation might occur for the custom at the time, it by no means signified any breakdown in the family as a social institution, since it was also a well-known practice in England, a vestige of the less personal but more integrated social structure of the Middle Ages. Linking together households of men of comparable rank—frequently of brothers or close cousins—merely reinforced the many other ties of each family to the community. When one Virginia gentleman sent a son or daughter into service at the plantation of another, it was evident that ancient tradition, not dire necessity, was at work.

In both law and practice the head of this unitary family, the director of its work and owner of its property, its social arbiter, and its political representative at the polls, was the husband and father. Within the household his wife shared the headship over the rest. If he were missing, she might assume his other prerogatives, even as a voter—though both widows and widowers were usually quick to remarry, as they virtually had to do if the family were not to be dispersed. Although law restrained the head of the family, like others in authority, from oppressing his dependents—from ill-usage or neglect of children, seduction of servant girls, or brutality toward slaves—in general a perfect identity between his interest and theirs was assumed to pervade their entire relationship.

Wherever spiritual and communal values predominated, notably among the Puritans of New England and the Quakers and German sectarians of Pennsylvania, the family maintained its customary integrity the longest. The affinity between church and state in seventeenth-century New England strengthened the clergy and the civil magistrates in their conservative supervision of family conduct as of other social matters.

The same tension between individualism and group compulsion that characterized the Puritan version of Calvinist theology carried over into family relations. The church was concerned both with salvation of the individual soul and with creation of a holy community. God called souls to salvation one by one, and, as far as fallible mortals could judge who among them were "saints," they received individuals into the church. On the plane of human love as well, seventeenth-century Puritans placed at least as high a value on the personal affection between husband and wife or parent and child—which they likened to God's love for man—as on the integrity of the family as a social entity. The Puritans found, nevertheless, sufficient scriptural warrant, in God's covenant with Abraham and his seed, for the family's corporate place in the church.

As in the Catholic and Anglican churches, Puritan church members had their children baptized in infancy, long before the latter could testify to their own conversion. It was the father's duty to lead his children, and also servants and other members of his household, in daily prayers, scriptural reading, moral admonition, and the catechism in order to impress on them a sense of their sinfulness and lead them to seek for signs of God's grace and their own salvation. A conscientious Puritan father missed no opportunity to awaken his children's divine apprehension, as Samuel Sewall's diary for 1689 indicates:

Sabbath, Jan. 12. Richard Dummer, a flourishing youth of 9 years old, dies of the Small Pocks. I tell Sam. of it and what need he had to prepare for Death, and therefore to endeavour really to pray when he said over the Lord's Prayer: He seem'd not much to mind, eating an Apple; but when he came to say, Our father, he burst out into a bitter Cry, and when I askt what was the matter and he could speak, he burst out into a bitter Cry and said he was afraid he should die. I pray'd with him, and read Scriptures comforting against death, as O death where is thy sting, &c. All things yours. Life and Immortality brought to light by Christ, &c. 'Twas at noon.[3]

Since scripture ordained proper family relations, the church enforced them on delinquent households as well as it could by public admonition, censure, or excommunication. Puritan churches excommunicated husbands for marital offenses and for overly "Rygarous and Cruell Correction" of servants—or rather for lying about it when so charged. A wife guilty of "reviling of her husband and stricking of him and other vild and wicked Courses" might similarly be cast out. The First Church of Boston admonished a certain Temperance Sweete "for having received into house and given entertainment unto disorderly Company and ministring unto them wine and strong waters unto Drunkennesse and that not without some iniquity both in the measure and pryce thereof."[4]

The family being the foundation stone of the Puritan commonwealth as well as of the covenanted congregation, the civil authorities also upheld the proper authority of parents and put down "Ill Discipline." The magistrates regulated potential as well as actual breaches of good family order. At the beginning of the Puritan migration in 1629, when many of the settlers were single young men, the Massachusetts Bay Company grouped them into artificial "families," each under the "watchfull eye" of a trustworthy head, "that soe disorders may bee prevented, and ill weeds nipt." As thousands of natural families arrived in the 1630s, the towns ordered single men and women to avoid "sin and iniquity" by "betakeing themselves to live in well Governed famillies." An ill-governed family was also subject to civil correction. It was the parents' duty to teach their children and apprentices to read and to catechize them in both religion and the civil law. If they did not, the town selectmen and constables might break up the delinquent household and turn the neglected children and servants over to more dutiful families. In the 1670s the Massachusetts General Court ordered the towns to appoint "sober and discreet persons" as tithingmen, each of them to oversee ten or twelve families. "Most of the evils that abound amongst us," a synod of ministers had warned, "proceed from defects as to family government."[5]

Such lamentation and regulation, instances of which occur also in the laws of colonies as diverse as Virginia and New York, may indicate a desperate, reactionary attempt to hold together a crumbling institution whch was rapidly losing its function as part of an organic society. Certainly there were always elders to complain of the unruliness of the young, even of "disorder and rudeness of youth in many congregations in time of the worship of God, whereby sin and profaneness is greatly increased"—and whereby God had been provoked, New Englanders feared in the late 1670s, to inflict King Philip's War on them.[6] But it should be remembered that the Puritan model for the family was much more rigorous, insofar as it was drawn from the Old Testament, than ordinary English practice. Provincial law ordained death for adultery and even for youthful disobedience—extreme penalties which, however, were never actually inflicted. Failure to live up to the exacting Puritan ideal was not necessarily degeneration of the actual, existing English institution that had been brought to America.

Sooner or later in every region the pattern of physical isolation of each farm or plantation household placed its members in a closer but somewhat uncertain relationship to each other. The family of the southern farmer or planter, whose purpose in growing marketable tobacco or rice and indigo was the most narrowly economic, probably felt the winds of change first and most severely. To the extent that its members were cut off from daily contact with the larger society, they may have been thrown in upon each other in a new, more modern sort of emotional interdependence. The places where many New England farm families lived in the eighteenth century were no less remote, but their abhorrence of idleness and the need for everyone to work kept them within familiar lines. The real staple crop of the ordinary Yankee farm—a "family farm" indeed—was likely to be its numerous children, for whom, from the age of six or seven, it could always supply a variety of useful chores in the fields or barnyard as well as flax spinning, wool combing, or the splitting of shoe pegs, and conscientious parents kept everyone "industriously implied."[7] The southern farmer had perhaps as many offspring but was made to feel less moral compulsion to keep them at work, as well as having less for them to do. He was preoccupied in raising a money crop for which the labor of half-grown children was not particularly useful, especially if there were slaves—and slave children— to be kept busy. White children in the plantation colonies could all too easily be permitted to grow up in idleness and ignorance of formal learning, compounded from generation to generation by the general lack of schools. By the time a boy was able to do a man's work, he was nearly ready to seek a farm and establish a family of his own—perhaps far from his parents' home—and bring up children in the same half-indulgent, half-heedless manner.

The availability of cheap land out toward the current frontier further impaired the old-fashioned structure of the family by permanently removing most of the new generation from their parents' immediate neighborhood. Even among the numerous brothers and cousins of one of the great families of the Virginia gentry, each of whom could build an estate of his own, there could be no single dominant head comparable to the English noble-man with his unchallenged inheritance, as eldest son, of both the title and the family estate. The English legal devices of primo-geniture and entail were available in Virginia for binding a family's land into a single indivisible inheritance. But it was seldom neces-sary to discriminate against younger sons in order to secure the position of the eldest. "Great clans like the Carters and the Lees, though they may have acknowledged a central family seat," it has been observed, "were scattered throughout the province on es-tates of equal influence."[8] The family tie that was so often a potent force in provincial affairs was a loose coalition of cousins rather than a single patriarchal interest.

The young colonial in his ambition for land and status may seldom have considered what the eventual consequences of eco-nomic progress would be for the stability of old-fashioned institu-tions like the family. Material considerations had always been part and parcel of marriage arrangements in England and seemed to be no different in America. One of Governor Winthrop's grandsons wrote to a brother in 1707,

If a man should be [so] unhapy [as] to dote upon a poore wench (tho' otherwise well enough) that would reduce him to necessety and visibly ruine his common comforts and reputation, and at the same time there should be recommended to him a goodly lass with aboundation of mony which would carry all before it, give him comfort, and inlarge his reputation and intrest, I would certainly, out of my sense of such advantage to my freind, advise him to leave the maid with a short hempen shirt, and take hold of that made of good bag holland.[9]

A young Englishman or woman expected to marry someone of similar social degree and the property to support it. In the colonies the simpler degrees of rank and the relative ease of acquiring modest wealth permitted the same proprieties to continue alongside fairly free personal choice for the young people.

The average age at which they married is an index of the easier circumstances of life in America. In England, where the ordinary method of limiting the size of families during hard times was to marry late, the trend from the mid-seventeenth to the mid-eighteenth centuries was upward, from an average age of twenty-seven to twenty-nine for men and twenty-six to twenty-eight for women. If Plymouth Colony was typical, the colonial rate of change was about twice as great and in the other direction, to an average age at marriage of twenty-five for men and twenty-four for women before the end of the seventeenth century.* The great longevity of seventeenth-century New Englanders by English standards could lead to an awkward situation if, as in Andover, Massachusetts, where the life expectancy of the original settlers of the 1640s was nearly seventy-two years, fathers held to the English practice of keeping legal control of the family property until old age or death. The young men of Andover, forced to await their full inheritance and lacking capital to buy land elsewhere, put off marriage until the age that had been usual in England. It seems likely, however, that the Plymouth experience was more typical, in other regions as well as in New England: a tendency to relax the prudence of the Old World and marry young without undue fear of having too many children to feed.

The crucial consideration for the parents of the bride and groom, whose consent the couple was still expected to obtain, was whether the dowry or "portion" that the other family could provide suitably matched what they could spare. The bridegroom's father usually contributed about twice as large an amount, in property or money, as the bride's, as was fitting if the new husband were to "be for himself" and establish his family on the same social level as his father.[10] Couples whose parents had little wealth or rank could scamp such niceties, and be none the worse off after a few years of their own hard work, but among people of substance a good deal of bickering generally preceded a betrothal. Samuel Sewall recorded in his diary the arrangements for his daughter's marriage to Joseph Gerrish:

---

* Presumably because of a typical frontier shortage of women at first, they were marrying at an average age of twenty in the early years of Plymouth Colony, so that the later figure of twenty-four was in a sense a reversion to English custom.

Dine with Mr. Gerrish, son Gerrish, Mrs. Anne. Discourse with the Father about my Daughter Mary's Portion. I stood for making £550 doe: because now twas in six parts, the Land was not worth soe much. He urg'd for £600. at last would split the £50. Finally Febr. 20. I agreed to charge the House-Rent, and Difference of Money, and make it up £600.[11]

Frank negotiation over such material inducements was necessary in arranging marriage treaties for the young men and women of families who, in each province, were accumulating wealth and proliferating into the sets of cousins that dominated provincial government as well as fashionable society and the chief economic enterprises.

It was over the matter of property, on the other hand, that the legal unity of the colonial family began slightly to crack. Under English common law the property interest of husband and wife was indivisible, but it was in the hands of the husband alone. That rule was giving way slightly in England, however, and the colonial courts went somewhat further in the course of the seventeenth century. They sometimes accepted property settlements agreed upon by a couple before marriage in order to safeguard the wife's separate interest. By the terms of one such agreement at Plymouth in 1667, the wife was "to enjoy all her house and land, goods, and cattles, that shee is now possessed of, to her owne proper use, to dispose of them att her owne free will from time to time, and att any time, as shee shall see cause."[12] Husband and wife could even make such a contract after the wedding (something inadmissible in England until 1879), not only if the purpose was to divide the property of a separated or divorced couple but also sometimes as part of a reconciliation agreement between them. In certain cases in the late seventeenth and eighteenth centuries the courts recognized the independent property rights of a wife who kept a shop to support her family in the overlong absence of her sailor husband, lest the errant husband should return and lay claim to the fruits of her enterprise. Apart from these few property matters, however, the legal identity of husband and wife continued unbroken in both the Old World and the New.

The legal and material particulars in which the colonial family deviated from English precedent should not obscure the fact that its structure did not change radically in a century and a half. So elemental a social institution survived the practical circumstances of a new country remarkably well. The only economic force strong enough seriously to disrupt its traditional integrity and the due subordination of its members to their head was the availability of cheap land, usually at some distance, for the rising generations. There must have been many mothers like the Plymouth woman in the 1670s who "Cryed and wrong her hands fearing that [her son] Joseph would Goe away."[13] But the dazzling opportunities for early independence did not as yet produce any overt rebellion of heedless or delinquent children or any mass outbreak of desertion and divorce.

If there was any basic type of American family that was literally shattered by the impact of new economic circumstances, it was the family—if indeed it can be called that—of the Negro slave. Since the Negro had been brought to America for purely economic purposes—those of others rather than his own—the members of a slave family could be separately disposed of, and the family's very existence abruptly cut off, for the economic advantage of the master, tempered only by whatever moral scruples he might have. The precarious situation of the slave family, deprived of its own freedom for the sake of the master's, was a portent, as yet no bigger than a man's hand, of how the thoroughgoing economic progressivism and individualism of the nineteenth century would undermine the integrity of families of every color. But in the slow-moving, socially conservative eighteenth century no such conclusion was yet apparent.

8. ESTABLISHED CHURCHES IN THE NEW WORLD

The church, since it has always believed that its spiritual concerns transcend other values of human society, is peculiarly exposed to the perennial preoccupation of men with merely earthly matters. North America was colonized during a European epoch of gradual "declension" from piety to worldliness, a time not so much of crisis for the church as of inertia, when the spiritual fires of the Protestant Reformation and the resurgent Catholic response to it were dying away. In spite of the colonists' attempt to perpetuate the beliefs and forms they brought with them, their circumstances in the New World also diverted them from spiritual values and undermined the authority of the church over society.

The colonial churches sloughed off a number of important functions that had been in their predecessors' charge in the old country. The reasons varied among different sects and in different colonies. On one hand, the New England Puritans deliberately stripped away "unscriptural" elements. On the other, the Anglicans of the southern colonies tried but failed to transplant the full episcopal polity of the Church of England. But the result for both of them, and for smaller bodies like the Baptists of Rhode Island and the Quakers of the Delaware-Susquehanna region, was the development of a common American form of ecclesiastical organization.

The "strong bent of their spirits" that led the first generation of Puritan colonists to establish a purified Church of England tended to diminish the formal status of the New England clergy. Since each local church was structurally independent—though presumably inspired by the same faith—the minister was ordained and appointed not by any bishop or presbytery of fellow clergymen but by the body of lay members. It was they, as a minister said, who were the "royal priesthood, all of them prophets, and taught of God's spirit."[1] Although it was God who called a man to the ministry and then only after a full university education, the "call" was voiced by the particular church that vested him with his authority. Control of the church property and the admission, censuring, and excommunication of members were also in the hands of laymen; how long the minister continued to serve them, for that matter, depended on how well he suited them as preacher and teacher, though in practice the relationship was almost always lifelong. The great authority wielded by the New England clergy of the mid-seventeenth century rested upon the common Puritan faith as well as upon "their character, and the love that they bore to their people and their God."[2] As long as the people shared that same wholehearted commitment, the Puritan minister would not feel the lack of a higher human authority to fall back upon.

The established church in Virginia, as in the other southern colonies and New York, was nominally episcopal, but in fact throughout the colonial period there was no bishop closer at hand than London. The Bishop of London was represented in the colonies from time to time by a "commissary," and the Virginians, unable in their early years to support a full episcopal establishment, later on were generally content to get along without one. Certain inconveniences resulted: American candidates for ordination had to go to England to seek out the indispensable bishop. But there were only about 150 colonial ordinands all told, almost all of them after 1750; the Anglican clergy in the colonies commonly were Englishmen or Scottish Episcopalians. The more frequent problem of appointing and disciplining parish priests, another of the proper functions of a bishop, had to be assumed by the provincial governor, who of course was a layman. Furthermore, in 1643 Virginia gave the laymen of the parish vestry the right to present a nominee for the governor to appoint. Although his flock could not formally dismiss him if he proved unsatisfactory to them, the vestry could virtually starve him out. By law the priest was entitled to his glebe or farm—of little practical value to him unless he could afford servants or slaves—and an annual tithe of a bushel of corn and ten pounds of tobacco from every man. Since the cash value of the tobacco dwindled over the years, it became customary for him to seek extra compensation from the vestry. Especially if they had neglected to present him for formal induction to begin with, they could easily reduce or even deny him this sum altogether. In parishes where this practice amounted to bargaining over an annual contract, the nominally episcopalian Virginians could speak as easily of "hiring" the priest as New England congregationalists spoke of calling a minister.[3]

Certain social matters in which the ecclesiastical courts of the Church of England had directly intervened were abandoned by the colonial churches to civil authority, in the Puritan colonies once again on principle and among Anglicans out of necessity. Among the Puritans, who celebrated only the "scriptural" sacraments of baptism and communion, marriage was a mere civil contract (although, oddly, a divine covenant as well). In the seventeenth century, marriages were regularly performed by magistrates without any religious ceremony. Although marriage was still a sacrament among Anglicans in America as in England, churches in the plantation parishes of Virginia were too dispersed for the reading of banns on three successive Sundays to serve its precautionary purpose—especially necessary in the case of servants who still owed time to their master and required his permission to marry. By 1642 the province therefore instituted a civil marriage license. In Virginia as well as in New England, furthermore, the church totally relinquished probate of wills to the county courts. In both regions also the civil authorities took over prosecution of moral offenders, though perhaps the ordinary Puritan's duty of neighborly "holy watching" made the dockets of the New England courts more crowded with such cases than was usual in Virginia.

Although the Puritan church had had its beginning in an attempted reformation of the Church of England, secularism and indifference steadily sapped the spiritual influence of the new establishment of the reformers in New England as well as that of the Episcopal church elsewhere. In the southern provinces the structural weakness of the Anglican church no doubt contributed to the general decline. The English cleric who would accept the poor living that a colonial vestry begrudged him was apt to be a man without prospects at home; in general such men would have been ineffectual pastors even if there had been enough of them to supply every parish in the country. The unusually conscientious clergyman who was so diligent as to take up the hard life of circuit-riding among several remote churches from Sunday to Sunday could hardly satisfy the spiritual needs of each of his flocks or, indeed, keep most of the scattered farmers and planters aware that they had such needs. The Anglican churches held to the old forms as well as they could, but most of them were perforce quite "low" in their simple ritual and plain architecture. They also practically denatured what was left of the old theology, since the gentlemen who served as vestrymen and churchwardens in the eighteenth century leaned toward Deism, the rationalistic religion of "Nature's

God" that was fashionable among their sort in Europe at the time.

Puritans were moving in the same direction, though by somewhat different stages. Not that the New England clergy greatly declined in quality: the scores of Cambridge masters of arts who accompanied the great migration of the 1630s were succeeded by graduates of Harvard (beginning in 1642) and Yale (from 1702), men educated on the same lines and prepared to explicate scripture with the same logical precision though not with much scholarly originality. The burden of their discourses bore increasingly, however, upon the sad declension of New England from its early piety and state of grace; by the 1670s the Puritan sermon, formerly a disquisition to the faithful, had become a jeremiad, a call to anxious backsliders as well as to the worldly to repent their sins. The prosecution of supposed witches at Salem in 1692 was an eleventh-hour attempt of both state and church to thrust back the devil and his servants and regain the divine favor with which the purer society of sixty years before had been graced. In the end the trials only compounded the moral confusion they had sought to purge: twenty persons who were too scrupulous to confess to sins of which they were innocent were convicted on "spectral evidence" and hanged, while others who cynically made public show of repentance saved their necks. As conservative in purpose as many later American reform movements, the witchcraft trials were also as radically reactionary in practically discrediting the clerical and civil authorities who had pressed them.

In their turn the thrice-reformed Quakers of Pennsylvania and New Jersey, who relied on a universal "inner light" of direct divine inspiration rather than on the sermons of an educated clergy or the stern justice of avenging magistrates, felt the same chilling atrophy of the spirit. Within a generation after the first settlement of Pennsylvania, their monthly meetings were regularly announcing their sad lapse from grace and seeking to recall them to their moral duty.

No doubt the passing of the generations was partly to blame. The farther the England of the Puritan reformers of the early seventeenth century receded into the past, the less clearly the New England-born remembered the earnest conviction, the persecution, and the self-denial of the fathers. John Winthrop's holy "city upon a hill," a beacon to mankind and a model of the purified church and society, was turning into the workaday province of hardheaded Yankee farmers, artisans, and merchants. In Pennsylvania too the perfervid Quaker evangelists of seventeenth-century

England, who had resolutely kept their hats on their heads in the presence of judge or bishop—and sometimes had run naked through the streets as a "sign"—were succeeded by the plainly dressed but comfortable and complacent Philadelphians of the mid-eighteenth century. As New Englanders and Pennsylvanians prospered in their worldly callings, the merely economic values of producing and accumulating the world's goods subtly displaced their spiritual vocation. The quandary in which success left the Quakers, many of whom had come out of the lower orders of English society, unaccustomed to the wealth that so many of them soon amassed, was perhaps more acute than it was for the descendants of the considerable number of Puritans who in England had been small merchants, respectable farmers, or even country gentry. No matter how confident the first Calvinists and Quakers had been that they could pursue their material concerns quite conformably to God's will, their earthly callings tended to cloud over the saving grace of the Puritan or the Quaker inner light.

The children of the original Puritan settlers found it hard to meet the requirement (dating from 1636) that, in order to qualify for church membership, they show convincing evidence of having experienced true conversion. It may be that the second generation was not as lax as they feared, but that conscience and uncertain recollection made them demand more of themselves than had formerly been insisted upon. In any case the churches faced the practical problem of a dwindling membership. If nonmembers or, for that matter, the baptized children of members could not find evidence of salvation in themselves, they could not join the *church* of convinced or "visible" saints but only the larger miscellaneous body of the *congregation*. Worse yet, their own children would be denied baptism altogether. It was likely that after another few generations of this withering away no church would be left, but only, as a historian has recently suggested, a "genealogical society of the descendants of the faithful."[4]

In each successive generation the New England churches devised fresh countermeasures. By the "half-way" covenant (as its opponents scornfully called it) certain churches permitted the baptized but unconverted simply to "own [consent to] the covenant"; their children—the grandchildren of full members—could then be baptized in their turn. By the end of the seventeenth century many of the grandchildren themselves were dissatisfied with this self-perpetuating half-way commitment, especially among the dispersed, struggling new settlements in the poorer inland parts east and west of the Connecticut Valley. In the Saybrook Platform of 1708 a synod of Connecticut churches abandoned strict congregationalism, vested the old occasional "consociations" of ministers with the superior authority of regular presbyteries, and proceeded to admit anyone, unless too obviously unregenerate, to full church membership. By this retrograde reform it was hoped that the sacrament of communion, like baptism, would be a means of bringing men to a state of grace and not simply the final seal upon the already proven salvation of a few.

None of these reforms sufficed to keep New England society safely under the domination of spiritual values. To open the communion table to all, though a useful means of filling the church rolls again, was merely to recognize that the lukewarm majority was preoccupied with secular matters. The Congregational churches, with or without consociations, of course survived and indeed multiplied as New England settlement advanced in the eighteenth century. So too did the Anglicans or Episcopalians in the South and here and there in New England, the Presbyterians (with the great Scotch-Irish influx into Pennsylvania after 1720 and the accretion of many of the Saybrook Platform consociations), the Quakers more modestly around Philadelphia, the Dutch Reformed of New York and East Jersey, and the scattering of Huguenot congregations as well as Sephardic synagogues in the major port cities. A remarkable array of ecclesiastical institutions for a new country, they all awaited some new dispensation of saving grace. But with the notable exception of the Great Awakening of the 1730s and 1740s—a new kind of spiritual reform movement which, since in a vital sense it marked the beginning of the next era for the churches, can best be put off for discussion along with the nineteenth century—colonial Americans continued to drift either into spiritual indifference or into the rationalistic religion fashionable in contemporary Europe.

9. COMMUNITIES IN DISPERSION

Whatever the import of rationalism or indifference for the state of the colonists' souls, a well-founded social community still clustered about each church or meetinghouse. The local community, like the family, has been in most ages an almost irreducible institution, resistant to structural change even under extreme pressure. Colonial America was not yet beset by any such radical force.

Although by European standards the local communities of British North America were dispersed and isolated, it took a century and a half for the colonists to penetrate one or two hundred miles inland, an advance slow enough to permit them to reproduce and sustain the old communal patterns to a remarkable degree. Each of those conservative communities, not excepting even the odd dozen commercial seaports, had a certain economic unity, whether it was organized around the nearly self-sufficient agriculture and handicrafts of the New England town or the nearly universal production of export staples by the counties of the South and the Middle Colonies. Most of them were also ethnically homogeneous. Although by the end of the colonial period more than a third of the white population was not of English descent, its distribution gave every region of settlement (though not every colony as such) a certain ethnic unity. Some of the minor ethnic groups—notably the French Huguenots, the Welsh, and the Jews—were more widespread but were also thoroughly Anglicized in fairly short order. Most of the other peoples—the Dutch of East Jersey and the Hudson Valley, the Pennsylvania Germans and Scotch-Irish, and the Scottish Highlanders of the North Carolina backcountry—kept more or less to their own districts. And in the local affairs that everywhere were the colonists' chief concern, the mother country's celebrated policy of salutary neglect permitted them to improvise new forms of the self-government for which the English parish, borough, and county had long been distinguished in the Old World.

There was a certain artificiality, to be sure, about the beginnings of the counties and parishes of the Chesapeake region. As early as the 1620s the rudimentary society of Virginia took on a random pattern of dispersed farmers and planters, each working for his own profit and shipping his tobacco hogsheads from a nearby landing. When counties were divided off after 1634, their only unity lay in the convenient access to a county court which they gave the planters of a district. The modest courthouse did not cause, however, an English county town to grow up around it. What went on in those crossroads hamlets was only what was significantly to pass into later American speech as "courthouse politics." In spite of the provincial government's occasional call for the building of boroughs and towns, even the eighteenth-century capitals of Williamsburg and Annapolis remained mere villages which bustled into life only when the assembly was in session.

The need of a dispersed society for administrative and judicial control, however, made the Chesapeake county a fair equivalent of its English prototype. Insofar as the magistrates, the eight to a dozen or more justices who made up the county commission of the peace, had any professional knowledge of the law—a few of them perhaps from study at the Inns of Court in London—it was no more extensive than befit gentlemen of their rank and local responsibilities. In the monthly courts and the quarter sessions they, or at least a quorum of four of them, dealt with a growing variety of criminal and civil cases and administrative affairs. Matters which in England were handled by other kinds of courts early fell into their hands: estates of orphans in 1643, probate of wills in 1645, and equity and admiralty jurisdiction in 1645 and 1658. They also enforced the regimen of local economic and social controls, some of which were familiar to English justices of the peace —market regulation of prices and weights and measures, tavern licensing, maintenance of public roads, bridges, and ferries—as well as others which American circumstances required, such as civil marriage licenses, registration of land titles, inspection of tobacco for export, and the bounty on wolves. The justices directly or indirectly selected the county clerk and the lesser officers who carried out their orders, and also the sheriff and the officers of the militia, who were customarily men of their own class. After 1661 the office of sheriff was rotated annually among the members of the court itself.

Since parish vestrymen and churchwardens were gentlemen of the same sort—perhaps justices or former justices as well—the functions of court and vestry in practice were often intermingled. The churchwardens not only looked after church property but also sent up indictments to be heard by the civil courts for moral offenses of the sort that in England had been under ecclesiastical jurisdiction: nonconformity, Sabbath-breaking, profanity, drunkenness, adultery, fornication, and bastardy; they had the duty, too often neglected, of recording marriages, christenings, and burials. Through court and vestry together the county gentry, true to their aristocratic aspirations, kept control of the local affairs of their otherwise somewhat amorphous communities. It can only be surmised whether the ordinary farmers, who in Virginia had no voice in electing justices or vestrymen, were comparably attached to local society. As in most hierarchical societies of the past, practically all surviving descriptions were written by members of the elite. But most of the small farmers who formed the bulk of the population were qualified by property ownership to vote for burgesses or deputies to the provincial assembly, and not until long after the Revolution did they begin to challenge the rule of the local planter oligarchies.

Although there were counties in New England too, their functions were more narrowly judicial; the primary political, economic, and social community was the kind of township, either urban or rural, which the first Puritan immigrants devised and gave the rather misleading name of "town." Having left England for religious and economic reasons of their own, they blended and adapted English village customs and the forms of manorial, parochial, and borough government to their new circumstances and special purposes. The chief resemblance between the local communities of old and New England lay less in specific political forms than in the maintenance of a certain social stability. In sixteenth- and seventeenth-century England this had been bound up in immemorial usages that in most places—all those that were not ripped up by enclosure or dislocated by the first onset of industrialization—changed almost imperceptibly. Although New England drew a variety of customs from the several kinds of English villages and boroughs from which the first emigrants came, homogeneity and common consent were deliberately fostered as a solid foundation for Puritan orthodoxy. After a generation or two the much adapted English usages were blurred into what seemed like antique Yankee custom. Like the other variant developed by the Chesapeake counties, it was carried on essentially unchanged into the nineteenth century.

The proprietors of new towns in seventeenth-century New England conformed them with remarkable fidelity, in spite of the pressure of economic change, to the tightly knit social pattern devised in the 1630s. Unlike the English village, whose huddle of cottages lay only half an hour's walk from its next neighbor, towns were roughly six miles square, each town center was several miles from the next one, and the original house lots around the meeting-house and common really were small farms—from four to twenty acres in Andover in the 1640s. On the other hand, since New England had done away with manors along with other feudal tenures, there was none of the English splitting of villages among different jurisdictions. Each town was a self-contained political as well as territorial entity that gave local society a focus that southern farmers and planters lacked.

Growth brought complexity to the town without destroying its basic pattern. As the population increased, new hamlets hived off at convenient spots within the township and grew into villages. Some, in time, were permitted to set up their own parishes and perhaps eventually, like Marblehead, which was originally a fishing outpost four miles from the Salem town center, were completely separated off as new towns. At the same time those towns that had chosen to begin farming on the communal open-field system were changing over to the other English pattern of detached, "enclosed" farms. As at each successive division of the outlying common more and more of the villagers dispersed to their own farmsteads of one to six hundred acres, the individual family tended to become more isolated from society even though the town as a whole was more crowded. By the middle of the eighteenth century the New England town was more like the local communities of other regions than it appeared to be. The tidy village around its common green still made the older towns picturesquely different, but most of the townsmen were scattered through the countryside like farmers elsewhere. In Vermont, settled late in the eighteenth century, many rural towns lacked even the appearance of a village center.

As some of the common economic and social functions of the New England town decayed in the course of the seventeenth and eighteenth centuries, its society was brought closer to the practical individualism of farmers and shopkeepers in other regions. From the start the arable fields and the meadows of every town were owned and worked as the property of individuals. In places which held for a time to the open-field system, however, the town directed the uses to which the owners could put their holdings. The passing of the seasons was marked by a series of town orders to plant this or that field and to let another lie fallow, to fence each of them off before planting and to open them for common grazing after the harvest. As long as some of the land of such a town remained unallotted, it was put to common pasture. The number of beasts a townsman could graze on the common was "sized" or stinted according to the amount of meadow he owned to provide hay for winter fodder, and the regulations were enforced by minor town officers like the hog-reeve and the pound-keeper. The hayward (hedgewarden), or fence viewer, oversaw the proper enclosing of the town pastures and the seasonal fencing of the common fields. But with the successive divisions of the commons and the general dispersal to enclosed farmsteads the public functions of the New England town contracted to those of local governments elsewhere. They were still numerous: maintenance of roads and bridges, regulation of markets, perhaps including price- and wage-fixing, the disposition of paupers and incompetents, organization and training of a militia company. For a time late in the seventeenth century the town designated the public tithingmen who supervised orderly Puritan family life. It also took over various practical matters that in England and the Anglican colonies belonged to the parish vestry, from building a church or meetinghouse to recording births, marriages, and deaths.

The same concern for social morality was expressed through education, another public function nearly unique to New England. New York and the southern colonies formally recognized a public responsibility to provide schools, but in practice they left formal education to family tutors and to the very few privately endowed or church-conducted schools; more often they simply neglected it. In seventeenth-century New England there was no lack of the piety and philanthropy that had inspired the founding of schools in England over the centuries. In the colonial economy it took time, however, to accumulate the private wealth for adequate endowments. The only ready capital was land, but by the same token almost any conceivable land grant would be worth too little to support good schools indefinitely. Yet the American-born generations would need a solid English education, from elementary literacy for all to the classical liberal arts for ministers and other gentlemen, in order to cultivate rational understanding as an aid to Puritan faith. The need for schools seemed the more urgent for the fear that the family, preoccupied as it was with the task of earning a living or making a fortune, would neglect even such instruction of the young as English schools had not had to concern themselves with.

The General Courts of the Puritan colonies—all New England but Rhode Island—therefore enjoined the towns to establish schools. In Massachusetts by the Act of 1647 a town of fifty families had to maintain an elementary school and if there were a hundred a Latin grammar school as well. The system was never perfected, and during the eighteenth century it fell into decay in poor, remote districts. The dispersion of the farming population away from the town centers made attendance difficult for many children, and the general withering away of religious zeal sapped their elders' incentive to impose traditional learning on them. A town might divide itself into several school districts in order to give children from outlying farms access to schooling, but if the town could support only one schoolmaster, each school would be open only a month or two in the year. As many as fifty towns in Massachusetts in the eighteenth century preferred paying an annual fine of £5 to the expense of keeping any school at all. The result was widespread illiteracy, less than in other regions but far more than the first Puritan colonists would have tolerated. On the other hand, enough of the system survived to carry the tradition into the nineteenth century and put New Englanders in the vanguard of the modern public school movement. In the meantime the school as a communal institution helped bind society together, generation by generation, in a common tradition of formal culture even after much of the original religious inspiration had been lost.

Economic individualism encroached most sharply upon the social community of the town through the business of land speculation. The question of the proper division of common land could turn the Puritan ideal of "joint consent" into bitter discontent.[1] As early as 1655 the original grantees of the Massachusetts town of Sudbury tried to prevent the young men, mainly their own sons, from using the town meeting to share out the undivided land among all inhabitants; the province managed to smooth over the affair only by granting the young dissidents the new township of Marlborough. Ultimately in many towns the originally exact identity between the board of proprietors of common lands and the town meeting of inhabitants was lost when the board, the descendants of the first settlers, kept the successive divisions of the commons in their own hands and required others to buy land from them. The community of Haverhill was badly riven in 1720 when certain freeholders, on the strength of having paid taxes for twenty years, claimed shares in the undivided common. The heirs of the original proprietors accused them of attempting to confiscate private property and even of fomenting revolution; after a bitter struggle in which each faction elected its own set of town officers, the General Court upheld the proprietary party.

In many towns settled in the late seventeenth and eighteenth centuries, the legal proprietors of the land included a number of absentee investors who were not inhabitants at all. When Worcester was resettled in 1684 after the devastation of King Philip's War, 400 of the 480 lots were divided equally between actual settlers and the company of "undertakers," or investors. (The rest were devoted to the usual communal institutions—church, school, cemetery, and mills—and to rewarding the lobbyist who had procured the grant from the General Court.) Such situations often set residents and absentees at loggerheads, each party arguing in terms of the highest moral principle even though one was no less addicted to land speculation than the other.

Conflict became endemic in those towns of western New England where the land had been entirely bought up by groups of Boston, Salem, or Connecticut Valley merchants and speculators for re-sale to settlers. The latter, as they came to control the town govern-ment, were tempted, in view of the traditional identity between political authority and the direction of other economic matters, to appropriate to themselves the proprietors' rights to the undivided commons. In most such cases, once again, the courts of the province legalistically sustained the proprietors, even when their land titles rested on nothing better than some dubious "purchase" from the Indians years before. Such decisions, even more than the lawsuits, measured the degeneration of Puritan social harmony into materialistic self-seeking. When conflict of that sort subsided on the last New England frontier, Vermont, it was because by that time the proprietors of new towns were land speculators pure and simple whose only interest was to sell off their holdings to settlers as fast as good business permitted and to reinvest some-where else.

Although the resident townsman was as avid for speculative gain as any absentee investor, the squabbles over land took place within communities that maintained remarkable stability throughout the colonial period. In the early years the common Puritan purpose had inhibited internal dissension. Until nearly the end of the seven-teenth century only church members, as "freemen," could regularly vote for the town's deputies to the Massachusetts General Court, but they were the great majority in the first generation of Puritan colonization. After 1647 virtually all other heads of families who were freeholders were admitted to full participation in the town meeting. When the new charter of 1692 shifted the basis for the provincial franchise from sanctity to property, once again most men qualified, and, as before, the town franchise was broader yet. Since town officers were elected annually and the monthly town meeting voted directly on local ordinances, the local political and social communities were more nearly one and the same in New England than in any other region.

"The democracy of the Massachusetts towns," it has recently been argued, "was a democracy despite itself, a democracy without democrats."[2] It was not for the sake of majority rule but rather in order to maintain the Puritan moral community that the towns enlisted the "prudent and amicable composition and agreement" of all independent men—of all those whose economic position gave them the freedom to exercise a will of their own in town affairs.[3] Because their purpose was to govern through consensus, the towns "warned out" or refused admission to the "contrarye minded," just as the province regularly expelled and sometimes hanged Quakers and other persistent interlopers before 1660 and never gave a warm welcome to foreigners, not even to fellow Calvinists like the Scotch-Irish Presbyterians and French Huguenots.[4] Quarrelsome factions inevitably roiled the local political and social waters: the rich and more respectable set themselves off from the ordinary farmers, while men dissatisfied with their portion, or lack of any, in divisions of the commons appealed to higher authority and perhaps withdrew in anger to found a new town of their own. But social classes and political factions, no less than church, family, or school, were only variations on the common Yankee tradition, operating within a communal structure that substantially endured for two hundred years.

Since the local social communities of other regions, unlike those of the New England towns or Chesapeake counties, were not regularly coextensive with the boundaries of local government, less can be gleaned about them from the provincial statutes, tax lists, county or township records, and other official documents. The welcome which the Middle Colonies extended to immigrants of various nationalities and religions soon established a highly mixed population in the bustling, already modern commercial cities of New York and Philadelphia and in smaller places like Lancaster, and a mosaic of ethnic groups from district to district in the countryside. The New Englanders who settled the eastern two-thirds of Long Island and the western arc of New York Bay introduced their familiar town organization and congregational churches. But among the Dutch, English, Welsh, Germans, Scotch-Irish, Huguenots, and others elsewhere across New York, New Jersey, and Pennsylvania, the "open-country neighborhood" (to use an anthropologist's term for their loosely settled townships) set the pattern of scattered homesteads which the later Middle West would follow—and into which both Southerners and Yankees sooner or later lapsed. Drawn from European traditions—of Celtic croft and family farm and upland German *Einzelhof*—far more ancient than either the open-field village or the county, such a community had no single center but only a number of crossroads hamlets. To these the outlying farmsteads might be variously linked in a loose, overlapping net of "neighbors, kindred, and fellow-sectarians."[5] In such localities the churches—parish, congregation, or meeting —were livelier communal institutions than the civil township, county, or borough.

Like the Puritans, the Quakers of West Jersey and Pennsylvania did not withdraw into monastic seclusion from the worldly community but sought to make the world conform to their spiritual ideal. As long as they dominated the two provinces through numbers and influence, the monthly and yearly meetings of the Society of Friends were virtually, though not formally, the civil government, and long after the influx of other people Quakers played a part in provincial affairs. But as far as possible the local Quaker congregation or meeting directly governed its own economic and social life. "In addition to nourishing the religious life and guarding the morals of its members," a Quaker historian observes, the monthly meeting "functioned as a dispenser of poor relief, a loan office, a court of arbitration in economic matters, an employment agency, and a source of advice to new arrivals on the management of their affairs."[6] It issued certificates sanctioning marriage between Friends, recorded births and deaths, settled civil disputes among Friends out of court, admonished parents and children to observe decent family relations, enjoined sober behavior and dress as well as honest business dealings, and disciplined any Quaker who transgressed the civil law. As a holy community the Society of Friends was literally Quaker society.

Many of the German sectarians who settled inland in Pennsylvania in the eighteenth century endeavored to withdraw far more completely from the profane world. Although they could not transplant the close-knit life of their Rhenish villages to a new country where a peasant family might buy a farm as large as several hundred acres, among the farmsteads of Berks and Lancaster counties the church bound the Mennonite or the Amish community together more securely than the mere fact of neighborhood could do. Certain German sects kept to themselves more strictly than others. The Amish were the most extreme. They had split from the Mennonites in the 1690s, a generation before their emigration began, in order to uphold their disciplinary doctrine of *Meidung,* the absolute shunning of the excommunicated member. In Pennsylvania they enhanced their social isolation by clinging to the seventeenth-century dress they had come in, modified only to abjure such worldly vanities as buttons and lapels. But even the less conspicuously "plain" German churches, the Moravians or United Brethren and the Lutherans, left little for civil government to do by way of ordering the life of their communities. In the German states the peasantry had been subjects of authoritarian governments in which they themselves played no part; in Pennsylvania they submitted willingly to their own church leaders and took as little notice of the state as possible. Although Benjamin Franklin and other Anglo-Pennsylvanians for a time feared them as a socially divisive element, by keeping almost wholly to themselves in their own well-ordered communities they proved a conservative influence.

In South Carolina the unusual centralization of government, including the judiciary, at Charleston, which was also the social capital, makes it harder to discover the nature of local community in the countryside. The counties were large, merely nominal districts. Parish vestrymen and churchwardens, elected by Anglican church members, performed the usual minor civil functions. The governor appointed justices of the peace who, with their constables, kept order in the district. The system suited the cosmopolitan planters of the low country well enough, and when small communities of Welsh Baptists, Irish Quakers, Germans, French Protestants, and Scotch-Irish settled in the backcountry around the middle of the eighteenth century, they were left to themselves.

The society of every colony displayed a provincial unity that transcended local attachments. Even in those colonies whose boundaries were most artificial and populations ethnically mixed, habituation to self-government over several generations added a common identity to their differences of cultural or social tradition. The various provincial governments, furthermore, were remarkably alike, whether the governor was appointed by the crown or by a lord proprietor (the latter only in Pennsylvania and Maryland by the mid-eighteenth century) or popularly elected (in Connecticut and Rhode Island). The governor's council, or upper house of the legislature, almost everywhere constituted a provincial oligarchy. In the assembly the deputies of the counties or towns, although perennially divided by a "milling factionalism that . . . at times reduced the politics of certain colonies to an almost unchartable chaos of competing groups," gradually built up a common American tradition of parliamentary privilege.[7] The Whig principles of the Glorious Revolution of 1688 seemed remarkably apposite to their resistance to the arbitrary but often ineffectual prerogatives of the governor. Although this constitutional pattern was most closely identified with the elite of wealth, standing, and influence, there survived a sense of broader purpose that harked back to a tradition of Puritan commonwealth, Pilgrim Old Colony, or loyal Old Dominion.

Since no intercolonial government existed, however, social community was also lacking. For all their similarities, the dozen continental colonies had no permanent official links with each other short of London. Americans spoke of England as "home" and of Virginia or Massachusetts as their "country." Even their external trade was more likely to be conducted with the British Isles or other distant parts of the empire, especially the West Indies, than with their neighbors up and down the coast. There were exceptions. Brothers and cousins of certain eighteenth-century merchant families branched out on their own in the ports of different colonies —the Amorys of Charleston and Boston; Edward Shippen of Philadelphia and also Boston and Newport for a time—and Quaker, Huguenot, and Jewish merchants wove intercolonial trading networks among their own kind. Carolinians who summered at Newport even formed a link with the Narragansett planters and Yankee mercantile gentry. But normally the planter aristocrats of one region had little contact with the merchant princes of another.

The tastes which the elite everywhere shared in law, education, books, portrait painting, architecture, music, and fashionable dress and manners—in everything, indeed, but religion—derived from London, their common imperial metropolis. The proper finish to the education of a southern planter's son was not to be gained at the New England colleges, no matter how closely their curriculum followed that of Cambridge and Oxford. Cultural links with the mother country in fact grew stronger in the 1750s and 1760s, when several hundred young Americans attended the English and Scottish universities and the Inns of Court. Colonial and British coreligionists—not only Anglicans but also Quakers, Congregationalists, and Presbyterians—maintained regular communication as well as communion. The twenty-one colonial Fellows of the Royal Society, from the younger John Winthrop in 1662 and William Byrd II in 1696 to Dr. Benjamin Franklin in 1756, encompassed nearly every American with a claim to scientific distinction. Franklin, in his youthful role as journeyman printer of Boston, Philadelphia, and London, also exemplified the English and intercolonial connections among artisans.

Most ordinary men, being firmly tied to their small farms, plantations, and shops, had no firsthand acquaintance with distant parts. Although the Yankee peddler was already known in the South, the appearance of his sloop up one of the tidal creeks did not endear his kind to the respectable. "Some of these Banditti," William Byrd complained in 1736 to a correspondent in Salem,

anchor near my estate, for the advantage of traffiquing with my slaves, from whom they are sure to have good Pennyworths. . . . I wish you would be so kind as to hang up all your Felons at home, and not send them abroad to discredit their country.[8]

Byrd's contempt for the sharp-dealing Yankee later hardened into a universal southern folk-belief. It was partly in order to impose unity of purpose on provinces as detached, though not yet fixedly antagonistic, as Massachusetts and Virginia that the master of Mount Vernon was appointed in 1775 to command the Continental Army of New England farmers, artisans, and no doubt a few peddlers.

Colonial Americans, provincial though they were in their subservience to English cultural modes and the English mercantile economy, belonged to an essentially self-contained and independent social structure. The English ties of American families, of the new communities named for old Billericay or Framlingham, and of the various provincial elites soon grew tenuous. Some of the first families of seventeenth-century Virginia stemmed from the English gentry, as indeed a few did in New England. The ancient county society of Kent, for instance, can be said to have "reproduced," by 1660, "its names, its attitudes, its literary interests, even its field sports, in the swamps of the Virginia creeks."[9] But a hundred years later, although plantation society displayed as formidable a network of cousins as any English county, genealogy practically stopped at the water's edge among the gentry of the Chesapeake or New England, as for humbler men. "It's so long since I came away," Benjamin Franklin's father, who had emigrated in 1683, wrote to a probable grandnephew in England sixty years later, "that I have lost the knowledge of all our relations."[10] In 1756 the famous son visited the ancestral village with the casual curiosity of a tourist.

Although an English education or a tour of diplomatic duty in London as agent for one of the colonies made William Byrd II or Benjamin Franklin as well acquainted there as in America, only a few North Americans—mostly South Carolinians—shared the West Indian sugar planter's ambition to retire to an English manor and purchase election to a seat in Parliament. The movement in the other direction was considerably greater. British colonial office-holders, from the royal and proprietary governors and army and naval officers down to customs agents, figured for a few seasons in the society of the provincial capitals and ports. The governor's court set the tone for the colonial gentry, and an occasional place-holder, such as Governor Spotswood of Virginia in the early eighteenth century, used his office to establish himself as a colonial landowner. But all in all very few persons had standing both in English and in American society.

Social isolation as such posed no threat to imperial loyalty. During the long century from the 1650s through the 1750s, when the rival European empires were almost continuously at war in North America as well as in the East and West Indies and in Europe itself, prudence cemented the colonial allegiance to the power whose ships and troops guaranteed Anglo-American security. Imperial rule, furthermore, rested lightly on the colonists. In virtually everything but external commerce and a few other economic matters, the provincial legislatures were free of British regulation or taxation. Indeed, because of private smuggling and the official evasions that distance, slow communications, and British dilatoriness made habitual, even colonial commerce, with the notable exception of tobacco exporting, went ahead almost as though it were free of the Acts of Trade and Navigation. For colonial social institutions—families, communities, churches, schools, colleges—there was virtually no imperial regulation to evade. To the contrary, it was the colonists who sought to maintain a familiar English social structure in the face of natural obstacles. The course of events that precipitated the American Revolution in the dozen years between 1763 and 1775 involved another matter altogether: whether the constitutional relationship of the provincial legislatures to Parliament would continue to be one of virtual equality or subside into an unwelcome subservience. Americans had no need, however, to fight for the long-established and unchallenged independence of their society.

Well before 1775 an American society was flourishing, in half a dozen variant regional forms, from the granite coves of New England to the brackish swamps of Carolina and Georgia. Enjoying manifold opportunities for individualistic economic enterprise, the social order was shot through with a restless mobility: men moving from place to place and from rank to rank, while a pervasive materialism began to whittle away at the foundations of the family, community, church, and other institutions of the social order. But that was only a beginning. The natural and social limitations that hedged in economic progress enabled change to take place within a social structure of fairly stable institutions whose ancient values were still substantially accepted by all. It was a hierarchical society, though one in which neither aristocrats nor poor men were as yet hopelessly removed from the broad middle class; a society engaged in settling a continent but still confined almost entirely to the contiguous communities of the Atlantic slope; a society of a dozen ethnic origins, almost all of which had accommodated themselves to the dominant Anglo-American culture. However mobile the individual colonist might be, however rapid and disorganizing his upward or outward movement, his place within the social order at any given time was fairly certain. The mobility of that society may reveal to us more than a few hints of the egalitarian revolution that was to come, but in its growing maturity it gave contemporaries no clue that it would not be solid and stable enough to contain progress and change indefinitely within traditional lines.

PART TWO

The Society of Individuals, 1775–1875

I. Economic Revolution

In less than two centuries the white settlers of British North America had established a new provincial branch of European society. Within the next century that still youthful but conservative social order was riven to the roots. The structure whose foundation had been laid by 1775 and which continued to rise for nearly another half century was broken off and never brought to maturity. By 1861, when it collapsed into civil war, it had lost almost all coherence. The social revolution was only half recognized at the time. Men continued to speak familiarly of such institutions as the community, the family, the church—although no longer of social classes—as though they were substantially the same as of old. Yet the disintegration of established forms went far beyond the political egalitarianism professed by the two generations who lived between 1776, when Thomas Jefferson declared that "all men are created equal," and 1832, when Andrew Jackson struck down the "aristocratic" Bank of the United States.

The prime engine of the social upheaval of the nineteenth century was less ideological than economic. The material progress of the country, hedged about in so many ways during the seventeenth and eighteenth centuries, now broke free from both natural and artificial restraints. Old limitations were transformed, indeed, into positive stimuli. By the early 1840s, it has been suggested with considerable reason, the economy reached the point of "take-off" where it began to generate its own further growth.[1] Many of the advances of the age—the rapid occupation of the West, massive foreign immigration, ruthless exploitation of natural resources, mass production of goods, speedy communications, and accumulation of capital for reinvestment—built upon the hesitant experience of colonial days. What was radically new, however, was the great acceleration in the rate of economic progress, so great that instead of buttressing the material foundations of American society, it shook apart the institutions of the old social order. Since the brand-new phenomenon of industrialization was now part of the process, furthermore, the economic revolution promised to keep on shaking up the structure of society for generations to come.

10. THE WESTWARD MOVEMENT

The economic revolution got under way, well before the end of the colonial era, in the oldest of all American enterprises, the occupying of the continent. Before 1730 the settling of each region had inched forward along a broad front of new farms, plantations, towns, and counties fairly contiguous with the seaboard communities. That first frontier had advanced, against the resistance of the terrain and the Indians, hardly a hundred miles in a hundred years. At that rate the distance to the Pacific might be measured in millennia. About 1730 there began, however, a new stage of the westward movement that would blanket the rest of the continent within another century and a half. Between 1730 and 1890 the frontier advanced not only rapidly but by enormous leaps and bounds, from remote and isolated districts, themselves only recently settled, to others even more distant. No mere stepping up of the gradual infiltration from the seaboard, this migration made physical mobility itself into a valued way of life. Even more important for nineteenth-century society, the perennial land rush so confirmed Americans in their earlier inclination toward the individualistic pursuit of material ends that they soon came to see their own society in terms of the single value—always necessary but hitherto ranked much lower—of economic progress.

Migration into the new West went through three overlapping phases. The first began in the 1730s, just as Georgia, the last of the seaboard colonies, was being settled, and it continued to the 1780s. The movement in fact was not westward but southward and northward into the "back settlements" or "up-country" of New England and the southern colonies. In the South it spilled out of the Delaware-Susquehanna plain about 1730 and down along the fertile but narrowing valleys between the Blue Ridge and the Alleghenies: across western Maryland in the 1730s, in Virginia up the Great Valley of the Shenandoah River in the 1730s and 1740s. Crossing east of the Blue Ridge between the 1740s and 1760s, this rising tide of "Greater Pennsylvanians,"

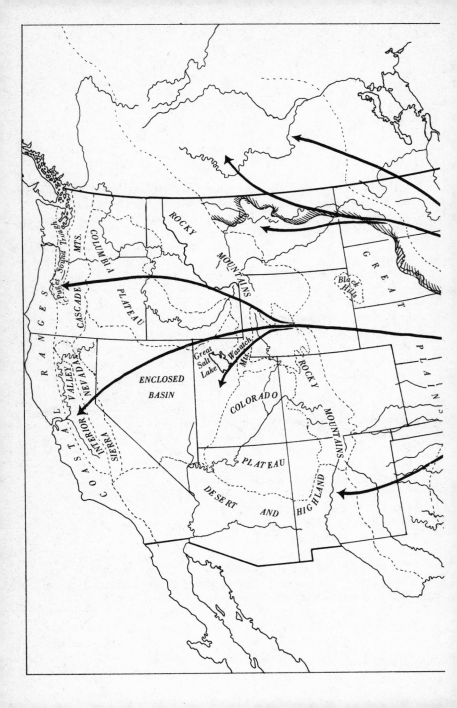

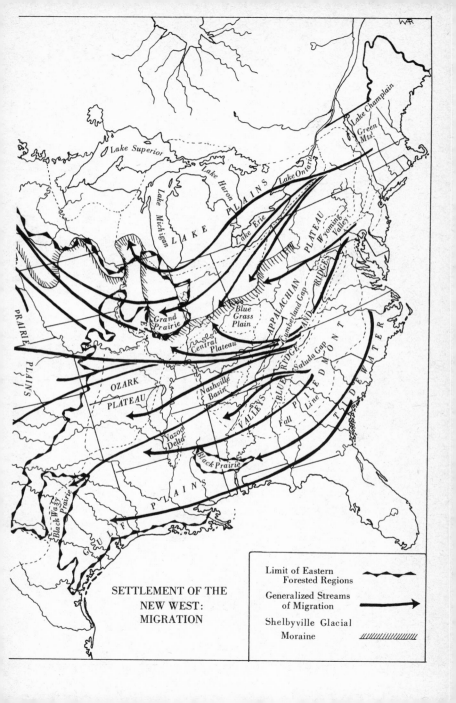

SETTLEMENT OF THE
NEW WEST:
MIGRATION

Limit of Eastern
Forested Regions

Generalized Streams
of Migration

Shelbyville Glacial
Moraine

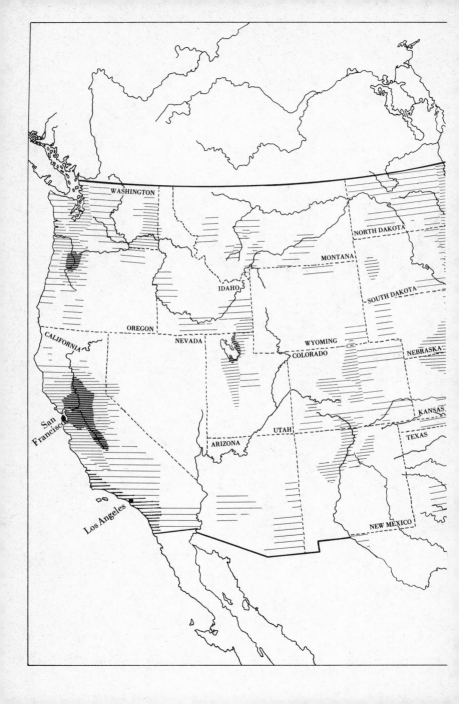

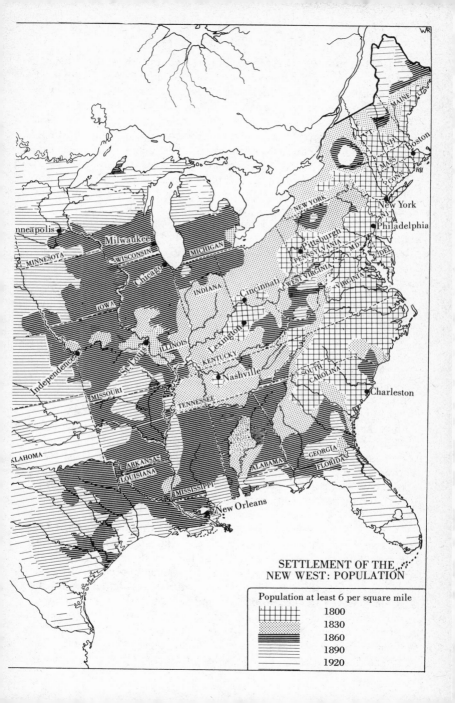

SETTLEMENT OF THE
NEW WEST: POPULATION

Population at least 6 per square mile
1800
1830
1860
1890
1920

joined by another wave from the Tidewater, filled the Virginia "south side" and the Piedmont of the Carolinas and Georgia. A new southern regional society rapidly took root along the seven hundred miles of the Great Wagon Road from Philadelphia, a society separated by the Blue Ridge and the Carolina pine barrens from the plantation society of the lowlands and divided within itself among the clannish settlements of Pennsylvania Germans, Scotch-Irish, Highland Scots, small groups of Welsh and Swiss Quakers, and a great many people of ordinary English descent. This "mixd Medley from all Countries, and the off Scouring of America," was set off both geographically and ethnically from the older seaboard societies.[1] Lying within the chartered boundaries of the Chesapeake and Carolina colonies and athwart their line of westward migration, the back settlements would in time be substantially absorbed into the society of the five southeastern coastal states, but in the eighteenth century they formed one great new inland region.

A new northwestern backcountry, more closely related to the society of the older regions, also materialized in New England in the eighteenth century. This Yankee frontier, a rough but not unfamiliar terrain peopled by the original Puritan stock, was distinguished mainly by its rapid pace of settlement and the great opportunity it opened for land speculation. Except for further settlement up the Maine coast, the new frontier was a branch of western New England, pushing up the Connecticut Valley and into the Berkshire Hills in the 1750s, through the Green Mountains to Lake Champlain in the 1760s and 1780s. Although the lake formed a natural extension of the Hudson Valley, New Yorkers arrived there after the New Englanders had preempted its eastern slope. By 1791, when Vermont was organized as the first inland state, the Yankees were ready to push on across the unsettled parts of upper New York State.

The second great phase of the new migration turned directly westward out of these same northern and southern back settlements. For a hundred years, 1770 to 1870, and across more than a thousand miles of mountain, plateau, and plain—penetrating the continent, that is, at ten times the rate of the colonial advance—the settlers moved in three broad, roughly parallel westward streams: northern, deep southern, and border. The border, or southern-upland, stream began moving first and reached the edge of the arid Great Plains, the Great American Desert of earlier maps, before the others. Out of western Pennsylvania and the southern backcountry it flowed, through Cumberland and Saluda "gaps" in the 1760s and 1770s, on down the valleys of the upper sources of the Ohio—the Holston, Clinch, and French Broad rivers, the Conemaugh and Monongahela, Kanawha and New—into the Appalachian and Central plateaus. By the 1780s the two most fertile districts, the bluegrass plain of Kentucky and the Nashville basin of Tennessee, were occupied, as well as innumerable mountain coves and patches of alluvial bottomland. As the Ohio Valley became the main axis of this migration after the Revolution, settlement proceeded both north and south of the river to the farther limits of the familiar upland country in northern Georgia and Alabama, in southeastern Ohio, and by 1820 in southern Indiana and Illinois. Across the Mississippi, beginning before 1803 when the whole of "Louisiana" was still Spanish or French territory and continuing down to the 1860s, the border migration worked its way up the Missouri Valley and across the Ozark Plateau to Kansas, where the forbiddingly dry Great Plains began. Men from this entering wedge of the frontier also moved onto the Texas prairies in the 1820s and 1830s and along the Oregon Trail over the plains and mountains to the Pacific Coast in the 1840s.

By that time these people whose German, Scotch-Irish, and Anglo-American grandfathers had set out from the colonial backcountry had merged their original ethnic differences; in turn they forgot their common border identity as they became citizens of nearly a dozen new states. Particularly because some of them lived in "slave" states and others on "free" soil, they did not think of themselves as fellow members of a single great inland region. Yet the career of one man like Daniel Boone—born in Pennsylvania in 1734, moving southwest up the Valley of Virginia to the Carolina frontier, northwest into the Kentucky bluegrass, and finally west to Missouri, where he died in 1820—spanned nearly its whole length.

The northern stream began to move westward in force a full generation after the border movement into the southern uplands. Already in the 1760s a few New Englanders had turned due west to certain isolated districts such as the Wyoming Valley of northeastern Pennsylvania and Cherry Valley in New York. Then in the 1790s a steady flow of wagons, sleighs, and boats carried New England people up the Mohawk Valley and turned the Appalachian districts of western New York and northern Pennsylvania into a new Yankee region quite distinct from the older parts of those states. Between 1800 and 1830 they occupied the plains of northern Ohio —and of Upper Canada or Ontario across Lake Erie—and pressed on until by 1850 a greater New England covered northern Ohio, Indiana, and Illinois and southern Michigan and Wisconsin. In a few districts already preempted in the 1820s by southern uplanders, especially between Lake Erie and Lake Michigan and in the lead mining region about Galena, Illinois, the American origins of this vast new northwestern society were more mixed. Taken altogether, however, by the 1860s a self-consciously northern province stretched from New York to the treeless prairies of Iowa and Nebraska, where, like the border province, it came up against the Great Plains.

The third stream of migration, from the plantation regions of the Atlantic slope, did not turn the flank of the Appalachian Plateau and begin to occupy the Gulf Plains until after 1800. Held at bay by the southwestern tribes until the War of 1812, white settlers swarmed in after Andrew Jackson's victory over the Creeks in 1814, and especially after the Indians were finally ejected from Alabama and Mississippi in the 1830s. By 1850 another major new province, the Deep South, encapsulating the old French enclave on the lower Mississippi, had been established across the Gulf Plains from Georgia to the edge of the Great Plains in Texas. A new West was complete. Like three tines of a pitchfork the northern, border, and southern migrations had pierced to the middle of the continent and established three regional societies far vaster than the old colonial regions from which they had sprung.

In 1850 the economic and social differences between the new regions, as they coalesced into the embattled South and North of the Civil War, were all too apparent. But certain general similarities underlay the Balkan complexity of sectional politics. Essentially common causes had impelled the rush of settlement into all the new regions and made each of them a prime exemplar of the "western" character of nineteenth-century America.

The rate of population growth was enormous in all parts of the country, although only New England kept adequate records of births, marriages, and deaths. As late as 1800 the annual birthrate was still more than 50 for every thousand people, and it was not at all extraordinary for a family to have seven or eight children. In Connecticut, the source of many of the migrants to northwestern New England in the late eighteenth century, more than one man could boast of a dozen children, some seventy grandchildren, and two or three hundred great-grandchildren. The population doubled every quarter century or less, "which increase (under divine benediction)," the governor reported in 1762, "we attribute to industrious, temperate life and early marriage."[2] Blessings on the same scale were counted in other regions in the eighteenth century, and in Pennsylvania and the southern backcountry the throng of immigrant Germans and Scotch-Irish augmented the natural increase. In turn the youthful settlers of the backcountry, both north and south, produced their own large families. Eight households in one Vermont town in the 1790s had 113 children among them, 99 of whom were young enough to be attending school together.

The youth of the migrants quickened the increase on each new frontier. Although there were graybeards who had spent their lives moving from frontier to new frontier, making a career of clearing and selling land, most of the migrants were the overly numerous sons and daughters of the latest pioneer generation. Three-fourths of those who went west from Vermont in the 1820s, when migration into the state had ceased and emigration was in full spate, were under thirty, and half were under twenty-five. During the first generation of settlement in one farming county of Wisconsin, between 1850 and 1880, the median age of the *working* population was twenty-nine at the start of the period and still only thirty-three at its close. The streams of migration across the country swelled into self-generating torrents as they rolled westward. As decade by decade the movement gathered strength and each generation of youthful settlers had to remove farther from their parents' neighborhood than the parents had done before, they grew more and more inured to the rigors of pioneering.

It was not the absolute numbers of young people crowding the soil so much as the wasteful agricultural practices, long since habitual among American farmers, that impelled so many to leave places that had been new in their own recent childhood. The ruination of tobacco fields in the Chesapeake region proceeded unchecked, in spite of the efforts of "improving" planters, as late as 1830. On every hand stretched the gullied "old fields" of stunted pines and broom sedge: "dreary and uncultivated wastes, a barren and exhausted soil, half clothed negroes, lean and hungry stock, a puny race of horses, a scarcity of provender, houses falling to decay, and fences wind shaken and dilapidating."[3] The remedies proposed by the reformers were fertilizer, diversification of crops, and more careful cultivation, all of which were beyond the means or the prejudices of ordinary farmers. Many of the latter instead sold out to large planters or, after 1840, to northern farmers who brought sufficient capital for such innovations. In the West they could start the cycle of soil destruction over again. "Ask those who have gone, or are going West, why they have left; or intend to leave their native hills," the editor of an agricultural journal observed in 1835, "and they will tell you 'the soil is worn out.' "[4]

For a time, early in the nineteenth century, prospects were better in the Piedmont of South Carolina and Georgia as farmers took up cotton growing. Formerly some long-staple cotton had been grown on the sea islands and coastal lowlands, but short-fiber or upland cotton became practicable only after the 1790s, when Eli Whitney devised a machine, or gin, to separate out the "sticky" green seeds without undue hand labor. Repeated crops of cotton wore out the thin soil of the Piedmont, however, within twenty-five years; it was said that the planters were baling up and selling their land in the form of lint. As early as 1815 there were men in this new cotton belt, as in the old tobacco lands, who were ready to move farther west.

No region was immune to soil exhaustion. In northern New England, where ten to twenty successive crops of wheat impoverished the thin forest mold on the granite slopes, the profitable course for the richer farmers in the 1820s was to buy up worn-out wheatland and turn to raising sheep for their wool; those who sold out moved west if they could. Other means of subsistence were also being pinched off: the wild game had been depleted, the marketable timber near the rivers had been cut off, and since deforestation made the streams no longer flow evenly throughout the year, the gristmills and sawmills were put out of business. Little room remained for enterprising young men.

The land system of the colonial, state, and federal governments whetted their desire to be off. The single-minded goal of economic progress, both public and private, shaped land disposal policy from 1730 onward. Although the old political forms of county and township were extended to the new West, they had degenerated into devices for promoting the quickest possible settlement.

The persons of influence who profiteered in the vast land grants of the colonies and then of the new states thoroughly debased the principle of aristocratic responsibility to society. When Governor Benning Wentworth of New Hampshire granted speculators some 130 townships west of the Connecticut River in the 1760s, the magnificent plan for doubling the size of the province was little better than a means to his own aggrandizement. (The only considerable revenue that an eighteenth-century governor received, except for what the assembly begrudged him in taxes, came from the sale of land and collection of quitrents on it.) Unfortunately for Wentworth, the Duke of York's proprietary charter of 1664 had clearly established New York's claim, confirmed by the British government as late as 1764, as far east as the Connecticut River. New Hampshire could dispute it on no better grounds than that New York had agreed with its other New England neighbors on a common boundary nearer the Hudson. But that arrangement had been based on the solid fact that Connecticut and Massachusetts had reinforced their own charter rights by occupation and long-continued possession of the area in question. Perhaps if New Hampshire mapped out townships in the territory west of the Connecticut, even though there were no inhabitants as yet, it too could make good its claim and thereby line the pockets of the several hundred land purchasers, among them members of the provincial council, the Wentworth family, and the governor himself. Besides charging an official fee of $30 for executing each of the town grants, Wentworth set aside lots for himself in each town, amounting in all to about a hundred thousand acres. In the end it required the rough-and-ready tactics of equally land-hungry Yankee farmers, marshaled during and after the Revolution in the guise of patriotic Green Mountain Boys, to give practical validity to the speculators' titles.

Official and private interests were similarly intermixed, though usually less fraudulently, in the land grants of other colonies. Speculation by the great did not, however, necessarily inflict oppression and extortion on the ordinary farmers who ultimately bought land from them. The traffic in frontier land would seldom bear exorbitant charges, since the prospective buyer could always go elsewhere. Speculators in Virginia in the 1730s asked £3 a hundred acres for land which had been valued, when still in the public domain, at only ten shillings, but the price was low enough to start in motion the great rush of backcountry farmers from Pennsylvania and Maryland.

Such western lands as the new state governments of the 1780s did not cede to the United States they put directly or indirectly into the hands of private speculators. On the pattern of the old baronial grants in the Hudson Valley, hundreds of thousands of acres in northern and western New York State were sold *en bloc* by both New York and Massachusetts, which had split their conflicting claims to ownership of the soil in 1786. Massachusetts' share, west of Lake Seneca, was resold in the 1790s to the Holland Land Company, a group of Dutch investors who retailed it in smaller parcels during the next forty years. The states of Virginia and North Carolina, in disposing of the entire acreage of their western districts of Kentucky and Tennessee, continued their old practice of selling warrants for small quantities of land, the purchasers to "locate" the actual tracts wherever they chose. By buying up warrants, speculators accumulated enormous holdings. To stimulate actual settlement both states stipulated, when turning over certain great expanses to promoters, that the latter bring in at least one family for every thousand acres, but such requirements were no easier to enforce than in colonial days. The most disreputable of all state land deals were the grants by Georgia of its Mississippi territory to the Yazoo Land Company between 1789 and 1795; in spite of the most blatant fraud and bribery, the transactions were upheld by the federal courts.

The Congress of the Confederation, having acquired most of the states' other western claims, also made a few enormous grants to speculative groups in the 1780s, particularly in southern Ohio. In all these ventures the speculator was as likely to fail as to succeed; even the celebrated financier of the Revolution, Robert Morris of Philadelphia, ended in debtors' prison in the 1790s. The riskiness of the business underscored the growing tendency of the age to hazard every other consideration for the hope of sudden wealth.

In 1785 Congress set up a system for disposing of the new national domain north of the Ohio, combining and regularizing certain features of the colonial and state systems. By surveying successive "ranges" of six-mile-square townships in advance of sale or settlement, the Land Ordinance made land titles as secure as in New England and avoided the confusion and litigation that had plagued the southern colonies. Every other tier was to be sold as entire townships, presumably to organized communities migrating in the old New England manner. In the next tier the thirty-six mile-square sections into which townships were subdivided could be sold to individual settlers after the southern custom. The speculator found scope for his business too, since few farmers could afford to buy a whole 640-acre section at the land office's price of a dollar an acre in gold, and of course the migrating community of farmers that conceivably could bid against him was already an anachronism even in New England. Indeed, since the land offices sold the new townships and sections at auction, well-capitalized companies could bid them up far above the minimum of a dollar an acre and corner the best tracts.

Over the next three quarters of a century the system was repeatedly amended in favor of the ordinary farmer. By 1820 the terms were fixed at a minimum of $1.25 an acre (an eighth or twelfth of the value of very ordinary land in the East) for a minimum purchase of eighty acres, only half a "quarter section." After 1841 squatters on the public domain were regularly permitted to preempt their quarter sections at $1.25 an acre without having to compete for them at auction; sales customarily were not opened, indeed, until such squatters had had several years in which to accumulate the necessary capital. Land not worth even the minimum price could be sold, under an act of 1854, at prices graduated downward to as little as 12½ cents an acre if unsold for more than thirty years. Finally in 1862 the Homestead Act simply offered a quarter section free to any actual settler.

The speculator found ways to make use of almost all the reforms or at least to evade them, since alongside preemptions and homesteads the open sale of land, at whatever price it might command, continued until 1889. The practical function of the federal land office in the nineteenth century was much the same as that of the provincial and state systems in the eighteenth: to encourage the most rapid possible exploitation of the public domain, whether by individual farm families, organized communities, wealthy planters, or merely speculative investors. Debates over land policy were conducted in terms of the conflicting economic interests of the speculator and the "actual settler," the partisans of each of course espousing the noblest social ends, but they were all agreed on the absolute desirability of economic progress.

As late as 1830 the Indian tribes on the frontier still impeded the westward movement, by deflecting the course of white settlement rather than by blocking it completely. The migration of the mid-eighteenth century had had to turn north and south into the backcountry of New England and the southern colonies largely because the western passes were still commanded by powerful tribes: in the north the Iroquois and Shawnees of the Mohawk and Ohio valleys; in the Gulf Plains the Cherokees and Creeks. Although most of the Appalachian Plateau was less promising terrain for farmers, the fact that the Shawnees and Cherokees seldom entered it except on hunting forays encouraged the southern backwoodsmen to move into Tennessee and Kentucky. In the 1760s, after the Seven Years' War, the British government attempted to stabilize the entire frontier, partly to compensate the loyal Iroquois and Cherokee allies of the crown. Further white encroachment was temporarily forbidden in the Indian country beyond a "Proclamation Line" along the height of the mountains, and two superintendents were appointed north and south of the Ohio to regulate the fur trade and prevent illegal settlement.

By 1768, however, the imperial government, having proved notoriously unable to tax the colonies for the maintenance of orderly Indian relations, abandoned the attempt and negotiated new Indian treaties moving the line farther west just ahead of the existing frontier of settlement. In 1774 the Virginians broke the Shawnee grip on the upper Ohio Valley, and during the Revolution the Iroquois, still faithful to the crown, together with the Shawnees in the Illinois country and the Cherokees on the southern frontier, were reduced by American forces. After the Iroquois ceded their New York lands and withdrew to small reservations or departed for Canada, the northern frontier lay open as far as Lake Erie.

The last serious armed Indian resistance east of the Great Plains was put down in northern Ohio in the 1790s and at the time of the War of 1812 in both the Northwest and the Southwest through defeat of the Creeks and of the confederacy led by the Shawnee Tecumseh. Over the next three decades the northern tribes withdrew farther west or onto reservations before the steady approach of white settlement. In the Southwest, however, most of the Creeks, Cherokees, Choctaws, Chickasaws, and Seminoles, having adopted many of the agricultural, social, and political devices of white civilization, were able to stand fast. It required the full weight—legal, extralegal, and illegal—of the federal government under the implacable old Indian-fighter Andrew Jackson in the 1830s, twenty years after his military victory over the Creeks, to force the bulk of the southwestern tribes to migrate to the edge of the Great Plains in Oklahoma. At once a tidal wave of farmers and planters, held back so long from the Gulf Plains, burst through to the Mississippi and beyond. Until the white frontier encountered the mounted warriors of the Great Plains in the 1860s, the red man posed only an occasional nuisance to the westward movement.

Beyond the circumstances in the older regions that determined who would go west, beyond the official land policy that encouraged men to do so, and beyond the clearing away of the Indian barrier lay the lodestone of the West itself. Although it presented an endless variety of topography, soil, and climate, the westward migrants were "not in search of the richest lands of the public domain," a recent study observes, "but merely the richest of the particular type of land to which they were accustomed back in the East."[5] Men who had been plowing the alluvial loam or the sandy upland soil of the Atlantic slope sought out similar places in the West, of course the better for an untouched layer of forest mold, in preference to potentially better but unfamiliar terrain where they would have to learn how to farm all over again. "Men seldom change their climate," the superintendent of the federal census of 1860 remarked, "because to do so they must change their habits."[6] The fact that migration moved westward in several parallel streams owed as much to this conservatism as to the obvious shortness of the journey between old and new regions in the same latitudes.

The cattle and swine herders and farmers of the border migration found in the Appalachian Plateau somewhat the same mixture of uplands and river bottoms that they had known among the ridges and valleys of the older southern backcountry. The limestone soil of the Kentucky bluegrass plain, the fertile Nashville and Huntsville basins, and the bottomlands of the Ohio and Missouri valleys gave new scope to old planters and to farmers striving to become planters. For ordinary men the rougher and poorer uplands, both north and south of the Ohio and up the Missouri, were good enough to begin with. Most of western New York was also Appalachian hill country, quite attractive to "the industrious yeomanry of Vermont and New Hampshire who wish for farms not lying edgeways," as a land company advertised.[7] After six generations on the granite slopes of New England they succumbed by thousands to the "Genesee fever" of the 1790s.

As the Yankee emigrants filled up New York, northern Pennsylvania, and the Connecticut Western Reserve of northern Ohio, the lake plains broadened out before them and merged into the prairie plains of the Middle West. "Here are mighty rivers, lakes, and forests," the report came back from Indiana. "Here are immense prairies, covered with immense vegetation. Here is a soil of inexhaustible fertility, capable of supplying all the reasonable or unreasonable wants of man."[8] During the last glacial age the "Wisconsin" ice sheet had ground down the limestone of the region into one of the largest and richest expanses of soil in the world. An earlier advance of the ice had pushed farther south, to the Ohio River, but in that southern third of Ohio, Indiana, and Illinois the additional millennia of weathering had leached out much of the valuable inorganic matter. The southern uplanders who for some time had been moving across the Ohio found the terrain acceptably familiar, and the New Englanders took possession of most of the richer area north of the Wisconsin or "Shelbyville" moraine. That line of glacial hillocks, although invisible on the political map of the states, fixed an approximate social boundary between the Border South and the North—in Illinois, most clearly, the lasting division between "Egypt" and the "Land of Canaan."

When in the 1830s the Yankees encountered the treeless and often marshy prairies that began in central Indiana and Illinois, they were discouraged at the absence of the hardwood forests that had always been the mark of good soil in the East, the arduous task of plowing the matted prairie sod, the lack of drinkable water and of wood for fences and buildings, the plagues of horseflies and mosquitoes, the ague or malaria, and the high winds and autumn prairie fires. Less fertile areas like the "oak openings" of southern Michigan and Wisconsin, so clear of underbrush that they called to mind an English park, were more familiar and easier to put under the plow. But further acquaintance with prairie soil and the invention of a suitable steel plow brought settlers swarming from all sides into the Grand Prairie of Illinois in the 1840s and on the still grander plains of Iowa, Minnesota, and eastern Kansas and Nebraska in the 1850s and 1860s. At the same time there were thousands who were willing to cross two thousand miles of plains and mountains to the Willamette Valley of Oregon in order to find the familiar sort of forested land.

The Gulf Plains presented fewer great expanses of excellent soil, although there were two good prairie regions much like those in the Northwest. South of the foothills of the Appalachian Plateau an arc of black limestone soil bisects central Alabama and northeastern Mississippi. Most of this Black Belt was a treeless plain when an early settler described it in 1821:

Fancy yourself for a moment in such a situation: before you a wide and extended meadow, to the right and left intervening strips of oaks and pines; proceeding onwards, the prospect seems terminated by the surrounding woods; anon, you catch a glimpse of the opening vista; and now again the prospect expands into the widespread horizon of an extensive prairie. These prairies are generally rolling, which is a great advantage, as otherwise they retain water, to the great injury of the crops; and as it respects the quality of the soil, it is generally admitted that it is the best the country affords.[9]

Between the black prairie and the Gulf lay red-clay hills and pine woods, poorer but still enticing to migrating farmers from wornout lands in the Southeast. The alluvial loam of the bottomland of the many rivers, especially the broad flood plain of the Mississippi, was also highly desirable. Before much use could be made of what was potentially the best region of all, the Yazoo Delta of western Mississippi, however, swamps had to be drained and levees built against flood, a work begun in the 1840s but not completed until much later. The second major prairie of the Gulf Plains was the "black waxy" of eastern Texas, the southern extension of the prairie plains of the Middle West. It gave less trouble than the Delta and was settled early by uplanders from Tennessee. Wherever the soil of the Gulf Plains permitted cotton to be grown, the spring rains, dry summers, and the nine-month growing season fostered the advance of plantations and farms.

As settlement proceeded in the vast reaches of both Northwest and Southwest, it stimulated still more migration from the East. In the 1820s the wheat crops of the Genesee Valley forced New England hill farmers to switch to wool growing or else to go west themselves. Between the 1830s and 1850s the center of the wheat belt followed the frontier across northern Ohio and southern Michigan to northern Indiana and Illinois and southern Wisconsin and Minnesota. Decade by decade, as the soil was worn down by repeated planting of wheat and became infested with plant diseases and insect pests, farmers abandoned wheat for sheep, first in New York and then in Ohio and Michigan, or moved still farther west with the wheat frontier. By the 1840s New Englanders were no better able to compete with western wool than with western wheat; this time many of them simply abandoned the hill farms which their people had settled only half a century before and joined still another wave of westward migration.

The cotton kingdom advanced in a similar fashion across the Gulf Plains between 1815 and 1860, but the new textile mills of Europe and New England provided markets for all the cotton that could be grown both on the older plantations of Carolina and Georgia and the new ones of the Southwest. After the first generation of settlement in each region the most successful cotton planters bought up much of the best land. The frontier business of herding cattle, sheep, and hogs on the unclaimed public domain was forced steadily westward or back onto inferior soil, but down to 1861 small cotton farmers continued to thrive alongside the great plantations.

For southern society the most portentous aspect of the expansion of plantation agriculture was the unexpected resuscitation of Negro slavery in the old tobacco and rice regions and its extension across the best soil areas of the new Southwest. Eastern slaveowners who sold out and bought new land in the West took their slaves along and found that each hand was worth half again as much in the new cotton fields. Since the international slave trade from Africa and the West Indies was prohibited after 1808 by act of Congress, there developed a brisk interstate business in Negroes. Between 1820 and 1860 some three-quarters of a million slaves were moved

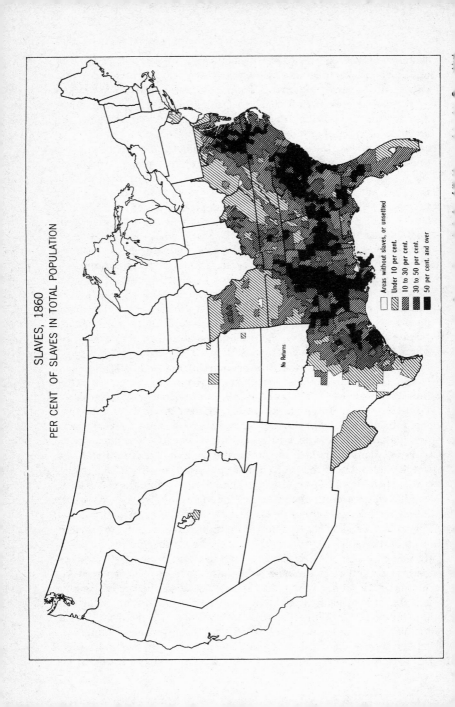

SLAVES, 1860

PER CENT OF SLAVES IN TOTAL POPULATION

Areas without slaves, or unsettled
Under 10 per cent.
10 to 30 per cent.
30 to 50 per cent.
50 per cent. and over

No Returns

from the southeastern and border states into the Gulf Plains. Somewhat more than half of them were taken there by their own migrating masters, the rest by commercial slave traders. Negroes rather than tobacco became the staple crop of many worn-down plantations in the Chesapeake region. As a Virginian confessed in 1832,

Virginia is in fact a *negro* raising state for other states; she produces enough for her own supply and six thousand for sale. . . . [The slave trade] furnishes every inducement to the master to attend to his negroes, to encourage building [i.e., breeding], and to cause the greatest possible number to be raised.[10]

The involuntary black migration entailed fewer physical horrors than the transatlantic "middle passage" of colonial days, but it manifested the same unconcern for any higher human value than the profits of a chain of economic enterprisers: slave breeders, slave merchants, slave drivers, and slave buyers.

The process of settling the western frontier was in many respects the force for individualism and egalitarianism, if not always actual equality, that Westerners themselves—most notably the historian Frederick Jackson Turner of Wisconsin in the 1890s—have liked to think it was. In every part of the new West, even in the Southwest of the Gulf Plains—a frontier of Negro slavery and quick wealth and abject poverty among white men—the frontier kept opening enormous fields for individual enterprise, individual fortune-building, and the rapid economic development of half a dozen vast new regions. Although most of the farmers, planters, and speculators who went west were seeking only a more comfortable place for themselves in the kind of society they had known back east, the revolutionary speed and breadth of their movement were bound to work equally radical changes in the structure of American society.

11. THE ATLANTIC MIGRATION

European immigrants joined the great rush to the new West. They were also part of another movement, one of the great folk-wanderings of history. The Atlantic migration of the nineteenth century had as radical an impact on American society as the frontier, although the ordinary immigrants to America, like most native Americans who moved west, were anything but radicals themselves. Most of them assumed that the material bounty of the New World would enable them to maintain their place in a society which, except perhaps for its easygoing manners, would be much like the society they had always known. Down to 1875 they were still coming, after all, from the same countries of Northwestern Europe that Americans had always come from. But the nineteenth-century immigrant usually found both the physical and the social environment of America disturbingly strange. The land itself had always been difficult for newcomers to cope with. Now its inhabitants were also unfamiliar. No longer were they so many transplanted Englishmen, Dutchmen, Irishmen, or Germans, but a composite, transmuted people with a national character of their own. The most massive infusion of foreigners could not turn this America once again into a province of Europe, nor could the newcomers merge unobtrusively into the new American society.

Forty years of intermittent warfare in the Atlantic world, from Lexington in 1775 to Waterloo in 1815, had reduced immigration to a trickle and isolated more than a generation of Americans from the homelands of their ancestors. During that span, when only a quarter of a million foreigners managed to cross the ocean, the American population more than tripled, from about 2½ million to some 9 million. Most of the old ethnic distinctions of colonial America dimmed and dissolved, or persisted as local oddities. By 1815 there were hardly any French, Dutch, Welsh, Scotch-Irish, or Scottish Americans who were recognizable as such or, apart from the pietistic communities among the Pennsylvania "Dutch," any Germans. The Anglo-American society into which most of the colonial stocks had merged had become, moreover, less specifically English, not out of any revolutionary rejection of the social and cultural example of the mother country but simply in the course of continuing to adapt to circumstances.

The new immigration was a prime mover in the economic progress of nineteenth-century America. From 1815 to 1875 more than 9 million immigrants arrived, a somewhat larger number than the whole American population of the earlier year; by the end of those two generations the old stock and newcomers together had produced a population of 45 million. The official statistics are inexact, but some 3 million emigrated from Ireland, nearly as many from Germany, more than 1 million from England, perhaps 200,000 from Scotland and 100,000 from Wales, and more than 250,000 from Scandinavia. Only about 1 million came from elsewhere than Northwestern Europe, and half of those were British North Americans of European origin.

The occupations, social characteristics, and cultural backgrounds of the immigrants were more important for America than their numbers. The categories into which the great majority fell reflected neither profound discontent with European society nor any compelling desire for the society of the New World. They emigrated for essentially economic, not social or cultural, reasons. Until about 1875, furthermore, economic dislocations in Europe drove far more of them across the ocean than were drawn there by specific American opportunities. Northwestern Europe was going through a lengthy upheaval in its agrarian and industrial systems, an upheaval that affected many more people than the few millions who emigrated. For every one who left, scores of others stayed behind and managed to find some new niche at home. Little direct evidence has survived of the particular motives of the persons who did emigrate. Ordinary emigrants seldom were articulate people, and many were illiterate: the fragmentary letters and journals they left are insufficient to confirm the circumstantial connection that seems to have existed between the broad economic changes of the time and the emigration of so many specific individuals.

The most widespread circumstance was the rapid growth of the population of Northwestern Europe after 1750, an increase beyond the capacity of the old economy to support or the old social order to contain. In 1750 the population of Europe was about 140 million; by the end of the century it was nearly 190 million; by 1850, almost 270 million. The countries that supplied most of the emigrants more than doubled their numbers during those hundred years, while others grew only moderately. Among the latter, France, which was more populous in the mid-eighteenth century than either England or Germany, grew only from 25 million in 1790 to 35 million in 1860. The German states numbered about 40 million by the latter date. The population of Sweden more than doubled, from 1½ million in 1750 to 3½ million a century later. The English rate of increase was almost twice as great: from about 5 million in 1750 to 8 million in 1800, 15 million in 1840, and 20 million by 1860. In Ireland, which may have had no more than 1 million people in 1700, there were 4 or 5 million by 1800 and by 1840 more than 8 million.

The chief reason that used to be given for the extraordinary multiplication of Europeans in that period was a decline in the death rate, particularly among infants, because of improved sanitation. The thesis now seems doubtful. The rural districts, which produced almost all the new population, benefited least from the medical advances of the age, and indeed as peasant villages grew more crowded, their crude notions of sanitation were likely to increase the death rate and cause the population to level off again. At least at certain times and places a rising birthrate made the greatest contribution. In part it reflected a lowering of the average age at which young people married, presumably encouraged by a more abundant food supply and a gradually improving standard of living. The same conditions also helped reduce mortality and stimulate fecundity. Many peasants, notably in Ireland, subsisted, however, on a single cheap new food, the potato; they profited little from the contemporary improvement of farming methods, and married early out of reckless despair rather than optimism about the future.

The century of Western European fertility and emigration was an age of general economic progress. The Industrial Revolution and the Agricultural Revolution together awakened in the larger population an expectation of a steady rise in the common level of material comfort. Measured solely in economic terms, the condition of the people would hardly have required many of them to leave Europe, except for victims of certain highly exceptional catastrophes, by far the worst of which was the Irish famine of the 1840s. But the effects even of beneficent economic changes are seldom simply economic. One by-product of the industrial and agricultural progress of the age was a splintering of old social institutions that cut individuals loose from their customary way of life into a new and often disconcerting kind of freedom. The advantage that America seemed to hold out to the ordinary emigrant was a happy combination of economic opportunity and social security. The liberal new economy which in Europe jeopardized a man's traditional livelihood and social status might, in the form which it took in the transatlantic land of liberty, grant him the freedom to conserve and perhaps improve on these customary things. In the end such immigrants, or their children, would be disillusioned in this hope. Economic individualism and social stability were as incompatible on one side of the ocean as on the other.

The Industrial Revolution got up steam in England in the mid-eighteenth century and spread across Europe and the United States in the course of the nineteenth. Most production for market formerly had been the work of handicraft artisans—literally "manufacturers." In many trades the master artisan was still proprietor of his own shop, and his workmen were either apprentices learning the trade or hired journeymen out of their apprenticeship but not yet masters themselves. Some trades, notably spinning and weaving, had already been reorganized by merchant capitalists who put out the wool or yarn to peasant families to be combed, carded, and spun or woven in their cottages and collected again for market. When entrepreneurs began to move production out of the cottage and into great "manufactories" in the late eighteenth century, so that the workers came to their work rather than it to them, the Industrial Revolution was in full swing. The capitalist who could organize and finance production and marketing on a large scale replaced the independent master artisan; factory machinery powered by waterwheels or steam engines replaced the old handicrafts; and the wage laborers who tended the machines could no longer reasonably hope to become proprietors themselves.

In the long run of a generation or two, factory production could be expected to provide a job and a profusion of goods for almost everyone. But in the displaced artisans' own lifetime the competition of cheap factory-made cloth, shoes, or pottery undermined their customary livelihood and the way of life that it sustained. Even by working longer and longer days they were hardly able to subsist. Scottish weavers in the 1820s had to sit at their hand-looms sixteen hours a day in order to eke out a wretched five or six shillings (less than $1.50) a week. For every one of the old master artisans who managed to become a factory owner or superintendent, factory competition drove many more out of business altogether. The factory that displaced the shop journeyman and the cottage weaver seldom seemed to them to be a satisfactory refuge. Not only was the wage of the semiskilled machine tender too low, but having expected to become their own masters or at least to direct the work of their own families, they were repelled by the inexorable discipline of the factory bell. The industrial employer for his part could find plenty of peasant laborers who would take the pay and who could be trained to do the work quickly enough.

An artisan might continue at his old trade and maintain his family's standing, however, by emigrating to America, still a technologically backward country, and setting up shop there. In the 1780s Parliament had prohibited emigration of skilled mechanics, but in 1825 the new liberal economics, coinciding with a swarm of "redundant" artisans, brought about repeal. In the next few years English handloom weavers left by the hundreds for America, many of them settling in Philadelphia, then as for a century before a center of their trade; where they continued the weaving of fine cottons and woolens as late as the 1860s. By the time American power looms finally captured their trade there too, the skilled immigrant handworkers were also passing from the scene.

The Irish or German journeyman who was similarly displaced by the competition of the English factories unfortunately lacked in his own country even the poor alternative of factory work. The linen spinners and weavers of Germany and Ireland were swamped between 1815 and 1845 by a flood of English cotton goods. Rather than turn to unskilled labor at whatever wages they could get, many of them joined their English fellow craftsmen in Philadelphia and other American towns.

The significance of these few thousand preindustrial artisans went far beyond their numbers. To emigrate in order to maintain one's trade and the social standing it had supported was exactly what the far more numerous agricultural emigrants, peasants and farmers alike, were doing. The peasants included, in fact, those part-time domestic craftsmen who had supplemented their wages in the fields by spinning, weaving, or shoemaking for merchant capitalists. At the same time that the Industrial Revolution pinched off that source of income, the Agricultural Revolution deprived many of them of their main livelihood and, worse yet, dissolved the old village communities to which they belonged. In 1750 the economy and society of rural England were still more medieval than modern. Only in certain villages of the Midlands had the enclosure movement of the century 1540–1640 broken up the old communal open fields and common pastures into a modern pattern of detached farms. In England as in most other parts of Europe the village still held all the vicissitudes of peasant life within its conservative orbit. It was too inefficient, however, to suit the enlightened "improving" gentry of the late eighteenth and early nineteenth centuries, for whom the higher rationality—and rents—of scientific crop rotation, machinery, fertilizer, and stock breeding put quite out of mind any lingering elegy for the old society of the manorial village. Sooner or later between 1750 and 1850, as the larger landholders of each locality secured from Parliament the right to enclose the open fields and commons, the English aristocracy took the final step to transform themselves from liege lords of men to mere landlords of acres.

The most grievous effect of the new enclosures, once again, was not economic dislocation but the uprooting of the old communal societies. Although every enclosure bill gave token assurance that each villager would receive the equivalent of his ancient rights, many mere cottagers, tenants at will, and small freeholders, who usually opposed the reform anyway, inevitably were squeezed out. The displaced could perhaps find other work and subsist somehow. Those who were dispossessed or who could not afford to hedge their small allotments might remain as wage laborers for the large farmers. Even if the district was converted from arable fields to a sheep run, unneeded laborers could usually find work in other parts of the country, since the reformers of the day put much former wasteland under the plow. The new factories also had places for "redundant" peasants, and for that matter if the villager stayed where he was and sank into indigence it was difficult for the parish authorities to shake off their legal responsibility to maintain him. Both before and after passage of the new Poor Law of 1834 the pauper's lot, to be sure, was as miserable as the ratepayers of the parish or poor-law district could make it in an effort to keep down the level of wages and to discourage applicants for relief. Occasionally the local authorities got rid of a few paupers by paying their passage to Canada or the United States, but most of the abjectly poor could not afford to migrate any farther than Manchester, Birmingham, or London to join the new urban proletariat. Wherever they went, their old communal roots were cut off.

The depth of the social revolution which all these economic changes entailed is suggested by the large number of substantial farmers among the transatlantic emigrants. They had shared for a time in the profits of the new "high farming" in England, or, elsewhere in Northwestern Europe, they had had some comparably reputable place in their village communities. During the Revolutionary and Napoleonic wars high prices for grain, cattle, and wool encouraged farmers to expand operations onto marginal land at high rents, but after 1815 production frequently exceeded demand. Rents went on rising upon each renewal of the farmer's lease, however, until English farmers by 1860 were paying perhaps thirty-five shillings (more than $8) an acre, one-fifth more than in 1815 and three times the figure of 1760. By 1860, that is, land in England rented for more than the outright purchase price of many "improved" farms in America and several times the federal land office's price for raw new land. Like the independent artisans who emigrated, many small farmers did not wait until the vise of high rent and low prices wrung them dry of capital and pinched their social status, but took passage for America to invest in land that promised better security. During and after the 1820s much of the emigration from all parts of the British Isles, including Ireland, was impelled by no catastrophe more imminent than the fear of declining into eventual poverty and degradation and jeopardizing the children's future.

From all parts of Northwestern Europe between 1815 and 1875 there came small or middling farmers who hoped to maintain their position—to improve on it if possible, to be sure, but essentially to conserve what they had and remain what they were. Although the Agricultural Revolution came to Germany somewhat later than to England, the growth of the peasant population of the southwest German states put pressure on land already as intensively worked as any in Europe. When a family's small holding was subdivided among several sons or when younger sons with no inheritance competed for available bits of land in the neighborhood, they were all threatened with an intolerable lowering of their economic and social condition. Many seized the alternative of emigration and a quarter section of cheap American land while they could still afford it.

These respectable classes were increasingly outnumbered after 1840 by a flood of steerage passengers who had already lost virtually all economic and social standing. Some were pauperized English cottagers, others were victims of local crop failures and sometimes near famine in parts of Germany and Highland Scotland, but the overwhelming majority were poor Irish cottiers. The prodigious multiplication of the Catholic Irish peasantry could lead to nothing but catastrophe. The improvidence with which young Irishmen married and rented a cottage plot was stimulated on one hand by an agrarian and political system which made these sub-subtenants of absentee and alien landlords despair of any self-improvement, and on the other by the ease of growing potatoes for any number of children to subsist upon. More and more land was taken up by smaller and smaller cottage holdings. Of the seven hundred thousand separate landholdings in Ireland by 1841, more than four-fifths were smaller than fifteen acres.

The cottier family—or perhaps several families in a single two-room cabin—grew potatoes and kept a cow for their own subsistence, raised a pig or two, the sale of which proverbially paid the rent, and found work where they could, the men sometimes in England or Scotland as "spalpeens" or migratory agricultural laborers and navvies on canal or railway construction projects. By 1840 many of them had brought their families over and settled down as the poorest of the new proletariat of industrial and casual laborers in the slums of Liverpool, Manchester, or Glasgow. For the time they could go no farther. The transatlantic steerage fare for a family, even at only a few pounds a head, was more than many an Irish laborer's wages for an entire year. Too many remained in Ireland without hope of regular work, although the new Poor Law of the 1830s, whereby surplus pauper laborers were to be systematically consigned to prisonlike workhouses, satisfied neither the inmates nor the ratepaying farmers and landlords. When the blight of 1845–1847 destroyed the potato, the last prop of the system, it seemed time for thoroughgoing agrarian reform in Ireland.

The potato crop had occasionally failed in the 1820s and 1830s, but the blight of the mid-1840s was nearly total. All across the country the potato patches, blooming one week, were "one wild waste of putrefying vegetation" the next.[1] Anything that could be eaten—cows, pigs, sheep, poultry, dogs, scarcely edible roots—soon disappeared. The British government's relief measures, restrained by the *laissez-faire* scruples of the age, were sorely inadequate, and since the export of grain was the normal basis of the Irish economy it was permitted to continue as usual. Everywhere there were people "like walking skeletons—the men gaunt and haggard, stamped with the livid mark of hunger—the children crying with pain—the women in some of the cabins too weak to stand."[2] Perhaps as many as a million died of starvation and disease.

In the late 1840s and 1850s another million and a half managed to get away to the United States and Canada, some assisted by remittances from relatives already there, others virtually deported at their landlords' expense. The landowner's answer to the old unprofitable use of the land was mass eviction of the peasantry, a reform that began in the depths of the famine and continued for some twenty years. In the three years 1849–1851 a quarter-million legal actions turned more than a million people out of their cottages, the cottages were forthwith pulled down, and the holdings were consolidated into more productive, although depopulated, farms and sheepwalks. At a cost of only £3 or £4 a head, at least some of the homeless and idle could be shipped off to America at no further expense to the district workhouse.

The mass of Irish emigrants of the 1840s and 1850s, together with much smaller numbers of destitute Germans, Scandinavians, and Scots who suffered the same potato blight—few of them lived as exclusively as the Irish on potatoes—were already bereft of either economic prospects or social standing in the old country. Unlike the ordinary emigrant farmers and artisans, they were driven forth by immediate disaster, sure not that there would be any work or place for them in America but only that neither existed any longer at home. The sheer number of people emigrating within a few years in such a desperate plight would make a radical impact upon American society.

A much smaller but no less important category of immigrants were attracted to America although they were already well enough adapted to the new industrialism of the Old World. They were factory, mill, and mine workers, most of them British down to 1875, whose skills the new industries of the United States also needed. Since America and Britain were going through approximately the same cycle of prosperity and depression, these fortunate emigrants threw over fairly satisfactory jobs at home in the expectation of still better ones abroad. As early as the 1790s the Lancashire cotton mill superintendent Samuel Slater and the Scholfield brothers from the woolen mills of Yorkshire placed the designs of the new English textile machinery at the service of New England capitalists; thirty years later both Slater and the Scholfields had become American millowners themselves. Between the 1820s and 1840s, after the repeal of British emigration restrictions and the full onset of American industrialization, thousands of experienced hands of all sorts crossed the ocean: Lancashire calico printers, Ulster and Scottish thread spinners, English and Scottish carpet weavers, Welsh, English, and German ironworkers, Scottish and English machinists, Sheffield cutlers, Staffordshire potters, slate quarrymen from North Wales and anthracite-coal miners from South Wales, Scottish and English soft-coal miners, Cornish copper, lead, and iron miners. For a generation or more in each industry, until America improved sufficiently on British technology, a quite ordinary immigrant collier or machine tender could expect the best wages in an American mine or factory and perhaps a foremanship or super-intendency.

It had been more than a century since many Europeans had emigrated for political or religious reasons, although the citizens of the independent United States liked to congratulate themselves that something more than the mundane push and pull of economic circumstances was at stake. Every European revolutionary up-heaval from the 1790s through 1848 did wash up a wave of refugees on American shores. Except for a handful of French émigrés in the 1790s, most of them were liberals or radicals whose causes had gone under: Irish rebels of 1798, liberals from reaction-ary German states, France, and Poland between 1815 and 1830, Canadian rebels of 1837, English Chartist democrats during the 1840s, and finally in 1848 several thousand Germans, Frenchmen, Hungarians, Italians, and Irishmen, the liberal-nationalistic "Forty-Eighters." Few in number, the refugees were distinguished for the educated, professional, and middle-class persons among them, liberal-minded individuals most of whom were predisposed to look with favor upon the American republic. Many quite ordinary young men fled Europe after 1848 for a political reason of their own: the military conscription which a number of countries were imposing.

For some hundreds or perhaps thousands of emigrants America seemed to offer both the space and the freedom they needed for their peculiar social experiments or religious refuges. Few of the phalansteries and other utopian communities that were planted in the 1840s and 1850s lasted long, since opportunities for private gain just outside their walls enticed away too many of their mem-bers. Colonies of German or Scandinavian peasant pietists, how-ever, like the Pennsylvania Dutch before them, flourished in all the midwestern states by dint of hard work, spiritual unity, and self-imposed isolation.

Like native Americans moving to the West in those same years, most immigrants from Europe were seeking the security of the familiar. Except at the extremes—the million-odd Irish famine refugees at one pole and the few thousand liberal revolutionaries and communitarian theorists at the other—the foreigners who came between 1815 and 1875 were not fundamentally discontented with the existing economic system or social order of their home-lands so much as with the precariousness of their place within it. Emigration held out the hope of securing and perhaps enhancing a man's fortune and good repute and those of his children after him. The kinds of opportunity varied. But whether the immigrant sought cheap and abundant land, the chance to carry on an obsolescent trade, or higher wages and advancement in the new industries, his goals were familiar and socially comprehensible. Such venturesome yet old-fashioned people seldom reflected, in deciding to emigrate, upon the fact that in its own way the American economy was already undermining the organic social pattern that most of them took for granted. Still less did they suppose that their own immigration would hasten the process.

Their plunge into the unknown began before they ever reached America. Merely to get there, once an individual or family had settled upon it, could be an unimaginable ordeal. There were discomforts enough, in the age of sail and the first steamships, for those farmers, skilled workingmen, or middle-class people who could afford regular means of travel: riverboat, stagecoach, or railway to the port; decent lodgings for the few days it might take to engage passage on a scheduled packet; four to six weeks on the North Atlantic in a vessel of less than a thousand tons burden; and finally a wearying succession of river, canal, and lake boats and railway cars to some likely town or farming district. But upon the growing majority of emigrants who were too poor for such luxuries, the journey inflicted a disconcerting series of trials of physical and moral endurance.

Travel to a port was perhaps merely tedious for people who had to walk, leading a bullock and cart piled high with boxes and children and pausing for spells of work along the way to make expenses. The pattern of seasonal migratory labor within the British Isles and on the Continent had already accustomed many— Irishmen in particular—to such travel, and no doubt some who set off for America got no farther than another village where there was work for them. Those who reached a port, which was increas-ingly likely to be one of the four—Liverpool, Le Hâvre, Hamburg, Bremen—where transatlantic shipping was becoming concen-trated, found themselves in a less tolerable situation. Peasant villagers were easily confused and demoralized while spending a

week, perhaps three or four, in sordid dockside lodgings, the unwitting prey of thieves and swindlers, until they found a ship that
would give them cheap passage to America.

Before 1840 all vessels with steerage berths for poor emigrants,
and many in the next two decades, were primarily freighters,
unloading staple North American cargoes of cotton, grain, tobacco,
timber, or fish and taking on European manufactured goods. The
latter being less bulky, the empty holds could be fitted out with
tiers of wooden bunks and profitably stuffed with human freight.
The fare, as low as £2 or as high as £5, depended on various
considerations: the number of emigrants who happened to be
seeking berths, the captain's impatience to clear for America, the
emigrant's preference for New York or Philadelphia over Halifax or
St. John as his destination, and the relative tolerability of the
lingering odor of cotton bales or salt fish. On even the better ships
which made a regular business of the emigrant trade after 1840,
several hundred people might be promiscuously packed into a
steerage hold measuring only 150 by 30 feet with 5 or 6 feet of
headroom. The emigrants had to crowd about open fires on deck
to do their own cooking, either of the ship's ration or provisions
which they had brought, mostly oatmeal in either case. During
heavy weather, when they were confined below deck for days at
a time, no cooking was possible, even if they had any appetite.
Herman Melville observed of one such emigrant ship, "To hold
your head down the fore hatchway was like holding it down a
suddenly opened cess-pool."[3] All too often "ship fever" raged
through the steerage, particularly among the debilitated Irish of
the famine years; one brig out of Sligo buried 108 of her 440
passengers at sea. Shipwreck was not infrequent. Of the seven
thousand emigrant sailings from the British Isles between 1847
and 1851, forty-four ships with more than a thousand lives were
lost at sea.

The crowding and discomfort of the steerage, although bad
enough to call to mind an African slaver, were less disturbing to
many than a degree of anarchy that no slaver could have tolerated.
"In the name of the grandfather," a Welsh emigrant complained
in 1856, "cannot anything be done to pack men and boxes in
order with the patience that the crew stow iron, lead, hemp, and
cotton? . . . As soon as they start stowing men everything becomes
a mess and the sailors bad tempered."[4] The most conscientious
and solicitous captain could do little more than see to it, as one said
in 1838, that "relations, friends, and persons from the same

neighbourhood" were given adjacent berths and that "the oldest
and most respectable married couples" were placed amidships to
keep the single men in the fore part of the hold decently away
from the young women.[5] Usually, however, the immigrants, most
of whom were strangers and even foreigners to each other, were
regulated only insofar as necessary to keep them out of the way
of the sailors working the vessel.

Steerage passengers were expected to regulate themselves, but
it was a rare company of them that had a common social and
spiritual interest such as had brought the *Mayflower* over in 1620
without loss of life or morale. A Cornishman who crossed in 1841
found "every man's hand against neighbor, and even friend, if
anything is to be got thereby."[6] Clergymen who happened to be
aboard an emigrant ship drew their coreligionists together at the
customary times of the day or week, but even though Catholic
emigrants did not invariably "take great pleasure in dancing Irish
jigs" on the deck above a Protestant service, the orderly communal
life which most emigrants had always known lay far astern.[7]

Although the great majority of immigrants landed in America
alive and well, the port where they happened to disembark was
yet another accident of transatlantic commerce: Boston for many
of the Irish famine refugees because it was the nearest and cheapest port in the United States; New York for Irish, English, and
continental Europeans arriving on ships in the Liverpool cotton
trade; Baltimore more usually if they came from Hamburg or
Bremen, and New Orleans for others embarked at Le Hâvre;
ports in the Maritime Provinces and Quebec for the poor Irish
who crowded into vessels in the timber and fish trades. Their reception ashore could be as unnerving as their departure, as a new
set of thievish dockside "runners" seized their baggage and offered
to "dollar" them out of their foreign money with little regard for
the state inspectors and agents of emigrant aid societies who first
appeared in the 1840s.

Many immigrants remained in the ports where they happened
to land only because they lacked funds to go farther. Unlike substantial farmers or skilled workingmen who had the means to
reach the destinations they set out for, poor immigrants simply
followed the water or rail routes as far as they could into the
unforeseen vastness of the continent and perhaps came to rest at
the transfer point—Buffalo, Detroit, Milwaukee, Chicago, Saint
Louis—where their funds ran out. It was largely through such
contingencies that Boston became an Irish center, that Germans

first deposited themselves at Baltimore, Cincinnati, and Saint Louis, and that by 1860 foreigners from every country of Europe made up 40 percent of the population of New York. Such places might have little demand for the labor of so many unskilled peasants, to whom nothing at all in the physical aspect of a great city was recognizable. Like Americans moving west, immigrants might have preferred more familiar surroundings. The hazards of immigration unfortunately withheld that source of security from them.

12. COMMERCIAL AND INDUSTRIAL REVOLUTION

The mass of emigrants who fled the insecurities of nineteenth-century Europe found life in America richer but hardly more secure. Between 1815 and 1875 the society of the United States was shaken by its own industrial revolution at the same time as it was enormously enlarged by the westward and overseas migrations. The peculiar American conjunction of several distinct sources of economic change, indeed, subjected American society to a uniquely revolutionary upheaval.

Commerce, although a long-established American enterprise, only gradually broke through its old colonial limits. For a generation after 1783, when American merchants lost their share in the British mercantile empire, they struggled to develop new lines of trade with continental Europe and places as distant as Canton. Since the Atlantic powers were at war during three years in every four between Lexington and Waterloo, there were new hazards to the direct trade which opened up with France, the Netherlands, and their Caribbean island colonies. During the 1780s and again after 1815 it was difficult for American traders, no longer accounted "English," to compete with British shipping and cheap British goods.

Both domestic and foreign commerce nevertheless reached an altogether new order of magnitude as the population expanded westward and the means of land and water travel were rapidly transformed. Turnpikes or toll roads, built by private joint-stock companies, were the rage of the 1790s and early 1800s, especially in the Northeast. The federal government undertook its own modest program of interstate "internal improvements," the greatest of which was the National Road westward from Cumberland, Maryland, which reached the Ohio River in 1818 and Vandalia, Illinois, by 1850. Roads proved unprofitable for long-distance freight wagons, however, and the turnpike boom gave way to a canal boom in the 1820s and 1830s. The busy canal network of

England had inspired a number of earlier American schemes, but none was successful until New York State built the Erie Canal, between 1817 and 1825, to connect the Hudson River at Albany with Buffalo and the Great Lakes. Nearly a score of similar public works were dug in the Northeast and Northwest, but none matched the Erie in length, revenue, or stimulation of local commerce.

The steam railway, an English innovation of 1825—the year the Erie Canal was completed—ended the canal-building era by 1840, when some 3326 miles of waterway, and already 3328 of railway, were in operation. By 1875, when the country had almost 75,000 miles of track, most of it in the North, the first transcontinental line had recently been completed across the Great Plains, through the western mountains, and over the deserts to San Francisco. Steamboats also appeared early on the rivers and lakes and in coastal waters. On the Atlantic, although the steamship could not compete with sail until the 1850s, lines of sailing packets were crossing on schedule as early as 1818, and in the golden age of sail between 1815 and 1860 the volume of foreign commerce and shipping more than doubled. The national economy was no less transformed by several commercial innovations of the period— the state-chartered banks and the money markets and stock markets of Boston, Philadelphia, and especially, as time went on, of New York—which conveyed capital where it was needed as easily as ships, boats, and trains conveyed goods.

Industrialization, a wholly new engine of economic progress, was the most revolutionary force of all, although in many fields of production the factory did not supplant old-fashioned methods until late in the nineteenth century. The American factory system followed the lines established in England: standardized, mechanized production; integration of various processes, especially those of carding, spinning, weaving, bleaching, and dyeing or printing in a single textile plant; a labor force of semiskilled machine tenders and a few highly skilled machine fixers, foremen, and technicians; a large capital investment; and the control of both production and marketing by a class of managers who were not necessarily technical experts. The first American factories were a few small cotton mills in southeastern New England in the 1790s. The rapid growth of the industry in the twenty-five years after 1815 made cotton textiles the largest category of manufactured goods; by 1860 the factory output of woolens was already half as great. A whole new machine tool industry grew up to outfit the textile mills with spinning "mules" and power looms and the railroads with engines. Ironworks were still charcoal-fired down to the 1840s, when they turned to anthracite coal and commenced to grow in scale as well as in number. As late as the 1860s some two-thirds of all manufactures, however, came from businesses that were not yet substantially industrialized, notably shoemaking, lumber, flour milling, clothing, and wagon building. The annual value of all American manufactures by 1875 was more than $3 billion, a fifteenfold increase since 1810 and a solid foundation for complete industrialization later in the century.

The old limitations on American economic progress were transmuted into positive stimulants between 1815 and 1875. The soil of the West, as it opened new opportunities for those who went there, also poured forth a flood of wheat, corn, beef, and pork which, together with fruit and vegetables from the older farming districts close to city markets, could feed as large an urban population as might develop. The cotton of the Gulf Plains and the wool of the North supplied two of the new industries more directly yet, although most of the cotton crop was exported to European mills. The land held other resources, some newly discovered and others long known but unworked in any quantity until this age of railroads and factories. Anthracite coal was sent down from the valleys of northeastern Pennsylvania by canal and rail to heat city homes and to fire factory boilers and blast furnaces. As cities and industry grew in the Middle West, the bituminous coal of western Pennsylvania, Maryland, Ohio, Illinois, and Missouri exceeded, by 1869, the tonnage of anthracite. The Northwest also contained rich deposits of iron, copper, and lead. The lead of the Galena district of Illinois and Wisconsin drew in a mixed population of English and American miners after 1815, well in advance of the farming frontier. By the 1840s copper and iron ore were coming down the Great Lakes from the upper peninsula of Michigan. The petroleum of northwestern Pennsylvania, discovered in 1859, led within a dozen years to a huge new oil-producing and refining industry stretching from Lake Erie to the Atlantic Coast.

Farthest away and richest of all, the gold of California, a region taken from Mexico in 1848, one year later turned the trickle of migration to the Pacific slope into a mass movement from every part of the world. During the next twenty years Colorado, Nevada, Arizona, Idaho, Montana, and Wyoming attracted their own gold and silver rushes. Each mining region of the Far West has cherished ever since the memory of the picturesque early years of Jackass Gulch and Hell's Half Acre when the miner was a solitary "prospector" panning for gold on a "claim," his right to it protected by no law but the rough-and-ready code devised by his own kind. In fact within a few years mining everywhere became a big business in the hands of big companies. By 1875 the combined annual product of the mines, oil wells, and refineries of the country was calculated at a third of a billion dollars. Even as prolific a people as the Americans could hardly make use of the full opulence of their new domain.

The floodtide of immigration in the 1840s and 1850s, together with a new American migration from the farms to the cities, turned the old chronic labor shortage into a sudden surplus. For a time the ports were swamped by thousands of poor foreigners unable to find steady work. Unemployment now became a recurrent problem, particularly during the general depressions which recurred every decade. As soon as good times returned, however, American employers could count, for the first time in two hundred years, on having plenty of labor on hand.

The most indispensable immigrants for American industrialization were the skilled workingmen from British and other European factories, mills, and mines. The first sixteen English coal miners in the Pennsylvania anthracite region, who arrived in 1827 carrying their own picks and shovels, were welcomed as "a very great acquisition to the number of our operatives, and . . . the commencement of a new era at our mines."[1] The surface quarries which had been cut only a few years before into exposed coal seams having been worked out, the foreign colliers were required to open underground shafts and drifts on the English system. In the same way a new cutlery works at Bridgeport relied on immigrants from Sheffield in the 1830s; as an emigrants' guidebook advised, "If from the factory of Rodgers, it is a sufficient introduction anywhere."[2] A New York manufacturer, writing to a Sheffield blade forger who was about to emigrate, requested him to "bring your hammers and other small tools and perhaps an Anvil or two."[3] Usually the immigrant needed to bring nothing more substantial than his skill.

Many working-class neighborhoods in American industrial towns, accordingly, were colonies of people from very particular localities of the Old World. Lancashire cotton printers came to new centers of their trade such as Lowell; thread spinners from the mills of Ulster and Paisley came to Newark, where the old-country companies had set up branches; iron puddlers and rollers from Germany and the English Black Country found work in Pittsburgh; Scottish and English "engineers" became American "machinists"; Staffordshire potters made Trenton and East Liverpool the American centers of their trade; Welsh colonies were settled in the hills of Vermont and Pennsylvania by slate quarrymen from North Wales, and Scottish villages by granite workers from Aberdeenshire in Maine, Massachusetts, and Vermont; Cornish tin and copper miners opened the Galena lead mines in the 1820s and the copper and iron mines of Upper Michigan in the 1840s. The list was long: the English, German, and French woolen spinners of Lawrence, the Kilmarnock and Kidderminster carpet weavers and Nottingham hosiery knitters at Philadelphia, the Macclesfield silk weavers of Paterson, English and German cutlers in Connecticut, English papermakers and glovers, and—all across the country when new mills and cities were going up—English and Scottish bricklayers, masons, and other building tradesmen. Within a decade or two, when each new industry had firmly established itself, the imported methods and machinery were improved upon by "Yankee ingenuity," that habit passed down from the days when labor had been scarce, so that the industry was freed from its initial reliance upon immigrants' skill. That later stage of the Industrial Revolution was reached so quickly, however, because so many skilled foreigners could be called in at the start.

Cheap manpower was also necessary in the early days of industrialization. An employer could recruit his dozens or hundreds of skilled men by paying them half again as much as they could get in Europe, but for the common labor in the factories, the canal and railroad projects, and the building trades thousands of men were needed at subsistence wages. The readiest source of such an industrial proletariat in the 1820s and 1830s was in the rural districts about the new mills and mines. As Yankee hill farmers gave up trying to compete with the prairie plains of the Middle West, many who lacked the means to go out there too went instead to the new factory villages of southern New England. The growth of factory production, for that matter, was a cause of their worsening economic position. Just as in Europe, merchant capitalists had organized a system of household industry whereby farm women and children turned idle moments to profit—perhaps $50 a year— weaving cloth or making shoes or straw hats. When factory competition undermined these domestic trades, many families lost the margin that had made subsistence possible and gave up farming for factory work. The shift from poor agriculture to poorly paid mill labor was somewhat eased by the rustic surroundings of the first mill villages, which were built around inland waterpower sites.

The labor system that attracted most notice at the time was a peculiarity of the cotton mills of Waltham, Lowell, and other places north of Boston. It proved easy to recruit the daughters of poor hill farmers for a few years' work, since the wages of two or three dollars for a seventy-five hour week seemed enough to help their families make ends meet back on the farm and perhaps to lay aside a dowry for themselves. The mill managers assured the parents that none of the notorious immoralities of English industrial slums would be permitted; the Lowell girls lived in dormitories supervised by respectable widows. Easily sent back home during a depression and quickly regathered when orders for cotton goods resumed, they were an ideally elastic labor force as well as world-renowned for their exemplary Yankee character and their literary effusions.

A more ordinary sort of labor, which the mills of southern New England and the Middle Atlantic states used from the start, displaced the Yankee mill girls in the 1840s. Whole families from farms that no longer provided either a respectable subsistence or the means to go west found work in a mill village for everyone down to the seven-year-olds. "In collecting our help," a Connecticut millowner said in 1827, "we are obliged to employ poor families and generally those having the greatest number of children . . . where their only means of livelihood has been the labor of the father and mother, while the children spent their time mostly at play."[4] Children who could work for a few dimes seemed an economic asset, not only to employers intent on cheap production but also to the parents; they could accept less than subsistence wages if their children contributed a pittance as well. In Rhode Island in 1853 there were nearly two thousand children under fifteen working in the mills; seven hundred of them were younger than twelve and sixty were under nine.

It was nothing new for a Yankee family to labor from dawn to dusk for a mere subsistence, and the astonishing "din and clatter" of a cotton mill, which seemed "such an atrocious violation" of the senses at first, could be endured along with the hot, humid, lint-laden air.[5] But as the machinery was improved in the 1840s and 1850s and more efficient production methods were devised, the pace of work grew incessant—perhaps four looms for a man to tend instead of two—and as his output increased, his daily wage could be reduced. Remonstrating or quitting might make it hard for him ever to find another job in the district. For people with a tradition of owning and running their own farms, no matter how poor, such conditions were hardly tolerable. Although few of them ever went on strike, as time passed people of their sort were less willing to join the ranks of mill labor.

The massive immigration of the 1840s and 1850s removed the need for them. Ports like Boston and New York, where penniless Irishmen and other peasant laborers landed, could put relatively few of them to work on the docks, streets, and land reclamation projects. But the surplus powerfully stimulated the growth of commerce and industry elsewhere. The "internal improvements" of the time, the canals, railroads, and river levees, had to be built by gangs of laborers, yet they ran through rural districts where there were few men to be hired. But in Boston or New York the contractors could recruit all they needed and perhaps more, in order to keep wages down to the suitably Irish level of $12 a month with board. As early as 1818 there were three thousand Irishmen digging the Erie Canal, and down to 1875 it was a rare construction gang anywhere in the Northeast or Middle West that was not Irish, from the pick and shovel men to the subcontractors bossing the job. In the South the same sort of Irish and German laborers, from the port of New Orleans, were preferred to Negro slaves for heavy and dangerous work on the levees and riverboats because, as a steamboat mate said, "The niggers are worth too much to be risked here; if the Paddies are knocked overboard, or get their backs broke, nobody loses anything."[6]

Industry also seized on the greenhorn peasant. In the cotton mills south of Boston poor Irish and English men, women, and children supplanted the original Yankees in the 1840s and enabled the industry to continue its rapid growth. Foreign visitors who came to view the intellectual mill girls of Lowell were surprised to find "a motley crowd of Americans, English, Scotch, Irish, Dutch, and French Canadians."[7] Irishmen also entered the coal mines as the laborers or "butties" of the skilled British miners. Since their wages were low by American standards, the immigrant mine laborers, navvies, loom tenders, and hod carriers contributed more to the growth of the American economy as producers than as consumers. But even poor foreigners had to eat, and it is true enough that mass immigration "helped to furnish the United States with both the manpower and the demand conditions for the great investment boom of the fifties."[8]

Before long the new continental economy, unlike the pinched affair of colonial days, was generating most of the capital for its own accelerated development. The first great ventures in textile manufacturing, such as that of the Boston Associates at Waltham and Lowell, drew on mercantile capital of the older sort, especially when foreign commerce became less profitable after the end of the Napoleonic era of neutral carrying or of privateering by American ships. The Lowells, Cabots, and other families who had risen to substantial commercial fortunes as recently as the Revolution now surpassed themselves in industrial wealth. Between 1816 and 1826 the cotton mills of the Boston Associates returned nearly 20 percent per annum on a half-million dollar investment. Competition pared the rate as time passed, but many cotton manufacturers who had begun with only $10,000 to $50,000 capital—in one case as little as $1100—enjoyed an annual profit of from 6 to 12 percent, and a few managed 25 percent.

A merchant like Moses Taylor of New York, who first established himself in the Cuban sugar trade, could turn to banking and thence to a variety of ventures in coal mining, ironmaking, and railroads. The young John D. Rockefeller, who began in 1859 as a commission grocery merchant and was soon carrying a $400,000 business on only $5000 capital, by 1863 was able to invest to even greater advantage in one of the comparably small new petroleum refineries at Cleveland. Pittsburgh ironworks, which could be started on $150,000 as late as the 1850s, regularly returned profits of 10 to 25 percent in good years and as much as 40 to 60 percent during the boom of the 1850s. An iron mill established about 1820 with an investment of $25,000 grew to the value of $500,000 by 1845 without raising any further outside capital. Similarly the surplus profits of one industry could be invested in another: thus coal mining might stimulate iron manufacturing, or ironworks finance new cotton mills. Foreign capital, largely British, also played a part, especially in the new railroad ventures, through investment in the bonds of the states or the private corporations that built them. But by the middle of the nineteenth century the young American transportation and industrial revolutions were essentially self-sustaining.

Government played its part in economic development. The first half of the nineteenth century saw the evolution of a progressive public economic policy, or rather the almost complete atrophy of the old social and spiritual considerations of the commonwealth. The eighteenth century's habitual permissiveness toward almost anything that would stimulate immigration and western settlement was now extended to the development of transportation and industry. The old commonwealth, in which private enterprise was expected to be regulated for the general welfare of society, dissolved into the nineteenth-century liberal state which recognized no common social purpose greater than the sum of the many private purposes of individual farmers, merchants, railroad builders, and industrial entrepreneurs. Each of them, and presumably the industrial workingman as well, was supposed to fit the image of the "common man," common in sharing with each of his fellow countrymen the free and equal opportunity to enrich himself by his own efforts. It was a rare American in that age who did not claim to be simply a "workingman."

The role of government was not, however, merely a passive one. The state governments promoted economic progress, particularly in the uncertain early years, through a combination of regulation, subsidy, and public works. The trend toward a liberal policy of *laissez-faire* was more apparent in the progressive dwindling away of almost all economically regressive legislation, that is, regulation aimed at social or spiritual ends, until little remained but a few vestiges of the old town market regulations. The first of a new set of laws intervening, all too feebly, in such social matters as the sale of liquor and the exploitation of child laborers were not passed until the 1850s and 1860s.

Most public regulation was intended solely to stimulate economic progress. The states, like the colonies before them, regulated weights and measures and inspected their staple exports in order to maintain their reputation for quality abroad. The small early factories did not need public capital, but applied as a matter of course for tax exemption, land grants, and water rights of the kind previously extended to local sawmills or gristmills. Canals and railroads were undertakings too vast, however, for the private enterprise of the time. They were also more clearly species of public utilities, akin to the roads for which government had always been responsible. Many of the early projects, notably the Erie Canal and the Baltimore & Ohio and Pennsylvania railroads, were built either by the state, by mixed public and private corporations, or by private ventures subsidized by the state. Those that were public works were not sold off to private investors until the early 1840s or late 1850s, times of depression when the shortcomings of their inexperienced managers and the growing adequacy of private sources of capital made it seem inexpedient for the states to own or operate them any longer. The one project that did enjoy solid success, the Erie Canal, remained the property of the state of New York.

Although down to 1862 the federal government never systematically subsidized commercial or industrial development as had been proposed by Alexander Hamilton in the 1790s and later by Henry Clay in his "American System," its inactivity was mainly due not to *laissez-faire* principles but to the fact that the state and private projects were adequate for the time. Whenever politically and economically expedient, Congress protected manufacturing by levying tariffs on foreign imports, subsidized the fisheries, gave public land to railroad corporations as capital for construction, regulated steamboat traffic on interstate waters, and established a central Bank of the United States. The precedents were always at hand for the great expansion in federal support of private enterprise that became politically practicable during and after the Civil War.

One state-established institution, the chartered corporation, as it evolved from its eighteenth-century public character into what by the 1850s was an essentially private institution, perfectly exemplified the triumph of a merely permissive and promotional economic policy over the old concept of public regulation. In 1800 an incorporated joint-stock company was still as much an instrument of the commonwealth as any incorporated town or city. In return for building and operating some useful public work such as a turnpike or bridge it was granted the special privilege of collecting tolls. But as the practical advantages of the corporate form for business became apparent, particularly as a device for selling shares of stock in order to raise the capital for the mammoth canal and railway projects, incorporation came to seem not so much a privilege granted in the public interest as a private right to be protected by the state.

In the 1830s the egalitarian demand inevitably arose that the right of incorporation be open to anyone who could use it. Corporations had hitherto been chartered by special act of the legislature. To prevent monopolistic privilege and make opportunity equal for all, reformers urged that anyone should be able to obtain a "general charter" by paying a nominal fee and subscribing to a few standard requirements. Most of the states adopted this reform by the 1850s. Although in fact most businesses were still incorporated by special acts, the idea was firmly implanted that incorporation was merely a species of public license for conducting private enterprise. The courts now usually accepted a state charter as a kind of private contract between the government and the corporation with which the state itself could not unilaterally tamper. Thus not only had economic ends come to overshadow the other traditional purposes of the commonwealth, but the commonwealth itself was held to exist for private economic convenience. Liberty had indeed become licensed.

Other economic reforms of the period were also pressed in the doubtfully relevant terms of equal opportunity for the common man. The political attack on the Second Bank of the United States, culminating in President Andrew Jackson's veto of its charter renewal by Congress in 1832, revolved around the supposedly "aristocratic" regulatory power of a central bank. To other bankers who operated under state charters, from the new financial center of New York City to impecunious western frontier towns, the central bank's prudent insistence that they keep their confusing issues of banknotes in line with their assets seemed like sheer hostility toward honest enterprisers, a hostility that they expected from Nicholas Biddle, the Philadelphia gentleman at the head of the Bank. Jackson, who impartially disliked all kinds of banks and subscribed to the simple doctrine of "hard money," shared the particular horror with which the state-chartered bankers regarded a "monster" bank that boasted of its power to regulate them. His veto message of 1832 bristled with the egalitarian prejudices of the yeoman farmer and artisan "mechanic." In the end a new set of state-chartered bankers—and the entrepreneurs and speculators to whom they extended easy credit in the form of their inflated banknotes—reaped the harvest of liberation from central economic control.

The idea that an egalitarian society necessitated an unregulated economy was the fundamental misconception of the age. By identifying the commercial and industrial entrepreneur with the yeoman farmer, the easy access to cheap land which generations of farmers had enjoyed could be equated to the much richer opportunities open to the new businessmen. But wherever opportunity to acquire land had in fact been no more than roughly equal, most men had gained little more from it than a modest material competence and respectable social standing. The nineteenth century moved on to make opportunity in commerce and industry as free as landownership. In the early years of industrialization the analogy might still apply; it might be almost as easy for a small entrepreneur, even an ambitious workingman, to enter one of the new businesses as for a farmer to take up new land in the West. Those individuals who succeeded in promoting banks, railroads, cotton mills, ironworks, or coal mines soon rose, however, to heights of wealth and power of an inequality quite unprecedented in the old agrarian-commercial America. But like western settlers and also European immigrants, businessmen did not anticipate how radically their ventures would subvert the society they had been used to.

"Things are in the saddle, and ride mankind."[9] By the middle of the nineteenth century the fastest possible economic development of the country had become the supreme practical value governing American society. Conventional homage was still accorded other values and institutions inherited from the old commonwealth as long as they did not stand in the way of material progress. But any remnant of a stable social order that threatened to check such progress—even if its own goal, like that of the Second Bank of the United States, was only a more moderate and steady rate of growth—was brought down by the popular cry of "aristocracy." The individualistic, egalitarian elements of colonial society and the early republic were adjusted to the purposes of the new entrepreneurs; whatever was not adaptable was denigrated or simply forgotten. The infinitely mobile economy of the mid-nineteenth century could thus be proclaimed as the legitimate heir of a society that had in fact been relatively stable and far more coherent. To assert, at any time thereafter, the absolute rights of private property against society—a radical heresy to earlier generations— would be taken for the very essence of American conservatism.

II. Social Disorder

The American economic revolution of the nineteenth century was so sweeping and so beneficent in raising the material standard of life that it obscured from view the social revolution that accompanied it. A people who made economic progress their pre-eminent value could discern only dimly the fundamental but far less salutary upheaval that was undermining the primary institutions of their social order. They were preoccupied with the tasks of economic growth: opening up the land and the other resources of the continent; gathering an industrial working class from Europe and rural America into new urban centers; applying a new technology to commercial transportation and industrial production. There was a further problem that Americans did not yet recognize. Since they saw fit to allow the economic revolution to move ahead under no tighter a rein than the slower and simpler farming and trading economy of the previous century had required, the consequent slackening of the strands that had bound the old institutions of society together seemed quite acceptable, even desirable. It was one thing, however, to free the individual enterpriser for the material development of the country. It proved quite another for the individual to get along without the non-economic values of life that had been embedded in the old social order.

13. THE ERA OF THE COMMON MAN

The final collapse, as it was supposed, of one ancient category of social institutions, the old hierarchy of ranks or classes, almost all Americans regarded as the peculiar triumph of the young republic. The egalitarianism of the age of Jefferson and Jackson was, however, more an article of faith, inspired by a state of affairs that was already passing away, than a sober description of the society that was coming into being. At a time when advancing the economic revolution was almost everyone's first thought, the popular notion of the society about them lagged so far behind actual institutional change as to be perennially out of date.

Such a lag in the general perception of things was nothing new. Colonial Americans had persisted in thinking of their society in English hierarchical terms even though property was far more equally distributed than in England. Now, just at the time when economic revolution was beginning to generate unprecedented extremes of wealth and poverty, they discovered the virtues of a broad-based society of "common men" and resolved to excise any remaining aristocratic imperfections from it. There was always some correspondence, of course, between the social egalitarianism of the "Jacksonian persuasion" and the contemporary class pattern. Certain practical economic circumstances, shaped in part by the egalitarian ideology itself, made the hope of a perfectly classless society credible. But essentially the new creed of equality reflected the practical circumstances of a simpler age, the era before the onset of economic revolution.

As late as 1832 the relative "equality of condition" among the American people struck Alexis de Tocqueville, that shrewdest of foreign observers, more forcibly than anything else he saw. "The more I advanced in the study of American society," he wrote, "the more I perceived that this equality of condition is the fundamental fact from which all others seem to be derived."[1] That practical equality went back several generations. Its most solid basis was the easy availability of land, reinforced by widespread economic opportunity of other kinds. The high incidence of landownership had made the suffrage fairly democratic long before the American Revolution. Although the Revolution itself was directly provoked by a different issue, the constitutional struggle between the prerogatives of the imperial and provincial legislatures, the lofty abstractions of the Declaration of Independence—"*all men* are created equal"—led Americans to reflect on the relative status of individuals as well. The Revolution was, as a recent student of suffrage reform says, "the turning point in the *conscious* democratization of ideas."[2] If all men were indeed created equal, then each should have a truly equal voice in electing public officials. By 1825 every state had adopted universal suffrage for white men, without even the modest property test of colonial days. No doubt because property had already enfranchised the great majority, there was little of the resistance to the reform that delayed it for another two or three generations in Europe.

As a social doctrine, the new egalitarianism was simple and coherent enough to conceal a certain inconsistency with the actual practice of the time. There were two parts to it which eighteenth- and much nineteenth-century experience seemed to prove compatible. The first was the concept of equal economic opportunity, the kind of individual liberty that colonial Americans had enjoyed in a modest way as proprietors of farms, plantations, small mercantile businesses, artisans' shops, and the like. They were content to see all kinds of economic opportunity thrown open in the nineteenth century, one may infer, because neither success nor failure had usually been excessive. The second concept, accordingly, was Tocqueville's "equality of condition," a modest and equitable leveling-up that assured the individual of what a later age would call social security.

A number of recent historians have described the character of this "Jacksonian" egalitarianism—a doctrine shared by men of both parties and all sorts and conditions. It harked back to the not wholly imaginary memory of an America of "simplicity and stability, self-reliance and independence, economy and useful toil, honesty and plain dealing" in an Arcadian "countryside of flocks and herds and cultivated farms, worked in seasonal rhythm and linked in republican community."[3] It was a nostalgic vision in which a primitive equality was assumed to have produced everything an honest man could desire. Perhaps no later age would ever quite recapture it. "We cannot help looking back, with sorrowful heart," a Pittsburgher was already lamenting in 1826, "on that time of unaffected content and gaiety, when . . . all was peaceful heartfelt felicity, undisturbed by the rankling thorns of envy; and equality . . . was a tie that united all ranks and conditions in our community."⁴ Sixty years later the reformer Wendell Phillips was still inspired by the vision, which he saw as an idealized New England town of the old days, "with no rich man and no poor man in it, all mingling in the same society, every child at the same school, no poorhouse, no beggar, opportunities equal, nobody too proud to stand aloof, nobody too humble to be shut out."⁵ Would not the same happy equality of condition and the same social harmony stretch on indefinitely into the future if free and equal opportunity were kept open for the common man? The common men of this popular ideology, neither very rich nor very poor, constituted the "people" of democratic oratory.

There were in fact a great many such men in America throughout the nineteenth century, middle-class proprietors of farms or shops whose condition was close enough to an equality to reinforce the ideal of democratic classlessness. As long as new land could be had fairly easily, it provided the means for self-advancement to farm ownership, and in the country towns it opened a field for small merchants, lawyers, and doctors, millers, wagonmakers, and harness makers. A few individuals would find much vaster possibilities to exploit in the West, but most men gained no greater success there than the middling competency and secure standing that their fathers' experience had taught them to expect.

Opportunity on the land was limited in some of the old ways in the first region settled west of the mountains, the southern uplands of the Appalachian and Ozark plateaus. Except in a few districts of Kentucky and Tennessee the upland frontiersman was never able to gain much more than a subsistence from the hillsides and patches of river-bottom land. The hill people grazed herds of cattle and hogs in the woods and drove them down to the eastern urban markets, south to the Gulf Plains, or up to the meat-packers of Cincinnati (the "Porkopolis" of the early nineteenth century), and they grew Indian corn and distilled some of it into a whisky of their own invention. But as the generations passed, for lack of richer opportunities most of them remained a race of fossilized frontiersmen (even to the log cabin), still recognizably Anglo-Scotch-Irish, independent and self-respecting, indeed a bit touchy in defense of their equal rights. Although many of them pushed on into the

Northwest across the Ohio, up the Missouri Valley, and on to Texas and other more promising regions, those who stayed behind formed as fiercely egalitarian a society as any in the nineteenth century and the closest, perhaps, to the common man of the Arcadian legend. Although historians have since demonstrated that other regions and classes also contributed to Jacksonian democracy, Andrew Jackson of Tennessee appeared so much the exemplar of this society as to give that movement a decidedly frontier coloration.

The place of ordinary farmers in the Gulf Plains before the Civil War has been obscured by the conventional tableau of great cotton and sugar planters and "poor whites." By any objective count the "plain folk"—the small planters and farmers of one or two hundred acres—were a majority in every county, even in the "black belts" of rich soil and plantation slavery, and in the less fertile hill country the great majority. Like the planters they grew cotton and corn, perhaps with the labor of a few Negro slaves. Although as livestock herders on the public domain many of them had to fall back steadily onto the poorer land of the Gulf Plains, they made the Southwest (including the upland plateau region) the chief cattle and hog section of America. The southern farmer veritably breathed equality and independence, as a large planter observed in 1860:

Though not so polished as the Southern Gentleman, and even, perhaps, a little blunt in manners, sometimes to rudeness, the middle-class planter is still no boor, but whole-souled, generous to a fault, and extremely hospitable, entertaining freely all strangers who neither look suspicious nor affect to put on airs of superiority. For, mark you, he is a man of the stoutest independence, always carries a bold and open front; asks no favors of either friend or foe, and would no sooner doff his hat to the Autocrat of the Russias, than to his poor neighbor . . . nor would he . . . insult the one any sooner than the other.[6]

The material base for his self-reliance began to erode, however, by the 1840s and 1850s, when the Gulf Plains had been substantially settled. Small farmers had less and less opportunity to improve or even maintain their position in competition with the great planters. Though there continued to be many times more farmers than planters, within a generation of the first settlements the best cotton land tended to be bought up by those who could afford it. One reason that the national political dispute over extending slavery into the western territories assumed extraordinary importance to the ordinary southern farmer in those years was his need for a never-ending supply of new land in order to ensure his continued opportunity to get ahead in spite of the trend of the times. And yet, since land engrossment did not have time to proceed very far before the Civil War, the antebellum "Old South," in the three or four decades that it lasted, never entirely lost the egalitarian character of a society of yeoman farmers.

The farmers of the Northwest had as great a wish to keep the trans-Mississippi territories free of slavery because so much of it was exactly suitable for their kind of agriculture, far more, indeed, than they managed to occupy until several decades after the Civil War. Since the Northwest Ordinance of 1787 and the Missouri Compromise of 1820 had excluded slavery almost from the beginning of settlement, the whole vast expanse north of the Ohio River and on beyond the Mississippi—together forming the later Middle West—appeared to be the land of perfect freedom and equality. Nowhere was economic opportunity more in accord with equality of condition. There were many districts like Trempealeau County, Wisconsin, settled between 1850 and 1880, which held out the chance to all comers, as the local editor wrote, to "obtain farms and become independent."[7]

The conditions of men in the Northwest were not literally equal. At no given moment was property in Trempealeau equally distributed; in both 1860 and 1870 one-third of the property holders owned two-thirds of the property, and indeed the richest tenth owned nearly two-fifths of it. These proportions were much like those to be found in long-inhabited rural regions of the East. In 1870 about a third of the farming population of the young states of Wisconsin, Minnesota, Iowa, Nebraska, and Kansas were laborers, and perhaps another third were tenants, many of them sharecroppers paying a third of their crop as rent. Tenancy first became common in the Northwest during the depression of 1837–1843, when few men could afford to buy land, and it was widespread by the 1850s.

But the economic distinctions that can be pieced together from the census returns do not define the social classes of the time. Among the landless laborers and tenants of one decade were many of the farm owners of the next. Laborers could make seventy-five cents to a dollar a day plus their board, and sometimes during planting or harvest as much as three or four dollars. Renting, too, even at $1.25 an acre, the same price at which land could be bought from the government, was a means of accumulating the capital necessary to improve and stock a farm—an expense several times the cost of the land itself. By paying a half-share of the crop on a rental-sales contract, some tenants earned full title to farms in only seven years. Abraham Lincoln observed in a speech to the Wisconsin State Agricultural Society in 1859:

Many independent men, in this assembly, doubtless a few years ago were hired laborers. And their course is almost if not quite the general rule. The prudent, penniless beginner in the world, labors for wages awhile, saves a surplus with which to buy tools or land for himself; then labors on his own account another while, and at length hires another new beginner to help him.[8]

Recent studies confirm the truth of the popular belief. In Trempealeau County, for example, while "the rich became somewhat richer, the poor became a good deal less poor."[9] Although every township had what the local editor could point to as its "highest social circles," class distinctions were minimal and, most important, usually temporary.[10] The "agricultural laborer" and the "domestic servant" of the census reports were simply the "hired man" and "hired girl." It was not surprising that they customarily lived as members of the farmer's own family, since many or most of them—two-thirds of the farm laborers in Trempealeau County in 1880—were in fact young relatives of his. As long as young men could expect to save enough from working for father, uncle, or a neighbor to buy cheap new land on the prairie plains, the egalitarian doctrine remained fairly close to the reality of the rural Middle West.

The upward-leveling effect of western land confirmed nineteenth-century Americans in their faith that they had a truly classless society or at any rate would have it soon. The existence of undeniable material differences, especially the impermanent ones between the older and younger generations, did not serve to establish distinct social classes. If classes supposedly did not exist, they could not be accepted as constituent institutions of American society; rank or degree was no longer an admissible principle for organizing or even thinking about the social order. Had the national economy remained on the modest agrarian and commercial level of 1775 or 1825, the belief might have proved workable indefinitely.

But in the radically altered context of the nineteenth-century economic revolution, which included industrialization, urbanization, and massive foreign immigration as well as the occupation of new farm land, social mobility all too often proved to be something other than a leveling force. Economic freedom in the new circumstances led, within a few decades, not to more perfect equality of condition but to enormously greater distinctions between rich and poor than the aristocratic society of colonial America had ever known. Economic classes existed in fact if not in popular social theory. But since the economic revolution which produced this practical inequality was conducted under the egalitarian banner of free enterprise and material progress for all, few Americans could quite permit themselves even to comprehend the nature of the problem. It was impossible to reform a defective class structure while denying that social classes existed.

Americans of course had been engrossed in the pursuit of wealth long before the Jacksonian era of egalitarianism. Tocqueville observed, after his visit in 1832, that he knew of "no country, indeed, where the love of money has taken a stronger hold on the affections of men and where a profounder contempt is expressed for the theory of the permanent equality of property."[11] The same individuals who fondly clung to the idea of a harmonious equality of condition—and in 1832 there was still a degree of truth to Tocqueville's assertion that "in America there are but few wealthy persons"—nevertheless grasped every chance to make the fortune that would lift them above the common herd.[12] The crucial point was that success should not be contrived through some artificial advantage in unequal laws but should be based upon individual talents, diligent application, and prudent calculation. It was not foreseen that economic opportunity itself in the new age of industrialism would be even less equitably distributed than the aristocratic privileges and official monopolies of the past.

Some who followed the streams of migration to the West found grounds on which to build far grander estates than a yeoman farmer's homestead. Large-scale cotton or sugar planting with slave-gang labor seemed quite in the old tradition of Chesapeake tobacco and Carolina rice, and for a double reason: the great colonial planters had been agricultural businessmen as well as landed gentlemen. The planters of the new Southwest carried over something of the eastern aristocratic tradition—some of them indeed were gentlemen from Virginia or Carolina—but this was diluted more than ever as they subjected soil, labor, and society to the economic ends of production and profit. By far the greater number of planters in the Gulf Plains, furthermore, were men who had climbed to that eminence; by no means were they transplanted eastern gentlemen. For every planter (defined as the owner of more than twenty slaves) who displayed the gentle breeding, classical education, and social conscience which had traditionally been expected, if not always attained, in the Old Dominion or the Carolinas, there were many more self-made men distinguished simply for the thousands of acres and scores or even hundreds of slaves which they had managed to acquire within ten or twenty years. The colonial founders of most of the old tobacco, rice, or indigo fortunes of the Tidewater and Piedmont had worked themselves up from small farming in much the same way. But in the richer and broader districts of good soil in the Southwest—the bluegrass plain of Kentucky, the Nashville basin of Tennessee, the Huntsville basin of northern Alabama, and the Black Belt, Yazoo Delta, and black waxy regions of the Gulf Plains—the field open to individual ability, hard work, careful management, or simply ruthlessness and luck was altogether dazzling. By 1860, taking the South as a whole, there were nearly 50,000 planters, some 1700 of whom owned not simply 20 but more than 100 slaves; a dozen had between 500 and 2000. The income of the 1000 richest families of the cotton states was perhaps as great as that of all the other 650,000 white families.

Inevitably many of the newly rich entrepreneurs of the cotton and sugarcane fields—entrepreneurs in spite of their peculiar relationship to their labor force—were more plutocratic than aristocratic: "cotton snob" or "Southern Yankee" was the ultimate reproach that a planter of the old school could hurl.[13] The cotton snob, as he was contemptuously described in 1860, was

a dirty fellow, who swears roundly, drinks deeply, boasts incessantly of his patrician blood, and is always in a snarl with every body and every thing. . . . He also seeks every opportunity to talk about "my niggers" (observe, a Southern Gentleman rarely if ever says *nigger*); endeavors to look very haughty and overbearing; sneers at whatever he considers low, and "their name is legion;" carries a cane not infrequently; affects a military step and manner, and tries to look daggers, bowie-knives, revolvers, blood and thunder, whenever or wherever he meets an abolitionist or a *nigger*.[14]

Given enough time, the truculence of the parvenus among the generation that appropriated much of the best soil of the Southwest might have mellowed into the assured gentility of sons and grandsons accustomed to wealth and standing, but the society of the "Old South" was cut off by the Civil War long before it could grow truly old.

In the North things seemed simpler. Northerners scorned the casuistry with which Southerners claimed all the virtues of aristocratic hierarchy and, at the same time, those of democratic equality among all white men. Was not the Northwest the true land of yeoman equality plain and simple? The conventional distinction that Northerners drew between the aristocratic and democratic societies of the two sections was less clear-cut, however, than they liked to believe. Here and there in the Northwest, particularly on the rich prairie plains, what amounted to a landed upper class quickly took root. Just as in the Southwest, some of the first settlers were substantial Easterners with capital to invest in the best available lands, an initial advantage that many of them maintained thereafter in spite of the generally upward-leveling effect of western land. Although the federal land system, from the Land Ordinance of 1785 to the Homestead Act of 1862, ostensibly favored the small farmer, down until 1889—when the new land was nearly gone— anyone could buy any number of acres he could pay for. Since the land office sold new tracts at auction, furthermore, large capitalists often commanded the best townships and sections. In the land boom of 1835–1837, when some 38 million acres of public land were sold, speculators seem to have bought three-fourths of the total amount. Eastern banks invested heavily; one group of bankers bought a third of a million acres, equivalent to fifteen townships, in eight states and territories. Twenty years later, in the boom of 1854–1858, speculators bought a large share of the 65 million acres of public domain that were sold. Throughout the years of settlement there were many great individual operators, such as John Gregg, who acquired 124,000 acres on the Illinois prairie, sold it off as quickly as possible, and still got an average of $5 an acre and sometimes as much as $10. Even under the Preemption Act of 1841 and the Homestead Act of 1862, the farmer, unless he got there first, could lose his chance to the speculative land engrosser. Large tracts were also granted in federal subsidies to the states and to railroad corporations, at whose prices the ordinary farmer then had to buy.

The kind of land speculation about which "actual settlers" complained was the private resale of land for as much as $7 or $8 above the government's minimum price of $1.25 an acre. That business had little effect, however, on the class structure of most new districts. However much the great speculators profited—a modest return of 5 percent was probably typical, and many lost everything in the panics of 1837 and 1857—not many of them, whether railroad companies, eastern banks, European syndicates, or individual investors, belonged to the local society at the scene of their operations. As absentee owners they simply drew off a certain increment from the struggling economy of a new district, as its citizens habitually complained.

Speculation also gave an opportunity, however, to many ordinary men who fell in with the bullish spirit that permeated the whole Northwest. During the great land booms it appeared that virtually everyone had turned speculator. As one of the early settlers of Michigan remembered the "land-fever" of 1836,

He who had no money, begged, borrowed or stole it; he who had, thought he made a generous sacrifice, if he lent it at cent per cent. The tradesman forsook his shop; the farmer his plough; the merchant his counter; the lawyer his office; nay, the minister his desk, to join the general chase.

The woods were full of men with maps and pocket compasses. "Who would waste time in planting, in building, in hammering iron, in making shoes, when the path to wealth lay wide and flowery before him?"[15]

A farmer might buy two or three quarter sections besides the one he intended to work, to resell at a tidy profit when the price rose, as usually it did. Or he lent his spare capital, on the security of a mortgage, to a neighbor who needed credit for land or improvements. In Trempealeau County no class either of debtors or creditors existed; borrowers and lenders alike were "a rough cross section of the . . . population."[16] Even more than in the eighteenth century, dealing in land and credit accounted for the success of a good many men who were only indifferent cultivators. Some of course were more successful than others, especially if they had been richer to start with; any rural county, township, or village soon knew them as the "first families" of the supposedly egalitarian community. "The successful land dealer of one generation," it has been observed, "became the banker, the local political oracle and office holder, or the country squire of the next."[17] But the business was so common that those who did best at it, as long as they were local residents and not absentees, inspired admiration in the ordinary farmer. Presumably nothing stood in the way of his someday doing as well himself, if not in the same place then in another new township farther west.

There were, in certain districts, men who bought great estates for their own use rather than for speculative resale. A number of livestock ranches (to use the later Great Plains term) of more than twenty thousand acres, raising cattle, corn, and hogs, were established on the Illinois prairies in the 1850s; one cattleman owned eighty thousand acres, the equivalent of four townships. Other landlords leased farms to tenants. But since farm labor and tenancy were regarded as means for poor men to rise to eventual proprietorship, even the greatest landlords were not supposed to constitute an established upper class. Land was the source of many midwestern fortunes, but only occasionally was it the foundation for permanent social leadership as it was in the plantation Southwest. In objective fact, in both regions alike land was a commodity which men acquired for economic exploitation of one sort or another, but only in the South was the great landowner expected to be attached to a particular estate and to derive his social rank from land—and "people"—in the antique feudal sense.

Far more scope existed in the Northwest, on the other hand, for the commercial business of towns and cities, places where profits from land speculation could be reinvested. Unlike the southern planters whose cotton bales or hogsheads of sugar or tobacco were handled by factors or brokers in a certain few large ports, the northwestern farmers marketed their relatively small crops of corn, wheat, sheep, hogs, or cattle through commission merchants and jobbers in nearby towns. From the first generation of settlement the villages, towns, and especially the burgeoning cities of the upper Mississippi Valley offered the enterprising merchant, shopkeeper, manufacturer, lawyer, and other business and professional men a wider opportunity for wealth and social standing than on the farm. The larger the place, the more exalted were the pretensions of its social elite. "We have our castes of society," it was said of Pittsburgh in 1826, "graduated and divided with as much regard to rank and dignity as the most scrupulous Hindoo maintains."[18] Such evidence of caste should not be accepted literally. The very contempt with which the wife of one storekeeper dismissed the wife of a somewhat smaller competitor—"she only belongs to the third circle of society"—suggests the tenuous and transitory nature of class distinctions even in the urban West.[19]

The social elites of new western towns modeled themselves on the richer but not much older upper class of the eastern cities at the hub of the transportation and industrial revolutions. There the rush of new wealth in railroads and manufacturing quite eclipsed the older commercial elite, most completely in New York, perhaps, as it overtook its rivals Boston and Philadelphia. Of course many of the old established merchant-aristocrats had also been new men as recently as the Revolution, when they had displaced still older families. But even when their predecessors had been conservatives who suffered exile and confiscation for their Toryism, the patriotic new men had continued in the old businesses and lived in much the same style. The rise and fall of individuals had not greatly altered the social structure. The advent of the industrialists and railroad men in the nineteenth century did not require actual ruination of the old mercantile elite, many of whom prudently put their commercial profits into the new enterprises.

But the magnitude of the new fortunes far outclassed anything seen in America before. In 1842 there were said to be fourteen millionaires in New York City alone. Although most of them were old-style merchants and real-estate speculators, during the next thirty years the foundations of the multimillion-dollar industrial fortunes of the late nineteenth century were put together in the cities of the Middle West and Far West as well as the East. Given the size of the new kinds of enterprise, the men who prospered in them swamped the older type in number as well as wealth. The "take-off" of the economy into self-accelerating ascent, which some historians place shortly after 1840, carried many a boy with no roots in the old mercantile elite to economic power and personal fortune. The year 1835, it has been calculated, was the most propitious in which a poor boy could be born if he was to aspire to great wealth; it was, indeed, the year of Andrew Carnegie's birth in a Scottish weaver's cottage. By any objective standard the upper reaches of the class structure were being considerably heightened, while at the same time the gentility of the new rich had never been less assured.

Neither the sheer wealth nor the origins of the new industrial elite were as significant for the American social order as the attitude which Americans, common men as well as rich men, held toward it. Successful merchants, bankers, railroad men, and industrial entrepreneurs could conceivably all have assimilated themselves into an aristocracy or gentry of the earlier American sort. But since social classes had gone out of fashion just at the start of the era of economic revolution, the new elite formed a mere plutocracy, distinguished only by wealth and the cultural façade it could buy. Ordinary men looked up to them not as a class that had prospered from the special circumstances of the time but as individuals superlatively endowed with personal virtues of the sort that commanded economic success.* When the great merchant-banker of Philadelphia, Stephen Girard, died in 1831, editors and memorialists attributed his vast fortune of $10 million solely to "his own industry, exertions, and enterprise."[20] He had begun as a "poor, outcast, ignorant, and wandering boy" and through "sobriety, prudence, economy, and industry" had climbed from "the lowest point of existence . . . to the highest."[21]

Popular repudiation of established privilege and monopoly in the Jacksonian 1830s promised to make self-help the unvarying rule for success. When John Jacob Astor, the fur trader and speculator in city blocks, died in 1848, leaving a fortune twice as great as Girard's, his humble origin seemed as remarkable as the wealth he had accumulated; even his notorious stinginess was not held to dim the brilliance of his career of magnificent acquisition. Not until 1877, the time of "Commodore" Cornelius Vanderbilt's death, did it begin to dawn on the reflective, after half a century of the general faith in equal opportunity for all—and in the trough of the worst depression of the age—that favorable circumstances perhaps had more to do with such success than superior individual character. The sharp-dealing railroad manipulator's egregious deficiency in the ordinary polite virtues no doubt contributed to the suspicion. But by that time a new, more systematic economic era of the twentieth century sort was also beginning to dawn. During the previous half century it had been supposed that the new barons of the industrial age were simply common men writ large, individuals uncommonly gifted with the economic virtues that the common man prized. Social class had given them no advantage, nor should their wealth preclude other worthy individuals from success in their turn.

At the other pole of the social spectrum those less than common men who did not prosper in the agricultural, industrial, and transportation revolution constituted a new peasantry and proletariat, real enough despite the fixed notion that no such European designations could ever apply to Americans. Euphemisms like "help," "hired men," even "poor whites," masked the objective situation. As long as it could plausibly be maintained that every American, no

---

* This doctrine has since acquired the name of "the Protestant ethic" and been traced back to the concept—which seventeenth-century Americans, especially Puritans and Quakers, shared with other Protestant Europeans of their time—that each man had a God-given earthly vocation which it was his duty to pursue. By the nineteenth century it had degenerated, however, into a merely secular ethic, divorced from higher spiritual or even social values, even though the name of God might still be invoked in its support.

matter how rich or poor, was a workingman with an equal chance in life, the existence of an inferior *class* seemed out of the question.

Down to 1865 Americans had to concede that the Negro slave was a manifest exception to the rule of equality. The castelike position of the Negroes became more rigidly fixed as the egalitarianism of the common white man flourished in the half century after the Revolution. Only in the northern states, where slave labor had never been essential to the economy and where few Negroes lived, could slavery be abolished or put on the road to rapid extinction. It was also kept out of the new northwestern territories and states over the objection of some—by no means all—of the settlers from the South. But Congress never forbade slavery in the southwestern territories, where the new states, as they were established by slaveowners and would-be slaveowners from the Southeast, legalized the "peculiar institution" as a matter of course.

Few Negroes, free or slave, escaped from the ironbound caste to which white opinion in all parts of the country had relegated them. Within the caste there were class distinctions of a sort. Free Negroes were a small minority. (For a master to manumit his slaves, even his own mulatto children, was increasingly unpopular and was even made illegal in certain states in the mid-nineteenth century.) Most of the free colored people lived in the cities, both north and south, tightly circumscribed within menial occupations and their own churches and rudimentary social institutions. It is doubtful that legal freedom made them materially better off than the higher ranks of slaves, the house servants of the great plantations, who scorned the white "poor buckra" as well as the uncouth black field hands. On large plantations and in southern towns there was a sort of middle class of Negro artisans—blacksmiths, carpenters, coopers, masons—perhaps hired out by their masters if slaves or working on their own account in town if freemen. But hardly any Negro was permitted to share in the ordinary economic opportunities open to the common white man or to assume a place in the professedly egalitarian white social order. Here and there an exception to the economic rule, even a Negro planter and slaveowner, could be found, but he had no place in white society.

There had been a certain economic logic to the existence of such a social caste in colonial days, when opportunity for the individual white laborer to become his own master produced a chronic shortage of crude labor that could be filled only by involuntary, perpetual servants. But the extension of Negro slavery across the Southwest after 1815, and the iron determination with which white Southerners of all sorts insisted on maintaining it, coincided with the beginning of massive foreign immigration and a national surplus of common laborers. Irishmen were indeed employed for heavy and dangerous work in the South in the 1840s and 1850s, since no one liked to risk the several hundred dollars invested in a slave.

By that time it was too late, however, for white Southerners to contemplate a new labor system; the slave might conceivably be displaced, but the whole black population could not be shipped "back to Africa" or any other remote place as various colonization schemes proposed to do as late as the 1850s. Unless the whole Negro caste could somehow be excised from white society—quite impracticable if only because the breeding, selling, and working of slaves were all as profitable as ever—any alternative to holding them in subjection, either as slaves or marginal freemen, was quite unthinkable to most people. No one proposed even so slight a reform as converting slaves into sharecropping tenants, although that sort of peonage quickly enough proved feasible when slavery was summarily abolished after the Civil War. To contemplate the least disturbance of the "peculiar institution" in the South conjured up the most dreadful nightmares of rapine and anarchy.

White fear of Negro violence was almost always grossly exaggerated. Generations of habituation to their allotted "place" had taught the mass of Negroes to endure the system as well as they could. Field hands may have doggedly offered a kind of passive resistance: it has been suggested that their proverbial laziness amounted to a labor slowdown and that their carelessness with tools and hard usage of mules and oxen was virtual sabotage. But in the nineteenth century there were no more than three outright Negro insurrections, each of which was confined to a certain limited locality in the old Southeast, and after Nat Turner's rising in southside Virginia in 1831 there were none at all.

Turner alone was enough to heighten the occasional alarms of the previous century into a constant dread. Southerners tightened their already stringent legal and extralegal system of militia patrols, bands of regulators or vigilantes, and Draconian corporal and capital punishments. Anything that might conceivably embolden a slave to slip the lines of caste—freedom of movement off the plantation, assembling in church or other large meetings without white supervision, working for wages with or without the master's permission, being taught to read and write—the southern states progressively (if somewhat selectively) interdicted. Free Negroes, who were always suspected, with reason in view of the Turner affair, of complicity whenever a slave uprising was rumored, were likewise hedged about with curfews, licenses and bonds for good behavior, and other petty restrictions. As the feeling grew in the South that the free Negro was a dangerous anomaly in society, his status was made more precarious; the burden of proof of his freedom was on the Negro if some white man claimed to be his owner.

The institution of caste in a free society, which had seemed a paradox at the time of the Revolution, required explicit defense in the professedly classless nineteenth century. The only explanation could be that Negroes were inherently so inferior that they did not belong to the race of men "created equal." And so most people believed. The abstract theories of the time—that Africans, as descendants of the pseudobiblical Ham, had been collectively condemned by God to be slaves; that the darkness of their skins also clouded their intellect; that they were childlike savages who needed unending generations of plantation training for civilized society; that, more like dogs than like white men, they were happiest when dependent upon a responsible master—no doubt were all rationalizations of the practical situation that provided the evidence for the theories. Negroes could not be treated equally because, as any common white man could see, they all too obviously *were not* equal.

Of course their practical inferiority had been imposed on Negroes during the same two centuries in which practical equality among most white men had gradually produced the doctrine of liberal individualism which the latter cherished. But to most people it did not matter that a Negro born in America in the nineteenth century was no more to blame for his degraded condition than a white man was entitled to congratulate himself on his boasted self-reliance. Logic could not lessen the general fear of anything that might upset the uneasy equilibrium of a society containing such disparate elements. That so glaring an inequity existed in an egalitarian society was a further source of the pervasive sense of instability that made honest democrats all the more determined to preserve and defend that same inequitable but fixed relationship. Even legal emancipation, when it was imposed as an unplanned contingency of civil war, could not erase the caste line running through the social order.

The presence of Negro slaves seemed to have some connection with the existence, also generally recognized as a southern peculiarity, of the depressed class of "poor whites." Identified in the early eighteenth century as the "lubbers" of the southeastern Tidewater, in the nineteenth they were known by various contemptuous names, as a planter observed in 1860.

In the extreme South and South-west, they are usually called Squatters; in the Carolinas and Georgia Crackers or Sandhillers; in the Old Dominion, Rag Tag and Bob-tail; in Tennessee and some other states, People in the Barrens—but everywhere, Poor White Trash, a name said to have originated with the slaves, who look upon themselves as much better off than all "po' white folks" whatever.[22]

Some of them seemed, especially in the eyes of the great planters who boasted of the same heritage, to be remarkably degenerate specimens of the southern Anglo-Scotch-Irish stock. The worst of them were described as "lank, lean, angular, and bony, with flaming red, or flaxen, or sandy, or carroty-colored hair, sallow complexion, awkward manners, and a natural stupidity or dullness of intellect that almost surpasses belief."[23] Long after the hopeful frontier era had passed, they existed on a pioneer standard of log cabins, hunting for game, and scratching out a few acres of corn.

All they seem to care for, is, to live from hand to mouth; to get drunk . . . ; to shoot for beef; to hunt; to attend gander pullings; to vote at elections; to eat and to sleep; to lounge in the sunshine of a bright summer's day, and to bask in the warmth of a roaring wood fire, when summer days are over.[24]

There may be some small degree of truth to the usual southern explanation for the indifference of this degraded class to material ambition. Like Negroes on one hand and southern gentlemen on the other, they were presumed to have inherited some of the inborn faults and virtues of their ancestors, in their case the unsuccessful freed servants, English convicts, and other dregs of the colonial immigration. But the circumstances of southern geography and society were more immediate causes of anyone's status than an untraceable and considerably mixed ancestry, whether of English "cavaliers," pauper-convicts, or, for that matter, captive African tribesmen. Much of the South was sandhill and pine-barren country, soon exhausted, gullied, and washed away by careless cultivation if not sterile to begin with. As the population of such districts grew, many small farmers took up very marginal land in misplaced confidence or eventually fell back onto it when the successful planters bought up the better tracts. Success followed success; failure and poverty became habitual.

Slave labor contributed to the economic advantage of the planter and of many ordinary farmers, and, since slavery was Negro slavery, it incapacitated the poor whites in both known and unsuspected ways. White wage labor was almost impossible in agriculture as long as it was identified as "niggers' work," and the alternative of industrial labor hardly existed as yet in the South. The more the owners of slaves and good soil thrived, the less chance their poor neighbors had to acquire the means to break out of their poverty. As an ultimate irony, though one quite unsuspected until the next century, the notorious listlessness, sallowness, and odd craving of the poor white "clay eater" were symptoms of anemia caused by hookworm, a parasite which enters the body through the feet and which had been endemic to the shoeless population of the Gulf Plains since first introduced in the persons of slaves from Africa. The "poor white trash" of the South were trapped in a vicious circle, made up of economic disadvantage, their own social attitude toward Negroes, and physical debility, only the first of which could have come from England with indentured servitude.

Although their squalor was an obvious anomaly in nineteenth-century America, no one was more insistent than they on the social doctrine of white equality and Negro inferiority. Especially because by any objective standard the superiority of their condition to that of the Negroes was highly doubtful, they were the most adamant defenders of slavery. As a poor Alabama farmer said in the 1850s of the blacks, "Now suppose they was free, you see they'd all think themselves just as good as we."[25] By the same token, in spite of the glaring inequality between great planter and poor cracker, both heartily assented to the dictum of the Louisiana editor who wrote in 1861: "The interest of the poor man and the rich man are the same in this country, one and indivisible. We have but two classes here, the white man and the negro."[26]

The North never adopted any one phrase like "poor white" for the new industrial proletariat, white and poor though they were. The mere wage earner was a workingman in a new sense: he was depressed as far below the common man of egalitarian dogma as the successful entrepreneur was raised above. Such workingmen were slow to recognize, however, that the gap was becoming permanent. In the industries to which the factory system and wage labor came earliest, cotton and woolen spinning and weaving, it was not until the 1840s, almost half a century after the first mills opened, that the operatives were seen to resemble the notoriously underpaid, overworked slum population of Lancashire and Yorkshire. Most other branches of manufacturing until 1850—some of them until 1875—employed more artisan-craftsmen or "mechanics" of the older type than semiskilled "operatives." In some of these, such as shoemaking and the men's clothing trade, which in 1850 had not begun to emerge from the domestic system, the independent artisan had already been degraded into—or more often displaced by—low wage earners working for a merchant capitalist. In certain others that were more fully industrialized—ironworks with their puddlers, hammermen, heaters, and rollers, the new machine shops, and mines and quarries with their several special trades—until well after 1875 a large proportion of the employees were highly skilled. Among still other workingmen, notably the printers and building tradesmen, such new machinery as was introduced did not greatly affect their status as craftsmen, though they complained of the intrusion of women compositors or other half-trained laborers. But the long-term tendency of industrialization was to rob skilled craftsmen of whatever degree of independence they had once enjoyed.

The low wages, long hours, and disagreeable working conditions, both in the new factories and among artisans with obsolescent skills, attracted attention at the time and have often since been described. Perhaps by some abstract calculus of dollars, time, and physical effort they were no worse than many farmers and journeymen had long endured. But in the circumstances of the time, particularly the common man's expectation of self-improvement, they bore heavily on any American. Hardly any but the highest-paid craftsmen made enough—$10 a week was the estimated requirement—to support a small family in frugal comfort. Anything over a dollar a day—$300 or $400 a year—was a "good" wage in the 1840s and 1850s; many semiskilled factory operatives made hardly half that much, and women clothing workers did well to get $1.50 a week. Working hours, even for children, lasted as long as daylight permitted, as they had for the less unremitting work of the farm. If toward the end of the period the hours were reduced to ten or eleven, the working pace in many industries was more than proportionately speeded up. No less important, the mass discipline that factory work imposed—the unvarying day's work, the myriad petty rules and pay deductions for infractions, the arbitrary authority of foremen and superintendents—seemed demeaning when set against the ideal of the independent artisan or farmer, whether or not the man who took a factory job had ever been so self-reliant himself.

Poverty and servitude were nothing new. But in the old days the man starting at the bottom—the servant or apprentice freed from his indenture, the peasant immigrant, or the farm boy setting off with little but his father's blessing—could reasonably hope to capitalize on his opportunities and raise himself to a fair equality of condition. Now both the obsolescent artisan and the semiskilled factory hand who supplanted him were reluctant to abandon that hope. The wall of economic immobility behind which the new wage-earning working class was becoming isolated had its loopholes, and sometimes there seemed to be more holes for the ambitious lad to pass through than wall to hold him back. There were always well-known exemplars, duly celebrated by the newspapers, of successful climbing out of honest poverty to well-merited fortune, presumably by dint of effort and force of character. In cold fact, as early as the 1870s, and quite probably at any earlier time as well, most of the leading businessmen were not onetime poor boys at all but rather the sons of somewhat lesser businessmen. But no matter that the meteoric rise of a Slater, Girard, Astor, or Vanderbilt was a rarity rather than the rule; anyone knew the names of scores of workingmen in his own bailiwick who had achieved moderate substance and status.

The sheer growth of the industrial economy kept opportunity open for ever-greater numbers of foremen, supervisors, and managers as well as a field for shopkeepers and other small businessmen. The egalitarian ethic of the time encouraged the workingman to answer opportunity when it knocked. An unskilled laborer could become a semiskilled operative, and the operative could acquire better-paid skills—or at least their sons could. There were limits to those prospects. As industrial machinery was progressively improved, in the long run it reduced the proportion of skilled hands, men whose job essentially was to do things the machines had not yet been perfected to do. That evolutionary process was not very far advanced, however, in the early decades of the Industrial Revolution, when whole new categories of machine-tending skills were continually being introduced, perhaps to remain in demand through the working life of the machine tenders.

The occupational mobility that kept partly open the class structure of industrial society demonstrated, all the same, the concrete reality that occupational classes did in fact exist. And for all the contemporary faith in the significance of upward mobility, recent investigation has shown that for the ordinary workingman success

was severely limited. Among the unskilled Yankee and Irish laborers who came to the small textile and shoemaking city of Newburyport, Massachusetts, between 1850 and 1880, only a minority
found a job and remained in town from decade to decade; virtually
none of them achieved anything more than a semiskilled job,
ownership of a mortgaged house or a nearby subsistence farm, and
a few hundred dollars in the bank, saved mainly against the day
when the principal of the mortgage fell due. The penny-pinching
required for a family to accumulate that narrow margin of security
entailed setting the children to work at an age when they should
have been in school and thereby jeopardized the rising generation's chances in life. By the standard of the egalitarian faith, that
was no success at all. "A few dozen farmers, small shopkeepers,
and clerks, a large body of home-owning families unable to escape
a grinding regimen of manual labor: this was the sum of the social
mobility achieved by Newburyport's unskilled laborers by 1880."[27]
But to the men themselves their small property betokened the
same sort of equality of condition that characterized the small
capitalist, the independent proprietor of a productive farm or
business, and made them true "common men."

The workingmen of the early industrial age refused to accept the
idea that most of them were permanently relegated to an inferior
status—that a workingman was *less* than a common man. Such
protests as were voiced by the few weak trade unions that existed
down to the 1840s implied that the "practical mechanic" might yet
shake off the "purse-proud employer" and escape "the disagreeable,
servile, and degrading status of the English laborer."[28] By the 1850s
it was becoming plain, the printers' union conceded, that "it is useless for us to disguise from ourselves the fact that under the present
arrangement of things, there exists a perpetual antagonism between
Labor and Capital . . . one side striving to sell their labor for as
much, and the other striving to buy it for as little, as they can."[29] As
late as the 1870s, however, the Knights of Labor, the first great
national labor federation, still hoped to establish producers' and
consumers' cooperative shops which would make the industrial
worker once more a kind of independent proprietor. Faith in the
universality of the American "common man" defied experience.

Or rather it was an older, pre-Jacksonian kind of experience that
still made men confidently deny the permanence of social classes,
especially those men for whom a middling equality of condition was
still a reality. The poverty in which many workingmen undeniably

were sunk did not, in middle-class opinion, constitute them a distinct class in society but only a number of individuals of less moral fiber and economic virtue than the self-made man of wealth. Since the days of the earliest settlements there had been ne'er-do-wells, loafers, and village drunkards who disqualified themselves for an honorable place in society. "If any continue through life in the condition of the hired laborer," Abraham Lincoln asserted to his audience of farmers in 1859, "it is not the fault of the system, but because of either a dependent nature which prefers it, or improvidence, folly, or singular misfortune."[30] The hundreds or thousands of "debased poor" in the slums of a nineteenth-century city seemed less a social class than a knot of perverse individuals. The most sympathetic reformer could say of the notorious denizens of the Five Points district of lower Manhattan in 1851, "They love to clan together in some out-of-the-way place, are content to live in filth and disorder with a bare subsistence, provided they can drink and smoke, and gossip, and enjoy their balls, and wakes, and frolics, without molestation."[31]

Presumably anyone of sound character could extricate himself from the ruck. As a New York judge lectured the officers of a journeymen-tailors' union, when fining them for conspiring to strike for higher wages in 1836, "In this favored land of law and liberty, the road to advancement is open to all, and the journeymen may by their skill and industry, and moral worth, soon become flourishing master mechanics," that is, employers.[32] Although within a few years the courts began to concede the economic morality of trade unionism, the door to the classless society was supposed to be as open to industrial workingmen as to other would-be proprietors of farms or businesses. One of the favorite fables of the 1860s, reprinted over and over by newspapers across the country, took to task the arrogant girl who "wouldn't marry a mechanic"; her snobbery was quite out of place in free America, where *everyone* was a workingman—and every workingman could rise to better things.[33]

The self-congratulatory Americanness of the egalitarian ethos was another reason for ignoring how the current situation contravened it. The new proletariat consisted largely of foreigners, many of whom, even after years in the New World, seemed still to belong to the class-bound societies of Europe. In providing the unskilled labor necessary for rapid industrialization, the massive immigration of German and Irish peasants in the 1840s and 1850s deepened the gulf between classes and yet made it plausible for Americans to deny that classes existed in their own society. Segregated, socially if not physically, by poverty, occupation or lack of one, outlandish language and behavior, and many of them by illiteracy and Catholicism, the foreign laborers were undeniably in America but not full members of American society. It was the same in Boston, New York, Baltimore, Saint Louis, or one of the smaller towns and country districts where the vicissitudes of making a living had taken them.

The social and cultural differences between these foreigners and Americans—even poor American workingmen—were substantial, beyond mere prejudicial discrimination, though there was plenty of that too. To the artisan displaced by industrialization a ready explanation for all his troubles was suggested by the sight of immigrants who, as one complained, "feed upon the coarsest, cheapest, and the roughest fare—stalk about in rags and filth—and are neither fit associates for American laborers and mechanics, nor reputable members of any society."[34] The economist Francis Bowen enunciated what employers believed to be the practical lesson of their experience with immigrants: "rude labor" had "incapacitated them for higher tasks. . . . Foreigners generally, and the Irish in particular, cannot be employed at all" in factories except "in the lower or less difficult tasks."[35] In Newburyport the unskilled Irishmen were much less successful at rising to skilled jobs than the former Yankee hill farmers who competed with them for work in the mills and who had little enough mobility themselves. Insofar as the American-born son of an immigrant peasant laborer was still identified as a kind of foreigner, he too suffered from many of the same disadvantages.

By no means all immigrant workingmen came to America as unskilled laborers; the thousands of experienced miners, mill operatives, and building tradesmen from Great Britain, Germany, and other industrial countries had the pick of many of the best kinds of jobs, and not a few of them managed to work their way out of the working class altogether. But most of them, even while enjoying a decent standard of living and the relative freedom of America from invidious class distinctions, persisted in thinking of themselves as members of the class into which they had been born. Unlike "the young American mechanic of ideas" with his individualistic concern for the promotion of "Number One," a Boston editor observed in 1877, the immigrant English workingman thought first of "association for the benefit of his class."[36] Respectable British and German workingmen, at whose foreign speech and manners Americans took no offense, perplexed them when they appeared in the character of trade unionists. Could they not just as well throw off their European class identity, to their own material advantage? Instead they organized class-conscious labor unions, ştriking for some small collective gain and attempting to induce others to join them; it was explicable only as "Anti-American" behavior.[37] "Whatever they might do in England," the striking mill hands of Fall River were warned in 1870, "interference with the right of free labor would not for an hour be tolerated in America."[38] Whether the immigrant was a craftsman able to join with others and defend the interest of his craft or only one of the faceless mass of peasant laborers, most Americans brushed his problems aside as extraneous to their free and equal society.

To deny that social classes existed in America was to slough off most of the old links between them, along with the old deferential manners. The existence of great wealth and poverty side by side need not in itself have disrupted the social structure. In the course of the world's history social stability has often enough proved compatible with either hierarchy or equality; colonial America struck a fair balance between the two. But to ignore the new extremes of social status—to assume, mistakenly as often as not, that economic opportunity was equally open to everyone and that it must inevitably lead to a more perfect equality of condition, from which all other social harmonies would flow—was to fail to see a need for any stable relationship between the various economic strata that in fact were taking shape.

The society of the plantation South was the great apparent exception—not alone in the planters' own estimation—to the general pattern of individualism or social irresponsibility. The great slave-owner's claim to old-fashioned gentility was warranted by his obligations toward his dependent "people." Historians will always argue over how conscientiously this black-belt *noblesse oblige* was performed. There were firm but kindly masters, admonishing their overseers against undue chastisement and humanely fostering the welfare of the sick and aged and the integrity of slave families, and there were others who condoned every imaginable abuse and were seldom called to account by law or public opinion. As much might be said of aristocrats in other hierarchical societies; it was not the human falling short of a social ideal that was peculiar to the planter. What was peculiar was the fact, already noted, that his "people" were not serfs or copyhold tenants or freeholding liegemen but chattel property, enslaved for the economic profit of the master, not a class within society but a caste—considered almost another species—beneath it. The social relationship between master and slave was incidental to the economic nexus.

Among the white social classes in the rural Deep South—the great planters, lesser planters and yeoman farmers, and poor squatters and crackers—social relations were uncertain partly for the *lack* of economic connections. Kinship among near and distant cousins, rich, middling, or poor, was commonly recognized, but insofar as all white men, as fellow members of the upper caste, thought themselves equally aristocrats, wealth and gentility no more made for social responsibility than poverty made for humble deference. If getting rich involved a planter in buying out his smaller neighbors, some of whom would have to fall back on poor land and sink into crackerdom, the planter as an economic individualist could be as callous as any other entrepreneur of the time. Although the colonial tradition of aristocratic leadership of county and state government was little affected, except in rhetoric, by the egalitarianism of Jacksonian democracy, it was not brought to bear on such private economic problems. Instead of leading directly to social disorder, however, the recognized gradations in the southern class structure —the color line in particular—were by tacit consent the very basis of southern social stability and political unity. Incipient class conflict among whites was muted before 1875 by the common racial prejudice and fear; so too was recognition of the need for a more coherent relationship between social classes.

In the rural Northwest, where fairly equal economic opportunity did foster equality of condition, the impermanent stratification of society, especially in the first generation of settlement, obviated the need to devise a harmonious pattern of class relations. Almost any man in his time might be farm laborer, tenant, and proprietor, debtor and creditor, mortgagor and mortgagee, and there were few paupers to be taken care of. The communities of the Middle West before 1875 had their own problems of social disorder, but not because of a faulty class structure.

In contrast to these agrarian regions, industrial society presented a problem of class relations almost entirely new to America. The terms "capital," "labor," and "middle class," to which Americans were becoming accustomed between the 1840s and 1860s, were economic categories. If, as the egalitarian faith had it, no individual was bound to any *social* class, the relationship between employer and employee was a matter merely of buying and selling a commodity, labor, at its current market price. A cotton mill superintendent at Fall River put it bluntly in 1855:

I regard my work-people just as I regard my machinery. So long as they can do my work for what I choose to pay them, I keep them, getting out of them all I can. What they do or how they fare outside my walls I don't know, nor do I consider it my business to know. They must look out for themselves as I do for myself. When my machines get old and useless, I reject them and get new, and these people are part of my machinery.[39]

The northern "wage-slave," southern critics caustically observed, was far worse off than the chattel slave, since his master took no responsibility for him in infancy, old age, illness, injury, or even on the job, except to pay him as little as possible for work acceptably performed.

Even that economic relationship was a limited one. The law prescribed no compensation for industrial accidents, unless the employer, and not the employee or any of his "fellow servants," could be proved, to the satisfaction of a jury, to have been the negligent party. If the job was particularly hazardous, the workingman was considered to have assumed its inherent risks when he accepted it. He was also expected to put something by for his old age out of his meager wages, even though long spells of unemployment during the recurrent dips in the business cycle made it difficult to subsist at all. The justification for this whole situation—not that anyone but proslavery casuists and a few lonely "labor reformers" questioned it—was that the workingman, like the farmer and everyone else in "free" society, was a freely contracting individual, free to accept the wages offered, free to look for work elsewhere, and free to rise by his own diligence and thrift out of the economic category of "labor" into that of "capital." As a Pennsylvania coal mine operator said in 1867, "Every man . . . must take care of himself."[40]

Traditional Christian charity withered in the parched soil of economic individualism. The doctrine of the stewardship of wealth —the duty of those whom God had favored with worldly riches to devote them to relieving the poor and to other "pious uses"—had lost its seventeenth-century meaning. Although it was unavoidable that obviously helpless widows, orphans, cripples, and the demented had to be relieved—that is, given just enough to keep them alive— the able-bodied man who had become a pauper out of failure to practice the virtues of industry and frugality in good times and bad was written off as "undeserving." The most sympathetic philanthropists exhorted the poor to seek "abundance and comfort" by eating frugal meals and abstaining from liquor or by taking up land in the West, "where, by honest industry, they may recover self-respect and independence."[41]* The cure for poverty lay not in the hands of the rich, however charitably inclined; it was up to the poor to cease being poor by accumulating property. Indeed, the only solution to the problems of the industrial working class was the dissolution of all such classes by everyone's pulling himself up to the great middle class of economically independent common men. But what was still reasonable advice for the farm boy in the West was resounding mockery for the industrial laborers to whom it was addressed.

In both the plantation South and the industrial North the pattern of classes, so universally misunderstood, was inherently unstable. The economic reality had departed too far from the social ideal of classlessness. Men of substance, both north and south, thought of themselves as conservatives because of their interest in the stability of property. But the right of the individual to acquire and possess property, although a usual element in orderly societies of the past, was now exaggerated out of all proportion to the other usual element of reciprocal responsibility between one class and another. As a social value, material progress—individual success and national expansion—had displaced considerations of the coherence and stability of the social order. One of the hinges of the old American society had been broken.

* The hundreds or even thousands of dollars that it cost to buy land, stock, and "improvements" for a western farm was of course prohibitive to men who spent their whole lives without ever seeing a fraction of such a sum. The poor laborers of the industrial districts, both native Americans and immigrants, had got where they were for lack of practical alternatives.

14. THE "COPARTNERSHIP
OF MARRIAGE"

The leveling of social classes, so Americans congratulated themselves, heralded a new liberal order of perfect freedom for the individual. They did not anticipate that economic individualism would subvert other fundamental social institutions that everyone professed to cherish: the family and the local community. As in every epoch there was a good deal of headshaking, on the part of supercilious foreigners and native Jeremiahs alike, over the sad falling away of husbands, wives, and children from the rectitude of more mannerly times. But it was assumed that the family as such would always function as an integral part of society, just as the community of village, township, county, or city would persist unshaken and even enhanced in spite of, indeed because of, its own undirected growth and the self-seeking of its members.

The familial revolution struck far deeper than contemporaries realized. As the larger society lost structural coherence, the family was cut adrift from its old institutional moorings. The loss of its function as a unit producing goods for the larger economy was apparent almost at once, especially as the factories of the Industrial Revolution rendered the artisan's household shop obsolete. But there were comparable kinds of disengagement from the larger social structure that were neither much remarked nor particularly missed. In law the family retained only a vestigial function in the political community: the duty, already obsolescent, to keep its own aged and other indigent members from becoming a burden on the public. The state in turn might attempt to safeguard the economic security of the family by legally exempting some small amount of property from taxation or attachment for debt. But the other legal and political reforms of the age, insofar as they affected the family, were such as to undermine its stability more than they shored it up. White manhood suffrage, by permitting any young man of twenty-one to vote, casually whittled away the old concept of the family as a political entity represented by its single head, the patriarchal husband, father, householder, and voter. To be sure, it could be assumed in the 1820s and much later in some parts of the country that a single man of twenty-one soon would have his own farm or household. But as more and more young men left the old rural communities for the distant West or went to the cities to seek a foothold in commerce and industry—and left behind, at least for a time, many of the young women—and as immigration likewise brought in a disproportionate number of males, the voter was less certain to be the representative elector for a family group.

Since in 1800 hardly a tenth of the population were church members, the great majority of families no longer stood in any special relationship, either by explicit covenant or out of inveterate habit, to a particular religious congregation or communion. Even the evangelical revivals of the next half century, seeking as they did to convert individual souls, might succeed only in intruding a source of dissension into any family. Again, the larger kinship groups that had been proliferating in the older colonial regions, when it had not been unusual for several degrees of cousins to be neighbors in the same township or county, were fractured by the accelerated pace and extended scale of migration and settlement. People whose forebears had lived in the same eastern district for three or four generations, long enough to become related to nearly everyone else, now uprooted themselves out of the lives as well as the neighborhood of their kindred, indeed even of their own parents. So thoroughly was the conjugal family disengaged from the crumbling old order—economic, political, ecclesiastical, and even cousinly—that the fact that it had once played so many public roles was virtually forgotten. Like the business corporation, the family had become a species of private enterprise.

Changes in the internal composition of the family were no less profound and almost as little noticed. The American family was steadily shrinking in size all through the nineteenth century. In 1800 perhaps as many as 55 children were born each year for every thousand people in the country, a birthrate almost impossible to surpass. Decade by decade it fell until by 1875 it was about 35 per thousand. The "fertility rate"* declined accordingly from more than seven children per family in 1800 to less than four and a half in 1875. By later standards those rates were still very high, but they had already fallen halfway toward the eventual low point of the

---

* A demographers' formula for the average number of children that would eventually be born to *all* the women who at a given time were of childbearing age.

1930s. As a clergyman lamented in 1867, "It has become the fashion for parents to be leading around a solitary, lonely child, or possibly two, it being well understood, talked about, and boasted of, that they are to have no more!"[1] By that time, when popular moralists were blaming the dwindling size of families on everything from tightly laced corsets to a vogue for illicit abortion, it was taken for granted that a family did not include unrelated young people—the cluster of servants, indentured apprentices, and others who had once been accounted virtual members. Thus it was considered worthy of special note that a farm family treated the hired man *like* a member. Evidently a basic change had long been underway to diminish the size and complexity of the family, so long, indeed, that even those who expressed alarm could not recall very precisely what sort of institution it had been in the days when the hired "servant" was included as a matter of course.

Disorganization of the internal structure of the family, like its contraction in size and detachment from the community at large, reflected the contemporary tendency for material values to undermine social institutions. The economic individualism of the time chipped away at fixed relationships between husband and wife, parents and children, brothers and sisters. Everyone seemed, by the 1860s if not before, to be looking out for his own satisfactions. Popular critics decried the self-indulgence with which the age was unaccountably afflicted, the taste for extravagant fashions among the wives, a premature addiction to luxury among children, and the invidious pride which the fondly doting husbands and fathers took in all this display. But if the universal pursuit of material self-interest sometimes ran to extremes in an increasingly affluent age, its most corrosive effect was not corrupt manners but rather the reduction of the many-sided practical relationships among the various members of a family to a simple matter of whatever sentimental affection each of them happened to feel for the others.

How satisfactory this might be depended on their individual needs and personal inclinations. Tocqueville saw in the new "democratic" informality a healthy untrammeling of natural affection, intimacy, and confidence, a deeper unity of heart and mind. Families whom other Europeans observed were less remarkable for such "paternal and filial affection," however, than for the matter-of-fact coldness which an Italian visitor reported in 1827:

In a large family the sons gather together at mealtime, each coming from his business; each enters the room, says not a word to father or brother; opens not his mouth, in fact, except to put something therein;

devours in a few instants the few ill-cooked dishes, and whoever is first satisfied, without waiting till the others have finished, rises, takes his hat and is off.[2]

Rather than a new phenomenon, it may be that such behavior was (if not simply too laconic for Italian taste) nothing but a relic of old-fashioned, stable family ties, unquestioned and on this occasion also unspoken among persons whom marriage and the happenstance of birth had thrown together. Or perhaps the members of that household were crudely displaying the individual ambition that even a family was now expected to foster in its sons, without as yet feeling the need to make up for such self-seeking by a stream of solicitous chatter.

The most important affections, it was generally agreed, were those between husband and wife. A couple formed their new family without necessarily regarding the economic interests, social status, or even the wishes of the older generation. Odd cases of parental pressure upon a daughter to marry for money or social standing— sometimes of her own too shrewd calculation—evoked cries of "legal prostitution" from popular sermonizers.[3] The withering away of the old "marriage settlement," commonly applauded for setting the pure affection of a young couple free from sordid pecuniary considerations, certainly freed them from having to succeed at once to their parents' social status. The new husband was now expected to carve out afresh his own family's place in the world. Accordingly the bridal dowry was seldom more than a token of parental affection, and the bridegroom's dowry, once the larger of the two, fell out of the negotiation altogether. Among ordinary people, as Crèvecoeur observed in New England, the change had come about by the late eighteenth century: "as the wife's fortune consists principally in her future economy, modesty, and skillful management, so the husband's is founded on his abilities to labor, on his health, and the knowledge of some trade or business."[4] Early in the nineteenth century it was commonly remarked that even the young man or woman with a substantial inheritance or "great expectations" was apt to pick a spouse without regard for a suitable match in fortune or social standing. "Fortune-hunters are despised here," a foreigner concluded in 1856.[5]

It was a curious thing to say of a society given over so wholeheartedly to the pursuit of individual economic success and private property. As against the personal calculations or desires of the particular man and woman, neither law nor public opinion governed marriage at all. Foreigners were startled at the informality with which a couple could buy a license and find a clergyman or justice of the peace to marry them, without having to publish banns, prove their parents' consent, or otherwise acknowledge that society had the least interest in their private contract. The "excessive readiness of the law in the formation of marriage," a Frenchman could only surmise in 1860, must have been "designed to increase the population, without regard to moral considerations or the future of the family."[6] The past of the family, as represented by the elder generation, at any rate could be ignored.

The multiple economic revolution of the age was the strongest corrosive of the old institutional links between the generations. Migration to farther and still farther wests removed many young men or couples from their parents' neighborhood and at length made their childhood associations strange to their own children. Migration from farm or village to an industrial city, though usually shorter in miles, still more abruptly broke the inherited pattern of life. Immigration from Europe, whether to farm or city in America, was a double amputation that made the old-country ways of grandparents, if indeed the latter followed along, unintelligible to their American-born grandchildren. The prime mover of all this migration was the hope of enhanced economic opportunity, particularly for the children, in order that an acceptable way of life, threatened by certain circumstances weighing on the old home, might be carried on in the new one. The more the migrants' sons and daughters improved on their parents' economic condition, however, the less relevance the parents' accustomed way of life bore to their own.

Even among people who remained in the same place, the rapidity of the change that the westward and cityward migrations and the Industrial Revolution worked in America made the society of any child's parents out of date by the time he was grown. He and his wife and children would have to come to terms with their own situation, whatever it might turn out to be. The young couple whom the age congratulated for consulting only their own affections and scorning the mercenary conventions of the past were, for all that, adapting to the radical new economy in order to win the kind of success it offered. Fortune hunting still went on, but without the old rules.

Even as the burgeoning economy permitted young people to fling off some of the old constraints, the new freedom imposed others of its own. To form a family was easy enough; the modest affluence that the young American had long since come to expect from landownership encouraged him to marry in his early twenties. Although a temporary shortage of women on a newly opened frontier might force him to delay a year or two, any girl in her teens who could get there could find a husband at once. But early marriage was not simply a matter of choice. The ordinary farm of the time required labor to work it, and most men had to generate their own labor force. For a farmer who had sunk all his small capital and credit into land, stock, and improvements, to hire labor was prohibitively expensive, since every farm laborer was looking for wages that would enable him to acquire a farm of his own, and to get married, as soon as possible. Each child, from the age of seven or eight to seventeen or eighteen, was an economic asset. "He must be a poor block indeed," it was observed in the 1840s, "who does not pay back into the common treasury more than he takes from it."[7]

The economic stringencies binding the industrial workingman were less unlike the rising farmer's calculations than appearances suggested. Wages in factories, mines, and construction gangs were set no higher than necessary to attract enough hands in an era of a growing surplus of labor—usually to provide a mere subsistence for a single man, or woman. Marriage was easy enough, but children were a mixed economic blessing. Like the farmer's children, they were completely dependent upon their parents only in their first six or seven years. For the next ten, as the little bobbin-doffers or slate pickers contributed their pittances to the household larder, the family economy increasingly depended on them.

The social dislocations of the mobile economy kept some people from marrying at all. The westward and cityward migrations from rural New England isolated many of the girls, both those who were left behind and those who went to work in the new textile towns. In terms of abstract statistics there no doubt were plenty of men looking for wives in both the rural West and the urban East, but many such were hardly acceptable as husbands. How many of the Yankee mill girls of early Waltham and Lowell ultimately devoted the savings from several years' labor to marriage and a family of their own, as was said to be their object, is unknown. It is fairly certain that they did not find suitable husbands among the poor Catholic Irishmen who were supplanting them in the mills in the 1840s. There were Yankee boys in the cities too. But young men of character who took to heart the precept to work, save, and make their fortunes in commerce and industry might put off marriage for years. Contemporaries who criticized the spinster aunt, with her "joyless and in many instances unsatisfactory" life of dependence in another's household, or the "confirmed" bachelor, "insensible of all the joys and comforts of matrimony," rather unjustly laid the blame on the selfish mania for luxury that they supposed, unaccountably, to have sprung up.[8] For all their nostalgia for a certain image of the old-time family, it did not occur to the critics to dissent from the general enthusiasm for the progressive economy that made marriage necessary for some but objectionable to others.

The capacity of the family to educate its children in either secular or spiritual learning, already considerably shallower than it once had been, now virtually dried up. Families in traditional kinds of enterprise were perhaps no worse off in this respect than before. The ordinary small farmer who still relied on his wife, sons, and daughters for the chores appropriate to each in fields, farmyard, or house, all together forming a working unit that produced its own subsistence and a modest cash crop, could pass on to the children the practical skills needed to carry on as earlier generations had done, even if no longer in the same place. Whatever instruction children could get at home in the rudiments of formal learning and the catechism depended on what the parents happened to retain from their own similar childhood, limited as many of them had been by the inadequate schools and religious indifference of the recent past. The family's role as transmitter of high culture was often enough summed up by the parlor display of the Bible, *Pilgrim's Progress*—one could do worse—and a few other inspirational, patriotic, or utilitarian books. There was an open field in the Northeast and Middle West for the contemporary movements to establish public elementary schools and Sunday schools to take up the job that the family had let lapse.

In the South the ordinary slaveless farmer had neither the education to instruct his sons in anything but "making" cotton and corn nor schools to do it for him. But it was not only the poor crackers who let their children grow up in "listless, aimless, and idle independence"; the sons of wealthy planters, attended by Negro servants and kept from the impropriety of manual labor, enjoyed much the same happy indolence.[9] They might, as in the eighteenth century, be tutored at home or sent off to school and college, perhaps in the North or in England. The crudity of the managerial methods of many cotton planters down to 1860 suggests that the sons did not learn enough from the fathers—many of whom were themselves new to the business—to improve much on their example.

As commerce and industry opened a wider choice of occupation to eastern farm boys, many of them rebelled against what Horace Greeley later recalled as the "mindless, monotonous drudgery" of their ancestral calling.[10] In early childhood they were no doubt happily oblivious of the fact that their parents could teach them little to prepare them for city life. But by the time a boy decided to give up farming for an urban or industrial job, he had to face the irrelevance of his familial upbringing to life in the modern world. However much affection he might feel for his family, the prospect of entering the radically changed circumstances of urban society inevitably cut him off from them.

The families of industrial laborers suffered the most obvious loss. There were jobs in a cotton mill for men, women, and children, but it was usually mere coincidence if parents and children happened to work together. The working family was not a work crew under the father's authority, as former generations had been in the artisan's shop, on a New England farm, or on an Irish croft or German peasant holding. In heavy industries without jobs for girls or women, the fathers and sons both might work, but usually not together until the boys were nearly men themselves. The coal miner's son of seven to fourteen years picked slate with a gang of boys in the coal breaker, sat by himself in the darkness tending a ventilation door, or drove a mule and "trip" of cars along the underground gangways without seeing his father from breakfast to suppertime. Far from serving an apprenticeship to his father's trade, many a working boy nursed the ambition, which the father could only approve, of rising above the father's occupation and the social standing that it held him to. There was little of the tradition of pride in a heavy, manly occupation that fathers and sons alike felt in the mining villages of a country like Wales, although many of the American miners had come from there. "Very few of the boys around the mines follow their fathers' occupations," a Pennsylvania newspaper observed in 1872:

The mines are supplied with hands from abroad, else they would be obliged to stop work altogether. . . . It is the miner's pride and ambition to have his sons occupy a better position than that of a miner. Many a time have we heard a miner devoutly say, "If God spares my life, my son shall earn his bread above ground!" Poor fellows! Often their lives are not spared; but even then, the widowed mother seems all the more determined that her son shall not follow the occupation and meet his father's fate. It is no uncommon thing to see a mother going about the streets of Wilkes-Barre from a machine-shop to a carpenter's shop . . . to a tinsmith or blacksmith's shop, trying to find a place for her boy to learn a trade, so that he may be kept out of the mines.[11]

The father's authority, relinquished to foremen during working hours, was compromised at home—although foreign-bred parents would insist upon due respect—by the high value which he himself soon learned to place on his sons' upward mobility in America. If the American-born child managed to rise above his father's status, as many did not, he would be content, knowing no other standard of achievement in life. The father could take pride in the neighbors' admiration for his son's success. But functional continuity between the generations, already interrupted by migration from Europe to America, or from farm to city, was now virtually sundered.

In middle-class families the headship of the husband and father, as sole provider, was still undisputed. Yet the nature of most modern businesses and professions, like most industrial labor, took him away from his family during ten or twelve working hours, six days a week, and tended altogether to dissociate his function in the productive economy from the household and the other concerns of his wife and children. Business and politics were becoming, more narrowly than before, the man's only sphere and hence the only manly activities. The conventional deference of the American husband toward his wife—"a sort of limitless respect and a boundless submission," it seemed to one European visitor—marked off her role as mistress of the household and custodian of such "intellectual culture and moral refinement" as the family was able to muster.[12] But for all the politeness and solicitude with which American men treated their wives, it was the opinion of one visiting Englishman —or perhaps of his wife, who accompanied him on his tour of the country in 1828—that there was no real companionship, mutual understanding, or even conversation between American men and women.[13] Oddly enough, foreigners also thought, the same husbands did not disdain to shop for groceries, set the fire in the stove, and "do a considerable part of the slip-slop work" about the house.[14] Respectable Americans nevertheless had no doubt that the home was the wife's proper place, as the shop or office was the husband's.

The narrowness of women's conventional sphere, against which a few of them were beginning to remonstrate in the 1840s, reflected the general withdrawal of the family from its former place in the outside world. The duties of the "home," which once had reached outward into the local community and its productive economy in various ways, had become circumscribed within the four walls of the household. Only the wife of a master of a great cotton or sugar plantation, which was still a self-contained community of slave quarters about the planter's house, still performed the manifold

duties of a mistress of numerous dependents. Indeed, it was because of "feudal" peculiarities of that sort that the planter seemed
quite different from other entrepreneurs of the time. No matter how
many employees a merchant or manufacturer had on his payroll,
only if he was one of the early or unusual kind whose house stood
overlooking an isolated mill or mining village did his wife have
much opportunity to play the role of benevolent lady of the manor,
if indeed she had any inclination for it. Her social duty, little
broader than that of any other housewife, was to her own ménage,
which might include a number of servants—probably a succession
of maladroit and impertinent Irish or German girls—but not any
recognized dependents on the far side of the tradesmen's entrance.

The legal inferiority of wives, suitable enough in the more complex family of the earlier age, grew irksome in the conjugal unit of
the nineteenth century. For the wife's identity to be legally merged
into that of her husband—"husband and wife are one, and that one
the husband" was the lawyers' maxim—began to seem both unjust
and impractical in an age of economic individualism.[15] The husband's ancient duty to keep good order by judiciously beating a
disobedient wife, as he might chastise a child, probably fell into
abeyance in the home long before it did in the courts; in the nineteenth century even a servant, if he was not a Negro slave, did not
have to put up with such treatment. A husband's absolute control
of his wife's property, which colonial law had chipped away in a
few particulars, succumbed to reform in several states in the 1840s
and 1850s. To give the wife the right to hold property in her own
name struck a congenial note among the economic individualists
of the time, though the immediate impetus for reform seems to
have been the panic of 1837, which demonstrated to many bankrupt businessmen the inutility of losing their wives' property to their
business creditors.

Most of the states also liberalized divorce to some degree, at least
by providing a general law under which one could sue for divorce in
the courts instead of having to seek a special act of the legislature.
Western states were the most liberal in admitting new grounds for
divorce; for several decades after the 1850s, when Indiana passed a
highly permissive law, the courts of the state attracted hundreds of
discontented spouses from other parts of the country. Its "divorce
mills" did not, however, make Indiana the paradise of free love
that eastern moralists suspected, nor was legal reform anywhere
the prime cause of family instability. In any case, few couples exercised the new option. As late as 1867 fewer than three divorces

were granted for every 10,000 people in the country, less than a thirtieth the number of marriages. But the option existed. Even the law was catching up with the practical reduction of the family to what a German immigrant in 1858 called "the copartnership of the American marriage."[16]

Material circumstances, quite without the aid of legal reform, sufficed to give American children a freedom over which European visitors wonderingly exclaimed. "The first impression produced by their manner," a Scotswoman observed in the 1850s, "is that they are brave, bright, pleasant, little 'impudent things.' "[17] The unremitting struggle of the father, whether businessman or workingman, for economic success or security, which regularly separated him from his presumably still affectionate wife, more obviously frayed the practical ties between him and his children. Neither father nor mother in many families had much time to supervise children, especially in the impressionable years between infancy and youth when, even on the farm, there was little work that they could do. "Baby citizens are allowed to run as wild as the Snake Indians," an Englishman remarked in 1855, "and do whatever they please."[18] Even further removed from their parents' oversight, though they were subjected to other disciplinarians, were industrial child laborers on one hand and middle-class schoolchildren on the other.

At the same time, the growing margin of material comfort permitted many parents to indulge childish whims. When "little creatures," as the Scottish lady observed with awe, were "trusted with cups of glass and china, which they grasp firmly, carry about the room carefully, and deposit unbroken, at an age when in our country mamma or nurse would be rushing after them to save the vessels from destruction," perhaps the relative ease of buying replacements was partly responsible for the parental laxity.[19] Permissive behavior at teatime could be traumatic for the Englishman who had to endure it:

The children's faces were dirty, their hair uncombed, their disposition evidently untaught, and all the members of the family, from the boy of six years of age up to the owner (I was going to say master) of the house, appeared independent of each other.[20]

But parents were not simply negligent. They deliberately fostered childish independence, at least in their boys, in the optimistic expectation that the rising generation would be the better able to improve on their parents' condition. "The idea instilled into the minds of most boys, from early life," *Harper's Magazine* remarked in 1853, "is that of 'getting on.' The parents test themselves by their own success in this respect; and they impart the same notion to their children."[21] They rejoiced in signs of manly self-reliance in the smallest toddlers. The Scottish lady remarked:

The parents, full of frank, simple emotion, bring their little treasures under notice and ask you with pride and joy, "Don't you think my Charley is a brave little fellow?" . . . If the children are not at home, you will be shown their pictures and told their histories. . . . They come, not with a "make your bow," or "courtesy to the lady,"—that is not re-publican fashion; but with a becoming courage, looking straight into your eyes, and extending the right hand for a cordial shake.[22]

As the children grew older, more and more matters were re-signed into their hands. Dances, parties, and other social affairs not only centered about the adolescents but were increasingly con-ducted by them. "Even in the serious decisions of life," a Polish resident commented in 1857, "children in America enjoy a fulness of independence not customary in Europe. They make freely the choice of their intimacies, then of their church, of their politics, their husbands and wives."[23] What he took to be forbearance, meekness, and a "yielding disposition" in the parents and sadly unfilial irreverence and arrogance in the young seemed to fit, how-ever, the confident American belief that economic opportunity lay within the grasp of the enterprising individual.[24] Since each new generation would grow up to live in a more advanced world than the parents had known, the young people would have to devise their own standards of behavior—presumably still including the Golden Rule as well as social equality.

Oddly enough, the more common it became to expect the youth-ful members of each family to make their own way in the world as individuals, the more they gave the outward appearance of merging the whole younger generation into that of their elders. "In America there is, strictly speaking, no adolescence," Tocqueville observed as early as the 1830s; "at the close of boyhood the man appears and begins to trace out his own path."[25] Freedom meant a kind of featureless assimilation into adulthood. "Children accus-tomed to the utmost familiarity and absence of constraint with their parents," the Polish observer wrote in 1857, "behave in the same manner with other older persons."[26] By the 1870s foreign visitors were puzzling over the "extinction of childhood" among young people who arrogated to themselves the independence and even the appearance of grown-ups.[27] So too an editor in Pennsylvania in 1875, recalling the days when boys were content to proceed gradually from aprons to "roundabouts," to do the family chores, play "town ball," shoot marbles, fly kites, skate and coast, and learn their lessons, was startled by the daily sight about town of beardless "miniature men" sporting "long-tailed coats, spring-bottom pants, and gay vest chains," affecting an awkward dignity, and looking for a "position" in business.[28] Females who ought still to be "little girls" were likewise on the streets in "long dresses and . . . all the pretensions of young ladies."[29] The blurring of distinctions of dress and behavior between the generations led foreigners to conclude that there were no children in America, nothing but "diminutive men and women in process of growing into big ones."[30] The older and younger generations no longer stood in any accepted relationship to each other but were simply equal individuals of different ages.*

To level children up to equal status with the adult Americans of the mid-nineteenth century was to add the eternal heedlessness of youth to the individualism of a society already tending toward excessive irresponsibility. Youthful liberty, although admirably go-ahead, often seemed to older people—Americans as well as European travelers—to have sunk "to insubordination and to violent revolts against superiors," as a college president complained after an outburst of undergraduate depredations about 1815.[31] No doubt college boys, who for four virtually adult years were bound down more rigidly by their archaic curriculum and petty parietal rules than anyone else but soldiers, prisoners, and slaves, were an unusually rebellious lot. But moralists then and later were also wont to grumble that children, when reproved by their elders, would boldly argue back or threaten to throw stones; that young people on steamboats monopolized all the seats, forcing invalids to stand; and that boys spoke slightingly of their father as "the governor" and their mother as "the old 'un."[32] The man who lamented that he had

---

* It is conceivable that the collapse of old distinctions between youth and adulthood which foreigners and nostalgic Americans thought they saw was in fact the preservation—a typical phenomenon in the New World—of an archaic European pattern. If the recent hypothesis of Philippe Ariès is correct, adolescents in medieval Europe had always been regarded simply as little men and women. American economic and social conditions may have permitted the perpetuation of that pattern—perhaps in an exaggerated form—well past the seventeenth century, when middle-class European youth had already begun to acquire the distinctively juvenile style of dress, schooling, and manners that they had by this later date.

been a child when children were nothing and was now an adult when children were everything was expressing more than the age-old grievance of elders. The youth, like everyone about him, was enjoined to be an independent, self-reliant individual, no longer responsible to society and its institutions—not even to his family—except as their economic advancement might be fostered by his own.

15. THE COMMUNITY AS REAL ESTATE

"The American," a Scottish visitor observed in the late 1840s, "exhibits little or none of the local attachments which distinguish the European."

His affections have more to do with the social and political system with which he is connected than with the soil which he inhabits. . . . In some parts of the Union the local feeling may be comparatively strong, such as in New England; but it is astonishing how readily even there an American makes up his mind to try his fortunes elsewhere, particularly if he contemplates removal to another part of the Union, no matter how remote, or how different in climate and other circumstances from what he has been accustomed to, provided the flag of his country waves over it, and republican institutions accompany him in his wanderings.[1]

It was a large statement to make of a people whose sectional differences had for thirty years past been leading them inexorably toward civil war. It could not have been made at all, however, much before the nineteenth century. The colonial American had identified himself with his particular province and local community at least as strongly as with his family or social class. In the nineteenth century many of the old differences persisted between the types of community—township, village, county, and city —that distinguished one region of the country from another, and indeed new regions, each with its own variants of these, were continually being settled. But underneath all the peculiarities of form, foreign observers and Americans alike also sensed a fundamental uniformity which they identified, and usually praised, in the political terms of legal equality, individual liberty, and "republican institutions."

The flag that flew everywhere to symbolize those beneficent principles nevertheless hid from view certain shortcomings of the liberty and equality that permeated the country. Like other institutions under the pressure of the economic revolution, local communities in all parts of the country were socially unsettled, so to speak, because of the manner in which their physical settlement was permitted to proceed. As long as economic progress was the prime value dominating these republican institutions, the communal stability upon which republican government was based stood in danger of derangement.

The continual fragmenting of communal structures never wholly atomized them into formless masses of unrelated individuals. But it produced a haphazard pattern of social groups, the "private circles" and "small coteries" which Tocqueville perceived would coalesce in an egalitarian society.[2] Just as the integrity of the family now depended on a fragile network of personal affection among its members, the mere physical propinquity of people who had chosen to become neighbors and fellow townsmen was too tenuous to bind them together into a stable community. Brilliant feats of material production and acquisition were accomplished with extraordinary dispatch in the booming towns and rural districts of the time, but the social needs of their citizens required something more substantial than the fortuitous groupings that economic circumstances brought together, perhaps shortly to disperse again.

During the half century after the American Revolution, communities in every part of the country continued to develop more or less along their old structural lines. A radical break did not come until the middle third of the nineteenth century, when the concentrated pressures of the multiple economic revolution grew too great for the old framework. By that time, indeed, the American community was ill-equipped to resist. Its members had long been more concerned with promoting economic development, in an age when such progress was held back by environmental circumstances, than with keeping up the old communal controls. After 1825, although Americans had not yet explicitly abandoned the principle of social control of the economy, both the local community and the state were too permissive to give much direction to the rush of economic change. That is not to say that settlement of new communities, whether freshly planted on the western frontier or superimposed on old eastern villages and cities, was entirely unplanned. Nineteenth-century public planning was designed first and foremost, however, to facilitate rapid development by private interests: real-estate promoters, land speculators, industrial entrepreneurs, and individual farmers and townspeople. What was left of the old-fashioned community's more specifically social values soon fell into abeyance.

Historians have demonstrated some of the social defects of the federal land system under which the new West was settled. Since

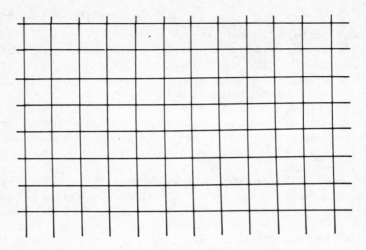

ABOVE ———— SECTION LINES, EXAMPLE AREA S.

BELOW ———— NUMBERED SURVEY UNITS, EXAMPLE AREA U.

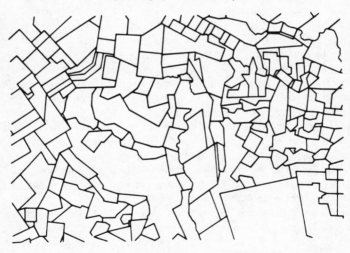

Figure 4. Basic Original Cadastral Survey Lines in the Example Areas. *Above:* Section Lines, Federal Rectangular Survey, 1819 (Northwestern Ohio). Each section = 640 acres. *Below:* Survey Units, Unsystematic Survey, 1798-1855 (Virginia Military District, West Central Ohio). (Reproduced by permission from the Association of American Geographers Monograph No. 4, *Original Survey and Land Subdivision* by Norman J. W. Thrower.)

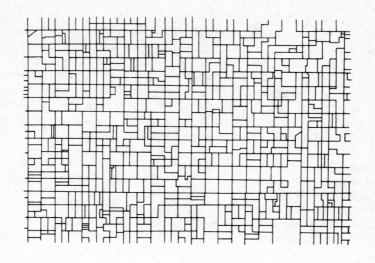

PROPERTY BOUNDARIES IN THE EXAMPLE AREAS c. 1875

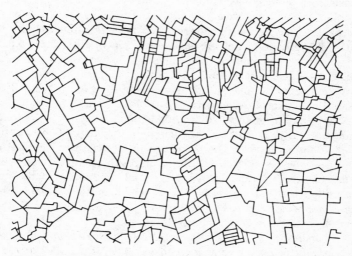

Figure 5. Property Boundaries in the Same Areas, 1875. (From Norman J. W. Thrower, *Original Survey and Land Subdivision,* p. 40. Chicago: Rand McNally. Association of American Geographers © 1966.)

speculators could buy and hold off the market as much land as they could pay for, the steady growth of some of the new townships and counties was hampered for a decade or two. Few have objected, however, to a more basic flaw in the system, since by that time it was the normal expectation of ordinary farmers everywhere: the isolation of each farmstead on its own 160-acre quarter section, more or less. Even those Westerners who were of New England origin were now several generations removed from the old communal agriculture and the village nestled about the meeting-house. In the South, of course, those English traditions had never been successfully transplanted, and the Middle Atlantic and Border regions had taken over, and carried westward in the course of settlement, the quite different Celtic or German pattern of self-contained farmsteads. Economic individualism was not only the American farmer's ingrained preference for himself, indeed, but supremely his contribution to the national ethic of the nineteenth century.*

It is true that farmers—and their nostalgic descendants—made a virtue out of such exceptions to the rule as the occasional coming together for a cooperative logrolling, barn-raising, or cornhusking party, social occasions that were made necessary precisely by the half mile separating neighbors. Cooperation in these heavy tasks was the more welcome for the competition between teams of volunteer house-raisers or for the rhythmic "corn songs" with which, like Gaelic cloth-waulkers, the huskers kept the work moving along, as well as for the rare opportunity for a horse race, a "rastlin'" or shooting match, or the fiddling and "double shuffling" of a rustic frolic.[3] It was the infrequency of communal festivity, however, that made it so memorable. The isolated daily life of farm families, occupied as they were with acquiring, improving, and working their detached properties, gainsaid the nominal community of the rural township. The half-dozen buildings at the unincorporated cross-roads hamlet or "center" of the midwestern township marked the final disintegration of the village tradition.

City planning was left almost entirely to real-estate promoters and private owners who paid even less heed than the farmer to

---

* The social significance of the *shape* of farms and townships under the right-angled federal survey is uncertain. The farmers came to accept geometrically square fields as natural enough, and the system seems to have been more convenient for conveyancing property without undue litigation than the irregular southern colonial system. Perhaps it was of some slight importance to the rural community that township boundaries under the federal survey were apt to coincide with certain property lines. See Figures 4 and 5.

social values. Their usual object was to lay out the greatest possible acreage in building lots and to sell them as conveniently and profitably as possible. The rectangular grid of the street plan of colonial Philadelphia, suitable enough on the flat peninsula between the Delaware and Schuylkill rivers, provided a simple pattern which later surveyors imposed on the most irregular sites. The "perfect regularity" that pleased the foreign visitor when he first saw it in Philadelphia gave a "disgusting appearance" by the time he reached western towns like Cincinnati, where the right-angled streets blindly labored up hills and crossed and recrossed streams.[4]

The most long-term planning had the most immediate objectives. As the New York commissioners observed in 1811, when marking off the rigid gridiron plan on the rocky slopes of the rural upper four-fifths of Manhattan Island, "Right angled houses are the most cheap to build, and the most convenient to live in."[5] By dividing off streets and lots far in advance of settlement they piously hoped to allay "the pernicious spirit of speculation," but their own chief argument for the plan was its utility for the "buying, selling, and improving of real estate."[6] The narrow frontage and awkward depth of city building lots were calculated with the same speculative yardstick.

How suitable a physical environment such a scheme would provide for the community in later years—whether indeed it might not cut roughly across natural ties of community and even neglect the comfort of individuals—was hardly worth taking into account. No plan could physically isolate city people in the manner of western farmers, but even on the reduced urban scale the rectangular ground plan lacked adaptable social dimensions. Since there were neither zoning nor building laws to control the uses to which property owners and developers could put the basic design, even pleasantly varied city plans usually were soon vitiated. The occasional blocks that in Philadelphia had been reserved for open squares most new towns sacrificed in short order to private buyers. Warehouses blocked off waterfronts, industrial works swallowed up residential streets, and projected parks vanished into still more building lots. The obliteration of topographical amenities under the unyielding mass of commercial and industrial structures was plain to be seen. Worse but less obvious was the built-in instability of random conglomerations of residential subdivisions, each designed by a speculative builder or by individual owners according to the demand of the moment. At best it would have been difficult to foresee a permanently satisfactory plan for any city, since within a few years a shifting population and someone's hope of momentary profit were likely to cause houses, blocks, and subdivisions to be converted to unanticipated uses for which they were worse suited than ever.

In short, the planning of rural and urban communities faithfully reflected the economic individualism of the westward and cityward migrations. Although most immigrants and native Americans had originally moved in order to maintain their accustomed social status against the pressure of economic circumstances, few of them either migrated or settled in the kind of organized groups within which that status would have counted for much. An occasional party of New Englanders did transplant themselves to the West under a communal and congregational covenant, formal or tacit, of the archaic Puritan sort. At least a few Southeasterners, as the North Carolina Highland names of the McRaes, McDuffies, McIntoshes, and McLeods of Greene County, Mississippi, suggest, went to the Southwest in loosely organized groups of very old neighbors.[7] Occasional parties of European sectarians came in order to isolate themselves in their own rural colonies. The vast majority of people moving into a new farming settlement or industrial town came as individuals, however, or in groups no larger than a few families. They might settle near old neighbors from whose letters they had heard of the place, but they did not bodily transfer sections of old communities.

Within any decade, furthermore, whether the community was a new western county or a growing industrial city in the East, it was not unusual for more than half the inhabitants counted at one census to move on elsewhere before the next. The poorest—the farm laborers and tenants looking for cheap land and the unskilled industrial workingmen seeking a living wage—were by no means the only ones to move in and out. In the one midwestern county where the statistics of movement have been thoroughly analyzed, a majority (though a smaller one) of the farm owners also left in each of the first two decades of settlement. Many of the skilled miners and factory workers whom an industrial center attracted from abroad were as quick to depart, perhaps for the homeland again, when a prolonged depression or strike threw them out of work. For the skilled and the unskilled, farmers and laborers, native Americans and immigrants, Northerners and Southerners and Westerners, continual movement had become quite unexceptional.

The ebb and flow of individuals was in itself not crucial for the social order of the fast-growing counties and towns. There had been colonial communities and, earlier yet, English villages many of whose people also were transients. Unlike the English villagers of that day, however, the modern American migrant seldom had any ties of family, community, or even economic organization to the place in which he settled until he formed them himself in the course of time—time which often enough was cut short by another move. The social groups that coalesced in every community, consisting of individuals unrelated before their arrival and likely to break off their stay at any time, were defined mainly by the circumstances of the moment.

In both rural and urban settlements everywhere but in the South the ethnic lines introduced by immigration from abroad most sharply defined the new social groupings. The hundreds or thousands of Germans, Irishmen, Englishmen, Scots, Welshmen, Dutchmen, Norwegians, Swedes, and Poles who filtered into a farming county or an industrial town were likely to come from various provinces of the old country. As they settled alongside a medley of native Americans, people of each general linguistic and cultural description fused into self-conscious national groups. Here and there a western township was occupied almost entirely by a single immigrant nationality, some indeed mainly by people from Posen or Silesia, Merioneth or Cardiganshire, Stavanger or Gudbrandsdal, as of course other places were by Vermonters or Southern Uplanders. But most localities filled up with a random conglomeration of individual families and small groups, drawn and held together more by the economic advantages of the place and by chance than by past connections. The little knots of relatives and former neighbors who had been attracted by the good reports of early comers to an American industrial center—from Preston to Fall River, Bradford to Lawrence, Wanlockhead to Pittston—were scattered among the usual miscellaneous population of the place.

The strongest bond among the members of a local ethnic group was the consciousness of what they were not. Surrounded by other kinds of people, the Irishman, Norwegian, or Yankee began to turn what had been a neutral circumstance, the customary common culture which everyone in his old community had taken for granted, into an exclusive principle of self-identification. Even the "old families" of the onetime market towns and ports that were being transformed by commerce and industry, the descendants of the original inhabitants of the place who still thought of themselves as the real community, became only the most eminent among a number of discrete ethnic groups. The cultural differences among all these groups were perpetuated by the practical circumstances that confined most peasant immigrants to poorly paid labor, offered a respectable standard of living to immigrants with industrial skills, and cast an aura of property and social eminence over "old stock" Americans and the other "Anglo-Saxons" among the immigrants. In spite of the prevalent distaste for fixed class distinctions, the rough coincidence between ethnic groups and the broad gradations of occupation, income, and wealth made the latter more binding than would have been likely in a homogeneous population.

Between the 1820s and 1850s a few of the largest cities began to develop a new pattern of residential segregation along ethnic and economic lines. As long as old commercial ports like Boston or Philadelphia had been small enough for everyone to walk to work, the greatest merchants had lived near their countinghouses and their employees and other ordinary folk. They might have country houses as well as townhouses, but they felt no compulsion to dissociate themselves physically from the neighborhood of their inferiors as long as everyone accepted that personages like themselves belonged to a higher order of mankind. It was in much the same fashion that the homes of owners and managers of cotton or iron mills in the early years of certain industrial villages overlooked from no great distance the works and the workmen's houses. The cities of the egalitarian nineteenth century obliterated, however, that age-old physical and social pattern. The new extremes of wealth and poverty, reinforced by ethnic distinctions, induced the rich and respectable to remove as far as possible from the old commercial and industrial center, which they abandoned to working-class slums. The distance might be measured more in social terms than in miles. Some moved no farther than a newly fashionable section of the inner city itself, such as the land which was reclaimed in the 1850s from the Back Bay of Boston Harbor, separated from the commercial hub only by railway lines and the new Public Garden that was added to the old Common; some Boston families, indeed, both of the old China trade and the new industrial fortunes, held onto old Beacon Hill as their bastion overlooking the city.

But increasingly such people were taking flight to the outlying fringes of the cities. The peripheral area which both in Europe and in the old America had usually been the ragged purlieus of a town, the refuge of squatters and outcasts—like the poor Irish shanty dwellers on the rocky ground on the upper edge of New York City before it was converted into Central Park—now became the desirable suburbs. Nostalgia for the rustic amenities of village and farm, the origins of most of the new city dwellers, whether Americans or immigrants, played some part in this. Perhaps too the egalitarian ethic made physical segregation more agreeable to people of property and status now that deference from their inferiors had gone out of fashion.

The flight to the outskirts was limited at first to the two or three miles that one could walk to work. But the advent of steam railways in the 1830s enabled those who could afford the daily round trip to live in the outlying country villages; more useful still, horse-drawn streetcar lines began to radiate in all directions in the 1850s and permitted businessmen and workingmen alike to disperse their homes as far out—up to four or five miles—as each could afford. By 1875 the new mobility had unofficially but quite clearly marked off every sizable city into residential districts whose social character was familiar to all, whether under graphic labels like Quality Hill or Shanty Hill or merely as the East Side, the North End, or the flats. Few districts kept the same character long; the fashionable street or subdivision of one decade might be passed by in the next and begin an unforeseen slide down the social scale toward shabby gentility and ultimate squalor. Even old inhabitants whose economic and social position was quite secure might repeatedly feel pressed to seek a new neighborhood as the old one lost its tone.

An entire community could fall into economic depression and stagnation with even more unfortunate social effects. One by-product of the rapid growth of the country and the sudden rise of new cities and regions, new industries, and new means of transportation was the continual exposure of established enterprises and communities to competition that they could not meet. Unpredictable economic regression was a major facet of unregulated economic progress. The port of Boston grew at the expense of its smaller commercial rivals of colonial days; those which could not save themselves with textile mills or shoemaking dwindled into somnolent villages as the docks decayed and the young people departed. The westward movement of wheat growing and then of sheep-herding from the New England backcountry to upstate New York and in turn to the plains of the Northwest undermined the Yankee hill towns when they had hardly attained economic maturity. The canals, railroads, and lake boats that brought western produce east, while stimulating towns at the junction and transshipping points, bypassed and undercut the farmers of the poorer valleys a little off the line. And even in the booming West and industrial East the unpredictable course of events blasted the hopes of certain communities and uprooted their people when other places beat them out in the competition to secure rail connections, factories, a college, or the county courthouse.

Since it was axiomatic that economic progress was all-important, unfortunate individuals and communities had to readjust to the new conditions as well as they could. Sometimes they managed to shift to a more profitable crop or manfacture, but once again they had no assurance of the length of the reprieve thus gained. In many cases the farmer, businessman, or workingman had no choice but to stagnate in an economic backwater or to move to some other place in the mainstream of progress. Local people of wealth who did not move away were likely to invest their capital in more promising places rather than risk it trying to rescue their own community. Economic regression was even less subject to social control than was economic progress. The stranded community suffered from the irony of the economic values of the time.

In the previous age men had turned without hesitation to government to protect as well as to help enrich their communities. But as the two generations between 1815 and 1875 grew habituated to the ideal of individual self-reliance, it came to seem inexpedient and then improper to rely upon the organized power of community or commonwealth for positive social ends. Just when local government everywhere was faced with far more complex problems than the old colonial towns, counties, and civil parishes had had to deal with, it was vitiated by the gathering distrust toward any concentration of public power. Individuals who were being carried along by the current of economic circumstances not only attributed their success or failure to the private economic virtues but also rejected public authority, the one organized counterforce that might have struck a balance between economic freedom and social stability. As we have seen, they had little more compunction than in colonial days about using government to stimulate economic progress, but they now quite lost sight of the social utility of the old kind of public regulation.

Far from literally withering away for lack of its old functions, local government was transformed, most rapidly in the cities, into the special concern of a new class of politicians who made a thriving private business out of public office. The popular distaste for aristocracy made the ideal of the disinterested, gentlemanly

magistrate unfashionable. Here and there a successor to that tradition managed to keep afloat on the turbulent sea of egalitarian
politics by playing the role of what has been called the "professional
gentleman democrat."[8] But whatever the personal origins of the
professional party organizers of 1825–1875, their business was to
win elections, to control the machinery of government if not to
hold office themselves, and to enjoy the perquisites.

The ordinary voter staunchly supported the ticket of one party
rather than another for a complex of reasons, most of them apparently unspoken, the most important of which often involved
nothing more or less profound than his own social identity. The
Democrats as a rule could count on the votes of the Catholic Irish
and the Germans (though after the crisis of the 1850s many of
the latter become Republicans); partly in reaction against them,
British and Protestant Irish immigrants were just as solidly Whig
and then Republican. The voter's economic class and social status,
which for the immigrant was usually related to his ethnic identity,
might be the decisive factor for the native American as well. Of
course in the democratic age after 1825 all politicians protested—
loudly and perhaps a little too much—that they were no respecters
of such invidious distinctions, and in fact either party, depending
on local circumstances, might rely on the support of the rich or the
poor, the businessman, workingman, or farmer. The most sophis-
ticated recent students of the formation of local Whig and Democratic parties in the 1820s can sometimes discover no better
explanation than "the imponderable element of personality."[9] And
party loyalty, once any individual was confirmed in it, was apt to
survive all his later mutations of wealth and status. For a man to
cleave to the lofty principles of the Democratic, Whig, or Republican party platform, as his father had perhaps done before him,
was to establish a social identity more solid than mere residence
in a community and more acceptable than class or ethnic labels.

After 1840, the year of the Whig log cabin and hard cider campaign when each party tried to appear more popular and democratic than the other, the social side of local party organization
grew more and more elaborate. Partisans set up liberty poles and
tried to chop down those of the other side; they paraded with torch-
lights and transparencies bearing party mottoes and wore symbolic uniforms, Wide Awake military caps for Lincoln in 1860,
leather capes for Grant or white ones for Greeley in 1872; they sang
such songs as "Ain't You Glad You Joined the Republicans" and
fired off cannon to mark election victories. Remarkably enough,

between 1840 and 1880, just when government was least effective in dealing with the critical issues of the country, a vast majority of the electorate—a higher proportion than before or since—regularly turned out to vote.

Local parties not only reflected the unsteady social groupings that made up the community; they themselves added a whole new set of groups to the mosaic. It was not particularly helpful that the rhetoric of their campaigns for local office usually expressed high-sounding national issues of uncertain local application: protective tariffs, the power of the Bank of the United States, the abstractions of "state rights," extension of slavery to distant territories, the march of freedom through the wreckage of the monarchies of Europe. Not that these were insubstantial matters, but arguing over them could only intensify the ethnic, religious, occupational, or simply factional divisions within the community. Politics of that sort was unlikely to resolve either the national issues or the disorder of local society.

It is difficult to describe the shortcomings of local government precisely because things not done leave few traces. Problems that had earlier been recognized as public responsibilities continued to be dealt with, but in old ways that now all too often were quite inadequate. New kinds of public problems were ignored as simply the private concerns of those involved, whether suffering victim or benevolent philanthropist. Relief of disabled paupers had been no great public burden in the seventeenth and eighteenth centuries. But the poor laws and the occasional almshouse, hospital, or orphanage had been designed for the unfortunates of small, stable communities. They could not begin to cope with the masses of helpless immigrants stranded in Boston, New York, and other ports in the 1840s and 1850s or with the families of laborers who were periodically thrown out of work in any industrial town. Nor did the authorities and the respectable taxpayers recognize a duty to take care of the family of any able-bodied individual whose failure to be self-reliant seemed to indicate a deplorable lack of character. Even to apply for poor relief was purposely made so shameful, for fear of discouraging the poor from seeking honest work, that anyone with the vaguest hope of finding a job avoided getting his name into the official reports and the annual statistics of the poor board. The nearly destitute men, women, and children whom any citizen could observe about him daily he could also deny to be a civic or social problem.

City governments that were almost always behindhand with

passable streets, sufficient water mains and sewers, and competent police forces—all within the accepted public sphere—were not yet prepared to take on regulation of private real estate, not even the noisome tenements into which poor laborers crowded from cellar to garret as fast as landlords could divide up old houses and speculative jerry-builders could insert still more buildings in the spaces behind and between them. Epidemics of cholera or typhoid fever occasionally aroused a city board of health to investigate the physical squalor of the slums, but the public outcry seldom outlasted the threat to the health of respectable people in other parts of town.

When these major nuisances were ordinarily considered to be beyond public regulation, it was hardly likely that much would be done to provide civic amenities. There were some notable exceptions, such as the reservation of land, usually outside the currently settled part of the city, to be developed as public parks. One of the first and the largest, Central Park in New York, was thus begun in the 1850s. But even the need for public recreation occurred to many city governments a generation after their handsomely landscaped "rural cemeteries"—for private graves—were laid out in the 1820s and 1830s.[10] If other civic institutions—libraries, concert halls, art galleries, and museums—existed at all, they were usually the result of individual bequests or voluntary associations organized for the purpose.

The mid-nineteenth-century American social order was one in which old communities were undermined by economic change and new ones were kept unsettled from the time they were "settled." It was a society in which the family was losing both its inner integrity and its place in the larger community, and where men denied the reality of social class distinctions even while the gap between wealth and poverty yawned in their face. Americans assured themselves that this liberal society was wholly desirable. The lack of social values that they had never known or perhaps had forgotten since their grandfathers' day did not seem outwardly to trouble them. Tocqueville, the conservative European, doubted how satisfactory the self-reliance of the professed individualist would ultimately prove to be. The democratic Americans, he observed,

owe nothing to any man, they expect nothing from any man; they acquire the habit of always considering themselves as standing alone, and they are apt to imagine that their whole destiny is in their own hands. Thus not only does democracy make every man forget his ancestors, but it hides his descendents and separates his contemporaries from him; it throws him back forever upon himself alone and threatens in the end to confine him entirely within the solitude of his own heart.[11]

Could so atomized a society ensure the stability and security for the lives of its self-reliant members that the institutional structures of the past had supported? In their national mood of boundless optimism few Americans bothered to ask the question.

III. Conservative Reaction

A people who place no great value upon social stability will find the problems of a disordered society hard to recognize and still harder to come to grips with. During the first three-quarters of the nineteenth century, Americans were far too busy pursuing material progress to recognize the signs of social breakdown all about them. The present was rich, the future promised to be richer yet, the slow-moving past was well behind them. What had been good in the vanishing past was whatever had led to their present freedom and affluence; any other values that society once had honored now seemed quaint, perhaps, but far too confining for an ambitious modern nation. The old hierarchy of social classes seemed well lost. What the family and the community had been was virtually forgotten even by those moralists who from time to time deplored their current state. European criticism of the general looseness of American society was curtly dismissed as proof that "no foreigner can ever be made to understand our character."[1] Freedom of the individual from the constraints of Old World, old-time institutions was the glory of the country and the meaning of its history.

When accused of believing only in the "almighty dollar," Americans warmly denied that they had no higher values than material production and accumulation. The cultural and spiritual ideals of their remarkably enlightened society, they confidently retorted, were as lofty as any. Not only social harmony but the most sublime poetry, art, and music, the profoundest theology, political economy, and natural and moral philosophy, and the best hope for universal salvation of the human soul would presently flow forth from the enterprise that was reshaping the continent. Free enterprise—the exercise of the economic virtues of hard work and thrift, free of archaic scruples—was supposed to be the best field for the flowering of human character and a harvest of every possible earthly felicity. There were no limits to that American dream. But they supposed, in effect, that somehow all the noblest achievements of mind and spirit were going to rise directly from the bounty of their fields, mines, and factories without their particularly needing to build or maintain any supporting structure of social institutions. Quite to the contrary, by their reading of their own experience of the old "monopolies" of established church, privileged upper class, specially chartered companies, and central banks, the very existence of strong institutions would inevitably encroach upon the common man's rightful share in the pursuit of public and private happiness.

The impact of their much-prized liberty on the structure of society nevertheless troubled Americans more than they were aware. They spent a great deal of energy in anxious groping, so it appears in retrospect, for some practical modern equivalent to the old organic society. The age is famous for its plethora of social and spiritual reform movements. But instead of thinking to devise an institutional structure able to subordinate economic means to higher ends, they increasingly equated social, cultural, and spiritual values to the economic freedom of the individual. Surely there was moral guidance enough for the future in their free, disestablished churches, the secular crusades to inspire the individual willingly to seek the right or sternly put down wrong, and the national faith in the manifest destiny of democracy in the world. In failing to see that freedom from institutional constraints might be the cause rather than the cure of their anxieties, they rendered most of their social reforms oddly self-defeating.

16. SOCIAL USES OF RELIGION

Although men continued to defer to the church as the overarching institution of society in the New World as in the Old, the decline in its spiritual authority had long been evident in every region of the country. Even in colonial New England and Pennsylvania, established to support true religion, the church had proved just as vulnerable to material preoccupations as the other basic institutions of the old social order. In spite of the Puritans' retreat to a presbyterian system of authority, and in spite of the efforts of the Society for the Propagation of the Gospel to maintain the influence of the Church of England, churches lost effective contact with the great majority of the population. Presumably it was well before 1800, the earliest date for which a general estimate can be made, that church membership fell below 10 percent of the adult population.

Much of the history of the church from the middle of the eighteenth century to the early twentieth is taken up with a long series of reactions to the dominant economic pressures of the age. Churches might seek to accommodate themselves to circumstances or somehow to resist them, but they had lost the autonomy necessary to rule the affairs of the world according to transcendent values of their own. Consequently their efforts often compounded the difficulty. On one hand, a materialistic ethic steadily filled the void of faith and displaced theology of any coherent sort. On the other, every attempt to revive spiritual values ended in fragmenting the church, the institutional foundation for those values, into "denominational" disunity.

There was no lack of bickering over theology in the course of the nineteenth century, but it had surprisingly little practical relevance to the church's role in the society of the time. The Deism inherited from the Enlightenment of eighteenth-century Europe caused a rationalist schism in only one orthodox communion, the onetime Puritan Congregationalists, and that mainly in eastern Massachusetts. By 1805 the lines were openly and irrevocably drawn (over the theological liberalism of Harvard), and in 1825 the seceding liberal congregations established the Unitarian Association. The Universalists, also rationalist but centered in up-country towns and villages of less social elevation, appeared about the same time. For all the fine distinctions that theologians might draw between the old Calvinist orthodoxy of divine predestination and the rationalist offer of salvation to virtually anyone who devoted himself to good works, they did not much affect the social attitudes and practical behavior of Congregationalists or Unitarians. For that matter, clergymen of most descriptions, not alone those of Calvinist origins, found that for the church to hold even the perfunctory attention of any considerable number of Americans it had to accommodate its doctrine, at least tacitly, to their optimistic, economically progressive individualism. A degree of Arminianism, or reliance on human effort to achieve salvation—a salvation which, furthermore, was measured in the worldly dimensions of a perfected human society—imbued the operative beliefs of people both inside and outside the churches.

An unanxious Christianity of that sort was most often found among the comfortable middle- and upper-class beneficiaries of commercial and industrial progress in the eastern cities. Thus in Hartford the minister reputed to be the acutest theologian of the age, Horace Bushnell, sought to reconcile Calvinism to the spirit of progress. A Yale graduate of rural and orthodox background, Bushnell found in the 1830s that the enterprising merchants in his congregation were impatient with the doctrine of human depravity if it meant that they themselves could not win an acceptable salvation. The congregation had split off in 1824, indeed, from another church whose minister they considered overly strict in such matters. By drawing heavily from the worldly side of the old doctrine of the calling or vocation, Bushnell formulated a concordat between Calvinist dependence on grace and the practical materialism of his hearers. It was above all a rational compromise, with a specifically economic rationale "making the unworldly spirit amiable." In part it involved mercantile figures of speech: God had invested in humanity with the confidence of "a banker whose fund is in"; "as certainly . . . as you succeed, you can be saved." More important, worldly success would come from practicing the virtues of "patience, frugality, temperance, and economy"; wealth was "a reward and honor which God delights to bestow upon an upright people." "Give me, then, as a minister of God's truth," Bushnell urged his comfortable flock, "a money-loving, prosperous and diligent hearer." The "mechanical hardness" of business, no matter how "eager and sharp," need not dull Christian charity, he suggested, since the businessman had the rare opportunity to sell shelf-worn, faded, or no longer fashionable goods to the poor at reduced prices. Bushnell evaded his own lingering doubts of the sufficiency of such Christianity by assigning economic and spiritual values to separate compartments of life. Business hours were ruled by "the laws of trade," that is, by economic self-interest; on the Sabbath the soul might "ascend to things congenial to its higher affinities."[1]

The economic gospel to which even a minister like Bushnell reduced the old social ethic of Puritanism increasingly pervaded more popular churches than his. Christian faith and worldly success were very nearly the same thing, in the opinion of a Methodist journal in 1866, since

> by virtue of the habits which religion inculcates and cherishes, our Church members have as a body risen in the social scale, and thus become socially removed from the great body out of which most of them were originally gathered. This tendency of things is natural and universal, and in its results unavoidable; perhaps we might add, also, not undesirable.[2]

Although few Protestant clergymen addressed themselves so baldly to reducing the vestiges of seventeenth-century orthodoxy to something palatable to the nineteenth-century world, the values of the marketplace had clearly infiltrated the church.

Many clergymen were not at all resigned to seeing orthodoxy eclipsed either by indifference or by liberal accommodation. Instead they launched, as early as the middle of the eighteenth century, what amounted to the first of the nineteenth-century reform movements. With the flaming arrows of a new evangelism they fought to revive the urgency of the old spiritual commitment, once more undimmed by material distractions. Revivalism, as its name implies, was an essentially conservative reaction. It was not the exclusive peculiarity of any region or class, but it usually appeared among people whose Calvinist traditions were strong enough to make them aware of how far they had lapsed and whose social circumstances were somehow unsatisfactory (though their economic prospects might be good enough). From 1720 to 1830 the places most affected were settled rural towns and country districts lying about a generation behind the current frontier of settlement. Thereafter revivalism spread into the eastern cities, perhaps especially among the many people of rural origin who were slow to become inured to economic individualism in the unsettling forms that it took in urban society.

The Great Awakening, as the earliest wave of evangelism came to be called, took nearly twenty years to gather head. In the 1720s Theodorus Frelinghuysen roused the somnolent Dutch Reformed churches of the Raritan Valley, a part of East New Jersey some fifty miles and several decades behind the frontier, and in the late 1720s and 1730s the enthusiasm was spread by Gilbert Tennent to the Scotch-Irish Presbyterians who had more recently settled in the neighboring districts of West Jersey and Pennsylvania. The interior of New England was next: at Northampton in 1734–1735 the preaching of Jonathan Edwards converted some three hundred souls, nearly the whole town—an unprecedented phenomenon among the descendants of the lukewarm Puritans for whom the Saybrook compromise with Presbyterianism had been devised. The spiritual contagion swept up and down the Connecticut Valley and throughout Connecticut and western Massachusetts. The blaze reached its height in 1740–1741, fanned by the preaching tour of the English Methodist George Whitefield through the colonies. (John Wesley himself had already visited Georgia a few years before.)

The evangelists spurned all those halfway compromises with spiritual indifference which Calvinists had been making for the past eighty years. They refused to concede to the person who had never experienced mystical assurance of God's grace any hope that he was not damned eternally; the most moral outward behavior and the greatest worldly success could in themselves make him no purer in God's sight than the proverbial whited sepulcher. In the most startling imagery they drove home to depraved human beings the sense of total dependence on God's will. To Edwards the unconverted sinner was a spider tossed onto a kitchen fire to be shriveled and consumed:

The God that holds you over the pit of hell, much as one holds a spider, or some loathsome insect, over the fire, abhors you, and is dreadfully provoked; his wrath towards you burns like fire; he looks upon you as worthy of nothing else, but to be cast into the fire; he is of purer eyes than to bear to have you in his sight; you are ten thousand times so abominable in his eyes, as the most hateful and venomous serpent is in ours. You have offended him infinitely more than ever a stubborn rebel did his prince; and yet it is nothing but his hand that holds you from falling into the fire every moment; it is ascribed to nothing else, that you did not go to hell the last night; that you was suffered to awake again in this world, after you closed your eyes to sleep; and there is no other reason to be given, why you have not dropped to hell since you arose in the morning, but that God's hand has held you up; there is no other reason to be given why you have not gone to hell, since you have

sat here in the house of God, provoking his pure eyes by your sinful
wicked manner of attending his solemn worship; yea, there is nothing
else that is to be given as a reason why you do not this very moment
drop down into hell.[3]

The demonstrable effect of the new "sensational" method of
preaching commended it to ministers impatient with the old-
fashioned didactic style. It was later recalled:

In many places, people would cry out, in the time of public worship,
under a sense of their overbearing guilt and misery, and the all-consum-
ing wrath of God, due to them for their iniquities; others would faint
and swoon under the affecting views which they had of God and Christ;
some would weep and sob, and there would sometimes be so much
noise among the people, in particular places, that it was with difficulty
that the preacher could be heard. In some few instances, it seems, that
the minister has not been able to finish his discourse, there had been so
much crying out and disturbance.[4]

"The greater [the] Number cried out of themselves and their
Vileness," one minister wrote, "the more I rejoyced in Hope of the
good Issue."[5]

The Awakening was not only the first revival of religion but
also the first in a long series of radically conservative reactions
against the main drift of modern American society. Revivalism was
perhaps the most conservative of all in seeking most explicitly to
restore the primacy of the highest spiritual values; it was reactionary
in the literal sense that those values had long since become archaic;
it was nonetheless radical in its novel means of preaching them. Like
the contemporary Methodists working among the new urban, industrial, and mining population of England, the evangelical "New
Lights" among the Congregationalists and the "New Side" among
the Presbyterians won their greatest response from people whose
social institutions had been somewhat disordered by economic
progress—progress from which, moreover, they were far less certain
to benefit than the enterprising merchants, planters, and land
speculators of the time. The cultural and institutional erosion that
successive migrations wrought in the society of new settlements
evidently troubled them no matter how committed they were to
worldly getting-ahead.

Puritans had always been aware of the temptation inherent in
the pursuit of wealth. "There is a venom in *Riches*," Cotton Mather
warned in 1727, "disposing our depraved Hearts to cast off their
Dependence on *God*."[6] Diligent pursuit of the earthly calling of the

merchant or farmer, though good in itself, always threatened to overbalance his spiritual vocation. "They will plead in defense of a Worldly Covetous spirit," another minister lamented in 1721, "under the colour or specious pretense of Prudence, Diligence, Frugality, Necessity."[7] The eighteenth-century descendants of the Puritans still assumed that the patently avaricious man must be damned. And yet every new settlement swarmed with land speculators, great and small men alike, each one avid for quick profit whatever it might cost the community in dissension, uncertainty, and anxiety.

The doctrine and style of preaching of the New Lights were both reassuring. The hearers sometimes responded on the spot to the preacher's adjuration "not to hunt for Riches, and Honours, and Pleasures in this World, but to despise them, and deny themselves," by making a communal bonfire of whatever fashionable clothing, jewelry, and wigs they happened to possess.[8] By some such show of repentance they could at least restore the sense of being a social community covenanted together in a common spiritual cause. For people whose communities were only half-formed and whose daily tasks on the farm or in the shop involved them in a highly unsocial economic struggle, a revival of religion could be enormously heartening.

Like many later reform movements, however, the Great Awakening ended by still further shaking up the social order. Instead of simply restoring spiritual strength to the church and good order to the community, it set new sects against the old ones. Some of the evangelists deliberately made themselves as obnoxious as they could to "unregenerate" clergymen, both the liberal rationalists who were moving toward Unitarianism and the passively orthodox Old Lights who of course considered themselves to be the true conservatives. Although most of the evangelical New Light and New Side preachers were as able and as well educated as any, the nature of their appeal —at once mystical and sensational—called into question the merely human learning of an "unconverted ministry." To Gilbert Tennent the latter were "Orthodox, Letter-learned and regular Pharisees," "blind Guides," and "dead Dogs, that can't bark." He likened the unconverted minister to "a Man who would learn others to swim, before he has learn'd it himself, and so is drowned in the Act, and dies like a Fool."[9]

Bad feeling between the two Congregationalist factions in western New England led many New Light congregations to throw off the authority of the quasi-presbyterian ministerial consociations—unless, with more guile than principle, they managed to capture the latter as well—and to withdraw as Separatists. Some began calling themselves Baptists. But since the existing Baptists of New England had lost the spiritual ardor of Roger Williams's day and generally took an Old Light position, two sects of Baptists—Separate and Regular—competed during the late eighteenth century, as well as the two factions of Congregationalists. The old Puritan order was truly being cast, as a moderate minister lamented in 1741, "into *Anarchy*, and *Confusion*"—even into sordid local disputes over paying taxes to support the church, disputes which could end only in partial disestablishment in the 1750s and 1760s as the dissenting congregations secured tax exemption.[10] Among the Presbyterians of the Delaware-Susquehanna region the formal New Side–Old Side schism lasted only until 1758. There was similar discord among Anglicans which did not, however, split off a separate Methodist church until after the American Revolution. Although by the 1750s the Great Awakening had spent its force, it proved difficult to restore the unity of the churches, doubly weakened as they were by rankling memories of the controversy and by the inevitable relapse of most of the converts into the usual indifference of the eighteenth century.

There remained a saving remnant, however, especially among the Presbyterians, Baptists, and Methodists who sent missionaries in the wake of the backcountry migration into western Pennsylvania, the Valley of Virginia and the Carolina Piedmont, and across the mountains into the Appalachian Plateau. The Presbyterians, who organized their first presbyteries beyond the mountains in the 1780s, dedicated themselves to redeeming the West from the heathenism into which those isolated places were falling. "I found scarcely one man and a few women who supported a credible profession of religion," one of the itinerant missionaries wrote of Kentucky. "Some were grossly ignorant of the first principles of religion. Some were given to quarrelling and fighting, some to profane swearing, some to intemperance, and perhaps most of them totally negligent of the forms of religion in their own homes."[11] Half of the frontier ministers themselves lamentably had to be disciplined at one time or another for intemperance, wrangling, licentiousness, or heresy.

Strong measures clearly were called for from the orthodox, the same measures that had prevailed two generations earlier. In Logan County, an upland district of Kentucky that was notorious for its gangs of lawless "rogues" and extralegal "regulators" or vigilantes, the impassioned preaching of James McGready began in 1797 to win great numbers of converts. "He would so array hell before the wicked," a fellow minister related, "that they would tremble and quake, imagining a lake of fire and brimstone yawning to overwhelm them and the hand of the Almighty thrusting them down the horrible abyss."[12] The crowds who flocked to hear what hope they might have of salvation, "struggling in the pangs of the new birth, ready to faint or die for Christ, almost on the brink of desperation," gave rise by 1800 to a new institution, the camp meeting.[13]

The great camp meeting at Cane Ridge in Bourbon County, Kentucky, in 1801 was the model for later western revivals. A crowd of ten to twenty-five thousand from near and far assembled in a large clearing in the forest. Eighteen Presbyterian ministers and an uncounted number of Methodist and Baptist preachers exhorted them in relays of half a dozen at a time for six days and evenings. The throng was swept by "a strange supernatural power." People wept, sobbed, shouted, and shrieked, to begin with, and then fell into the uncontrollable contortions that revivalists soon came to recognize and classify: the "falling exercise," in which the sinner lay rigid and unconscious on the ground; the "rolling exercise," in which he thrashed wildly about; the "jerks," in which his head snapped involuntarily from side to side; and the "barks," which caused him to bay like a hound, sometimes going as far as the exercise known as "treeing the devil." Perhaps three thousand souls were converted, or "brought to the ground," at Cane Ridge.[14]

Within a few years the Great Revival spread throughout the Southern Uplands and into the Northwest, bringing tens of thousands into the Baptist and Methodist churches. Although the Presbyterians had started it, emotional evangelism did not comport very well with the Calvinist tradition that clergymen should be classically educated, systematic theologians and logical preachers. The camp meeting came to be more typical of Baptists and Methodists, many of whose preachers the Presbyterians scorned as "illiterate exhorters."[15] An early settler in Michigan described the inspired but untrained preacher "with the dress and air of a horse-jockey, who will rant and scream till he is obliged to . . . dry the tears which are the natural result of the excitement into which he has lashed himself." But there were also ordinary men who had earnestly pored over the Bible and who could deliver "a good plain practical discourse."[16]

As long as frontier society remained dispersed over great distances, the itinerant Methodist or Baptist preacher was a familiar figure, riding from settlement to settlement, ministering to a circuit of churches, and calling for converts wherever he could find anyone to hear him. As revival followed revival in various parts of the West down to the 1850s, the Methodists and Baptists became the principal churches of the Mississippi Valley.

Although frontier revivalism slackened in the 1830s, the movement had already spread back to the older regions. Revival meetings were as commonly held in huge tents at regular camp grounds near large cities, or in city churches, as in isolated settlements. Some of the greatest of the "sensational" preachers were pastors of churches in Boston and New York. For several decades the whole country, indeed, was periodically swept by tidal waves of conversions, notably in 1830–1832, 1842–1843, and finally in 1857–1858. Although the last of these began as a laymen's movement and took the clergy by surprise, never again were Americans susceptible to revival on a national scale.

The sequence suggests that revivalistic religion embodied a popular reaction to the peculiar social circumstances of the early nineteenth century. It was not the mere orgy of stentorian haranguers, hysterical women, and sexual license under the trees at which Old School critics darkly hinted, nor did the New School adequately explain it by simply asserting that once again "the Lord worked like himself in power."[17] All those people who panted for conversion, whether in the Appalachian backwoods or a city church, belonged to the first generation or two to undergo revolutionary economic change and dislocation of the social order. Isolation of the individual, whether because of sheer distance from his neighbors in a rural settlement or the strange anonymity of life in one of the crowded new commercial or industrial centers, made men and women crave the intensely communal experience of the revivals, especially the protracted camp meetings. "When they congregate on these exciting occasions," a western preacher observed, "society itself is to them a novelty, and an excitement."[18] To be "found" by Christ among the throng could be equally satisfying to people who had moved into the unfamiliar life of a city and felt oddly lost in the crowd.[19] In either sort of place the evangelist's urgent preaching revived the old Protestant tension—and hope of striking a balance—between the covenanted community and the individual seeking "union with Christ." At the same time, since the revivalists called on the individual to bestir himself to seek salvation (even though God alone could grant it), the doctrine of conversion accorded, in a sense, with the self-reliance in economic matters which the new age inculcated. Perhaps one's spiritual and earthly call-ings could be reconciled after all.

The Americans who lived between the revivals of 1801 and 1858 were not so far advanced into the modern world, however, that they could not respond to the simplified but still roughly orthodox doctrine which most of the revivalists preached. Although they had grown up in an age increasingly engrossed with material progress, they retained a sense of the old supernatural values and remembered the theological terms in which their Protestant ances-tors had expressed them. Their optimism over western expansion, industrial growth, and the universal opportunity to get rich was counterbalanced by the old pessimism about human nature and human self-sufficiency and by a lingering apprehension that life held some higher purpose than making money. They had seen enough of modern society to be disturbed by its uncertainties with-out as yet becoming inured to social disorganization, or "pluralism," as it would one day be called, nor reacting against it with no loftier gospel than one drawn from its own economic values. A revival, one of the new preachers wrote in 1833, could dispel "chill-ing selfishness, or hateful discord, or unblushing crime" and restore "the social virtues" to a community.[20] The anxiety of the penitent who came forward to the "anxious seat" or "mourner's bench" was for the state of his society as well as that of his own soul.

For all the social and theological conservatism of the revivals, evangelism inadvertently splintered once again the institutional integrity of the church. Some denominations profited of course: the Baptist and Methodist churches, being evangelical sects by origin as well as by current practice, held together in spite of the rapidity of their expansion across the vast distances of the West. But the question of the propriety of revivalism divided the older churches more bitterly than in the 1740s. To orthodox Calvinists the "new measures" of Charles G. Finney, as he preached through upper New York State in the late 1820s, smacked of the old Arminian heresy of free will and a salvation to be won by mere human effort. To exhort sinners to strive to be converted came close to saying that they were free not only to choose between heaven and hell but even to achieve personal perfection here on earth. The outspoken temerity of Finney's doctrine of "Perfectionism," with its optimism about the ease with which "disinterested benevolence" could drive out selfishness, seemed to the orthodox of the 1830s and 1840s as heretical as the Unitarian rationalism on their other flank; were not revivalism and Unitarianism guilty of exactly the same overweening human presumption? In defense the revivalists could point not only to the spiritual exaltation of their converts but also—as though they had calculated how best to impress that expansive age—to their success in winning such numbers of converts as orthodox clergymen seldom saw. Finney adjudged that Christ himself had not done better at the job of conversion, though the difficult "circumstances under which he labored" had of course to be conceded.[21]

No denomination was immune to the controversy. Hardest hit once again were the Presbyterians, already split by all the secessions of the past two centuries in Scotland, Ireland, and colonial America. A Kentucky presbytery controlled by the revivalists withdrew in 1810 as the Cumberland Presbyterian Church; congregational but hopefully ecumenical groups calling themselves Disciples of Christ or simply the "Christian Church" emerged between 1809 and 1830. From 1837, when the General Assembly expelled nearly six hundred churches for unorthodoxy, until 1869, the main body of Presbyterians was divided into separate Old and New School denominations. However radical the evangelicals appeared to the others, all these groups were fundamentally conservative in their common spiritual commitment. They succeeded mainly in further dissipating, however, the influence that the church could exert upon the other affairs of mankind.

To proliferate new sects might of course have been to disseminate religion into every neglected corner of society. And in fact the evangelical factions from various denominations cooperated in their missionary work abroad and in the new West, in Bible societies, and in the Sunday School movement. They could even avow in so many words the "conservative" hope of securing general agreement on certain Christian essentials in spite of all the sectarian forms.[22] But another sort of enervation accompanied the schisms. In their urgency to make faith simple and compelling, the revivalists drifted away from substantive theology of any coherence and complexity. As a Lutheran clergyman wryly observed of the new measures in 1843, they might cause the sinner to "get religion," but what got the sinner was not religion as the orthodox understood it.[23] Rather like their rationalist opponents, the Unitarians, revivalists tended to slough off theological rigor in order to find some sort of faith palatable enough to the secular-minded to keep them in the church.

The spiritual mission of the revivalists, conservative as it was in intent, could be accounted a success; slowly but steadily the proportion of church members in the adult population rose from the meager tenth of 1800 to perhaps a fifth by 1875. But the church was inexorably losing its capacity to impose spiritual values on society in any clear and coherent form. It responded in various ways to the economic preoccupation of the time: rationalists acquiesced in it; revivalists tried to divert attention from it; the orthodox went on intoning dogma handed down from other times and places. They were bound to be frustrated in their common yet disunited reaction against the main cause of instability in a society they could no longer control.

In one region—the backcountry of New England and the Yankee-settled districts of upper New York State—men who clung to spiritual values were inspired to break entirely with old institutions and create the first indigenous American sects. The region had been swept by revivalism so often and with such heat that by the time the climax was reached, between 1825 and 1837, upstate New York was known as the "burned-over" district. Although the Yankee anxious over the state of his soul behaved more circumspectly than the Southern Uplanders of Cane Ridge, the old Puritan fire of 1630 and 1740 still smoldered in him, whether he now counted himself a Congregationalist, Presbyterian, Baptist, or a churchless disciple of some popular rationalist like Tom Paine or Ethan Allen. Literacy and the habit of thinking in terms of biblical history and theological categories predisposed him toward religious speculation about the problems of earthly existence.

Northern and western New England and upstate New York had reached a critical point in the 1820s. Settled in the course of the accelerated frontier migration since 1730, the district had reached a certain level of economic maturity, and some parts had even begun to decline in competition with the still newer and much richer lands of the Northwest. Although many farmers promptly moved on to Ohio, Michigan, and Wisconsin or back to the eastern cities, while other men in a few key towns along the Erie Canal battened on the traffic in western wheat and wool, the backcountry people who hung on were restive. Farm life was easier than in frontier days, especially for the women, but the dispersed society of the isolated rural townships provided few diversions from the dull daily round. Many of the social disadvantages of the remote frontier persisted, without the old frontier confidence that economic opportunity would continue to widen. Left behind by agricultural, commercial, and industrial progress, the region was ready for its own peculiar response to the liberal nineteenth century.

Several new sects that had begun elsewhere had already been

attracted to the region. The Shakers, a millennial, perfectionist, communist group who relied on direct revelation somewhat as the Quakers did, came from England in the 1770s under their prophetess Mother Ann Lee, whom they believed to be Christ returned in female form. If the deity was bisexual, it followed that women were the equals of men; the Shaker doctrine of celibacy was imposed on both alike. (They perpetuated their communities by adopting orphans as well as by attracting converts from the region.) Another Quaker variant, the Community of the Public Universal Friend—the latter divine personage being their founder, Jemimah Wilkinson—settled in western New York in the 1780s. Although such movements were planted close to the frontier of the time mainly because land was available there, their success at winning adherents among the local Yankees foreshadowed the homegrown sects of the next generation.

The Mormon church was the first of these. Its prophet, Joseph Smith, was born in Vermont in 1805 to a poor farm family who moved to Palmyra in western New York in 1816, at the end of the Yankee migration to that district. Like many others, the family belonged to no church; the father professed a simple rationalism, the mother had something of a mystical bent. Young Joseph Smith became engrossed in the local pastime of digging for Indian relics in the mysterious ancient mounds of the neighborhood. In 1827, according to his account, an angel revealed to him certain golden plates buried in a nearby hill and provided him with "seer stones" through which their Egyptian characters could be readily translated. As dictated by Smith, the Book of Mormon explained the Indians, in biblical language, as one of the Lost Tribes of Israel who had defeated a rival tribe and buried them in the local mounds. The same sort of explanation for the mounds, fortifications, copper breastplates, and other strange artifacts of the region had already occurred, in simpler form, to a number of individuals whose acquaintance with antiquity came mainly from the Old Testament. There were more timely matters as well. The Book of Mormon reflected "every error and almost every truth discussed in New York for the last ten years," a hostile critic observed in 1832:

infant baptism, ordination, the trinity, regeneration, repentance, justification, the fall of man, the atonement, transsubstantiation, fasting, penance, church government, religious experience, the call to the ministry, the general resurrection, eternal punishment, who may baptize, and even the question of freemasonry, republican government, and the rights of man.[24]

Although the Church of Jesus Christ of Latter-Day Saints, which Smith and a few followers founded in 1830, was a distinctive phenomenon of the time and the region, its doctrine of continuing revelation—with a very ordinary young man like Joseph Smith as "Seer, a Translator, a Prophet, an Apostle of Jesus Christ, and Elder of the Church through the will of God the Father and the grace of your Lord Jesus Christ"—was too heretical for most Yankees to tolerate.[25] In 1831 Smith and about a hundred followers prudently removed to Kirtland in the old Connecticut Western Reserve of northern Ohio, where for the next six years they collected converts from their old region and from Europe. Few converts ever came in, however, from among the ambitious but conventional people of the new Middle West around them. In fact, the farther west the Mormons went, the more they were persecuted. Driven out of Ohio in 1837, they settled on the far frontier of Missouri only to be expelled by the militia the next year.

Regathering on the Illinois shore of the Mississippi at Nauvoo, where they had a few years' respite, the Mormons sent out missionaries, prospered as more converts joined them, and received through their leader a divine revelation sanctioning polygamy. Joseph Smith, who within a few years had forty-nine wives—some of them linked to him only spiritually—was by no means the libertine that his critics alleged. With his Yankee conscience he was no hypocrite seducing girls in the frenzy of a camp meeting. Like John Humphrey Noyes, who developed his own doctrine of "complex marriage" at the strictly regulated Oneida community in western New York, Smith made novel sexual arrangements moral —someone was sure to find polygamy preferable to prostitution and even the derided spinsterhood of the time—in terms of Old Testament precedents and a more "eternal family organization."[26] But polygamy inevitably brought still harsher persecution down upon the Mormons. Smith was arrested in 1844 for forcibly suppressing antipolygamist Mormons, and while held in jail he was lynched by a mob of outraged citizens.

In 1846–1847 his successor Brigham Young, another native of Vermont, led fifteen thousand of the Mormons a thousand miles west of the intolerant midwestern settlements to the deserts of the Enclosed Basin between the Rocky Mountains and the Sierra Nevada. There the elaborate Mormon hierarchy, consisting of president, apostles, patriarchs, high priests, seventies, elders, bishops, priests, deacons, and teachers—a far more thoroughgoing theocracy than the old Puritan commonwealth had ever been—

directed settlement with a regard for social order that fully reversed the liberal economic individualism of the persecuting society from which the Mormons had fled. Salt Lake City and the other towns, or "stakes," were laid out in a remarkable return to the spirit of the old New England system. Each family was given a house lot in a compact village and, depending on the number of members, an outlying tract of ten to eighty acres to farm. Although the church had no legal title to bestow, the settlers abided by its arrangements. When a federal land office was finally opened in 1869, the Mormons managed to adapt the 160-acre homesteads of the federal survey to their quite different pattern. The church also devised an irrigation system, something quite unknown in the East or in Western Europe, to bring water down from the Wasatch Range and distribute it equitably and economically. The watermaster, a communal officer, was a desert version of the old Yankee fence viewer. For a few years in the 1870s, when the church reorganized the economy of Utah on a semicommunistic basis, Mormon society went even further beyond Puritan precedents.

Every other aspect of Mormon life was likewise directed by the hierarchy. Missionaries were sent to the East and to Europe, especially England, Wales, and Scandinavia, where they converted thousands to the Mormon faith and to the prospect of owning land in Utah. The church lent converts their Atlantic fare, chartered ships to bring them across as "a Family under strong and accepted discipline, with every provision for comfort, decorum, and internal peace," as a Parliamentary committee reported in 1854, and sped the immigrants on to Utah by rail, wagon train, and sometimes handcarts.[27] In the same manner the church closely supervised the institution of polygamy for the sake of spiritual and social ends. Since "plural marriage" was permitted only to church members who could support more than one family, no more than one man in twenty practiced it, and most of those had only two wives. Mormon polygamy may be considered a system of eugenics, engaged in by the morally and materially most fit. The church forbade use of tobacco and stimulating drink, down to tea and coffee; at the same time it sponsored literary societies and, unlike many evangelistic sects, condoned social dancing. For all its peculiarities, Mormon society was Puritan society reborn: an orderly, hierarchic commonwealth in which both economic enterprise and social institutions were communally regulated for the sake of spiritual values. Since, furthermore, the harsh natural environment of Utah required disciplined cooperation as never before in American history, the

Mormon commonwealth was able to fend off indefinitely the individualistic secular disorder into which Puritan society had fallen.

The Mormons' old region had not seen the last sectarian novelty when Joseph Smith left Palmyra in 1831. In that same year William Miller, a Vermont Baptist farmer, became convinced that Christ was about to return to earth; the date, he calculated, would be March 21, 1844. By 1842 his followers all over the Northeast were preparing for doomsday. A comet in 1843 seemed to confirm his prophecy. Converts sold their farms or shops, put on "ascension robes," and gathered on the hilltops on the appointed night ready to be swept up into heaven. When another terrestrial day dawned, Miller set about correcting his computations and shortly announced a new date. Not even a second anticlimax discouraged all the Millerites, or Seventh-Day Adventists, as they called their new sect.

Spiritualism was another phenomenon of the burned-over district. In 1848 two country girls claimed to have heard mysterious rapping noises, supposedly communications from the spirit world. In spite of the objections of physicians and scientists, the North went through a prolonged fad of "Rochester rappings," seances, and table-tipping experiments among the million and a half persons who were said to be convinced spiritualists in the mid-1850s. By that time, however, the old Yankee backcountry had generated almost its last spiritual novelty. Its people had either gone west, moved to the cities that were industrializing the region, or reconciled themselves for better or worse to their circumstances.

Another wellspring of division in the church had opened in the Northeast by that time: the massive immigration which added a whole new range of ethnic churches to the denominational spectrum. The churches of the immigrants were exceptionally conservative. To be sure, the newcomers had been uprooted by economic change in their homelands and attracted to America by economic opportunity; their presence further stimulated the American economic revolution. But, if anything, they expected their improved economic circumstances to allow them to perpetuate the old familiar institutions and folkways, and of all the elements of old-country society transplanted to the New World the church was the hardiest. Its forms were designed to be established wherever the faithful might be, and since its creed provided a spiritual leaven to the grossly material ends of immigration itself, the church served as a focal point around which ethnic communities could coalesce and maintain their identity in the midst of an American society where everything else was in flux.

Most of the principal American denominations having also originated in Europe, some of the immigrants' churches were nearly their exact counterparts in both doctrine and polity. There was little to distinguish most English Methodists and Nonconformists or Scottish and Irish Presbyterians from their American coreligionists, whose churches they usually joined. (Oddly, the small sect of Primitive Methodists, though originally an American movement carried to England by missionaries, came to consist mainly of English immigrants.) On the other hand, Anglican working-class immigrants sometimes formed parishes of their own, especially if there were too many of them to fit easily into the local congregation of prosperous American Episcopalians, where they might be "made to feel the difference between a good coat and a poor one," as a Lancashire cotton mill hand in Fall River said in 1871.[28] Or theological differences might be the sticking point. The German and Scandinavian Lutherans, arriving in great numbers after the late 1830s, found that the American Lutheran church, established by their countrymen in the previous century, had slipped too far down the way of modern liberalism to suit them. Each nationality ultimately organized one or more separate synods of its own— the Germans first in 1847, the Swedes in 1860, the Norwegians in 1870—and managed to stave off change well into the twentieth century.

Catholic immigrants lacked the easy option of schism. Down to the first American provincial council of bishops in 1829 the Catholics were a small group—though nine of the ten episcopal sees had been organized since 1807—mostly of colonial ancestry and Gallican liberal in tone, with an appropriately French element in the hierarchy. Many Catholic churches had picked up the American Protestant practice of vesting the parish property in the hands of lay trustees rather than those of the bishop; here and there, laymen were even demanding a voice in selecting the priest. After 1829 nearly twenty years of interdicts and excommunications were required before all the recalcitrants could be brought into line with universal Catholic polity.

The flooding in of millions of Irish and German immigrants, however, was already swamping the original character of the church in America. German Catholics were relatively liberal, but the arch-conservatism of the much more numerous Irish made Catholicism from 1840 until after 1875 the most thoroughgoing of all counters to the American tendencies of the time, alike condemning liberalism, evangelism, orthodox Calvinism, and secular indifference. As

Irishmen rapidly came to dominate the hierarchy, along with a few notable converts to the certainties of Roman orthodoxy, they more and more explicitly rejected the liberal society that surrounded them. Catholic social doctrine exalted harmony and stability, precisely the qualities that American society not only lacked—most clearly in its multifarious ethnic and religious groups—but boldly repudiated on principle. The Irish peasant to whose frustrating life in Ireland his religion had given meaning—a hope of a better world beyond the grave—found it no less consoling among the confusions of urban and industrial America. The priest, having also been the only popular leader of the downtrodden Irish peasantry, easily took up the same role in the immigrant community. The Catholic church which each Irish neighborhood built and clustered about was perhaps the most perfect example of the central place that the church assumed in every ethnic community.

The medley of devoutly conservative foreign churches in an American city or farming district was something less than a conservative force for social stability. Although all such denominations were opposed to the material values that permeated society, each one inevitably was made aware day by day of the obvious differences among them and was bound to consider all the others to be in error. Some of the distinctions, they had inherited from the distant past; others sprang from the practical circumstances in which their communicants found themselves. The starkest expression of the social disjunctions and cultural dissimilarities among the various immigrant groups and between them and native Americans thus issued from the very institution that professed the most transcendently universal values.

On balance the problems of economic change and social disorder were more aggravated than relieved by the multiplicity of denominational efforts to reinstate spiritual values. Even the one avowed attempt to reunite all Protestants in a single, simply "Christian" church succeeded only in adding one more separate institution, under that ironically all-embracing name, to the list of competitors. By 1875 there were at least ten separately organized denominations of Methodists, seven of Baptists, ten of Presbyterians and other Reformed churches, half a dozen kinds of Lutherans, the rationalistic Unitarians and Universalists, two sects of Quakers, the united but never wholly unitary Episcopalians and Roman Catholics, and a score of minor sects, mostly of remote ethnic derivation, that had survived from the eighteenth century or had recently arrived in the nineteenth. The church had been exploded into the denominations. However the latter might react against the runaway material progress and social fragmentation of the time—the same forces out of which so many of their own divisions had sprung—in their internecine clamor they could hardly hope to make their properly spiritual values prevail.

17. MORAL VOLUNTARISM

Erosion of the established institutions of the old social order—class, family, community, and church—did not also remove the needs which they had existed to satisfy; it could only leave them unsatisfied. A disordered society being unable to resolve its own disorder, new institutions suited to the times had to be devised. Although contemporaries seldom expressed it that way, Americans throughout the nineteenth century were in effect casting about for social institutions with two essential qualities: consistency with the revolutionary new individualism of private economic enterprise, and yet the capacity to cope with the social anxieties that were by-products of that same economic revolution. The answer was the voluntary association, an institution which existed because its members chose to create and sustain it.

The voluntary association came on the stage as the institutions of the old establishment receded. A prototype familiar to all was provided by the denominational sects which had succeeded the established churches of colonial America. During the half century between 1783 and 1833 the proliferation of competing sects made separation of church and state a practical necessity in every state where the Anglican or Congregational church had been established by law. Disestablishment in turn removed the last legal checks both to further sectarian schisms on one hand and on the other to sectarian cooperation in missionary associations, the American Bible Society (1816), the American Tract Society (1825), the American Sunday School Union (1824), and local societies for the reformation of morals. Now that everyone took free choice of a church for granted, no one was likely to question his right to choose among secular associations.

The way toward voluntarism was also pointed in the 1790s by the rapid (though quite unforeseen) evolution of the first modern political parties, organizations which were made necessary by the absence of a ruling aristocracy or of an all-powerful government under the new federal Constitution. By Tocqueville's time, a generation later, political parties were "only a single feature in the midst of [an] immense assemblage of institutions."

Americans of all ages, all conditions, and all dispositions constantly form associations. They have not only commercial and manufacturing companies, in which all take part, but associations of a thousand other kinds, religious, moral, serious, futile, general or restricted, enormous or diminutive. The Americans make associations to give entertainments, to found seminaries, to build inns, to construct churches, to diffuse books, to send missionaries to the antipodes; in this manner they found hospitals, prisons, and schools. If it is proposed to inculcate some truth or to foster some feeling by the encouragement of a great example, they form a society. Wherever at the head of some new undertaking you see the government in France, or a man of rank in England, in the United States you will be sure to find an association.[1]

A few special kinds of associations, besides the business corporations, contributed directly to the progressive economy. Societies to encourage manufacturing—notably Alexander Hamilton's Society for Establishing Useful Manufactures, which built a cotton mill at Paterson—seemed a promising device at the end of the eighteenth century, but industrialization eventually developed on other lines. Merchants dealing in certain commodities banded together in state and national associations early in the nineteenth century to advance their special interests, and promotional groups propagandized for railroads and other "internal improvements." Local agricultural societies sought to improve the level of farming practice by holding annual exhibitions or fairs, awarding prizes, reading papers, and publishing journals, but since most of their members were gentlemen farmers or simply gentlemen, neither their meetings nor their hortatory "tomato papers" had much practical effect. State medical and bar associations and local societies of scientific, musical, esthetic, and literary societies functioned on the border between material advantage—of the country and of their members—and the disinterested elevation of professional ethics or cultural standards. Such self-constituted groups felt that they were thoroughly in tune with the universal spirit of progress, although the lawyer or doctor whom they accused of unethical practice or quackery—or was he simply a bold experimenter?—could also appeal to the democratic principle of free individual enterprise.

Movements for reforming society were a special province of voluntary associations. Each group conceived of its cause as the vanguard of the progressive, egalitarian, individualistic, and optimistic spirit of the times. The injustice and oppression that aroused their indignation, compassion, and fervor seemed to be vestiges of an imperfect but now outworn age. Individuals who were held down, whether by oppressive institutions like chattel slavery or imprisonment for debt, by lack of schooling and other opportunity, or even by their own vices, could be pictured as having been deprived of the freedom that every man should enjoy. To free the slave, the ignorant, the intemperate, seemed to promise the perfection of American liberty. In a fundamental sense such schemes involved, however, something other than the ultimate refinement of a liberal social order. Like most of the religious movements of the time, they now appear to have marked an implicitly conservative reaction against the anxieties engendered by the disorders of libertarian society. The reformers sprang from the same social generation, so to speak, as the revivalists, the Mormons, and the Irish Catholic immigrants: people not yet sufficiently habituated to the nineteenth-century economic ethic to have lost sight of the higher values of social stability and of equitable relations, as well as equal conditions, among men.

Several common threads ran through all the social reform movements. Since the same kinds of people—often the same individuals—involved themselves in a variety of reforms, they have been lumped together as "humanitarian reformers," or as one of the more lighthearted of them put it, "the Lord's chore boys."[2] The reforming impulse was strongest among those New Englanders and people of Yankee stock in New York State and the Northwest who had abandoned Calvinist orthodoxy, whether for Unitarian rationalism, evangelical perfectionism, or romantic transcendentalism; in a secular age their Puritan inheritance might well incline some of them toward social reform. In the Middle and Southern Atlantic states the Quakers, few as they were, had long and earnestly concerned themselves with the social disorders of slavery and war. American reformers of almost every kind also drew inspiration from contemporary European liberalism. And yet for all the modern liberal reinforcement of the old Protestant urge to do good, reform was far from the universal "ferment" that most subsequent accounts have pictured. Nowhere in the United States did more than a small minority actively "come out" for the reordering of society.

Until recently, historians have usually agreed with the reformers that the substantial evils of that day were quite sufficient explanation for the rise of movements to correct them. But without charging those earnest men and women with cant and hypocrisy, as their opponents often did, it has been suggested that their personal circumstances, perhaps as much as those of the society about them, may have inclined them toward reform. A number of the leaders of the antislavery movement in New England in the 1830s, in particular, seem to have belonged to "a displaced class in American society," young men and women of respectable lineage, educated to lead society like their ancestors the merchants, clergymen, and magistrates of the old elite.[3] A moral crusade on behalf of the southern slaves may have appealed to such persons, quite subconsciously, as a way to recover leadership from the crass new set of industrialists who were usurping it. The fact that almost the only industrialists in New England at that time were the cotton manufacturers, whose supply of raw material was produced by slave labor, also made abolition of slavery a not illogical cause for anyone so discontented. The movement "offered these young people a chance for a reassertion of their traditional values, an opportunity for association with others of their kind, and a possibility of achieving that self-fulfillment which should traditionally have been theirs as social leaders."[4]

The heavy incidence of reform sentiment in the backcountry of New England and western New York has likewise been attributed, along with the evangelistic revivals and novel sects of that spiritually burned-over district, to the small farmers' unrest over a stagnating economy and backward society—although neither the reform agitation nor the religious excitement took very precise aim at any such conditions. At least it is certain that humanitarian reform did *not* flourish among people who were profiting or expecting soon to profit from the new kinds of economic development: the frontier farmers and speculators of the new West and the manufacturers, bankers, railway promoters, and other rising entrepreneurs of the industrial Northeast.

Some recent historians, quick to defend the purity of the reformers' motives, have objected that vague, subconscious anxieties are impossible to document and, far worse, that even to consider the personal anxieties of abolitionists must be to imply that slavery was no genuine moral issue and should never have excited them. We need not choose, however, between canonizing the reformers for selfless zeal and damning them for unworthy status-seeking. A measure of each may well have been present, since both sets of motives, after all, stemmed from the same basic situation. Enslavement of a race of men for the sake of profitable tobacco or cotton production; the precarious position of an old social elite during an industrial revolution; the racking uncertainty which pervaded a whole society engaged in rapid economic growth and sometimes equally rapid decline—each of these was an aspect of the general subversion of spiritual and social values by radical material progress.

Whether he or anyone else recognized it, the man who was pressed by one such situation and joined a movement to reform another was simply hacking at a different head of the selfsame hydra. Indeed, he might suffer from no discernible personal dislocation at all and still, feeling the tensions of the social disequilibrium around him, address himself to setting right some injustice suggested to him by his inherited moral scruples, a foreign example, or his own observation. It is significant that although slavery was the oldest and worst injustice in American society, no concerted movement to abolish it arose until the 1830s, not long after American society commenced its headlong slide into a whole complex of derangements.

Some other, less complicated problems than slavery were apparent to anyone in an egalitarian age. Europeans and Americans alike were shaking off the old callousness toward the deaf, the blind, and the insane; compassion extended even to duly convicted criminals penned up in noisome jails and prisons. It was a great merit of that optimistic age of material progress and economic individualism—though perhaps not as great a merit as it thought— to believe that everyone should have an equal opportunity to share in it. Insofar as the belief derived from the widespread equality of opportunity in colonial America, it was related to the conservative reaction against the current falling away from the old order, even though the disorder had been fomented by ideas deriving from that same equality.

To release the deaf and the blind from their physical bondage, New England philanthropists in the 1820s and 1830s experimented with new European methods for their education and, supported first by voluntary associations organized for the purpose and then by the state governments, established the first schools for them. Startling successes with such unfortunates led in the 1840s to the first state institutions for mental defectives as well. The insane were also rescued from the jails, poorhouses, and garrets where they had usually been left to abuse and neglect. The first private and state asylums, established between 1815 and 1840, were inspired by European experimenters, certain benevolent Quakers, and a few leading physicians. In the 1840s a shocking series of reports by a Quaker lady, Dorothea L. Dix, drawn from her two-year investigation of how even the enlightened state of Massachusetts maltreated the insane, touched off a national movement for mental hospitals which won over most of the state governments by 1860.

Penal reform became an urgent matter in the late eighteenth century, when imprisonment was substituted for the bloodthirsty old code of capital and corporal punishment for most crimes. Philanthropic groups, the first of which was the Philadelphia Society for Alleviating the Miseries of Public Prisons (1787), sought to rehabilitate prisoners instead of simply punishing them. As long as delinquent debtors, persons awaiting trial, and even homeless children were locked up together with convicted felons of all kinds and both sexes, the jails and prisons clearly were breeding new criminals and hardening the old. Two standard designs for prisons were proposed in the 1820s and adopted by New York and Pennsylvania and then a number of other states. Both systems put prisoners in separate cells and gave them work to do. The Pennsylvania system permitted no contact with the outside world or with other prisoners; work, Bible-reading, and remorse were to lead to regeneration. The New York plan, which allowed prisoners to work together but not to speak, was adopted by most of the states by the 1840s. Its cheapness—prison workships produced more than isolated individuals could—commended the silent system perhaps more than the discovery that it was less likely to drive prisoners insane than the near-solitary system. Between the 1820s and 1840s the first reform schools were also established to teach delinquent children "the habits of industry and the principles of religion."[5]

These clearly humanitarian causes of educating the handicapped, curing the insane, and reforming criminals and juvenile delinquents had nothing to overcome but public inertia and indifference. Certainly a humanitarianism that promised that dependent individuals would pay part of their keep accorded well with the current faith in hard work and frugality. But at the same time the reformers were coming to see that, just as the concerted effort of society might put opportunity within the reach of such persons, social disadvantages were perhaps to blame for their plight in the first place. Among the many poor immigrants in the jails and asylums of New York and Massachusetts in the 1840s and 1850s, environmental causes were particularly evident. As a commission on the insane asylums of Massachusetts reported in 1855:

Being in a strange land and among strange men and things, meeting with customs and surrounded by circumstances widely different from all their previous experience, ignorant of the precise state of affairs here, and wanting education and flexibility by which they could adapt themselves to their new and unwonted position, they necessarily form many impracticable purposes, and endeavor to acomplish them by unfitting means. . . . Their lives are filled with doubt, and harrowing anxiety troubles them, and they are involved in frequent mental, and probably physical, suffering.[6]

No one was ready, however, to combine such casual observations about particular kinds of unfortunates into a general prescription for social reform. It would take decades—until long after 1875—before the puzzlement of volunteer philanthropists over the inadequacy of their patchwork reforms would lead them to suspect that the whole social order was fundamentally unhinged.

Even the reformers who probed most deeply into the nature of contemporary society—the abolitionists, the advocates of public schools, and the temperance crusaders—did not explicitly question its dominant values. Like other humanitarians, they sought to liberate individuals from bondage. Whether it was chattel slavery, illiteracy, or alcoholic tastes, were they not being denied equal opportunity to share in the general progress of the country? Reform so conceived seemed to stand in the forefront of progressive liberalism. But there were still deeper implications in the reformers' own conception of what they were about. Just as their discontent was too profound and their motives too conservative to be explained only in terms of the idealism and compassion they felt, so also the means that they adopted to make their reforms effective went far beyond their libertarian rhetoric. Sceptics then and since have thought it unduly perverse of professed libertarians to resort to compulsion in order to set men free—most egregiously, perhaps, to deny them free choice of what to drink. It was no great paradox, however, to employ the classic instrument of public regulation for the conservative end of restoring stability to some corner of society. The old principle of regulation for the general welfare of the commonwealth had become so attenuated since the eighteenth century as to lead the humanitarians, like other reformers of the time, into confusion as to how best to apply it. But their flights of libertarian rhetoric need not drown out forever the inherently conservative and sometimes literally old-fashioned character of the measures they proposed.

Clearly the public education movement had to establish a new set of institutions, a system of elementary schools, which could assume some of the disciplinary functions that the family, church, and community had abdicated. Now that parents were almost wholly preoccupied with getting on materially, it was indeed necessary, if the cultural inheritance of the race were to be passed on to children in the thousands of scattered, loosely organized communities of the rural West and urban East, to plant a school in each of them. In a country where only the sale of public land and taxes on real estate could provide enough capital to endow and maintain so many schools, the latter would have to be publicly established. Although the Puritans had anticipated the need in the seventeenth century, the common school system of the New England towns had since deteriorated, and in other sections, particularly in the South, no adequate system had ever existed.

The campaign of the 1830s and 1840s to drive home the urgent need for state-supported schools was conducted by hundreds of local associations throughout the North. But it was most purely a New Englanders' reform movement; the most influential reformer, Horace Mann, could speak between 1837 and 1848 with the constituted authority of the secretary to the Massachusetts State Board of Education. The common school tradition, however eroded, still manifested the conscientious Yankee's unwillingness to bury mind and soul in the pursuit of wealth.

The learning that educational reformers now prescribed for schoolchildren departed somewhat from the predilection of the old "grammar school" for Latin and Greek as preparation for a gentlemanly course in the liberal arts. Following the progressive European ideas of the time, they introduced English grammar and literature, modern history, geography, and other "practical" matters into the old curriculum. Presumably making "A" stand for "apple pie" rather than "Adam" made spelling more relevant to children in a secular age, but it was a limited concession to utilitarianism. The principle remained intact that the school was distinct from the marketplace: that even the most practical life required cultural values beyond what might be useful in any trade or profession. It was beginning to be recognized, furthermore, that educating children in a common culture was socially valuable in instilling into a mobile, heterogeneous population a sense of loyalty to a single national society. "Our policy as a State," the Indiana superintendent of public instruction said in 1853, "is to make of all the varieties of population among us, differing as they do in origin, language, habits of thought, modes of action, and social custom, one people, with one common interest."[7]

The reformers somewhat obscured their essential conservatism when they invoked current material values in order to secure the support of various interest groups. On one hand, they professed sympathy for artisans and laborers who complained that it was "the neglect of education" that made possible the "perverted system of society, which dooms the producer to ignorance, to toil, and to penury, to moral degradation, physical want and social barbarism."[8] Free, universal public education, together with free land, would fulfill the faith of the age in equality of economic opportunity and of social condition. In effect, schools would rescue the workingman by educating his sons into the middle class of small proprietors. The reluctance of most workingmen to give up their old expectations and move toward labor unions of the modern, class-conscious sort owed something to the popular faith in education which the reformers encouraged.

A few businessmen of the time took that line seriously enough to fear that schooling would deprive them of a reliable labor force. "The only way to get along with such ignorant people," one gentleman asserted in 1833, "is to keep them from mischief by keeping them constantly employed."[9] But the advocates of public schools warned employers and taxpayers that a far greater danger lurked in "besotting vices and false knowledge" that bred disrespect for the rights of property and could turn the country into "one vast moral desert."[10] If businessmen were vaguely uneasy over the moral implications of the economic revolution that they were conducting, they had the reformers' assurance that popular ignorance was the real social malady and the public schools its sovereign remedy:

When . . . boys come up into the ranks of apprentices and journeymen, without the intelligence or moral restraint which a good education would have supplied, and are found at the head of mobs, and strikes, and trades unions; speech-makers at riotous assemblies, and ringleaders of agrarian and atheistical clubs; when war is made upon the peace and order of communities, and law, with all its forms, and sanctions, and ministers, is set aside; and especially when the hand of their lawless violence is laid on the mansions, and luxuries, and treasure-houses of the rich; the arm of power must be raised, and held up by military force; the police dockets must be crowded; and . . . our prisons and penitentiaries will overflow, and the public purse be emptied for the support of their degraded and miserable tenants. . . . Under such institutions as ours . . . not a child can come to years of maturity, uneducated, without harm to us—to you—to the whole republic.[11]

The educated laborer, working "more steadily and cheerfully, and therefore more productively," "more disposed to respect [his] superiors" and "to look upon the distinctions of society without envy," would be immune to incitement by trade-union organizers, ambitious politicians, and other "crafty and aspiring demagogues" and "lewd fellows of the base sort."[12] Elementary schoolbooks like Noah Webster's "blue-backed speller" accordingly inveighed that it was "the meanest of all low tricks to creep into a man's inclosure and take his property" and that poverty was due to the fact that beggars "would rather beg than work."[13] "The greatest part of life,"

Webster advised his little readers, realistically enough for that epoch, "is to be employed in useful labors. . . . Man has but little time to spare for the gratification of the senses and the imagination. . . . Let it then be the fit study of your early years to learn in what consists *real worth* or *dignity of character*."[14] It may be that reading moral tales illustrative of the economic ethic of diligence and frugality helped to keep fresh the new generation's hope of lifting themselves above their fathers' economic and social problems.

The public school reformers promised workingmen and people of property alike more than any school could accomplish. Although they achieved more in less time than the other reformers, they made only a step toward universal education. By 1860 the states of the Northeast and Middle West, but only North Carolina in the South, had established elementary school systems, lengthened the school year, provided decent buildings, and introduced standard textbooks. No state, however, at a time when it seemed necessary for children to labor in industry, went so far as to compel attendance. Nor did the hundred new public high schools, most of them in New England, begin to supplant the six thousand private academies of varying size and dubious quality across the country. The substantial taxpayers of the South, which had nearly half of the private schools, were content to send their sons there; the northern reformer's economic arguments for educating lower-class children bore no relevance to Negro slaves and poor whites, whom no amount of schooling would have made more useful to the plantation economy or less menacing to the stability of southern society. In 1850, accordingly, some 20 percent of the whites of the South were illiterate, as against only 3 percent in the Middle Atlantic states and less than 0.5 percent in New England.

It was relatively easy to resort to the power and resources of the state to establish and administer a school system, a reform that almost anyone could accept less as social compulsion than as liberation of the individual for his own advancement. In that respect public schools were analogous to the public subsidies to canals, railroads, and other "internal improvements," the permissive laws for chartering business corporations, and other legislative instruments for releasing the economic energy of private entrepreneurs.

The goal of the antislavery movement, on the other hand, smacked of a wrongheaded illiberality. Since the abolitionists were a small minority of the northern population—once again, mainly certain kinds of New Englanders and Northwesterners of Yankee stock—most Americans thought their insistence on immediately freeing the southern slaves a dangerously eccentric notion, harmful to the security of the already free white people of another section of the country than their own and subversive of the stability of society everywhere. The earlier plan of the American Colonization Society (1817) not only to free slaves but to get rid of Negroes in general by sending them to Africa or Central America was far more widely supported, at least in principle, throughout the antebellum period. But abolitionism, at once the most high-minded and the most surely self-defeating of all the humanitarian movements, posed insoluble inconsistencies between its underlying social goal and the practical measures it proposed. Although the American Anti-Slavery Society (1833) claimed a quarter of a million members in some 1350 local societies by 1838, the active abolitionists never mounted to more than a coterie of a few thousand people, split into factions after 1840 in their frustration and disagreement over how to proceed. The place that sectional polemics assigned them between 1831 and 1861, when Southerners imagined them to be a vast northern conspiracy against southern society, was always grossly exaggerated.

No one, not even the abolitionists themselves, recognized the essentially conservative direction of their social movement. In the view of most people in their own part of the country the doctrine of immediate emancipation of the millions of slaves quite unnecessarily threatened to undermine the stability of society. From the perspective of the late twentieth century it appears that slavery itself, because of its fundamental inequity and violation of human dignity, was inherently unstable and hence potentially far more disruptive than the abolitionists who sought to excise it from society. But to most Northerners and Southerners alike, slavery was customary, familiar, and, given the general belief in the Negro's natural inferiority, a not unreasonable arrangement for fixing the proper place of the African race in a white man's country where, we may add, so little else was fixed. To propose freedom and equality for Negro slaves seemed a fanatical prescription for social chaos. Things were precarious enough for most people without that.

Those who were fortunate or sanguine enough to trust the beneficence of the economic revolution and the drift of social change wasted no time on the moral crusade against the plantation labor system. Perhaps human slavery was an awkward anomaly in the middle of the egalitarian nineteenth century, but one did not need to batten upon Negro slavery as directly as the planter, merchant, or textile manufacturer to accept the mounting output of cotton bales, cotton exports, and cotton cloth as evidence of national progress. If Americans ever reflected that slavery had been introduced, two hundred years before, for the sake of the same sort of economic progress, the thought failed to shake the modern liberal faith that the largest possible production of goods, by whatever sort of labor, would somehow foster the most equitable distribution of wealth as well. Slave labor seemed essential to the spread of tobacco, cotton, and sugar growing across the Southwest, to the expansion of American exports and the consequent accumulation of capital, and to the industrialization of the Northeast—all crucial to rapid economic development and everyone's hope of success. Anyone, even a Southerner like Hinton Helper in 1857, who ventured to argue that slavery was an economic disaster to the country, got very little hearing except among those already converted to abolitionism by noneconomic considerations. It seemed obvious to most people that since the slaves were noted for neither diligence nor thrift, it was the nature of Negroes to require masters and overseers to hold them to their necessary tasks. The argument that it was slavery that made Negroes work-shy, rather than age-old African laziness that necessitated slavery, once again persuaded only the already convinced.

If any of the planters, businessmen, farmers, and workingmen who threw themselves into the national pursuit of economic development had the faintest sense that the greater danger to social stability was ticking away in their own daily activity, they easily satisfied themselves that the immediate menace lay rather in the machinations of abolitionists and other irresponsible tinkerers with existing arrangements. Southerners, the ordinary slaveless farmer perhaps even more than the slaveowning directors of the system, conjured up a chimera of Haitian horrors that would surely erupt upon the slightest relaxation of the slave codes of their states. Northeastern workingmen, especially the poor Irish laborers of the new urban proletariat, could picture only too vividly a flood of freed Negroes streaming north to push them off the bottom rung of the ladder of jobs and social respectability. Northwestern farmers, standing with the Free Soil party of 1848 or the Republicans after 1854 against extension of slavery into the western territories, were determined to keep slaveowners and Negroes alike from occupying land they wanted for themselves. When even the antislavery movement was thus shot through with anti-Negro prejudice, outright abolitionists were hardly more tolerated on free soil than in the slave states. Ordinary outraged Americans in the 1830s man-handled William Lloyd Garrison in Boston and lynched Elijah Lovejoy at Alton, Illinois, and Irish laborers in Boston and New York set upon fugitive slaves and free Negroes in the 1850s and 1860s, just as the Yankee peddler traveling in the South ran the constant risk of being taken for an abolition agent inciting slaves to rebel or run away.

Frustrated by such overwhelming odds, the small bands of aboli-tionists could hardly foresee the changed circumstances in which their moral cause might suddenly prevail. Carried headlong by their heated version of the libertarian rhetoric of the age, they saw neither use nor right in expecting the established institutions of church and state, or even voluntary associations like their own, to produce any practical amelioration of the slave's lot. We may now think that the debility, at that time, of all institutions—eco-nomic, social and political—was reason enough for reformers to despair of enacting and then administering any careful plan of gradual emancipation. But instead, sharing the common faith of the time in a merely permissive individualism, the abolitionists felt, as Wendell Phillips observed in 1852, positively "bullied by institutions."[15] Neither churches nor political parties seemed any-thing but temporizers with the stark oppression of human slavery. One wing of the abolition movement, represented by Garrison, the artisan-editor of the *Liberator* (most of whose one or two thousand subscribers were uninfluential free Negroes in northeastern cities), saw so little hope of inducing the federal government to impose abolition on the slave states that they went to the opposite extreme of publicly burning copies of the Constitution, which by implication recognized the legality of slavery, as "a covenant with death and an agreement with Hell."[16]

But to renounce existing political institutions for falling short of the higher law of God, nature, or the Declaration of Independ-ence was to despair of the only practical means for the desired reform. And so the abolitionist campaign of moral imprecation accomplished little but confirmation of the general belief that they were the worst sort of radicals, bent only on destruction. In the end it was not the years of agitation but the agony of civil war that convinced most Northerners that slavery itself had been the great disrupter of the Constitution, the Union, and the fabric of American society. Only at the point of federal bayonets could the coercion that had been altogether beyond the command of the antislavery reformers be exerted to put an end to slavery.

The humanitarian amalgam of underlying conservative motives, foursquare libertarian rhetoric, and ambiguously compulsory methods emerged most clearly—almost in caricature—in the temperance movement. Once again the immediate evil to be exorcised was real enough. Americans had always been hearty drinkers, and since the eighteenth century, when they had turned from the beer of English tradition to distilled spirits—New England rum and Scotch-Irish rye or corn whisky—they had become heavy drinkers as well. "In my childhood," Horace Greeley recalled of the rural New Hampshire of the early nineteenth century,

there was no merry-making, there was no entertainment of relatives or friends, there was scarcely a casual gathering of two or three neighbors for an evening's social chat, without strong drink. Cider, always, while it remained drinkable without severe contortions of visage; rum at all seasons and on all occasions, were required and provided. No house or barn was raised without a bountiful supply of the latter, and generally of both. A wedding without "toddy," "flip," "sling," or "punch," with rum undisguised in abundance, would have been deemed a poor, mean affair, even among the penniless; while the more fortunate and thrifty of course dispensed wine, brandy, and gin in profusion. Dancing—almost the only pastime wherein the sexes jointly participated—was always enlivened and stimulated by liquor. Militia trainings—then rigidly enforced at least twice a year—usually wound up with a drinking frolic at the village tavern. Election days were drinking days, . . . and even funerals were regarded as inadequately celebrated without the dispensing of spirituous consolation.[17]

It was calculated in 1810 that there were some fourteen thousand distilleries in the country, annually producing the equivalent of more than three gallons for every man, woman, and child. Liquor was cheap, lightly taxed, and obtainable everywhere from inns, taverns, and grocery stores regulated only by the old licensing laws, applied now more for the sake of public revenue than of public order.

Drunkenness became apparent as a public problem in the crowded cities of the nineteenth century—explosively among the Irish laborers with their *shebeens* and street brawls, more decorously in the *Lager-Bier* gardens of the Germans. An English immigrant wrote home in 1830, accurately enough, "Give my very kind love to Father, and tell him if he was here he could soon kill himself by drinking if he thought proper."[18] Liquor seemed to be the cause of far worse evils than disorderly conduct in the streets. Humanitarians who investigated the inmates of prisons, asylums, and poorhouses deduced that alcohol accounted for most crime, insanity, and poverty. Of six hundred men in one New York prison in 1833, two hundred significantly were reported to be drunkards and only nine-teen total abstainers. At the very least, habitual intoxication seemed destructive of the habits of hard work and thrift in terms of which Americans defined character and which they expected would lead to economic independence for those who practiced them. That the same economic individualism was making a greater contribution than alcohol to the social disturbances of the time was of course less apparent. But if the temperance reformers attacked the alcoholic symptoms of public disorder instead of its basic cause, at least they were laying hold of one immediate problem that required regulation.

The problem was taken in hand by a typical complex of voluntary associations, and they quickly ran through the usual cycle from voluntarism to compulsion. The American Temperance Society (1826) pledged its members, of whom by 1831 there were 170,000 in twenty-two hundred local branches, mostly in New England and the Yankee parts of New York and Ohio, to forswear hard liquor. The society claimed to have prevailed on forty factory owners to forbid their workmen to drink spirits and on uncounted numbers of farmers to cease paying their farm hands in whisky. "Temperance hotels" attracted a good business, college boys took the pledge, New Year's toasts became unfashionable, and 130 distilleries were reported shut down in New York State alone. The distillers and liquor dealers remonstrated that, far from freeing anyone from bondage to alcohol, temperance fanatics were high-handedly infringing their property rights and, most inequitably, proscribing the common man's tot of rum or whisky but not the rich man's glass of wine.

Like true egalitarians the reformers responded by anathematizing wine and beer as well. A new society, the American Temperance Union (1836), exacted a million pledges of total abstinence from alcohol in any form. Children were enlisted to march and sing in a Cold Water Army, and the Washington Temperance Society (1840) of reformed drunkards evangelized the hard-core tipplers, through lectures in the "off-hand, direct, bang-up style," to swear off all "spirituous or malt liquors, wine, or cider."[19] Science and scholarship were invoked, from "well authenticated" accounts of drunkards who had died by spontaneous combustion to retranslation of biblical wine into grape juice. The heart of a sentimental age was melted by "the simple tale of the ruined inebriate," ballads like "Father, Dear Father, Come Home with Me Now," and the highly moral drama "Ten Nights in a Bar-Room."[20] The crusade had a certain effect. By the middle of the century it had implanted a general belief that abstinence from alcohol was a prime moral principle.

The campaign of moral suasion sadly failed, however, to keep most of the converts from backsliding. By the late 1830s the reformers began to call on the state governments for regulation, or rather, since carefully administered public regulation had gone out of fashion, for simple, outright prohibition. Between 1839 and 1847 nine northern states complied by giving their towns or counties the "local option" of forbidding the sale of liquor within their boundaries. Finally in the 1850s Maine and then a dozen other states, all but two of them in the North, prohibited the liquor trade entirely. Like the antislavery movement, the temperance men could hardly envision any more complicated system of regulating evil than simply forbidding it to exist.

Prohibition collided squarely with the liberal individualism of the age. In most of the "Maine law" states, as soon as the moral fervor of the temperance campaign subsided, statutory interference with the right of the individual to drink was either ruled unconstitutional by the courts or rescinded by the legislature. Some kinds of people, indeed, had always stubbornly denied that drinking was any sort of moral issue. Most immigrants, Englishmen as well as Irishmen and Germans, clung to their own drinking customs. Those of the foreigners who were Catholics could take a theologically as well as ethnically conservative line. The reformers' notion of Demon Rum—that is, that alcohol itself was the devil—was simply "the ancient manichaean heresy that evil is a positive principle and not merely the privation or abuse of power."[21] (Catholics likewise held that sin inhered not in slavery as such but only in certain masters' abuse of their authority—and, worse yet, in the abolitionists' conspiracy to upset the precarious stability of American society.) Against such a coalition of conservatives and liberals the odds for the prohibitionists' imposing their moral principle anywhere for long were exceedingly slim.

However ill-considered and inconsistent the humanitarian reformers' methods for bringing about moral regeneration, their melange of teetotalism, public schooling, and equitable treatment of prisoners, handicapped persons, and slaves—and also pacificism, woman's rights, "rational" reform of the starchy diet and cumbersome dress of the time, and a dozen lesser causes—amounted to an implicit modern equivalent for the rigorous ethical code of their ancestors. Although no doubt they believed, honestly enough, that they were marching in the vanguard of freedom, with no motive but zeal for the perfection of human liberty, like old-fashioned conservatives they were ready to resort to public compulsion whenever necessary to establish their moral standard. As professed libertarians, however, the reformers found it difficult to conceive of any continuing system of institutional restraints upon the evils of slavery or drink; even the idea of *compulsory* schooling they approached quite gingerly. To make schools available to all who wanted the opportunity was at least a useful first step in freeing future generations from ignorance. But when they proposed not to work toward gradual amelioration of social problems but rather to abolish slavery out of hand or simply prohibit the liquor trade, they stultified their own purpose. Well before the Civil War their humanitarian crusades were dead or dying, clearly not exhausted by the greater fervor of the war, as has sometimes been argued, but smothered by their own ineffectuality and by the moral indifference of a new generation. Americans, who after 1858 never again were swept by any one great evangelical revival, were growing too remote from the old Calvinism and from an organic social order to suspect that a society blessed with the material fruits of economic individualism might conceivably stand in need of fundamental reform.

Far more numerous than all the social reformers together, many quite obscure men whose ordinary occupations and condition left neither time nor inclination to concern themselves with the plight of slaves, drunkards, or the ignorant nevertheless reacted in their own way against social disorder and the cultural and spiritual emptiness of their own lives. Certainly there is a striking coincidence in the appearance, at the same time as the humanitarian reform movements, of another, even more elaborate set of voluntary associations, the secret fraternal orders and lodges. They continued to flourish, furthermore, long after most of the reformers had disbanded. Perhaps because fraternal lodges neither had nor claimed any substantial function outside the lives of their own members, they have usually been dismissed as the harmless addiction of a somewhat addled "nation of joiners"—altogether too trivial for serious explanation. Their arcane rituals, preposterous titles, and bizarre uniforms have seemed at best the froth on the liberal, pluralistic society of nineteenth-century America. But for every man or woman who joined a movement to improve or reform that broader society, there were scores or hundreds who withdrew into one of the secret societies.

During the first half century of the new republic, a secret society was apt to excite suspicion that an aristocratic cabal was afoot against the liberty of the common man. As long as American society still hung in the balance between the hierarchic, communal order of the eighteenth century and the egalitarian individualism of the nineteenth, the popular fear that self-constituted groups might seize and manipulate the established organs of economic, social, ecclesiastical, and political power was not wholly fanciful. Since an increasingly English sort of aristocracy seems to have been consolidating its position in late colonial government and society, the republican future was not ensured simply by winning independence from Great Britain. In the popular uproar over the Order of the Cincinnati in the 1790s and the Masons in the 1820s, the common man, who felt no need to organize voluntary associations of his own as long as the traditional family, community, and commonwealth seemed fairly stable, expressed his uneasiness over the pretensions of self-established and exclusive groups. The Cincinnati (1783) were regular officers of the Revolutionary army and were to be succeeded by their eldest male heirs. However patriotic their credentials, they appeared to be establishing a kind of hereditary nobility based on primogeniture and arrogating to it a privileged position in the state; the prominence of members of the order in the new federal government of the 1790s gave a certain substance to the notion. Like the Federalist party, however, the Cincinnati withered before the egalitarian winds of the early nineteenth century, not to be revived until another change in the social climate.

Although there had been American lodges of the Free and Accepted Masons since about 1730, when the order was introduced from England, by 1800 they had only about three thousand members. The Masons were a truly voluntary association with no taint of hereditary exclusion—indeed, their liberal, bourgeois principles, which made them suspect to reactionary European governments in the age of the French Revolution, were quite unexceptional in the United States. In many places, however, the lodges appeared to consist preponderantly of merchants, lawyers, and other eminent gentlemen, just the sort who, in the hierarchic society of colonial days, might well have constituted a local oligarchy. Rumors that they swore sacrilegious oaths and performed mock religious rituals offended the evangelical churches to which the common man was becoming attached, and the members' fondness for hinting broadly at their influence upon government—especially the courts—seemed to fit the "monarchical" titles borne by their officers. When in 1826 one William Morgan, a poor artisan of Batavia in western New York and the author of a pamphlet exposing Masonic secrets, suddenly disappeared and his abductors escaped due punishment for kidnaping and murder, popular indignation set the Yankee burned-over district aflame once again.

The agitation coincided with the coalescing of new political parties around certain factional leaders, each of which was casting about for an attractive set of principles. The common man's alarm over the Masonic order—"an institution which has so long intruded upon the equal rights of the people," in a Vermont editor's words—furnished a plausibly egalitarian cause around which the Anti-Masonic party soon organized against the no less egalitarian coalition forming around Andrew Jackson (a Mason as well as a military hero).[22] For a few years after 1826 the anti-Masonic campaign caused a sharp decline in membership in the order. Even the original college fraternity, Phi Beta Kappa (1776), made haste to mollify the common man by dropping its veil of secrecy.

But by the 1830s, when the new Whig party, which absorbed most of the Anti-Masons, was vying with the Jacksonian Democrats for the vote of the common man, secret societies likewise took care to proclaim their devotion to democracy and, to the general satisfaction of Protestant clerics, the conventionality of their religious opinions. Like the granting of corporation charters to bankers and businessmen, admission to a fraternal order now was ostensibly open to every man who met a few minimal qualifications. Although in fact the Masons continued to attract men from a somewhat higher social class than the other orders which sprang up on all sides, the specters of aristocracy and monopoly had been sufficiently exorcised from the public mind for the fact to cause no further alarm. The common man no longer feared that private groups of ordinary democratic Americans like himself could seize the centers of power when, he was confident, power had been safely returned to "the people."

Fraternal lodges proliferated most exuberantly in the towns and cities of the industrial age. Not only was lodge-going much easier for urban people than for farmers, but the novel anonymity of city life seems to have pressed them harder—not least the former country folk among them—than the physical isolation that American farmers were used to. Although both city and country people professed to see exactly the same virtues in individual freedom, the city dwellers now swarmed into the refuge which the secret society offered from its uncertainties.

Many of the new orders, like the Masons before them, were introduced by immigrant members of the English "friendly societies." The Odd Fellows, thus planted at Baltimore in 1819, were too plainly plebeian to excite suspicion of the anti-Masonic sort. By 1843, when the American branches seceded from the parent order in England, the Independent Order of Odd Fellows had some 30,000 members, most of them in the eastern cities; twenty years later there were 135,000. By 1875 a large part of the urban male population belonged to a labyrinthine prolixity of competing orders: Foresters (1832) and Druids (1834), both originally English; Red Men (1834), Heptasophs (1852), Knights of Friendship (1859), Knights of Pythias (1864), Elks (1866), Mechanics (1868) and United Workmen (1868), Knights of the Mystic Chain (1871), Knights of the Golden Eagle (1873), Knights of Malta (1874). Protestant immigrants might be admitted to some of these orders, perhaps with their own lodges of *Freimaurer, Rothmänner,* or *"der deutschen Odd Fellows."*

The immigrants, who had been accustomed to a more tightly knit communal life than almost any American could now recall, were quick to adopt the fraternal form of the American voluntary association in order to bind together their local ethnic communities against the unpredictable looseness of life in America. Besides the usual congeries of independent groups—Caledonian Society or *Männerchor,* Yeagers or Napper Tandy Rifles—each immigrant people founded its own national fraternal order: among Irish Catholics, the Ancient Order of Hibernians (1836); Jews, the Independent Order of B'nai Brith (1843) and the Free Sons of Israel (1849); Germans, the Sons of Hermann (1840) and the Order of the Harugari (1847); Welsh, the True Ivorites (which they brought from the old country in 1863); Protestant Irish, the Loyal Orange Institution (also a branch of the parent order, 1867); Englishmen, the Sons of Saint George (1870); and the Order of Scottish Clans (1878).

A voluntary association of this sort had almost no discernibly practical functions. At most the lodge provided its members with rudimentary mutual benefit schemes of burial insurance, soliciting contributions or levying a small assessment to pay for a brother's funeral. But insurance against the cost of dying was perhaps the least of the human needs that economic individualism left unfulfilled. Like the religious and humanitarian movements of the time, the fraternal orders defined their main purpose as moral or spiritual. The ethical values expressed in their mottoes and precepts were conventionally vague: honesty, unselfishness, loyalty, friendship, brotherhood. Some orders—the Rechabites (1842),

Good Templars (1847), Sons of Temperance (1851), and, among the Irish, the Catholic Total Abstinence Union (1872)—put absolute sobriety at the head of the list. But most of the fraternal principles were broadly social values of the sort that the larger society, obsessed with the narrowly economic virtues of production and accumulation, had practically abandoned. The members of a lodge were sworn, for that matter, to nothing more public-spirited than practicing the ethical code of their order among themselves, leaving outsiders to their own voluntary devices.

But in their narrowness lay a larger significance. The brotherhood of the fraternal lodge harked back almost atavistically—certainly not consciously—to communities of roughly the size and character which men until recently had always known, from the prehistoric hunting band to the medieval farming village or artisans' guild. The grand exalted titles of the lodge hierarchy, even though their holders might be elected annually, supplied not simply honorific status but a sense of precisely the kind of established order that modern society had repudiated. The dramatic ritual and flamboyant costumes with which each order expressed its corporate sense, although incongruously embroidered on some theme from the Old Testament, the legends of King Arthur or Robin Hood, notions of Indian tribal lore, or, among the immigrants' orders, a more or less adulterated version of their national folklore, also had an esthetic appeal to men who disregarded art and literature as too impractical for everyday life. The straight-faced claim to a prescriptive antiquity for the "ancient" order of this or that—that the Masons dated from the building of Solomon's temple or that the Knights of Pythias had been organized by Pythagoras—would be senseless except in the conditions of instability and impermanence which were cutting the individual off from whatever line of tradition, European or American, his own past might in other circumstances have handed down to him.

In any of its myriad forms the voluntary association was more than a novelty suited to the new age of economic individualism and social pluralism. For all their liberal rhetoric, each of these self-constituted groups of moralizers, particularly the reform societies and the fraternal orders, stood in reaction against the social, cultural, and spiritual inadequacies of the nineteenth century. Ineffectual or insubstantial though they might be, they had at least begun the evolution of new institutions and a new community capable of satisfying eternal human needs in forms suited to modern society.

18. LIBERTY AND UNION

To the generation that lived through the Civil War only an unshakable faith in the providential destiny of the country made it credible that the embattled sections, parties, economic classes, ethnic groups, and other fragments of American society shared an essential unity. They were all too painfully aware of the conflicts that filled the newspapers, the political forums, and eventually the military cemeteries. In particular, the major geographical sections of the country were ineluctably turning into hostile nations. During the forty years between the Missouri Compromise of 1820, which barred slavery from the farther northwestern territories, and the final debacle of southern secession and civil war in 1860–1861—both episodes involving much the same issues—men had come to believe that an economic and social conflict of the most fundamental sort dissevered the "slave" South from the "free" North and a still somewhat amorphous West.

The continual political battles and campaigns were impossible to ignore. Since the inception of the Federal Union in 1789 it had provided an arena in which hostile partisans, based on the states, could coalesce, contest elections, and work up the sectional and class feelings of the day into urgent public issues. No doubt such staple matters as tariff protection for industry, federal subsidies to "internal improvements," and currency and banking arrangements were genuinely important to the material welfare of each section or class. But the struggles over them were too inflated for the narrow frame within which they took place. Whether government actively assisted the merchant, farmer, and entrepreneur, as Whigs proposed, or simply set their enterprise free from old constraints, as Democrats insisted, the first order of business was the rapid development of the economy. To the equally rapid unsettling of the institutional structure of society that accompanied the economic revolution, politics and government paid less and less attention. Worse yet, even though political debate ranged no farther than certain narrow economic bounds, in so volatile a society conflict of any sort was likely to prove explosive.

There were certain social and cultural controversies of the time which intruded into politics but which, since they had little economic importance, have until recently been dismissed by historians as of no practical substance whatever. In particular the nativism or anti-Catholicism of 1829–1856 used to seem like nothing more than malevolent bigotry. But the "Protestant crusade" against popery, like the revivals, the new sects, the moral reform movements, and voluntary associations in general, embodied far more than an irrational animus. Even when it took the form of a native-American political movement, it was no mere eruption of xenophobia. The most fundamental problems of the time were involved. Although the economic, social, and cultural gulf between native American Protestants and Catholic immigrants was only one manifestation, it cried out for a heroic remedy. Like the poisonous dispute that was estranging the South from the rest of the Union, its practical consequences were all too real, at the same time that it pointed to some still more basic derangement of American life. As symptoms of a common disorder, the ethnic and sectional controversies were connected at a number of practical points, so that it was not wholly unreasonable for nativists to suppose that a cure for one might also relieve the other.

Of nativism pure and simple, that is, hostility to foreigners as such, there was remarkably little until long after the Civil War. The fusion of colonial ethnic stocks had produced a recognizably American national character which, though not uniform everywhere, was clearly different from that of the contemporary Englishman, Scotch-Irishman, or German. But Americans continued to welcome immigrants both as a necessary element in the country's material growth and as prime witnesses to the beneficent liberality of the republic. The empty West and the new factories and mines needed labor, and every foreign laborer who came soon learned that Americans liked to hear that their free institutions were indeed the hope of the downtrodden common people of the corrupt Old World.

Even when immigrants organized themselves for essentially foreign purposes—to raise money for the relief of famine victims in the homeland or of destitute fellow countrymen stranded in American ports, to support the European liberal revolutions of 1848, or simply to celebrate one of their innumerable national holidays— Americans could easily identify such causes with their own, contribute cash or encouragement, and even join in toasting Daniel O'Connell or Queen Victoria, as the case might be. Although the immigrants' churches, *Turnvereine* and Highland-games societies, ethnic fraternal orders, and militia companies of Yeagers or Hibernia Greens all made their foreignness conspicuous, the sight of their parades and picnics was not much odder than some of the native American's own voluntary associations whose basic forms most of the immigrant organizations were copying. Suspicion arose only if the exotic trappings were such as to call to mind the monarchical and popish Old World which immigrants ought, presumably like the ancestors of the native Americans, to have left thankfully behind them. But usually the ethnic differences in the population, like those between classes, regions, sects, or individuals, although they were adding to the aimless heterogeneity of American society, did not provoke open conflict. The continual murmur of social dissonance seldom rose to a deafening pitch.

In an age of spiritual uncertainty when frantic revivals of religion and the inspired founders of new sects were further splitting the churches and denaturing old Protestant creeds, the sudden enormous growth of the indivisible Catholic church summoned up fears that were as old as the Reformation. Perhaps because there never had been more than a few Catholics in the country—some seventy thousand, less than 1 percent of the population at the end of the eighteenth century, with only seventy priests and a single bishop—Protestants had had little occasion to update the legendary picture of indulgence sellers, corrupt priests and nuns, and the burning of heretics and Bibles by the Inquisition. Self-doubt over materialism and sectarian divisions among the heirs of Luther and Calvin could be swallowed up in the greater terror of popery, and preachers of every sect joined in denouncing the Scarlet Woman, the Man of Sin, the Whore of Babylon.

Even before the massive immigration of Irish and German Catholics, the ancient Romish phantom was given flesh. In 1829, when the American bishops, already grown in number to ten, met at Baltimore in the first provincial council ever held in the country, the splendid spectacle of prelates who were also good Americans, which Catholics had expected to allay Protestant prejudice, instead suddenly revived it. Here was a truly monolithic, impenetrably secret, and flagrantly hierarchical institution, far better organized to seize power than Masons or anti-Masons, abolitionists or slave-owners, Whigs or Democrats.

Unfortunately the bishops in their conciliar decrees chose to denounce "unauthorized" translations of the Bible, Protestant "perversion" of the public schools, and the ordinary American practice, into which some Catholic congregations had been falling, of placing

the parish property in the hands of lay trustees. The suppression of "trusteeism" by the church in the course of the next twenty years was condemned by Protestants as a chain of "tyrannical and unchristian acts, so repugnant to our republican institutions"— altogether "a singular specimen of papal authority exercised over the people of a free country."[1] Perhaps it was none of the Protestants' business whether laymen or bishops held title to Catholic church buildings. But when poor Catholics spurned the King James Bibles which the interdenominational Bible societies offered them, when candidates for local office promised Catholic voters that Bible-reading in the public schools would be discontinued, or when European Catholic missionaries arrived to undermine Protestant America (or was it that the Christianity of the new West and the new cities, the special targets of Protestant and Catholic missionaries alike, was already highly uncertain?), the Roman Antichrist seemed poised to subdue the republic with "ignorance, priestcraft, and superstition."[2] Violent reaction was certain whenever the traditional fears happened to be crossed with practical economic and social grievances for which Catholic immigrants could be blamed.

The tide of antipopery sermons, tracts, pamphlets, books, and newspapers that began to rise in 1829 soon overflowed from print into action. The first and perhaps the worst single eruption occurred in 1834 among Protestant laborers in Boston who believed that Irish immigrants were taking their work and depressing their wages. The mob attacked not the Irishmen themselves but a convent school conducted by the Ursuline Sisters. The fact that some upper-class Protestant families sent their daughters to be educated by the nuns proved less than no deterrent to the rioters. The convent had become the local symbol of Romish corruption and power because of certain alleged revelations of inhuman discipline and priestly indecencies there and finally the escape of two inmates, one a servant girl and the other a teaching nun. Although the latter soon returned to her duties, rumor had it that she was now a prisoner in the dungeon which was popularly understood to be a regular appurtenance of convents. Without waiting for a state commission of investigation to issue its refutation of the whole story, the mob marched on the buildings and burned them to the ground. The few rioters who were tried were promptly acquitted, and the "escaped" servant girl's rather dull account of various past penances, published under the adequately suggestive title *Six Months in a Convent,* enjoyed a brisk sale.

Others soon improved on her model. In 1836 a certain Maria

Monk, claiming to be another runaway nun but actually a former inmate of a Catholic asylum for "fallen women," published her *Awful Disclosures of the Hôtel Dieu Nunnery of Montreal.* Her tale of priestly lechery, threats of execution, and infanticide was flatly disproved by a committee of Protestant clergymen, and Maria herself continued on her career of bastardy and pocketpicking until her death in prison. During the next twenty-five years, however, some three hundred thousand copies of the *Awful Disclosures* were sold. A flood of imitators further embellished the ancient tradition with such titles as *Priest's Prisons for Women, The Escaped Nun,* and *Open Convents, or, Nunneries and Popish Seminaries Dangerous to the Morals and Degrading to the Character of a Republican Community,* all purporting to reveal how "unmarried foreign priests" methodically debauched respectable young women and appropriated their property.[3]

The public, anxious not only for the virtue of its daughters but also, we may surmise, for the stability of the republican community in an age of economic individualism and unregulated immigration, began to find more tangible signs of subversion and sedition. The liberality with which municipal or county judges turned fresh immigrants into voters raised the specter of Catholic domination of local governments and school boards. Foreign laborers, particularly the Irish canal and railroad gangs, some of them Catholic and others Protestant, were already notorious for their brawling, outlandish factions of Corkonians, Far Downs, and the like. The same sort of loyalties, baffling to respectable Americans, drew together groups of casual laborers, native or immigrant, in the poorer parts of the cities. The turbulence of their raffish versions of the voluntary association, each tied to some political faction, is suggested by the names of thirty gangs which flourished in Baltimore in the 1850s: the Rip Raps, Plug Uglies, Black Snakes, Tigers, Rough Skins, Red Necks, Thunderbolts, Gladiators, Ranters, Eubolts, Little Fellows, Ashlanders, Screw Bolts, Junior Mount Clares, Stay Lates, Hard Times, Dips, Wampanoags, Blood Tubs, Bloody Eights, Double Pumps, Calithumpians, Ferry Road Hunters, Gumballs, Peelers, Pluckers, Shad Roes, Bloats, Eighth Ward Black Guards, and the Butt Enders.[4]

Like some of the only slightly more respectable militia and fire companies in the cities, such spontaneous groups were ready to hand for the purposes of the rising political bosses of the working-class wards. Although most of these organizers were native Americans, they seemed to respectable citizens, as to the liberal *Nation* in 1866, to be "keen, shrewd, cunning, unscrupulous" manipulators, "who have thoroughly trained themselves to the art of cajoling the Irish" and "who use their ignorance as a stepping-stone to power and plunder."[5] The great public issues of tariffs, banks, and the like which honest citizens debated meant little to immigrant workingmen. Irish Catholics and Germans, who generally adhered to the Democratic party in the 1830s and 1840s, did so less for its lofty principles than for such fortuitous reasons as the fact that British and Irish Protestants usually were Whigs.

Few immigrants of any nationality came from the classes that had a voice in the politics of their homelands. Conceivably some of the Irishmen had been in the habit of being "voted" by their landlords in Ireland and came to America with a certain aptitude for machine politics; their first experience in ward politics was as "voting cattle" and strong-armed "shoulder hitters." Elections in the Bloody Ould Sixth Ward on the lower East Side of New York in the 1840s frequently broke up into riots between the (Irish Catholic) Spartan Band and the (Irish Protestant) Faugh-a-Ballaghs. Although the immigrants had not yet learned to use the leverage of their numbers to secure office or other advantages for themselves, it was easy for respectable people to blame election frauds, intimidation at the polls, and the growing venality of politics on the presence of ignorant foreigners rather than on the Americans who took advantage of it. "How is it possible," Samuel F. B. Morse asked in 1835,

that foreign turbulence imported by ship loads, that riot and ignorance in hundreds of thousands of human priest-controlled machines, should suddenly be thrown into our society and not produce here turbulence and excess? Can one throw mud into pure water and not disturb its clearness?[6]

To combat such highly organized antirepublicanism called for counterorganization. The first nativist political parties appeared in New York, Philadelphia, and other cities about 1835, but none of their candidates for local office were elected. In 1841 Catholics in New York made a political issue of the practice of reading the Protestant Bible in the public schools and, when the Democrats hedged in fear of losing the Protestant vote altogether, the Catholics organized a separate party which gave the election to the Whigs. Such demonstrations of Catholic influence rekindled the old "No Popery" excitement. In 1844 an American Republican party won elections in New York and Philadelphia, and in the latter place riots between Protestant and Catholic mobs led to several church-burnings. For the next few years, however, the anticonspiratorial crusade was taken over, fittingly enough, by a set of secret fraternal societies: Native Sons of America, Order of United American Mechanics, Guards of Liberty, and the like. Sworn to an even more impenetrable secrecy than the Masons or Odd Fellows, whose quasi-religious forms they imitated, they exalted patriotism as the highest morality. Less nativistic than anti-Catholic, most of them welcomed foreign-born Protestants into their ranks. The so-called American Protestant Association, indeed, consisted mainly of Irish Protestants or Orangemen.

The popular sense of imminent peril reached a crisis in 1853, when a papal nuncio, Cardinal Gaetano Bedini, arrived to extinguish the last sparks of parochial trusteeism and to convey the Holy Father's blessing to the faithful. But might not his real mission be to destroy republican liberty, just as the church, and Bedini in particular, so it was said, had helped suppress the Italian liberals of 1848? Various renegade priests and Protestant agitators like John Orr, known as the Angel Gabriel for his white robe and brass horn, followed Bedini's progress from city to city. Riots broke out afresh, priests were tarred and feathered, a dozen churches were burned, mobs once again stormed convents to liberate "captive" girls, and a few legalistically minded persons brought suit to emancipate nuns from their bondage. The height of patriotic fervor was reached by the mob that seized a block of marble which the pope, like other diplomatic well-wishers, had contributed to the building of the Washington Monument, and pitched it into the Potomac River.

By that time anti-Catholicism was part and parcel of the deadlock between North and South that had developed since 1846. The immediate sectional issue was whether the federal territory in the West would be opened or closed to slavery. By the compromise of 1820 the larger part of the old Louisana Territory, to the north and west of Missouri, was closed; only the limited area south and west of Arkansas was open. In 1848, just when the frontier settlement was about to move beyond the first tier of new states west of the Mississippi River, the spoils of the Mexican War were added, an enormous territory stretching from the Rio Grande and the Rocky Mountains to the coast of California, most of it open to slavery if the line of 1820 were extended through it. But was that simple arrangement any longer acceptable? Since 1820 Americans had grown restive toward all kinds of restrictions on economic progress. Whatever had been intended in 1820, the absolute ban that the Missouri Compromise had set against extension of the slave-labor system north of 36° 30′ was now an anachronism.

Three new political doctrines on the territorial question, all of which, in the mid-nineteenth century manner, were equally promotional or permissive from the point of view of one economic interest or another, were advanced by representatives of North and South and also the Border region. Southerners, following the constitutional logic elaborated by John C. Calhoun in the 1840s, argued for free extension of their peculiar institution wherever a master took his slaves; the federal government, as territorial "trustee" for the states, had no right to restrict, indeed had the duty to protect, the property rights of citizens from the slave states no less than those of others. If, as some Southerners hoped, the United States were to annex still more of Mexico and also Central America and Cuba—all likely places for plantations—the trusteeship rule would presumably apply there too. To Northerners, however, the proposal to admit slavery into territories from which it had long since been barred, or even to extend the 36° 30′ line to the Pacific, would effectively delimit their own opportunities for farming and commerce. To take the other tack and exclude slavery from all the newly acquired territories, as David Wilmot's unsuccessful "proviso" of 1846 proposed, would considerably enlarge the Northerners' economic options. A third and still more timely, because entirely permissive, basis for sectional compromise was advanced by politicians like Lewis Cass and Stephen A. Douglas under the democratic name of "popular sovereignty": let the actual settlers of a territory choose between opening the way for those who wished to use slave labor or keeping the ground clear for "free" farmers, tenants, and wage laborers. What could be more liberal?

The drift of legislation during the early 1850s was along the presumably permissive line of popular sovereignty. The Compromise of 1850, after balancing admission of the new "free" state of California and the removal of slavetrading from the federal capital against a new, more stringent law for federal recapture of fugitive slaves, went on to organize the new territories of New Mexico and Utah without specifically either admitting or excluding slavery. That was sufficiently like Douglas's doctrine to allow him to claim it as a precedent for his bill of 1854 to organize territorial governments for Kansas and Nebraska. Since those areas had been part of the old Louisiana Territory, the popular sovereignty prescribed by the Kansas-Nebraska Act wiped out the line which the Missouri Compromise had drawn between free and slave territory.

For more than a generation almost the entire expanse now at issue had been reserved for free white farmers, and they were ready to claim it. But the tacit understanding in Congress in 1854 was that Kansas, the area directly west of the border slave state of Missouri, could be claimed instead by slaveholders moving up from the lower Missouri Valley and elsewhere in the South.

The surge of northern indignation, already set in motion by the Fugitive Slave Act of 1850 with its distasteful apparatus of federal marshals, mandatory service in slave-catching posses, special commissioners, and summary trials for suspected runaways, now swept up thousands of men who had neither moral compunction about slavery nor compassion for Negroes but who saw their own freedom being reduced by government rather than enlarged. To be sure, the new act gave both free-soil and proslavery farmers alike the legal right to try to capture Kansas for themselves. But popular sovereignty, although in accord with the economic policy of the time, had the peculiar inadequacy of a merely permissive policy. What it permitted to the majority it denied to the minority. At what point in the settlement of the territory should it be determined which faction of the people should exercise sovereignty, in the name of the whole, over the question of slavery? Who, indeed, among so many newcomers, should be counted as "the people"? In spite of the clumsy maneuvers of President James Buchanan, that "northern Democrat with southern principles," nothing was clear, after three confused years of rival constitution-making, referendum and counterreferendum, and savage guerrilla warfare, except that Kansas could not, after all, either be voted or dragooned into the ranks of slave territories and future states. Ironically, the particular economic venture that Douglas's territorial bill had been designed to bring about, construction of a transcontinental railroad through Kansas, instead was delayed for another decade.

In 1857, when Kansas was still hanging in the balance, the Supreme Court in the case of the Missouri slave Dred Scott, whose master had once taken him north into Minnesota Territory and back, adopted Calhoun's doctrine that Congress could not exclude but must instead guarantee the security of private property in slaves throughout the federal territories. Logically enough the Missouri Compromise, repealed three years before, must have been unconstitutional from the start, and neither the slavery-exclusion clause of the Wilmot Proviso nor the popular sovereignty principle of the Kansas-Nebraska Act was any better. To Northerners the Dred Scott decision seemed to prove once and for all that an insidious "slave power" conspiracy against the legitimate ambitions of free farmers had captured all three branches of the federal government. Indeed, since Dred Scott had been taken not only to a federal territory but also to the free state of Illinois and yet was still a slave, might not the Court's logic soon lead it to deny the northern *states* the right to interfere with slave property brought in from states where it was legally established? It even began to seem possible that the argument of certain Southerners that slavery was the best conceivable arrangement for any and all laborers might shortly be put into practice throughout the country. Wherever slavery might be established, the system that was thoroughly permissive toward slaveowners would be thoroughly restrictive toward ordinary men, whether they hoped for farms or shops of their own or simply for freedom from the competition of slave labor. In the cities in the late 1850s there was as much talk of the principle of Free Labor as of Free Soil.

The Supreme Court was no more able than Congress or the president to dispose of the issue of slavery—or, rather, to enlarge the economic options of slaveowners and would-be slaveowners without constricting those of free farmers and workingmen. In the end a government which had abandoned most of its regulatory functions for the sake of encouraging and promoting economic development managed only to exacerbate other fundamental problems. Politicians whose main function was to win elections preferred to ignore such problems, and when pressed to act could only blunder between the irrelevant and the impractical, however ironbound their constitutional logic. To reduce public policy to a choice between permissive and promotional economic measures was ultimately to fail to mediate between the genuine economic interests of different sections. Far worse, it blew up their differences into an insoluble confrontation between what each side believed to be the most sacred moral principles.

As the political dispute over extension of slavery into the West drifted toward catastrophe between 1846 and 1860, it seemed ever more clear that profound differences between the structure of society in the North and the South must lie at the root of the trouble. "A separate people," the English novelist Anthony Trollope called the Southerners in 1861, "dissevered from the North by habits, morals, institutions, pursuits, and every conceivable difference in their modes of thought and action."[7] The nation, as both Abraham Lincoln and the southern polemicist George Fitzhugh essentially agreed, had become "a house divided against itself."[8]

Northerners and Southerners agreed that they differed; they disagreed only in their valuation of the peculiar character of either section. Most Northerners were confident that they exemplified the good old Yankee virtues of political liberty, economic opportunity, and social equality for the common man, native or foreign-born, who enjoyed free scope for his enterprise, initiative, and hard work, whether in old-fashioned farming or commerce or the new fields of industrial manufacturing, mining, and railroads. The Yankee half of the nation, in short, was a liberal society. Southerners saw only the dark side of those same northern traits. The enterprise of the northern farmer, merchant, or manufacturer was inspired by mere greed; his vaunted individualism was a shabby excuse for selfish irresponsibility toward his dependents; his high-sounding principle of equality concealed the most heartless exploitation of undeniably inferior classes; diligent only at moneygrubbing, he neglected the nobler values of art and literature and even gracious manners. If, as it was supposed, the Yankees had inherited these unlovely traits from boorish "Roundhead" or "Saxon" ancestors, even that poor heritage was being debased by promiscuous immigration. The liberal society was spawning, furthermore, a swarm of fanatical reformers bent on multiplying its defects. "Free Society! We sicken of the name," an Alabama editor expostulated in 1856. "What is it but a conglomeration of greasy mechanics, filthy operatives, small-fisted farmers, and moon-struck theorists? . . . That is your free society!"[9]

Although few Northerners were ready to accept this southern caricature of themselves, many felt a certain fascination for the contrastingly conservative character of southern society as Southerners envisioned it. The key figure in this well-composed picture was the slaveowning planter. A worthy heir of "Cavalier" and perhaps Norman ancestors, the planter was frankly an aristocrat, true to the code of his class in selflessly accepting the burden of responsibility both toward his slaves, as his immediate dependents, and toward the whole community of his neighborhood, county, and state. His well-chosen library, the classical education which he considered appropriate for his sons, his elevated yet nobly condescending manner, all evinced his inbred superiority to considerations of mere material gain. At the same time, since the ordinary slaveless farmer—even the poorest of the propertyless poor white trash—was neither a Negro slave nor usually in any other sort of economic dependence on the planter, he too could be accorded a place in the broader aristocracy of all white men. Jacksonian egalitarianism in its southern form stressed the equal superiority of all white men, with the planter *primus inter pares*. So ingeniously contrived a social hierarchy, in which any white man could rank himself as high as he liked, obviously had no need for the crank reformers who infested the North.

Northerners were repelled as well as attracted by this Cavalier ideal. On one hand it obviously contravened all the liberal virtues: for all his whiteness the southern poor white was nonetheless hopelessly sunk in his poverty; the Negro slave was the helpless prey of the economic necessities if not the vices of his master; and slave and poor white alike were practically denied an opportunity to improve their material and social condition. Such a caste-ridden society could only vitiate its own hope of progress. Even the planter, though no doubt superior in his "feudal" way, suffered from the vices of aristocracy. Habitually tempted to self-indulgence, he seemed to lack the steadfastness of purpose that carried the Yankee forward; vacillating and irresolute in practical matters, he could be wild, vindictive, and self-destructive, especially when his code of honor impelled him to resort to the duelling ground. His leisured patronage of polite literature and his other affectations of culture, like his mercurial temperament, appeared somewhat effeminate to the hardheaded Yankee who admired genteel culture as an ornament in his wife and daughters but felt it hardly a proper business for men.

Repelled or attracted by the conservative southern Cavalier, virtually everyone believed in his existence. The novelists and publicists who built up the image, between 1820 and 1860, included Northerners like James Kirke Paulding and Harriet Beecher Stowe as well as Southerners like John Pendleton Kennedy and William Gilmore Simms. The evidence is highly inferential, but the alacrity with which the reading public of all sections accepted the fictional planter-aristocrat as veritable fact, a figure as credible as Scott's Highland clansmen or Dickens's cockneys, suggests that it answered a general if unspoken need of the time. Even while enjoying the great desideratum of economic progress, all parts of the country sensed the obscure and undefinable uncertainties and anxieties of a disordered society. At many points they can be seen to have been casting about for some principle or institution which might restore a tolerable balance between progress and order. The Arcadian ideal of a pastoral republican community which the 1820s and 1830s thought somehow to perpetuate in the new age of westward expansion and industrial revolution was proving less and less credible in any section. No figure or institution in the North, where farmers, merchants, manufacturers, social reformers, and even clergymen saw themselves as champions of individual freedom, appeared stable enough for the purpose. But it was easier to distill another agrarian ideal out of the memory of the eighteenth-century gentry of the Chesapeake and lowland Carolina and identify it with the existing cotton planters of the new Sou⁺hwest.

The Cavalier ideal was highly acceptable to the planters themselves, just as the model of the English squirearchy had been to their colonial predecessors, precisely because it justified and somewhat moderated the actual rawness, crudity, and ruthlessness of the plantation as an exploitative enterprise. The only essential way in which cotton planting differed as a business from cotton shipping or cotton manufacturing—or even from wheat growing, sheep grazing, and land speculation—was its anachronistic link with romanticized tradition. It was the planter as landed gentleman rather than as exploiter of soil and labor who captured the popular imagination. Unsympathetic travelers' accounts and troublesome statistics were not lacking to cast doubt on the notion. Sometimes even the most perfervid champions of the South lamented, with a South Carolina editor in 1851, that they were surrounded by a society "of speculators, of calculating traders and narrow reasoners, who would never venture one blow for honor or independence, if that effort brought hazard or danger."[10] But Northerners and Southerners alike evidently needed to believe in the existence of *some* conservative, steadying element in American society. The circumstance that the only figure who seemed convincing, the gentleman-planter, was specifically southern, just as his Negro slave was the only plausible American counterpart to a feudal serf, was fatefully significant. Because of it the societies of North and South came to seem fundamentally different—one egalitarian and liberal, the other feudal and conservative—even though it was their actual common preoccupation with material progress and their common social anxiety that impelled them to imagine that they had nothing at all in common.

To find the reassuring stability of a traditional institution in the striving slaveowner of 1820–1860 was perhaps conservative in impulse. But like most of the other conservative impulses of the time it succeeded only in magnifying superficial differences and making existing conflicts worse. If southern society was inherently as peculiar as it was believed to be, if it exemplified principles diametrically opposed to those of the North—benevolent feudalism against liberal individualism, responsible aristocracy against leveling equality—the national house must verily be divided against itself.

There was a good deal more to the issue between the sections, accordingly, than the debate of the 1850s over the abstract morality of slavery and the practical treatment or mistreatment of slaves. When men spoke of the "free" society of the northern states, they meant something much broader than the mere absence of slavery: not only the whole liberal complex of economic individualism and social egalitarianism but even the welter of religious, social, and political movements that were confusedly reacting against it. In the same way "slave" society signified not simply legal establishment of a peculiar labor system in certain states but an orderly social system which safeguarded the interests of all classes, the slaves in particular, since they were cared for, according to Fitzhugh, under what amounted to the highest form of socialism. As an ethical system neither section's abstract and somewhat fanciful notion of the absolute worth of its own economic and social arrangements ranked with the loftiest concepts of moral philosophers. But once the existing society of North and South took on the aura of uncompromising moral rectitude, even though its members were driven to it by gnawing moral self-doubt, the lesser economic and political controversies of the time were exalted into the irrepressible conflict about which men were beginning to speak.

By the 1850s Americans were used to the idea that the country staggered on the brink of disintegration. Revivalists and reformers all along had been darkly hinting at moral declension and social decay, but now the political fabric itself was starting to rend. The old Whig and Democratic parties, splintering on sectional lines into proslavery and free-soil factions, lost what little capacity they had for mediating public controversy. Some new unifying principle was desperately needed, one that could at least divert attention from the otherwise irreconcilable differences between North and South.

One patriotic issue came ready to hand. Immigration, like slavery, was intimately involved in the social disorder of the time. A foreign quarrel might well busy giddy minds, especially one that entailed no diplomatic or military danger. Foreigners were undeniably at the gates and some already within the walls of the national citadel. They were only poor Catholic immigrants, but a crusade against them, such as the "patriotic" societies had been waging for several years, might reunite Americans of all sections. Who would not enlist to repulse the priest-led battalions in their

campaign to capture the eastern cities, preempt the western terri-
ories, undo the Reformation, and subvert republican institutions
generally?

One of the anti-Catholic secret societies, the Order of the Star-
Spangled Banner, founded in New York in 1849, revived the political phase of the nativist movement in 1853 under the form of a new
American party. The feigned inscrutability of the members won
them the name of "Know-Nothings." Their platform was plain
enough: "The grand work of the American Party is the principle of
nationality. . . . We must do something to protect and vindicate it.
If we do not, it will be destroyed."[11] That something had to be done
was only too true. All that the Know-Nothings could propose, however, was to withhold naturalization and the ballot from immigrants
until—like everyone born an American citizen, equitably enough—
they had been in the country for twenty-one years, to exclude
foreign paupers altogether, and forbid landownership by aliens
(thereby denying control of the West to the Catholic church). Nothing so illiberal or impractical as excluding the masses of ordinary
immigrant laborers was suggested. Scotching the foreigners' political
power would suffice to dispel the menace of popery without retarding the economic progress of the country, and at the same time the
patriotic endeavor would renew the common dedication of all sections to the Union.

The elections of 1854 in the North and the Border states showed
the promise of the nativist party in local coalition with one or another faction of Whigs, Democrats, or Free-Soilers: they actually
carried Massachusetts, Pennsylvania, and Delaware. The next year
they also captured New York, three more New England states, and
Maryland and Kentucky on the Border, made a strong showing
across the South from Virginia to Texas, and gained a balance of
power in the Northwest between the Democrats and the new Republican party. The presidential election of 1856 could be expected
to save the virtue and integrity of the republic everywhere.

In the event, 1856 demonstrated what a disorganized society had
so often demonstrated before: that even the most deeply conservative and widely shared motives, when expressed by a haphazard
plurality of groups in terms of their conflicting traditions, beliefs,
and circumstances, are likely to lead to a radically disruptive end.
The Know-Nothings, like the country they wished to reunite, were
as disunited as they were patriotic.

In no two sections of the country were they the same. In New
England political nativism had been growing since 1848 alongside

the new Free Soil party that had been organized by a coalition of reformers from both the old Whig and Democratic parties. Winning a legislative majority in Massachusetts in 1851 and 1852, the reformers enacted a mixed bag of humanitarian and egalitarian measures: prohibition of the liquor trade, a "personal liberty" law to block federal pursuit of fugitive slaves, and a Jacksonian general-charter law for business incorporation. In 1853, however, the new state constitution which they had drawn up to perpetuate the reform era was rejected by a countercoalition of "conservative" Democrats, with their Irish Catholic supporters, and regular or "cotton" Whigs.

The Catholic voters were conspicuously the immovable barrier to reform, hardened by the invective of Catholic spokesmen against the Free Soil coalition: "With the cant of religion and morality on their lips, its leaders are . . . infidels and blasphemers, as well as traitors and disorganizers."[12] These Yankee heretics evidently combined a disgusting sentimentality toward freed Negroes with a malignant animus against poor Irishmen. To the reformers, not surprisingly, nativism now appeared simply a matter of freeing American affairs from the intrusion of such illiberal foreigners, a reform urgently needed if they were to prevail against slavery, rum, or monstrous monopolies. First as Know-Nothings and then as Republicans they maintained their political coalition through the 1850s. When the Kansas-Nebraska Act of 1854 polarized opinion in New England still more sharply, they were able to retake Massachusetts and hold it until 1858. They speedily reenacted prohibition, disbanded the Irish militia companies (which had proved only too dependable at securing the shipment of fugitive slaves back South), and introduced a twenty-one-year naturalization bill. In seeking to impose a purer and more coherent political order on society, they were fundamentally as conservative as the most orthodox Irish Catholic believer in social stability. But one of the two versions of social conservatism could prevail only by embittering the other.

Southern Know-Nothings had their own reasons for disliking foreigners. Turbulent Irishmen and destitute newcomers of any kind were as troublesome in New Orleans as in Boston, but, infinitely worse, the liberal Germans had the effrontery to introduce the antislavery movement not only into the city but also into the cotton fields of the Texas prairies where they had settled. Immigrant radicalism, as Southerners saw it, was a greater threat than popery, which at least was above suspicion on the question of maintaining stable social institutions, the peculiar institution of slavery in particular. In the old French parts of Louisiana, indeed, a number of native-American Catholics, among them a priest, were leaders of the American party. Southerners counted themselves fortunate that the great majority of immigrants, whether Catholics or freethinkers, avoided the South; on the other hand, they deplored the economic advantage that foreign labor gave the rival North and West. All in all, the nativists of the South were primarily defenders of slavery rather than of white homogeneity. As the national Whig party broke up after losing the election of 1852, the American party furnished an unimpeachably southern haven for former Whigs, many of whom were cotton planters and merchants closely tied to northern markets. By avoiding the sectional extremism of the Democratic "fire-eaters," they could hope to associate defense of southern society with patriotic defense of the Union.

In the Middle Atlantic and the Border states the American party, in motives as in geographical situation, stood midway between the extremes of North and South. Since their cities, from New York, Philadelphia, and Baltimore to Louisville and Saint Louis, battened on commerce with both sections, while their countryside was the likeliest battleground in case of civil war, nativism appealed chiefly as a means of diverting overwrought partisans on both sides from the slavery issue. Rather than fusing either with proslavery or antislavery factions of the old parties, nativists ran their own American ticket with some success. New York and Philadelphia, like Boston or New Orleans, furthermore, were afflicted with practical disorders in which immigrants were always involved. Twenty years of crowded poorhouses, election riots, church burnings, and political campaigns over Bible-reading in the public schools had made poverty and popery seem substantially the same issue. In the Border slave states of Maryland and Missouri, in addition, the large number of German immigrants were as suspect for their liberal ideas as in the Deep South.

All the inconsistencies between Know-Nothingism in New England, the South, and the Middle States were reflected among adherents of this party of national unity in the Northwest. Although Yankee farmers in Wisconsin or Illinois opposed extension of slavery into the West just as German immigrants did, they had no use for infidel freethinkers, anti-Sabbatarians, and lager beer drinkers. On the other hand, some German liberals who lived in places where they were surrounded by Irish Catholics became Know-Nothings. In other places even Irish Catholics sometimes joined the American party out of hatred for those "foreign anarchists" and "universal republicans," the "Damned Dutch."[13]

The national convention of the American party in 1856, the year it expected to win the presidency, unmasked the hopelessness of a patriotic coalition of antislavery Northerners, proslavery Southerners, Middle Atlantic and Border equivocators, and, reducing to absurdity the common principle of nativism, a number of foreigners and Catholics. Unable to secure an unequivocal platform plank in favor of restoring the Missouri Compromise line limiting extension of slavery, the northern antislavery elements walked out and went over to the new, unambiguously free-soil Republican party. The mainly southern remnant of the Americans nominated Millard Fillmore, whose campaign harped on simple Unionism rather than nativism but carried only the state of Maryland. The party held a balance of power in Congress during 1857–1859 but never seriously pressed for restricting free immigration or easy naturalization.

The fire had gone out of political nativism as soon as it proved its uselessness for diverting the country's attention from the sectional controversy. Instead of galvanizing the Union in common cause against foreigners or Catholics, the nativists had succeeded only in stirring up another source of ill feeling among ethnic groups, as the Republicans, with their prominent contingent of former Know-Nothings, discovered when they lost most of the German districts of the Northwest in 1860. Only the fact that the opposition to the Republicans was split, among Constitutional (proslavery) and National (popular sovereignty) Democrats and the Constitutional Union remnant of the American party, permitted the election of Abraham Lincoln. That a merely sectional, minority candidate could triumph was partly the result of the nativist, anti-Catholic attempt to save the Union.

The Civil War which soon followed marked the high point, or rather the nadir, both of social disorder and of the sort of conservative reaction that so often redoubled it. In the winter and spring of 1860–1861, before the "Black Republican" president-elect could take office, seven of the fifteen slave states, from South Carolina to Texas, seceded from the Union, organized their own militant Confederacy, and rallied the laggards by cannonading one of the last two Union outposts in the South, Fort Sumter in Charleston harbor. Four of the remaining slave states of the upper South promptly fell into line. The reaction of the North was no less vigorous. Although most Northerners, like the new administration, had expected somehow to maintain the Union without coercion, they rushed to enlist in numbers far beyond Lincoln's call for 75,000 three-month volunteers and then for 50 three-year regiments.

Men in both sections suddenly felt personally involved in the most urgent situation. Shaken by the economic revolution that they all desired and by an insidious social revolution that they hardly comprehended, both Northerners and Southerners were struggling to defend what each conceived to be the essentials of their social order. The election of a Black Republican, it seemed to white Southerners generally, threatened to lay the ax to Negro slavery, the taproot of their society. Ten years earlier the veteran Kentuckian Henry Clay, in urging the national compromise of 1850, had already sounded the tocsin: "habit, safety, property, life, everything is at hazard."[14] Now all the compromises negotiated since 1787 had collapsed, jeopardizing slave property itself—the only device Southerners could imagine for keeping relations between the two races from boiling over, as the Alabama secessionist William L. Yancey warned the Democratic convention in 1860, in a "great heaving volcano of passion and crime," the twin West Indian horrors of racial massacre and racial amalgamation.[15] During the subsequent campaign southern "fire-eating" newspapers had fanned these always smoldering fears by trumping up highly circumstantial stories of servile rapine, poisoned wells, and other long-expected outrages in farthest Texas and other vulnerable if remote places. The *Charleston Mercury* conjured up a nightmare of "pillage, violence, murder, poisons and rape . . . with the demoniac revelry of all the passions of an ignorant, semi-barbarous race, urged to madness by the licentious teachings of our Northern brethren."[16] The sober fact was that Lincoln, although firmly committed to the quintessential Republican policy of keeping slavery out of new federal territories, was no more disposed than most other Northerners to abolish it in the states where it had always been established. But to Southerners such considerations seemed trivial in the face of the incalculable peril to which "Northern Republican license" exposed what one newspaper called the "social security" of the South.[17]

For their part the northern volunteers who sprang to arms, rather to their own surprise, were responding not to any call to make the continent safe for liberal democracy, certainly not to free black men from slavery, but to Lincoln's invocation of the overarching abstraction of the Union, the ultimate American symbol of political and social stability. In view of the novelty, as recently as 1789, of a continental union embracing New Englanders, Virginians, and

Carolinians, men might well congratulate themselves on its weathering the storms of seventy years. During the past thirty years, however, egalitarian democracy had been steadily reducing the actual government of the Federal Union to a far feebler instrument of economic or social control than had been envisioned by the gentlemen of the mercantilist age who drafted its Constitution. The closer to absolute inanition that government was brought and the less effectual it became for any public purpose but the common man's drive for unbridled economic opportunity, the more that venturesome but anxious individual put his trust in the abstract idea of the Union—not simply a government to which every man belonged as an individual citizen, but a half-mystic essence in which all distinctions of sectional interest, religious creed, ethnic origin, partisan advantage, and material self-seeking were ultimately merged. Community, family, church, the old elites, and the organic structure of society itself might crumble into individualistic disarray; evangelical revivals, humanitarian reform crusades, fraternal rituals, and patriotic oratory all fell short of restoring the ancient certainties; but the Constitution and the Union would surely endure. Somehow the indestructible framework so marvelously devised by a convention of republican demigods would keep American society safe from the consequences of economic, social, and political disorder: "Liberty *and* Union, now and forever, one and inseparable."[18]

The paralysis of federal authority while one after another of the Gulf states seceded in the winter of 1860–1861 reflected the general incredulity in other parts of the country that the old sentimental rhetoric of Union would not once again prevail. Horace Greeley could airily bid the cotton states to "go in peace," since he expected them to return as soon as they, like South Carolina in the tariff-nullification crisis of 1832, had registered their political point.[19] Beyond Lincoln's vague inaugural appeal to "mystic chords of memory" that might "yet swell the chorus of the Union" he had no practical plan but to resupply the two off-shore southern forts still in the Union's hands as symbols, at least, of its perpetuity.[20] When at last, in the name of southern rights, the Charleston batteries opened their cannonade and violated the Union itself, nothing was secure.*

* In the Southerners' own view they too were defending the true Union of 1776 and 1787. The Confederate constitution, which almost exactly copied that of the United States, provided for admission—or in effect readmission—of the other states in due course. Most of the southern "Unionists," upon whose loyalty Lincoln had relied, adhered to the Confederacy, but they did not thereby cease to be Unionists.

By April 1861 there was no higher moral cause for Americans, Northerners and Southerners alike, to defend than the stability of their own society, whether shaken, as Southerners imagined, by a dread abolitionist conspiracy or, as it seemed to Northerners, by the rebellion of a sinister "slave power." For four desperate years each side was forced to rally and regroup as much of its long-neglected institutional structure as a war for so conservative an end might require. Both the United States and the Confederate States had in particular to reinvoke the onetime authority of government, civil and military, though the liberal habits of both sections, especially the South, usually made it less than adequate even for the immediate military effort and allowed the war to drag on through four years and nearly three-quarters of a million lives.

The endless fascination which the Civil War has always held for Americans, like the inordinate difficulty for historians fully to plumb the depths of its causes, is sometimes ascribed to the essentially aberrant character of the whole sectional controversy as the one great American tragedy, the single irremediable catastrophe in a national success story. But if instead of any sudden reversal in the course of American history the coming of the war is seen as the culmination of a mounting failure to maintain a stable social structure, the abiding popular sense of its crucial importance becomes much more comprehensible. Perhaps even the different standard interpretations of the causes of the war, each of which centers upon one or another quite real facet of the situation—constitutional ambiguity, the "imbecility" of blundering politicians, the conflicting economic interests or the social incompatibility (so it was supposed) of the different sections, the moral fanaticism of abolitionists and southern fire-eaters—all may fall into place within this longer perspective of national failure.

The national successes had been mainly material: westward expansion and the building of cities, the commercial and industrial revolutions, the accumulation of wealth, both national and personal. The failures were social, cultural, spiritual, and finally political in the most profound sense, the dark side of the same material success story. Because of a certain chain of circumstances the ultimate breakdown occurred along the sectional fault line rather than at all the others. When at last in 1861 it came to civil war, the fight was not a general melee among planters and farmers, agrarians and industrialists, capital and labor, middle class and working class, political parties, ethnic groups, Protestants and Catholics, fathers and sons, or Easterners and Westerners, although all of them had a part in the general atomization of society. The Civil War was fought between Northerners and Southerners, but even they were also fighting against a common enemy which challenged both sections alike with the most profoundly moral problem of the time, the instability of society itself. Each blamed the other for the social insecurity from which both suffered. Of all the variant names that have been attached to the war, each representing a theory of its origins and essential nature—War of the Rebellion, War Between the States, War for Southern Independence, the Second American Revolution—none strikes quite to the heart of its character, on the rebel side as on the Yankee, as a war for social security, a civil war in the deepest sense.

More sharply than all the lesser spasms of blind reaction, of conservatism gone wrong, in the course of the nineteenth century, the Civil War only compounded the prevalent confusion. Of course the eventual Union victory meant that an essential first step toward a better order could be taken. Behind the immediate threat both to southern institutions and to the Union had lain the intractable, two-hundred-year-old social dilemma of Negro slavery. It had been the first and remained the worst instance of placing economic values—specifically the demand for a labor force adequate for the most profitable production of tobacco, rice, and latterly sugar cane and cotton—ahead of all considerations of social stability, cultural homogeneity, and spiritual welfare, not only of the Afro-Americans but of the whole of American society.

Halfway through the war, in 1863, the year which began with the Emancipation Proclamation and ended with the Gettysburg Address, it became apparent to most Northerners that preservation of the Union from endlessly recurrent disaster would require what only a few moral fanatics had hitherto contemplated, the outright abolition of slavery throughout the country, together with whatever other reforms might serve to secure government "of the people, by the people, and for the people" of the reunited nation. The economic advantages in permitting some men to own others had been bought too dearly for the Union and for American society. In due course after the end of the war in 1865 slavery was constitutionally abolished, without compensation to slaveowners even in the loyal Border states.

The Thirteenth Amendment, however, was somewhat like Andrew Jackson's vigorous veto of the rechartering of the Bank of the United States thirty years before, in that it removed one system of institutional control, slavery, without putting anything positive in its place.

Even after ratification of two more amendments proclaiming his equal civil and political rights, the Negro remained fixed in a caste beneath the rest of society. Although the Republican majority in Congress subjected the governments of the lately rebellious states to a "radical reconstruction," or at least a military occupation, even the Radical wing of the party halted well short of inflicting the kind of social revolution that southern white men had fought for four years to stave off.

Military defeat had heightened, if anything, southern determination to hold onto what remained of the only social order they had known. The Negro freedman was kept almost as firmly in his "place" as he had been under slavery. In various parts of the South he was tolerated as a voter as long as both parties hoped to manipulate his vote. But any greater assertion of social equality or political independence was apt to bring down upon the freedman a new version of the old patrollers, the night riders of the Ku Klux Klan. Even the "reconstructed" state governments of northern carpetbaggers and southern blacks and whites, during their few years' tenure, did not attempt, except temporarily in a few places, to give the freedman practical hope of economic equality with landowning white farmers or to free him from white social supremacy.

Most Negroes exchanged chattel slavery for the precarious tenure and hand-to-mouth existence of sharecroppers. In law the tenant on shares was a freely contracting individual who might be on his way toward landownership, as most white tenant farmers always had been. In hard fact the sharecropper's livelihood still depended on the will of the plantation owner, who no longer could be held, however, to the old slaveowner's social code of responsibility toward his "people." Although the black sharecropper was on an economic level with many poor white men who were falling into the same virtually perpetual peonage, the latter grew the more adamant in insisting upon their social superiority to all Negroes. The war, in shattering the economy of the South and disrupting the only social structure that it had known, had failed to put anything more stable in place of the old "peculiar institution" than a mock-individualistic form of racial caste. Northerners had managed to preserve the Union, but Southerners also won their goal of stabilizing relations between the races on much the old basis. Unfortunately the new stability was as ill-designed to endure as the old had been.

Neither side had as yet established a fundamentally stable basis for the security of the American social order. A greater battle than any Bull Run or Gettysburg remained for them to fight, a battle to recast their economic system, their government, and their social structure on lines they could not yet perceive. Thomas Carlyle had a glimmering, as early as 1850, of what those lines would be. Material wealth—"cotton crops and Indian corn and dollars," even the admirable "roast-goose with apple-sauce for the poorest working-man"—was not a sufficient national product. "No," the conservative Scotsman had prophesied, "America will have to strain its energies in quite other fashion than this; . . . she will have her own agony, and her own victory, but on other terms than she is yet quite aware of."[21] Delphic criticism from the sort of European whose eyes were fixed on intangible values of mind and spirit would never be quite intelligible to liberal Americans in their implicit faith in the infinite beneficence of material progress. Not until the final quarter of the nineteenth century were many of them ready to consider what those other terms might be.

PART THREE

The Reconstituted
Society, 1875–1945

I. Economic Progress and Reform

In 1876, as Americans by the millions repaired to Philadelphia, the birthplace of the republic, to see the international exposition which celebrated the end of a century of independence, nothing displayed in Fairmount Park suggested to them that in the next century they would turn away from their past course. Nor in fact would they explicitly repudiate, during the next two or three generations, the goal of material progress fittingly symbolized by the locomotives and the mammoth stationary engine in Machinery Hall. Even the silent wheels and unsmoking chimneys of the depression of 1873–1879, which reached its lowest point in the unemployment, destitution, strikes, and rioting of the year after the centennial, could not shake their confidence that the national productive mechanism, industrial and agricultural, promised the best as well as the fullest life for the common man.

That personage, who confidently identified the independence of the United States with his own freedom from governmental restraint, had for some time been laboring to build a modern industrial system on the patternless plan of economic individualism, a principle derived from the earlier experience of yeoman farmers, handicraft artisans, and petty merchants. As the inadequacy of this procedure began to grow evident, Americans cast about for some way to regulate economic enterprise without retarding further material growth or throttling the freedom of the individual. The impetus for regulation came at first from the businessmen, workingmen, and farmers who were bearing the brunt of the economic struggle; ultimately the ordinary middle-class common man went so far as to call up the dormant regulatory power of government in order to defend his own liberty against the power of those same newly organized economic interests. As late as the 1930s this many-sided search for economic order, essentially conservative though it was, proceeded under the individualistic banner of "liberalism."

The freedom which was sought was in most respects not that of the age of Andrew Jackson and Abraham Lincoln, though the new reformers invoked their names rather than those of Alexander Hamilton or John Winthrop.

19. THE FARMERS' LAST FRONTIER

By 1875 each of the three streams of the westward migration of the past century, having advanced across nearly the whole of the prairies, was beginning to spill over onto the "Great American Desert," the three- or four-hundred-mile wide belt of the Great Plains that banded the country from Canada to the Gulf of Mexico. Only two large regions of well-watered prairie remained unbroken by white settlement: one in the Red River Valley just beyond the Old Northwest, the other to the southwest in the Indian Territory (Oklahoma), a patchwork of some twenty tribal reservations closed to white farmers by federal treaty. The Great Plains, besides being even flatter and more treeless than the prairies, lacked the minimal twenty inches of annual rainfall necessary for farming on European or eastern lines.

Exactly where the prairies stopped and the Great Plains began was uncertain; a cycle of unusually wet years in the early 1880s tempted farmers onward, only to be driven back by drought after 1887. Until the twentieth century, when the technique of "dry farming" was developed and strains of Russian wheat were introduced, the Great Plains were most adaptable to cattle herding. The cattlemen who had made use of the open range of the southeastern backcountry in colonial days and then of the Old Southwest, came into their classic element from Texas northward to Montana and across the Canadian border between 1865 and 1885. Taking over Spanish lingo along with the Mexican longhorn cattle of Texas, the cowboy-*vaquero* now rounded up his stock into a *corral* rather than a "cowpen," roped steers with *la riata*, and wore *chaparajos* as well as Colt's .45 revolver from Connecticut. But the changes were more picturesque than real. Almost everything in the cattleman's system of exploiting the Great Plains, except perhaps his extralegal concept of "range rights," he had brought along from the older frontiers; even an innovation like barbed wire, invented and manufactured—like his windmills and revolvers—in the industrial East, soon permitted ranchers and then farmers to divide up the open range with fences after the eastern fashion. Although the peculiar topography, climate, and vast extent of the Great Plains gave off a romantic haze which lingers yet over that ultimate frontier, the enterprises in which cattlemen and farmers engaged were only the last chapter, if also the richest, in the old story of appropriation and exploitation of the soil of a continent.

Like settlers on earlier frontiers, most of the farmers of the farther prairies and plains came from what had been the Northwest, including Ontario, or the Southwest of the previous generation. In the 1860s more people migrated to the new regions from Ohio than from any other state; in the 1870s and 1880s Illinois sent the largest number; in the 1890s Kansas, only forty years earlier the goal of westward migration, in turn became its main source. Although Easterners might think of these frontiersmen as moving merely from one part of the West to another, the distances from Illinois to Nebraska or from eastern Kansas to Dakota were measured in hundreds of miles, and in any new settlement the medley of people who had come from different districts accentuated the physical isolation now habitual in American rural society.

The inveterate migratory habit was not simply the eternal "westering" of poetic reminiscence; the practical circumstances that had led their grandparents from Vermont to Michigan or from the Carolinas to the Gulf Plains still operated on this generation. Although farmers were now more often drawn west by the richness of prairie soil than driven there by literal exhaustion of the older land, the heedless old pattern of two or three decades of steady cropping, followed by erosion, insect pests, and plant diseases, put the farmers of the older Midwest—and their still numerous sons— at something of the same disadvantage in growing wheat or corn as that from which New Englanders and New Yorkers had previously suffered. With each advance of the wheat belt toward its ultimate dual concentration in western Kansas and the Dakotas, the Old Northwest fell back on sheep raising, dairying, and truck farming as New England and New York State had done before. The displacement of crops displaced labor as well, sometimes because the new crop required less attention than the old, oftener because it was easier and safer to follow the familiar crop westward than to learn to handle new ones.

Since the Europeans who joined the last phase of the westward movement of farmers had, like their predecessors, no experience of pioneering, they usually preferred to take up partly improved land behind the actual frontier. Most of them came from the same old countries of Northwestern Europe, though from somewhat different regions; most had been farmers or peasants; and usually the causes of their emigration were much the same as before: overpopulation in their old districts, changes in agriculture and the agrarian social order, and occasional crop failures, all of which threatened to undermine their customary economic position and social status. No new catastrophes remotely comparable to the potato famine of the 1840s occurred to dump masses of destitute and degraded peasants in American ports; the population of Ireland had shrunk to economical proportions, and by 1881 the Irish peasantry finally gained legal security of tenure. Irish emigration continued by tens of thousands each year, but since the newcomers usually joined the hundreds of thousands who had gone before, only a few became farmers in the West.

British farmers and farm laborers continued, however, to emigrate in force; together with a much larger number of industrial workingmen they made the 1870s and 1880s the greatest epoch in the long history of British emigration to the New World. The English farmer, who had feared foreign competition ever since the protective Corn Laws were repealed in 1848, saw the threat materialize at last in the 1860s and 1870s as wheat from the American West poured into European markets. A succession of even wetter than usual harvest seasons at the end of the 1870s drowned the last doubt of many English farmers about emigrating and reestablishing themselves in Canada, Australia, or the United States.

German emigration, also at its peak in the 1880s, was similarly spurred on by the competition of American wheat, as well as by the old phenomena of minute subdivision of peasant landholdings and decline of household industry in southwestern Germany and the new one of peasant land hunger in West Prussia, Pomerania, and elsewhere in the northeast, a region long since preempted by great estates and large-scale cultivation. Peasants who were determined to maintain or improve their condition continued to look abroad. The Prussian system of three-year military conscription, now extended over the new German empire, gave young men a still more pressing reason to leave. Smaller groups of Germans came from Russia, where their eighteenth-century ancestors, many of whom had been pacifistic sectarians like the Pennsylvania "Dutch," had settled along the Volga and in the Crimea. Withdrawal of their military exemption in 1871, on top of the usual land hunger and other economic discontents of the time, induced some fifty thousand "Volga Germans" to transfer their colonies to the American plains, where their Russian wheat proved ideally suited to the dry climate.

Crop failures in Norway and Sweden in the late 1860s and a perennial shortage of arable land for the numerous sons of farmers added two new major components to the ethnic mosaic of the American West. Many crofters and landless laborers, who were the hardest pressed, managed to emigrate; altogether in the 1880s more than 1 percent of the Norwegian population left the country each year, and three-fourths of 1 percent of the Swedes. A steady flow of people out of the rural districts of Western Europe, comparable in the course of time to the sudden depopulation of Ireland in the 1840s and 1850s, had been made quite normal by the prospect of a better, more secure living in the far Midwest.

The inducements to immigrants were painted in bright colors, sometimes a trifle larger than life, by land companies and by the western states. The federal Homestead Act of 1862 had ostensibly opened the public domain as a free gift to families who would undertake to farm quarter sections of 160 acres for five years. But until 1889 the land office auctions also proceeded with no restriction on the size of tracts that speculators might buy. Certain Indian reservation lands were also put on sale, and millions of acres more were given to the new western railroads, in order to subsidize rapid construction, and to the states, both east and west, to endow their new "agricultural and mechanical" universities. The states and railroads threw their land onto the market to be turned into cash as quickly as possible. Altogether after 1862 the federal government disposed of more than half a billion acres of the public domain through direct sale or through subsidy and eventual sale, nearly seven times more than was granted in free homesteads—and even a good many of the latter were fraudulently acquired by speculators for resale. Of some 33 million acres still unoccupied in Kansas in 1883, less than one-third was open to free entry by homesteaders, and that almost entirely in the arid western end of the state.

Historians have censured the government for failing to treat the homesteading farmers with the full liberality intended by Congress in 1862. As in other sectors of the economy, however, it may be that the government was excessively liberal in encouraging rapid economic development both by small farmers and by great land speculators. Any planning for the future welfare of western rural communities was certainly not the work of the federal land office, which left homesteaders to their own devices—or to those of hired "landlookers"—in finding a suitable quarter section. On the other hand the railroads and the land companies, some of which held the greater part of whole counties, introduced more planning into western settlement than anyone had done in the previous hundred years.

Although the land sellers' planning was designed to enhance their profits, often enough their interests coincided with the ambitions of prospective buyers. The railroads had to balance the probable returns from high land prices against the advantage of filling the vast reaches between the Midwest and the Far West with enough settlers to produce profitable freight for them to haul. Never before had immigration recruitment been so well organized. The different lines placed agents throughout the eastern states and across Europe as far as the Volga; the Northern Pacific alone was represented in hundreds of towns and villages in the British Isles, Germany, Switzerland, Scandinavia, and the Netherlands, and of course at the immigration stations at New York and elsewhere, offering cheap steamship and rail passage and accommodations at special reception hotels in Minnesota or Iowa. The railroad agents organized parties of Swedish, German, or American farmers—sometimes a group of old neighbors whose minister doubled as railroad agent on commission—and dispatched them west by trainloads in "emigrant cars." The fare for cut-rate "land exploring" tickets might be credited against the price of a farm. Railroad land ranged from $2.50 to $8.00 an acre—in Kansas in the 1880s the average was $3.25—and payment could be stretched out over ten years. Each of the western states, in an effort to outdistance its neighbors, added its own posters, maps, and brochures to those of the railroads and the land companies.

As social planning, all this activity was of course more promotional than public spirited. None of the interested agencies, including the federal land office, had a goal much beyond wringing the quickest possible cash return from land sales and freight rates in the new rural townships, counties, and towns of the plains. Their neglect of the quality of the social relationships that might develop in those far-flung settlements was, like the plains frontier itself, a final flowering of a way of thinking that had become habitual to Americans.

The western farmer, like the old southern tobacco or cotton planter, had left self-sufficient "family farming" far behind him. Except in out-of-the-way districts that had been bypassed by the westward march of progress, or among immigrant families who for a time sought only the security of working, women as well as men, in their own fields, the farming business required substantial capital investment, mechanized production, transportation connections to distant markets where prices were unpredictable, and a force of casual wage laborers. Although in his own mind the farmer represented all the personal and communal virtues of the yeoman proprietor of a much earlier generation, he had become a kind of capitalist and industrialist, on as large a scale as he could manage, different from other businessmen mainly in the absolute degree to which he was vulnerable to the vagaries of the unsystematic economy.

The scale of farming operations constantly grew. While the farm population of the United States increased only by some 50 percent between 1875 and 1915 (roughly from 20 to 30 million), the acreage under cultivation doubled, and production of most staple crops more than doubled; once established on the western plains, wheat production tripled. Machinery accounted for much of this increased yield, of grain in particular. Although most of the basic devices—steel plows, disc harrows, grain planters, reapers, binders, and threshing machines—had been invented two or three decades earlier, they became essential for profitable agriculture during the acute labor shortage of the Civil War years and the subsequent era of expansion onto the western plains. The old machines were improved, and new ones invented: gang plows turning sixteen furrows behind a steam tractor, huge combine wheat harvesters, corn shuckers (though not yet corn or cotton pickers), cream separators and testers. By 1900 one man could harvest as much grain as twenty in his great-grandfather's day, and a farmer could plant practically his entire acreage in wheat instead of the eight or ten acres formerly possible with hand tools.

Grain growing on that scale called for a greatly expanded labor force at planting and harvest, supplied in part by a new army of migratory workers who moved northward from Kansas to the Dakotas each season with the crops. These rural tramps, a pest to railroad brakemen as they traveled about in empty boxcars, formed an agricultural proletariat such as no earlier farming frontier had seen. In the older sections of the country, farm laborers were now commonly regarded as an economic and social class distinctly below the landowning farmers who employed them. The truck farms and orchards of the East were worked by gangs of foreign laborers, recruited in the cities and hired out by the same sort of agents that supplied railroad construction labor. A Connecticut farmer in 1887 succinctly indicated how far the social status of farm labor had fallen: "If you hire this class of men, there is one thing you must not do. Don't go into the field with them to work." Farmers in New

England no longer spoke of them as "help" in the old fashion, but simply as "labor."[1] At the other end of the country, on the fruit and vegetable farms and wheat ranches of California which had always been worked on a large scale, the employers of Chinese and Japanese coolies never used any of the egalitarian Yankee euphemisms for labor. In the cotton South, of course, the old economic distinctions between the Negro slave caste and the poor whites were simply merged into the common form of sharecropping tenancy; the sharecropper, black or white, in his unshakable indebtedness to the landlord or storekeeper who exacted a lien on his share of the crop, was less a tenant than a dependent laborer.

On the midwestern prairies and plains the old social egalitarianism persisted, partly because most of the migratory harvest laborers were native Americans, including small farmers and lumberjacks whose own work happened to be slack during the wheat harvesting season. The ordinary farmhand, who was still likely to be a farmer's son himself, continued to be "admitted to the family table upon the same plane of equality," it was observed in Minnesota in 1900, and to "partake of the same social conditions, practically, [as] a member of the family."[2] But by 1900 it also had to be admitted that fewer and fewer young men had much practical hope of rising appreciably through farm labor:

Twenty-five years ago . . . a man generally worked upon the farm for the sake of getting a little money with which to buy some new land for himself and become a farmer. . . . But now that lands can not be had at $1.25 per acre, or $5 per acre, there seems to be a decided tendency for the farm laborer, if he is unmarried, to work for money without a very definite object, and this money is likely used for whatever his fancy dictates, most likely for a horse and buggy of his own.[3]

Although no one was likely to revive the European word "peasant" for anyone with those middle-class tastes, it became ever clearer as the twentieth century advanced that most agricultural laborers— whether immigrant or native American, migratory or settled, eastern, midwestern, southern, or far western—belonged to a distinctly inferior social class as well as an occupational category. Since that was hardly acceptable to most American farm boys, many of them who were not lucky enough to inherit a farm simply shook the dust of the back roads from their heels and joined the search for more promising work in the city.

The capital investment required for commercial farming increased beyond anything that a laborer could reasonably hope to save. Far beyond the $500 or $600 which the land itself might cost, and which some land companies represented as the entire sum that was necessary, it was estimated in the 1870s that it took from $1500 to $2500 to start farming in Kansas, Nebraska, or Minnesota with any practical hope of success, and perhaps twice as much before the farm was properly stocked and developed. The long deflationary cycle between 1873 and 1897 increased the financial burden. Like other entrepreneurs, many commercial farmers had to borrow capital, which they usually secured by a farm mortgage, a device common since the great boom in western settlement in the 1830s; by 1900 about 30 percent of all American farms were encumbered by mortgages. The farmer whose mortgage debt in effect kept growing, while the price he got for his corn, hogs, or wheat kept falling, felt he had a special grievance. Of course what he had to buy to keep his farm in operation—farm machinery in particular—was relatively cheap. Like all American machinery, however, the reapers and binders were lightly built, expected to wear out or rust away in a few years, and repeatedly had to be replaced by improved models.

As a fast-growing branch of the old business of western land speculation, mortgage-lending remained in private hands in spite of occasional proposals to liberalize the Homestead Act by offering federal loans to farmers at a low interest rate. Interest charges, nominally limited by state law to between 7 and 10 percent, were pushed as high as 20 percent through various technicalities. The mortgage lender, usually not a villain of the sort that stalked the stage in contemporary melodrama, was more apt to grant extensions of time in the hope that the farmer might repay principal and interest than to foreclose hastily (or to ruin the farmer's beautiful daughter), but the payments eventually had to be met. Basic land and property taxes, which were as low as the functions of local government were few, were no great burden. Counties, townships, and even individual farmers sometimes borrowed money, however, with which to induce railroad promoters to build branch lines into their district, and whether or not they eventually got their railroad, they would have to pay off the bonds or mortgages they had committed to the project.

The commercial farmer's need for transportation to take his goods to distant markets was as great as that of any industrialist. Although the western railroads had their own interest in getting the empty plains settled and producing freight, it would not have been worth the effort for an ambitious farmer or cattleman to go to such remote places, however rich the soil or luxuriant the prairie grass, if there were no means of sending his wheat, corn, or steers to where they were in demand. The four "transcontinental" lines connecting the Mississippi Valley with the Pacific slope, and half a dozen other railways, laced the western plains with the heavy steel rails and outsize locomotives and freight cars capable of carrying all the grain and livestock the new farmers and ranchers could produce. On the Great Lakes and the Atlantic, iron steamships now joined in flooding the East and Europe with the western staples. At terminal points the lofty grain elevators, first seen in the 1850s and 1860s, entirely displaced manual handling of wheat and corn. The physical identity of any individual farmer's shipment was submerged under a standard classification system well suited not only to massive production but also to speculation by the dealers in "futures" in metropolitan commodity markets such as the Chicago wheat "pit."

The ultimate markets for the bulk of midwestern flour and meat, as for southern tobacco and cotton, were the burgeoning cities both of America and Europe. Between 1875 and 1915, while the population of the United States only doubled, that of "urban" places (over 2500 persons) quadrupled and that of cities of over 100,000 grew by nearly six times. Exports of American agricultural products, growing faster yet, reflected both the continuing urbanization of Western Europe and the European farmer's inability to compete with the harvests of the midwestern United States and of Australia, Argentina, and Canada as well.

Enmeshed as western farmers and cattlemen now were in a national and international business, they gained no exemption from risks that had always been peculiar to farming. These were compounded, indeed, by the natural hazards of the western plains. When a series of wet years ameliorated the climate on the cattleman's and farmer's frontier of the early 1880s, the larger their optimistic investment in land and stock the greater and quicker their profits usually proved. But just when they had convinced themselves that their own settlement—and the smoke and whistling of the trains—had brought about a permanent increase in rainfall, a still longer dry cycle burned up the crops, starved the cattle, and depopulated whole counties and brand-new towns. Within five years of the onset of drought half the settlers of western Kansas pulled back eastward, and the state temporarily lost nearly two hundred thousand people. Even in good years the wind across the treeless plains might whip up prairie fires in the fall, blizzards in winter, dust storms in the spring, and clouds of locusts or "grasshoppers" in summer, any of them capable of ruining a farmer's calculations for the year and of driving his wife quite distraught, isolated and already disheartened as she might well be at trying to make a home of a one- or two-room hut built of blocks of prairie sod. The old-fashioned family farmer with his near-subsistence agriculture and his more dependable local market had usually survived his bouts with nature until a better year; the combination of the natural scourges of the Great Plains and hard times in distant markets made farming on the last frontier the most risky business of any during the worldwide cycle of depression between 1873 and 1897.

Back when farms were small and the costs of settlement moderate, the fact that many farm operators were tenants—some of them literally sharecroppers even in the Old Northwest—had seemed less significant than their expectation of buying land of their own. But in spite of the tradition that a farmer should eventually be a landowner, farm tenancy had kept increasing ever since the 1830s in the new prairies of the West as well as in older districts. After 1875 the expense of entering mechanized, commercial agriculture raised an ever-higher barrier against the old upward mobility; a tenant farmer needed the new machinery as much as anyone. Rents were rising: landlords demanded perhaps two-fifths of the crop from the sharecropper instead of the customary third, or perhaps simply a cash rental of $1.50 or $2.25 an acre.

Tenancy was so fast becoming normal practice that by 1900 more than 40 percent of the farmers of several of the young prairie states were renters. Some of them no doubt still were men on the way up, and others perhaps earned a decent income without particularly seeking to own the land they worked, but there was reason behind the general fear in the Midwest that the tenant farmer was falling into as hopelessly inferior an economic class and dependent social status as southern sharecroppers or tenants back east. By 1930 some 42 percent of all American farms were operated by tenants, including more than half of those in the South, a third across the older states of the North, and a quarter of those in the West. It is true that simply to equate the growth of tenancy with impoverishment, social degradation, and political subservience was to fail to take account of all the other agrarian societies where, as in England, the etymologically synonymous words "farmer" and "tenant" connoted nothing of the sort. But Americans, given their different history, might well take a gloomy view of the decline in landownership.

In spite of their peculiar complex of problems, farmers in the West and elsewhere persisted, like other entrepreneurs of the time, in the optimistic habit of speculation, buying and selling real estate in confidence that, whatever else happened, in the long run the land itself would keep on rising in value. That miracle, which had sustained American farmers in their careless agriculture for two hundred years, did not altogether fail them now. The demand for land among the hopeful thousands who kept moving west confirmed the optimism of those who were already there and had improved land to sell. After prosperity returned in 1897–1913 and during the First World War, they seemed to have won their gamble with nature and international markets. It was a period which they would recall, when depression and drought returned in the 1920s and 1930s, as their golden age.

20. CAPTAINS OF INDUSTRY
AND ARMIES OF LABOR

The farmer was now a species of businessman; the businessman had long thought of himself as a practical individualist like the old yeoman farmer, though now engaged in the novel enterprises of industrialization, railroading, or commercial speculation. Most businessmen continued, until as late as the 1930s, to subscribe to some version of the nineteenth-century doctrine of free enterprise and *laissez-faire*. During the last quarter of the century, indeed, theorists formulated new, "scientific" theories to support the old practical economic ethic of hard work and accumulation for reinvestment. But the business of operating a modern economy according to the will or whims of thousands of individual competitors and the haphazard pressures of unregulated markets proved as chancy for businessmen as for farmers.

Like the westward movement of the farming frontier, industrialization proceeded from fits of overoptimistic expansion to bouts of depression and retrenchment and then, since the other natural resources of the continent were even more abundant and accessible than the soil, on again to renewed bursts of growth. Neither the wartime dislocation of the economy during 1861–1865 nor the acute depressions of 1873–1879, 1883–1886, and 1893–1897 held back the captains of industry and finance for long. During the forty years between 1872 and 1913 the manufacturing production of the country multiplied by six, the output of mines by ten, and the mileage of railway track by five. As early as the 1880s industrial production surpassed agricultural production and in several major lines overtook the British.

Factory methods substantially replaced most of the handicraft manufactures that were still being carried on just before the Civil War: shoemaking and garment making (both stimulated by the war), flour milling, wagonmaking, woodworking and metalworking generally, and meat-packing. Exploitation of newly discovered resources like petroleum and aluminum; new inventions, some of them European, like the Bessemer and open-hearth processes for cheap steelmaking; and a combination of tariff protection and growing domestic demand for previously unsuccessful manufactures like silk and tinplate—all added to the number as well as the scale of modern industries. Electricity, usually generated by steam engines or turbines, helped quadruple the power applied to manufacturing during the last quarter of the nineteenth century, though by freeing such devices as sewing machines from the cumbersome shafts, belts, and pulleys of the old-fashioned factory it also gave new life to "domestic" manufacturing of clothing within the household—usually now in fact a city tenement.

Sweatshops and sweated labor apart, the scale of production of the average factory grew rapidly: cotton mills by about a third, shoe factories to twice the old output, steelworks by an almost immeasurable factor over the old iron furnaces. The growth of cities of course was closely bound to this industrial growth. Industry went through its own westward movement, moreover, as Pittsburgh, Cleveland, Chicago, Saint Louis, Milwaukee, Minneapolis, Kansas City, and their satellites and smaller competitors rivaled and sometimes supplanted eastern cities as centers of steelmaking, oil refining, milling, or meat-packing. The "New South" had its own steel town of Birmingham, and cotton mills along the inland rapids, or fall line, of the southeastern rivers transformed poor farm families into poorly paid machine tenders, as the New England mills had done earlier, and began to draw the textile industry away from New England itself.

As in the spread of rural communities across the new West, public policy of the permissive, promotional kind into which the country had drifted in the mid-nineteenth century stimulated the processes of industrialization and urbanization. Neither federal, state, nor local government ever wholly abdicated its "police power" over private property or its theoretical responsibility for the general welfare of the commonwealth. But nearly everyone now agreed that the commonweal was best served by permitting private enterprise the greatest possible freedom. The essential role of the state had been reduced, by 1875, to keeping out of the way of the common man's economic opportunity and, on the other hand, actively enlarging the options open to enterprise. As a recent student of the policy of both the legislatures and the courts sums it up, "The law provided an open field (assured broad markets), legal instruments (the corporation and manifold tools of contract, especially the devices of corporate finance), legal subsidies (grants of land and public credit, and currency inflation and deflation), and then substantially stood aside."[1]

The legislative devices that politicians argued most about, notably the land grants to western railroads and tariff protection for "infant industries" (even after some of the latter had grown quite middle-aged), were perhaps not the most important factors for economic growth. There was also the tacit acquiescence of federal and state judges, when applying constitutional, statute, or common law to a steady procession of specific cases, in the self-evident, eternal verity of "business principles," that is, the practical methods into which businessmen had fallen since the 1830s. The most explicit application of that mid-century economic ethic came late, in the 1880s, when a majority of the Supreme Court concluded that the "due process of law" of the Fourteenth Amendment—which in fact had been intended, as part of the postwar Reconstruction of the South, to guarantee the civil rights of all "persons," black or white, to life, liberty, and property—should also protect incorporated business enterprises from "unreasonable" public regulation, unreasonable, that is, when measured against business principles.

The astonishing rate of economic growth thus favored by public policy enabled a population only twice as large in 1913 as in 1875 to produce fully five times as much a year. Such abundance kept improving the middle-class standard of living even while building up a national capital investment substantially free, by the turn of the century, of further need to seek foreign investors. There seemed no end to the benefits that society might hope to obtain from the industrial cornucopia.

No one appeared to prosper more than businessmen themselves, especially the captains of industry and finance, so generally looked up to and only occasionally condemned in the 1880s as overmighty "robber barons." The unsteady advance of the national economy, however, made business success almost as incalculable a proposition as farming on the Great Plains. Although even in the worst years the proportion of businessmen who failed was a good deal less than the 95 percent estimated by alarmists, the latter were right enough in asserting that capitalists were in as "precarious a position as other classes in the community."[2] The Philadelphia shipbuilder John Roach testified in 1883: "Capital is very timid, and there are few persons who know the excitement and fear that exists among capitalists today . . . owing to the unsettled conditions of things."[3] As shrewd and successful a man as John D. Rockefeller of

Standard Oil later summed up his career as "work by day and worry by night, week in and week out, month after month."[4]

As long as businessmen, and most other Americans with them, put their faith in a "law of free development" that excluded any kind of public or private regulation that did not promise to make it freer yet, life would remain precarious. The unsystematic economy not only made the success of legitimate ventures highly uncertain, but it whetted the greed and cunning of all the "mere money-getters and traders" who flourished, as a critic observed in 1886, by means of "sharp practice, by chicanery, by circumventing the laws, by monopolizing the national heritage, by gambling on the stock exchange, by making 'corners' in food products, by wrecking railways, by watering stocks" and innumerable other refinements of the classic forestalling, engrossing, and regrating which the law had once sought to suppress.[5]

One of the least stable conditions confronting the industrialist was the rapidly changing composition of his labor force. The sheer number of nonagricultural workers increased some four times between 1875, when there were already as many of them, 7 million, as there were of farm laborers, and 1913, when fewer than 12 million people worked in agriculture and more than 27 million in other occupations, including 11 million in manufacturing and mining. The quantitative growth was welcomed as warmly as all the other statistics of national progress. By the late 1880s, however, rumblings of discontent began to be heard over the quality of the foreigners in the labor force of most of the important industries of the country. The Irish Catholic peasants and their children never ceased to trouble some people's minds as they had in the 1850s, but they had at least become accustomed fixtures, and many of them within a generation or two climbed from "shanty Irish" squalor to "lace-curtain" respectability. Their places at the bottom were taken by other kinds of peasant immigrants. Although for twenty years after 1875 most of the new arrivals came from the same countries of Northwestern Europe as before, the number of Slavic, Mediterranean, and other new people rapidly increased from the late 1860s onward: Czechs, Poles, Italians, Slovaks, Ruthenians, Lithuanians, Croats, Slovenes, Serbs, Bulgarians, Greeks, Syrians, Russians, Eastern European Jews, Chinese, and Japanese.

A majority of the annual immigration by 1896 and fully seven-eighths by 1914, these were the "new immigrants" against whom, as we shall see, the nativist campaign of the early twentieth century was aimed—peoples whose languages, customs, and physical appearance were obviously unlike those of the old immigrants and Americans of Northwestern European descent, and whose inferiority supposedly was demonstrated by the sordidly materialistic reasons for which they came to the United States. Since almost all of them settled in cities, especially in the slums abandoned by other people, they seemed unnatural to Americans, who continued to claim for themselves the moral superiority of the old yeoman farmer's life even while hastening to abandon it. Above all, the new immigrants seemed lacking in character. "Beaten men from beaten races," the economist Francis A. Walker called them; Professor Woodrow Wilson agreed, in 1902, that they were "men of the lowest class from the south of Italy and men of the meaner sort out of Hungary and Poland, men out of the ranks where there was neither skill nor energy nor any initiative of quick intelligence."[6] In time of stress, at any rate, it was easy to lay the blame for labor troubles, and for almost any other disturbing aspect of society, on these new immigrants' lack of moral fiber.

But in fact the economic and social circumstances of the newcomers from Southern and Eastern Europe were strikingly similar to those of the Northwestern Europeans who had come and were still coming down to 1914. The new nationalities' main reasons for emigrating were indeed materialistic, as Americans suspected, but the idea that most earlier immigrants had been pilgrims in quest of religious and political freedom was a romantic fancy of their descendants. Altogether the new arrivals of 1875–1914 were much the same sorts of people, from much the same spectrum of peasant and artisan occupations and classes—of course in terms of their own countries' economy and social order—as the generality of "old" immigrants from England, Ireland, Germany, or Scandinavia. Their discontent with the old country arose from economic maladjustments comparable to those through which Western Europe had passed a little earlier. Two of the actual differences in their economic situation were, if anything, to their advantage: no European catastrophe on the scale of the Irish famine of the 1840s occurred to drive masses of them forth on pain of starvation; and the advanced level which American industrialization had reached now made it much easier to find work than when the shiploads of poor Irish and German peasants had been cast ashore in American ports.

It was, on the other hand, to the relative disadvantage of the Italian or Polish peasant that when in the late nineteenth century a great increase in the rural population overcrowded the available land, neither the old-fashioned agriculture nor the underdeveloped industry of their countries could provide work enough. Between 1865 and 1910 the population of Italy grew about 35 percent, that of Austria (including Bohemia and part of Yugoslavia) about 40 percent, that of European Russia nearly doubled, and some of the lesser Slavic peoples multiplied even faster. Population growth in Southern and Eastern Europe during those years exceeded that of Germany in the nineteenth century, matched that of England, and indeed had been surpassed only by the Irish before the potato famine. The causes of this growth are obscure, but certainly the birthrate reached new peaks, each of them followed within thirty years by comparable spurts in emigration.

There was little land at home for the surplus children. Although serfdom had been abolished earlier in the century in the countries where it had still existed, legal freedom did not usually make the peasant a landowner. The government of united Italy broke up ecclesiastical estates in the south, but for three-fourths of the peasantry the reform amounted to exchanging one absentee landlord for another. In Poland toward the end of the nineteenth century, great estates averaging 1400 acres were calculated to take up two-fifths of the land; the usual peasant holding was smaller than 20 acres, a sixth of the peasantry had less than 4 acres, and another sixth had no land at all. In the Austro-Hungarian empire about a third of the land was occupied by estates larger than 250 acres, and half of all landholdings were smaller than 5 acres. Even in Russia, where most of the great estates were sold in the half century after emancipation of the serfs in 1861, so many peasants were seeking land that the average peasant holding shrank to about 7 acres. Wherever the peasant had the customary right to subdivide his holding among his sons, the larger number of heirs now led, as it had earlier in southwestern Germany and elsewhere, to the farming of plots too minute for a family's expected standard of living. Fourteen acres were estimated to be enough in Galicia (Austrian Poland), but four-fifths of the agricultural holdings were smaller than 5 acres. Even in Finland, where there were relatively few large estates, two-fifths of the farms were smaller than 8 acres.

The backwardness of farming practices held the peasant in an archaic vise. It was observed in Italy about 1880 that even the most equitable subdivision of a peasant holding among, say, three sons might split it not into three but rather nine parts, in order that each son might have his due portion of arable field, of meadow, and of chestnut grove; he would then have to spend half his time going from one fragment to another. Since plows and hoes and methods of mowing, threshing, and winepressing had scarcely been improved since Roman times, it was hard for the Italian peasant, a third of whose land lay fallow every year for lack of fertilizer, to wrest from it any sort of respectable livelihood. Only in regions exposed to Western European influence, notably Finland, was agricultural reform the force that uprooted peasants, expelled some of them from the countryside entirely, and sent a considerable number abroad. Elsewhere not innovation but economic stagnation recruited the emigrants.

"While the grounds of emigration are in the main economic," an American observer of the Slavic exodus remarked in 1910, "it is a mistake to suppose that poverty is its cause in the sense that the greater the poverty of a man or district, the greater the impulse to emigration."[7] To undertake as radical and expensive a project as emigration required both initiative and capital, neither of which the landless laborers at the bottom of peasant society were likely to have. Nearly two-thirds of the peasantry of southern Italy and Sicily were day laborers: they had to go daily to the marketplace to hire themselves for a pittance, paid perhaps in kind rather than cash. Such men rented a hut and a plot of ground barely large enough to feed their families, and for many of them, as for the old-time Irish cottier, it was the yearly pig that paid the rent. There had been many desperately poor Irish cottiers in the earlier waves of emigration to America, but that was only because of the peculiar coincidence of famine and wholesale eviction, a massive upheaval fortunately not repeated anywhere in Europe in the late nineteenth century.* A good many agricultural laborers did manage to get to America—perhaps as many as two-fifths of the Finnish emigrants and a majority of the Russians, Hungarians, Italians, and some others. But even these were unlikely to be the most abjectly dispirited persons, resigned to habitual degradation.

Whatever the "new" emigrants had been—peasant landowners and tenant farmers or merely laborers—like most of those who had come before they were apt to be people of at least a little respectability who would exert themselves to stave off losing it. The same American observer perceived this in 1910:

---

* Here and there minor crises still occurred. In Italy and Greece, where landowners had taken advantage of a blight in the vineyards of France and turned grain fields and olive groves over to grapes or currants, great distress occurred among the peasantry about 1890 after the French wine industry recovered. Large-scale Greek emigration to America dated from that episode.

The peasant with mortgage payments which he could not meet or with children for whom he could not provide an adequate patrimony, saw himself face to face with an intolerable decline of social status for himself or for his children; namely, reduction to the position of a propertyless day laborer. This is the sting which induces many a man among the Slovaks, the Poles, the Ruthenians, to fare over seas or to send out his son to the new land from which men come back with savings. . . . It is when the habitual balance of family budgets is disturbed that a sense of poverty incites to emigration.[8]

Laborers who already enjoyed a relatively decent wage level were similarly impelled to emigrate in order to augment it. "It is significant," a contemporary historian of the Italian emigration wrote, "that emigration should not have originated where misery was greatest. It began where there was the chance of saving enough money for passage fares and has maintained itself where wages were at a medium level."[9]

An agricultural laborer or son of a peasant proprietor who worried over an impending slippage in his family's standard of living and social status did not at first think of the remedy of crossing the ocean. Although mines and factories in Italy or Poland were still too few to offer something better, right across the border in France, Switzerland, Germany, or Austria there was plenty of work in the harvest season and on railway construction gangs. Of the tens of thousands of Italians and Poles who went abroad to work each year, many eventually settled into the working class of such places as Marseilles and Lyons, as the Irish had done in Liverpool and Glasgow. Toward the end of the nineteenth century many Italians were venturing as far as Brazil and Argentina, perhaps shuttling home again to get two seasons of summer work in the year.

Migratory workers or "birds of passage" from Italy and Poland appeared in the United States each year from the 1870s onward. They were a considerable puzzle to Americans. Since typically their purpose was to maintain their families on their bit of land in the old country, it was plain enough that they were interested in America only for the money they could take back. In the 1880s shocking cases came to light of Slavic laborers struck down by scurvy because of unwillingness to squander their wages on decent food, or uncared-for in illness or death by fellow countrymen who were equally avid to save every possible penny: "dead man no good" was said to be the laconic explanation for such callousness.[10] But in spite of the migrants' lack of commitment to any American institution but the dollar, their attitude toward the society of their old homeland and their own place in it was quite conservative. The same may be said of the French Canadians who moved back and forth between Quebec and New England all through the latter half of the nineteenth century and who seemed alternately useful and alarming. They were valuable enough as cheap labor—"the Chinese of the Eastern States"—but for a long time they remained more attached to their own overpopulated province than to American society.[11]

The great majority of the new immigrants expected from the first to transfer their families and fortunes to the New World. Sooner or later many of the birds of passage also settled into regular work and brought their families and friends over to join them. In spite of the growing distaste and even alarm of the Americans into whose mining or factory towns they crowded, their essential object still lay within the conservative pattern of most earlier immigrants: to find security for their accustomed standard of living and the social status which had been based upon it in the old country. An industrialized America seemed to present the best chance for economic security at least.

The only large group of emigrants who had no choice but to flee were the Eastern European Jews, beset by Russian persecution after 1880 as well as the usual economic pressures. They were as unusual recruits to American society in their time as the Irish famine refugees had been in theirs. Unlike the so-called *Sephardim* (Spaniards) and *Ashkenazim* (Germans) of the earlier Western European Jewish immigration to America, the Yiddish-speaking Jews differed, in far more than religion, from the peoples among whom they lived—the Slavs of Poland, Galicia, Lithuania, White Russia, and the Ukraine. In the late Middle Ages the rulers of Poland had offered their ancestors freedom from persecution if they would leave Germany and help establish commerce and manufacturing, but more recently their situation had deteriorated along with the political fortunes of Poland itself. The Jews of Western Europe in the nineteenth century were much better off. They had the same economic and political rights as other citizens, they generally spoke the language of the country, and in effect they were only Germans, Dutchmen, or Englishmen of a peculiar kind. Most Eastern European Jews, on the contrary, were limited to certain commercial and working-class occupations and still spoke their old medieval Yiddish (*jüdisch*) dialect of German crossed with Hebrew and Aramaic, which, even with more or less of an admixture of Slavic words, set them off as a separate people.

After 1835 the Russian government hemmed them into the Pale

of Settlement—Russian Poland, Lithuania, White Russia, and the Ukraine—and in the 1870s and 1880s, having stirred up the credulous peasantry against them, it rapidly forced those Jews who still lived in rural districts to crowd into urban ghettos. There they were pressed by the same sort of population growth that was undermining the economic security of the Slavic peasants. In Galicia by 1900 there was said to be one Jewish peddler, with a stock of goods worth perhaps $20, to every ten peasants. Although Jews made up about a quarter of the factory labor, discrimination and the industrial backwardness of Eastern Europe denied most of the others that modern alternative. Where modernization of commerce and industry did occur, indeed, it only displaced Jews from their archaic role as small merchants and handicraft artisans. Among those who were not yet reduced to the habitual destitution of the *schnorrer* (beggar) or *luftmensch* (who lived on air), the fear of slipping into helpless poverty would have induced a very large emigration even without the special horror of the violent *pogroms*. The imminent danger to life and limb, added to the endemic anxiety over economic insecurity, caused the unparalleled emigration to the United States between 1880 and 1914 of about a third of the 6 million Jews of Eastern Europe.

Although the pressures in the Slavic and Mediterranean countries upon peasants, artisans, laborers, or peddlers to emigrate had as little to do with the specific needs of American industry for labor as the forces which had driven most of the earlier emigrants from Northwestern Europe, as soon as the new immigrants set forth on the journey they were no longer entirely victims of chance. The wooden seats of third-class railway carriages were hard traveling, but the once tedious journey to a transatlantic port was cut short. The steamship lines, spurred by keen competition for the highly profitable emigrant traffic and by stricter governmental regulation of ocean shipping, did away with the worst abuses of former days. At Liverpool, where emigrants formerly had to fend for themselves while finding a ship, three lines now maintained cheap hotels where they could pass the few days until a liner sailed. The usual fare of about $30 was almost as low as it had ever been, and rate wars between the lines occasionally cut it in half. Instead of weathering a month or more at sea, ships crossed in some twelve days by 1880 and steadily less time thereafter. Although by first-class standards the steerage still seemed indecently overcrowded, dirty, and conducive to disorder if not gross immorality, disease and death were no longer to be expected on shipboard; as early as 1867–1872, when iron steamships generally replaced wooden sailing ships, the mortality rate among steerage passengers was suddenly halved.

At the American ports the states and after 1891 the federal government maintained immigration stations—notably Castle Garden, succeeded by Ellis Island, at New York—which kept at bay the runners and swindlers who had once preyed on the greenhorns. Instead immigrants found agents of factories, mining companies, and construction contractors looking for men ready to go to work.* As soon as a man knew where to go to find a job, he could get there by the cheap "emigrant cars" on the railroads. In a fortnight a man could leave his Sicilian or Polish village and start work in an American mill town or mining patch; it was only now, indeed, that the "bird of passage" could flit back and forth each year.

It remained true, even in an era when the ordinary immigrant could deliberately choose his destination and determine how long he would stay, that relatively few foreign workingmen could find in America the kind of work for which they had any training. The director of the census succinctly observed in 1874:

Viewed in respect of their industrial occupations, the foreigners among us may be divided as those who are where they are, because they are doing what they are doing; and those who are doing what they are doing, because they are where they are. In the former case, occupation has determined location; in the latter, location has determined occupation.[12]

Old-country occupations continued to determine New World location very precisely for skilled miners and factory operatives who were lured from the industrial districts of Western Europe by the higher wage level of America; during a depression they could just as easily return home, whether they were also unemployed there or not, since the European cost of living was disproportionately lower. Between 1875 and 1914 over 40 percent of the British emigrants to the United States, nearly 30 percent of the Germans, and some of the Belgians, Frenchmen, Scandinavians, and northern Italians were skilled workmen; their absolute numbers were much greater than in the earlier stages of American industrialization.

---

* In the 1880s it was generally supposed that "contract labor" accounted for many of the new immigrants, and in 1885 a federal law was passed against the practice. Almost the only contract laborers whom American employers literally recruited abroad, however, were a few highly skilled workmen. There was little need to go so far for ordinary hands when the latter presented themselves so freely on American soil.

In the 1880s the immigration of miners, textile operatives, stonecutters, iron and steel workers, machinists, and building tradesmen from those countries reached its peak. New, more specialized branches of established American industries were also launched with cadres of skilled foreigners: Scottish gingham weavers at Fall River; English, Scottish, and German weavers of upholstery and drapery fabrics at Philadelphia; Nottingham and Darvel lace-curtain weavers in Pennsylvania and Connecticut; and plush and velvet weavers and finishers who followed the earlier silk weavers from Macclesfield to Paterson. Substantially new industries were established, notably window and plate-glass making in Pennsylvania, Indiana, and Missouri with English, Belgian, German, and French crews, and the tinplate works (for the now ubiquitous tin cans) in western Pennsylvania and the Midwest, to which the workmen, machinery, and even the millowners themselves came from South Wales, the former center of the industry. As long as American industry needed European skills, the immigrants who brought them were acknowledged to be a kind of "aristocracy" among wage earners.

The ordinary unskilled laborer might choose to go to the Scranton coal mines or the Chicago steel mills in response to a labor agent's handbill or the advice of some friend or relative already there; otherwise the job at which he might be set to work had as little to do with his old-country experience as the early cotton mills of Lowell had had to do with crofting in Ireland. He might become wonderfully handy at shoveling coal, carrying the hod, or routine machine tending, but he could always be replaced by someone else with only a few days' experience. Like the skilled immigrants, such laborers formed an economic class and at the same time a medley of ethnic groups which varied from industry to industry and place to place.

Ethnic identity and occupational categories often coincided as they had among Negro slaves or among the Irish peasants who had swarmed into the lower ranks of New England mill hands, Pennsylvania miners, laborers and ironworkers, and canal and railroad construction gangs earlier in the century. Irishmen were still coming in at the bottom in the 1870s and 1880s and even later. Now, however, the new immigrant nationalities increasingly filled that role: French Canadians and Portuguese islanders in the New England textile mills, Slavs and Finns in the mines, steel mills, and lumber camps of the upper Midwest, Italians as outside labor at coal mines, Chinese in the railroad construction gangs of the Far West and Italians, Slavs, and Greeks in those of the East and Midwest, and Eastern European Jews as the sweated labor of the half-factory, half-tenement garment trades of New York. Although the new immigrants shared a low occupational level, in their own estimation they did not form a common social class. Even in industries like coal mining where men of different ethnic groups worked side by side and perhaps lived as neighbors, when away from work and in their own churches and social groups they identified themselves as Poles, Lithuanians, or Slovaks. Their proletarian fellow feeling was as broken as their English.

To men of the nationalities that had arrived earlier this hotch-potch of new peoples appeared to be crowding into their recently captured niche in the American economy. In the long run, the continual growth of the industrial labor force actually propelled a good many of the onetime Irish or German peasants, or their sons, upstairs into skilled and supervisory jobs or out of the manual working class altogether. By the end of the nineteenth century the Irish-Americans no longer were lumped together in any industry as a class below workingmen of British, German, or American parentage; all the "old" immigrants—however recently some of them had arrived—could join in complaining of "the foreign element which crowd our country."[13]

The new ethnic striations running through the industrial working class were no more impermeable than the old ones. Besides the continual movement of individuals or families from one place to another, the new groups were in continual upheaval, as Polish or Slovak neighborhoods in a mining town gave way to Russians or Bulgarians and as Italians and Portuguese followed French Canadians into the cotton mills. Individuals managed to rise out of the working class, though they usually climbed on the backs of their own fellow countrymen. The notorious *padroni*, or bosses of construction gangs of Italians, Greeks, or some other single nationality, like the entrepreneurs of the garment trade among the Yiddish-speaking Jews of New York, found small-scale contracting a lucrative field for their old-fashioned sort of individual enterprise.

The technologically advanced industries generated much deeper changes. The chronic labor shortage of the older America having habituated manufacturers to economize on labor, they now fully exploited the double advantage of labor-saving machinery and a plentiful supply of cheap labor to tend it. In much the same way that the first factories had undercut the old handicraft artisans, the introduction of complex semiautomatic machinery left little room for the skills that the British or German operatives had brought from the old country. Lancashire "mule" spinners and cotton weavers were made obsolete overnight in the 1890s by the ring frame and the Northrop loom. At Fall River, when some of them were "making trouble," the millowners simply "started right in and smashed up a room-full of mules with sledge hammers" and were pleased to be able to put "ring-frames run by girls" in place of the old hands and machines.[14] Coal-cutting machines and dynamite similarly displaced the old miners and their picks and black powder about the same time. In the steel mills the change began as soon as Bessemer converters were built in the late 1860s, since they were as strange to European ironworkers as to Americans; during the next thirty years other innovations steadily did away with the old manual methods of puddling iron, charging furnaces, and rolling rails. The tinplate works of the 1890s improved so quickly on the imported Welsh machinery that within the decade it was unnecessary to import any more Welsh workmen. In time most American employers concluded that the skilled immigrant, however superior he might be in "cleanliness and fineness of work," was too slow to adapt to the ongoing technological revolution.[15]

For the same reasons the skilled immigrants were growing dissatisfied with American working conditions between the 1870s and 1890s. Wages were higher than in the old country, but the pace of work was faster; American cotton weavers in the 1870s operated four looms instead of the two that were customary in Lancashire. Overly sanguine expansion of productive capacity, notably in the coal mines, meant frequent layoffs even in good times; as an English miner in Pennsylvania complained in 1885, "a miner only gets an opportunity to work a few months in the year and consequently has to work all the hours God sends—in fact, make a beast of himself or else starve."[16] Pittsburgh steelworkers, standing a twelve-hour daily "turn" in the 1890s and twenty-four hours every other weekend, were better paid than in England at the cost of being "used up" by the time they were forty.[17] When technological advances permitted employment of quickly trained Poles or Italians at lower wages as well as a general speedup, the British or German immigrant was apt to leave the industry, if he could not move up to a foreman's job, and perhaps go back to the old country.

Immigration of skilled Northwestern Europeans did not altogether cease—most of the British who came around 1910 were skilled—but the new nationalities far outnumbered them. By 1914 Southern and Eastern Europeans made up two-thirds of all the anthracite mineworkers, "old" immigrants only a tenth. Although the remaining Englishmen, Scots, Welshmen, Germans, and Irish-men in a coal mine, cotton mill, or steel plant usually held the best jobs, the thousands of their working-class countrymen who now emigrated to Australia and elsewhere probably were glad enough to avoid being submerged in the new American industrial proletariat of outlandish foreigners. As an Englishman observed at Scranton in 1913, "It goes against the grain in an English-speaking man to fetch and carry for a Slovak or a Pole."[18]

The drastic reduction of immigration by law, soon after the First World War, was a result of much the same "Anglo-Saxon" pre-judice among old-stock Americans and "old" immigrants. By any economic calculation, however, the industrial boom of the 1920s was a fairly reasonable time for the country to decide to pinch off the supply of cheap, unskilled foreign labor upon which it had de-pended since industrialization began. Technology was enormously expanding the productivity of labor. While between 1915 and 1945 the American population multiplied by 70 percent, the national product had tripled as early as 1929; after the depression it recov-ered to about the same level in 1940 and then doubled again during the Second World War. Although some older manufacturing indus-tries like textiles, foodstuffs, and even iron and steel fell behind that rate of growth, several newer ones—notably automobiles, the re-fining of gasoline to run them, and chemicals—forged far ahead. As more and more processes were mechanized, the productivity of labor in manufacturing and mining more than doubled. By 1929 an industrial labor force only one-seventh larger than that of 1915 was required; at 14 million in 1945 it had still not had to grow more than a third in the whole thirty years. Among nonindustrial workers, although for the first time the number in agriculture was absolutely declining (to less than 10 million), the number in "service" occu-pations doubled, from 6 million in 1915 to 12 million in 1945. Within another few years the bulk of the labor force would be composed of these technicians, white-collar clerks, and others who produced nothing tangible enough for an old-fashioned working-man to have considered worth a day's pay.

The industrial economy of 1915–1945 still needed, however, a steady supply of strong backs and hands that could be quickly set to work at unskilled and semiskilled jobs. While most of the nearly 20 million foreigners who had arrived during the previous genera-tion were still on hand to fill the various kinds of industrial jobs that had fallen to them, the wartime demand for labor, just when massive immigration was cut off, set new currents of migration in motion. Southern Negroes had been moving north in increasing numbers since 1890, but the first great black exodus from the cotton states, a movement of the sort that poor Irish laborers had once feared would immediately follow the abolition of slavery, set in at last during the First World War. White farmers, both northern and southern, such as had been going to the cities in all parts of the country since the Industrial Revolution began, also answered the new call for labor. But even greater numbers of Negro field hands and sharecroppers were displaced by a chronic depression in cotton growing just when northern employers found their supply of Italians, Slavs, and Greeks cut off.

Between 1914 and 1930 some 2 million Negroes moved to the cities, most of them to the largest cities of the North, in particular New York, Chicago, Philadelphia, and Detroit. Even the depression of the 1930s did not reverse the current of black migration, as it did the trickle of foreign immigration that had been coming under the restrictive law, and during the Second World War well over a million more Negroes came north and to the West Coast. Before 1914 only a little more than a tenth of the nearly 10 million black Americans had lived outside the South; by 1945 a third out of some 13 million did so. Equally useful as labor though harder to trace, as a new yet very old native-American ethnic group in midwestern cities, were the white Appalachian uplanders whose old-fashioned "hillbilly" rusticity fit them for urban society no better than the Negroes of the Deep South.

During both World Wars the federal Department of Labor recruited Mexicans for agricultural work in the Southwest; afterwards many of the contract laborers, and not a few others, managed to remain illegally in the United States at the urging of their employers. Western congressmen like Senator Patrick McCarran of Nevada, a chief defender of the principle of excluding "inferior races" from the country, managed until 1954 to keep the government from effectively sealing the Mexican border against the "wetbacks" who swam the Rio Grande in response to western farmers' demand for labor and dislike of red tape. Puerto Ricans, who had been granted American citizenship in 1917, followed the established trade routes to New York, as so many European immigrants had done but as only citizens were still free to do; their numbers increased even during the Great Depression. Until the 1960s, when economic conditions improved in Puerto Rico, they formed the one substantial and growing foreign-language group in New York, settling mainly alongside the Negroes of Harlem. By the middle of the twentieth century the American industrial labor force and urban population was still as divided along ethnic lines as in the nineteenth century, but on the lower occupational levels the Irish, Italian, Slavic, and Eastern European Jewish immigrants of the earlier day had been replaced by black and white Southerners and in certain places by Mexicans and Puerto Ricans.

The greatest ethnic group of all between 1875 and 1945, the Americans who were in no sense exotic—the thoroughly urbanized people whose fathers or grandfathers the Industrial Revolution had drawn from their farms or had engulfed in their handicraft shops —tended to maintain their advantage over immigrants of all sorts. The higher the echelon of industrial occupations, the more solidly "old stock" it was likely to be. Among the leading managers in textile manufacturing, railroading, and steel in the 1870s, nine-tenths were American-born, almost all of them in fact of native-American parentage as well. The rest were foreigners only in that they or their fathers had come from Northwestern Europe more recently than the ancestors of the out-and-out natives. Thirty years later, except for a few more sons of "old" immigrants, the same native-American hegemony prevailed in business. Of course only a few Americans, however lengthy their ancestry, managed to become company presidents and directors, but such was the proper goal for the young man whose speech, businesslike appearance, and moral fiber fitted him for a clerkship on the bottom rung of a company's ladder of white-collar positions. In spite of the unquenchably nostalgic myth of free opportunity, in any established industry by 1900 the best road to success no longer began with a mechanic's training on the factory floor, where in any case the old-time craftsman was being superseded by a polyglot crowd of foreign laborers.

More than a few old-stock Americans perversely rejected the goal of success in business. An alarming number of men—at times approaching one percent of the adult male population and a still higher proportion of the American-born of the North and West— dropped out of the working class by becoming tramps. The phenomenon of tens of thousands of idle men begging or pilfering their way around the country, a nuisance to the railroads, a terror to timorous housewives, and a target for the choicest editorial imprecations, first appeared during the depression of the 1870s. Many of them then and later were simply unemployed workingmen looking for jobs. Going on tramp from one job to another, indeed, had always been a regular phase of the training of the journeyman printer or building tradesman and a way of matching the supply of labor in his craft to local demands. Wanderlust, or "hearing the bluebird whistle," was nothing new in America.[19] But an army of fifty to one hundred thousand "professional" tramps, as they were estimated in the 1890s, was quite another matter, not easily explained away by a supposed predilection of old soldiers for bivouacking in the open, the handiness of railroad boxcars, or some sudden simultaneous deterioration in the character of so many individuals.

The typical tramp, according to a survey of police chiefs about 1890, was an unmarried man under forty, American-born or perhaps Irish or English (tramps of the same sort had also become common in Great Britain and Europe). He claimed to be skilled in some trade and would stoutly swear that he was looking for work—though not on the day he happened to be arrested for vagrancy. Conclusive evidence has vanished along with the classic tramp himself under the wave of affluence since 1940, but he may have been, among other things, a man who in an earlier day would have had at least the expectation of becoming an independent artisan or farmer and who now was unable or unwilling to adapt to wage labor, the inexorable discipline of the factory, and the company of greenhorn immigrant laborers. For all his rags and irresponsibility he, like so many others of the time, perhaps represented a conservative predilection for an older, more satisfying order of society, could that somehow have been sustained in the new industrial economy. Instead both the tramps who rejected the new order and all those workingmen who cast themselves into it—native Americans and immigrants, blacks and whites—added to the fragmentation of the working class and the general incoherence of American society.

21. THE SEARCH FOR
   ECONOMIC SECURITY

The derangements which the unregulated, uncoordinated economic revolution had brought about were far advanced by 1875— they had already contributed to several depressions and a civil war and would shortly sound the first fire bell of class warfare—but for a generation or more hardly anyone had tried to pull together an American economic *system* worthy of the name. If there is any reason beyond the symbolic to date a new era in American history from the centennial decade, it is the appearance in the 1870s, from at least three directions, of the first fumbling attempts to organize institutions that might impose some effective order on the economic base of society.

Western and southern farmers, united in the Granger movement, called on the state governments to regulate the rates charged by the railroads and grain elevators that linked their farms to their now distant markets. A variety of workingmen sought to extend a controlling hand over their own wages and hours by organizing the first halfway effective national federation, the Knights of Labor. With much more telling effect, certain combinations of businessmen strengthened their hand against the vagaries of the free, unregulated marketplace, in which, as one of them said in 1883, there was "no steadiness, no system, no fixedness for anything."[1] Intent upon their own purposes, men of those three economic classes could hardly divine that the ultimate result of their efforts would be to integrate them all into a general system less vulnerable to cyclical spasms or to periodic deadlocks between the economic interests of the sections or classes of the country. But even though the industrialist, the workingman, and the farmer each remained intent on securing his own narrow advantage, each could also see, as did the liberal *Nation* in the trough of the depression winter of 1877–1878, that "security is necessary to prosperity."[2]

Partly because only businessmen actually succeeded in wringing much profit or security from their new organizations, it was hard for anyone to conceive that they might be the entering wedge of a

general movement toward system and order. Most businessmen, for
that matter, imbued as they were with the liberal economic doctrine
that had come down to them from the previous generation, rather
misrepresented the nature of the reform they were undertaking. It
has been suggested, indeed, that the very certitude with which
they explained the level of prices, wages, and interest rates, booms
and panics, success and failure, as the ineluctable operation of
eternal natural law may have been a way of reassuring themselves
that some sort of orderly system, however abstractly theoretical,
must govern the marketplace. Other people, having so often heard
them preach that, as Joseph Medill of the *Chicago Tribune* put it
in 1883, "under the fixed laws of trade, of supply and demand, the
employer has really little more control over prices . . . than over the
winds and the weather," were understandably indignant when
certain businessmen were discovered organizing, or conspiring, to
control prices and profits themselves.[3] The Jacksonian feeling
among ordinary Americans that organized controls are somehow
unnatural, whether manipulated by businessmen or government, is
of course far from dead even today.

Whatever the broader public implications of business consolidation might eventually prove to be, the consolidators themselves
viewed it from behind the narrow blinkers of private enterprise
and self interest. The immediate problem before them usually
seemed to be overproduction: they had optimistically built oil
refineries, opened coal mines, and laid railroad trackage far beyond
the capacity of the market, especially during the long years of
depression. In their incessant straining to accumulate capital for
still further expansion, neither the businessmen nor the economists
of the time, nor even the most frugal workingmen, considered the
larger problem of underconsumption by the families of underpaid
laborers. Rather than seek ways to raise demand to absorb the
abundance that they already could supply, they set to work to cut
supply down to the meager existing demand. The possibility of an
economics of abundance through high wages occurred only to a
few cranks.* Businessmen clung to an economic theory drawn from

* Colonel J. A. Price of Scranton, in an address to "the more intelligent
of the laboring men" in 1876 "denied that there was such a thing as over
production; there are not wheels enough in America to produce more than
can be consumed. . . . The man who claims that there is over production
regards the producer as nothing but a producer, throwing out of the argument that every producer is a consumer. . . . The corporations begin to
economize at the wrong end. To recover losses they cut down wages the first
thing, seeming not to know that they are crippling their own bodies."
Scranton *Daily Times,* November 26, 1876.

a bygone age when both capital and labor had been in short supply.

Their own remedies inevitably required, however, new kinds of organization and regulation. The "trust movement," as it came to be opprobriously known, developed several organizational devices to accomplish its immediate ends. Although not without isolated precedents early in the century, the pools or gentlemen's agreements of the 1870s began the first sustained series of experiments. Certain groups of competing railroads, any one of which had the capacity to supply the cities of the East Coast with all the anthracite coal or kerosene they needed, found it more convenient to share the traffic, assuring each line a dependable daily number of cars at moderately profitable rates. The six anthracite railroads got control of the mines as well in the 1870s, limited production of hard coal, and kept the price at a level that could support remunerative freight rates. Rockefeller's Standard Oil Company contrived a succession of pooling agreements with the Lake Shore, Erie, Pennsylvania, and Baltimore & Ohio railroads in the course of the 1870s. As a large shipper of oil eastward from its refineries in Cleveland, Standard could exact rebates on its own shipments and even drawbacks on those of its competitors; by 1879 it had compounded its advantage into a monopoly of nine-tenths of the refining capacity of the country.

Pools were legally unenforceable, however, and almost impossible to maintain; as soon as they forced prices up, someone was sure to break away from the agreement, quietly lower his prices, and try to capture all the business for himself. Standard Oil adapted the conventional legal device of trusteeship into a much tighter mechanism for unified control of its associated companies in several different states. As the system was perfected in 1882, nine individual officers, as trustees, held the stock of all the companies in trust for the latter's stockholders, who received trust certificates in exchange. Seven years later New Jersey enacted a permissive charter law allowing one corporation or "holding company" to own outright the stock of other corporations; this gave Standard Oil and a great many other "trusts" a still surer means of control. By 1904 some three hundred combinations were said to control more than five thousand plants in "practically every line of productive industry in the United States"; fully 95 percent of the railway lines were in the hands of half a dozen consolidations; and most of the public utilities of the country had also been interconnected under private control.[4] At a time when the total national wealth had only recently reached $100 billion, the consolidated businesses of the country were capitalized at more than a fifth of it. The purposes of the consolidators were mixed: on one hand, efficiency, abundance, and even lower prices through the "vertical" combination of processes, from the extraction of raw materials to marketing the finished goods; but often enough, as hostile critics alleged, monopoly sheerly for the sake of holding production down and prices up.

Until well into the twentieth century the trust movement was almost the only source of effective economic regulation. It could exert only very partial control over a continually expanding economy, in which new competitors kept appearing in old industries like oil and steel, and whole new ones such as electricity and automobiles sprang up almost overnight. What was sometimes called the "business community," split as it actually was between small and large concerns, "Main Street" and "Wall Street," the regional interests of Northeast, South, Midwest, and Far West and the conflicting claims of railroads and shippers, importers and tariff-protected manufacturers, bankers and borrowers, never was in much danger of consolidation into any single great trust, not even the "money trust" of metropolitan bankers that excited public alarm in the first decade of the twentieth century. But since businessmen of one kind or another were leading the way toward a system of economic regulation, they were not wholly disingenuous in casting themselves in the role of trustees disposing wisely and firmly for the general weal.

The earliest organized challenge to the hegemony of the businessman came from his own workingmen. Although trade unions of the modern sort, demanding a voice in setting wages and hours rather than abolition of wage labor altogether or a return to the good old days of the independent master artisan, had appeared as early as the 1850s and 1860s, almost all of them had been short lived. The labor movement began to be effective only after the failure, in the 1880s, of the Knights of Labor, the first general federation of unions, either to supplant the wage system with cooperative workshops or to secure better terms within it. The leadership and many of the rank and file of the craft unions of the American Federation of Labor, which rose as the Knights fell, were skilled European immigrants of the sort who held the better jobs and yet had always thought of themselves as members of a working class of wage earners.

"Business unionists," as they came to be called, did not seek entire control of working conditions, nor was their intervention unwelcome to all employers. In a few old-fashioned skilled trades like iron molding and hatmaking in the last third of the century, joint agreements between the manufacturers' associations and the unions proved satisfactory to both sides in maintaining prices and wages alike. For a few years around 1870 the anthracite mine operators and mine workers managed to cooperate in limiting production for their mutual benefit, though as soon as the railroad pool got control of the industry it let the union destroy itself in the long strike of 1875. As late as 1900 a few big businessmen still saw an advantage in admitting labor to a share in an organized system. A number of industrialists joined with certain labor leaders in a National Civic Federation to promote such cooperation. Since they included the banker of bankers, J. Pierpont Morgan, who was the dominant power over the anthracite railroads, the hard-coal industry suddenly and surprisingly was induced to accept arbitration of the United Mine Workers' strike of 1902 and establishment of a joint conciliation board for the future.

Most employers felt only consternation at this precedent for dividing control of their stockholders' property with organized labor. For some time their way of thinking had been moving away from any sort of shared control. In 1903 the National Association of Manufacturers launched a campaign for the open or nonunion shop, ostensibly to protect the individual laborer's "right to work" unmolested by union organizers and strike agitators. By that time the process of replacing skilled "old" immigrants with machinery and inexperienced "new" immigrant laborers had gone far enough for many industries to fall into line with the NAM. In 1892 the Carnegie Steel Company, the nucleus of the forthcoming "steel trust" of 1901, had led the way by locking out and crushing the old-line union of puddlers, rollers, and other obsolescent craftsmen. Rapidly losing their own niche in industry, by 1910 the craft unions of the AFL, few of which were either able or willing to bring the unskilled newcomers into all-inclusive "industrial" organizations, had clearly failed to enlist nine-tenths of the wage earners of the country. The NAM claimed credit for thus endowing the self-reliant workingman with "freedom of contract"—nothing less, it asserted, was "consistent with American manhood"—and saw no inconsistency in summing up the cause of its own success "in one word—Organization."[5]

Employers who insisted upon undivided control of their sectors of the industrial economy did not, however, use it simply to grind the face of labor. Partly to allay public scepticism of their role as self-appointed trustees for the general welfare and the liberty of the individual, and partly to keep their own employees from organizing as a hostile interest, corporate business after 1897 developed a program which has been aptly described as "welfare capitalism." As represented by the employer, most of the new arrangements were designed to demonstrate that the identity of interest between capital and labor had diminished not a whit since the days when master and journeyman toiled side by side in the workshop. But one could doubt whether it was old-fashioned "loyalty" or simply dependence which the employer most sought to inculcate. The need for company hospitals, factory first-aid rooms, and safeguards against hazardous machinery was clear enough. The old-age pension plans, first begun by certain railroads in the 1870s but not adopted by many manufacturing industries until after 1910, had the practical effect, since pensions were paid only to employees of fifteen, twenty-five, or even thirty years' service, of tying them to the company and preventing an uneconomical rate of labor turnover. In any case, as late as 1932 only 14 percent of the retired wage earners of the country, still mainly railroaders, were eligible for pensions.

Again, profit-sharing plans for wage earners, known as early as the 1880s but not widely adopted until the 1920s, were supposed to give capital and labor a common incentive. Workingmen tended, however, to regard their share in the company's profits simply as wages always owed to them but previously unpaid. Even the movement of efficiency engineers for "scientific management" would benefit the individual worker, it was argued, since his pay would rise as he proved his competence at tasks calculated by the stopwatch instead of "the whim of a foreman."[6] To the employee the standard working routines and production quotas smacked of a speedup more than of efficient use of "time and motion." Mechanisms for "industrial democracy" were another enthusiasm of employers, especially in the 1920s, purporting to give employees a voice in adjusting working conditions and other matters of proper concern to them. In the eyes of organized labor, however, these "shop committees," "works councils," and "employee representation plans" were nothing but company unions, mere devices for keeping workingmen subservient to the boss in every important respect. Although the intention of the employer was benevolent enough from his viewpoint, the practical effect was to impose his conception of system and order upon his employees.

As long as Americans generally regarded the leading industrialists and bankers as uncommonly successful practitioners of the universal economic ethic of hard work and frugality, they assumed an identity of interest between big business and the public welfare. By the late 1870s, however, just when the trend toward business consolidation was setting in, the common man was beginning to suspect that the enormous success of a figure like "Commodore" Cornelius Vanderbilt had stemmed less from the practice of proper business principles than from adroit manipulation of highly favorable circumstances, foremost among which was, as one of his obituarists put it, "the old democratic notion that everybody should be allowed to do anything short of direct robbery or murder without let or hindrance from the Government."[7] Nor did it seem entirely acceptable to allow the captains of business to devise and operate their own regulatory system for the country. However necessary or inevitable the consolidation of industrial units into larger and larger "trusts" might be, the resulting concentrations of private power called to mind the state-established monopolies that had been put down, presumably for the sake of the liberty of the common man, earlier in the century. Now it might be necessary to reawaken the latent public power of government against these newfangled, self-established monopolists. Whether the proper goal of governmental interference should be simply to set the common man literally free once again, or instead to merge the trusts into a broader, more truly public system of organized control, remained in doubt well into the twentieth century.

The first concerted appeal for public intervention arose, late in the nineteenth century, from those quintessential common men the farmers, mainly in the Midwest and South. In an era of depression they had second thoughts about free enterprise, in their state of all too "perfect" competition—and perfect helplessness—as individuals supplying a world market. Although they too could organize, as they did in the Granges of the 1870s and the Alliances of the 1880s, they were even less able than the labor unions to bring pressure directly to bear on their oppressors, as they considered the railroads to be. But since a railroad, however private its management, was a kind of public highway—and indeed most of those built between the 1830s and the 1870s had had some sort of public subsidy—it seemed no great breach of the principle of economic liberty for public authority to regulate their freight rates. Not all the state railroad commissions of the 1870s were set up in response to the farm vote, but those in the farming states of the Midwest and South were the most fully empowered to fix legal rates, prohibit discriminatory practices, and punish violators. But most railroad traffic was an interstate matter for federal regulation, as the Supreme Court ruled in 1886. The next year Congress created the

Interstate Commerce Commission, lacking effective power but setting a precedent at least for a national system of ongoing economic regulation.

The Farmers' Alliances and the mainly agrarian People's party of the 1890s demanded a great deal more: outright federal ownership of railroads and telegraph and telephone lines, federal "subtreasuries" to make low-interest loans to farmers on the security of their stored surplus crops, an income tax, and other measures designed to right the balance between the "capitalists" and the "people." The sudden return of farm prosperity in 1897 put the Populist program in abeyance for thirty years as farmers sought to ensure their future by organizing their own cooperative marketing associations. In the 1920s a new cycle of agricultural depression led them once more to call for public regulation.

Public opinion—that is, the conventional opinion of the middle-class majority, the now largely urban heirs of the Jacksonian common man—lagged as usual behind the new developments. It impartially deprecated almost every form of organized economic control: the "anarchism" of the labor movement, the "agrarianism" or communism of the farmers' new political platforms, the new "feudalism" of the barons of consolidated big business. Only in order to suppress these threats would respectable middle-class people accept the need to revive the long disused power of government. Regulation of railroads by the Interstate Commerce Commission, the first federal board of its kind, could therefore be cautiously begun in 1887. More typical of that time, the overly general Sherman Anti-Trust Act of 1890 simply forbade any and all "combinations in restraint of trade." The army was called out to break the great Pullman strike on the railroads in 1894. Nothing more seemed to be required in 1896 than to elect the good gold-standard Republican William McKinley and so quash the unsound notions of foreign radicals and the obstreperous western "sons of the wild jackass."

And yet the most unquestioning, unreflective believer in the egalitarian dogma of his father's day had to admit that "freedom of opportunity" was not after all leading triumphantly to equality of material condition or to social classlessness but instead to greater extremes of wealth and poverty than American society had ever known. More than half the national income, it was estimated in the 1890s, was going to an eighth of the families of the nation; the richest hundredth, indeed, skimmed off a full quarter, considerably more than what was left for the whole lower half of the population.

Half the accumulated wealth of the country was estimated to be in the hands of the leading 125,000 families, who were calculated to be worth, on an average, more than a quarter-million dollars apiece. Altogether the upper eighth owned nearly seven-eighths of the wealth, leaving only one-eighth to all those "middle-class" (averaging $1500) and "poorer" ($150) families who together constituted fully seven-eighths of the people. By either yardstick, income or wealth, nearly half the population could be said at best to be living in virtual poverty.[8] The *New York Tribune*, seeking to reassure the public that things were not in fact a great deal worse, demonstrated in 1892 that there were *only* four thousand American millionaires, a third of them based on industry, another third on commerce, railroads, and banking, and an eighth on the classic enterprise of real-estate speculation—though hardly any on cultivating the soil. But such figures, even from a traditionally Republican supporter of free enterprise like the *Tribune*, were alarming to most people.

Although the general fear of agrarian and working-class rebellion subsided after the return of general prosperity in 1897, the redoubled pace of business consolidation continued to alarm the middle-class half of the American people. After 1901, when the "progressive" Republican Theodore Roosevelt succeeded to the presidency, Americans rapidly came to agree that government would have to expand its regulatory functions. The precedents being so far beyond recollection as to seem virtually nonexistent, this essentially conservative idea seemed as radical an innovation as the billion-dollar monopolies at which it was principally aimed. Andrew Jackson's old argument with the Second Bank of the United States had to be rehearsed all over again: should the trusts be regulated by a continuing public agency, or would it not be safer simply to annihilate them once and for all?

The businessmen who had been leading the consolidation movement since the 1870s were not blind to the possible advantages of governmental interference with what they were used to thinking of as their absolute right to control company property on behalf of the stockholders. A sympathetic government might well help to systematize and stabilize the economy in ways quite acceptable to them, and even if politicians had as little sense of business principles as businessmen suspected, a diverting show of public authority might outmaneuver the rising challenge of outright socialism. Public opinion clearly had to be cultivated. To go on ignoring vulgar curiosity about the "private" business of a gigantic corporation, as had been Rockefeller's practice at Standard Oil, now seemed a source of dangerous misunderstanding; to damn the public after the fashion of William Vanderbilt could be self-destructive. The public relations consultant now set up shop to relieve businessmen of the dangers of a bad press. The railroads were persuaded that an accurate account of an accident was usually less shocking to the public than gory newspaper rumors. By no longer sedulously concealing even his benefactions—which in fact had always been munificent—John D. Rockefeller outlived the public impression of the 1890s that Standard Oil was an all-devouring octopus. The private pension plans and other schemes for the welfare of employees likewise contained a prudent element of good public relations. Perhaps the great middle class could be systematically controlled, though less directly than labor, by judiciously playing on their good will as well as their fears and biases.

Democratic government might contribute more directly to the efforts of businessmen to control the economy. If the fulminations of progressive politicians could be diverted against Roosevelt's somewhat shadowy "malefactors of great wealth" and away from the substantial businessmen upon whom the progress of the nation depended, governmental regulation might be quite useful. The small businessman welcomed a degree of trust-busting against the more powerful of his competitors; shippers of freight, especially those too small to extort rebates for themselves, approved of governmental regulation of railroad rates; the metropolitan banker and the "country" or western banker were each attracted by proposals to reestablish a central bank, as long as it would control the other kind of bank more than his own. On the other hand, businessmen had no use for governmental competition with private business; the postal savings banks (1910) and the parcel post system (1912) were anathema to bankers and express companies. Nor could most businessmen see any validity to such reforms as wage and hour laws that were designed to aid economic classes other than their own.

A judicious measure of governmental regulation of one's own business might be tolerable if it promised to enhance the businessman's own efforts at control. The railroads generally accepted the Interstate Commerce Commission and the legislation of 1903, 1906, and 1910 which enlarged its authority over freight rates; if their independence was somewhat circumscribed, the legal rate schedules freed them from importunate demands of large shippers for discriminatory rebates, drawbacks, and other costly favors. For all the conservationist rhetoric against waste of the country's natural resources by the lumbering, mining, and other great "interests," it was the latter who favored public reservation of mineral and timber lands and administration of water supplies for electric power or irrigation; the common man who would have liked to become a mine operator or timber baron saw little opportunity for himself unless the government continued to permit free access to all sorts of land. Bankers, after eighty years of jerking along without a central bank, generally recognized the need for the Federal Reserve Act of 1913, which struck a balance between unified control and the local interests of each of the twelve districts into which it divided the country. The Clayton Anti-Trust Act of 1913 contributed to business stability by defining, as the Sherman Act of 1890 had not done, exactly what kinds of unfair competition would be put down by government, and the Federal Trade Commission, launched in 1914 with a business-minded membership, set about reinforcing, in the broader context of the public interest, the self-regulation toward which the trusts had been working for forty years.

These progressive reforms were less basic than they were popularly supposed to be. Businessmen still tended to regard government not as a structure overarching all particular interests but as merely one more great combination with which bargains might be struck—and one which, since unfortunately it consisted of political adventurers rather than practical businessmen, sometimes seemed to deserve prosecution under its own antitrust acts. In a sense they were right; big business, government, and for that matter the common man were more alike than different in their basic commitment to economic values. Neither progressive government nor the middle-class public opinion which supported it fundamentally disputed the values of production and acquisition to which business was dedicated. Public economic regulation might now be required as well as public subsidy, but few Americans doubted that all government needed to do was to tune up the productive mechanism and work out a set of equitable arrangements for distribution of the goods it poured out.

Although things were as firmly in the saddle as ever, progressivism seemed to be a profoundly moral movement. When the middle-class descendant of the Jacksonian common man took up the progressive cry against the trusts, he considered his goal to be nothing less than the establishment, as the Kansas editor William Allen White put it, of "a just and righteous relation between men."[9] The just society, ever since Jacksonian egalitarianism had become the kernel of the national democratic ethos, had been defined as that which left the individual most free, and the freedom the individual most prized was the economic liberty to choose among and pursue his opportunities for self-advancement. By the early twentieth century big business appeared to be reducing opportunity for "the man on the make," as Woodrow Wilson aptly renamed the common man. At least until 1912, the year of Wilson's election to the presidency, middle-class progressives were more taken with the prospect of righteously "busting" the trusts into small, competing fragments than with mere regulation of a few ever-bigger businesses.

On every hand there were signs, not always recognized as such, that economic opportunity was far from equal for great numbers of people. Some practical inequalities still seemed easy to explain away. After the failure of southern Reconstruction in the 1870s, white Americans almost unanimously concluded that the Negroes, having been presented with constitutional and legal equality, had proven themselves as a race forever incompetent to make proper use of it. Perhaps the failure of many of the "new" immigrants from Southern and Eastern Europe to lift themselves quickly out of penury and squalor was also due to some insurmountable inferiority, stemming either from the economic, cultural, and political backwardness of their feudal homelands, which their children perhaps could overcome in time, or, less hopefully, from certain innate and ineradicable physical and mental defects of their race. There were shiftless people everywhere—the anarchic army of tramps, the shanty dwellers on the wrong side of the tracks, degenerate folk like the Jukes family, made a byword by anthropologists for their supposedly inbred criminality, and even, in spite of the recent discovery of their endemic hookworm and anemia, the classic poor white trash of the rural South—but it was easy to blame their condition on a simple lack of the gumption to answer opportunity when it knocked on their doors.

It was harder for respectable middle-class people to explain why even the most sedulous application of the economic ethic of "forecast, industry, thrift, and honesty" no longer ensured independence and security.[10] Most of them had suffered no absolute decline in standard of living, status among their neighbors, or self-esteem. In a practical way they were no doubt aware of the fact, which historians and sociologists have since reduced to statistics, that their sons enjoyed an enormous advantage over immigrant, working class, and farm boys in the race for business success. But the shopkeeper or small merchant or manufacturer also felt a diminution in his status relative to that of the "big boys" of industry and finance.

Wall Street called the tune to which the small entrepreneur danced, the trusts effectively controlled the new man's entry into established industries and his chance of success there, and even the most promising career for his son was likely now to begin on the bottom rung of some corporation's hierarchy of what a later generation would call "organization men."

Professional men saw still less promise for their own independence and prestige. For the lawyer the most glittering reputation was no longer to be made in independent practice, with its ideal of professional responsibility and perhaps an accompanying influence in public affairs, but instead as a member of a metropolitan law firm counseling one or another of the great corporations, if not, indeed, as a mere staff employee of one of the latter. Perhaps those who succeeded as corporation lawyers felt most acutely of all that their profession had become a business with no loftier ethic than the cash nexus. Clergymen of middle- and upper-class churches, such as had been trying for the greater part of the nineteenth century to find some viable accommodation between religion and the material values of their parishioners, began to feel that the overwhelming victory of big business amounted to their own defeat. Other professional men who were demonstrably on the rise could be just as anxious about their status as those who felt themselves slipping. College professors, perhaps because they were beginning to claim their "academic freedom" from dictation by businessmen-trustees, also began to change from habitual defenders of the status quo to almost automatic critics of a culture dominated by big business.

Resentment against the near billionaires of corporate finance and industry was sharpest among some of the heirs and successors to the preindustrial gentry of merchants and landowners, men whose wealth now would be accounted only moderate. While old elites had always displayed a decent aloofness toward the newly rich, ever since the 1830s the magnitude and the rawness of new money had particularly affronted the authentic gentlemen of Boston, New York, or Philadelphia, and of course the plantation South, the more so as any attempt of theirs to remain exclusive was overborne or simply ignored by those who followed the new, purely pecuniary standard. Thus the ornate new Metropolitan Opera House, with its Diamond Horseshoe tier of boxes, was intended in 1883 to eclipse the hitherto fashionable New York Academy of Music, and the extravagant banquets, balls, and palatial seaside "cottages" of the New York "Four Hundred" consigned to near oblivion those scions of older lineage who disdained to marry or be absorbed into this crass new "Society." Old-fashioned gentlemen who were still ready to undertake the burden of civic leadership found that the egalitarian ethic, having set private entrepreneurs free to become plutocrats if they could, had long since excluded confessed "aristocrats" like themselves from their onetime role as custodians of the public welfare. An occasional figure like Charles Francis Adams or Hamilton Fish ornamented the embassy or cabinet to which he was appointed, but few of their sort could win election to responsible office. Now all at once such men found progressive allies and even willing followers among the same middle class of common men who had so recently dethroned them.

"Progressivism, in short," Richard Hofstadter concludes, "was to a very considerable extent led by men who suffered from the events of their time not through a shrinkage in their means but through the changed pattern in the distribution of deference and power."[11] Stirrings of the same sort have been detected among other reformers: the abolitionists of the 1830s; the Liberal Republicans or "mugwumps" who attempted to displace President Grant in 1872 and, through reform of the federal civil service in the 1880s, to break up the collusion between party bosses and big business. Progressive rhetoric was "democratic"—the cure for the ills of democracy was said to be more democracy—and many more people than the middle and old upper classes responded to it. Still speaking in the egalitarian phrases which came readily to the lips of all practical politicians, the progressives promised, to farmers and workingmen as well as to the main body of their middle-class followers in both the Republican and Democratic parties, that the individual's economic opportunity would be unobstructed by powerful monopolies. The neo-Jacksonian rhetoric obscured the fact that many of the leaders of the movement represented a new version of the old pre-Jacksonian elite. Although it was in the name of the people that they sought to control the overmighty plutocracy, their new measures amounted to restoration of the sort of regulatory commonwealth in which gentry like themselves had ruled before the industrial era.

The resemblance of progressive government to a refurbished mercantilist state was heightened by the renascence, therefore, of a somewhat covert but authentic political elite. Those who strove for places in this new governing class were themselves too steeped in egalitarianism, or perhaps too prudent, to cast themselves in the aristocratic role undisguised, and some of them would have been less than convincing successors to Winthrop or Washington. Businessmen having been in the vanguard of the movement toward system and control since the 1870s, some of them helped extend it from business into government. George Perkins of United States Steel and the House of Morgan organized Roosevelt's Progressive party candidacy of 1912; more typically, a number of progressive city governments were led by men like Tom Johnson, the Cleveland streetcar "traction" magnate and mayor. But in general the business leader was too narrowly concerned with profit and loss, even as a gauge of the general welfare of society, to act the disinterested aristocrat. Johnson appeared in public office, indeed, as a reformed or maverick businessman, and Perkins's frankly unregenerate character as a trust magnate made him seem a strange bedfellow in the Bull Moose party.

Most people, not appreciating the delicate gradations within "big business" and "Society," failed to distinguish between the gentleman of antique pedigree and the merely plutocratic businessman. The former was nevertheless the more credible of the two as a progressive leader. To be sure, America was not yet wholly ready to accord the "patrician reformer," as he has since been characterized, an indefeasible claim to leadership.[12] Although Theodore Roosevelt's ancestry in the landed merchant-gentry of old New York was no secret to the public, his ambition to belong to the actual ruling class of the country as well was considerably enhanced by the guises of western cattleman, bear slayer, boxer, and Rough Rider which he delighted to affect. His "Square Deal" brand of progressivism called to mind not Hudson Valley patroonships but the most egalitarian, hyperindividualistic of all frontier images. Like other patrician reformers, Roosevelt also disguised his claim to the aristocrat's ancient political function by the conventional assertion that he was not a "politician"—not, that is, one of those self-aggrandizing creatures who served a degraded party machine rather than the public weal—and that his reforms far transcended partisan politics. Roosevelt had actually had sense enough to begin his career, in the highly partisan 1880s, on a solid base of party regularity, but he was the more effective a politician, in the broader, old-fashioned sense of the word, for seeming not to be a professional politician at all.

Later in the twentieth century, as Americans grew accustomed to authentic gentlemen in politics and government—with such names as Taft, Stimson, Harriman, Clark, Rockefeller, Stevenson, Scranton, or Kennedy—the egalitarian and apolitical disguises could be dropped. Franklin Roosevelt, though misunderstood by the businessmen who called him a "traitor to his class" (presumably their own), enjoyed receiving the torchlit homage of his neighbors on his victorious election nights, as the "Squire of Hyde Park," the village near which his familial estate lay but which he by no means owned as an archetypical squire should. There was no inconsistency, furthermore, from either his own viewpoint or the perspective of past aristocracies, in his open alliances with the machine bosses, those *condottieri* whose bands of retainers made up the local Democratic organizations of the rural South and the urban North. Thirty years earlier, however, the elitist nature of many of the progressive leaders had been too novel to be safely revealed in either of those ways.

A third element in the new political elite, one which first appeared in the progressive years, was altogether too new to suggest even the remotest precedents. Scientific and technical experts—political scientists and sociologists as well as natural scientists and engineers—commanded a thoroughly modern sort of respect from the common man. If a proposed reform could be labeled scientific, no matter how untried or even near quackery it might be, it was assumed that the democratic majority would rationally accept it. The "scientific" program of engineers like Frederick W. Taylor for rationalizing the management of labor, of professional foresters and mining engineers for conservation of natural resources, of race-minded anthropologists for restriction of immigration, of social workers for systematic philanthropy, of political scientists for efficient government, of the pragmatic philosopher John Dewey for "progressive" education, and of other self-professed experts for compulsory "eugenic" sterilization of the unfit, for prohibition of alcohol, and for purifying politics itself—whatever the scientist proposed was assumed also to be the democratic program, that is, the most individualistic, libertarian, egalitarian, and altogether progressive arrangement.

According to this popular rhetoric, the scientist or engineer who sought to apply the abstract standards of his profession—with uncompromising rigor for all their newness—was diametrically opposed to the self-aggrandizing trust magnate. The economist Thorstein Veblen best expressed the distinction that most progressives drew: the captain of industry—or "Captain of Solvency"—was interested only in pecuniary profit; the engineer, in efficient workmanship and production for use.[13] But if the scientist or engineer subscribed to a higher ethic than the businessman, it was no more than a higher materialism, a more rational—if not necessarily more disinterested—version of the ingrained popular idea that all important values of life would flow straightway from a perfected system of production and distribution of goods. The manipulator of trusts, after all, regarded business consolidation as a way toward more efficient organization of his industry and a more rational economy. Some of the professional experts of the time were more like such "practical" businessmen than others, but even social workers, sociologists, and political scientists, who had to deal with actual men and women rather than that machine-tending, resource-using abstraction "economic man," put their faith in an equitable distribution of material wealth as the moral basis for rebuilding society.

This basic materialism, tinctured with a trace of the more expansively social and spiritual values of the remote past, did fire a kind of moral idealism among middle-class progressives. Having called government in to safeguard their own individual economic liberty against domination by the trusts, they began to recognize that poor working people, if they were truly so depressed as to lack economic opportunity, might also expect more from the state than an abstract "right to work" at whatever was offered them. Down to 1917 only a beginning was made toward the welfare state. Most Americans were still reluctant to admit that not all able-bodied men could fend for themselves unaided; it was feared, indeed, that preferential "class legislation" would only demoralize the beneficiaries into settled indigence and dependence. Even when the middle-class majority of the public took up progressive reform, labor leaders knew the depth of their prejudices too well to rely much on public regulation to assist their members; to think of workingmen collectively, as the unions did, still seemed unmanly and demeaning to most other Americans. It was becoming clear, however, that for the growing majority of ordinary industrial laborers neither individual nor collective efforts at self-improvement were adequate; something had to be done for them.

The first steps were halting enough. By 1917 the federal government and forty states required that compensation be paid the injured workman or his survivors. Although doing away with the impractical common-law requirement that the victim prove that neither he nor any "fellow servant" was to blame and that in accepting the job he had not "assumed" the risk of such accidents, the new system had practical limitations of its own. The prescribed payment hardly covered most cases, yet it absolved the employer of further claims, and about a third of all industrial employees still were not covered at all. For two peculiarly vulnerable kinds of workingmen, the merchant seamen and the railwaymen, federal acts in 1915 and 1916, at the end of the progressive period, forced some useful improvement in the terms of labor. As for state regulation of hours and working conditions, even the most rudimentary law was likely to provoke the Supreme Court, with its majority of mid-nineteenth-century-minded justices, to rule it unconstitutional for tampering with the "freedom of contract" of (as in the Lochner case of 1905) some overworked baker and his liberty-loving employer.

It was somewhat easier for the public conscience to accept state protection of women and children than of men. Toward the end of the nineteenth century more than half the states prohibited labor in mines and factories by children—usually defined as under twelve years of age—or a working day of more than ten hours for older ones, but even those minimal regulations were feebly enforced and easily evaded by parents who did not make enough to live without their children's wages. By 1914 nine states had enacted the proposal of reformers to raise the minimum age to a certified fourteen in manufacturing and sixteen in mining, to reduce the daily hours of older youths to eight, and to prohibit any night work. The act of Congress of 1916 on the subject was ruled unconstitutional by the Supreme Court two years later, however, as not involving a federal matter.

Between 1896 and 1917 more than half the states also limited the hours of women workers. Although infringement of the individual liberty of women was only slightly more tolerable to the Court than the statutes affecting men, it led to the novel sight of the justices' pondering sociological evidence, first introduced in a brief by Louis Brandeis in 1908, in addition to the usual abstract constitutional doctrine and conventional economic theory. It had become necessary even for gentlemen steeped in the economic individualism of their youth to listen to higher considerations than those of cheap production of goods, remunerative use of available labor and capital, or even the freedom of any man, woman, or child to make a little money.

The brief but intense American experience of war in 1917–1918 suddenly galvanized the country's hesitant advance toward a systematic economy under public authority. The demand of wartime mobilization for economic controls—to set priorities for industrial production, allocate and fix the price of staple crops, coal, and other raw materials, standardize products, supervise collective bargaining between capital and labor, and temporarily nationalize the railway, telephone, and telegraph systems, as well as to enforce conscription and impose a graduated income tax—went far beyond the progressive reforms. The hastily contrived complex of regulatory boards and administrations, operating amid the feverish patriotism of the time and a good deal of volunteer suppression of suspected dissidents, amplified to a deafening crescendo the movement of progressivism against economic disorder.* The wartime system so far exceeded anything that the country was ready to support in peacetime that in the haste to dismantle it after 1918 government pulled back as much as it could into a preprogressive "normalcy."

The normality of the last quarter of the nineteenth century, although not remembered for the fact in the 1920s, had included a certain amount of groping after devices for economic control, and the "New Economic Era" of old-fashioned business principles which was supposed to have dawned in 1921, after the twenty-year interval of antitrust agitation, resumed the forward movement toward business consolidation. By the end of the decade the two hundred largest companies were calculated to control nearly half the corporate wealth of the country, nearly two-fifths of the business wealth, and a fifth of the entire national wealth. If the current rate of expansion were to continue, within another twenty years they would have more than half the national wealth. "Welfare capitalism" for labor was also extended, notably into plans for distribution of company stock among employees and for more elaborate arrangements for "industrial democracy" (or company unions); partly as a result the trade union movement could make no headway in spite of the generally brisk demand for labor.

Although businessmen resisted even the feeblest suggestions for further governmental regulation—a proposed constitutional amendment to empower the federal government to regulate child labor in industry was condemned as socialistic "nationalization" of children and rejected by thirty-five state legislatures—they were content to see the existing regulatory agencies continue, suitably adapted to the New Era. The Federal Trade Commission acted upon less than a tenth of the complaints of unfair competition presented to it, few of which had anything to do with the causes of "trust" consolidation, and the courts reversed half the orders that the com-

---

* Those intellectual reformers who flung themselves into the war effort were not as false to the nature of progressivism as alleged by critics who took the libertarian rhetoric of the previous two decades at face value.

mission did issue. The Department of Commerce, under the self-styled "rugged individualist" Herbert Hoover, actively fostered voluntary cooperation by trade associations in industries not already pulled together by holding companies. Although the farmers, caught once again in a cycle of overproduction and ruinous prices, had their own organized political force in the congressional Farm Bloc, its bills for federal dumping of surplus crops abroad smacked of preferential "class legislation" and twice ended in a presidential veto.

The great majority of Americans, still middle class in fact or in aspiration, put the doubts of the progressive generation behind them as they looked to corporate enterprise for the thoroughly up-to-date opportunities that it seemed to offer the individual. Investment in corporate stock was never as widespread as businessmen liked people to think, and even in companies where it was, the more diffuse or "democratic" the ownership pattern the easier it was for an organized minority of large stockholders to control the management. But the ordinary man was able to persuade himself that at last he had a way to become an independent proprietor of sorts, a stock dividend collector and bond-coupon clipper if no longer a free farmer or business entrepreneur. At all events the business system in which so many felt they had a share was providing full employment, raising wages, reducing hours, adding to its own system of welfare, extending consumer credit through the installment plan, improving the general standard of living, and presumably leading to the long-desired equality of opportunity for everyone—even the industrial workingman—to become middle class. The dream of the Jacksonian common man, it seemed, was about to be realized, substantially as he had expected, through free industrial enterprise.

The suspicion among surviving progressives that the process was not working in so happy a direction became a ghastly certainty when the New Era of business hegemony evaporated in the Great Depression of 1929–1938. Mass unemployment, low wages, and absolute loss of control over working conditions were less than surprising to workingmen, who had endured them all during the recurrent depressions of the past century; the farmers, for their part, had fallen out of the New Era almost before it began. But for the middle-class majority of small business and professional men, white-collar clerks, salesmen, and salaried office workers, for careful savers caught by a tidal wave of bank failures, for people who had ventured into debt to acquire houses and goods, and even for many property owners—especially, perhaps, the recently hopeful investors in now-depreciated or worthless corporate stock—the depression completed the revolution which the progressive era had begun in the American attitude toward public authority and economic order.

The libertarian, ruggedly individualistic rhetoric which President Hoover doggedly expounded for three years after 1929—while he was gingerly intruding the camel's nose of government under the free-enterprise tent—only quickened the impatience of people of all kinds to have done with nineteenth-century scruples and to revive the wartime powers of government for the duration of this new national emergency. And this Franklin Roosevelt proposed to do in the "hundred days" of hasty legislation that set up the New Deal in 1933. To be sure, the reaction of not a few reputable middle-class people—certainly of many businessmen annoyed at the disrepute into which business principles had fallen—was to blame Roosevelt's complex of bureaucratic meddlers, machine politicians, and unbusinesslike academics for clogging the "natural" processes of economic recovery. Although at least a few of the disillusioned adopted one of the literal absolutisms, fascist or communist, that they often accused the New Deal of promoting, most Americans waited to see whether a moderate degree of public intervention might not yet rescue capitalism and substantially reopen economic opportunity to all.

The ordinary individual was beginning to get a new sense of the kind of opportunity or economic liberty that might be practically open to him in a system dominated by great corporate structures, including government as well as big business and organized labor. During the depression the old concept of "opportunity" rapidly merged into the newly popular idea of "security." The change in usage was perhaps mainly verbal, a tacit scaling-down of the exaggerated expectations of the common man of the nineteenth century or the 1920s to something like what all along had been his real prospects. Most men, native Americans or immigrants, had had the practical opportunity to get either land or a job, to improve a little on the material condition and social status of their farmer or peasant fathers, to set aside a competence, and to live out a secure old age as master of their own house. The inspiring instances of enormous success, especially in new businesses, were real enough, but the more typical businessman considered himself successful if he managed to stave off bankruptcy during slumps and make a modest fortune during boom times. Although "conservative" opponents of the New Deal damned such fainthearted ambition as unmanly and un-American, after the drastic experiences of the 1930s most people understood well enough that, as an automobile worker put it, "if you're secure, then you're getting ahead."[14]

The New Deal economic program was shot through with the same equivocality, particularly at the outset. In a campaign speech in 1932 Roosevelt dwelt, like a businessman of the 1880s in one of his more anxious moments, upon the need to retrench, consolidate, and administer an industrial system "overbuilt" far beyond the demand for its products, and upon the problems of an economy too constricted any longer to offer opportunity for the "independent business man" or even the security of a farm for a family's subsistence. On the other hand, Roosevelt proposed to increase consumption of goods by enlarging the purchasing power of the people; if effected in good egalitarian fashion by "an economic declaration of rights, an economic constitutional order," such a program could reprime the pump of unlimited economic growth.[15]

Unfortunately the discouraging inability of the New Deal in the next five years to push "recovery" back up to even the economic level of 1929 seemed to confirm the forebodings of stagnation. The first great "effort to stabilize for all time the many factors which make for the prosperity of the nation," in Roosevelt's words, were the labyrinthine "codes of fair competition" which the National Recovery Administration required hundreds of industries to draw up in 1933 and then struggled to enforce.[16] The NRA bogged down in unwieldiness even before 1935, when the still backward-looking Supreme Court, with unintended mercy, ruled it unconstitutional. In a less sweeping but more useful and lasting way, the government established new supervisory commissions and strengthened the old ones inherited from the progressive era in order to regulate particular economic institutions, notably the stock market, holding companies in public utilities, and the banks.

Although the NRA seemed to prove that the kind of regulation that organized business had been trying to impose on itself ever since the 1870s was unworkable even with public compulsion behind it, government managed to cooperate to better effect with the efforts of farmers and workingmen to regulate their own economic circumstances. What the trusts had done for themselves the government now assisted the farmers to do. The Agricultural Adjustment Administrations of 1933 and 1938 (the first was struck down by the Supreme Court in 1936) made it possible, by means of prohibitive taxation, enabling loans, outright subsidies, and other devices applied with the consent of a majority of the growers involved, to limit production of corn, wheat, cotton, tobacco, and other commercial staples and maintain prices at parity with the "fair" level of the prosperous years 1909–1914.*

The National Labor Relations Board (1935), although imposing no particular standard of wages or hours, prevented the employer from interfering with the organizing of trade unions acceptable to a majority of his workingmen. Collective bargaining suddenly was possible in certain major industries, notably automobiles, for the first time, or, in others like steel, after a generation of the "open shop." With that official support the Committee for (later Congress of) Industrial Organization (1935), led by men who had long been restive in the craft-minded American Federation of Labor, organized unskilled as well as skilled hands in all the major industries by 1941. For the first time in American history the labor movement was a solidly established structure. Employers bitterly complained that their own freedom of speech was being "regimented" by the government and their property rights obliterated by such union tactics as the sit-down strike, just as nonagrarian interests could not understand why farmers should be cosseted at public expense. But by 1941 there stood three great economic groups, business, labor, and agriculture, each organized in its own interest with more or less governmental assistance, where formerly there had been only "big business."

Many, perhaps most, of the victims of the depression were people whom no democratic government could render capable of organization and self-regulation. Small, subcommercial farmers, sharecroppers, and farm laborers derived little from the AAA's largess; neither the AFL nor the CIO could do much for casual laborers, domestic "help," irregular wage earners, and people too old to work; small businessmen felt merely harassed by official bureaucracy, whether of the NRA or the NLRB; how and to what end could the great mass of middle-class individuals and individualists organize themselves? The danger seemed imminent in the mid-1930s that the disaffected and unassociated might, not unlike such people in Germany and Italy, be swept up by one of the authoritarian, half-populist, half-fascist demagogues of the time who were grandly promising to institute "social justice," to "share our wealth," to provide $200 every month to the elderly or "thirty dollars every

* The resemblance to the "just price" of early colonial times is highly suggestive of the nature of the basic direction of twentieth-century reform. "Parity," indeed, went rather beyond the "just price," which had been based on unimpeded supply and demand, to suggest that farm products had a certain inherent value whatever the state of the market.

Thursday" to the unemployed.* On the fringe there lurked a number of small but virulently anti-Semitic, Negro-baiting groups such as the Silver Shirts and the Black Legion. As it turned out in the presidential election of 1936, the dismal failure of the Union party, a coalition of such extremists, demonstrated the difficulty of anyone's rallying the unemployed, the aged, the bigoted, and the disaffected under one banner.

But by 1936, partly in response to the radical-populist threat, the federal government was already laying the foundation for a welfare state which could regulate the economic circumstances of individuals unable to control them themselves. The programs specifically designed for depression relief, notably the Works Progress Administration's make-work projects for the unemployed and the Civilian Conservation Corps' work camps for idle youth were hopefully designed to be only temporary. But a complex of permanent federal institutions was also devised to assure a minimal economic security to various sorts of people. The Fair Labor Standards Act of 1938 set a minimum wage and a basic forty-hour working week for the one or two million of the unskilled industrial workers who were not yet organizable into labor unions; it also abolished, at last, child labor in industry. The Home Owners' Loan Corporation salvaged a fifth of all urban homes from imminent mortgage-foreclosure between 1933 and 1936, and by 1940 loans underwritten by the Federal Housing Authority financed repair of three million dwellings and construction of more than half a million private homes and three hundred rental projects. Between 1935 and 1937 the Resettlement Administration assisted some ten thousand poor farm families to move to more promising land, and after 1937 the Farm Security Administration, by making low-interest loans of the kind that homesteaders had wanted in the 1870s, cut back the incidence of farm tenancy for the first time in nearly a century. The Tennessee Valley Authority, in the course of generating electric power and controlling floods and soil erosion, began to draw the southern Appalachian upland folk out of their economic stagnation of the past century and a half.

The Social Security system (1935) was the most pervasive of all. By 1940 some 2 million old people and 1 million poor children were receiving small federal pensions or aid, more than 50 million wage and salary earners and their employers were contributing to an-

---

* These were the rallying cries of Father Charles E. Coughlin, the "radio priest," Senator Huey P. Long, the red-neck dictator of Louisiana, Dr. Francis Townsend of Old-Age Revolving Pensions, Limited, and one of the latter's rivals in California.

nuities payable after sixty-five, and most working people could expect modest benefits during spells of unemployment. All this was only a beginning. As the welfare state stood at the end of the New Deal years, it was a loose patchwork offering niggardly benefits at best and almost nothing at all to agricultural laborers, household workers, the unemployable, and anyone too poor to pay for medical care; they still had to turn to the old-fashioned local public charity that the depression had proved entirely inadequate. But at least an organized system of public regulation now existed, and the concept of public responsibility for the commonweal was alive again.

Out of the pragmatic confusion of the New Deal and the wreckage of its abandoned experiments there remained in 1940 a functioning system. For all the fulminations of businessmen against its bureaucratic paperwork, the new economic system, as Walter Lippmann had foreseen in 1934, was not a totalitarian "directed economy" but rather a "compensated economy," retaining private initiative as far as possible but when necessary committing the state to "redress the balance of private actions by compensating public actions."[17] A few years after the end of the New Deal, economists could begin to draw a rough sketch of how the balancing and compensating mechanism worked. It was a system of "countervailing powers": of consolidated big businesses, some of them effectively checking each other; of labor unions solidly entrenched and with five times as many members as in the 1920s; of commercial farmers likewise organized both economically and politically; of "big government," the federal regulatory agencies in particular, redressing the balance of power among "big business," "big labor," and "big agriculture" and guaranteeing the welfare of other classes unable to countervail on their own.[18] The five-wheeled vehicle lumbered creakily along, and some economists objected that its counterweights were not really in balance at all, but it seemed to provide sufficient stability for further progress without continually breaking down into general depressions like those of the nineteenth and early twentieth centuries.

The Great Depression and the New Deal quickened the practical trend toward a controlled economy that businessmen had begun in the 1870s and progressive reformers had stimulated thirty years later. The rhetoric of business leaders about freedom of contract and of progressives about freedom of opportunity had still reflected the economic liberalism of the mid-nineteenth century; New Dealers too, although they talked more of regulation for the economic security of the individual, thought of themselves as "liberals" and their opponents as "conservatives." In spite of outraged accusations of dictatorship from champions of the old free enterprise such as the wealthy individualists of the Liberty League, the New Deal also reflected the American past in its preference for a loose, experimental, pluralistic system rather than any of the totalitarianisms of the contemporary world.

For latter-day liberals, however, true economic freedom or opportunity for the individual inevitably had to rest upon a solid institutional base of public regulation. Indeed, though New Dealers seemed unconscious of the fact, there had been a time in the preindustrial past when Americans, before they committed themselves to free private enterprise, had taken for granted the ancient principle of public regulation on behalf of the economic welfare of individuals and commonwealth alike. Not until well after the New Deal reforms had been accomplished, however, did it occur to historians to compare the new regulatory system to the old mercantilism. The two proved to be astonishingly alike. Since some such systematic interaction between government and economic affairs had been accepted in most societies down through all the ages until the liberal nineteenth century, the New Dealers would have had a doubly better claim to the name of "conservatives," had they thought to make it, than those who sought only to perpetuate the anarchic arrangements of the mid-nineteenth century. But since they supposed that they lacked precedents in American history, most New Dealers defended their successful experiments simply on the pragmatic ground that trial and error proved that they "worked," a standard which convinced their political opponents that they were wholly unprincipled radicals. If Franklin Roosevelt saw a deeper meaning when he announced in 1936, "I am that kind of conservative because I am that kind of liberal," it escaped everyone else at the time.[19]

In a still broader sense the new economic system, as far as it went, was quite in line with the main thrust of American history ever since the seventeenth century: its basic concern was to add another material value—the equitable distribution of goods—to that of adequate production. The New Dealers' version of the "American dream" was still solidly economic. Insofar as they recognized, perhaps a little more than the progressives before them, that they might serve other and even higher values—the stability of a well-founded structure of social institutions, the creative excellence that a vital cultural tradition could sustain, or a moral climate conducive to spiritual salvation of the immaterial soul—

they evidently still expected these good things to flow forth once the economic system was perfected. They established, accordingly, a "social" security system to pay money to aged or unemployed individuals; they did not direct it specifically to problems of social relations like the disintegration of the kind of family to which individuals had once belonged. Except for a few eccentric communitarian projects for self-supporting villages of handicraftsmen or collective farmers and for "suburban resettlement" of slum dwellers in a few experimental "Greenbelt towns," they did not specifically seek to tighten the links of social community once again. The emphasis lay rather on the utility of the inhabitants' physical surroundings and on their means of support. So too the cultural projects—the touring stock companies of the Federal Theater Project, the professional concerts and community music groups, the post-office murals, and the series of American Guide books—were justified on the ground that actors, musicians, painters, and writers had "to eat just like other people," and were abruptly cut off along with the other make-work projects of the WPA when prosperity returned.[20]

Between the 1870s and the 1940s the American social structure continued, in a still materialistic age, to be a more or less fortuitous by-product of economic processes. The institutional reforms which the trust movement, progressivism, and the New Deal effected in the economy inevitably made their impact on social institutions as well. But when development of an organic new economic system had to proceed by such fits and starts toward its dimly perceived goal, the social order that rested on it was bound to be an even more haphazard accretion of vestiges of outmoded institutions, reactions to the economic impetus of the times, and the confused hubbub of reformers and counterreformers.

II. A Personalized Society

The effort of progressives and New Dealers to perfect American freedom by subjecting the economy to regulation was not as absurd as it seemed in the 1930s to the Liberty League and other surviving champions of untrammeled free enterprise. By ensuring the individual a degree of material security, the new economic structure which the "trusts," the labor unions, various agrarian crusaders, and the state were building between 1875 and 1945 might conceivably liberate him for other kinds of self-fulfillment than economic success. The new economy could also provide the material foundation for a new social structure. If society were made stable enough to assure the individual a reasonable security of status—a fair certainty of what to expect from his community, family, and other associations—he might be freed from the excessive anxiety that had harried so many kinds of people into reactionary movements in the nineteenth century. Unfortunately the confusion of purpose that had usually made those movements ineffectual, and sometimes self-destructive, persisted in the twentieth century. As late as 1945, social reformers preferred to think of themselves as only an advanced variety of the old "liberals"—as seekers after new means for equality of economic opportunity and material condition in the Jacksonian tradition—and shut their eyes to what a thorough-going program of truly *social* security might entail.

Change in the structure of society accordingly lagged farther behind the practical changes in the economic system than at any time since 1607. It had taken decades, sometimes generations, for the triple economic revolution—migration to the West and into the cities, massive immigration from abroad, and industrialization—to erode the old primary institutions of society. It took even longer for the reformers of the twentieth century, under the spell of their own libertarian rhetoric, to address themselves to the task of reintegrating the social structure or any of its institutions. Not until the New Deal system of organized, countervailing economic powers had been in operation for some years did it dawn on social critics that the rootlessness of the modern individual—*anomie* and "alienation" were soon the fashionable words—might be as destructive of his true freedom as cutthroat economic competition had ever been. Throughout the progressive-liberal decades the same theorists, reformers, and practical businessmen who were successfully refloating the long-derelict economic commonwealth continued to drift out into the unfathomable waters of social individualism and pluralism.

They even did a good deal of hearty rowing with the antisocial current. As uneasy as reformers felt about the symptoms of disorder in the modern world, in the twentieth century their prescriptions for its cure became more explicitly radical than before. This was a novel twist in the history of reform. For all the talk in previous generations about economic individualism, any signs of the dissolution of the ancient institutional bonds of community, family, or church, if noticed at all, had usually been viewed with alarm. It had been assumed, in particular, that the *normal* family or community was as well-founded as ever; the odd ones that obviously failed to live up to the norm were regarded as delinquents to be corrected rather than as portents of a new order. Now, however, what had been deplored as defective practice was turned into a positive principle.

The argument now ran that the good society, like the good economy of about 1850, was that which set the individual free from institutional constraints, whether public or private. Even while in their economic affairs Americans were progressively repudiating the maxim that the best government governs least, they took to preaching permissiveness as the right principle for their social institutions. The progressives and liberals of the twentieth century, who were foremost in refastening public restrictions upon the individual's freedom of economic contract, at the same time abandoned, in theory at least, the little that remained of the old social sanctions against free choice in personal relations.

New declarations of social independence were heard on all sides. Like the egalitarian doctrine of 1776, they only made explicit a practical state of affairs that had long existed. And like that earlier recognition of political democracy, the new emphasis on free personal relations as the basis of society sometimes led to disconcerting consequences. Whether the new personalism amounted to elevating the American concept of individual liberty from the material level to a higher social, cultural, and spiritual plane, or only a new misreading of the American economic experience, was still not at all clear by 1945.

22. VICTIMS OF INDIVIDUALISM

The old-fashioned or "classical" liberals of the nineteenth-century type, having no idea that the country was already in process of turning to a system of private and public regulation, continued to subject the social order to the peculiarly corrosive effects of economic individualism until well into the twentieth century. As reformers or antireformers, in their unwitting disregard of the inadequacy of individual self-help and official *laissez-faire* they could not begin to conceive that the individual might have a need for a more organic social structure. Their attempts to deal with, or to ignore, certain social problems after 1875 played an ominous prelude to the more explicit social individualism, personalism, and privatism that was shortly to become the dominant theme of American society, although few at that time could detect the dissonant overtones.

The liberal reformer, like most Americans of the time, was far readier to demand a rigorous individualism of others than of himself. As we have seen, any group in a position to defend itself against the uncertainties of the unsystematic economy set up organizations of its own—trusts, trade unions, Granges, fraternal lodges, political machines—even while decrying others for doing the same thing. Trust consolidators insisted that their laborers be free from trade-union organizers; Grangers called for antitrust laws; urban taxpayers organized to protest the wastefully corrupt machinations of party bosses who helped propertyless slum dwellers in return for votes. Anyone might feel the need for his own kind of association and yet suspect that any other kind subverted the liberty of its own members as well as threatening his. In this unsettled climate of practical consolidation and libertarian rhetoric, people who were unable to organize effectively in their own interest were unfortunate indeed. To certain groups of that sort—Indians, Negroes, and "new" immigrants in particular—even the most earnest solicitude of the overly doctrinaire spelled social destruction.

The Indian, earliest victim of American progress, once again was the most vulnerable to the new developments. No longer able to hold back the white frontier nor even to protect the limited areas reserved under the federal treaties of the previous hundred years, the tribes that now survived in the West entered what liberal reformers intended to be the final phase of "savage" society. Tribal society had been highly communal; by comparison, Anglo-American society, as early as the Indians' first contact with it in the seventeenth century, was shot through with individualism. Since then cases of successful adaptation to white society had been rare. They were not particularly welcome to the whites when they did occur. In the eighteenth and early nineteenth centuries the Cherokees, one of the five great tribes of the Old Southwest, not only converted to Christianity but devised their own alphabet, published newspapers, conducted schools, drafted a constitution and a legal code, and even operated cotton plantations with Negro slaves. Their success unfortunately made the forcible removal of the "Five Civilized Tribes" to the remote Indian Territory (Oklahoma) in the 1830s seem the more necessary to the white men who wanted their land. In spite of that piece of calculated brutality the five tribes quickly resumed their remarkable line of progress in adapting white techniques to their own purposes.

Like other eastern Indians now on reservations in the West, however, they remained tribesmen who used land communally for both agriculture and hunting, not as so many absolute owners but simply as members of their "nation." Out beyond them on the Great Plains and in the Rocky Mountains the last "savage" Indians still roamed undisturbed by white civilization until the coming of the overland migrants of the 1840s, the gold seekers of the 1850s, and the railroad builders of the 1860s. The skirmishes between the wild tribes and frontier army units after the Civil War led to the final effort by the government, during the next twenty years, to remove them all to reservations in Oklahoma, Dakota, and elsewhere. Although Congress discontinued the ancient practice of negotiating formal treaties with Indian "nations" in 1871, they still had to be dealt with as tribes rather than as so many individuals.

The helplessness of reservation Indians at the hands of the federal Indian Bureau and its private contractors—the source of one of the blackest scandals of the Grant administration in the early 1870s—was doubly shocking to eastern liberals. A popular account of the red man's accumulated wrongs, Helen Hunt Jackson's *Century of Dishonor* (1881), inspired the founding of the Indian Rights Association. But the most sympathetic white people were fettered by misconceptions. Much as they deplored the whole sorry history of ill-usage by white men, the reformers felt that

the Indians had made themselves unduly vulnerable by their inability, as tribal communalists, to compete on equal terms with
enterprising white cattlemen or farmers.

The more successful the communal Indian economy, in fact, the
shorter it seemed to fall of the liberal ideal. The Cherokees, most
of whom were farmers, owned tens of thousands of horses, cattle,
and hogs, and as Senator Henry L. Dawes of Massachusetts wonderingly observed in 1883, "there was not a family in that whole
nation that had not a home of its own. There was not a pauper in
that nation, and the nation did not owe a dollar. It built its own
capitol, and it built schools and hospitals." But the senator perceived
a fatal flaw.

They have got as far as they can go because they own their land in
common. It is Henry George's system, and under that there is no enterprise to make your home any better than that of your neighbor's. *There
is no selfishness, which is at the bottom of civilization*. Till this people
will consent to give up their lands, and divide them among their citizens
so that each can own the land he cultivates, they will not make much
more progress.[1]

In order to "stimulate within them to the very largest degree the
idea of home, of family, and of property"—identified by another
senator as "the very anchorages of civilization"—Congress in 1887
passed the general Indian Allotment Act and in 1898 a similar act
for the Five Civilized Tribes.[2] The reservation lands of each tribe
would be divided into 160-acre homesteads; after a twenty-five-year
period of federal guardianship, while the Indian was learning to
farm, the allotment would become his private property.

The eastern idealism behind these acts was matched by western
land hunger; in Oklahoma lay the last unexploited expanse of the
lush prairie plains. After the Indian allotments had all been parceled
out, there would remain millions of acres to be thrown on the
market. The proceeds would enrich the tribal trust funds, held for
them by the government, but the land would pass irrevocably into
the hands of the white purchasers. Since many Indians carelessly
selected poor farming land for their allotments—or had it selected
for them if they refused to comply with the acts—many of the best
tracts went onto the auction block. Furthermore, while the Indian
owners could not sell their allotments for twenty-five years, white
speculators or "grafters" were able to lease them for a pittance and
rake off all the profit to be made by rerenting to farmers or stripping
the timber and other resources. Grafters also made free with the

forty-acre allotments of Indian orphan children, whose guardianship the local probate courts assigned them by the dozen. Ostensibly
to stimulate the individual Indian still further as a self-reliant
property owner, an act of 1907 apportioned half a billion dollars
from the tribal trust funds, some of which had been enormously
enriched by the recent discovery of petroleum in Oklahoma. The
squandering of these riches on Pierce Arrow hearses and ill-suited
mansions provided many amusing accounts of what must have
seemed undeniably individualistic behavior to readers of the Sunday
newspaper supplements.

The impatience of speculators with the twenty-five-year waiting
period finally led to an act of 1908 permitting a "competent" Indian
—casually defined as anyone who had less than half Indian blood or
who had gone to elementary school—to sell his allotment at once.
Many nominally qualified allotment owners promptly fell into the
clutches of swindlers who, perhaps after getting them drunk,
conned them into signing away their land, or married them only in
order to abscond with the property, or were made their legal heirs
in exchange for a small pension to be paid during the rest of what
in some cases proved to be a remarkably short life. The liberal lesson
in individualism had turned out to be an economic disaster for the
communally minded aborigines. "It is an absolute and utterly hope-
less task to make them understand it," one of their own lawyers
sighed; "their heads are not built right."[3]

By 1928, four decades after the original allotment act, the
Indians had lost 90 million of their 140 million tribal acres, a third
of the remainder was leased to white men, and two out of every
three Indians possessed only fragments of poor land or none at
all. No less disastrous was the inadvertent destruction of their
tribal governing councils, their religious forms, and even, among
the Five Civilized Tribes, the schools and other institutions of white
society that they had already adopted. It appeared to a different
kind of reformer in 1928 that the liberals of the 1880s, in assuming
that "some magic in individual ownership of property would in
itself prove an educational, civilizing factor," had succeeded only
in shattering a social structure whose nature they no more understood than an Indian tribesman understood theirs.[4]*

---

* In the Indian Reorganization Act of 1934, the most successful of the
few explicitly social reforms of the New Deal, the federal government undertook to mend the ravages of the individualistic policy of 1887. If they wished,
tribes could reorganize under their own largely self-governing councils, hold
their lands in common, repurchase lost land with federal grants, conduct
tribal cooperatives for farming, cattle herding, fish canning, or other appro-

Excessive disorganization made American Negroes as vulnerable to white individualism as the too communal Indians. Not since the slave trade wrenched their ancestors out of West Africa had they had an adequately communal society of their own. Nor, as a caste first of slaves and then of depressed freedmen, had they been part of even the loosely organized white society above them. The only social institutions that most of those living at the end of the Civil War had known were the working community of the plantation slave quarters set up by the white master, the church which they modeled on such observation of white churches as they were permitted, and a far less stable family than the master's, since his economic interests had always had to be served first. But although no tightly knit Negro community existed for the liberal reformer of the late nineteenth century to break down, neither was it likely to occur to him that anyone—whether black or white—needed help in building one up. When all that the individual white man was supposed to expect from society was a negative freedom from legal barriers to his self-improvement, nothing more positive was likely to be provided in support of the Negro.

The constitutional amendments and civil rights acts of the Reconstruction period had sought little more for the freedman than an abstract legal equality in the courts and at the polls. The states, like the federal government under the original Bill of Rights, were simply forbidden to "deprive any person of life, liberty, or property, without due process of law," to deny him "the equal protection of the laws," or to abridge his "privileges and immunities." Neither state nor federal government was to deny a citizen's right to vote "on account of race, color, or previous condition of servitude."[5] It did not yet seem proper, on behalf of the freedman any more than of any other individual, to implement such negative injunctions by a system of administrative regulation; even the limited assistance of the federal Freedmen's Bureau (1865–1872) was abandoned as soon as the immediate postwar emergency seemed to be over. In the name of libertarian principle, moreover, the Supreme Court in 1883 struck down the last Reconstruction statute, which had attempted to give Negroes equal access to privately owned inns, theaters, and "public" conveyances: "*individual* invasion of individual rights is not the subject-matter of the amendment."[6]

---

priate enterprises aided by federal loans, reopen schools, and preserve their traditional religion and culture. Three-quarters of the 325,000 Indians elected to reorganize under the act despite the outrage of the Indian Rights Association over the heathenism and communism which old-fashioned liberals, now self-styled conservatives, were always quick to detect in the New Deal.

Throughout the following decades the occasional Republican bill that sought only to make the southern states comply with the Reconstruction amendments was defeated by an alliance of southern stonewalling, liberal aversion to "force," and general indifference to the Negro's special need for protection.

That need grew, however, for the amount, if not the kind, of solicitude that the government was devoting to the Indian. The white South was settling its former slaves into a new version of the old racial caste. Although legally the freedmen were now at liberty to move about, almost all of them remained as a kind of peasantry in the plantation regions; few ventured farther than the nearby cities of the industrializing "New South." A few basic social advantages accrued from legal freedom: the churches and lodges that comprised almost the only Negro communal institutions were freer of white surveillance, and the black farmer's wife and children could no longer be casually taken from him and sold. But the precarious tenure of the sharecropper or laborer left his family's economic security every bit as vulnerable to the interest of landlord or employer as it had been under slavery. Even as late as the First World War, when northern demand for labor and the depression in southern agriculture induced the first great emigration of Negroes out of the old black belts, the direction and rate of their movement were governed by no plan but the immediate needs of their new employers and the remonstrances or cajolery of their old ones.

In the politics of the South the Negro was likewise used for the convenience of various white factions. From Reconstruction days until the 1890s they sought to manipulate his vote; when that no longer seemed useful, they tacitly agreed to disfranchise him altogether by certain disingenuous requirements—that he prove his literacy or pay a poll tax—from which white men, liberally enough, were usually excused. At the same time state and municipal lawmakers in the South, responsive to lower-class white discontent in an age of democratic Populist and progressive rhetoric, imposed on the Negro a pattern of physical segregation—in trains, streetcars, sidewalks, parks, theaters, hotels, hospitals, libraries, schools, and even cemeteries—such as had not seemed necessary back in the days when slavery made the inferiority of Negroes indisputable. "It took a lot of ritual and Jim Crow," a southern historian observes, "to bolster the creed of white supremacy in the bosom of a white man working for a black man's wages."[7] The Supreme Court, in a series of cases in the 1890s, refused to recognize that publicly segregated schools or railway cars were inherently unequal or that white officials discriminated against Negroes in court or at the polls, as long as the southern states maintained the fiction of a technical equality.

Lynch law reinforced the public ordinances. Although the volunteer regulators or vigilantes who had policed the South and other regions in their frontier days were now quite rare, the Ku Klux Klan and several other self-constituted groups sprang up to terrorize black men who showed signs of discontent with their inferior social "place." The Negro's physical place was of less concern to white men who had always used his labor, but the swelling migration of black laborers into southern cities was part of a generally unstable economic and social situation that stirred up white mobs to assault the colored sections of New Orleans (1900) and Atlanta (1906). As Negroes also moved north into formerly "white" jobs and neighborhoods, the same white terrorism erupted from time to time, at its worst in New York (1900), Springfield, Illinois (1908), and, during the confusion of the two wartime migrations, at East Saint Louis (1917), Chicago (1919), and Detroit (1943). Except for the militant polemics of small groups of Negro intellectuals like the National Association for the Advancement of Colored People (founded in 1910), Negroes themselves sought no more than a tolerated niche within the white-dominated economy and the equal protection promised them by the law; even the NAACP devoted itself mainly to securing abstract justice through the courts. The slightest practical improvement in jobs or housing was sure, however, to seem a threat to white supremacy or at least to the uncertain status of numbers of apprehensive white people.

For all the obvious oppression at the hands of southern public authority, private hostility in the North, and the lynching parties and street mobs of both sections, liberal reformers could excuse their neglect of the Negro by regretfully concluding that the innate unworthiness of his race accounted for the low worth accorded him by society. As early as 1877 the Republican *New York Tribune* decided that although Negroes had been given "ample opportunity to develop their own latent capacities" during the dozen years of Reconstruction, all they had demonstrated was that "as a race they are idle, ignorant, and vicious."[8] By the end of the century it was generally believed that "the new negro" was "less industrious, less thrifty, less trustworthy, and less self-controlled than was his father or his grandfather."[9] For the next forty years few white men were ready to concede the possibility that the Negro's proverbial lack of ambition, his sullen manner, and reckless and sometimes criminal behavior, especially in the tenement neighborhoods of northern cities, might be the product of segregation itself.

Reformers still assumed that nothing more positive was called for than removal of the sort of legal disabilities that the southern states inflicted. In spite of the shift among progressives and New Dealers away from economic individualism to the regulatory welfare state, little was done to rescue the Negroes from their submerged social caste and nothing at all to encourage them to build up their own social institutions. Some of the economic reforms of the time helped Negroes as farmers or laborers. But the cotton subsidies of the AAA somehow failed to pass through the planter's fingers to his tenants; federal encouragement of trade unions did the least good to unskilled labor; domestic workers were excluded from the minimum wage and Social Security systems. After two New Deal administrations the most advanced reformers were still concerned above all with improving the material welfare of the individual. There was no doubt that most Negroes, like other disadvantaged persons, desperately needed any general labor and welfare laws that could be devised to enhance their economic opportunity and security. But neither public authority nor black Americans themselves seemed prepared, as late as 1945, to grapple with the fundamental disability that had been fastened on the Negro race through three hundred years of legal and economic change: the suppression of his common humanity, and of the potential for its expression in a stable social structure, by the rigidity of his unfree caste in an overly free country. Liberal reformers—both the old free-enterprisers and the new advocates of regulation—could usually persuade themselves, even though their own social structure was progressively breaking down, that an inferior caste was still what the Negro deserved.

A similar indifference and neglect on one hand, or a peculiarly obtuse sort of benevolence on the other, was visited upon poor immigrant peasants, artisans, and laborers, more and more of whom after 1875 were coming from remote and unfamiliar parts of Europe and the Far East. Somewhat like the aboriginal Indians in having known the emotional security of communal traditions, they could easily be confused by the liberal expectation that anyone would be happy to abandon such things in exchange for the material chances that America offered. The immigrants' experience also somewhat resembled that of the poor Negroes in that any failure to take advantage of those opportunities was usually blamed on some defect of their character. Unfortunately, whether the individual "new" immigrant succeeded economically or failed, he was likely to be upset by the looseness and uncertainty of social relationships in America. In a country where reformers and most of those whom they proposed to assist were tacitly agreed on the prime importance of the economic nexus, even the most benevolent were slow to recognize that the poor immigrant's chief problem might lie beyond poverty and might even be aggravated by the best attempts to relieve his physical distress. For all their talk of reform, Americans could hardly conceive that social demoralization among the foreigners might be an acute symptom of an organic disorder in the larger society.

Although a movement to restrict immigration arose in the 1890s and at length culminated in the quota acts of 1921 and 1924, as late as 1917 the popular and official policy of the country was to leave the door open almost as wide as ever. The nearly continual demand for industrial labor, skilled and unskilled, ensured that a liberal policy based strictly on economic considerations would prevail. Individual immigrants might be excluded, under acts of 1882, 1891, and 1903, if infected with certain diseases, suffering from such defects of character as would presumably unfit them for productive labor and self-support, or adhering to anarchism or other objectionable political beliefs. But anyone sound of limb and moral principle was free to come. Only one economic interest group, organized labor, regularly opposed the liberal policy, and it was too weak to obtain any substantial reform. To most people—including those industrial workingmen whom the groundswell of new immigration helped lift to better jobs—the foreign labor supply seemed as useful as ever, and the liberal tradition of free opportunity for the individual immigrant persisted through the progressive period in spite of the general trend toward a regulated economy.

Until the First World War most Americans remained vaguely sanguine about the social and cultural aspects of immigration, if they thought about them at all. Although the customs and peasant culture of Italians or Poles were far more alien to them than those of the Irishmen and Germans of an earlier day, surely the country could count on the alchemy of the republican melting pot—"the admirable assimilation processes of our orderly freedom," as a progressive (more complacent than such reformers were about most other matters) put it in 1909.[10] Presumably the foreigner still came not only to work but to submit himself to the New World transmutation of base metal into gold, in social as well as material terms. But the old faith in the melting pot rested on two premises that had always been dubious and had been growing steadily more so ever since 1815: that the typical immigrant had specifically intended to exchange the society and culture of the old country for American ways, and that American economic individualism would in itself provide an adequate social and cultural pattern for him. There was little substance to the first notion beyond the fact that after a time in America most immigrants ineluctably shed many of their old-country ways; the second evaporated in the course of the nineteenth century as the fire of economic change melted down the old American social structure along with that of the immigrants. The social dislocation suffered by almost any ordinary European who plunged into so inchoate a society was at least as acute as the difficulty of earning a livelihood. But to Americans it seemed that the chance for material success was virtually all anyone could properly ask of society.

As the latest to arrive at the foot of the economic ladder, the Southern and Eastern Europeans had trouble enough simply making a living and finding a decent place to live. As the newest members of the industrial proletariat of machine tenders and casual laborers, they could seldom avail themselves, until the 1930s, of either the mutual self-help of trade unions or the ministrations of welfare state and welfare capitalism. They were sure to be found crowded into those older city districts which had already degenerated into slums in the decades of poor Irish and German immigration. They and their children had the smallest opportunity to rise above semiskilled labor and escape the slums. Although every nationality could point to its successful individuals, the typical way up was an enterprise that involved exploitation of less fortunate fellow countrymen, such as subcontracting on construction projects or in the garment industry, banking and brokerage in remittances to the old country, or liquor dealing and saloonkeeping. The general coincidence between the newer ethnic groups and the lower occupations and tenement districts—even though it was less complete than Americans often supposed—made the social and economic problems of the "new" immigrants appear to be one and the same. As respectable citizens took for granted the daily sight of Polish mine workers, Jewish garment workers, or gangs of Italian railway trackmen or street laborers, and habitually avoided the squalid "foreign" parts of town, foreignness and poverty came to seem inseparable.

If the immigrant felt something lacking in America, it was not simply that the streets after all were not paved with gold; economic security rather than riches had been his practical goal in coming and usually remained his hope. But whatever he had heard of American freedom and opportunity, he had not anticipated that so many familiar elements of old-country society would be missing. In an American city he could preserve only fragments of the sort of parish, village, or family that he was used to. The old rites and holidays which his church still celebrated were now quite detached from the seasonal round of peasant life and labor. His family was reduced to the conjugal group of husband, wife, and young children, severed from most of their kindred by their changed circumstances as well as by distance. His ethnic "neighborhood" had little more cohesion or tradition than could be mustered by fraternal lodges and other voluntary associations on the American plan. Weak as they were, such institutions played an essential social role in his life. Toward relieving the immigrant's economic distress the church or lodge could give only a bit of mutual aid in time of sickness or death and nothing at all toward improving his basic position in the economy, a position imposed from outside the ethnic group. But these struggling versions of old-country social institutions could at least do what they had been doing ever since the 1820s: reassure the individual of his social identity and moral worth as a member of some collective entity more coherent and less confusing than the atomistic society at large.

Americanization, it has been argued, was fostered by the immigrants' own social institutions, since they were modeled on American voluntary associations. But the process was neither as automatic nor as beneficial to the foreigners as Americans assumed. A member of the local chapter of the Ruthenian National Union or of the *Società Italiana Umbria di Mutuo Soccorso e Protezione* became accustomed to American voluntarism when he paid his mutual insurance assessment at the weekly lodge meeting or contributed to the support of his no longer established church. What such associations institutionalized, however, was his social isolation within a particular ethnic enclave. An Italian could hardly join the Sons of Kosciusko, or a Pole the Knights of Garibaldi, in the way an American might be both an Odd Fellow and a Knight of Pythias. No doubt each fraternal order hoped to celebrate its common Americanism when it turned out to parade on Washington's birthday or the Fourth of July, but the observer who took the existence of such patriotic rituals for granted was apt to be more forcibly struck by the exotic banners and regalia of each group passing by. It was usual, for that matter, to assign the immigrants' societies to a separate division of the parade, somewhere behind the American lodges, "patriotic" societies, veterans' associations, and so on.

At most the immigrant's own institutions tempered the shock of his plunge into the icy waters of American social disorder. American preference for the figure of the melting pot suggested that the transformed foreigner would be received with rather more warmth. For not a few individual immigrants, and for still more of their children whose ties to their parents' "foreign" voluntary associations and to old-stock American society were equally tenuous, the American norm of individual self-reliance could mean literal demoralization: "the decay of the personal life-organization of an individual member of a social group."[11] As the contemporary sociologists who investigated the Polish immigrants pointed out,

an individual who, like the peasant, has been brought up as a member of a permanent and coherent primary-group and accustomed to rely for all regulations of conduct upon habit and the immediate suggestions and reactions of his social milieu, . . . lacks the necessary preparation to construct for himself a new life-organization with such elements as abstract individualistic morality, religious mysticism, and the legal and economic system which he finds in America.[12]

Coming from the far denser society of the peasant village or the veritable ghetto of the Yiddish *shtetl*, where work, family, religion, and community had been inextricably bound together, the immigrant whom American disorder and uncertainty had "demoralized in any particular line—family life, economic relations, community relations—soon [lost] moral self-control in general, all his institutional attitudes [being] more or less dissolved."[13] The immigrant stood in greater danger than other Americans of falling, not necessarily into indigence and economic dependency, but into an overly individualistic sort of personal irresponsibility and antisocial delinquency, perhaps ending in crime or insanity.

Only a few Americans saw the "immigrant problem" as more a social than an economic matter. By far the most advanced in this respect were the volunteer residents of the "social settlement" houses of the 1890s and after, the young people of the "better classes," many of them fresh from college, who sought to open a channel between the mainstream of modern life and the backwaters of the city slums, as certain English prototypes were already doing. But at Hull House in Chicago, the College Settlement in New York, South End House in Boston, and a hundred others the problem of bringing together "the masses and the classes" was compounded by the wide variety of language groups in the slums and the foreignness of their churches.[14] The settlement workers were sympathetic and acute enough to recognize the inherent worth of the foreign cultures. They soon learned to question, furthermore, the individualistic, materialistic drift of the turbulent American mainstream that they represented; "the test which they would apply to their [own] conduct," as Jane Addams observed at Hull House, "is a social test."[15]

These cultural missionaries to the slums could see the quandary that their effort to introduce the immigrants to their own rational, middle-class way of life placed them in. On one hand they were eager to provide libraries, lectures on polite literature or political economy, meeting rooms for social clubs, playgrounds, kindergartens, and day nurseries for the infants of working women, and classes for adults in music, art, and domestic science. At the same time they perceived in the old-country attitudes of the immigrants highly attractive elements of a more communal society, a richer culture, and an immemorial tradition. They cultivated the immigrants' self-respect by incorporating their old-country holidays, celebrations, folk customs, and languages into the life of the settlement house. It was there that the old insistence upon melting down alien cultures in an unalloyed native-American pot began to give way to a sense of the potential worth of "immigrant contributions" of "color, gaiety, and self-expression" to the prosaic daily life of America.[16] In the same way the YMCA and the city churches which sought to draw the urban masses into their "institutional" programs of English classes, gymnasiums, and welfare work gradually learned to resist the temptation to proselytize among their new Catholic, Jewish, and even foreign Protestant neighbors.

Although settlement workers could not wholly shake off a certain air of benevolent condescension, they did not make the mistake of reducing the immigrants' social and cultural needs to a matter of wages and rents alone, as did those other progressives and socialists who derided settlement houses for "relieving an infinitesimal fraction of misery."[17] At the same time, however, the door into middle-class society which the settlements tried to open for immigrants and other slum dwellers, particularly the youth, was ultimately that of self-help and personal advancement. The industrious, thrifty, single-minded individual was encouraged to get ahead on his own—and in so doing to break away from the communal and cultural traditions of his own people.

Help for far greater numbers than could be reached by the settlement houses was offered by the new welfare programs of government and industry, but they too did little to relieve the economic plight of ordinary poor immigrants and still less to resolve their social dilemma. The half-dozen states with major ports of entry, after turning immigration control over to the federal government in 1891, eventually created new bureaus to shield resident aliens from swindlers, dishonest "bankers," and medical quacks, regulated or operated employment agencies, and set up night classes in English at the public schools. But these official programs were as limited in conception as in scale. Progressive reformers might speak of "social" conditions as the basic cause of poverty and insecurity, but in practice they looked no further than remedies for the inadequacies and inequities of the system of material production and distribution. When government had provided for better wages and working hours, compensation for industrial accidents, and basic standards for tenement housing, their reforms were complete.

In much the same way the "welfare capitalism" of the period—the company pension and profit-sharing schemes, the safety programs, and the like—failed to look beyond the economic interests of workingmen. When after 1910 some corporations sponsored English classes for their immigrant employees, they usually discouraged the odd instructor who introduced anything beyond precepts of safety and efficiency into the lessons. Only a very few companies went further. The Ford Motor Company, in conjunction with its new "five-dollar day" in 1914, set up a "sociological department" to investigate whether each employee's personal habits and household decencies merited such largess. While the workingman and his family could endure the intrusion for the sake of the paycheck, the company's solicitude did little to shore up the family as a social institution.

The "social workers" of public and private charitable agencies who day by day had to deal with the urban and immigrant poor only gradually gave up the urge to apply the dogmas of middle-class economic individualism to every problem. Well into the twentieth century their chief aim was to pare applications for relief down to the smallest possible number of the acceptably frugal "deserving poor"; the rest they regarded not as victims but as perpetrators of their own poverty. In the course of ascertaining that lack of a father's income, or bad health, or wretched housing entitled this or that family to so many dollars for so many weeks, they no doubt passed along a certain amount of useful advice to the poor; in time their accumulated experience was consulted by New Dealers groping for some new line for basic reform. But when even seasoned social workers retained a narrow economic outlook toward the poor, the judges and other public officials who saw only the more demoralized, delinquent, and criminal sorts of immigrants were almost sure to treat them—men, women, and children—as individuals of defective character rather than as members of broken or half-formed social institutions that desperately needed shoring up.

The peasant society of the old country had taken for granted the integrity of the whole complex of institutions to which the individual belonged. In America, however, the immigrant wife found that she could have her husband haled into court for any ill-treatment; the judge, whose standards of decent behavior were not those of the old country, would casually "step between husband and wife and arbitrate between their personal claims as those of separate individuals."[18] Like other Americans, of course, judges and social workers professed to honor the integrity of the family, but they measured it in terms of the "well furnished and cleanly kept house" of the investigator's report and the legal contract which a man and woman had freely entered into and then carried out in a manner satisfactory to both parties.[19] Such an official standard was too narrow altogether. "My people understand two things, kindness and force," an Italian woman of New York objected in the 1920s; "the rational, temperate attitude of the Americans does not move them."[20] However good the intentions of the American functionary, he was likely only to confuse still further any immigrant whose economic difficulties and social demoralization had already brought him to official attention. "After a careful study of many hundreds of cases," the sociologists of the Polish peasant immigration concluded in 1920, "we have found not a single instance where official interference strengthened the conjugal bond."[21]

The inevitable misunderstanding between the poor foreigner, victim of an immense social displacement, and the best-intentioned institutions of an individualistic society was never wholly resolved. Changing circumstances eventually removed the problem, mainly by removing most of the immigrants. In 1914 the European war fortuitously blocked off further mass immigration; the stoppage was written into law shortly after the war and then sealed by the Great Depression and the Second World War. As the number of foreign-born in the population steadily dwindled, the children and grandchildren of the "new" immigrants of 1875–1914 assimilated the individualistic expectations of American society. The typical second-generation youth, in summarily rejecting the folkways of his green-horn parents, made the most pervasive of all "immigrant con-tributions" to American life, by replicating in extreme form the basic social discontinuities of American individualism.

For him and most of his descendants there was no turning back, no matter how the well-bred young ladies of the settlement house enthused over the picturesque old folksongs and dances. Unlike the Indians, with their obstinate tribalism, and the Negroes, still immured within the three-hundred-year-old wall of caste, the chil-dren of the newer European immigration outdid, if anything, the older American stock in seeking to take advantage of the ethos of opportunity and self-advancement. Now highly mobile individuals, they left far behind them any sense that a more organic society than that which they found around them might provide a more satisfac-tory social life. As late as 1945 there were few Americans, liberal reformers or anyone else, who would argue differently.

23. "CONGERIES OF SOCIAL ATOMS"

Having lost touch with the established social structures of other times and places, Americans at the end of the nineteenth century could suppose that their own institutions best exemplified, at least in embryo, the true principles from which a satisfactory common life should grow. Nearly a hundred years had passed since they had convinced themselves that a society without exclusive or even distinguishable classes—a society such as they supposed had existed in certain parts of America, at least, sometime in the recent past and as they hoped would soon exist in all perfection again—was the most harmonious and truly communal of all possible societies. In their general faith that virtually every individual had a free and roughly equal opportunity to better himself, they imagined that they had already nearly achieved that good society. They assumed, moreover, that the working relationships between men with different economic functions—between capitalist and laborer, industrial monopolist and the "common man" who owned his farm or shop, debtor and creditor, producer and consumer, even master and slave—were also the most important social relations. They still spoke of other institutions—"community," "family," "church," though not social "class"—as though they were what they always had been, but man as a social animal they subordinated to economic man.

The absence of any solid structure of social organization did induce a certain countervailing ethos of self-restraint and self-discipline among citizens determined to "succeed." But such an ethos only intensified the dominance of strictly economic considerations. Well into the twentieth century, reformers strongly committed to new measures of economic organization and control and to more equitable distribution of wealth felt little compulsion to deal directly with the social structure, defective though it was. Economic reform would presumably take care of any imperfections in society.

Oddly enough, when the twentieth century did hit upon a more specifically social norm—a social democracy (as that word was extended) of self-reliant individuals, bound together only by a network of voluntary personal relationships—it resembled the vanishing economy of free private contract more than the new one of public control. The crumbling of old social institutions that had been going on inadvertently was now accepted as right and proper as well as inevitable. The social institutions of the new age were to be simply the sum of the personal ties among their individual members. The "church of one's choice," the family held together mainly by the inclination of its members; the suburban community of physically detached houses and socially isolated households— such anti-institutions, long since foreshadowed in fact, now became the asocial norm for American social aspirations.

"Community," in the prevailing usage, was taken to mean little more than the local class structure, or the relative lack of one. Down to 1875 it had been plausible to explain away the erosion of other aspects of the ancient communal structure as the healthy eradication, through the democratic effect of economic individualism, of the remnants of European aristocracy. Of course no one could be entirely sure whether the desired liberty and equality or some new version of the old class distinctions would prevail. The harmonious society of responsible, independent equals always seemed to be receding into a hazy Arcadian past, of uncertain date, such as reformers had been invoking since the 1820s. It seemed, to an editor in Illinois in 1915, that those happy, democratic times, when "old and young, church members and worldlings, saints and sinners, bank presidents and laborers, society belles and kitchen maids" had mingled freely, lay no further back than the 1890s.[1] Like earlier moralists in the same vein—or like decriers of "status seeking" in the 1950s—he placed it in his own childhood, when everything had seemed simpler and more secure. To restore some such happy democracy had been the announced aim of most reformers. In order to realize the "American dream" (as it came to be called in the twentieth century) that the good society would emerge or reemerge in due course if men could produce enough goods and contrive to distribute them equitably, Populists, progressives, and New Deal liberals all sought as a first order of business to assure everyone the opportunity to rise in his occupation and acquire property. The fact that it had been precisely the liberal economic individualism of the nineteenth century that permitted the anarchic social disorder that often disturbed them—notably including the exaggerated differences of economic class—did not yet trouble many reformers or popular moralists.

From 1875 onward one could well believe that the chief impediment to the social harmony which Americans had long pursued was the alarming outbreak of class warfare between the "armies of labor" and the "captains of industry." There had been rumors of war in the 1840s and 1850s, after the first massive immigration of poor laborers who were neither British in origin, Protestant in religion, nor, it seemed, safely republican in their political prejudices. But class conflict did not explode until the depression of 1873–1879. Since by that time Irish and German workingmen were no longer so strange and only a few of the "new" immigrants from Southern and Eastern Europe had yet appeared, it was hard to blink the fact that the turbulence was the work of a rebellious American working class, something hitherto believed impossible in a free country. The strikes and rioting along the railroad lines and throughout the industrial districts all too clearly made a mockery of the hope of communal harmony.

The depression lasted so long and destitution was so deep and widespread that it was equally remarkable how long it took for the desperation and disaffection of working people to boil over. The early demonstrations by thousands of the unemployed in Chicago in 1873 ended without securing them any special public assistance; one at Tompkins Square in New York the next year brought only a clubbing at the hands of the police. It took two years of wage reductions and layoffs before the underpaid cotton operatives of Fall River and anthracite miners of Schuylkill County went out on the long and bitter strikes of 1875 in which their unions ultimately were shattered. Here and there by 1876 the cry of "work or bread," sometimes sharpened by a threat of looting or even of an assault on the city council, intimidated the authorities into providing a temporary dole or a few make-work projects. But usually neither the paltriness of such relief nor the ill grace of property-owning taxpayers at having to provide it interrupted the patient "quietness and perfect good order of people thrown out of work and all but starving" which an editor observed at Scranton. The faith of the unemployed seemed as strong as his that "the chief influences of American life are wholesome and vital, and tend to national prosperity."[2]

On several of the northeastern railroads in July 1877 an impulsive strike by trainmen against a wage reduction touched off the most shocking clashes of the decade. Most, however, of the dozen major riots between Baltimore and Saint Louis either were provoked by half-trained militiamen, called in by panicky state officials to "restore order," or were the work of anarchic mobs of hangers-on, many of them tramps and mere boys. Of the twenty-four persons killed in the astonishing pitched battle at the Pittsburgh roundhouse, four were militiamen from Philadelphia (three of whom were workingmen themselves) and only three were striking railwaymen. Before the uproar subsided, as it promptly did upon the arrival of a few regiments of the regular army, the complacency of a good many middle-class people had been badly shaken. Sober Christian editors of denominational journals felt driven to call for "the club of the policeman, knocking out the brains of the rioter," and if necessary "bullets and bayonets, canister and grape," and the Gatling gun. "Let the mob know," the *Congregationalist* sputtered, "that for it to stand one moment after it has been ordered by proper authorities to disperse, will be to be shot down in its tracks."[3] Both the mob violence and the middle-class bloodthirstiness that it had excited soon died away, however, though the depression dragged on another two years.

As each upturn in the business cycle in the 1880s and early 1890s collapsed, within three or four years, into a new depression, the fright of 1877 was repeated. The apparent causes seemed contradictory. Sometimes blame for the restiveness of the working classes appeared to lie with foreign agitators, notably the anarchist orators at the Chicago Haymarket on the night in 1886 when a bomb killed seven members of the police battalion that marched on the crowd. Sometimes the public sensed that the horny-handed mechanics had the right of it—the Carnegie steelworkers besieged by Pinkerton agents at Homestead in 1892, or, two years later, the strikers who felt as oppressed by the "model" company town of Pullman as by conditions in the carshops there. Public sympathy for the underpaid workingman at the outset of a strike was apt to turn, as disorders inevitably followed, into a muddled concern for the property rights of capital. Whichever side seemed right in principle, it was accepted that the turbulence of industrial communities was essentially a matter of economic class conflict.

That the ordinary American apprehended that something more elemental was wrong with society is perhaps indicated by his quickness to detect "anarchism" at the root of the trouble. He meant specifically such professed anarchists, usually foreigners, as Johann Most of the "Black International" of the early 1880s, or the Haymarket orators, or Leon Czolgosz, who assassinated President McKinley in 1901. In the twentieth century the scapegoat figure of the alien anarchist gave way to the alien socialist or communist; during the depression of the 1930s and even as late as the 1950s many were ready to accuse "international communism" for making poor people imagine that they belonged to an oppressed lower class. The reality of such specters was always highly exaggerated. The armies of labor of the 1880s and 1890s in fact were a straggling corporal's guard of trade unions, and all the actual anarchistic or communistic conspirators of the time could have bivouacked in a medium-sized garret. For that matter, even the captains of corporate industry who sometimes shared the popular opprobrium were more like bushwhacking soldiers of fortune than a general staff.

Quite another kind of anarchism—less violent but far more productive of disorder—surrounded Americans on every side, in the economic individualism that they prized so highly. The gulf between economic classes was only one of its consequences. By the last two decades of the nineteenth century a few original theorists like Henry George and Edward Bellamy were proposing fundamental reforms of the whole system—the virtual expropriation of speculative profit or the nationalization of both capital and labor—and Protestant churchmen were beginning to redirect their "home missionary" efforts away from the unchurched frontier and into the class-riven industrial cities. The enormous popularity of their lengthy books indicated a general apprehension, looking far beyond the specific arguments for the "single tax" or a socialist "ethics of wealth," that the basic structure of American society was far too anarchic.

The main thrust of progressive and New Deal reform between 1900 and 1940 remained simply neomercantilist, however, and seldom looked beyond economic readjustments to a fundamental reconstruction of the social commonwealth. Usually the line of social reform ran in the opposite direction altogether. The selfsame business or professional man or workingman who was beginning to see advantages in submitting his economic affairs to an organized system of controls, the same ordinary Americans who deplored anarchism and the very idea of class conflict, now threw over what was left of the old organic community in favor of the new social norm of free personal relations. The building of a new economic system was paralleled by the further fragmentation of social communities into what by 1923 a sociologist could describe as "not much more than a congeries and constellation of social atoms."[4]

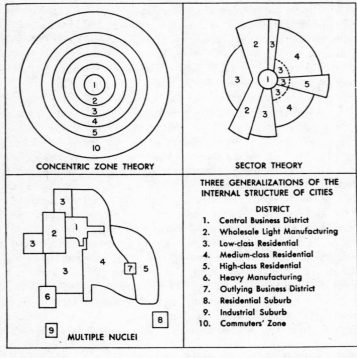

Figure 6. Generalized Structure of Cities. (From "The Nature of Cities," by Chauncy D. Harris and Edward L. Ullman, *The Annals of the American Academy of Political and Social Science,* CCXLII, 1945.)

The pattern of urban residential segregation along class and ethnic lines which had begun to take shape earlier was intensified in the age of the "new" immigration after 1875. As the horsedrawn streetcar gave way to the electric trolley car in the 1880s, and the latter to automobiles and buses in the twentieth century, individuals and their families were able to move outward from the centers of the cities as they moved upward in occupation, income, and wealth. Since there were as many variations of the pattern as there were cities, no one schematic description fits them all. (Figure 6.) It was a rare city whose zones neatly ringed the central business district in a sequence from slums outward to the farthest commuters' suburb. The upper-class sector might still begin almost downtown, as on Beacon Hill in Boston, or at only a short remove, like the Gold Coast along Lake Michigan on the near North Side of Chicago, and some of the poor residential and industrial sectors pushed far out from the center along a number of separate lines. Usually the socioeconomic categories were physically interspersed, according to the vagaries of the city's uneven economic development, into a random pattern of "multiple nuclei."[5] In any case, the districts identified in one decade with this or that economic class and ethnic coloration were apt to change by the next into something rather different and by local estimation usually much worse.

The half century after 1875 was the classic era of the city slum and the ethnic ghetto. Twenty families might now be crowded into the five- or six-story, dumbbell-plan buildings with which speculative landlords contrived to cover almost the entire surface from street to street. The tenements of the "new" immigrant groups or the Negroes were far more concentrated within certain blocks or sections of a city than the shanties, cellar dwellings, and derelict houses of the poor Irish and other old ethnic groups thirty years before. There were only a few ghettos in the strict sense, districts exclusively inhabited by a single ethnic group, though these were the more conspicuous for it: such sections as the lower East Side of New York and the near West Side of Chicago, where the Yiddish-speaking Jews made the word "ghetto" doubly fitting; the North End of Boston, now suddenly turned Italian; southwestern Milwaukee as it came into the "almost exclusive possession" of the Poles.[6] Even there, what Americans took to be undifferentiated "races" were sharply subdivided; old-country distinctions persisted among the Russian, Galician, Rumanian, Hungarian, or Levantine Jewish *lansleite* who predominated in certain "neighborhoods" of the lower East Side or the *paesani* whose parochial *campanilismo* made the Chicago

"Little Hell" into "a mosaic of Sicilian villages."[7] For a time the transplanted parish churches or orthodox synagogues and the American-style fraternal lodges of such subghettos reproduced something of the familiar old-country community amid brick and asphalt.

Only one ghetto was vigorous enough to create a viable, growing culture of its own—the Yiddish community of lower Manhattan. Its concentrated numbers heightened the singularity of the mixture of religious and ethnic self-consciousness that Jews had brought from Eastern Europe. Respect for intellect and scholarship—at least of certain traditional kinds—and the circumstance that Jewish intellectuals as well as artisans and peddlers had fled the Russian *pogroms* made the lower East Side unique. No other urban immigrant district produced anything comparable to the New York Yiddish theater, Yiddish journalism and literature, and indeed the creation of a standard Yiddish language out of the various East European "jargons." By comparison the smaller Jewish ghetto of the Chicago West Side, in the 1920s, seemed "provincial and sectarian," perpetuating itself for a time but "not capable of collective action on a larger scale."[8]

The many ghettolike slums, during the thirty or forty years when fresh arrivals were pouring in, retained a degree of communal coherence against great odds that was rare in the American society about them. Even the casual violence and occasional criminality—neither of which was as common as newspaper stories led respectable citizens to believe—usually were confined within the old-country ethnic lines. For all the sensationalism of the newspapers over the periodic revelations of the Mafia or the Black Hand between 1890 and 1910, Sicilian extortionists preyed mainly on fellow Sicilians until prohibition opened wider opportunities in bootlegging illegal liquor in the 1920s. Even then, the gangster or racketeer was less likely to be an immigrant whose style of life had been formed in the old country than an American-born and half-Americanized Italian, Irishman, or Jew, like Al Capone, Dion O'Banion, or Jake Gusick of the Chicago "syndicates."

Long before the passing of their own generation, the immigrants of the ghettos and slums were caught up in the same rush of continual change that had kept all American communities in motion in the nineteenth century, from the cotton planter's Old South to the cowboy's Great Plains. Within fifty years the near North Side of Chicago, as a sociologist surveyed it in 1929, had changed hands half a dozen times:

Fashionable residential streets have become the heart of the rooming-house district; rooming-houses have become tenements; tenements have been reclaimed for studios and shops. Group has succeeded group; the world of fashion has become the world of furnished rooms. The Irish Kilgubbin has become the Swedish Smoky Hollow; the Swedish Smoky Hollow, a Little Sicily; and now Little Sicily becomes a Negro quarter.[9]

New immigrant nationalities followed old ones. In the 1890s Italians took over sections like the Irish "plains" of Lawrence, "Old Dublin" in Rochester, and Greenwich Village, which as late as 1893 was the partly white, partly Negro "American ward" of New York City.[10] Native Americans also drifted into the slums. Southern Negroes were only the most conspicuous, especially those whose coming to New York turned recently fashionable Harlem into the classic black ghetto between 1905 and 1920.

Many other kinds of Americans—"the criminal, the radical, the bohemian, the migratory worker, . . . the unsuccessful, the queer and unadjusted"—came in search of more than cheap lodgings. Far from preferring the security of an archaic kind of community, as immigrants generally did, many of the lodgers in cheap furnished rooms were the sort who, in fleeing to the city from farms and small towns, brought along the old ingrained individualism of rural America. If they did not succeed in their material ambitions, the habit of social isolation all too easily became the mere anonymity of the lonely roomer and, at its worst, the helplessness of the derelict on "skid row." The very antithesis of society, a Chicago rooming house was a place, it was observed in 1929, "where people are constantly coming and going, where they live at best but a few months, . . . where no one knows anyone else in his own house, to say nothing of his own block, . . . where there are no groups of any sort."[11]

The luckier or more enterprising who did succeed in finding a place in the business life of the city were hardly better off in terms of social involvement. The respectable apartment dweller might exhibit any amount of "etiquette, urbanity, sophistication, finish," but he was notorious for not knowing much more than the names of the other families listed on the mailboxes in the lobby—indeed, he seemed proud of it.[12] "Urbanity" among modern American city dwellers, sociologists observed, masked an absolute lack of the close institutional relationships of the burghers of earlier ages.

In a few districts partly reclaimed from the slums, notably Greenwich Village after 1912, urban individualism of an extreme sort created a kind of antigroup life among the aspiring artists, poets, novelists, free-lance intellectuals, and hangers-on who flocked there. Although they declared a rebellion against what they conceived to have been the oppressiveness of Victorian society and its "genteel" cultural tradition, as an avant-garde they were only a little ahead of all those Americans who were turning the disorderly side of Victorianism into a new individualistic norm. They had chosen a fitting locale for it. To outsiders it might seem that Greenwich Village was a single distinctive community. In fact, like other poor districts—the lower East Side of Manhattan or the Chicago near North Side—it was partitioned off by invisible ethnic walls, separating the few remaining old American, Irish, or German inhabitants from the Italians, Slavs, Jews, Greeks, and Syrians who were pushing in, and the latter from the anonymous lodgers, derelicts, and self-conscious bohemians. In some places, along Lake Shore Drive in Chicago or the East River in New York, the mansions and fashionable apartment houses of the extremely rich and respectable abutted upon the tenements of their incongruous neighbors.

No district of a city retained its character long. Within ten or twenty years of the formation of the "new" immigrant slum neighborhoods, the individualism that drew native Americans to the lonely bed-sitting rooms, apartments, and bohemian garrets of the city was also drawing immigrants and their children out of the slums into "zones of emergence" or districts of "second settlement," as sociologists variously called them. A taste of economic success whetted the foreigner's ambition for still better things—as an Italian woman in Brooklyn said in the 1920s, "Isn't that why everybody moves?"—especially in view of the crowds of poor Bulgarians or Syrians or Negroes who now were pushing into their old neighborhoods.[13] The sheer physical growth of the city hastened change. Factory districts encroached upon the old tenement neighborhoods, and construction of new avenues, bridge and tunnel approaches, or subway lines cut through them.

The settlement house workers who saw the neighborhoods repeatedly break up could tell themselves that it all betokened the Americanization, the self-help and sense of individual responsibility, that they had all along hoped to foster. The success of upward-striving and outward-moving individuals, whether Italians or Poles, "swell" Jews or lace-curtain Irish, seemed to prove that economic opportunity was still open to everyone. Were not the former slum dwellers going where "the air is brighter, cleaner, and more vibrant; sunshine falls in floods rather than in narrow shafts; there is not

so much dust and smoke; the streets are quieter; there is less conges-
tion and more evident freedom of movement"? The immigrants'
drive for homeownership, in the opinion of their old patrons of the
settlement houses, was not only "extremely valuable training in
acquisition" but a "great educational force . . . automatically inter-
esting the owner in government, neighborhood, and the general
community situation as nothing else does." The farther the new
district was from the slums, in that point of view, the greater "the
cultivation of real society," a society, that is, in which "each community . . . has its own banks, department stores, small shops and
other business enterprises . . . keeping up the local social life."[14]

And yet communities organized upon that materialistic principle
seemed oddly unsatisfying to the Americans who had gone into the
foreign quarters and glimpsed something more truly communal
there. To be sure, not all the worthwhile elements of the slum neighborhood were abandoned in the move; former residents kept re-
turning to the churches and ethnic organizations that remained, and
still relied on the familiar stores of "their block" for old-country
foods.[15] But ultimately their emergence into American respectability
gave cause for regret to anyone who recognized the deficiencies of
American society in the foreign light of the social organism of
ghetto life. The children of Yiddish-speaking Jews who had succeeded, by the 1920s, in moving from the East Side of New York up
to the Bronx or from the Chicago West Side out to Lawndale—the
Deitchuks of *Deutschland,* as the latter appeared to the envious ones
they left behind—nevertheless formed a new, hybrid sort of ghetto.
They had taken along their synagogues and ethnic associations, yet
old-countrymen and Yankees alike were dismayed by the type of the
hyper-Americanized *allrightnik,*

playing baseball, great fight fans, commercial travelers, clean-shirted,
white-collared, derby-hatted, creased-trousered. The women are stylish
and stout, white-skinned, long-nosed, bediamonded; social workers,
actresses, stump speakers, jazz dancers, with none of the color and the
virtues of their erstwhile bearded, bewigged parents.[16]

More often the life of the "streetcar suburbs," as old Bostonians
observed it in Cambridgeport, Roxbury, and Dorchester just before
the First World War, was merely "deadly commonplace." Too many
new neighborhoods where rising Jews or Italians had moved in on
the heels of the original Yankee, Irish, German, and English families
now presented "a dull monotony of tenements broken by certain
streets of utterly unindividualized cottage houses." In spite of a con-

centration of Irish names in one place and Italian, Russian Jewish, or Slavic ones in another, it was easy "to discard old loyalties, to take no part in the local life, to cut oneself off utterly from one's fellows."[17] As more and more families emerged from the slums, the inner suburbs grew more crowded but less neighborly; physically they too slipped into slumdom as old single houses once again were partitioned off into cramped apartments:

The garden setting of the street often disappeared under the feet of running children; back yards and porches filled with the overflow and trash from the houses; planted playgrounds required tar to support increased use; and the large country parks grew to weeds because of lack of time and interest among their new users.[18]

The best solution that apprehensive older residents could hit upon was yet another move outward toward the spacious suburbs: "To be lived well life cannot always be passed in crowds."[19]

At the ends of the trolley car lines which laced each metropolitan area after the 1880s and the electric rapid-transit railways which soon extended beyond their boundaries, along the paved avenues, boulevards, streets, and lanes which private automobile owners required after 1920, there agglomerated the new suburban communities of the twentieth century. The individuals who chose to live in the "safe, sanitary environment [of] new houses in styles somewhat in keeping with their conception of family life, and temporary neighborhoods of people with similar outlook"—or similar incomes—thought that they were now fairly immune from further movement and social flux.[20] Some suburbs happened to be built around the nucleus of an old rural village, whose name and traditions, such as they were, fostered the illusion of communal stability. Such quaint survivals seemed to have a pleasing connection to the lives of the new proprietors of the place, since so many of them were grandchildren of uprooted farmers and peasants who had never wholly come to terms with either the unanticipated pressures or the social and cultural potential of the raw new cities. A man could feel he had regained true neighborliness by moving out to the "bedroom suburb" and commuting back to the city each day to work.

It was a neighborliness in the modern mode, however, of personal relationships between individuals rather than of shared communal functions. The families of adjacent householders could hardly help becoming acquainted with each other, but beyond the conventional pleasantries and occasional annoyances of life among the unfenced lawns, garden plots, and detached houses the suburban neighborhood was riven by much the same sort of social isolation and anonymity as a block of downtown apartment houses. The deeper associations were not among neighbors so much as among persons whom the happenstance of occupation, hobbies, and "volunteer work" brought together and who had little in common beyond that interest.

Personal associations of that sort were formed in groups, but most of these were not integral institutions of the local community. The church services, the meetings of clubs, benevolent societies, or study groups, and the "sports events" which the suburban resident attended might be scattered over a number of localities as far from home as the city to which he commuted to work. The complex of voluntary associations was not unimportant in his social life, but since each of his neighbors belonged to some different set, it was far more diffuse than the old-fashioned territorial community. The one clearly communal institution was the public school, which served from time to time as a meeting place for adults as well as children. The "neighborhood school" was situated in a neighborhood, but if anything it was the school, its Parent-Teacher Association, and the "school spirit" generated by its athletic rivalries that drew the neighborhood together into a semblance of social cohesion.

There was little else to do it. Whatever sense of achievement or security an individual or family might derive from settling in so unsettled a place, the suburb was not as different from the districts they had fled as they liked to think, especially since within another few years they were likely to move farther out in quest of better arrangements, perhaps to escape once again the deterioration setting in where they were. "One is tempted to conclude," a sociologist observed of the suburbs of the 1920s, "that they can have no character which is not described in terms of change."[21] Whether in city or suburb, apartment or detached villa, among brick and asphalt or clapboard and shrubbery, everywhere but in the old foreign-occupied slums, the nature of modern urban life was essentially uncommunal.

To the liberal reformers of the late nineteenth century and to the progressives of the twentieth alike, the central problem of the urban community seemed to lie in the structure of municipal government. In 1888 the English Liberal James Bryce, the most systematic analyst of American life since Tocqueville, adjudged city government to be "the one conspicuous failure of the United States."[22] Municipal reformers, from the high-minded gentlemen who turned the Tweed Ring out of power in New York City in 1871 down to the journalistic "muckrakers" after 1900, laid the blame on the bizarre fragmentation of authority that was typical. The city council usually consisted of two overly large houses, at odds with each other as well as with the mayor. Since the latter's department heads were separately elected or perhaps appointed by the governor of the state, they were not responsible to him. The arrangement seemed designed to allow officials both to evade the responsibility for frugal management of public affairs that the old liberals expected of them and to thwart the sort of action that the new progressives considered useful. Coming out of the prewar Irish gangs, the organizers of the urban political machines established the new type of leader: Hughey McLaughlin in Brooklyn, Martin Lomasney in Boston, Mike McDonald and then Bathhouse John Coughlin and Hinky Dink Mike Kenna in Chicago. Although William Marcy Tweed, the most notorious of the postwar bosses, was not Irish, within a few years of his overthrow he was succeeded by Honest John Kelly. The brassbound wheels of city government required the grease of their kind of corruption if they were to turn to any positively useful purpose at all. On one hand, the boss and his henchmen provided slum voters with simple amenities like bathhouses, found some of them jobs on the public payroll, and assisted the peddler or peanut vendor to get a license. On the other, these peanut politicians, as honest middle-class citizens called them, accepted bribes from businessmen for public utility franchises and lesser favors and raked off graft from contracts with public suppliers.

No old-fashioned liberal and few progressives were ready to acknowledge that the machine boss answered any legitimate social need whatever. The typical urban reform group consisted of middle- and upper-class property owners and businessmen, usually operating, at least before 1900, under some such self-righteous name as "taxpayers' protective league." Their goal was to wrest political control of the city from the "professional politicians" and to vest it in the same "nonpolitical" hands—their own—that held the economic reins. In taking direct control of municipal affairs they sought not so much to carry out more honestly the manifold functions of the bosses and wardheelers as to eliminate them altogether.

Reform rhetoric of course had to ring democratically in the progressive twentieth century. Proposals to augment the power of the mayor or, better still, to replace him with a professional city manager operating on prudent business principles were represented as simplifying the lines of executive responsibility to "the people." Arrangements for securing a safe majority on the city council by electing councilmen "at large" rather than by wards—most of the more populous wards now being inhabited by unpropertied and otherwise unreliable people—were put forward as more truly representative. New procedures that would enable a well-organized and well-heeled minority, like the reform group itself, to initiate legislation by petition, call for a referendum to approve (or reject) some public measure, or secure a "recall" election to remove an objectionable judge from office all were advertised as "direct democracy."

Such devices could not absolutely guarantee the hoped-for result, but they at least temporarily delivered certain cities from the slum-based rule of machine bosses and secured the interests of the respectable folk in the outlying wards and indeed in the suburbs outside the city proper. Not all progressives were so devious, or rather so limited in their conception of the economic and social functions of government. By the 1930s the leaders of the New Deal were co-operating freely with the urban machines as well as more directly providing welfare services for the poor, the slum dweller, and the property owner dispossessed by the depression. But nothing was done, even by this new Democratic alliance, to bind together the various self-segregated, income-graded pseudoneighborhoods of a metropolitan area into an organic community.

The most substantial urban reform that progressives and New Dealers undertook was, quite typically, an attempt to solidify the material foundations of city life. The first requisite seemed to be to stabilize the uses to which real-estate developers could put the land and buildings of particular districts. There was no way to restrict movement of individual families from the country to the city or from the slums to better neighborhoods, nor did anyone propose, in an age which still prized economic opportunity above all, to try to do more than channel the flow. But by statute and city ordinance the existing pattern of industrial and commercial districts and areas of apartment buildings or detached houses, however haphazard it was in origin, could be frozen into "zones." The individual who achieved a middle- or upper-class income could then buy property in a neighborhood matching his social status without undue fear that the place would be invaded at any moment by factories or by folk less reputable than himself. Economic mobility could thus be contained within at least a rudimentary kind of communal structure. In New York, which passed the first zoning law in 1916, the shops and residences of midtown Manhattan were saved from the hitherto irresistible northward advance of the garment industry. During the next fifteen years nearly a thousand other cities adopted zoning codes, which usually limited both the character and the size of new buildings in each zonal category.

Regulation of building standards had in fact begun much earlier, though at first it was directed only against the physical dilapidation of the slums. The early reformers in New York unwittingly, in 1867, inflicted the "dumbbell" tenement house on the next generation of city poor, a prize-winning model that proved ironically lacking in light, air, living space, and sanitation. When in 1901 New York finally adopted an adequate building code, it was too late to affect the endless blocks of "old law" tenements. By 1910 philanthropists and real-estate developers, inspired by recent English experiments, were laying out near New York and Boston the first planned "garden cities"—dispersed, economically self-sufficient communities with space for greenery and other amenities. During the real-estate boom of the 1920s, unfortunately, the idea of the garden suburb was debased in many places to a builder's slogan for promoting quite ordinary new subdivisions. The "Greenbelt" suburbs which the New Deal built in three metropolitan regions in the 1930s housed only 2267 families, a measure of how little in the way of basic planning even the reformers of the time were ready to undertake. The United States Housing Authority did conduct a much larger program, supplemented by projects in which certain great insurance companies invested, of replacing whole blocks of ill-designed and now dilapidated old buildings in the slums of New York, Chicago, Memphis, San Antonio, and many other cities, large and small.

By 1945 the new high-rise "superblocks" were beginning to generate their own social problems. They were better designed, more solidly built, and equipped with more playgrounds, grassy lawns, and other physical conveniences than the old tenement blocks. But, as we shall see, instead of inducing the growth of communal neighborhoods, they plunged the slum dwellers—who increasingly were rural southern Negroes instead of European immigrants—into a starker form of the social isolation and anonymity which middle-class apartment dwellers had elected for themselves.

It had been a long time since the model American small town or rural village—the settled, fairly stable, self-contained, practically egalitarian and democratic community of the backcountry of colonial New England or the Delaware-Susquehanna region—had existed in anything like its original form in any part of the country. Only vestiges of it were still to be found after 1875, either in declining eastern townships riddled by out-migration or in thriving places in the Midwest where people continually came and went; by

1945 hardly anything but nostalgia was left. Nostalgia had a life of its own, however, as the sociologists who investigated Candor, a town of 2500 in the old "burned-over" district of western New York State, discovered in the 1940s. People there still saw themselves in the good old image. Candor was the exemplar, they would assert, of

a wholesome friendly place, the best place to bring up children, and made up of ordinary people, just folks, trying to make their community a better place to live. Nobody here has to worry about having friends, all you have to do is be friendly yourself. No problems are too big for [Candor], it's the outsiders that cause all the trouble. People here have a lot of community spirit, you can always get people to take part, but usually the busiest people are the most reliable. One thing about [Candor], nobody is excluded, this is a democratic town. Anybody who tries to run things gets pushed down, but fast. If you join clubs you can learn things and have a lot of fun too. Everybody was invited and fun was had by all.[23]

To small-town folk their habit of "inoffensive stylized humor, standardized greetings which are given the appearance of intimacy by the cheerfulness with which they are spoken, and the sheer volume of talk devoted to the weather and jokes," echoed their essential social equality.[24] Their township and school board elections exemplified democratic self-government. Their way of life, they were satisfied, embodied a purer culture and a higher morality than the notorious corruptions of the cities.

If there was any residual truth to this description, if the values of the villagers and farmers of such a place were less materialistic and self-seeking than elsewhere, it was mainly for lack of opportunity. The economic progressivism and individualism of American city dwellers had been derived, after all, from their own rural and small-town background. Every small place hoped to grow larger; every rural township dreamed of converting fields to city lots. The common talk was "of population growth and rising real-estate prices, . . . of industrialization, of exploitation of local mineral resources, of improved transportation, and of trade-at-home, home-town loyalty as keys to 'progress.' "[25] Unfortunately most of the "booster" schemes to amass local capital or entice outside investment for such ends were likely to fail in an age of big business controlled from big cities. Candor had achieved its largest population by 1880 and its greatest prosperity a decade or two later. In the automobile age many of the inhabitants were actually commuters who belonged to the economy of nearby industrial cities where they could find jobs.

The most enterprising individuals left such places altogether, leaving them, it was said as early as 1912, no better than "fished-out ponds populated chiefly by bull heads and suckers."[26] The physical decay was plain enough: the "empty store buildings—some with broken windows—vacant lots on Main Street, [the] unpainted, warped, and dying lumber in sagging business houses."[27] Even where the village or hamlet was not abandoned altogether—as more than two thousand had been in Iowa alone by 1930—the place sadly belied the ostensible values and ambitions of its inhabitants. Old-fashioned economic opportunity was not to be found there. A minimal security, inferior to the rising standard expected elsewhere, was best assured by giving up impractical ambitions and withdrawing to a subsistence farm or some other economically marginal existence.

By any objective measurement the social structure of a small town in the modern age was wildly at odds with the image of the egalitarian, democratic community of "just plain folks." Among the villagers of Candor it was easy enough for sociologists to discern a number of distinct, practically exclusive economic classes. Some of these in fact were recognized in colloquial speech. There were the "old aristocrats," a dozen families whose prescriptive claim to leadership in the community was based on what had been leading businesses two or three generations earlier and on safe investments since. A middle class, almost half the population, consisted of businessmen, commercial dairy farmers, and professional men who, though fairly well fixed, were far less free of the constraints of the national economy than they liked to think. Another fifth of the people were struggling either to get ahead in small businesses or farms of the old-fashioned sort or simply to keep up respectable appearances; a few had lapsed into fecklessly eccentric behavior, keeping innumerable pets, compiling baseball records, collecting things. The bottom tenth, the "shack people," were declassed, virtually segregated casual laborers, people without ambition, incentive, or firm social ties even among themselves.[28]

Small-town culture, for all the talk of its superior merits, was increasingly permeated with the catchphrases and stock ideas of the national magazines, the programs of urban radio stations, and Hollywood movies. Success in local politics and government similarly depended on outside connections, if any could be found, to the remote bureaucracies of state and nation which local people professed to despise. All in all the small town's claim to moral superiority was an expression of helpless reaction against its unmanageable circumstances, an act of self-deception that removed any real hope of controlling its own situation. Most small-town people energetically practiced the old economic precepts of hard work, self-reliance, careful calculation, and thrift, but to the outside observer the only practical use of such busywork was to avoid having to recognize the emptiness of the nostalgic vision of continual progress within an eternally neighborly community.

As late as 1945, in short, Americans had not yet begun to reflect that a satisfactory social community—urban, suburban, or rural—would require something beyond economic progress or economic security. They thought the battle had been won when the warm sun of individual success drew individuals up from the immigrant neighborhoods of the squalid urban slums into the middle-class respectability of the detached apartment dweller or suburban householder. Even in laying out a new suburb or subdivision, they tacitly assumed that the half-settled, half-unsettled villages and townships of the nineteenth century were the most suitable models for social community in the twentieth. Understandably, since they were still engaged in the struggle for economic security—a struggle ominously thrown back, as late as the 1930s, by a ten-year depression—they were preoccupied with laying material foundations. It was reassuring to believe that the complex of local economic functions, lubricated by superficially intimate and cheerfully egalitarian manners, in itself comprised a satisfactory communal structure. Not until the next generation, as Americans grew accustomed to economic security and even affluence, would they clearly recognize a communal need for something loftier than economic progress and privatism.

24. THE COMPANIONATE FAMILY

The American family, as European visitors saw it at any time between 1875 and 1945, appeared to be a decaying institution. "Home life is less known in the United States than in any other country," a Frenchman wrote in 1895. "A thousand signs indicate . . . disintegration of the domestic hearth."[1] And yet to an American woman a few years later it seemed no less certain that the families of her acquaintance possessed unique virtues. "In no country," she asserted, "does the cozy home life of the bourgeoisie—the scramble intimate of children, and family pets, and elders—so thoroughly permeate its middle and upper classes as in the United States."[2] Not that the French critic wholly disagreed; the family certainly still existed in America. But it was more apparent to the foreign critic than to the American that the family had become a kind of voluntary association, held together by little more than the preferences of each of its members.

The American family appears to be more than anything else [he observed] an association, a sort of social camp, the ties of which are more or less strong according to individual sympathies, such as might exist between people not of the same blood. I am certain . . . that the friendship of brother and sister, or sister and sister, is entirely elective. So it is with the relations between father and son, mother and daughter.[3]

No longer was the family expected to transcend mere personal intimacy, to endure in spite of the likes and dislikes of its members, or to outlast any one generation.

Foreign observers had been remarking upon the institutional breakdown of the American family for a hundred years past; now many Americans ceased bothering to deny it. Unacquainted with any other sort of family than that in which they and most of their parents and grandparents had grown up, they were smitten by the supreme virtue of its "scramble intimate" as a new, thoroughly up-to-date norm. In turning the loose practice of the nineteenth century into a social ideal for the twentieth, they inevitably made the practice itself looser yet.

The new-model family was best exemplified by the urban and especially the suburban household that had achieved physical and social detachment from its neighbors in the half-community, half-encampment where it had driven in its stakes. To belong to such a place, however, was virtually to have no social place at all, since it furnished almost no channel through which the family could join with others in the achievement of common ends. It had neither the collective agriculture of a peasant village, the social fellowship of the proverbial town pump and marketplace, any highly developed cultural tradition for its members to express, nor the spiritual unity of an established parish. The modern family could take no regular part in such functions even if its members wished. Whatever their economic, social, cultural, or spiritual aspirations, they took it for granted that the family could do little to satisfy them.

Long before 1875 the occupations of most individuals had been practically severed from their family connection. It no longer struck anyone as odd that men left home daily to work in factories or offices, that wives might also go out to earn their own wages, or that sons usually expected to follow some other occupation than their father's. This detachment of the family from the productive economy seemed not simply inevitable but positively desirable. Even if it was no longer an article of faith that the successful man owed everything to his own hard work and prudent calculation, his family was supposed to contribute nothing more to his success than the determination to forge ahead on his own. Presumably it it was not family influence but only this parentally instilled "inner direction" (as a later sociologist would call it) that accounted for the practical fact that the son of a business or professional man, in the 1870s and in the 1920s, enjoyed so great a lead in the race for success that none but the most exceptional farm or working-class boy could overtake him.[4] And in fact in the new bureaucratic economy there could seldom be a direct institutional link between boyhood upbringing and the business in which a man made his career. Except for the youth who inherited a "family business" owned and operated by his father or father-in-law—a less and less likely circumstance in the age of corporate enterprise and hired managers—family background endowed him with little more than a set of abstract attitudes. Since the family, like other social institutions, was now based upon personal affection, it did not in itself exhibit the best model for a modern business career of impersonally "manipulating people and things," a virtue that a recent student attributes to it.[5]

As preparation for all sorts of industrial and commercial occupations increasingly went by default to schools and colleges and the business corporations themselves, the least intrusion of the family into the process suggested that nepotism—presumably uneconomic as well as unfair—was at work. It was too much to suppose that sons regularly inherited their fathers' ability and interests. "When a rising man is given an administrative job and a chance to choose men for other jobs," an anthropologist observed in 1942, "he does not, if he is an American, fill those jobs with members of his family —such conduct is left to those who have never left their foreign neighborhoods, or to the first generation."[6] The thoroughly American, middle-class father was not supposed to pass on his occupational advantage to his son: as for all those other sons who were pushing their way up and out of "foreign" neighborhoods, few of them had much desire for their fathers' occupations or social standing. The welfare of any man's family obviously depended on his getting on in his job, but getting on through his father's "pull" was now as unacceptable as it was unlikely.

The ever-widening range of jobs for women outside the household came to be accepted as the chief gauge of their independence from the old-fashioned family. Not only were some entirely new occupations consigned to them in the late nineteenth century, notably that of telephone operator, but they rapidly took over work formerly done by men, such as stenography, and at least a few young ladies took up the practice of medicine and other masculine professions. State regulation of women's working conditions in industry somewhat reduced their desirability as cheap workers, but perhaps it also made wage labor somewhat more attractive to them. In any case, more women were working for wages every decade. Where in 1870 only 15 percent of the women of the country had been "gainfully employed," thirty years later 21 percent were working, and by 1940 nearly 30 percent. By that time the workingwomen also composed 30 percent of the entire labor force of the country.

Since the proportion of the workingwomen who were wives also rose, from 15 percent in 1900 to 35 percent in 1940, it was clear that the modern woman could still get married and establish a family, of course one of the modern sort. Sometimes young women seemed to be rebelling against the family altogether—in 1901 a women's magazine writer described their letters to her as "a volcano of seething unrest."[7] But they were rejecting only the peculiarly constricted family life of the mid-nineteenth century, when womenfolk had had to withdraw into a career of mere housekeeping as the household itself lost its old place in the agricultural or industrial economy and the social community outside its walls. The household did not regain a place as an integral institution of the productive economy even though a woman could now spend five or six days a week at some job quite detached from it—a job, for the typical middle-class workingwoman, that was also considerably inferior to her husband's occupational level.

Legal abolition of industrial child labor progressively removed children from almost all sectors of the productive economy. In 1900 a quarter of all boys between ten and fifteen and a tenth of the girls of the same age worked for wages. By 1920 those fractions had been cut in half, by 1930 halved again, and by 1940 virtually wiped out. Henceforth young people would not leave the family to go to work until near the end of adolescence. It was no longer possible however, to return children to their premodern economic relationship to their families. The modern family had little for them to work at. In sustaining the constitutionality of the new legislation on the very old grounds of the general interest of the commonwealth, the state courts that went so far as to declare that "the right to the labor of the child is not a vested right in the parent" were at least incidentally taking a very pragmatic view of the situation.[8] A family could not even be expected to train its children for jobs in the fast-changing economy as the farmer or artisan had been able to do long ago. The modern institutional alternative of course was the school. Passage of state laws against child labor was shortly followed by the first effective enforcement of compulsory school attendance, both in the two-thirds of the states that had nominally required it before 1900 and in the others that ordered it later. An increasingly elaborate succession of elementary, secondary, and vocational schools, colleges and professional schools took up the training function that the family perforce had abandoned.

The family was also poorly adapted for carrying out political, religious, and even social purposes. Ever since the 1820s, when all white men were given the vote, the basic political integer had been the individual, rather than the householder as representative of his family. The movement of 1875–1920 for woman suffrage proceeded with almost no consideration of its fundamental implications for the family. Although most opponents of the reform were voluble enough over the danger that voting would "unsex" wives and mothers, only a very exceptional one explicitly invoked the principle, as a delegate to the New York constitutional convention of 1894 did, that "the unit in this State is not and should not be the individual, but . . . the family," and even he was more concerned to preserve the precarious internal unity of the family than to restore it as the basic constituent element of government and politics.[9]

At no point in the new era of progessive reform did the state pay much attention to the family as such. Limiting the working hours of women in industry or removing children from factories and compelling them to attend school of course affected the life of many particular families and no doubt often, as reformers argued, materially improved it. Operation of the reforms was entrusted, however, not to the family—how many fathers had sworn to the justice of the peace that their nine-year-old boys were twelve and ready for working papers?—but instead to schools, juvenile courts, welfare agencies, regulatory commissions, and other special new institutions. At most the family was a passive beneficiary of a state which worked through instrumentalities of quite other kinds.

Other established institutions relied less and less on the family. Even though the ordinary churchgoer practically inherited his religious affiliation as a kind of "birthright" from his parents, most Protestant churches had long since shifted the care of religious instruction, charitable works, and even private devotions from the hands of the family into those of Sunday schools, Dorcas societies, and other subgroups of their own. Likewise the voluntary associations to which individuals belonged—Boy or Girl Scouts, women's clubs or businessmen's luncheon clubs, lodges and college fraternities, and the rest—were organized far less in terms of family affiliation than of common age groups, occupations, and other personal categories.

In fact the family was now too narrowly constituted to keep up old ties of extended kinship. The very popularity of the "family reunion" of far-flung cousins, many of whom otherwise hardly knew of each other's existence, only underscored the opinion of a French visitor in 1892 that the "American of Anglo-Saxon origin" quite lacked "that large family feeling which characterizes certain European peoples; he is not bound to folk of his own blood by any special connections."[10] Beyond his wife and children and his own parents' family, as sociologists later pointed out, he had only "cousins," "relatives," and "in-laws," each of whom was bound to him not according to precise degrees of blood relationship but simply by whatever personal affection he and they might feel for each other.[11]

There were exceptions among old-fashioned kinds of people. Not yet wholly "Americanized" immigrants were more closely united among themselves, perhaps, the more they were practically cut off from their European kin. Old-style "family farmers," if they were not repeatedly on the move, set great store by kinship, particularly in the South. Propertied families of old local elites still cherished antique pretensions to dynasty. Most up-to-date Americans could see little more than sentimentality, however, in the conservative point of view which the Hegelian philosopher William T. Harris advanced in 1876 (in defending the practice of the public schools of Saint Louis of providing German-language instruction for children of immigrants):

The consciousness of one's ancestry and the influence derived from communication with the oldest members of a family is very potent in giving tone to the individuality of youth and ripening age, and indeed even to a community or people as a whole. This continuity of history is a kind of solid, substantial ground for the individual and from its soil spring up his self respect and aspiration. It is to be looked upon rather as a calamity than otherwise when a community is increased by the immigration of a class of people who have no desire to preserve a close communication with the mother country.[12]

The American who took grandfatherly ramblings about his ancestors too seriously, like the immigrant who hesitated to cast off his old allegiance, would be suspected of a lack of republican self-reliance.

No matter how free a family might be of other social institutions, past or present, it needed some internal coherence if only to rear children fit to take their part as individuals in the larger society. For that residual task—which Americans took for granted would remain its irreducible, inescapable one—the usual nuclear or conjugal unit of husband and wife and minor children was perhaps well enough adapted as long as the larger society was governed by the economic individualism of the nineteenth century. The family's internal structure, the network of interrelations among its various individual members, had accordingly grown quite casual and often, in the opinion of old-fashioned European visitors, startlingly loose.[13] * Many young people who emerged from such families

* In this respect the kind of poor Negro family that both black and white students of the time considered to be typical was an extreme case of the general American type rather than something quite different. The notorious looseness of marital ties among ordinary Negroes, the large proportion of unmarried couples and of broken liaisons, the "healthier and more reasonable" attitude toward sex (as some by 1910 were beginning to defend it), the number of mothers who worked outside the home, leaving their children practically to bring themselves up in the neighborhood, the lack of private "home life": this set of mores was farther advanced, in the oncoming twentieth-century sense, than that which the typical white family had yet reached. The pressure of economic circumstances upon Negroes having been unusually extreme ever since the days of slavery, the institutional integrity of family life had broken down among them much earlier than in the white community. Eventually the latter would find attractive something of the same sort of loose arrangements.

around 1900 had a "curious sense that they had practically brought themselves up."[14] That might be an advantage for forging a career and getting on in the highly mobile, rapidly changing industrial economy of the time. But a family that lacked the capacity to instill any higher social, cultural, or spiritual purpose was not wholly satisfying to the very children about whose success it was most concerned. Although the young twentieth-century rebels against the middle-class "Victorian" family thought of it as overly patriarchal, authoritarian, and oppressive, especially toward its women and children, it is probably truer to say that in its structural looseness and detachment from broader social, cultural, and spiritual purposes it was simply "repressive."[15] Like most other nineteenth-century institutions, that is, it was too content with mere absence of constraint to open the way to rewarding social relationships or cultural self-expression—to anything, indeed, but the single-minded pursuit of material success.

Perhaps only a few unusually reflective young people at the turn of the century had the sense of "mysterious inner paralysis" which has been detected between the lines of their letters and diaries.[16] Ordinary Americans, even if they could not conceive of any better internal structure for the family, were increasingly able to recognize what it had become and to accept that as normal. No one gained a general hearing for any new institutional arrangement of a sort to match the business consolidation and governmental regulation of the progressive era. It is not surprising that, at a time when many big businessmen and progressive politicians were still briskly asserting the outdated rhetoric of economic individualism, the twentieth-century social norm of intimate personal relations between individuals seemed to suit the family well enough. By that standard its already loose and often unstable structure could be validated without in fact having to be greatly reformed.

Intimacy soon took on meanings, however, about which the previous age had preferred not to speak too explicitly. Before 1910 no more than a handful of emancipated spirits, in making "a kind of religion" of personal relations, were beginning to exalt sexual intercourse as the most personal of all—and as the source of all other relationships between individuals.[17] By the 1920s a great many more flaunted the same banner of emancipated speech and behavior. They were a good deal less revolutionary than they and those they shocked liked to think. Rather than simply overthrowing Victorian "Puritanism" and introducing an essentially new pattern of love and marriage, they were content to see the family complete its practical detachment from the larger society—begun even before the nineteenth century—and to make a supreme virtue out of personal affection.

Popular moralists of the 1920s and 1930s, convinced that a social revolution was indeed going on, singled out the motion pictures as the source of excessively "romantic" expectations in the young. But courtship and marriage had been reduced to the personal concern of each couple long before "Hollywood." Courtship now consisted of nothing more formal than a succession of agreed-upon "dates." Marriage was in a sense displacing the family itself; a husband and wife now referred colloquially to their "marriage," implying not so much a fixed social institution as a special arrangement between two people who had "fallen in love." If thereafter they fell out of it again, what they were likely to say had gone on the rocks was again their marriage, a relationship more or less separable from their other personal relationships with their children and their in-laws.

The parents of a young couple usually played no more than a ceremonial role in arranging the marriage, mainly that of providing a suitably elaborate reception on the day of the wedding. That was the palest vestige of the old protracted negotiations over a "settlement"; not in several generations had it been expected that dowries should be large enough to start the new family off on their parents' social level. A German wryly observed in 1877 that if a suitor were to broach the subject of any such subvention to an American father, the latter would inquire sharply whether he was proposing "to marry his daughter or his property."[18] The prudence with which young people of so many former times and places had put off marriage and parenthood was now thrown to the rising winds of material affluence and social individualism. The average age at marriage, which was unaccountably two or three years higher in 1890 than it had been in 1860, fell again between 1890 and 1940, from twenty-six to twenty-four for men, and from twenty-two to twenty-one and a half for women; within another few years it would fall even more. This was reflected in the increase in the annual number of marriages, relative to population: fluctuating between 77 and 96 for every 10,000 persons during the generation before 1890; from 90 to 120 in various years thereafter and, immediately after the end of the Great Depression and the Second World War, as high as 162—"a period of the most rapid family formation in [American] history."[19] By the late 1940s fully 70 percent of all American adults were married; fully 90 percent, indeed, had been married at some time in their lives.

Freedom of personal choice was still more clearly asserted by divorce. The annual divorce rate, which had been minuscule at the middle of the nineteenth century, steadily rose to 10 per 10,000 population in 1914, about 17 in 1929, and in 1946, again just after the depression and the war, an astonishing rate of 44, fully a fourth of the record marriage rate of the time. The growing readiness of discontented spouses to free themselves, most of them to try again sooner or later with another partner, was not due to liberalization of the divorce laws of the various states. (Reno became the chief national divorce mill after 1900 not because Nevada loosened its requirements but because the Dakotas had tightened theirs a little.) The reformers who sought to safeguard the beleaguered American home by promoting a uniform divorce code for the country ignored the practical attitude that, as a recent historian approvingly puts it, "easy divorce is the only policy consistent with the aspirations of a freedom-loving people."[20]

Most couples of course stayed together or at least never got a divorce—nineteen out of twenty in 1880, nine out of ten in 1910, and three out of four as late as 1945—and lived most of their lives within families of the kind that now seemed normal. How their style of married life should be described depended on one's point of view. Foreign visitors usually were struck by the equality and independence of the American wife. An Englishman concluded, as early as 1880, "Married ladies have equal or even greater license than the unmarried. They do as they like, and go where they like, having no fear of their husbands before their eyes."[21] At the turn of the century a French visitor interpreted the "mutual respect for personality" displayed by American husbands and wives as a mutual craving for independence "or at least the constant repression of every wish to invade or to penetrate the intimacy of the self."[22] Americans themselves—among them the leading historian of the family in 1919—believed that their system of "reciprocal enlightened loyalty" gave the surest "guarantee of general happiness."[23] Though the promise often proved rosier than the actuality, on balance it was still possible thirty years later to represent the ideal modern marriage as

an intimate community of two persons within which they gratify their desires for marital happiness and companionship; . . . family and home are their strongholds always. . . . In any circumstance the present companionate family is what most of them desire; few would care to revive, even if they could, the earlier large farm family with its greater cohesion but also its larger neglect of personality of its members.[24]

The combination of "constant companionship, mutual loyalty, and sexual gratification" upon which urban middle-class husbands and wives commonly set the highest value—and to which families of recent foreign origin or rural background also at least partially adjusted—was the more attractive when set against the uncertainties of the disjointed society about them. "Marriage and the family," a sociologist observed in 1953, was the most available way for them to "organize and give quality to their existence."[25] The fact that the economic system made husband and wife practically independent of each other most of the day—he at his distant work, she perhaps at a job of her own or freed at any rate from the old confining household tasks by modern electrical "appliances"—only intensified their need to cultivate their relationship with each other as the most intensely personal one open to them. Under the pressure of such demanding expectations, it was perhaps surprising that more marriages were not propelled straight into the divorce court. The same basic cause that created this intensity of expectation—the lack of other primary social institutions offering any greater emotional security—may have helped to keep husbands and wives together in spite of their disappointments; where else could they turn?

In a rapidly changing society the relations between parents and children, past infancy, were chancy at best. Husbands and wives, being each other's close contemporaries, at least shared the values of their time. But the children of each new generation were more likely than the last to reject their parents' values as laughably outdated. Perhaps the apparent changes from one generation to the next were largely an illusion created by the acceleration of technological progress on every side: the rapid advance from horsecars to trolleys to automobiles and airplanes intensified the impression of a radically new mobility, and the sudden advent of movies and radio broadcasting separated the young even more sharply from parents who perhaps had hardly ever seen a play or vaudeville show. The major social change after 1900 may have been simply the conscious acceptance of conditions long established: the progressive disintegration of a common social structure, the substitution of personal relationships as the prevailing norm. But to those who first accepted that standard as a revolutionary dispensation, the gap which they felt yawning between them and their predecessors was no less real for being mainly a state of mind.

The new intensity of affection which parents expected to feel for each of their children perhaps accounted for their giving birth to proportionately fewer of them every decade. Between 1800 and

1875 the annual birthrate had already fallen off more than a third, to about 35 births per 1000 population; by 1900 it was below 30; by 1920 at about 25; and at its lowest, in the trough of the depression in 1933, under 17. Accordingly, where four or five children had been usual in a family in 1875, by 1900 there were three or four and by the 1930s hardly two. Since of course at any time there were improvident or old-fashioned people—recent immigrants, "family" farmers, poor Negroes—who persisted in having as many children as ever, the contraction of the urban and suburban middle-class family was sharper yet. Perhaps the 485 families living in twenty-two apartment houses in New York in 1900 who were found to have only 54 children, one for every 9 families, represent an extreme case, but a doctor on the respectable upper West Side had some reason to conclude that "having a family is not an American ideal."[26] By the 1940s most white urban Protestant and Jewish couples and, in spite of the strictures of their church, a good many Catholics had evidently chosen to have fewer children than their parents had had—though some of them no doubt had rather more, given the persistence of practical misinformation about methods of contraception, than the number they had intended.

Popular moralists at the turn of the century denounced the decline in the birthrate as "race sterility" and "race suicide," to be accounted for only by the physical or moral decay of the once virtuously prolific American people. Some critics saw it as yet another deleterious contribution of the Slavic, Italian, and Jewish immigrants, whose improvidently large families must, by some "rule of nature," have discouraged native Americans from attempting to keep pace: "the higher the animal," one editor loftily aphorized, "the lower the birth rate."[27] Others blamed the distractions of modern life, especially the vogue of subjecting the tender intellects of girls to the rigors of higher education at the expense of their nerves and their fitness to be wives and mothers. All in all, an unsympathetic college president (and psychologist) wrote in a women's magazine in 1910, "It does not seem to be entirely certain that the human race can permanently survive and flourish in this country."[28]

Although the decline in childbearing was indeed largely a matter of deliberate choice, that moral issue was already an old one in America. The late-Victorian laws against "obscene literature" took particular aim at the confidential volumes which, ever since the 1830s, had been offering wives and husbands technical advice on contraception—some of it physiologically quite erroneous—and also the moral arguments that so many of them evidently were seeking. In the early twentieth century both aspects of the subject were brought into the open by plainspoken advocates of "birth control." The children of families of every class had become, in economic terms, only an expense to their parents. Besides the effect of the child-labor laws, neither large-scale farming nor the ordinary middle-class household any longer gave children much real work to do. And now practical caution began to be reinforced by a revised standard of private morality. As early as 1903 an ordinary Methodist clergyman could admonish his flock, and have it printed in the local paper, that among the personal rights of children was the right not to be born into a family unable to maintain them. "Parents must be able to properly support a child or it is a crime to bring them into being."[29]

"It can not be doubted," a sociologist pronounced in 1919, "that America has entered upon 'the century of the child.' "[30] Most foreign travelers would have dated the beginning of that epoch much earlier. "The family, which is a monarchy in the old world," a Frenchman wrote in 1883, "has become, like everything else, a republic in the new. The father is not a king; he is simply a president."[31] (It was still the era of weak presidents.) Fathers and mothers alike were used to the idea of nurturing the individuality of each child as their equal, soon to become their better. They were not wholly unaware that such treatment, extravagant by old-fashioned standards, could mislead children into outright antisocial behavior. The youth whose elders put his convenience, ambitions, and advantage before their own might easily get the notion not so much that they were equipping him eventually to excel them, but that he already possessed "some mysterious attribute, something," an editor mused in 1895, "that commands our service." Parental cosseting all too often produced not simply precocity but the "downright impudence" of arrogant and willful children who would "race and tear and yell . . . like hoodlums" at public gatherings and then "resent any restraint upon their actions."[32]

In fact, however, the youth of that time was taking one more step toward establishing a condition of complete equality, even indistinguishability, between the generations. "Spoilt, capricious, precocious little old men and women," an Englishwoman thought them in 1887.[33] The forwardness of American youth seemed the obverse, an Englishman speculated in 1900, of an odd air of childishness among American adults—"a want of discipline, an incapacity for ordered and corporate effort."[34] The relationship between the generations was not, however, simply a matter of spinelessness on one side and rebellion on the other, but an aspect of the general attrition of old social distinctions. Like other primary social categories, neither age nor youth much cared now to be confined within a straitjacket of formal manners. Nor did all foreign observers dislike what they saw. As the English reformer George Holyoake sympathetically noted in 1881, the young people of America, being "more self-acting" than children reared under the "somewhat domestic paternalism" common in England, often manifested a charmingly "affectionate and intelligent obedience."[35] Now and then visitors were also disarmed by the easy, unconstrained air of equality, even in public, which American parents and children so obviously took for granted. One might like it or not, but childhood no longer was sharply set off from adult society.*

This state of affairs, which had been generated earlier in the nineteenth century by a combination of parental indulgence, ambition for the self-reliant youth, and mere negligence, was formalized in the twentieth as yet another version of the doctrine of personalism. Although this too was less a practical revolution than a new application of the old libertarian rhetoric, the youth of each successive decade prided themselves on having left that much farther behind them the oppressively patriarchal Victorian family, as they supposed it to have been. The modern relationship between parents and children, like that between husbands and wives, could now, at any rate, be frankly recognized as one of personal affection and sympathy—"a spiritual and psychic association of parent and child based on persuasion," as one authority put it in 1904.[36] As in economic and political matters, however, the precise interpretation that the reforming expert of one day placed on this development differed considerably from that of the next. A "progressive" emphasis on childish spontaneity gave way in the 1920s to a fashion for "behaviorism," a rigorously unemotional training in essential habits that was somewhat mistakenly deduced from experimental psychology. By the 1940s the pendulum had swung back to development of personality through free play of "natural" affections, a basically intuitive regimen in which the child was to set his own pace and direction.

Every family had to work out whatever adaptation of such irregular rules it could manage, creating its own "private family culture."[37] White middle-class families, who had established the new

---

* See, however, p. 216n. of the present book. If perhaps American children had *always* been regarded in a sense as little men and women, they had not formerly been exalted into the practical equals or even superiors of their elders.

norm of emotional warmth and calculated permissiveness, no doubt came closer than others to living up to it. Although poor Negroes had arrived at something like it long since, their families of course were not regarded as being in the least comparable. Many working-class parents, less cut off from Old World attitudes, may have wrung a certain satisfaction out of imposing a traditional authority on their children, a satisfaction such as eluded them in subordinate occupations and the inchoate society outside the home. But by the 1940s the majority subscribed to a standard American doctrine of child-rearing. As a sociologist summed it up, the "socialization" of the young "should proceed leniently at the start, but, as they grow up and can understand, their discipline should progressively tighten until at the end they develop, it may be hoped, into secure adult persons."[38]

That fond hope was all too often sadly frustrated. Even when parents had dutifully absorbed the popular manuals of Dr. Gesell and Dr. Spock, there remained a puzzling vagueness about the precise steps by which authority over the child's actions was to pass from his parents to himself. Young people probably still exhibited, at each stage of the process, much the same mixture of arrogant irresponsibility and sober self-reliance as they had in the less analytical nineteenth century. Both the self-possession and the bumptiousness of the younger generation were of a piece with their elders' assumption, drawn from their own childhood, that every individual ought to proceed as quickly as possible to the responsibilities as well as the privileges and perquisites of adulthood. But evidently this inheritance from the practical behavior of the nineteenth century was not altogether satisfactory. By the 1940s sociologists were remarking, rather ominously, on the distinctive "youth culture" that had for some time been coalescing among adolescents. Not only was it cutting them off from adult society, but "this youth culture, with its irresponsibility, its pleasure-seeking, its 'rating and dating,' and its intensification of the romantic love pattern" seemed, disconcertingly enough to social individualists, to bear "the marks of reaction to emotional tension and insecurity."[39]

The adolescent's own social goal was still, however, to achieve "maturity" by his elders' current definition of that happy condition. What had changed was the accepted definition: from membership in a multipurpose social institution to full enjoyment of a set of warm personal relationships. Since the mature young person of course expected to marry, within a very few years, he began early to sort out his relationships with his contemporaries, particularly of the opposite sex. Oddly enough, the closer his ties to his parents the likelier it was that the shift to the new set would involve too great a wrench for either him or them to accept with equanimity. Perhaps coming of age had always been difficult. But now it demanded more of the adolescent than he could confidently supply. Moralists had some reason to fear that the current juvenile social conventions, in particular the hothouse forcing process of dating, grossly overemphasized the superficial virtues of "physical charm, friendliness, self-assurance, and gaiety," all mere "assets of personality" rather than of matrimonial stability.[40] But the young people were less peculiar specimens of their time than they appeared. As long as the family, like other primary social institutions, was expected to rest mainly on personal affection between autonomous individuals, the rites of dating and the rest of the youth culture fit the larger social pattern well enough.

Now that Americans gauged the success of any family by the elusive standard of its members' happiness and sense of individual fulfillment, the institution was all too easily overburdened. No longer an integral unit of the system of economic production or of the larger social structure, it was inadequately buttressed to support the emotional stress that, precisely because its members lacked other institutional outlets, they commonly loaded onto it. The husband and wife, sons and daughters, who depended so heavily on "social interaction with each other," it was observed in 1953, "react constantly to each other's love, or discontent, or anxieties, or aches, and breathe the emotional atmosphere of the home which these create."[41] Since it was the function of the companionate family to relieve all the stresses, social as well as personal, for which the modern world provided no other regular outlet, the one that succeeded was a success indeed. But families whose "intimacy [became] suffocating, their demands unbearable, and their expectations too high to be easily realizable" were all too likely to proceed relentlessly toward the utter wretchedness of divorce, unfilial contempt, and aggrieved but helpless isolation.[42] Whether the fortunate outnumbered the unfortunate is hardly calculable.

25. CHURCHES AND THE AMERICAN WAY

In view of the enormous growth in church membership between 1875 and 1945, one might reasonably have expected that the spiritual influence of the church over other institutions of society would mightily increase. By 1900, for the first time since the nadir of indifference a century before, more than a third of the adult population of the country had formally joined churches, and by the 1940s more than half. Almost everyone, indeed, was prepared (in response to an inquiry in the mid-1950s) to identify himself in religious terms: 68 percent as Protestants, 23 percent as Catholics, and 4 percent as Jews. Fully three-fourths of those who were asked also regarded themselves in some sense as regular members of churches or synagogues. In no other country of the modern world did the established churches or any major sects manage even to hold their own against the scholarly "higher criticism" of the Bible, the prestige of natural science, and the pervasiveness of popular disbelief. In America the churches somehow flourished in spite of an even more thoroughly secular cast of mind.

The upsurge in church membership by no means halted, however, the steady erosion of the old spiritual authority of the church. Indeed it was partly because most denominations demanded so little of the communicant that so many people could find a church of some sort to take them in. That they flocked into churches, when they had no lack of other organizations to join, suggests that something beyond the churches' lack cf theological rigor attracted them, something considerably more immediate than the creed, ancient or up to the minute, to which they formally subscribed. Creeds, theologies, and liturgies could of course provide sanctuary from the turbulent world. At one time they had also given direction to earthly concerns. But now for many people the church evidently was less a refuge from the world or a source of spiritual means of dominating it than a way for the individual to place himself in secular society. Now, indeed, that the churches were less able than ever to set a spiritual course of their own—when they were bobbing along in the wake of the economic and social preoccupations of the age—they seemed more attractive than ever before.

In the final quarter of the nineteenth century, when most Americans still thought of the Catholics and Jews among them as alien folk, it could be assumed that the country was essentially Protestant, none the less so for the division of Protestantism into half a dozen major denominations and scores of minor ones nor for the loud remonstrances of a few village atheists and agnostic lecturers of the old rationalist school. In old-fashioned rural districts and out-of-the-way towns where immigrants were few, and few of them were not also Protestants, that assumption was fair enough. But in the mainstream of change, especially in the booming industrial and commercial cities all across the North and West, Protestant churches were rapidly becoming the preserve of the middle and upper classes. "Go into an ordinary church on Sunday morning," a clergyman acknowledged in 1887, "and you see lawyers, physicians, merchants, and business men with their families . . . but the workingman and his household are not there."[1]

As the downtown sections of cities filled up with a medley of immigrant laborers, all but a few Protestant churches followed the exodus of their members to the suburbs. Seventeen Protestant churches abandoned lower Manhattan between 1868 and 1888 while some two hundred thousand immigrants, mostly Catholics and Jews, were crowding into it; one downtown ward in Boston in the 1880s had twenty-two thousand people but no longer a single Protestant church. By the same token, three-fifths of the Protestant church members of Pittsburgh were business and professional men and their families, although their sort composed only a tenth of the population of the city.

No church deliberately excluded honest sons of toil or the "deserving" poor. Respectable Protestants were quick to assert, however, that it was the fault of the poor themselves that they were both poor and unchurched. If men who were still manual laborers had been the churchgoing sort, "instead of giving so much of their time and earnings to saloons, or to labor associations," the Congregational weekly unctuously advised in 1894, "we are persuaded they would find themselves less frequently pinched by poverty and less in want of real friends than they now are."[2] After all, the greatest "sleeping partner in any business," the same paper had announced in 1876, was "the Almighty"; small wonder, the clergyman who investigated the economic status of Pittsburgh Protestants concluded, that "evangelical Christianity pays!"[3] Such profane dogma had been heard before, but now its smug postulates were too deeply engraved to be missed by the Protestant workingman who made bold to enter a city church only to be thrust "into nooks and corners."[4] According to Samuel Gompers, many of whose British and German lieutenants in the American Federation of Labor were at least nominal Protestants, trade unionists in the 1890s were convinced that the "real God" of the churches was "the almighty dollar."[5]

Although the purer scriptural idiom that had once come so readily to mind was fading out of daily use, there were still many Americans who defied the practical materialism all around them. Their impulse to preach a strictly spiritual gospel seldom led now to the founding of new sects. There were a few small groups of millennialists on the old lines, notably the Jehovah's Witnesses (beginning about 1879). Only one new faith, Christian Science, matched the triumphs of the Mormons and Millerites of the 1830s and 1840s. Mary Baker, the founder of Christian Science, came, like Joseph Smith and William Miller before her, from the run-down backcountry of northern New England. The difficulties of her life—not only poverty but an obscure "nervous" debility—she was inclined to interpret in spiritual terms, especially after treatment by one of the mesmerists fashionable in the 1840s and absorption in the spiritualist craze of the next decade. In the late 1860s, after the death of the "mental healer" who had been treating her, she evolved a healing technique of her own. Moving to Lynn, she gathered about her a band of followers, mainly working people, some of whom paid her a fee for training as practitioners. Her doctrine, published in 1875 as *Science and Health,* quite rejected the science and the general materialism of the day; since matter itself was an illusion, disease could be nothing more than a state of mind induced by one's belief in it, or perhaps by the "malicious animal magnetism" of others.

Mrs. Eddy, as Mary Baker was known after her third marriage, incorporated the Church of Christ, Scientist, in 1879. In Boston, where she moved three years later, she attracted a congregation of a more prosperous class of people than she had begun with. It was not in that material sense that Christian Science was essentially a conservative movement—nor in the circumstance that Mrs. Eddy died a millionaire in 1910—but rather in a doctrine that did away with material values altogether. Fittingly enough, the Mother Church in Boston maintained hierarchic control over the local "branches" of the sect. Its conservatism of course ended like that of so many others who had chipped new denominations away from the already shattered institutional fabric of American Protestantism.

As Quakers, Baptists, and other inspired sectarians had done before, Christian Science carried the individualistic implications of the Protestant Reformation squarely into modern society by emphasizing the believer's personal relationship to God, with no other local intermediary, at any rate, than the deputed "reader" from Mrs. Eddy's book and its *Key to the Scriptures*.

Spiritual individualism had been practiced by many evangelical sects long before Americans created a whole way of life based on personal relations. But where the idea of the inner light or the priesthood of all believers had seemed dangerously radical to the hierarchically established churches of the seventeenth and eighteenth centuries, now only the simplest possible relationship between man and God was intelligible to earnest Protestants of a great many denominations. Under the name of fundamentalism one more effort was made, literally as well as colloquially conservative in its spiritual purpose, to boil the old creeds down to a few essential articles of faith that even a theologically illiterate generation could comprehend.

A simplistic fundamentalism considerably antedated *The Fundamentals*, the series of pamphlets published in 1910 that gave the movement its modern name. As early as 1864 certain quite orthodox Presbyterians and Episcopalians, organized as the National Reform Association, had sought to restore the United States to divine favor —upon which the Civil War had thrown some doubt—through the simple device of a "Christian amendment" to the Constitution, naming Jesus Christ as supreme ruler. In proposing to establish what would amount to a state religion, the movement had been too extreme even for the age that first put "In God We Trust" on the coinage. The similar failure of efforts to ignite another great national revival like that of 1858 tempted evangelists to strip the essentials of belief down to a few compelling formulas.

The Fundamentals encapsulated Christianity in five points. First and foremost was the literally infallible authority of the Bible; upon it depended the other four—Christ's virgin birth, His atonement for human sin, the Resurrection, and the second coming—and everything else in creation. The variety of Bible Leagues, Bible Crusades, and other new institutions in which fundamentalism was soon incarnated for once did not split off more denominations; rather they constituted the right wing of most of the existing Protestant churches. Fundamentalism was strongest among Baptists, Methodists, and other dyed-in-the-wool evangelicals, but Presbyterians and even Episcopalians were thrown into turmoil in the 1920s by this

latest reformation. As in so many conservatively inspired movements in the past, fundamentalists considered themselves to be the
champions of the true orthodoxy, to the great annoyance of the
older orthodox church people.

The essential conservatism of fundamentalism, social as well as
spiritual, lay in its unquestioning certitudes, as the reflective on
either side of the issue in the 1920s recognized. To the young social
liberal Reinhold Niebuhr (who was soon to define a rigorously neo-
Calvinist theology) the "frantic orthodoxy" of the fundamentalists
sadly revealed the depth of their need to paper over the anxieties
and the scepticism of the modern world.[6] The leading theologian
of fundamentalism, the Presbyterian J. Gresham Machem, agreed:
people who were weary of the modern church, shot through as it
was by "the turmoil of the world," were seeking a faith that might
allow them "to forget for a moment all those things that divide
nation from nation and race from race, to forget human pride, to
forget the passions of war, to forget the puzzling problems of industrial strife, and to unite in overflowing gratitude at the foot of
the Cross."[7]

Usually the stridency with which fundamentalists hurled themselves into the "war" against modernist clergymen—whom they
denounced as scoundrels, hypocrites, seducers of the young, and
latter-day Tom Paines—was hardly calculated to subdue turmoil.[8]
The campaign of the 1920s to extirpate teaching of Darwinian
evolution from the public schools brought to a focus the contempt
of the "old-time religion" for liberal reformers as well as for natural
science and scholarly interpretation of biblical texts. In other
respects the antagonists were oddly related. The antievolution laws
passed by eight southern states were as democratic as any of the
"liberal" regulation of the progressive era; in Arkansas, indeed,
Darwinism was banished by popular referendum. But the test case
of the Tennessee statute in 1925, the trial of the biology teacher,
John T. Scopes, further embittered the two branches of reform, as
William Jennings Bryan, the old populist-progressive Democrat and
spokesman for biblical literalism, debated to the death—his own—
against the celebrated liberal-progressive and agnostic Clarence
Darrow. As so often before, the sharpest conflict was between men
seeking, in their different ways, a higher moral principle for society.

The evangelical revivalism that had been the classic instrument
for that same end from the 1730s through the 1850s was now in
sad decline. Beside an Edwards or a Finney the new preachers were

a race of calculating pygmies. The businesslike revival campaigns of Dwight L. Moody, beginning in the mid-1870s, accompanied by the sentimental hymns of his associate Ira Sankey, attracted few but the already converted and the traditionally pious. As the twentieth century advanced, they in turn were succeeded first by such panderers to the maudlin and credulous as Billy Sunday, the former baseball professional who boasted that he didn't "know any more about theology than a jack-rabbit knows about ping-pong" but was taking "trail-hitters" to glory at only "about $2 a soul," and then by Aimee Semple McPherson and other bizarre cult-leaders of the restless California of the 1920s and 1930s.[9] Even the two soberly evangelical groups, the Young Men's Christian Association and the Salvation Army, both English in origin, exemplified in spite of themselves the decline of revivalism in America. The YMCA grew rapidly after its introduction at Boston in 1851—it had branches in twenty-five cities by 1875 and nearly five hundred by 1900—but by the 1920s it almost completely de-emphasized evangelism in favor of deflecting young men from urban temptation—many of them were fresh from the farm—by supplying cheap but decent lodgings, gymnasiums, and reading rooms. The Salvation Army, whose brass bands and street preaching to "rumdom, slumdom, and bumdom" startled respectable people when it first appeared in 1879, also kept abreast of the times after 1889 by progressively expanding its welfare services.[10] By the 1920s even the most resolute evangelists had learned that modern Americans of almost all sorts preferred a gospel of substantial good works.

Earthly conduct had always been a concern of the church. The strictest Calvinists of the seventeenth century had recognized the validity of "works," insofar as these proceeded from faith. They had also held the church responsible for overseeing the ethical behavior of men in their material vocations. The "social gospel" which the leading wing in most of the major Protestant denominations preached between 1875 and 1945 was inspired less by any coherent theology, however, than by the progressive middle-class revulsion against economic inequities. In tackling the demoralizing physical condition of the slums, the "institutional" church remained downtown and tried to entice its foreign neighbors into its library, classrooms, and gymnasium (if not its sanctuary). Even congregations that had fled to the suburbs were likely to hear a good deal about the social responsibility of Christians from their ministers and their denominational hierarchies. The Federal Council of the Churches of Christ in America was founded in 1908 mainly to encourage and coordinate the work of the major Protestant denominations for "economic democracy."[11]

"On the whole," a recent study concludes, "it is safe to say that the churches have *reflected* the secular conscience; they have neither led nor followed as a rule."[12] At each point in the course of the twentieth-century movement to reform the economic and political systems much the same arguments were heard from the pulpit as from other rostrums. No progressive or New Deal measure would have turned out very differently had there been no such clerical urging. The social gospelers, indeed, were a minority of the clergy in every Protestant denomination; fundamentalists and other "conservative" churchmen—socially as well as theologically conservative, in the colloquial sense—refused to interject the church into political reform. Probably most of those clergymen who were reform-minded heard a good deal of grumbling in their own congregations over the unseemliness of intruding religion into the practical affairs of the world. But in a basic sense the liberal and conservative clerical positions on social reform were alike in reflecting mundane values of society rather than imposing any more elevated spiritual purpose upon it.

The central place of the church in almost any immigrant community—whether a Protestant congregation or, more often now, a Catholic church or Jewish synagogue—made its function more specifically a social one than in the old country, even if it had been state-established there. The parish church or synagogue was a good deal more important to some ethnic groups, indeed, than it had been in Europe. Italian Catholic immigrants soon shed their anti-clerical tradition, and the orthodoxy of Eastern European Jews became less simply a matter of the dietary rules of *kashrut*. The growing urge of immigrants toward religious affiliation, like that of native Americans, reflected the needs of their social situation. How well the immigrant church could fill those needs in its own terms was doubtful. Even in reacting against the individualism or personalism of American society, they were altered by it.

At the end of the nineteenth century the American Catholic church passed through what one of its own historians has called its "great crisis."[13] At issue was a doctrine or tendency, significantly defined as "liberalism" or "Americanism," which its largely foreign-born opponents condemned as rank heresy. The liberals, mostly American-born or American-reared, sought to adapt the church to American society in order ultimately to reconcile all Americans, in spite of their current religious, ethnic, and economic divisions, to the eternal spiritual values of the universal church. Liberal Catholicism was, in short, another instance of an essentially conservative reform movement that perforce took on the libertarian coloration of the nineteenth century. This time the result was near schism even in the highly organic structure of the Catholic church.

As early as 1858 American-born Catholics had voiced their discontent with the "foreign" character that Irish and German immigration had given their church. In that year Isaac Hecker, a second-generation German convert and Redemptorist priest, gave up his missionary work among German immigrants and founded the new Paulist order to carry out what Rome agreed was the basic mission of the church anywhere: conversion of the country to the true faith. In America, Hecker argued, that could not be done unless the church was as fully American as it was Irish in Ireland or German in Germany. Without compromising essential articles of faith, it should conform to the social and political institutions of the country. By the 1880s a great many children and grandchildren of the earlier immigrants, including a number of prelates, had accepted that practical analysis.

The most indefatigable Americanizers were Archbishop (later Cardinal) James Gibbons of Baltimore and Archbishop John Ireland of Saint Paul—both Irish in origin and both ruling over archdioceses somewhat apart from the main centers of the "new" immigrant Catholics. No old-time Fourth of July orator was more extravagant in praise of political democracy; was not the Catholic church peculiarly "the Church of the people"?[14] They welcomed the separation of church and state in America, since it left the church much freer for its spiritual mission than in those European countries where the state continually interfered with the established church. They were surprisingly ready, for Catholic prelates, to accept the beneficence of human progress in general. Archbishop Ireland wholeheartedly endorsed the watchwords of the modern age: "knowledge," "the amelioration of the masses," "material comfort," and the egalitarian aspiration "towards a perfect civilization, towards the enjoyment of God's gift in full measure, and by the largest number of God's children."[15] What more could be said to allay old Protestant fears of political subversion and conflicting allegiances and perhaps eventually reconcile America to Rome?

Although Gibbons prevailed on the Third Plenary Council of the American bishops, in 1884, to endorse democracy and the other civil institutions of the United States, equally eminent conservatives like Archbishop Michael Corrigan of New York, American-born but immediately responsible for the care of "new" immigrants, excoriated this "liberalism" as a theological and practical menace. How could democracy be compatible with the hierarchic polity of the church? How could what was notably the church of the poor carry out its spiritual mission in a country whose Constitution cut it off from the state as a source of subsidy? Most important, were not the liberal paeans to material progress and the perfectibility of society through knowledge and effort gross examples of human presumption? And in practice would not liberal tinkering with old ecclesiastical forms repel the immigrants—German, Polish, Italian, French Canadian—who had accounted for the gratifying expansion of the Catholic church in America in the course of the nineteenth century?

The dispute focused on a few specific issues. Catholics were no longer united on the question of the prohibition of liquor. In the 1870s, when Protestant reformers revived the temperance movement, conservative Catholics denounced once again the vain hope and theological impropriety of attempting to purify human behavior by prohibiting a supposedly evil substance like "Demon Rum," or more specifically the beer, schnapps, whisky, and wine of the immigrants. Now, however, liberal Catholics broke away to join the dry crusade. They were particularly chagrined over the middle-class Protestant impression that Catholics were nothing but drunken foreigners. Advertisements for the "celebrated St. Vincent beer," brewed at a German abbey in Pennsylvania, hardly helped.[16]

A much more disturbing problem to the liberals, as to Protestant social gospelers, was the bitter class conflict of the 1880s and 1890s between labor and capital. If the church were to persist in its reactionary fear of trade unions, the many Irish and German-American union men would feel driven to abandon it. Fortunately the liberal leaders helped prevail upon Pope Leo XIII to issue, in 1891, the encyclical *Rerum Novarum*, sanctioning the right of working-men's associations, as "societies in the full sense of the word," to assist "each individual member to better his condition."[17] On the other hand, the conservatives got Rome to silence Father Edward McGlynn, who had disobeyed Archbishop Corrigan in 1886 by campaigning for the agrarian reformer Henry George when he ran for mayor of New York.

The old issue of the relationship of Catholic parochial schools to the public school system was revived by the Third Plenary Council's injunction to every parish to establish a school for its children. On that mandate liberals and conservatives could agree. But the liberals, in their zeal to reassure Protestants that the education given by Catholic schools was as patriotic as any, not only acknowledged the legitimacy of public schools but were willing for the latter to teach the majority religion of the country, "be this religion as Protestant as Protestantism can be."[18] Their plan for the state to pay for and administer the parochial schools as well (except for specifically religious instruction) caught the liberals, however, in a withering cross fire from both anti-Catholics and conservative Catholics. Although certain schools in Ireland's diocese had already tested this "Faribault plan," the Protestant uproar in 1890 over Catholic intrusion into "the little red schoolhouse" brought it to nothing.

On the question that came closest home to the Catholic laity, the structure of the parish in which they lived and worshipped, the conservatives were the innovators. Actually their problem was more one of ethnic relationships than of ecclesiastical polity. The earlier immigration had given a decidedly Irish cast to most parishes and, by the 1880s, to the hierarchy as well. The Americanized church for which the liberals argued appeared to other Catholics, both old-stock Americans and non-Irish immigrants, to be in fact altogether too Hibernian. Even before the coming of the French Canadians, Italians, and Poles, a good many German Catholics were muttering over the Irishness of their priest or bishop and the practical interdiction of the German language from parochial affairs. The problem seldom arose in the "German triangle" between Cincinnati, Milwaukee, and Saint Louis, but in other regions it constantly threatened to alienate Germans from the church. And they of all people always had at hand the alternative of an ethnically and liturgically conservative Lutheran church.

In 1890 the St. Raphaelsverein, a Catholic emigrant aid society meeting in Switzerland, rashly ventured to advise the church on the American parish question. A certain German philanthropist, Peter Paul Cahensly, had persuaded the society that Catholic parishes in the United States, and even dioceses, would be better organized along ethnic or linguistic lines rather than in the usual territorial divisions. Germans might then have a German priest and bishop; Italians, Italian; Poles, Polish; and no doubt Irish, Irish if they wished. Each parochial school, bringing up children in the language of the home, would safeguard their loyalty to the church from the demoralizing effect of too rapid Americanization. To a considerable extent the residential pattern of many cities had already made St. Patrick's the predominantly "Irish church," St. Nicholas's or St. Joseph's the German parish, and St. John the Baptist's French Canadian. But to impose Cahensly's plan for "poll parishes" as a formal principle would cut squarely across the universality of the Catholic church; to the dismay of the liberal leaders, moreover, the mere word of it outraged the nationalistic sensibilities of most Protestant native Americans. The fury of the press in 1890, already aroused over the liberals' school plan and now redoubled by the conservatives' parish scheme, could not be assuaged by the most patriotic flights of Archbishop Gibbons's oratory.

The continuing wrangle within the church was smoothed over in 1899 by the papal letter *Testem Benevolentiae*. Although it condemned a doctrine known as "Americanism" or "liberalism," it gave latitude to the liberals to explain that somehow this referred really to a doctrine of certain *French* Jansenists that had unfortunately acquired those names; the Pope himself went to some length to express his entire approbation of "the characteristic qualities which reflect honor on the people of America" and on their laws and customs.[19] But it was all too plain that for a long time to come neither Rome nor American Protestant opinion would permit any Catholic accommodation with the public schools. And as for making Catholic parishes instruments for rapid Americanization, the church quietly allowed the *de facto* ethnic parishes to continue and provided a special "mission" church for each new foreign-language community until such time as the immigrants or their children had become English-speaking and ready for the ordinary single, territorially based parish church.*

Protestants, noting that Rome had practically, if not formally, overruled the liberal Catholics on both the specific issue of parish organization and the general one of modernization, persisted in regarding the Catholic church as a reactionary monolith in every respect—economic, social, political, ecclesiastical, and theological. Nevertheless an element analogous to the liberal-Protestant social gospel movement continued to grow within it. The National Catholic Welfare Conference, organized in 1919, worked during the next three decades for much the same economic reforms as the Federal Council of Churches.

No immigrant religion was immune to the tension between liberalization and a heightened conservatism. Descendants of the Spanish and German Jewish immigrants of colonial days and the

---

* It was already too late to prevent certain Polish clergymen and their congregations, mainly in industrial centers where they were thrown together with almost every possible variety of fellow Catholics, from breaking away, between 1897 and 1907, and organizing a separate Polish National Catholic Church—the only major schism in the history of Catholicism in America.

early nineteenth century were now in most respects only marginally distinguishable from people of other long-settled denominations. Newly arrived Jews from Western Europe, most of whom by 1875 had acquired much the same modern outlook, joined them in founding Reform temples of the sort that had first appeared in the 1840s and 1850s. Besides abandoning elements of ritual and dietary law that seemed unadaptable to the modern world and introducing sermons, choirs, and other forms customary in Protestant churches, Reform Jews endorsed a program of social amelioration and economic welfare, first enunciated by their rabbis in the Pittsburgh Platform of 1885. A still more liberal outgrowth, the Ethical Culture Society (1876) went so far as to shed its Jewish identity almost altogether and to become, at least in religious terms, virtually indistinguishable from Unitarianism. At the same time, however, the flood tide of Yiddish-speaking Jews from Eastern Europe set their own orthodoxy squarely against what they regarded as the shocking laxity of Reform Judaism. Many of them were more insistent than they had been in the Russian or Austro-Hungarian empires that as little as possible be conceded to the pressures of the Babylon in which they found themselves. After 1885 a third, "Conservative" sect provided a compromise position for Jews from both the old and the new migrations.

The Orthodox synagogue and the Reform temple, the fundamentalist and liberal Protestant churches, and the conservative and liberal Catholic factions were all alike in resisting in one way or another the practical materialism of American society. At the same time their very existence in America was a result of material circumstances—industrialization, the growth of cities, and their own immigration. One sort of church or synagogue might blindly reject the individualism or personalism of modern society; another sought to harness those values for the collective welfare of mankind. But neither the liberal nor the conservative factions could shape their environment as much as it was constantly shaping them and their children.

The increasing importance which so many individuals evidently placed on belonging to a church, or at least on identifying themselves as Protestant, Catholic, or Jewish, is as hard to explain in terms of the economic and social platforms that various churches endorsed as it is in terms of their formal creeds. Certainly most of the worldly goals of social gospel Protestants, liberal Catholics, and Reform Jews could have been gained more directly—as in the end they were gained—through secular institutions. Their theological opponents—the fundamentalists, conservatives, and orthodox—usually avoided applying religion to such matters at all. And then there were a great many persons whose religious affiliation was only nominal and for whom the church no longer was a compelling guide to the life around them. On the face of it, the apparently overwhelming commitment of Americans, of all people in the modern world, to religion and the church was truly extraordinary.

The general circumstances of American society suggest that an important function of almost any church—the main function for many, perhaps most, of its members—was to confer an acceptable social identity upon otherwise rootless, detached individuals. The church had always been a nuclear institution in American communities, from the earliest colonial settlements to the latest prairie township or urban slum neighborhood. Whatever it had been in the old country, in America the church necessarily took on a great many functions that had a very tenuous tie with religion. In the mid-1920s the seventeen Protestant churches of Webster Groves, a suburb of Saint Louis, operated "thirty-two women's societies, nine men's brotherhoods, ten young people's societies, six Boy Scout troops, one Camp Fire Girls group," and twelve other organizations—eight for children and four for adults—as well as the usual Sunday schools.[20] Many a Catholic priest in the late nineteenth century expostulated against his congregation's irreligious enthusiasm, as he saw it, for "church picnics" and the other "social events" on the usual American Protestant plan, to which the ladies' sodality or the young people's catechetical class had become addicted. In the end, however, the narrowest traditionalist had to accept such "church functions" and try to turn them to proper uses.

Under the aegis of the church, foreigners could safely engage in old-country customs that Americans might otherwise not have tolerated. A country which venerated the image of Pilgrims tramping through the snow to the meetinghouse, muskets in hand, could hardly deny anyone the freedom to belong to his own church. Anti-Catholicism was a still older tradition, but it was directed against whatever the Vatican might be plotting rather than the right of Catholic immigrants to worship as they wished. If on the other hand the immigrants or their American-born children fell away from the strictly spiritual concerns of their churches, that too was familiar enough to Americans. When individuals of the rising second generation shrugged off their religious duties along with the rest of the foreign culture of their "greenhorn" parents, they might well feel that they had become "100 percent American." But that was not always the end of it. As Marcus Hansen observed in 1938, "What the son wishes to forget the grandson wishes to remember."[21] By the time an ethnic group had passed beyond any imputation of "un-Americanism," the most acceptably American social category by which the individual could identify himself was not his ancestral nationality and its folk-culture—which in any event was substantially lost and irretrievable—but rather his religious affiliation.

With each new generation, furthermore, the old ethnic groups were becoming intermingled and losing their separate identities. How this happened is revealed by the marriage records of New Haven between 1870 and 1940. From decade to decade a diminishing proportion of persons of British, German, Scandinavian, Irish, Italian, or Polish origin married within their own ethnic groups, declining to less than half of the Germans and Scandinavians by 1930 and of the Irish by 1940. In 1940 a very great majority, however, were still choosing a wife or husband from among their coreligionists: 94 percent of the Jews, 84 percent of the Catholics, and 80 percent of the Protestants. In this, no doubt, the church's ancient concern for the sacrament of marriage played a part. But in an age when any couple could dispense with the religious ceremony if they chose, the church as a social institution was bringing men and women of Irish, German, Italian, Polish, and French Canadian origin together in a single Catholic "melting pot"; Protestant British, Scandinavians, Germans, and most native Americans formed another; the Eastern and Western European ethnic strains among the Jews, a third. Instead of the common melting pot which earlier Americans had envisioned, there were at least three separate ethnic crucibles for the white population in any locality, and sometimes an Eastern Orthodox one as well. The new ethnic alloys were likely to persist indefinitely.

The religious identity and ethnic parentage of any individual did not necessarily make his practical religion much different from other people's. Religious affiliation perhaps seemed a less invidious way to define who he was than his social class, one more relevant to modern life than his ethnic ancestry, and something easier to speak of than the sacrosanct matter of income or wealth. In any case he was subscribing to a common social ethic. By the 1950s certain critics who particularly valued the old orthodoxies were lamenting that all creeds had been submerged in the vacuous "civil religion" known as "the American Way of Life."[22] That this at least filled the place of religion was clear enough, one conservative observed, "for one's ultimate, over-all way of life is one's religion."[23]

No latter-day theorist had yet appeared to define the American Way of Life coherently, in spite of the frequency with which it was invoked. But it clearly included the general belief in political democracy, equality of economic opportunity, and material progress— the optimistic, secular idealism that looked forward to eventual perfection of human society by human effort. Although another current name for it was "the Judaeo-Christian tradition," it contained a good deal of cant that at one time every church would have condemned as grossly heretical. In the harshest view its pervasive materialism, when set against "the fundamental presuppositions of both Judaism and Christianity," could only be consigned to outer darkness as a "particularly insidious kind of idolatry."[24] At best it glowed with the generalized religiosity of President-elect Dwight Eisenhower's remark of 1952: "Our government makes no sense unless it is founded on a deeply felt religious faith—and I don't care what it is!"[25]

By that time a host of critics, some speaking from "neo-orthodox" reconcilations of old spiritual values to the modern world and some clinging to the orthodoxies of former centuries, had begun to be heard. And indeed the religion of Americans had never been uniformly reduced to the sanctimonious platitudes of a merely materialistic "way of life." There were always exceptions: unquestioningly devout wives and mothers who had been girls in Ireland, Italy, or Poland and some at least of the sons and daughters whom they hoped to dedicate to the priesthood or the sisterhoods; the *Hasidim* and other strictly Orthodox Jews among the new waves of refugees from Eastern Europe; many outwardly unremarkable persons in whom the spiritual fire of the old evangelical sects or the still older churches of the original Protestant Reformation steadily burned. But down to 1945 these represented remnants from a rapidly receding past, "saving remnants" perhaps, but ultimately certain, if things continued to go as they had for two centuries, to see following generations subside into superficially variant forms of the blandly moralistic common religiosity.

To most people that end seemed not only inevitable but right and proper, like the dissolution of the old organic community or family. The "American Way of Life," after all, was the faith of modern uncommunal communities and personalized families. It was an appropriately denatured religion—but still reassuringly a sort of religion—for a people who conducted their daily life on the material standard of equal opportunity for success or security and on the social standard of agreeable personal relations.

26. SOCIAL CONTROL AND
SOCIAL ADJUSTMENT

Unfortunately the disorder into which economic individualism threw American society in the mid-nineteenth century was no less unsettling and irksome when rechristened "personal freedom" in the twentieth and sanctified as a kind of national religion. In the fast-changing nineteenth century the individual could never be certain, for all his inherited moral precepts and egalitarian dogma, what to expect of his neighbors, his children, his church, and least of all his supposedly equal fellow citizens. In the twentieth century he did not banish the old sources of anxiety when he enshrined the cult of personal relations in his detached suburban home, his companionable family, and the church of his choice. Americans still lived in a state of social insecurity, and it was as certain to produce extreme reaction now as in the days of the revivalists and sectarians, the abolitionists and fire-eaters, the Anti-Masons, the Know-Nothings, and the Cold Water Army. Indeed, the Christian Science and fundamentalism of the dawning new age were highly reminiscent of earlier responses to similar circumstances. More characteristic of the twentieth century, the major economic and political reform movements, from progressivism to the New Deal, welled up out of the same kind of social discontent as much as from the more "practical" economic abuses against which the reformers took direct aim.

Logic and symmetry perhaps should have suggested to twentieth-century reformers that after they had reorganized and regulated the economic system there would remain the parallel task of restructuring the social order. But the idea hardly occurred to them. If the announced goal of their new economic order was a new form of individual liberty, was not the voluntaristic social ideal of personal relationships that was already coming in just the sort of thing that was wanted? Efforts to reform society between 1875 and 1945 consequently were afflicted more acutely than ever by the old inconsistency between the conservative impulse toward organic system and the overt individualism of the reformers' libertarian rhetoric. Most of their specific remedies, like those of earlier times, were essentially on the conservative side, but since they were seldom addressed to the basic sources of anxiety, they usually did not go beyond seeking to suppress the symptoms of the disorder.

The moralistic personal code which the late Victorian era heavy-handedly fastened upon the confusions of the time was the most general reaction. The Victorian proprieties, as contemporaries were well aware, were accorded more lip service than implicit obedience. But an impossibly spotless standard was not simply the hypocritical tribute to virtue paid by an era of red-light districts, "gambling hells," and bawdy burlesque shows. Blameless personal conduct could serve to ease consciences for excessive self-seeking in everyday business affairs. By the twentieth century, when public and private regulation had reentered the marketplace, there occurred an equal and opposite relaxation of the Victorian mores—and even a "rebellion" against what was supposed to have been their ironclad rule. The new, explicitly permissive doctrine of personal fulfillment would hardly have been bearable, however, in the anarchic 1870s and 1880s, when only an assurance of personal rectitude could make the uncertainties of life tolerable to many individuals. As it was, all the evangelistic exhortations of the YMCA, the Christian Endeavor Societies, or the temperance leagues, calling on the individual to pledge himself to personal purity, seemed sadly insufficient, especially in the raw new cities, to save young men from the temptations on every side.

As early as the 1820s and 1830s some of the New England states enacted laws to suppress the sale of obscene or indecent books and pictures and other alleged pornography. In 1842 Congress began to interdict the mailing of such matter and in 1873 extended the law to cover advertisements for it; shipment of contraceptive devices was specifically banned. To Anthony Comstock, the Connecticut farm boy who single-mindedly served for forty years as the special agent of the Society for the Suppression of Vice (1873) and also of the Post Office Department, the enemy was simply lust:

Lust [he wrote in 1880] defiles the body, debauches the imagination, corrupts the mind, deadens the will, destroys the memory, sears the conscience, hardens the heart, and damns the soul. It unnerves the arm, and steals away the elastic step. . . . The family is polluted, home desecrated, and each generation born into the world is more and more cursed by the inherited weakness.[1]

Comstock's attempt to eradicate every form of obscenity inevitably slid into crude excesses of its own. By the time of his death in 1915 he was notorious for his inability to discriminate between "a frankly pornographic book and a sociological or medical publication of educational character," between a masterpiece of the nude figure and what he called "lewd French art," between a hack pornographer and George Bernard Shaw, whom Comstock dismissed as an "Irish smut dealer."[2] His campaigns bore some of the credit for removing the most tasteless lures to prurience from the advertising columns of the "family newspaper." But the growing permissiveness and frankness of the twentieth century in matters of personal behavior was a more basic cause of the general disappearance of such vulgarities—and of the general ridicule of "Comstockery."

Moral compulsion was always more acceptable when tinctured with an element of libertarianism. The movement for woman suffrage appeared, indeed, to be entirely liberal in principle—a final extension of egalitarian democracy. At the same time its proponents sought from it a most conservatively moral result. From 1869 and 1870, when the territories of Wyoming and Utah gave women the vote, down to 1920, when woman suffrage was written into the federal Constitution, political equality for women was confidently expected to bring their purifying influence to bear on a system of politics notoriously in need of it. Like the democratic argument for other electoral reforms in the progressive era, the suffragists' rhetoric was most persuasive at times and places where respectable middle- and upper-class reformers, proposing to cleanse the political stables, were actually seeking to wrest control from the hands of elements whom they considered to be corrupt. To enfranchise women would presumably first of all enfranchise the wives, sisters, and aunts of reputable, responsible property owners, thereby doubling their votes as against those of unmarried, unstable young men, unsettled migrant laborers, naturalized but un-Americanized foreigners (whose womenfolk's place was in the home even on election day), and other unreliable elements.

The character of Wyoming society when women were given the vote there in 1869 suggests that the reform was "a civilized reaction to frontier rowdiness." Similarly in polygamous Mormon Utah three years later it seems to have been "a politically expedient and efficacious method of bolstering the voting strength, social values, and organizational structure of the regime in power" against the growing challenge of the "Gentiles"—ordinary miners, traders, railroad men, and the like—who were infiltrating the holy community.[3] The fact that by 1900 Colorado and Idaho, also in the new West, were the only states to join Wyoming and Utah in adopting woman suffrage reinforces that conclusion. It was not so much that frontier individualism led directly to political equality, as was usually supposed at the time, as that frontier disorder provoked conservative reaction. In the early twentieth century, when "women were increasingly . . . looked upon as custodians of public as well as private morality," all but one of the ten Pacific and Rocky Mountain states—and Kansas—gave them the vote.[4] Finally, in the atmosphere of moral fervor created by the First World War the same western expedient for imposing order on unruly miners and cowboys was adopted, in the form of the Nineteenth Amendment, as a likely antidote to urban and industrial disorder as well.

Much the same line of moral reform was traced by the temperance or prohibition movement, which reemerged out of the collective anxieties of the 1870s and triumphed, also just after the First World War, in the passage of the most extraordinary of all constitutional amendments. In 1874 the Woman's Christian Temperance Union burst upon the country in a spontaneous campaign of prayer meetings, often held within the "saloons" themselves, and set off on the old crusade, exhorting drinkers to free themselves from bondage to alcohol and at the same time calling for state laws which would allow them no choice in the matter. The movement was pushed to ultimate success by the Anti-Saloon League, founded in 1893, a federation mainly, as time went on, of local church committees. It was fitting, at a time when so many clergymen were preaching that moral character consisted of the practical virtues of hard work, thrift, and prudent calculation, that sobriety should seem to be almost the whole of piety. Although preachers no longer dwelt much on the old notion that a demon inhered in the rum itself, it was certainly sinful for liquor dealers to tempt men into drunkenness, improverishment, and helplessness. To the sober and successful the "drink-sodden, muddled and fuddled proletariat" seemed to menace the property and sound government upon which free society, like individual opportunity, was based.[5]

In due course after 1900 the dry crusade became one facet of the "progressive" middle-class fear of the twin specters of plutocratic domination from above and a socialist uprising from below. To many people who considered themselves progressives, prohibition was the linchpin of modern reform:

We are spending our lives, many of us [a social-gospel clergyman wrote in 1908], in the effort to make the world a little better and brighter for those that shall come after us. . . . We are tired of poverty, of squalor, of ignorance and dullness and stupidity, of the wretchedness of women and the degradation of men. Our hearts bleed when we look upon the misery of child life. . . . We want to change all this. We want to open out life and liberty to all the sons of men. We want to make possible for all a life in the whole, the good and the beautiful. . . . And the common sale of intoxicating liquors renders our work a thousand times more difficult.[6]

The liquor industry was undeniably one of the biggest businesses of the country. Ranking fifth in invested capital, it was concentrated in the hands of about a hundred brewers and the "whisky trust." In alliance with the trade associations of wholesale and retail dealers, the liquor manufacturers were openly engaged in lobbying against state regulation and in stimulating the popular thirst. Through their working-class customers in the saloons, who now included hard-drinking Poles, Finns, and Slovaks as well as Irishmen and Germans, the industry was tied up with the urban political machines that manipulated their votes. In the South, so prohibitionist-progressives argued, it was "the primitive negro field hand, a web of strong, sudden impulses," and perhaps the disreputable poor white as well, who had to be denied access to strong drink. Through prohibition, they promised, the alarming incidence of rape, and "the mobs, lynchings, and burnings at the stake" which so often followed, might be averted.[7]

The Anti-Saloon League at first sought nothing more than regulation of saloons by the state, but like its predecessors it advanced by 1907 to demanding absolute prohibition, either within entire states or at the "local option" of city or county governments. In 1875 there were four rural states—Kansas and the three of northern New England—that had already resorted to prohibition. Although only one more, North Dakota, had joined them by 1900, thirty-six had authorized local option and four imposed high license fees on saloons. Before the end of the progressive era twenty-six states had gone totally "dry," and Congress had forbidden (1913) interstate shipment of liquor into them. Here too the First World War furnished the moral zeal to make the reform nationwide by means of the Eighteenth Amendment, but the essential legal change had been substantially achieved already.

The general endeavor to impose a moral code on society would have been more influential in everyday life had there been some prescriptive civil tradition to invoke beyond that of the self-perpetuating moralism of the reform movements themselves. Unfortunately the American tradition was inherently libertarian and antitraditionalist. The national mythology told of Founding Fathers who had been nonconformists, revolutionaries, and self-governing frontiersmen. Apart from conventional Fourth of July oratory, indeed, Americans in their habitual present- and future-mindedness usually ignored the past. In particular they had never had much patience with the individual who rested his claim to superior morality or social position on pride of ancestry rather than on his own achievements. But toward the end of the century, as the accelerating pace of change propelled each new generation far beyond the world familiar to its predecessors, it also impelled many individuals to seek some secure grounding in family tradition. Precisely when massive immigration and the low native birthrate were rapidly reducing the "old-stock" majority among the general population, certain people were struck by the notion that they were the unique inheritors, guardians, and preceptors of the patriotic and moral traditions of the country.

For the first time it became acceptable to band together in societies based upon exclusive, hereditary distinctions of the sort that a century earlier the Order of the Cincinnati had come to grief for asserting. As recently as the late 1860s and 1870s a similar organization of Civil War officers and their descendants, the Loyal Legion, had likewise failed to grow, although the all-inclusive Union veterans' organization and pension lobby, the Grand Army of the Republic, was in process of enrolling its eventual four hundred thousand members. In 1883, however, the founding of the Sons of the Revolution, an association limited to male descendants of Revolutionary soldiers, opened a new era of "patriotic" societies: the schismatic Sons of the American Revolution (1889), the Society of Colonial Wars (1892), the Society of Mayflower Descendants (1894), the Order of Founders and Patriots (1896), and groups of self-styled descendants of Indian chiefs, Magna Carta barons, and the like. Even the Order of the Cincinnati at last began to revive.

The societies that were open only to men attracted no more than a few thousand members; like certain other kinds of moral-reform movements of the time, the hereditary society was preeminently a ladies' affair. Suddenly in the 1890s there burst forth, Athena-like, the Daughters of the American Revolution (1890), the Daughters of the Revolution (1891), the Daughters of the Republic of Texas (1891), the Colonial Dames (1894), the Daughters of the Cincinnati (1894), and the Daughters of Holland Dames (1895), the vanguard of a host of others. Given the lack, in a republic, of a herald's office, each group had to establish its own standards of attestation. The systematic study of genealogy, almost unknown in the previous generation except in odd corners of New England, accordingly became a prime concern of public libraries, newspaper columns, quarterly journals, and an army of professional compilers of family trees.

As men and women anxiously ransacked courthouse records and dusted off family Bibles to prove their personal fitness to join one of these novel groups of traditionalists, they were confident that, in the words of the founder of the SAR in 1889, they were simply carrying out "every citizen's duty to give some part of each day to patriotic work."[8] Supposedly it was the series of national celebrations, from the centennial of 1876 through the Columbian Exposition of 1893, that had awakened their fervent patriotism, interest in history, and pride in being scions of the Fathers. But the "patriotic work" of the hereditary societies consisted very largely of inventing forms, conventions, and rituals to embody the tradition they sought to invoke. The most important was the cult of the American flag, including Flag Day, school flag-salutes, the pledge of allegiance to the flag as well as to the republic, and laws against "desecration" of flags, all of which were innovations of the 1890s. Now for the first time the cloth itself became the object of veneration, unlike the casually symbolic or merely official usage of earlier days. (Surviving veterans of the Civil War expressed puzzlement over all "these mysterious flag gesticulations.")[9] The patriotic societies also busied themselves with commemorating centennials, demanding that the history taught in schools be suitably inspirational, and, as a sceptic summed it up in the 1930s, "preserving old farmhouses near spots where historic incidents took place, or marking trees underneath which generals are supposed to have paused for a drink."[10]

All the Fourth of July oratory of the whole first century of the republic had not led Americans to go the length of such elaborate ritualism. Evidently it was now important to a good many people's self-esteem not only to wrap themselves in the flag but to claim a special right to do so. To anyone anxious about his place in the confusing scheme of things the thought of sturdy pioneer and patriot ancestors could be reassuring. Genealogy, as the novelist Winston Churchill observed in 1917, was "a hobby almost amounting to an obsession, not uncommon amongst Americans who have slipped downward in the social scale. . . . This consciousness of . . . descent from good American stock that had somehow been deprived of its heritage, while a grievance to [them], was also a comfort."[11] The patriotic societies seem to have recognized that their reason for existing went beyond the claims of ancestry and might even be compromised if they promiscuously admitted applicants who lacked other social qualifications. The head of the DAR in 1891 urged the necessity to "entrench ourselves within the charmed barriers of Revolutionary descent *and* of social consequence."[12] Precisely because the fifty thousand ladies of the DAR in 1906 were no more than a tiny fraction of the living descendants of the prolific Revolutionary generation, they could assure themselves of the entire reputability of anyone whom they might encounter at chapter meetings or national conventions.

It was recognized at the time that this exclusive patriotism was specifically a reaction against the "new" immigrants on the part of white, "Anglo-Saxon" Protestants (though the latter would not be grouped under their own ethnic sobriquet of "wasp" for another fifty years). As the head of the SAR recalled in 1914, "Not until the state of civilization reached the point where we had a great many foreigners in our land, where we realized the necessity of stirring up a love of country and a spirit of patriotism among our people, were our patriotic societies successful."[13] As he indicated, the societies' part in the national resurgence of nativism, which had been quiescent since the Know-Nothingism of the 1850s, was not simply a matter of blind xenophobia. The heritage of the DAR, a state regent of the order reminded them in 1894, was after all "the estate of constitutional liberty," entrusted to them as stewards for their "adopted brothers and sisters" from abroad as well as for their own posterity.[14] Although it was tempting to many native Americans, as it had been in the 1850s, to blame all the social anxieties of the time on the mass of foreigners in their midst, their first remedy was not to cut off further immigration or to impede naturalization but to ensure—sometimes by sponsoring classes in English and "civics"—that immigrants were speedily converted into good Americans as much like themselves as possible. Even the outright immigration-restrictionists, for that matter, professed to be champions of true freedom against the overly free entry of foreigners who might endanger it.

Since restrictionists and Americanizers were the negative and postive wings of a common moral crusade, in time they tended to coalesce. If foreigners after all proved unadaptable to Americanization, further immigration would have to be cut off. But exactly what sorts were undesirable was uncertain between 1875 and 1920. The initial impulse of nativists in the 1870s and 1880s was to exhume the specter of the antirepublican minions of the Vatican, whom cartoonists still stereotyped as incorrigibly Irish with their whisky, shillelaghs, and monkeylike visages and their illiberal animus against the little red public schoolhouse. Several anti-Catholic secret orders which had been moribund since the 1850s suddenly came to life again; new ones were organized by Orangemen and English immigrants; and in the early 1890s a wholly new group, the American Protective Association, spread like wildfire out of the Midwest into the East. Like the Know-Nothing party before them, the APA by 1893 seemed about to capture a balance of power in local politics. The frenetic antipopery campaign convinced the fearful that every Catholic church basement would momentarily disgorge armed legions to begin "Rome's usurpations" at last.[15] Within another year, however, the excitement burned back to the old bedrock of latent Protestant distrust. Irish immigration was falling off sharply; many Irish-Americans had achieved a certain social respectability and were even known as "liberal" Catholics; and at the same time the new Italians and Poles in the Catholic ranks somehow did not seem menacing in the old Irish way.

Antipopery gave way to an animus more congenial to the secularism of the twentieth century, a fear of foreign economic and political doctrines. The violent strikes of the mid-1880s and early 1890s led a startled public to conclude that some sort of imported radicalism must be fomenting lower-class insurrection in a country that had been thought immune to the class strife of Europe. The foreign danger was now envisaged not as a reactionary Catholicism but as some such inflammatory social doctrine as anarchism or communism. Down to 1903 the aim of reformers—and of the first restrictive federal legislation—was to keep out or deport individual anarchists and other undesirable persons and not, except for the Chinese in 1882, to exclude whole races or nationalities.* After all, the most notorious foreign radicals, the Chicago Haymarket "rioters" of 1886, could not properly be said to have sprung from the innately "communistic and revolutionary races" to which the editor of a trade journal assigned them. Being in fact German or English in origin, they must have been descended, according to the popular anthropology of the time, from the founders of Anglo-

---

* In response to West Coast demands, Chinese immigration was severely restricted by Congress in 1882 and that of the Japanese by the "Gentlemen's Agreement" with Japan in 1907.

Saxon liberty, "the tribes that met under the oak trees of old Germany to make laws and choose chieftains."[16]

Down to 1920 an unseemly cloud of illiberality hung over proposals for explicitly excluding certain races or nationalities, other than the special category of Orientals. But to ban illiterates, as Congress tried to do three times after 1897, was an acceptable way to accomplish the same end. For an immigrant to be able to read his own language seemed, particularly to the Boston gentlemen of the Immigration Restriction League (1894), not at all an illiberal requirement to make of a prospective American, even though it was fully expected that in practice many more of the old Northwestern Europeans than of the new nationalities would qualify. Restrictionists failed to foresee that almost anyone who was determined to enter the country could learn to read—and so it turned out when the literacy test of the act of 1917 failed to check resumption of mass immigration after the war.

Some more reliable shibboleth had to be found. Was it likely that the faceless millions of Mediterranean, Slavic, and Jewish immigrants who were pouring in, with their thoroughly alien cultures, could ever be assimilated into American life as Englishmen, Germans, or even Catholic Irishmen had been? It was all too easy to blame the "new" immigrants for the very existence of the slums, the strikes and strikebreaking, the juvenile delinquency and adult crime, and the machine politics which yielded so grudgingly if at all to progressive reform—and with which foreigners were indeed involved in one way or another. But even though one was convinced that republican liberty depended upon a rigorous exclusion policy, it was awkward to deprive so many individuals of the right to emigrate, a freedom as old as Jamestown and Plymouth.

A generation that respected science could find an acceptable formula. Just as the Jacksonian common man had accepted learned theories of Negro inferiority in order to justify slavery, the contemporary anthropological concept of hereditary racial characteristics was now popularized and fused with the older notion of the special "manifest destiny" of the Anglo-Saxon peoples. If one could believe that the Sicilian peasant or the Jew from a Polish ghetto belonged to a race innately unfit for the sacred trust of American liberty, the moral dilemma of trying to save freedom by restricting it was resolved. This notion was immediately attractive to a number of gentlemen of the old upper class, in Boston and New York in particular, the class which had lost its dominant political influence in the nineteenth century (and from which now also came the "patrician" progressives who were pressing the reform of a variety of political and economic matters). Several of them between 1910 and 1920 published popular books of amateur anthropology to spread the idea of the supremacy—physical, cultural, political, and moral—of the Nordic "white man par excellence" over Alpine and Mediterranean races; free immigration of the latter would end, they warned, in eventual "mongrelization" of the country.[17]

All this was still awkward to write too explicitly into American law. Worse yet, a good many of the "inferior" types were already voters whom congressmen preferred not to antagonize with invidious legislation. But could not a façade of equitable treatment be run up to conceal practical discrimination? On the gratuitous supposition that the existing American population had already struck the best possible balance of "races," Congress in 1921 imposed annual quotas, based on the census, on immigration from every country. The quotas were revised in 1924, and five years later, after a special commission conducted learned research into the surnames in the census of 1790 and into the records of later immigration, the national quotas were finally fixed. The total annual quota immigration was set at 153,000, more than two-fifths of which could be British and Northern Irish, one-sixth German, and one-eighth Southern Irish, but only one-twenty-fifth Polish or Italian.* In fact, however, the practical effect of the law upon immigration down to 1945 was far less than that of the depression, the war, and the failure of Western Europeans to fill their allotted quotas even in good times. Popular attachment to the racial principles of the 1920s—and persistence of the vague popular anxieties they reflected—nevertheless kept a version of the act in force until 1965.

Some of the same reformers, once again buttressed by the theories of European and American scientists, argued that even among superior races the poor heredity of certain individuals was a major cause of the ills of society. If criminality, pauperism, feeblemindedness, insanity, epilepsy, and such psychological "complexes" as "constitutional psychopathic inferiority" and "moral imbecility" ran in families, nothing short of eugenic sterilization would prevent endless generations from jeopardizing "progress and true social development."[18] The eugenicists did not go so far as to reject the progressive theory that defective environment might bear some of the blame for social problems. Heredity and environment presum-

---

* Special categories, however, such as close relatives of immigrants already resident in the United States, could enter outside the quotas, considerably expanding the "new" immigrant proportion of the whole.

ably reinforced each other. If slums nurtured congenital defectives, then to impose sterilization on the latter was no less progressive or liberal than to deal with their housing by city ordinance. There was a "vast difference," a progressive editor in Milwaukee argued in 1913, "between liberty in the sound, normal being and liberty in the abnormal, degenerate, defective being."[19] Anyone who objected to compulsory sterilization, a physician concluded, was making an "absurd fetish of 'personal liberty.' "[20]

Between 1907 and 1917 sixteen states, at the urging of many of the "best people"—the same sort who were seeking to displace their irresponsible social inferiors from political influence through municipal reform and woman suffrage—provided for sterilization of various categories of presumably hereditary defectives.[21] But the reformers had grossly overshot the mark. Of the thirty states which passed sterilization laws by 1932, only half a dozen applied them to anyone but certain inmates of state institutions. For other persons the laws were only permissive, and in fact not one state applied them systematically enough to make a valid test of their eugenic effect. The laws were a dead letter by the 1930s, the theory behind them scientifically discredited and also distasteful to the second thoughts of the public.

Whether or not immigration quotas or sterilization laws had the desired effect, the moral reformers of the 1920s continued to act as if the perfect society was as attainable through legislation and private effort as the New Economic Era seemed to be. The "drys" and even many reluctant "wets" assumed at first that the prohibition amendment and an act of Congress were all that was needed to wipe out the liquor business. Perhaps the "fight for civilization" could shortly move on to abolish smoking—or rather the most insidious form of it, the cigarette, which supposedly led in a "logical and regular series" to drink and opium—and likewise to suppress jazz, that "sensual teasing of the strings of physical passion."[22] The cause was especially strong among fundamentalist church people in the rural South and lower Midwest. Like the old "regulators" and vigilantes, a new Ku Klux Klan (1915) lashed out in a fit of volunteer zealotry against Catholics, Jews, and "uppity" Negroes as well as against the wets and others of dubious morality.

Hardly any infraction of the village code [a historian notes] seemed too petty for intervention. An undertaker refused the use of his hearse to a bereaved family unable to pay cash in advance; Klansmen drove him out of town. A businessman failed to pay a debt or practiced petty extortions; Klansmen tarred and feathered him. A husband deserted his family, or failed to support it, or maintained illicit relations with women, or gambled too much; Klansmen paid him a minatory call. A widow of doubtful virtue scandalized the neighbors; Klansmen flogged her and cut off her hair.[23]

But even if the Klan had not collapsed from corruption among its officers in the mid-1920s, there was little hope that any rigorously "moral" regime could be successfully clamped onto American society. The same looseness of social structure that provoked these anxious attempts at social suppression made both official and volunteer regulation ineffectual. The federal prohibition agents of the 1920s went to outrageous extremes to entrap would-be drinkers; a leading "dry" proposed poisoning industrial alcohol so that those who ventured to drink it might fittingly commit suicide. The moral fanaticism that had produced prohibition set up an enormous opportunity for petty hoodlums and racketeers to make a big business out of bootlegging illegal liquor and operating "speakeasies"— those old Irish dens which now attracted drinkers of all classes. These illegal enterprises vastly multiplied the opportunities for corruption of urban government. Prohibition also provoked an equally extreme moral counterreaction, in the name of "personal liberty," among all those—including many who had never drunk before—who were determined to behave as they pleased. Consequently the outright repeal of the Eighteenth Amendment in 1933, although it also owed something to the economic urgency of the depression, was as absolute as the amendment itself. But simply to withdraw the police power of the federal government was to leave a matter of general social importance to the uncoordinated laws of the forty-eight states and thousands of cities, counties, and townships. "Wet" moral absolutism now overshot the mark of personal liberty as badly as the "drys" had that of social order.

All in all, there was only one established American institution in which social reformers and the state could effectively join forces: the public school. At the very time, a century before, when both churches and business corporations had been practically disestablished as instrumentalities of the state, the public had nevertheless accepted the argument of reformers that the utility of education for advancement of both society and the individual, together with the lack of private capital for endowments, required public authority to maintain a school system. But compulsory public education was incomplete, in spite of the laws which most of the northern and western states enacted in the late nineteenth century—the others did so by 1918—until they also removed children from the industrial labor force in the first third of the twentieth. To get virtually all children into school was the foundation of the school as a primary institution of society. Not until then could it fulfill the hope of earlier reformers to integrate society by imparting a common culture to children of every class, ethnic origin, or religion.

Until well after 1900 most children's formal education ended before they completed the six years of elementary schooling. Public secondary schools were established at an astonishing rate across the North and West and increasingly in the South as well, and yet as late as 1930 fewer than half the children between fourteen and seventeen were attending high school. In 1945 the figure was still only three-fifths. Those who left school earliest tended to the the children, mostly the sons, of the ethnic groups and social classes that presumably most needed the homogenizing and leveling-up process of the school. Graduation from high school or even junior high school (the institution that now replaced the old grammar school) was still apt to compound the advantage of children of the already favored social classes. The same sort of inequity may have been fostered by the tradition of local control of schools, which survived imposition of statewide standards for attendance, teacher training, and curriculum. With the growth of self-segregated urban and suburban residential districts, the local schools tended to perpetuate the peculiar character of each into the next generation.

The content of public education almost everywhere around 1900 was adapted to the economic and social values which middle-class parents conventionally expected schools to implant in the young. Progressive educators complained that schoolbook tales of individual self-help in bucolic settings were irrelevant to the lives—and the comprehension—of the immigrant slum children who had to read them. But if classroom drill had been geared too closely to the economic and social circumstances of various kinds of pupils, it would have been untrue to the old hope that education would help everyone lift himself to a happy middle-class equality of condition. Advocates of manual training and other sorts of vocational education had to deny that they were patronizing some inferior class of pupils: would not such practical subjects broaden *everyone* as much as six years of Latin or algebra? The old curriculum was also leveled to common social ends. Much of the history, literature, and "civics" that was taught in schools everywhere, as well as the patriotic exercises that were coming in after 1890, served as a kind of simplified public creed, the only state-established discipline of indoctrination outside the army and navy. In that sense the neighborhood of the "neighborhood school" was perhaps the nearest equivalent to the old English civil parish, and the public school itself was the true "parochial" school. Indeed, as keeper and official inculcator of the amalgam of economic and "idealistic" values later to be identified as the American Way of Life, the public school was the closest approximation to an American established church.

Of course it was primarily the children of a community or district, not the general population, whom the school organized into a social group for indoctrination in a common culture. Except for the hierarchy of school board, superintendent, and teachers, those adults who were not parents of a school child—and so were not recruited into the desultory proceedings of the local Parent-Teacher Association—had little part in the institutional life of the school. But since for more than a hundred years Americans had had such extravagant expectations of the social utility of education, they seldom hesitated to interfere with the day-to-day activities of the local school. In particular the self-commissioned patriots of the DAR and its sister organizations and, after the First World War, the American Legion and other veterans' associations maintained surveillance of teachers and textbooks for any lapses from the "Americanism" that they were expected to pass on to the young. Always aiming to be constructive, these organizations also preempted schoolrooms after hours for the "Americanization" classes in which immigrant workingmen struggled with first-grade primers ("I am a yellow bird. I can sing. I can fly. I can sing to you.") and learned the conventional attitudes toward the Constitution and the flag.[24]

The great hope that education would improve everyone's prospects in life, a hope which could induce roomfuls of grown men to attend to whatever lessons were offered them, was shared by all the native and foreign-born Americans who regarded individual economic opportunity as the prime social value. If "progressive" educators and those other pedagogues who regarded themselves as traditionalists agreed on anything, it was that education must be relevant to "the actual activities of mankind" outside the school, the most real of which was the business of making a living.[25] As late as the 1920s the successful businessman was still apt to boast fondly that he had risen by pure self-help, unaided either by family or by any school less common than "the University of Hard

Knocks, Horse Sense, and Practical Experience—college colors, Black and Blue."[26] When such men sent their own sons to college, however, they were conceding that as far back as their grandfathers' time most of the leading business executives of the country were men who had gone to high school, and many of them to college, and that higher education had now become the main route to success. By 1945, after the truly hard knocks of the depression and the wartime revival of industrial and military opportunity for the educated, and training programs for many who were not, the economic and social function of schools on every level had become indisputable. More than three-fourths of the postwar business leaders had attended college, and more than half had graduated; hardly a twentieth had not gone to high school.

A danger had always lurked in the popular faith in equality of economic opportunity through education. It was not only that the schools were tempted to reduce the inherited common culture of the country to a few "cultural subjects," impatiently tolerated and apologetically taught. In seeking to promote cultural conformity and social homogeneity for the sake of an unfettered individualism, the public school, like the larger society, found difficulty in rising above the lowest common level. In the end the individual might gain nothing but a nodding acquaintance with poetry, music, history, or "general science" and a practically irrelevant certification for some job. An education directed too narrowly at freeing the individual to get ahead might prove to be no education at all.

In any case, it was difficult to prepare students for a future economy and society which no one could accurately predict. The new breed of progressive educators of the 1890s and after, like the economic and political reformers of the time, tried to strike a balance between the old libertarianism and a new social organicism. The school itself should constitute "an embryonic *community* life," as John Dewey put it in 1899,

active with types of occupations that reflect the life of the larger society, and permeated throughout with the spirit of art, history, and science. When the school introduces and trains each child of society into membership within such a little community, saturating him with the spirit of service, and providing him with the instruments of *effective self-direction*, we shall have the deepest and best guarantee of a larger society which is worthy, lovely, and harmonious.[27]

A harmonious community of self-directed individuals: it proved hard for lesser minds than Dewey to avoid falling off the knife-edge into either stultifying group-conformity or wildly undisciplined permissiveness.

Progressive education was alternately and sometimes simultaneously damned for both kinds of excess. In the 1920s the free "expressionism" of the "child-centered school" was the more popular dogma among reformers. "Every child is born with the power to create," one of them announced in 1928; "the task of the school is to surround the child with an environment which will draw out this creative power."[28] Unfortunately the withdrawal of the old ironbound discipline all too easily lapsed into mere neglect; such education could entirely "misconceive," as Dewey himself objected, "the conditions of independent thinking."[29] It soon appeared "in too many classrooms," a later critic has observed, that "license began to pass for liberty, planlessness for spontaneity, recalcitrance for individuality, obfuscation for art, and chaos for education—all justified in the rhetoric of expressionism."[30] At the other extreme, that of meeting "the common needs of life in society," lay the danger—to a normal-school teacher in 1918 the hope—of reducing education to preparation for that narrow world within which "housewives, wage earners, consumers, and retail hardware dealers" conducted "the actual activities of mankind."[31] By the 1940s that meager ideal had frozen into dogma, the doctrine of "life adjustment" which was briefly fashionable until it revealed its essential mindlessness—and uselessness to the individual even for getting ahead economically.

Dedicated reformers were not the only source of change. Most ordinary schools, which remained under the control of local boards of untheoretical laymen, resisted drastic reform in either of the progressive directions. But schoolchildren themselves carried through an unsponsored school reform that put an odd version of both the social and the individualist ideals of progressive educators to their own ends. The round of "social activities" that centered in the school, and that could drive both academic subjects and pedagogic objectives right out of any child's head, were more likely to consist of sports, clubs, dramatics, newspapers, yearbooks, dances, and "dating" than of any serious preparation for rebuilding the larger community outside. Or rather they prepared the boy or girl well enough for a larger society whose adult members now saw no need for any institutional structure beyond whatever network of personal relations they managed to weave among themselves.

By the time, in the 1940s, that one in six Americans between eighteen and twenty-one were proceeding from high school to college, it was taken quite for granted that the average college student grudgingly endured "cultural subjects" for the sake of "socializing," making "social contacts," and in particular finding a husband or wife. Although the "academic department" in which he chose to "major" might bear little practical relevance to his future chances in business or even a professional career, the pattern into which "campus life" had haphazardly fallen could hardly have been better designed to prepare him for American society in the era of personalism. Society had casually assigned to the schools and colleges, which had always had substantial cultural ends of their own, the social function of furnishing as many young people as possible with the ticket of admission to a career in the industrial economy. The young who trooped through such schizoid institutions simply turned them to their own trivial but truly "social" ends.

Neither the logic and compassion of a Dewey nor the good-natured gregariousness of the young were able to make schools and colleges any better instruments for social control than the fretful reforms of the prohibitionists, restrictionists, ritualists, and volunteer censors of the age. The efforts of all such reformers together, whether intended to be repressive or permissive, failed to build an organic social order remotely comparable to the new economic system which, half by design and half through fortuitous circumstance, had been set in operation by 1945. If a stable structure of social institutions were to arise on that material foundation, its design was also likely to owe as much to chance as to the misdirected efforts of self-proclaimed reformers.

27. THE VOLUNTARY ORDER

The up-to-date American who liked to think of society as simply the sum of the personal relationships among self-determining individuals like himself nevertheless continued, as in the nineteenth century, to need organized institutions of some sort to mediate between him and the mass. Earlier generations had devised associations whose membership and very existence was entirely a matter of choice. In the course of the nineteenth century, voluntary associations of a great many kinds had sprung up to perform a variety of social and cultural functions and occasionally some local economic or political task that government was no longer equipped to do. Any new movement for civic reform was sure to be taken in hand by a special association; the disestablished church and the socially detached family also resembled voluntary associations. In the twentieth century this practical voluntarism was turned into an explicit principle: the church of one's choice, the companionable "marriage," the community that one moved into by free choice and left again as soon as he could afford it.

But freedom of choice among institutional affiliations was less than a satisfactory fulfillment of the ideal of individual freedom. Anyone might find, to be sure, greater spiritual comfort in the church of his choice and more good fellowship in his lodge hall than was possible for him as an isolated individual. But a literally voluntary association was inherently too tenuous an arrangement to assure him the fullest freedom to attain whatever kind of personal satisfaction he was seeking from it. If such private associations were to survive in the first half of the twentieth century, they had to modify the principle of voluntarism and in practice become as solidly established as the guilds, chartered communities, and even the universal church had been in the Middle Ages. By 1945, accordingly, they formed a framework for the sort of organic social structure that modern Americans thought they had abandoned— one which, when they began to be aware of it a few years later, would perturb most of them as a quite un-American "establishment."

For a time the simpler associations of earlier years continued to flourish. Secret fraternal lodges were still as popular as they were superficial. For all their elaborate ritual and costume, their official hierarchies, solemn moral precepts, fanciful traditions, and burial insurance schemes, their only indispensable function was simply to give the individual at least one highly organized social group to belong to. As an anthropologist observed in 1942:

The tie of common membership, flat and without content as it is, bolstered up by sentimental songs which no one really likes to sing but which everyone would miss if they weren't sung, has an intensity of its own; an intensity measured against the loneliness which each member would feel if there were no such society.[1]

The older fraternal orders—Masons, Odd Fellows, Red Men, Knights of Pythias, Elks, and the rest—proliferated new lodges across the country, and by a sort of spontaneous generation dozens of new orders sprang into being, among them the Loyal Order of Moose (1888), the Fraternal Order of Eagles (1898), the Order of Owls (1904), and the Fraternal Order of Orioles (1910). Old orders in turn begat new affiliates. The Ancient Arabic Order of the Nobles of the Mystic Shrine for North America (1870) served as the mock-Islamic "playground of Masonry," and the "fun-loving" among the Pythians spun off the Dramatic Order Knights of Khorassan (1894).

There was potentially some sort of lodge for everyone. Although the Catholic church still refused to share its spiritual authority with any such "blasphemous imitations" as these arcane secular bodies, its own authentic antiquity and hierarchic structure did not entirely satisfy the social needs of American Catholics.[2] The Catholic Knights of America (1877), the Knights of Columbus (1882), the Catholic Order of Foresters (1883), and several other orders were therefore set up on the same lines as their rivals but safely under clerical supervision. Since Negroes were generally excluded from the ordinary orders, they organized their own lodges of Masons, Odd Fellows, or Elks, indistinguishable in substance, or the lack of it, from those of the fraternal white men who scorned to admit any tie with them. Immigrants of the new nationalities, like the older groups already on the ground, poured what they could of their own genuine tradition into the same forms: the Czech-Slavic Benevolent Society (organized in 1854 but large and influential only after 1880), the Polish National Alliance (1880), the Lithuanian Alli-

ance of America (1886), the Ukrainian National Association
(1893), the National Croatian Union (1894), the Grand Carniolian
Slovenian Catholic Union (1894), the Spanish-American Alliance
(1894), the Japanese Association of America (1900), the Serbian
Beneficial Federation (1903), the Russian Brotherhood Association
(1903), the Slovak Catholic Sokol (1905), the Pan-Hellenic Union
(1907); by 1940 there were more than sixty ethnic orders.

The mass organizations of war veterans, from the Grand Army
of the Republic (1866) and the United Confederate Veterans
(1889) to the Veterans of Foreign Wars (1899) and the American
Legion (1919), resembled the immigrant societies more than they
sometimes supposed. The old *esprit de corps* which they nostal-
gically commemorated was seldom felt in American civil society.
From time to time the camaraderie of the local "camp fires" or
"posts" was exploited by ambitious organizers and leaders for
political ends, and the pensions which their persistent lobbying
secured attracted many members. But the rank and file stayed
together for different reasons of their own. It seems likely, as an
anthropologist later concluded, that those old soldiers "who have
the fewest ties among themselves—those whose poverty-stricken
way of life admits of few associations—cling longest to this common experience."[3]

The old fraternal orders rapidly expanded their "practical" functions, in particular by regularizing their insurance plans. In fact,
whole new orders were created expressly to provide the workingman's family with cheap, reliable insurance such as commercial
companies did not yet offer. In the wake of the first fraternal-insurance order, the Ancient Order of United Workmen (1868),
there followed a long procession of others with splendidly solvent
names: the Knights of Honor (1873), the Royal Arcanum (1877),
the Knights of the Maccabees (1883), the Modern Woodmen of
America (1883), the Royal League (1883), the Empire Knights
of Relief (1889), the Knights and Ladies of Security (1892), the
Tribe of Ben-Hur (1894), the Royal Neighbors of America (1895),
the Prudent Patricians of Pompeii (1897), the Praetorians (1899),
the Homesteaders (1906). In 1886 sixteen such orders federated
into a National Fraternal Congress; at its peak in the 1930s, nearly
ninety orders belonged. By the latter date, indeed, there existed
some 120 fraternal-insurance societies, with more than 7 million
members and assets of nearly $2 billion. Yet what was observed of
the principal Polish-immigrant order in 1920 was true of the lot,
that the main function of a mutual-insurance scheme was

to stabilize and extend a social cohesion which otherwise would manifest itself only irregularly and within narrower limits. . . . It introduces a regularity and continuity into the successive meetings, gives a definite purpose for each meeting, calls for a certain division of work, prevents up to certain limits personal disagreements from breaking up the association, and counteracts very efficiently individual indifference and anarchy, since a member cannot cease to participate even temporarily in the association without losing all his rights and thereby all the contributions which he has already paid.[4]

As commercial insurance became available to more kinds of people in the twentieth century, the fraternal orders could hit upon few other practical functions to justify their existence. They systematized charity within their own ranks by supporting homes for aged or ill members and orphans of members, but when it came to sponsoring worthy causes outside the walls, such as hospitals for crippled children, an *ad hoc* foundation could serve just as well— and usually did. But in keeping up with changing times, the lodges did not lose their chief reason for being. Their popularity, especially among men on the middling and slightly lower levels of society, had never rested on tangible services. As long as the everyday world lacked discernible order, moral certainty, and even much color or drama, the more important to the lodge member were the hierarchic ranks, the quasi-religious pledges and oaths, the venerated if not exactly venerable traditions, the intricate rituals and flamboyant sashes, helmets, or fezzes, and the whole "great humanitarian cause of the Moose" or whatever.[5] For half a century after 1875 that social need was enough to keep the fraternal orders growing—125 new orders in the 1880s, 350 more in the 1890s, 6 million members by 1900, and, at the zenith about 1925, some 800 distinct orders, tens of thousands of local lodges, and perhaps 35 million members.

That was their heyday, however, as an organizing force in American life. The decline that became apparent in the next decade was blamed at the time on the depression and on the movie-going, joy-riding, and radio-listening that supplanted the simple diversions of an earlier day. More fundamental forces were also at work. Other kinds of voluntary associations, far from declining, now multiplied and flourished because their social functions were more substantial than the rituals, oaths, and "fun making" of the fraternal orders.

The economic-reform programs of the many farmers' and workingmen's organizations of the 1870s and afterward were so obviously important, in fact, as to obscure their equally solid and far more readily attainable social purposes. The Patrons of Husbandry, or "Grange," (1867) and the Noble and Holy Order of the Knights of Labor (1869) began by imitating the rituals and socializing of the fraternal orders of that time, and it would be difficult to say that the secret oaths of the Knights (before 1882) or the monthly Feast of Pomona in the Grange hall were less important in their members' lives than such matters as wages or freight rates. But they went considerably beyond the ritualistic fraternalism of the lodges. The midwestern farmer and his family, it was recalled several decades later, desperately needed to escape periodically from their

lonely and monotonous life, the lack of opportunity for social contact and exchange of ideas. . . . Farms were so large that the nearest neighbor was generally at least half a mile away; cities were few and far between; and the crossroads villages, even when accessible, offered no better amusement than lounging in a grocery store or saloon.[6]

Mechanized farming on the endless prairie seriously reduced the need for the neighborly cooperation and jollity of the old logrollings, cornhuskings, and the like. In their place the libraries, musical programs, debates, and lectures at the Grange hall continued long after agrarian reform had passed into the hands of other agencies.

Labor unions too, even after they shed fraternal trappings for more businesslike procedures, were natural social communities for fellow workers as well as agencies for collective bargaining or political lobbying. However the middle-class public might frown on the class consciousness of the labor movement, unions sprang, as a recent student has observed, from "a spontaneous, unorganized assertion of a common purpose, by men who asked only for what they had to have if they were to remain men: recognition as members of a society, a fellowship in common duress."[7] In their combination of substantial economic and social purposes, the farmers' and workingmen's organizations pointed the way to the typical voluntary associations of the twentieth century.

The women's clubs which also appeared in the last third of the nineteenth century were a thoroughly new type of voluntary association. Women's auxiliaries to the fraternal orders were already common enough—Daughters of St. George, Ladies of the Maccabees, Companions of the Forest. But after 1868, when a group of New York ladies, indignant at their exclusion from a dinner for Charles Dickens, founded Sorosis as an organization of their own, independence of the narrow world of masculine attitudes became the banner of a national women's movement. By 1890 this coalesced into the General Federation of Women's Clubs; within ten years it embraced some 800 local clubs, with 150,000 members; by the 1930s there were some 15,000 clubs and 2 million members.

Women's clubs took the broadest view of their social and cultural responsibilities. "We have art clubs, book clubs, dramatic clubs, pottery clubs," a member wrote in 1880. "We have sewing circles, philanthropic associations, scientific, literary, religious, athletic, musical, and decorative art societies." To a wondering French-woman in 1895 it seemed that "the absence of men would make French women feel . . . as if they were eating bread without butter."[8] American clubwomen no doubt prided themselves on being less single-minded. One club in its first five years of "study and con-versation" managed to "embrace Greece, Rome, Italy, England, and France, with their traditions, history, literature, art, and govern-ment." Others took on the whole "History of Civilization," paying due attention to such salient phases as "Wife Capture and Slavery" and matters as diverse as "electricity, literature, and parliamentary law." From Arkansas an Edelweiss Circle reported:

For but a brief year has this "round table" group of women climbed the rugged sides of the mount of knowledge, and even now are plucking the dainty flower of culture from literature's lofty peak. Its success is assured by the earnest, faithful and persistent work of its members. The Intellectual Development of Europe . . . has been the basis of study for the past year.[9]

In many towns during the progressive era the local women's club took the lead in the cause of civic reform—improvement of sanitation or the schools, abolition of child labor and reduction of workingwomen's hours, conservation of natural resources, food in-spection, and the like. They still found time to debate such topics as "Is housework incompatible with the higher life?" and among their other civic crusades they called on Congress to designate a national flower (the mountain laurel), demanded that the Buster Browns and Happy Hooligans of the comic strips be "purified," and denounced (in 1914) "slit skirts, transparent gowns," and "im-modest dancing."[10] Perhaps the ladies exhibited a good deal of ingenuous sentimentality; nevertheless the goals of public morality, cultural self-improvement, and social responsibility were sub-stantial ones. As long as American men persisted in putting busi-ness and politics ahead of such unremunerative matters, there was hardly anyone to take up the latter but their hitherto sheltered womenfolk.

In the case of the professional associations that rapidly emerged in the 1890s and after, material advantage and social and cultural considerations were closely joined. The earlier societies of lawyers, doctors, architects, or engineers had been small groups organized to "elevate" their professions. By admitting only the "better" sort, they could both set an example to the democratic army of half-trained practitioners and also close ranks against unregulated quacks, shysters, and jacks-of-all-trades.[11] The new professional associations followed a different, ostensibly more egalitarian course. By freely admitting as many licensed lawyers or doctors, practicing engineers, architects, or teachers, as possible, the leaders in each profession hoped to bring the influence of the group more effectively to bear on marginal members, and in due time to force up the standards for admission to the profession.

At the same time all such organizations were concerned to maintain or to establish their members' professional independence. The lofty rhetoric of their campaigns to formulate and impose codes of ethics on themselves somewhat masked this main underlying purpose: to avoid complete domination by the business corporations or the regulatory progressive state in whose bureaucracies more and more of them had to function. "Professionals desire peer-group control," a recent student observes, "rather than public, client, or employer control. . . . Cohesion is necessary to attain control; control is necessary to attain cohesion. . . . The professional association and its impersonal code stand as a buffer between the individual and those who might otherwise dictate to him."[12] Advantageous as the new economic system was to them, the free practice of a profession according to its own ethical standards—as well as an individualistic dislike of dictation—were all too easily undermined by it.

Although medicine, law, and certain other professions found it convenient to enlist the state to examine and license new practitioners—bar associations, indeed, became in this respect quasipublic institutions—they succeeded in keeping public authority at arm's length. The American Medical Association (1849, federalized 1901), believing that "socialized medicine" would destroy the doctor's professional integrity, managed to fend off any sort of federal health insurance until as late as 1965, fully thirty years after the New Deal had put old-age pensions and unemployment relief under the Social Security system. Schoolteachers, many of whom in the nineteenth century had been underpaid and treated like hirelings, gradually established a claim to professional respect from the public, if not a great deal more salary from the state, through their mammoth federation, the National Education Association (1870, reorganized 1920). Within a mere twenty-five years the American Association of University Professors (1914) virtually demolished the absolute authority previously exercised by the businessmen and clergymen of college boards of trustees; the contractual position of the college teacher was transformed into an inherent status—significantly for the future of society in general —fixed by the extralegal but nonetheless effective concepts of academic freedom and permanent tenure. To seek knowledge and disseminate it freely the protection of a well-knit institution was required.

The victories of other professions were usually less sweeping, but each association turned what had been a mere category of competing individuals into something remarkably like the craftsmen's guild, with its chartered privileges, of the organic society of medieval Europe. Their institutional forms were obviously drawn from more recent models; at their state and national meetings they enjoyed, with due professional decorum, all the gregariousness and conviviality of a convention of Elks or American Legionnaires. The *esprit de corps* of the associated dentists, mining engineers, or archaeologists was considerably enhanced, however, by their code of professional ethics and the popular respect for the special mysteries of their profession.

Even the solid businessman, whose social instincts formerly were satisfied at work or at most at the lodge hall, now sought to generate a sense of ethical service to society. The founder of the first of the businessmen's luncheon groups, the Rotary Clubs (1905), conceived of their function in fairly narrow, nineteenth-century terms; they would re-create among modern businessmen the friendliness and good fellowship that supposedly had flourished among the village grocers, millers, and dry goods merchants of simpler times. The vision of small-town tradesmen competing like a band of brothers was perhaps only the latest version of the myth of a vanished Arcadia. But as "service" clubs Rotary, Kiwanis (1914), the Lions (1917), and by 1930 some twenty-five other federations soon undertook public responsibilities as well. Their campaigns to collect toys for poor children at Christmas, to beautify the local railroad station, or to raise money for scholarships and hospitals may merely have put an ethical gloss on the careers of men who still placed profit and loss first during business hours. But important as they implicitly believed the production, wholesaling, or retailing of goods to be, business lacked the bonhomie of their club luncheons and the energetic benevolence of their after-hours good works. Like the old Puritan merchants, they were trying to reconcile buying and selling to more pious uses. The higher ideal was celebrated in songs, pledges, and other rituals that embodied just enough fraternal hugger-mugger to enhance the sense that the businessman too had his ethical standards, over and above the starkness of "business principles." The service clubs, it was observed in the 1930s, had conferred on business

something of the noncommercial character of the practice of medicine, the ministry, and schoolteaching. Through its theology and ritual it asserted that the wholesale selling of coal, the practice of embalming people, keeping a store, are worthy undertakings somewhat on a par with seeking a cure for cancer, the conversion of heathen, and the instruction of youth.[13]

More exclusive than any fraternal lodge—most service clubs admitted only the proprietor and one or two officers of a company— but at the same time far broader in their practical involvement with society, the service clubs flourished as the secret orders declined. The membership of all the clubs (a million and a half by 1959) was never more than a small fraction of the numbers who had belonged to fraternal lodges at their zenith. It was significant, however, that an institutionalized social ethic was now professed by the kind of entrepreneurs who had always exemplified the distinctively free and open economic virtues of American life.

The ordinary American of the mid-twentieth century was likely to belong to voluntary associations of several kinds. All of them indulged in rituals that were merely symbolic of the social integrity of the group, but more than ever such private organizations carried the weight of the cultural, philanthropic, and even spiritual concerns of American society—of nearly everything that was neither narrowly economic nor technically governmental. In the single small industrial city of Newburyport about 1940, with a population of less than twenty thousand, there existed some 800 different associations, of which 357 were stable enough for their activities to be classified by visiting sociologists. More than a third of the people of the place took part in them, averaging two memberships apiece. In a two-year span these groups met nearly six thousand times. A fifth of the meetings were primarily ritualistic exercises of a quasi-religious or patriotic nature; another tenth were occupied with socially unifying activity such as "breaking bread" together and as many more with technicalities of organization and rule-making. But the other three-fifths of their scheduled activities were devoted to matters of some substance: dramatics and other exhibitions of "talent"; speechmaking; athletic games and other contests; instruction in arts and crafts and the like; and of course fund raising for a variety of worthy causes.

Not everyone in town was equally involved. Ordinary working-men and poor immigrants—together amounting to more than half the population of Newburyport—took little part, except in the strictly ethnic clubs and lodges. Since old-stock or thoroughly Americanized people did not belong to these groups, the lower class was as isolated from respectable society as ever. Among the middle classes the most binding social structure was the network of their individual memberships in service clubs, professional groups, civic associations, country clubs, patriotic and historical societies, church associations, and, on the lower margin now, the old fraternal lodges. Together with churches, neighborhoods, and families in their tenuous modern form, such institutions made up very nearly all the social order that America had.[14]

By 1945 the voluntary association had fully developed what Tocqueville had perceived in simpler form more than a century before. "Pursuing in common the object of their common desires," Americans had hit upon "the only means . . . of acting" in an individualistic society.[15] Since Tocqueville's time they had grown so accustomed to that sort of social "democracy" as to believe that voluntary personal relations among individuals constituted the best possible social cement. But in practice the social relationships they devised were not simply the result of personal choice or rational calculation. Far from being purely voluntary, these relationships followed a discernible pattern of organization; they were the loosely interlocking parts of a complex system that for all its inefficiency and absentmindedness would be recognized, a few years later, as an "establishment."

Attached as twentieth-century Americans were to personalism as an integrative social principle, they could hardly conceive of any blueprint for their society comparable to the one they had designed since 1875, by force of necessity, for their economic system. Nevertheless by 1945 the myriad of substantial social, cultural, and spiritual purposes to which the voluntary association of Tocqueville's day had been adapted bore out his dictum: "If men are to remain civilized or to become so, the act of associating together must grow and improve in the same ratio in which the equality of [material] conditions is increased."[16] Although the personalized, voluntaristic social structure of the mid-twentieth century was still far from the sturdiest edifice that the new economic system could support, the materials for a more organic society were beginning to fall into place once again.

Epilogue and Prologue

28. IN QUEST OF THE GREAT
SOCIETY: SINCE 1945

After more than a century of lurching back and forth between booms and depressions, peacetime laxity and the rigors of war, individualistic disorder and anxious social conformity, Americans only gradually sensed that in the new stability of their economic system they now had a base for a comparably stable social order. It had been so long since the country had known what an organic social structure was like that any sign of such a thing aroused more alarm than hope. Whatever had been wrong with the easygoing individualism and pluralism of the last few generations, at least it was familiar; what nameless evils might be expected from an all-enveloping, all-powerful "establishment"?

The fact that the channels of the bureaucratic corporations and the regulatory state were now leading not to economic stagnation but rather to a new wave of national growth and individual mobility should perhaps have reassured Americans that stable structures and systems need not constrict individual freedom unduly. Government now played an increasingly complex role in maintaining the new prosperity. For all the radical reputation of the New Deal, many federal agencies were still engaged in carrying out the old Whig-Republican policy of stimulating and subsidizing economic expansion. Although Congress no longer provided magnificent land grants or overly protective tariffs and the courts were less permissive toward business enterprise than formerly, the massive public investment in the cold war against the Soviet Union after 1946, including development of nuclear power and scientific penetration of extraterrestrial space, was a public works program on a scale totally eclipsing the antidepression measures of the New Deal. Some concluded that without that extraneous factor all the regulatory devices of the progressives and the New Dealers would not have prevented another relapse into depression.

But within the context of the "defense"-stimulated economy the means now existed to moderate both booms and incipient "recessions." The industrial-financial machine now was literally equipped with a governor to steady the business cycle, a stabilizer to keep the economy on an even keel. The mechanism included, in the Federal Reserve System, an improved model of the classic central bank, and now there were also federal and state commissions to supervise nearly everything from labor relations to the stock market. Most important, the accepted theory of regulatory taxation was flexible enough—when the inertia of government and the taxpayers permitted—to counteract either inflation or deflation of credit. Since the American welfare state lagged behind the "cradle to grave" systems of most other modern countries, it effected only a very moderate redistribution of the national wealth, but it helped to match demand for goods to the capacity of farms and factories to turn them out. Corporate business improved its own regulatory devices, furthermore, through decentralization of its bureaucracy as well as through further consolidation of ownership and management.

Prosperity after 1945 enabled most individuals to advance steadily in occupational status, income, and property. Although the frontier was long since gone and immigration continued to be sharply restricted, the never-ending relocation of the industrial labor force confirmed Americans in their migratory habits of the past two hundred years. Each year some 30 million people—one family in five—changed their place of residence. Although three-fifths of the movers remained within the same county and another fifth within the state, probably the number of long-distance migrants was greater than ever before. Rural Southerners, both black and white, continued to respond to the call of the cities for labor after the war, especially since cotton-cultivating and picking machines were replacing many of them anyway. Refinements in older kinds of agricultural machinery and methods drove many small farmers to abandon wheat, corn, and hog raising on the midwestern prairies and plains to the new type of fully mechanized commercial operators. Some of the latter were "suitcase farmers" who also packed up and left, at least in the off-season, for the city or the Florida beaches. The industrial labor force also was more mobile than ever, as whole new major industries sprang up— plastics and synthetic fibers out of the chemical industry, itself an earlier twentieth-century creation; jet aircraft and space rocketry out of the exigencies of wartime—and created new industrial concentrations almost overnight. As new centers grew, old ones declined; coal-mining regions decayed and lost population as petroleum and natural gas were piped throughout the country for industrial and domestic fuel.

Changes within each economic sector were equally unsettling. "Automation," the nearly final phase of the technological side of the Industrial Revolution, displaced unskilled and semiskilled labor, wiping out the hoped-for jobs of many new migrants from the country, especially Negro men, even before they arrived. On the other hand, anyone already qualified for the white collar of a salaried professional, technical, or clerical position could rise as the proportion of such middle-class workers in the labor force increased; in the 1950s it was more than four times as great as in 1875. Where skilled workingmen were still in demand, on the other hand, their state-protected unions won them higher wages than many schoolteachers and other marginally professional men who wore white collars and "business suits" to work. As the "gross national product"—the new indicator of general well-being which everyone anxiously watched from year to year—ballooned from $355 billion in 1945 to $932 billion in 1969, it seemed that the economy must have a comfortable berth for everyone who was willing to work.

The old Jacksonian faith in individual opportunity was preached with renewed fervor. The National Association of Manufacturers confidently assured the young that "your opportunities will be limited only by your vision of what your future may become, your abilities and how you use them, your character and your determination." And in fact if all the newly created professional, technical, and clerical positions were to be filled, promising individuals had to be recruited from below. Fortunately on the lower economic levels a relatively high birthrate had produced plenty of prospective applicants.

Opportunity was far from equal for all, to be sure. The boy who took a laborer's job in industry upon leaving high school was unlikely to rise out of the working class—especially in the automated industries where wages were high but skilled jobs and foremanships were few. The ordinary wage earner still daydreamed about becoming the independent proprietor of a small shop, service business, or even an old-fashioned farm, and perhaps as many as a fifth of the workingmen of the country actually would try such a venture at some time in their lives. But the modern small business—an automobile dealership or filling station, for example—was not in fact independent of the great corporations, and the chances against success were great. At any one time, consequently, the number of small businessmen who had once worked for wages was likely to be equaled by that of workingmen who had once been businessmen of some sort.

The only reliable way for a working-class boy to surmount the middle-class occupational barrier was to begin his career beyond it. The usual credentials for that were educational, that is, some sort of diploma to attest to having attended college. It was far oftener the children of workingmen than workingmen themselves, accordingly, who took part in the surge of individual mobility that statisticians discovered in the 1950s. Although sons of businessmen and professional men were still far more likely to go to college, the availability of schools and colleges to others had already made a perceptible change among the upper echelons of business leadership by the 1950s. Whatever a young man's origins, once he had qualified to start on the bottom rung of the executive hierarchy of a great corporation he could make ability and hard work play the the role assigned them by popular tradition. If he was the son or grandson of one of the "new" immigrants who, half a century before, had been stuck fast on the lowest occupational and social level, his chances for material success were immeasurably better than theirs in spite of a certain residue of the old ethnic prejudices.

"In the broadest sense," a study of the origins of contemporary business executives concluded in 1952, "American society is not becoming more castelike; the recruitment of business leaders from the bottom is taking place now and seems to be increasing. . . . Our society, although much like what it has been in past generations, is more flexible than it was."[1] Fifteen years later a much broader study likewise found "no indication of increasing rigidity in the American occupational structure"; to the contrary, the practical opportunities both for an individual to rise and for his sons to surpass him were somewhat greater than in 1945.[2] As the glaring exception to that rule, the ordinary Negro was held back partly by the modern shortage of unskilled jobs but far more by ancient social prejudice. Even when a black man managed to obtain the requisite education for a white-collar job, he was not as likely as a white competitor to be promoted further on his merits. Color was not the only such barrier. The lowest economic quarter of the population, which included many other inhabitants of "pockets of poverty"—Appalachian uplanders, southwestern Indians and Mexican-Americans, the demoralized remnants of onetime immigrant groups left behind in the slums, persons stranded in once thriving but now depressed industrial centers—fell below the material standard now deemed tolerable. But that gauge (the equivalent of a 1960 family income of $4000) had risen considerably since the days, only thirty years before, when fully two-thirds of the population—twice the "one-third of a nation" that Franklin Roosevelt in 1937 had called "ill-housed, ill-clad, and ill-nourished"—had not been that well off.[3]

The general concern for economic security, born in an era of depression, continued to deflect part of the national income downward in the new age of affluence. The system of federal supervision of labor relations continued—although in 1947 the rights of union organizers under the National Labor Relations Act of 1935 were somewhat curtailed—and organized labor fully shared in the new prosperity. Successive increases in the federal minimum wage and its gradual extension to almost all categories of casual labor took care of practically everyone who could find regular employment. Although the Republican administration of 1953–1961 was uninterested in extending the regulatory powers of the federal commissions, business and government continued to exert the established progressive and New Deal controls. In spite of further mergers and consolidation of holding companies, the single-minded pursuit of higher profits and lower wages that had characterized the old trusts was now held in check. The federal income tax, held until 1964 at the high level of wartime, redistributed through public agencies and public expenditure on the cold war a considerable share of what would once have remained in the hands of the middle and upper classes. The Social Security system of old-age and unemployment insurance was only grudgingly extended to domestics and other neglected categories of labor, and hospital and medical insurance was not added until 1965, and then only for the aged. But the fact that the New Deal's rudimentary welfare state was gradually enlarged under the political banners of Democrats and Republicans alike confirmed the return of American society to the old ideal of commonwealth.

Affluence made it clear for the first time in more than a century, however, that not even the most equitable distribution of wealth would suffice to establish the good society. As more gaps of that sort in the economic system were filled—by the "urban renewal" of slum housing, by training or retraining of labor to meet current demands, by the federal "War on Poverty" among the whole neglected bottom quarter of the population in the mid-1960s—the more uncertain the adequacy of material welfare appeared for the commonweal in the largest sense. Various classically conservative doctrines, invoking spiritual, cultural, and social values beyond economic opportunity or security, began to attract hearers. The quest for material success, no longer unquestioningly accepted as the most meaningful pattern for the individual, was now subordinated to such values as his social dignity, cultural self-expression, and even spiritual enhancement. All those good things evidently were not going to flow, without considerable further effort, from the cornucopia of the gross national product or any number of cases of individual economic success.

What part could the old primary institutions of society—church, community, and family—take in that effort? Reinhold Niebuhr and a few other churchmen, inspired partly by European theologians and partly by the inadequacies of the progressive "social gospel," had already begun to develop modern versions of Calvinism and other old orthodoxies, and after 1945 their "neoorthodoxy" became widely fashionable. By no means denying the need for economic reform, they preferred to relate any sort of social gospel to a systematic theology such as most American church members had long ignored. Instead of following the vaguely benevolent materialism of the "American Way of Life," these conservative critics called on the church to lead and guide society, as it had failed to do for two centuries past, along the more rigorous lines of its own doctrine. At the same time the "interfaith" or ecumenical movement, to which the Vatican and most American Protestant and Jewish leaders subscribed, sought to give a more concrete institutional base to the "Judaeo-Christian tradition." How these clerical movements could build on the existing denominational structure remained in doubt. When old creeds were translated into modern idiom, believers found them unfamiliar, and nonbelievers found them hardly more credible than before. The interfaith programs and successive mergers of rival denominations, as they brought the church a little nearer its ancient institutional unity, also lessened the social significance of anyone's identifying himself in terms of religious affiliation. Whether eventually reunited, reindoctrinated, or both, the church might conceivably find itself as unpopular among the great majority as the established churches of modern Europe.

In fact little had changed. The church was still divided into some two hundred of the old denominations, each of the dozen largest having more than a million members. Membership figures were deceptive, since a good many among the unprecedented 64 percent of the adult population who belonged to churches (in 1962) were not perceptibly swayed by profound faith or by systematic theology, orthodox or neoorthodox. Even if they had all been zealots, the churches would have found it difficult to impose spiritual values upon American society, given the constitutional interdiction of any state-established religion. The actual combination of denominationalism and spiritual indifference still made the First Amendment the only practical arrangement, as it had been in 1791. Any hint of a link between church and state aroused the fury of the religious and irreligious alike. On one hand, militant libertarians, usually supported by the courts, insisted that prayer and other religious forms be excluded absolutely from the public schools. On the other, most church members still hotly resented the minister who tried to apply spiritual doctrines too directly to public policy. In spite of the scores of thousands for whom church membership represented a place in the social order, the church could do little to direct the reconstruction of society.

What Niebuhr called "the doctrine of salvation by bricks" inspired after the war the first massive effort to rebuild the cities, the communities whose structural deficiencies had long been most obvious.[4] Certainly no material reform was more urgent than the physical reconstruction of the moldering slum blocks at the core of every city. "A decent home and a suitable living environment for every American family," the Federal Housing Act of 1949 announced, were essential both for the local community and for the national "growth, wealth, and security."[5] But public policy, by making urban renewal almost entirely a matter of land clearance and rebuilding, inadvertently disrupted the existing social communities of the slums and scattered their individual members as heedlessly as the old-fashioned private real-estate developers had done. The one virtue of slum life had been the social cohesion that the "neighborhood" sometimes attained; the tenement dwellers, especially if they had been *paesani* or *lansleite* in the old country, could make something familiar out of the most unlikely slum block or street. Although the English model for urban planning made a special point of transferring the whole slum community intact when a fresh "new town" was built, in America the old community was usually knocked apart along with the old buildings. The slum-clearer, a reporter observed in 1958,

uproots all the people in the neighborhood, good as well as bad. He tears down the churches. He destroys local business. He sends the neighborhood lawyer to new offices downtown. The clinic and the synagogue move to the Bronx. . . . The old-timers are driven from their run-down flats and their ancient brick houses [to] a worse flat in a tumble-down on the edge of the new ghetto-to-be.

In two or three years the new "superblocks" on the old site were occupied by "hundreds and thousands of new faces, often of a race and nationality different from that which lived there before."[6] Since one purpose of urban renewal was to put some of the land to more profitable uses than rental housing, hardly half of the dispossessed could have squeezed into the typical new housing project even if they could afford the higher rents.

Those who moved into the transformed district of self-contained superblocks, with their limited-access streets, "sheltered greens," and high-rise apartment houses, found that social community was no part of the urban rebuilder's plan. The simplest communal self-regulation now became ludicrously awkward, whether it was a matter of keeping an eye out for the children on the asphalted playground outside, fending off casual malefactors in the maze of corridors, stairwells, and elevators, or simply passing the time of day with the neighbors. The project dwellers suffered all the disadvantages of apartment anonymity with none of the compensations that such an unsocial existence held for the rich or the bohemian. By 1954, when the Federal Housing Act was amended, it was becoming clear that it might be easier on the inhabitants, as well as cheaper, to rehabilitate old houses that were not totally "blighted" beyond repair. But not until the 1960s was conservation of the existing social communities of such districts recognized as valuable in its own terms. The problem was more complex, however, than in England or most other countries. Given the transitory character of American communities of every sort, from the farming townships of the nineteenth century to the suburbs of the twentieth, no pattern that might be proposed, either by private developers or public planners, could foresee the succession of economic classes and ethnic groups that might move in and out from decade to decade.

Since in most of the largest cities the slum population increasingly consisted of Negroes—and in some places Puerto Ricans or Mexicans as well—the old hardships were unrelieved by the hope of individual mobility that American society had held out to European immigrants. Racial caste, the time-encrusted obverse of the coin of individual opportunity, prevented the colored tenth of the population from being melted away in the crucible where the distinctive character of most white ethnic groups had gradually been dissipated. At the same time the black ghetto lacked the cohesive conservatism of the old immigrant neighborhood. Negro Americans after all were Americans of the sixth, eighth, or tenth generation.

Their segregated caste, surrounded by the individualistic, libertarian society of white America, was not the stable element in the social order that "conservatives" had long supposed it to be; actually and potentially, it was far more explosive, disruptive, and literally radical than the transitory clannishness of the old immigrants. A truly secure society requires some reasonable equity for all its members. But for Negroes, segregated housing and schooling and occupational discrimination subtly prolonged the system of caste repression. If the stigma of color was forever to bar the mass of poor Negroes from the education and the jobs for which their individual talents might have suited them, from living wherever they could afford the housing, and from acceptance on their merits as individual members of society, even the best-planned public housing would succeed only in "immuring the slums" within permanent ghettos.[7]

For the first time since the short-lived Reconstruction after the Civil War, public authority undertook to "desegregate" Negroes and to integrate them into the general community. The public agencies in which the reform commenced in the late 1940s, notably the army, were more intent upon improving their own operating efficiency than upon social consequences. The decisive turning point was the Supreme Court's mandate to the public schools in cases decided in 1954 and 1955. Jettisoning the pious hope of 1896 that a "separate but equal" education would be adequate for Negro children, the Court announced its expectation that school boards would now proceed "with all deliberate speed" to provide black and white children the same education in the same schoolrooms. The injunction had to be reiterated in suit after suit against school boards, mainly in the South, in the next dozen years, without in fact securing more than token compliance in most districts there. In northern cities, as the new black ghettos congealed, schools that had long been open to all were inadvertently made all black or all white. In order to break up the pattern, so that Negro children could eventually be treated as individuals, some cities experimented with the "positive discrimination" of sending them by the busload across town to be distributed among the "white" schools.

At the same time the federal government sought, by statute as well as civil suits, to assist Negroes to break through the public segregation and disfranchisement—"Jim Crow"—which state and local law, mainly in the South, had imposed since the 1880s. Southern black people by that time needed little encouragement to demonstrate that they would submit no longer. The example of

Rosa Parks, a black woman of Montgomery, who one day in 1955 simply balked at a bus driver's order to give up her seat to a white person, touched off a decade of bus boycotts, restaurant "sit-ins," "freedom marches," electoral registration drives, and other tactics of the prayerful "non-violence" that was disconcertingly difficult for white Southerners to combat or circumvent in the old ways. With the help or at least the blessing of federal authority, the demonstrators and litigators liberated the public facilities of one southern town after another from "white only" ordinances, rallied Negro voters to reenter southern county politics, broke down restrictive residential "covenants" in northern cities and suburbs, and so revised once again the old unwritten code of social relations between the races.

What remained was still a racial code. The lines of caste survived legal abrogation of Jim Crow laws as they had earlier survived abolition of slavery. In particular, since the generality of whites abhorred the thought of intermarriage as strongly as ever, that ultimate solvent of other ethnic distinctions was quite unlikely to cause either Negroes or the "Negro problem" to disappear. By the mid-1960s, as frustrated Negroes, burning and looting white-owned stores in the ghettos of a dozen major cities across the country, reversed the old meaning of "race riot," black militants were proposing, instead of integration, the alternative of mutual withdrawal of the two races. It was the same idea upon which both whites and blacks had fallen back during earlier times of frustration: a black society, an "Afro-American" culture, "black capitalism," and perhaps even a black region separate from white America. It was uncertain, however, whether the new slogan of "black power" and the white backlash that it provoked would ultimately produce an American form of *apartheid* or instead force the Negroes' way into the larger community on their individual merits after all.

Far less attention was paid to an equally fundamental and more general question—the adequacy of that larger community for either whites or blacks. Even if Negroes gained opportunity and mobility as members of white ethnic minorities ultimately had done, any social structure built around that prime value was likely to be as shaky in the future as in the past. Integration into a society whose other parts were essentially unintegrated—nowhere more so than in the loose suburban communities where most Americans aspired to live—created peculiar frustrations of its own. As critics pointed out, to their own astonishment, middle-class families attained suburban isolation at the cost of giving up a controlling influence over the behavior of their neighbors and even their own children; the security of their dearly bought home itself always seemed vulnerable to the incursions of other restless strivers, desirable or undesirable, white or black. Life there might be more anxiety-ridden than in the crowded neighborhoods one had worked so hard to escape from. At best, suburban life was too often pervaded by a feeling of aimlessness, apart from keeping up material appearances, a new sort of "low-keyed unpleasure" for lack of the cultural vitality that immigrant groups had maintained for a time in the slum neighborhood or the rural township.[8]

It was hard to hit upon a workable structure for the concept of "community" that Americans rediscovered in the 1960s. What was left of the organic communities of the remote European or colonial past was too desiccated to flourish again. Hardly a vestige remained of the self-contained communes of which the state had once consisted. In the eighteenth century it had been taken for granted that townships or counties, as communities greater than the sum of their individual inhabitants, were the proper political units to be represented in the legislature. But now, when in the interest of more perfect democracy the federal courts required, on the principle of "one man, one vote," that state electoral districts be redrawn to give each an equal number of voters, liberals and so-called conservatives alike adopted any argument that seemed expedient except the old one that the community rather than the individual was the basic political entity. New kinds of communal structures were no easier to conceive of. The federal program of the mid-1960s for a Great Society only tinkered with urban communities when it added new welfare agencies for the poor and tidied up junkyards and other obvious eyesores.

The family was still less adaptable to the purposes of the mid-twentieth-century commonwealth. After the decades in which equality between husband and wife and permissiveness toward children had become the norm, the new vogue of "togetherness" in the 1950s no more than hinted at a change of direction. That advertising catchphrase perhaps played upon a general uneasiness about the disintegration of the family as an organic institution, but it was hard now to envision a family satisfactorily held together by anything but the personal affections of its individual members. Most of the half-sentimental, half-commercial devices for shoring up the institution—Mother's Day (originated in 1908 and, with the cordial support of the florists, now universally observed), a less insistent Father's Day, awards for the mother or father "of the year"—actually singled out one or another of the individual members of the family for obeisance. Every day was the child's day, since the family's proper goal was still held to be his advancement or, as it was now called, the self-fulfillment of his potentiality for life and growth—in either case to be determined ultimately by himself.

The general affluence of the 1950s and 1960s made that goal ever more attainable. Young men and women rushed into marriage a year earlier, on the average, than before the war, and the annual marriage rate, after a sudden postwar surge, kept up to its pre-depression level. The divorce rate also leveled off by the mid-1950s at 23 per 10,000 population, or one divorce to every three or four marriages. For nearly twenty years after the war the birthrate also remained about as high as it had been a generation earlier (as many as 23.5 births per 1000 population in 1957). It had suddenly become fashionable, to the chagrin of surviving feminists, for young women to aver no loftier ambition than having "lots and lots of babies" on whom to lavish affection. Accordingly the fertility rate also recovered to more than three and a half children for every woman of childbearing age. The "baby boom" which shortly crowded the schoolrooms helped increase the national population in 1967 to the 200 million that prewar demographers had not expected until the end of the century.*

Since half of that population was younger than twenty-eight, the self-differentiation of a "youth culture" which sociologists had already perceived in the 1940s now became the alarming "generation gap" of the 1960s. Young people, affecting a style of apathetic conformity in the 1950s and then of unkempt rebelliousness a decade later, flaunted as a badge the novel term "teen-ager," which earlier generations of adolescents would have hotly resented. In the mid-1960s, as great numbers of "the kids" passed beyond their teens and yet remained in the nonage of college or graduate school, they announced their settled distrust of almost everyone over the age of thirty.

At every age beyond the cradle, indeed, it was now accepted that young people, the rebellious no less than the apathetic, were governed more by a self-imposed conformity to the culture of their particular "peer group"—each such group being little different from all the others—than by any standard handed down from

* By 1965, however, the birthrate again fell below 20 for the first time since the Second World War, and after 1967 it was lower than it had been in the trough of the depression.

their parents. The adults who sought to maintain some control over the young usually did so in the guise of teachers rather than as parents and elders. Children's after-school and vacation time was relinquished by middle-class families to a swarm of camp counselors, scout leaders, Little League baseball coaches, and other experts in making organized play palatable to youth. By the late 1950s some of the elders, themselves progressively reared not long before, were objecting that it all amounted to a new form of the industrial child labor that their generation had abolished. Such systematic training as children got for their own imminent married life was acquired outside the family in school courses in "domestic science," "sex education," or simply "marriage." At the same time their mothers struggled to keep up to date, as their grandmothers and great-grandmothers had done before them, with the current books and articles of experts in child-rearing—or rather in what behavior to expect from their children at each age.

Deplored though the generation gap was by popular moralists who survived from the previous epoch, in effect the teen-agers and subteen-agers were defining a novel sort of relationship between youth and adulthood, in which each age grouping had a more distinct role than Americans were familiar with. Formerly, children had hastened to become young adults as soon as possible. But now the generations were virtually two separate, self-constituted institutions of society.* Where in the nineteenth century the youth had been regarded as in a sense the superior of his own parents, who hoped he would soon excel them in material success, now his whole generation was treated as a kind of privileged guild. They were not only indulged in their own wishes but even rather patronized, somewhat in the manner that had already become customary among the middle and upper classes in nineteenth-century England. By the mid-1960s teen-agers were going so far as to cling to, or rather to flaunt, wantonly childlike fashions in dress such as their immediate forebears would have scorned to wear at the same age. There might be, however, a certain stability in their status as members of a constituent institution of the new social establishment. They came and went with an evident sense of privileged immunity from the bodily jeopardy in which their combination of disingenuous appearance and provocative manners would once have placed them. Inevitably, their elders often read the new signals wrong. When

---

* Retired "senior citizens" were now also set apart as a third group on the far side of adulthood, somewhat to the dismay of those survivors from an age that had honored the self-reliant individual.

they saw only truculence behind youthful beards and outlandish clothing, or when they on the other hand hastened to put on the same short pants or skirts, they were perhaps less up to date than they thought. Their generation had been the last, after all, to accept a common standard of dress and behavior for old and young alike.

At no point did ordinary Negroes appear to be farther outside white society than in their family structure, or rather the lack of one. An excessive looseness of conjugal ties among them, and their somewhat haphazard rearing of children, had originally been induced by slavery, a system which stripped their ancestors of the complex familial patterns of Africa for the sake of exploiting their labor. The consequences lingered on in the mid-twentieth century for much the same reason: denial of full access to middle-class occupations and respectability. And yet the Negro family had never been altogether removed from the American norm. If anything the contrary was the truth: the Negro family had always been a virtual prototype of what the general norm was now coming to be. The practical dominance of economic values in American life had affected the ordinary white family as well as the black, though in obviously different ways and to a smaller degree. Of course most white families had prospered materially as most Negroes had not. But the difference was mainly one of timing. The peculiarity of the Negro family lay in its having had to fall back upon the personal affections of its individual members for each other, for lack of a stable institutional structure, so much earlier than the white family as to create the settled impression that the two were utterly dissimilar.*

By the 1960s, as the racial question once more claimed the country's attention, it was suddenly recognized that the condition of the "typical" Negro family was highly relevant to the unsatisfactory state of the whole society. On one hand, certain sociologists seized on devices for strengthening the Negro family as keys to a general reordering of interracial relations, though at the same time they rather airily assumed that the ordinary white family would provide a suitably patriarchal model—and militant Negroes indignantly spurned the idea as another imputation of black inferiority. Many middle- and upper-class people, on the other hand, were no longer shocked at the legendary looseness of Negro family

---

* The parallel had been apparent a century earlier to Harriet Beecher Stowe, whose design for *Uncle Tom's Cabin* was intended to reveal to white wives and mothers, North and South, that they had special grounds for sisterly compassion toward slave women.

life, since it was virtually only an exaggerated version of the personal—especially the sexual—relations of the general twentieth-
century norm. White people had been accepting elements of black
culture as their own since the beginning of the century, when
ragtime and jazz had filtered "up the river" from their disreputable
colored origins. By the 1960s the whole popular culture of the
country was shot through with colloquialisms and humor of a kind
that most white people had hitherto encountered only at second
hand in the pages of *Uncle Remus.* All in all, it was an awkward
time for even the most sympathetic of reformers to suggest that
the Negro ought to play "ole man Hunter fum Huntsville" and
seek out a no longer existent white kind of family to imitate.

It hardly occurred to reformers to try to enlist the ordinary
middle-class family as an instrumentality of the larger social structure. The state still dealt not with families but with individuals,
whether as voters and taxpayers or as clients and dependents of
its welfare agencies. The public welfare system, like other economic institutions, tended to weaken the family still further as a
social entity, notably by refusing to support destitute children unless the father was absent from the household. The public and
private "family planning" or birth-control clinics, which it was
proposed to expand, sought to inculcate modern middle-class notions of the small family among poor Negroes and other people
regardless of whether their chief satisfaction in life had perhaps
been to have children. In any case, now that three-fourths of the
families of the country had escaped from the poverty that justified
any public attention at all, the family was about the least adaptable
institution for general social reform, either as instrument or
object.

More than ever the primary institution for maintaining or for
reforming American society was the voluntary association. Family,
community, and church had all been reduced to virtual subspecies
of it, distinguished from other forms mainly in the fact that membership was still determined for most people by parentage and
early environment. That is, the individual had to choose whether
to shake off his connection with them, rather than choosing to
join them as he did other private associations. But his freedom of
choice among institutions of any kind was narrowing. The literally
voluntary association, the spontaneous creation of the nineteenth
and early twentieth centuries, was now either disappearing or
hardening into a component of a social structure in which the status
of each individual could be fairly well predicted.

The very substantial cultural, social, civic, and economic functions of the new associational establishment are indicated by the names of thousands of private groups that crowd the nearly six hundred pages of the 1959 edition of the *Encyclopedia of American Associations;* they include many national federations a full list of whose local branches would fill several more such volumes. More than a hundred of the old-fashioned fraternal orders were still active, about seventy-five ethnic societies (mainly among the nationalities of the "new" immigration of 1880–1925 and after), nearly three hundred "Greek letter" student fraternities and sororities, and about a hundred varieties of "patriotic" and war veterans' associations. It was as puzzling to the outsider as ever to discern the practical purpose of these groups, whose main function, as in the nineteenth century, was simply to give their members something to belong to. But the bulk of the *Encyclopedia* was filled with societies devoted to the whole range of private, secular, "non-profit" activities with which Americans busied themselves, and in fact to some of their public, religious, and economic concerns too. There were trade associations and chambers of commerce; agricultural and horticultural federations; labor unions and professional societies; associations of scholars, scientists, engineers, technicians, civil servants, and military officers; groups dedicated to the advancement of public health and social welfare or to discussion of civic and international affairs; athletic associations and leagues of hobbyists.

Perhaps the most characteristic institutions of the age were "the foundations," the nonprofit trusts into which many of the great industrial fortunes had been diverted since the nineteenth century. Like the medieval church, they claimed exemption from public taxation or regulation as they interposed the weight of their professional expertise, social conscience, and overwhelming largess into whatever area of American life they chose to investigate, benefit, or reform. With their permanent endowments and investments, salaried staffs, and systematic impressment of unpaid "volunteers" for the never-ending chore of further fund raising, the foundations signaled that the age of literal voluntarism was at an end.

In the longest perspective, nineteenth-century *Gesellschaft* (association) was being reconverted into a new form of the *Gemeinschaft* (community) of the Middle Ages; the liberal society of freely contracting individuals was giving way to a "postmodern" society in which everyone's status was fairly well defined although not literally fixed. Technically, just as no one was compelled to follow a particular occupation, the individual businessman, doctor, lawyer, or professor was not dragooned into joining a professional association, nor was the workingman forced to take an active part in his trade union, but none of them could any longer function independently of the regulatory hand of the institution. No boy was legally coerced into becoming a Boy Scout or a Little League shortstop, and any mother or father conceivably could refuse to attend meetings of the Parent-Teacher Association, to tramp about the neighborhood soliciting contributions for incorporated worthy causes, or to allow the Red Cross to drain off his or her blood by the pint. But certain social duties, carried out through customary institutional channels, were now virtually obligatory for every individual of reputable social standing. By the mid-1960s reformers were attempting to extend the network of quasi-public associations—under the libertarian name of "participatory democracy"—down through the bottom levels of society, so that the poor and socially deprived could control their own situation just as other classes were doing.

Even if a congeries of associations of this sort included everyone, it would not necessarily mesh in a finely calibrated social reciprocating-engine. Each fraternal order, professional association, cultural society, or service club was quite independent of all the others. Such institutions were linked only in the persons of individual members who happened to belong to more than one of them. It was unlikely, moreover, that the Rotarian would also join the American Philosophical Society or that a United Automobile Worker would frequent the Army and Navy League, to say nothing of a member of the League of Women Voters turning up to make an earnest speech at the Odd Fellows' lodge hall. When their conventions overlapped, the Knights of Columbus and the Organization of American Historians could rub shoulders in a hotel lobby and yet exhibit total indifference, even incredulity, to the possibility that they both belonged to the same larger establishment. In a social structure consisting of a plurality of such institutions, the pattern of affiliations that the individual had chosen at any given point in his life was apt to be too loose to liberate him from the old anxieties over status that had kept him from devoting his social energies to more substantial or valuable aspects of life. The "pseudo-intimacy" that bound together the modern family, community, church, or voluntary association was all too often, as a sociologist observed in 1953, "morally empty and psychologically baffling."[9]

By the 1950s the crystallization of the general social structure had proceeded just far enough to ruffle libertarian instincts inherited from the anarchic nineteenth century. Social scientists, popular moralists, and best-selling novelists joined in decrying the "organization man," the "man in the gray flannel suit" edging his way up the bureaucratic hierarchy of big business, the middle-class "status seeker" wallowing in the cultural inanities of suburbia or farther "exurbia," and an interlocking "power elite" of big businessmen, politicians, the military "brass," and the manipulators of the "mass media" and popular entertainment. Even the child was now revealed to be "other directed," seduced by the meretricious values of his little peer group and no longer guided either by ancient tradition or by the self-reliant "inner direction" which Victorian parents had sternly instilled.[10] It was all so strangely un-American that the foreign term "establishment" had to be borrowed from the rather different social context of England to sum it up. Although critics usually traced all this no farther back than 1940, significantly enough the best of them found the most relevant text to be Tocqueville's analysis of American democracy over a hundred years before. Many of the current abuses which they condemned—especially the "tyranny of the majority" in social and cultural matters—were indeed vestiges of the stress to which the economic individualism of the Jacksonian decades had first subjected society. Insofar as it was still necessary to work out a common standard for a coherent society among the remnants of the old miscellany of ethnic groups, denominational churches, unstable communities and families, and voluntary associations, it was as inevitable in the 1950s as in the 1830s that Americans would spend much of their time and energy in anxiously watching, consulting, and censuring each other. Too much of American life had consequently not yet risen above the low common denominator that had worried Tocqueville. The rising note of discontent with so mediocre a standard in the 1950s and 1960s perhaps indicated, however, that Americans were already building something better upon it.

But old anxieties were not dead yet. The political phenomenon of "McCarthyism," which boiled up in 1950, may mark the end of a century of nervous conformity rather than, as some feared, the beginning of one. Liberal critics at first deplored it as a contemptible attempt to "escape from freedom" into totalitarian tyranny. How could Senator Joseph R. McCarthy attract so enormous a following, with his wild accusations that the State Department or the army had been taken over by communists and fellow travelers, unless the liberty-loving American of old had unaccountably degenerated into an abjectly "authoritarian personality," characterized by "conventionality, rigidity, repressive denial, and the ensuing break-through of [his] weakness, fear, and dependency"?[11] But conceivably, red specters apart, there was something in the liberty that Americans traditionally loved that made them fearful. As a number of sociologists, historians, and journalists soon suggested, the popular uproar over "communists in government" opened an outlet for the anxieties of many insecure people in a still unstable society. It was tempting for the latter to believe that some conspiratorial clique must surely be responsible for whatever it was that was making them uneasy.

By any other accounting the McCarthyites were an oddly mixed lot. To the descendants of certain immigrant nationalities, now "Americanized" and prosperous where once they had been disdained, it could be gratifying to hear an Irish Catholic senator assert that it was not, after all,

the less fortunate, or members of minority groups who have been selling this nation out, but rather those who have had all the benefits the wealthiest nation on earth has to offer—the finest homes, the finest college educations, and the finest jobs in the government that we can give.[12]

Did it not seem likely that the fault lay not simply with the universal uncertainty of life in a loose social order but with certain "Anglo-Saxon," Protestant liberals? That sort still looked almost as monolithic, domineering, and unapproachable as in the days of other people's immigrant grandfathers. The old charge of un-Americanism could now be flung back in the teeth of "the American respectables, the socially pedigreed, the culturally acceptable, the certified gentlemen and scholars of the day, dripping with college degrees." Worst of all were the supercilious "intellectuals," loosely defined to include "lawyers, doctors, bankers, teachers, professors, preachers, writers, publishers." Quite conceivably they were all, as far as an ordinary plain-thinking man could see, fellow travelers in the cause of "Godless atheistic communism."[13]

At the same time many comfortably middle-class "Anglo-Saxons" succumbed to a curiously similar anxiety over what the recent rise of the onetime minority groups portended for them. Was not their own relative slippage in status the result of the collectivist and hence virtually communistic welfare state created by New Deal liberals? On the other hand, for a man to *rise* too rapidly in status, as students of anti-Semitism were discovering, could be as unsettling and productive of paranoia as to fall. One might manage to win a magnificently old-fashioned fortune in some highly speculative business, such as Texas gas and oil, and fret the more about holding on to it as he contemplated the "confiscatory" potential of the welfare state. In the background in the same years, of course, there were undoubted communists on the march in Eastern Europe, China, and Korea to add credence to McCarthy's allegations.

It was thus less surprising than first appeared that such superficially unlike, even formerly antagonistic, people should merge their social insecurities into McCarthy's coalition of the disgruntled. The senator offered reassurance to each by fixing the blame somewhere else. "To the status-deprived," a sociologist observed, "he is a critic of the upper class; to the privileged, he is a foe of social change and Communism."[14] The senator's briefcase full of "documents" which purported to prove that one thing at least was certain—even if it was *treason*—somehow seemed reassuring in an uncertain time. McCarthyism, like so many political, religious, or social reform movements in the previous two hundred years, was as conservative in its followers' yearning for security as it was radical in its leader's reckless language.

But if McCarthy's popular success was "best understood," as another sociologist concluded, "as a symptom of the strains attendant upon a deep-seated process of change in our society," it was for much the same reason that his meteoric career suddenly burned out in 1954.[15] When his daily televised hearings revealed McCarthy himself to be a cynical opportunist, a nihilist, a "seditionist" and "enemy of the established order" rather than one who would make it more secure, most of his followers abandoned him.[16] What his opponents had all along called his "witch hunting" did in fact end much like the self-destructive reaction of overly zealous conservatives in the troubled Massachusetts Bay Colony of 1692.

Could some other plausible demagogue of more durable character than Joseph McCarthy yet muster all the detached, fearful individuals of the country into a single political force? Such anxieties had burst forth over and over again. They had been a leading element in the evangelical revivals, novel sects, and humanitarian reform movements of the early nineteenth century, the embattled causes of southern secession and the Union, and such latter-day phenomena as Populism and progressivism, fundamentalism, the Anti-Saloon League, and the Immigration Restriction League. They were never, of course, the only element in those otherwise highly varied popular effusions, nor were they the sole impetus for McCarthyism. But as long as the social order continued to be too disconnected to contain the pressure of economic change and individual mobility, Americans could expect to have among them a mass of anxiety-ridden, more or less demoralized individuals who would respond to anyone who plausibly promised to restore law and order by dealing forthrightly with traitors and criminals, rotten apples and effete snobs. And yet every demagogue who failed in his efforts to exploit such fears was a gauge of the growing stability and good order of the new social establishment.

In its first 360 years American society had almost boxed the compass. The seventeenth-century English pattern of perpetual change within a reasonably stable order had shifted to the haphazard individualism and personalism of the nineteenth and early twentieth centuries; latterly a point of fair equilibrium had been sighted through all the complexities of the age of technology and mass communications. If the log of a past voyage may be helpful in plotting a future course, the American experience at least refurbishes the truism that man is indeed a social animal. As such he has open to him the alternatives of a satisfactory or an unsatisfactory structure for his society. The precise form of the social structure—small or large, rural or urban, egalitarian or hierarchical—is perhaps unimportant. But whenever Americans have acted as though they had a third option of no fixed structure at all, the resulting social disorder has proved intolerable to them no matter whether, as in the nineteenth century, they called it individual self-reliance or, in the twentieth, by such names as pluralism, voluntarism, and personal affection. Social institutions may be good or abusively or neglectfully bad, but at times when Americans have simply flung institutional constraints aside, even in the honored name of pioneer individualism, free enterprise, and opportunity for all, they have found the consequences unacceptable.

The belief that individual liberty could best be secured by a merely negative freedom from institutional bonds was illusory. In fact the traditional institutions of society—the family, the community, the church—have never ceased to exist in some form throughout American history, though at times they have been poorly organized to carry out their essential purposes. Nor have social classes ever disappeared, for all the strictures of Jacksonian-populist egalitarianism. It was precisely between the 1830s and the end of the century, when Americans most liked to think they were achieving a classless society, that the actual classes became more widely separated by wealth and poverty, more irresponsible and inadvertently abusive, and in sharper conflict than at any other time. Accordingly it was about 1850, not 1950 as latter-day critics have supposed, that "status seeking" first got out of hand. The individual borne along by the tidal wave of change in modern society has always worried about what his status in it would prove to be, but that concern need not always be the nearly universal obsession that it became in the mid-nineteenth and early twentieth centuries. A society of some structural strength can vouchsafe the individual a certain sense of assurance, as well as reasonable hope of beneficial change, as he goes about his affairs.

The 1950s and 1960s rang with echoes of the habitual individualism of the disorderly past. Self-styled conservatives, predictably enough, exhorted the middle classes to cut back the income tax, dismantle the welfare state, and leave the poor to look after themselves. But now latter-day liberals called on the "organization man" to fight against his own corporate bureaucracy and to devote more time to being a pal to his children. A "new left" arose crying that the youth should "do his own thing," cultivate personal sensitivity toward every other individual, and somehow find spontaneous community under the old black banner of anarchism. Black militants aroused Negroes to cut adrift from white society; resentful whites lashed back in the name of the "law and order" that had safeguarded property rights—and little else—in the nineteenth century. Some responded to the general advice to "turn off" and "drop out" of existing institutions rather than attempt to make them more answerable to the social needs of man. That there were designedly or unwittingly abusive aspects of the current "establishment"—from the archaic lines of racial caste to the postwar complex, already self-perpetuating, of military policy-makers and the masters of industrial technology—men of good will could hardly deny. But simply to break down institutional constraints upon the individual was likely, as the American nineteenth-century experience had demonstrated again and again, to prove self-destructive and self-defeating for him.

Fortunately the curious cycle through which American society had passed in its first 360 years left a growing sense that the good society could not be built merely by cutting the individual adrift from all institutions and structures. At best, too much of his energy and attention had had to be devoted to keeping the society going at all. At worst, the detached individual had become fearful, embittered, and unable to look beyond material success to any higher value of life. For a higher freedom—liberation of his energy and talents for cultural and spiritual self-fulfillment—evidently the support of a stable, well-founded social structure was as necessary as the checks and balances of the new economic system. By the late 1960s Americans were perhaps closer to ensuring the individual a positive and many-sided liberty than at any time in at least a century and a half. If in their perennial aspiration toward a great society they could keep a reasonable balance between change and order, economic mobility and social stability, they might yet bring about the new birth of freedom, the city upon a hill, the beacon to all mankind, of the long-troubled American dream.

Notes

FOREWORD

1. Richard Hofstadter, *The American Political Tradition and the Men Who Made It* (New York, 1948), p. x.
2. Louis Hartz, *The Liberal Tradition in America: An Interpretation of American Political Thought since the Revolution* (New York, 1955); Daniel J. Boorstin, *The Genius of American Politics* (Chicago, 1953); David M. Potter, *People of Plenty: Economic Abundance and the American Character* (Chicago, 1954); Oscar Handlin, *The Uprooted: The Epic Story of the Great Migrations That Made the American People* (Boston, 1951); John Higham, *Strangers in the Land: Patterns of American Nativism, 1860–1925* (New Brunswick, 1955); David Donald, *Lincoln Reconsidered: Essays on the Civil War Era* (New York, 1956), ch. 2; Richard Hofstadter, *The Age of Reform: From Bryan to F.D.R.* (New York, 1955).
3. John Higham, "Beyond Consensus: The Historian as Moral Critic," *American Historical Review*, LXVII (1962), pp. 609–625.
4. Rowland Berthoff, "The American Social Order: A Conservative Hypothesis," *ibid.*, LXV (1960), pp. 495–514.

PART ONE: The First American Society, 1607–1775

I. ORIGINS

Chapter 1. Foundations of Settlement

1. *Troilus and Cressida*, Act I, Scene 3. See E. M. W. Tillyard, *The Elizabethan World Picture* (London, 1943), p. 7.
2. Peter Laslett and John Harrison, "Clayworth and Cogenhoe," in *Historical Essays Presented to David Ogg*, ed. H. E. Bell and R. L. Ollard (Cambridge, 1963), p. 181.
3. W. G. Hoskins, *The Midland Peasant: The Economic and Social History of a Leicestershire Village* (London, 1957), p. 196.
4. Laslett and Harrison, "Clayworth and Cogenhoe," p. 181.
5. Bernard Bailyn, *The New England Merchants in the Seventeenth Century* (Cambridge, Mass., 1955), pp. 10–11.

II. THE LIMITS OF COLONIAL PROGRESS

Chapter 2. The Land

1. Josiah Strong, *Our Country* (New York, 1885), p. 153.
2. David M. Potter, *People of Plenty: Economic Abundance and the American Character* (Chicago, 1954).
3. Carl Bridenbaugh, *Myths and Realities: Societies of the Colonial South* (Baton Rouge, 1952), p. 127.
4. Allen W. Trelease, *Indian Affairs in Colonial New York: The Seventeenth Century* (Ithaca, 1960), pp. 169–170.
5. Richard S. Dunn, *Puritans and Yankees: The Winthrop Dynasty of New England, 1630–1717* (Princeton, 1962), p. 12.
6. E. R. R. Green, ed., *Essays in Scotch-Irish History* (London, 1969), p. 80; Conrad M. Arensberg, "American Communities," *American Anthropologist*, LVII (1955), p. 1154.

Chapter 3. Labor

1. Ansley J. Coale and Melvin Zelnick, *New Estimates of Fertility and Population in the United States* (Princeton, 1963), p. 35.
2. Abbot Emerson Smith, *Colonists in Bondage: White Servitude and Convict Labor in America, 1607–1776* (Chapel Hill, 1947), p. 60.
3. Wesley Frank Craven, *The Southern Colonies in the Seventeenth Century, 1607–1689* (Baton Rouge, 1949), p. 402.
4. Thomas J. Wertenbaker, *The Planters of Colonial Virginia* (Princeton, 1922), p. 126.
5. *Ibid.*, p. 136.
6. Carl Bridenbaugh, *Myths and Realities: Societies of the Colonial South* (Baton Rouge, 1952), p. 63.
7. Arthur W. Calhoun, *A Social History of the American Family* (New York, 1917), I, p. 205.
8. Smith, *Colonists in Bondage*, p. 286.

Chapter 4. Wealth

1. Robert E. Brown, *Middle-Class Democracy and the Revolution in Massachusetts, 1691–1780* (Ithaca, 1955), p. 16.
2. Charles S. Grant, *Democracy in the Connecticut Frontier Town of Kent* (New York, 1961), p. 53.
3. George Louis Beer, *The Origins of the British Colonial System, 1578–1660* (New York, 1908), p. 243.
4. Louis B. Wright, *The First Gentlemen of Virginia: Intellectual Qualities of the Early Colonial Ruling Class* (San Marino, Calif., 1940), p. 56.
5. Bernard Bailyn, "Politics and Social Structure in Virginia," in *Seventeenth-Century America: Essays in Colonial History,* ed. James Morton Smith (Chapel Hill, 1959), pp. 98, 100.
6. Carl Bridenbaugh, *Myths and Realities: Societies of the Colonial South* (Baton Rouge, 1952), p. 57.
7. *Ibid.*, p. 65.

8. *Ibid.*, p. 115.
9. *Ibid.*, p. 69.
10. *Ibid.*, p. 64.
11. M. Eugene Sirmans, *Colonial South Carolina: A Political History, 1663–1763* (Chapel Hill, 1966), p. 60.
12. Bridenbaugh, *Myths and Realities*, p. 11.
13. Grant, *Democracy in . . . Kent*, p. 46.
14. Bernard Bailyn, *The New England Merchants in the Seventeenth Century* (Cambridge, Mass., 1955), p. 101.
15. Frederick B. Tolles, *Meeting House and Counting House: The Quaker Merchants of Colonial Philadelphia, 1682–1783* (Chapel Hill, 1948), p. 95.
16. Grant, *Democracy in . . . Kent*, pp. 44, 53.
17. Bridenbaugh, *Myths and Realities*, p. 15.
18. Leonard Woods Labaree, *Conservatism in Early American History* (New York, 1948), p. 29.
19. Susie M. Ames, *Studies of the Virginia Eastern Shore in the Seventeenth Century* (Richmond, 1940), pp. 18–19.
20. Sumner Chilton Powell, *Puritan Village: The Formation of a New England Town* (Middletown, Conn., 1963), p. 96.
21. Bailyn, "Politics and Social Structure," p. 91.
22. Labaree, *Conservatism in Early American History*, p. 44.
23. James B. Hedges, *The Browns of Providence Plantations: Colonial Years* (Cambridge, Mass., 1952), pp. 6, 23, 28.
24. *Ibid.*, pp. 75–80.
25. Bernard and Lotte Bailyn, *Massachusetts Shipping, 1697–1714: A Statistical Study* (Cambridge, Mass., 1959), pp. 56–73.
26. Carl Bridenbaugh, *The Colonial Craftsman* (New York, 1950), p. 156.
27. Aubrey C. Land, *The Dulanys of Maryland* (Baltimore, 1955), p. 108.
28. Bailyn, *New England Merchants*, p. 105.

Chapter 5. Commonwealth

1. E. A. J. Johnson, *American Economic Thought in the Seventeenth Century* (London, 1932), p. 94.
2. *Ibid.*, p. 218.
3. Richard B. Morris, *Government and Labor in Early America* (New York, 1946), p. 61.
4. Johnson, *American Economic Thought*, p. 129.
5. Morris, *Government and Labor*, p. 75.
6. Bernard Bailyn, *The New England Merchants in the Seventeenth Century* (Cambridge, Mass., 1955), p. 49.
7. *Ibid.*, p. 42.
8. *Colonial Laws of Massachusetts* (Boston, 1887), p. 5.
9. Morris, *Government and Labor*, p. 69.
10. Johnson, *American Economic Thought*, p. 230.
11. *Winthrop's Journal "A History of New England," 1630–1649*, ed. James Kendall Hosmer (New York, 1908), I, p. 132.

III. THE FIRST AMERICAN SOCIETY

Chapter 6. Rank and Degree

1. Charles S. Sydnor, *Gentlemen Freeholders: Political Practices in Washington's Virginia* (Chapel Hill, 1952), p. 61.
2. Bernard Bailyn, "The Origins of American Politics," *Perspectives in American History*, I (1967), pp. 100–101.
3. William Smith, the New York lawyer and historian, in 1757, quoted in *ibid.*, p. 65.
4. Louis B. Wright, *First Gentlemen of Virginia: Intellectual Qualities of the Early Colonial Ruling Class* (San Marino, Calif., 1940), p. 331.
5. Ann Hulton, *Letters of a Loyalist Lady* (Cambridge, Mass., 1927), p. 105.
6. Frederick B. Tolles, *Meeting House and Counting House: The Quaker Merchants of Colonial Philadelphia, 1682–1783* (Chapel Hill, 1948), pp. 111–112.
7. Louis Morton, *Robert Carter of Nomini Hall: A Virginia Tobacco Planter of the Eighteenth Century* (Williamsburg, 1941), pp. 104, 110.
8. William A. Reavis, "The Maryland Gentry and Social Mobility, 1637–1676," *William and Mary Quarterly*, 3rd Ser., XIV (1957), p. 422.
9. Leonard Woods Labaree, *Conservatism in Early American History* (New York, 1948), p. 111.
10. Charles S. Grant, *Democracy in the Connecticut Frontier Town of Kent* (New York, 1961), p. 162.
11. Samuel Eliot Morison, "Precedence at Harvard College in the Seventeenth Century," *Proceedings of the American Antiquarian Society*, New Ser., XLII (1932), pp. 371–431; Clifford K. Shipton, *New England Life in the Eighteenth Century: Representative Biographies from Sibley's Harvard Graduates* (Cambridge, Mass., 1963), p. xxvi.
12. Carl Bridenbaugh, *Cities in the Wilderness: The First Century of Urban Life in America, 1625–1742* (New York, 1938), pp. 98, 411, 413; *Journal and Letters of Philip Vickers Fithian, 1773–1774: A Plantation Tutor of the Old Dominion*, ed. Hunter Dickinson Farish (Williamsburg, 1943), p. 35; Morison, "Precedence at Harvard," pp. 415–416.
13. Labaree, *Conservatism in Early American History*, pp. 5, 10.
14. Sydnor, *Gentlemen Freeholders*, p. 63.
15. E. A. J. Johnson, *American Economic Thought in the Seventeenth Century* (London, 1932), p. 96.
16. Marcus Wilson Jernegan, *Laboring and Dependent Classes in Colonial America, 1607–1783* (Chicago, 1931), p. 196.
17. *Ibid.*, p. 178.
18. Robert H. Bremner, *American Philanthropy* (Chicago, 1960), p. 15.
19. Carl Bridenbaugh, "The New England Town: A Way of Life," *Proceedings of the American Antiquarian Society*, New Ser., LVI (1946), p. 27.

Chapter 7. Well-Governed Families

1. James Truslow Adams, *Provincial Society, 1690–1763* (New York. 1927), p. 86.
2. Edmund S. Morgan, *The Puritan Family: Essays on Religion and Domestic Relations in Seventeenth-Century New England* (Boston, 1944), p. 38.
3. *Ibid.*, p. 81.
4. *Ibid.*, p. 83.
5. *Ibid.*, pp. 84, 85, 88.
6. Arthur W. Calhoun, *A Social History of the American Family* (New York, 1917), I, p. 117.
7. *Ibid.*, p. 124.
8. Bernard Bailyn, "Politics and Social Structure in Virginia," in *Seventeenth-Century America: Essays in Colonial History*, ed. James Morton Smith (Chapel Hill, 1959), p. 111.
9. Morgan, *Puritan Family*, p. 21.
10. John Demos, "Notes on Life in Plymouth Colony," *William and Mary Quarterly*, 3rd Ser., XXII (1965), p. 294.
11. Morgan, *Puritan Family*, p. 41.
12. Richard B. Morris, *Studies in the History of American Law* (New York, 1930), p. 136.
13. Demos, "Plymouth Colony," p. 281.

Chapter 8. Established Churches in the New World

1. Samuel Eliot Morison, *Builders of the Bay Colony* (Boston, 1930). p. 106.
2. *Idem.*
3. Wesley Frank Craven, *The Southern Colonies in the Seventeenth Century, 1607–1689* (Baton Rouge, 1949), p. 180.
4. Edmund S. Morgan, *Visible Saints: The History of a Puritan Idea* (New York, 1963), p. 128.

Chapter 9. Communities in Dispersion

1. Sumner Chilton Powell, *Puritan Village: The Formation of a New England Town* (Middletown, Conn., 1963), p. 118.
2. Michael Zuckerman, "The Social Context of Democracy in Massachusetts," *William and Mary Quarterly*, 3rd Ser., XXV (1968), p. 535.
3. *Ibid.*, pp. 532, 539.
4. *Ibid.*, pp. 536, 537.
5. Conrad M. Arensberg, "American Communities," *American Anthropologist*, LVII (1957), pp. 1153–1155.
6. Frederick B. Tolles, *Meeting House and Counting House: The Quaker Merchants of Colonial Philadelphia, 1682–1783* (Chapel Hill, 1948), p. 65.
7. Bernard Bailyn, "The Origins of American Politics," *Perspectives in American History*, I (1967), p. 50.

8. James Truslow Adams, *Provincial Society, 1607–1763* (New York, 1927), p. 205.
9. Peter Laslett, "The Gentry of Kent in 1640," *Cambridge Historical Journal*, IX (1948), p. 160.
10. Carl Van Doren, *Benjamin Franklin* (New York, 1938), p. 3.

PART TWO: The Society of Individuals, 1775–1875

I. ECONOMIC REVOLUTION

1. W. W. Rostow, *The Stages of Economic Growth* (Cambridge, Mass., 1960), pp. 7–9.

Chapter 10. The Westward Movement

1. Carl Bridenbaugh, *Myths and Realities: Societies of the Colonial South* (Baton Rouge, 1952), p. 131.
2. *Public Records of the Colony of Connecticut* (Hartford, 1880), XI, p. 630.
3. Avery O. Craven, *Soil Exhaustion as a Factor in the Agricultural History of Virginia and Maryland, 1606–1860* (Urbana, 1926), p. 84.
4. *Ibid.*, p. 122.
5. Frank Lawrence Owsley, *Plain Folk of the Old South* (Baton Rouge, 1949), p. 56.
6. *Ibid.*, p. 55.
7. Lewis D. Stilwell, *Migration from Vermont* (Montpelier, 1948), p. 120.
8. *Ibid.*, p. 183.
9. Thomas Perkins Abernethy, *The Formative Period in Alabama, 1815–1828* (Montgomery, 1922), p. 22.
10. Lewis Cecil Gray, *History of Agriculture in the Southern United States to 1860* (Washington, 1932), p. 661.

Chapter 11. The Atlantic Migration

1. W. A. Carrothers, *Emigration from the British Isles* (London, 1929), p. 187.
2. Edith Abbott, *Historical Aspects of the Immigration Problem: Select Documents* (Chicago, 1926), p. 117.
3. Herman Melville, *Redburn, His First Voyage* (Boston, 1924), p. 244.
4. Alan Conway, ed., *The Welsh in America: Letters from the Immigrants* (Minneapolis, 1961), p. 28.
5. Edwin C. Guillet, *The Great Migration: The Atlantic Crossing by Sailing-ship Since 1770* (New York, 1937), p. 16.
6. Arthur Cecil Todd, *The Cornish Miner in America* (Truro, 1967), p. 44.
7. Guillet, *The Great Migration*, p. 71.

Chapter 12. Commercial and Industrial Revolution

1. Pottsville (Pennsylvania) *Miners Journal*, June 16, 1827.
2. Rowland Berthoff, *British Immigrants in Industrial America, 1790–1950* (Cambridge, Mass., 1953), p. 70.
3. *Idem.*
4. Norman Ware, *The Industrial Worker, 1840–1860: The Reaction of American Industrial Society to the Advance of the Industrial Revolution* (New York, 1924), p. 75.
5. *Ibid.*, p. 106.
6. Frederick Law Olmsted, *The Cotton Kingdom: A Traveller's Observations on Cotton and Slavery in the American Slave States*, ed. Arthur M. Schlesinger (New York, 1953), p. 215.
7. Ware, *Industrial Worker*, p. 153.
8. Brinley Thomas, *Migration and Economic Growth: A Study of Great Britain and the Atlantic Economy* (Cambridge, 1954), p. 96.
9. Ralph Waldo Emerson, *Poems* (New York, 1904), p. 78.

II. SOCIAL DISORDER

Chapter 13. The Era of the Common Man

1. Alexis de Tocqueville, *Democracy in America*, ed. Phillips Bradley (New York, 1945), I, p. 3.
2. Chilton Williamson, *American Suffrage from Property to Democracy, 1760–1860* (Princeton, 1960), p. 76. Emphasis added.
3. Marvin Meyers, *The Jacksonian Persuasion: Politics and Belief* (Stanford, 1957), p. 17.
4. Richard C. Wade, *The Urban Frontier: The Rise of Western Cities, 1790–1830* (Cambridge, Mass., 1959), p. 203.
5. Stephan Thernstrom, *Poverty and Progress: Social Mobility in a Nineteenth Century City* (Cambridge, Mass., 1964), pp. 33–34.
6. Daniel R. Hundley, *Social Relations in Our Southern States* (New York, 1860), p. 84.
7. Merle Curti, *The Making of an American Community: A Case Study of Democracy in a Frontier County* (Stanford, 1959), p. 117.
8. Abraham Lincoln, *Collected Works*, ed. Roy P. Basler (New Brunswick, 1953), III, pp. 478–479.
9. Curti, *Making of an American Community*, p. 445.
10. *Ibid.*, p. 110.
11. Tocqueville, *Democracy in America*, I, p. 51.
12. *Ibid.*, I, p. 52.
13. Hundley, *Social Relations*, ch. 3–4.
14. *Ibid.*, pp. 170–171.
15. R. Carlyle Buley, *The Old Northwest: Pioneer Period, 1815–1840* (Bloomington, 1951), II, p. 155.
16. Curti, *Making of an American Community*, p. 157.
17. Paul Wallace Gates, "The Role of the Land Speculator in Western Development," *Pennsylvania Magazine of History and Biography*, LXVI (1942), p. 333.

18. Wade, *Urban Frontier*, pp. 203–204.
19. *Ibid.*, p. 204.
20. Sigmund Diamond, *The Reputation of the American Businessman* (Cambridge, Mass., 1955), p. 7.
21. *Ibid.*, p. 15.
22. Hundley, *Social Relations*, p. 257.
23. *Ibid.*, p. 264.
24. *Ibid.*, pp. 262–263.
25. Frederick Law Olmsted, *The Cotton Kingdom: A Traveller's Observations on Cotton and Slavery in the American Slave States*, ed. Arthur M. Schlesinger (New York, 1953), p. 225.
26. Roger W. Shugg, *Origins of Class Struggle in Louisiana: A Social History of White Farmers and Laborers during Slavery and After, 1840–1875* (University, La., 1939), p. 20.
27. Thernstrom, *Poverty and Progress*, p. 163.
28. Norman Ware, *The Industrial Worker, 1840–1860: The Reaction of American Industrial Society to the Advance of the Industrial Revolution* (New York, 1924), pp. xiv, 202.
29. *Ibid.*, pp. xix–xx.
30. Lincoln, *Collected Works*, III, p. 479.
31. Robert H. Bremner, *From the Depths: The Discovery of Poverty in the United States* (New York, 1956), p. 5.
32. John R. Commons, *The History of Labor in the United States* (New York, 1918), I, p. 410.
33. Curti, *Making of an American Community*, p. 110.
34. Ray Allen Billington, *The Protestant Crusade, 1800–1860: A Study of the Origins of American Nativism* (New York, 1938), p. 334.
35. Thernstrom, *Poverty and Progress*, p. 101.
36. Rowland Berthoff, *British Immigrants in Industrial America, 1790–1950* (Cambridge, Mass., 1953), p. 88.
37. *Boston Herald*, March 8, 1877.
38. Berthoff, *British Immigrants*, p. 96.
39. Ware, *Industrial Worker*, p. 77.
40. Rowland Berthoff, "The Social Order of the Anthracite Region, 1825–1902," *Pennsylvania Magazine of History and Biography*, LXXXIX (1965), p. 267.
41. Bremner, *From the Depths*, pp. 37, 38.

Chapter 14. The "Copartnership of Marriage"

1. Arthur W. Calhoun, *A Social History of the American Family* (New York, 1919), III, p. 239.
2. *Ibid.*, II, p. 131.
3. *Ibid.*, II, p. 215.
4. *Ibid.*, II, p. 28.
5. *Ibid.*, II, p. 29.
6. *Ibid.*, II, p. 40.
7. *Ibid.*, II, p. 22.
8. *Ibid.*, II, pp. 199, 203.
9. *Ibid.*, II, p. 349.

10. Lewis D. Stilwell, *Migration from Vermont* (Montpelier, 1948), p. 160.
11. Wilkes-Barre *Record of the Times,* February 21, 1872.
12. Calhoun, *Social History of the American Family,* II, p. 91.
13. Basil Hall, *Travels in North America in the Years 1827 and 1828* (Edinburgh, 1829), II, pp. 150–157.
14. Calhoun, *Social History of the American Family,* II, p. 112.
15. *Ibid.,* II, p. 95.
16. George M. Stephenson, "Nativism in the Forties and Fifties, with Special Reference to the Mississippi Valley," *Mississippi Valley Historical Review,* IX (1922), p. 200.
17. Calhoun, *Social History of the American Family,* II, p. 55.
18. *Ibid.,* II, p. 53.
19. *Ibid.,* II, p. 55.
20. *Ibid.,* II, p. 65.
21. Irvin G. Wyllie, *The Self-Made Man in America: The Myth of Rags to Riches* (New Brunswick, 1954), p. 9.
22. Calhoun, *Social History of the American Family,* II, p. 67.
23. *Ibid.,* II, p. 70.
24. *Idem.*
25. Alexis de Tocqueville, *Democracy in America,* ed. Phillips Bradley (New York, 1945), II, p. 192.
26. Calhoun, *Social History of the American Family,* II, p. 70.
27. Richard L. Rapson, "The American Child as Seen by British Travelers, 1845–1935," *American Quarterly,* XVII (1965), p. 521.
28. Scranton *Daily Times,* January 11, 1875.
29. *Ibid.,* June 9, 1879.
30. Rapson, "American Child," p. 521.
31. Oscar Handlin, ed., *This Was America: True Accounts of People and Places, Manners and Customs, as Recorded by European Travelers to the Western Shore in the Eighteenth, Nineteenth, and Twentieth Centuries* (Cambridge, Mass., 1949), p. 143.
32. Calhoun, *Social History of the American Family,* II, p. 67.

Chapter 15. The Community as Real Estate

1. Allen Nevins, ed., *America Through British Eyes* (New York, 1948), pp. 260–261.
2. Alexis de Tocqueville, *Democracy in America,* ed. Phillips Bradley (New York, 1945), II, pp. 215–216.
3. R. Carlyle Buley, *The Old Northwest: Pioneer Period, 1815–1840* (Bloomington, 1951), I, pp. 315–327; Frank Lawrence Owsley, *Plain Folk of the Old South* (Baton Rouge, 1949), p. 113.
4. John W. Reps, *The Making of Urban America: A History of City Planning in the United States* (Princeton, 1965), p. 294.
5. *Ibid.,* p. 297.
6. *Ibid.,* p. 299.
7. Owsley, *Plain Folk of the Old South,* p. 70.
8. Sam B. Warner, Jr., *The Private City: Philadelphia in Three Periods of Its Growth* (Philadelphia, 1968), p. 80.

9. Harry R. Stevens, *The Early Jackson Party in Ohio* (Durham, N.C., 1957), p. 151.
10. Reps, *Making of Urban America*, ch. 12.
11. Tocqueville, *Democracy in America*, II, p. 99.

III. CONSERVATIVE REACTION

1. Basil Hall, *Travels in North America in the Years 1827 and 1828* (Edinburgh, 1829), II, p. 182.

Chapter 16. Social Uses of Religion

1. Barbara M. Cross, *Horace Bushnell: Minister to a Changing America* (Chicago, 1958), pp. 37, 44–46.
2. Henry F. May, *Protestant Churches in Industrial America* (New York, 1949), p. 62.
3. Perry Miller, *Jonathan Edwards* (New York, 1949), pp. 145–146.
4. C. C. Goen, *Revivalism and Separatism in New England, 1740–1800: Congregationalists and Separate Baptists in the Great Awakening* (New Haven, 1962), p. 18.
5. *Ibid.*, p. 19.
6. Richard L. Bushman, *From Puritan to Yankee: Character and the Social Order in Connecticut, 1690–1765* (Cambridge, Mass., 1967), p. 188.
7. *Idem.*
8. *Ibid.*, p. 192.
9. Goen, *Revivalism and Separatism*, pp. 49–50.
10. Bushman, *From Puritan to Yankee*, p. 209.
11. Leonard J. Trinterud, *The Forming of an American Tradition: A Re-examination of Colonial Presbyterianism* (Philadelphia, 1949), p. 268.
12. Catherine C. Cleveland, *The Great Revival in the West* (Chicago, 1916), p. 45.
13. *Ibid.*, p. 57.
14. *Ibid.*, pp. 99–101.
15. John Allen Krout and Dixon Ryan Fox, *The Completion of Independence, 1790–1830* (New York, 1944), p. 175.
16. Caroline M. Kirkland, *A New Home, Who'll Follow?, or, Glimpses of Western Life* (New York, 1850), p. 202.
17. Cleveland, *The Great Revival in the West*, p. 67.
18. R. Carlyle Buley, *The Old Northwest: Pioneer Period, 1815–1840* (Bloomington, 1951), II, p. 459.
19. Timothy L. Smith, *Revivalism and Social Reform in Mid-Nineteenth Century America* (Nashville, 1957), p. 143.
20. Perry Miller, *The Life of the Mind in America: From the Revolution to the Civil War* (New York, 1965), p. 143.
21. Cross, *Horace Bushnell*, pp. 54–55.
22. Miller, *Life of the Mind in America*, pp. 70–72.

23. Sidney Mead, "Denominationalism: The Shape of Protestantism in America," *Church History*, XXIII (1954), p. 308.
24. Whitney R. Cross, *The Burned-Over District: The Social and Intellectual History of Enthusiastic Religion in Western New York, 1800–1850* (Ithaca, 1950), p. 145.
25. Fawn M. Brodie, *No Man Knows My History: The Life of Joseph Smith the Mormon Prophet* (New York, 1946), p. 84.
26. *Ibid.*, pp. 185, 297.
27. Charles Dickens, *The Uncommercial Traveller* (New York, 1910), p. 201.
28. Massachusetts Bureau of Statistics of Labor, *Second Annual Report* (1871), p. 486.

Chapter 17. Moral Voluntarism

1. Alexis de Tocqueville, *Democracy in America,* ed. Phillips Bradley (New York, 1945), II, p. 106.
2. Bronson Alcott, quoted in Arthur M. Schlesinger, *The American as Reformer* (Cambridge, Mass., 1950), p. 13.
3. David Donald, *Lincoln Reconsidered: Essays on the Civil War Era* (New York, 1956), p. 33.
4. *Ibid.*, p. 35.
5. Alice Felt Tyler, *Freedom's Ferment: Phases of American Social History to 1860* (Minneapolis, 1944), p. 288.
6. Edith Abbott, *Historical Aspects of the Immigration Problem: Select Documents* (Chicago, 1926), p. 615.
7. Merle Curti, *The Social Ideas of American Educators* (New York, 1935), p. 62.
8. *Ibid.*, p. 89.
9. *Ibid.*, p. 88.
10. *Ibid.*, p. 58.
11. *Ibid.*, pp. 83–84.
12. *Ibid.*, pp. 78, 83, 93.
13. *Ibid.*, pp. 33–34.
14. Tyler, *Freedom's Ferment*, p. 264.
15. Stanley M. Elkins, *Slavery: A Problem in American Institutional and Intellectual Life* (Chicago, 1959), p. 175.
16. Russel B. Nye, *William Lloyd Garrison and the Humanitarian Reformers* (Boston, 1955), p. 143.
17. Tyler, *Freedom's Ferment*, p. 310.
18. Marcus Lee Hansen, *The Immigrant in American History* (Cambridge, Mass., 1942), p. 109.
19. John Allen Krout, *The Origins of Prohibition* (New York, 1925), pp. 183, 187.
20. *Ibid.*, pp. 189, 231, 251.
21. William G. Bean, "Puritan versus Celt, 1850–1860," *New England Quarterly*, VII (1934), p. 77.
22. David M. Ludlum, *Social Ferment in Vermont, 1791–1850* (New York, 1939), p. 98.

Chapter 18. Liberty and Union

1. Ray Allen Billington, *The Protestant Crusade, 1800–1860: A Study of the Origins of American Nativism* (New York, 1938), p. 40.
2. *Ibid.*, p. 119.
3. *Ibid.*, pp. 310, 361.
4. *Ibid.*, p. 420.
5. Edith Abbott, *Historical Aspects of the Immigration Problem: Select Documents* (Chicago, 1926), p. 650.
6. Billington, *Protestant Crusade*, p. 198.
7. Anthony Trollope, *North America* (Philadelphia, 1862), II, p. 55.
8. Harvey Wish, *George Fitzhugh: Propagandist of the Old South* (Baton Rouge, 1943), pp. 104–105, 150–157.
9. *Ibid.*, p. 211.
10. Avery O. Craven, *The Growth of Southern Nationalism, 1848–1860* (Baton Rouge, 1953), p. 115.
11. John Higham, *Strangers in the Land: Patterns of American Nativism, 1860–1925* (New Brunswick, 1955), p. 4.
12. William G. Bean, "Puritan Versus Celt, 1850–1860," *New England Quarterly*, VII (1934), p. 76.
13. Carl Wittke, *Refugees of Revolution: The German Forty-Eighters in America* (Philadelphia, 1952), p. 182.
14. Holman Hamilton, *Prologue to Conflict* (Lexington, Ky., 1964), p. 54.
15. Craven, *Growth of Southern Nationalism*, p. 329.
16. Norman Graebner, ed., *Politics and the Crisis of 1860* (Urbana, 1961), p. 132.
17. *Ibid.*, p. 112.
18. Glyndon G. Van Deusen, *The Jacksonian Era, 1828–1848* (New York, 1959), p. 43.
19. David M. Potter, *Lincoln and His Party in the Secession Crisis* (New Haven, 1942), p. 52.
20. *Ibid.*, pp. 319 ff.
21. Thomas Carlyle, *Latter-Day Pamphlets* (New York, 1901), pp. 20–21.

PART THREE. The Reconstituted Society, 1875–1945

I. ECONOMIC PROGRESS AND REFORM

Chapter 19. The Farmers' Last Frontier

1. LaWanda F. Cox, "The American Agricultural Wage Earner, 1865–1900," *Agricultural History*, XXII (1948), p. 100.
2. Paul S. Taylor, "The American Hired Man: His Rise and Decline," *Land Policy Review*, VI (1943), pp. 12–13.
3. *Ibid.*, p. 12.

Chapter 20. Captains of Industry and Armies of Labor

1. James Willard Hurst, *Law and the Conditions of Freedom* (Madison, 1956), p. 82.
2. Edward C. Kirkland, *Dream and Thought in the Business Community* (Ithaca, 1956), p. 8.
3. *Ibid.*, p. 25.
4. *Ibid.*, p. 9.
5. Rowland Berthoff, "The 'Freedom to Control' in American Business History," in *A Festschrift for Frederick B. Artz*, ed. David H. Pinkney and Theodore Ropp (Durham, N.C., 1964), pp. 159–160.
6. Edward N. Saveth, *American Historians and European Immigrants, 1875–1925* (New York, 1948), pp. 40, 142.
7. Emily Greene Balch, *Our Slavic Fellow Citizens* (New York, 1910), p. 50.
8. *Ibid.*, pp. 49–50.
9. Robert F. Foerster, *The Italian Emigration of Our Times* (Cambridge, Mass., 1924), p. 104.
10. Rowland Berthoff, "The Social Order of the Anthracite Region, 1825–1902," *Pennsylvania Magazine of History and Biography*, LXXXIX (1965), p. 287.
11. Marcus Lee Hansen, *The Immigrant in American History* (Cambridge, Mass., 1942), p. 170.
12. Edith Abbott, *Historical Aspects of the Immigration Problem: Select Documents* (Chicago, 1926), p. 367.
13. Rowland Berthoff, *British Immigrants in Industrial America, 1790–1950* (Cambridge, Mass., 1953), p. 58.
14. *Ibid.*, p. 36.
15. *Ibid.*, p. 85.
16. *Ibid.*, p. 53.
17. *Ibid.*, p. 67.
18. *Ibid.*, p. 133.
19. Scranton *Daily Times*, November 24, 1880.

Chapter 21. The Search for Economic Security

1. Edward C. Kirkland, *Industry Comes of Age* (New York, 1961), p. 81.
2. *Ibid.*, p. 210.
3. Edward C. Kirkland, *Dream and Thought in the Business Community* (Ithaca, 1956), pp. 22–23.
4. Harold U. Faulkner, *The Decline of Laissez Faire* (New York, 1951), pp. 161–162.
5. *Ibid.*, p. 296; Albion Guilford Taylor, *Labor Policies of the National Association of Manufacturers* (Urbana, 1928), p. 52.
6. W. Jett Lauck and Edgar Sydenstricker, *Condition of Labor in American Industries: A Summarization of the Results of Recent Investigations* (New York, 1917), p. 238.
7. Sigmund Diamond, *The Reputation of the American Businessman* (Cambridge, Mass., 1955), p. 65.

8. Charles B. Spahr, *An Essay on the Present Distribution of Wealth in the United States* (New York, 1896), pp. 69, 128–129.
9. Walter Johnson, *William Allen White's America* (New York, 1947), p. 129.
10. Diamond, *Reputation of the American Businessman*, p. 53.
11. Richard Hofstadter, *The Age of Reform: From Bryan to F.D.R.* (New York, 1955), p. 135.
12. Eric F. Goldman, *Rendezvous with Destiny* (New York, 1953), p. 18.
13. Thorstein Veblen, *Absentee Ownership and Business Enterprise in Recent Times: The Case of America* (New York, 1923), pp. 113–114.
14. Ely Chinoy, *Automobile Workers and the American Dream* (Garden City, N.Y., 1955), p. 125.
15. Richard Hofstadter, *The American Political Tradition and the Men Who Made It* (New York, 1948), p. 326.
16. *Ibid.*, p. 329.
17. Arthur M. Schlesinger, Jr., *The Politics of Upheaval* (Boston, 1960), p. 399.
18. John Kenneth Galbraith, *American Capitalism: The Concept of Countervailing Power* (Boston, 1952), ch. 9–10.
19. *The Public Papers and Addresses of Franklin D. Roosevelt* (New York, 1938), V, p. 390.
20. Robert E. Sherwood, *Roosevelt and Hopkins: An Intimate History* (New York, 1948), p. 57.

II. A PERSONALIZED SOCIETY

Chapter 22. Victims of Individualism

1. Angie Debo, *And Still the Waters Run* (Princeton, 1940), pp. 21–22. Emphasis added.
2. D'Arcy McNickle, *They Came Here First* (Philadelphia, 1949), p. 264.
3. Debo, *And Still the Waters Run*, p. 131.
4. McNickle, *They Came Here First*, p. 290.
5. Amendments XIV and XV.
6. Alfred H. Kelly and Winfred A. Harbison, *The American Constitution: Its Origins and Development* (New York, 1948), II, p. 491. Emphasis added.
7. C. Vann Woodward, *Origins of the New South, 1877–1913* (Baton Rouge, 1951), p. 211.
8. *Ibid.*, p. 216.
9. *Ibid.*, p. 354.
10. Charles J. Bonaparte, quoted in John Higham, *Strangers in the Land: Patterns of American Nativism, 1860–1925* (New Brunswick, 1955), p. 118.
11. William I. Thomas and Florian Znaniecki, *The Polish Peasant in Europe and America: Monograph of an Immigrant Group* (Boston, 1920), V, p. 165.

12. *Ibid.*, V, pp. 167–168.
13. *Ibid.*, V, p. 169.
14. Robert H. Bremner, *From the Depths: The Discovery of Poverty in the United States* (New York, 1956), p. 62.
15. Jane Addams, *Democracy and Social Ethics*, ed. Anne Firor Scott (Cambridge, Mass., 1964), p. 14.
16. Grace Abbott, *The Immigrant and the Community* (New York, 1917), p. 276 (I have to thank Elizabeth Durham Rostberg for this reference).
17. Bremner, *From the Depths*, p. 65.
18. Thomas and Znaniecki, *Polish Peasant*, V, p. 266.
19. *Ibid.*, p. 310.
20. Caroline F. Ware, *Greenwich Village, 1920–1930: A Comment on American Civilization in the Post-War Years* (Boston, 1935), p. 168.
21. Thomas and Znaniecki, *Polish Peasant*, V, p. 265.

Chapter 23. *"Congeries of Social Atoms"*

1. Lewis Atherton, *Main Street on the Middle Border* (Bloomington, 1954), p. 279.
2. Rowland Berthoff, "The Social Order of the Anthracite Region, 1825–1902," *Pennsylvania Magazine of History and Biography*, LXXXIX (1965), p. 290.
3. Henry F. May, *Protestant Churches and Industrial America* (New York, 1949), pp. 92–93.
4. Robert E. Park, Ernest W. Burgess, and Roderick D. McKenzie, *The City* (Chicago, 1925), p. 107.
5. John Sirjamaki, *The Sociology of Cities* (New York, 1964), p. 197.
6. Bayrd Still, *Milwaukee: The History of a City* (Madison, 1948), p. 268.
7. Harvey Warren Zorbaugh, *The Gold Coast and the Slum: A Sociological Study of Chicago's Near North Side* (Chicago, 1929), p. 180.
8. Louis Wirth, *The Ghetto* (Chicago, 1928), pp. 225–226.
9. Zorbaugh, *Gold Coast and Slum*, p. 235.
10. Donald B. Cole, *Immigrant City: Lawrence, Massachusetts, 1845–1921* (Chapel Hill, 1963), p. 69; Blake McKelvey, *Rochester: The Quest for Quality, 1890–1925* (Cambridge, Mass., 1956), p. 154; Caroline F. Ware, *Greenwich Village, 1920–1930: A Comment on American Civilization in the Post-War Years* (Boston, 1935), p. 11.
11. Zorbaugh, *Gold Coast and Slum*, p. 235.
12. *Ibid.*, p. 82.
13. Ware, *Greenwich Village*, p. 29.
14. Robert A. Woods and Albert J. Kennedy, *The Zone of Emergence*, ed. Sam B. Warner, Jr. (Cambridge, Mass., 1962), pp. 34, 39, 40.
15. Ware, *Greenwich Village*, pp. 99–100.
16. Wirth, *The Ghetto*, p. 248.
17. Woods and Kennedy, *Zone of Emergence*, p. 108.

18. Sam B. Warner, Jr., *Streetcar Suburbs: The Process of Growth in Boston, 1870–1900* (Cambridge, Mass., 1962), pp. 161–162.
19. Woods and Kennedy, *Zone of Emergence*, p. 127.
20. Warner, *Streetcar Suburbs*, p. 157.
21. Harlan Paul Douglass, *The Suburban Trend* (New York, 1925), p. 164.
22. James Bryce, *The American Commonwealth* (London, 1888), II, p. 281.
23. Arthur J. Vidich and Joseph Bensman, *Small Town in Mass Society: Class, Power, and Religion in a Rural Community* (Princeton, 1958), p. 305.
24. *Ibid.*, p. 310.
25. Atherton, *Main Street on the Middle Border*, p. 353.
26. *Ibid.*, p. 254.
27. *Ibid.*, p. 352.
28. Vidich and Bensman, *Small Town in Mass Society*, pp. 29, 52.

Chapter 24. *The Companionate Family*

1. Arthur W. Calhoun, *A Social History of the American Family* (New York, 1919), III, p. 195.
2. *Ibid.*, III, p. 196.
3. *Ibid.*, III, p. 168.
4. David Riesman, *The Lonely Crowd* (New Haven, 1950), p. 15.
5. William E. Bridges, "Family Patterns and Social Values in America, 1825–1875," *American Quarterly*, XVII (1965), p. 9.
6. Margaret Mead, *And Keep Your Powder Dry: An Anthropologist Looks at America* (New York, 1942), p. 31.
7. Harold U. Faulkner, *The Quest for Social Justice, 1898–1914* (New York, 1931), p. 167.
8. Grace Abbott, ed., *The Child and the State: Legal Status in the Family, Apprenticeship and Child Labor* (Chicago, 1938), I, pp. 325–326.
9. Constitutional Convention of the State of New York, *Revised Record* (Albany, 1894), II, p. 544 (I have to thank Aileen S. Kraditor for this reference).
10. Calhoun, *Social History of the American Family*, III, p. 168.
11. Talcott Parsons, "The Kinship System of the United States," *American Anthropologist*, XLV (1943), pp. 24, 26.
12. Saint Louis School Board, *Report* (1876–1877), p. 175 (I have to thank Joyce Rittenhouse Parker for this reference).
13. W. E. Burghardt DuBois. *The Negro American Family* (Atlanta, 1908), p. 42.
14. Christopher Lasch, *The New Radicalism in America, 1889–1963: The Intellectual as a Social Type* (New York, 1965), p. 141.
15. *Ibid.*, pp. 85, 142.
16. *Ibid.*, p. 142.
17. *Ibid.*, p. 101.
18. Calhoun, *Social History of the American Family*, III, p. 213.

19. John Sirjamaki, *The American Family in the Twentieth Century* (Cambridge, Mass., 1953), p. 55.
20. William L. O'Neill, *Divorce in the Progressive Era* (New Haven, 1967), p. xi.
21. Calhoun, *Social History of the American Family*, III, p. 119.
22. *Idem.*
23. *Ibid.*, p. 130.
24. Sirjamaki, *American Family*, pp. 102–103.
25. *Ibid.*, p. 57.
26. Faulkner, *Quest for Social Justice*, p. 164.
27. *Scranton Republican*, October 12, 1899.
28. G. Stanley Hall, quoted in Calhoun, *Social History of the American Family*, III, p. 235.
29. *Scranton Republican*, December 21, 1903.
30. Calhoun, *Social History of the American Family*, III, p. 131.
31. *Ibid.*, III, p. 145.
32. *Scranton Republican*, February 5, 1895.
33. Calhoun, *Social History of the American Family*, III, p. 146.
34. Richard L. Rapson, "The American Child as Seen by British Travelers, 1845–1935," *American Quarterly*, XVII (1965), p. 533.
35. Calhoun, *Social History of the American Family*, III, p. 153.
36. O'Neill, *Divorce in the Progressive Era*, p. 176.
37. Sirjamaki, *American Family*, p. 81.
38. *Ibid.*, p. 130.
39. Parsons, "Kinship System," p. 33.
40. Sirjamaki, *American Family*, p. 73.
41. *Ibid.*, p. 114.
42. O'Neill, *Divorce in the Progressive Era*, p. 6.

Chapter 25. Churches and the American Way

1. Arthur Meier Schlesinger, *The Rise of the City, 1878–1898* (New York, 1933), p. 332.
2. Aaron Ignatius Abell, *The Urban Impact on American Protestantism* (Cambridge, Mass., 1943), p. 64.
3. Henry F. May, *Protestant Churches and Industrial America* (New York, 1949), p. 51.
4. Abell, *Urban Impact on American Protestantism*, p. 6.
5. Charles Howard Hopkins, *The Rise of the Social Gospel in American Protestantism, 1865–1915* (New Haven, 1940), p. 85.
6. Paul A. Carter, *The Decline and Revival of the Social Gospel: Social and Political Liberalism in American Protestant Churches, 1920–1940* (Ithaca, 1956), p. 56.
7. *Ibid.*, p. 57.
8. Norman F. Furniss, *The Fundamentalist Controversy, 1918–1931* (New Haven, 1954), p. 37.
9. William G. McLoughlin, Jr., *Billy Sunday Was His Real Name* (Chicago, 1955), pp. 103, 116, 123.
10. Schlesinger, *Rise of the City*, p. 336.

11. Herbert Wallace Schneider, *Religion in 20th Century America* (Cambridge, Mass., 1952), p. 78.
12. *Ibid.*, p. 76.
13. Thomas T. McAvoy, *The Great Crisis in American Catholic History, 1895–1900* (Chicago, 1957).
14. *Ibid.*, p. 116.
15. *Ibid.*, p. 100.
16. Colman J. Barry, *The Catholic Church and German Americans* (Milwaukee, 1953), p. 193.
17. *The Great Encyclical Letters of Pope Leo XIII* (New York, 1903), pp. 239, 243.
18. John Tracy Ellis, *American Catholicism* (Chicago, 1955), p. 109.
19. *Ibid.*, p. 119.
20. Harlan Paul Douglass, *The Suburban Trend* (New York, 1925), p. 207.
21. Marcus L. Hansen, *The Problem of the Third Generation Immigrant* (Rock Island, Ill., 1938), p. 9.
22. Robert N. Bellah, "Civil Religion in America," *Daedalus*, XCVI (1967), p. 1.
23. Will Herberg, *Protestant–Catholic–Jew: An Essay in American Religious Sociology* (New York, 1955), p. 89.
24. *Ibid.*, p. 102.
25. *Ibid.*, p. 97.

Chapter 26. Social Control and Social Adjustment

1. Heywood Broun and Margaret Leech, *Anthony Comstock: Roundsman of the Lord* (New York, 1927), pp. 80–81.
2. *Ibid.*, pp. 185, 224, 230.
3. Alan P. Grimes, *The Puritan Ethic and Woman Suffrage* (New York, 1967), pp. 46, 76.
4. *Ibid.*, p. 83.
5. James H. Timberlake, *Prohibition and the Progressive Movement, 1900–1920* (Cambridge, Mass., 1963), p. 16.
6. *Ibid.*, p. 34.
7. *Ibid.*, pp. 120–121.
8. Wallace Evan Davies, *Patriotism on Parade: The Story of Veterans' and Hereditary Organizations in America, 1783–1900* (Cambridge, Mass., 1955), p. 215.
9. *Ibid.*, p. 220.
10. Charles W. Ferguson, *Fifty Million Brothers: A Panorama of American Lodges and Clubs* (New York, 1937), p. 207.
11. Davies, *Patriotism on Parade*, p. 49.
12. *Ibid.*, p. 82.
13. *Ibid.*, p. 48.
14. *Ibid.*, p. 49.
15. John Higham, *Strangers in the Land: Patterns of American Nativism, 1860–1925* (New Brunswick, 1955), p. 85.
16. *Ibid.*, pp. 138, 143.
17. Madison Grant, quoted in *ibid.*, pp. 156, 272.

18. *Ibid.*, p. 152; Rudolph J. Vecoli, "Sterilization: A Progressive Measure?" *Wisconsin Magazine of History*, XLIII (1960), pp. 191, 193–194.
19. Vecoli, "Sterilization," p. 200.
20. *Ibid.*, p. 197.
21. *Ibid.*, p. 202.
22. Andrew Sinclair, *Prohibition: The Era of Excess* (Boston, 1962), pp. 180, 181.
23. Higham, *Strangers in the Land*, p. 294.
24. Lawrence A. Cremin, *The Transformation of the School: Progressivism in American Education, 1876–1957* (New York, 1961), p. 73.
25. *Ibid.*, p. 199.
26. F. W. Taussig and C. S. Joslyn, *American Business Leaders* (New York, 1932), p. 302.
27. Cremin, *Transformation of the School*, p. 118. Emphasis added.
28. *Ibid.*, p. 207.
29. *Ibid.*, p. 234.
30. *Ibid.*, p. 207.
31. *Ibid.*, pp. 195–196.

Chapter 27. The Voluntary Order

1. Margaret Mead, *And Keep Your Powder Dry: An Anthropologist Looks at America* (New York, 1942), p. 37.
2. Charles W. Ferguson, *Fifty Million Brothers: A Panorama of American Lodges and Clubs* (New York, 1937), p. 302.
3. Mead, *And Keep Your Powder Dry*, p. 35.
4. William I. Thomas and Florian Znaniecki, *The Polish Peasant in Europe and America: Monograph of an Immigrant Group* (Boston, 1920), V, pp. 108–109.
5. Noel P. Gist, *Secret Societies: A Cultural Study of Fraternalism in the United States* (Columbia, Mo., 1940), p. 134.
6. Solon Justus Buck, *The Granger Movement: A Study of Agricultural Organization and Its Political, Economic, and Social Manifestations, 1870–1880* (Cambridge, Mass., 1913), p. 279.
7. Frank Tannenbaum, *A Philosophy of Labor* (New York, 1952), p. 66.
8. Arthur Meier Schlesinger, *The Rise of the City, 1878–1898* (New York, 1933), p. 143.
9. Sophonisba P. Breckinridge, *Women in the Twentieth Century: A Study of Their Political, Social and Economic Activities* (New York, 1933), p. 20.
10. *Ibid.*, p. 30.
11. Corinne Lathrop Gilb, *Hidden Hierarchies: The Professions and Government* (New York, 1966), p. 31.
12. *Ibid.*, pp. 53–54.
13. Ferguson, *Fifty Million Brothers*, p. 98.
14. W. Lloyd Warner, *American Life: Dream and Reality* (Chicago, 1953), pp. 196 ff.

15. Alexis de Tocqueville, *Democracy in America*, ed. Phillips Bradley (New York, 1945), II, p. 107.
16. *Ibid.*, II, p. 110.

Epilogue and Prologue

Chapter 28. *In Quest of the Great Society: Since 1945*

1. W. Lloyd Warner and James C. Abegglen, *Occupational Mobility in American Business and Industry* (Minneapolis, 1955), pp. 35–36.
2. Peter M. Blau and Otis Dudley Duncan, *The American Occupational Structure* (New York, 1967), p. 424.
3. Dixon Wecter, *The Age of the Great Depression, 1929–1941* (New York, 1948), p. 124.
4. Jane Jacobs, *The Death and Life of Great American Cities* (New York, 1961), p. 113.
5. Scott Greer, *Urban Renewal and American Cities: The Dilemma of Democratic Intervention* (Indianapolis, 1965), pp. 4–5.
6. Harrison E. Salisbury, *The Shook-Up Generation* (New York, 1958), pp. 79–80.
7. Greer, *Urban Renewal*, p. 16.
8. David Riesman, "The Suburban Sadness," in *The Suburban Community*, ed. William Dobriner (New York, 1958), p. 377.
9. Robert A. Nisbet, *The Quest for Community: A Study in the Ethics of Order and Freedom* (New York, 1953), pp. 31, 52.
10. David Riesman, *The Lonely Crowd: A Study of the Changing American Character* (New Haven, 1950), p. 9.
11. Theodor W. Adorno *et al.*, *The Authoritarian Personality* (New York, 1950), p. 971.
12. Daniel Bell, ed., *The New American Right* (New York, 1955), pp. 210–211.
13. *Ibid.*, p. 211.
14. *Ibid.*, p. 214.
15. *Ibid.*, p. 138.
16. Richard H. Rovere, *Senator Joe McCarthy* (New York, 1959), pp. 213, 215.

Bibliographical Essay

To limit a bibliography of American social history to definitive or even merely systematic works would take only a few disconnected pages. At the other pole, a list of all the books and articles that might supply data for a survey of the field would run on indefinitely, since historians have usually admitted social matters into their work for some marginal relevance to the main story of economic, political, or intellectual developments. The most useful compromise seems to be to include studies of various sorts that have made some solid contribution to coherent understanding of this overly incoherent branch of history.

The thirteen volumes of *The History of American Life*, edited by Arthur Meier Schlesinger and Dixon Ryan Fox (New York, 1927–1948), exemplify both the stimulating promise and the indifferent performance of the social historians of their time. Schlesinger's own volume in the series, *The Rise of the City, 1878–1898* (1933), is typically rich in research but diffuse in organization and superficial in interpretation. The volumes by James Truslow Adams, *Provincial Society, 1690–1763* (1927), and Dixon Wecter, *The Age of the Great Depression, 1929–1941* (1948), stand out, the former for cogent insights, the latter for reintroducing the political matters that had been banished from the rest of the series. Although the new, more analytical generation of social historians has not yet undertaken a joint project of its own, several recent series with different orientations have not overlooked analytical social history. Among the nine volumes so far published of the *History of the South* (University, La., 1947–   ), those by Wesley Frank Craven, *The Southern Colonies in the Seventeenth Century, 1607–1689* (1949), and C. Vann Woodward, *Origins of the New South, 1877–1913* (1951), are indispensable. Edmund S. Morgan, *The Puritan Dilemma: The Story of John Winthrop* (Boston, 1958), and Robert H. Wiebe, *The Search for Order, 1877–1920* (New York, 1967), similarly distinguish themselves from their companion volumes in other recent series. The New American Nation series (New York, 1954–   ), the most ambitious multivolume project now going forward, so far has included no social history of comparable merit.

Economic historians are necessarily concerned with the foundations of the social structure, particularly in a new, developing country. The companion volumes of Lewis Cecil Gray, *History of Agriculture in the Southern United States to 1860* (Washington, 1932), and Percy Wells

Bidwell and John I. Falconer, *History of Agriculture in the Northern United States, 1620–1860* (Washington, 1925), continue to be invaluable. In the nine-volume *Economic History of the United States* (New York, 1945–   ), the most useful for the social historian are George Rogers Taylor, *The Transportation Revolution, 1815–1860* (1951); Fred A. Shannon, *The Farmer's Last Frontier: Agriculture, 1860–1897* (1945); and Edward C. Kirkland, *Industry Comes of Age: Business, Labor, and Public Policy, 1860–1897* (1961). Among several recent extended essays on the whole course of American history, the most relevant is also an economic interpretation, William Appleman Williams, *The Contours of American History* (Cleveland, 1961).

The most useful place to begin the study of American society is the preliminary analysis of the structure of seventeenth-century English society by Peter Laslett, *The World We Have Lost* (London, 1965). Partly because English society, in its colonial branches as well as in the mother country, had not yet lost the organic character of medieval institutions, several recent studies of colonial localities have achieved an exceptional degree of analytical coherence. Predictably enough, New England has been best represented: Darrett B. Rutman, *Winthrop's Boston: Portrait of a Puritan Town, 1630–1649* (Chapel Hill, 1965); Emery Battis, *Saints and Sectaries: Anne Hutchinson and the Antinomian Controversy in the Massachusetts Bay Colony* (Chapel Hill, 1962); Sumner Chilton Powell, *Puritan Village: The Formation of a New England Town* (Middletown, Conn., 1963); Charles S. Grant, *Democracy in the Connecticut Frontier Town of Kent* (New York, 1961); Richard L. Bushman, *From Puritan to Yankee: Character and the Social Order in Connecticut, 1690–1765* (Cambridge, Mass., 1967); and Robert J. Taylor, *Western Massachusetts in the Revolution* (Providence, 1954).

The colonial South has been harder for social historians to pull together. The wide-ranging essays of Carl Bridenbaugh, *Myths and Realities: Societies of the Colonial South* (Baton Rouge, La., 1952), present an enlightening comparison of what is known of the regional societies of the Chesapeake, lowland Carolina, and the backcountry. There are several good local studies: Susie M. Ames, *Studies of the Virginia Eastern Shore in the Seventeenth Century* (Richmond, 1940); Richard Maxwell Brown, *The South Carolina Regulators* (Cambridge, Mass., 1963); and Thomas Perkins Abernethy, *Three Virginia Frontiers* (University, La., 1940).

The geographical and social mobility of the nineteenth century has too often been simply described by historians, and the resulting social disorder mirrored in the rambling structure of their books. A few have managed to turn mobility and instability into a tight analytical principle: Roger W. Shugg, *Origins of Class Struggle in Louisiana: A Social History of White Farmers and Laborers during Slavery and After, 1840–1875* (University, La., 1939); Oscar Handlin, *Boston's Immigrants, 1790–1865: A Study in Acculturation* (Cambridge, Mass., 1941); Frank Lawrence Owsley, *Plain Folk of the Old South* (University, La., 1949); and Whitney R. Cross, *The Burned-Over District: The Social and Intellectual History of Enthusiastic Religion in Western New York, 1800–1850*

(Ithaca, 1950). Two exceptionally useful studies of westward migration are Avery O. Craven, *Soil Exhaustion as a Factor in the Agricultural History of Virginia and Maryland, 1606–1860* (Urbana, 1926), and Lewis D. Stilwell, *Migration from Vermont* (Montpelier, 1948). The classic study of the social consequences of natural environment, Walter Prescott Webb, *The Great Plains* (New York, 1931), exaggerates the extent of innovation on that frontier.

Historians of the societies of particular times and places have inclined toward one of two poles: either they have been content to assemble a vast miscellany of details or they have reduced the social structure to one of its parts: the ladder of economic classes and the vertical mobility of individuals upon it. The former approach lacks focus, though through it vast mines of useful data have been uncovered: Carl Bridenbaugh, *Cities in the Wilderness: The First Century of Urban Life in America, 1625–1742* (New York, 1938), and *Cities in Revolt: Urban Life in America, 1743–1776* (New York, 1955); R. Carlyle Buley, *The Old Northwest: Pioneer Period, 1815–1840* (2 vols.; Indianapolis, 1950); and Everett Dick, *The Sod-House Frontier, 1854–1890: A Social History of the Northern Plains from the Creation of Kansas and Nebraska to the Admission of the Dakotas* (New York, 1937), and *The Dixie Frontier: A Social History of the Southern Frontier from the First Transmontane Beginnings to the Civil War* (New York, 1948).

To concentrate on classes and economic mobility, on the other hand, makes social history manageable but far too circumscribed. One highly useful study is Jackson Turner Main, "The Distribution of Property in Post-Revolutionary Virginia," *Mississippi Valley Historical Review*, XLI (1954), pp. 241–258, but the same author's *The Social Structure of Revolutionary America* (Princeton, 1965) fails to advance the subject beyond the theme of relative material equality that has become conventional among eighteenth-century historians since its political significance was pointed out by Robert E. Brown, *Middle-Class Democracy and the Revolution in Massachusetts, 1691–1780* (Ithaca, 1955). Several articles by Paul W. Gates, summarized in "Frontier Estate Builders and Farm Laborers," in *The Frontier in Perspective*, ed. Walker D. Wyman and Clifton B. Kroeber (Madison, 1957), pp. 143–163, correct the overemphasis of earlier historians on the leveling effect of frontier land.

The relationship among economic class, social status, and political influence, clearest in the seventeenth and eighteenth centuries, has been effectively delineated in several brief books and articles in recent years: Charles S. Sydnor, *Gentlemen Freeholders: Political Practices in Washington's Virginia* (Chapel Hill, 1952); Bernard Bailyn, "Politics and Social Structure in Virginia," in *Seventeenth-Century America: Essays in Colonial History*, ed. James Morton Smith (Chapel Hill, 1959), pp. 90–115; William A. Reavis, "The Maryland Gentry and Social Mobility, 1637–1676," *William and Mary Quarterly*, 3rd Ser., XIV (1957), pp. 418–428; James Henretta, "Economic Development and Social Structure in Colonial Boston," *ibid.*, XXII (1965), pp. 75–92; and the general essays on the colonial upper class by Leonard Woods

Labaree, *Conservatism in Early American History* (New York, 1948).
The leadership of the colonial merchant class is displayed in all its
facets—social, economic, political, and cultural—by Frederick B.
Tolles, *Meeting House and Counting House: The Quaker Merchants of
Colonial Philadelphia, 1682–1783* (Chapel Hill, 1948); Bernard Bailyn,
The New England Merchants in the Seventeenth Century (Cambridge,
Mass., 1955); James B. Hedges, *The Browns of Providence Plantations:
Colonial Years* (Cambridge, Mass., 1955); and Leila Sellers, *Charleston
Businessmen on the Eve of the Revolution* (Chapel Hill, 1934). Several
biographies of colonial planters are also highly pertinent: Aubrey C.
Land, *The Dulanys of Maryland* (Baltimore, 1955); Louis Morton,
*Robert Carter of Nomini Hall: A Virginia Tobacco Planter of the Eight-
eenth Century* (Williamsburg, 1941); and David John Mays, *Edmund
Pendleton, 1721–1803* (Cambridge, Mass., 1952). Although the ordinary
workingmen of colonial America inevitably remain more obscure, the
circumstances of the mass of indentured servants, mainly in the seventeenth century, have been pieced together by Abbot Emerson Smith,
*Colonists in Bondage: White Servitude and Convict Labor in America,
1607–1776* (Chapel Hill, 1947), and those of both bond and free
laborers, mainly in the eighteenth century, by Richard B. Morris, *Government and Labor in Early America* (New York, 1946).

In colonial America the lower classes had a certain place in the
social structure, a status they later lost, as a comparison of Carl
Bridenbaugh, *The Colonial Craftsman* (New York, 1950), with Norman
Ware, *The Industrial Worker, 1840–1860: The Reaction of American
Industrial Society to the Advance of the Industrial Revolution* (New
York, 1924), makes clear. For the egalitarian nineteenth century, social
historians have almost entirely reduced the theme of economic class
to that of the upward mobility of individuals. The faith of that age in
economic opportunity produced the odd rationalizations of actual class
distinctions which are analyzed by Sigmund Diamond, *The Reputation
of the American Businessman* (Cambridge, Mass., 1955). The actual
working of "social mobility" has been measured most precisely, for men
who became business leaders, by a number of demographers and
sociologists: William Miller, ed., *Men in Business: Essays in the History
of Entrepreneurship* (Cambridge, Mass., 1952), pp. 193–211, 286–305;
F. W. Taussig and C. S. Joslyn, *American Business Leaders: A Study in
Social Origins and Social Stratification* (New York, 1932); W. Lloyd
Warner and James C. Abegglen, *Occupational Mobility in American
Business and Industry* (Minneapolis, 1955); and Seymour Martin Lipset
and Reinhard Bendix, *Social Mobility in Industrial Society* (Berkeley,
1959). The best recent studies by historians—Merle Curti, *The Making
of an American Community: A Case Study of Democracy in a Frontier
County* (Stanford, 1959), and Stephan Thernstrom, *Poverty and Progress: Social Mobility in a Nineteenth Century City* (Cambridge, Mass.,
1964)—necessarily include many other matters, the evidence for which
remains, however, more "impressionistic" than systematic. Impressionism
may be inevitable. The random method and frivolous tone adopted by
Dixon Wecter, *The Saga of American Society: A Record of Social
Aspiration, 1607–1937* (New York, 1937), is fair enough in an account

of the upper class in the deranged social order of the late nineteenth century.

The structural question in which earlier historians customarily were most interested, the development of governmental institutions, is still basic for any study of society in the seventeenth and eighteenth centuries, the age of the omnicompetent mercantilist state. The four magisterial volumes of Charles McLean Andrews, *The Colonial Period of American History* (New Haven, 1934–1938), are overly confined to technical details of constitutional and legal organization and regulation. But the compact study by E. A. J. Johnson, *American Economic Thought in the Seventeenth Century* (London, 1932), is quite explicit about the social purposes of governmental regulation, as is Morris, *Government and Labor* (cited above, p. 504). The seeming minutiae of Beverley W. Bond, Jr., *The Quit-Rent System in the American Colonies* (New Haven, 1919), and Roy Hidemichi Akagi, *The Town Proprietors of the New England Colonies: A Study of Their Development, Organization, Activities, and Controversies, 1620–1770* (Philadelphia, 1924), remain essential for an understanding of the active erosion of social community by public economic policy in the colonial period. Among a growing number of articles by younger historians that reexamine colonial government from the perspective of social structure and social control, two in particular should be cited: Kenneth A. Lockridge and Alan Kreider, "The Evolution of Massachusetts Town Government, 1640 to 1740," *William and Mary Quarterly*, 3rd Ser., XXIII (1966), pp. 549–574, and Michael Zuckerman, "The Social Context of Democracy in Massachusetts," *ibid.*, XXV (1968), pp. 523–544.

The history of reciprocal relations among economic classes—mainly in the form of public and private charity, or the lack of it—has only begun to be investigated, notably in the brief general survey by Robert H. Bremner, *American Philanthropy* (Chicago, 1960), and his nineteenth-century study *From the Depths: The Discovery of Poverty in the United States* (New York, 1956). In many places the poor of course were identified with certain immigrant ethnic groups; immigration history has usually not gone beyond the peculiar experiences that set the foreigners apart from native Americans. Oscar Handlin, *Boston's Immigrants* (cited above, p. 502), remains the unique study of mutual acculturation, though the theme of ethnic interaction is also dealt with by Theodore C. Blegen, *Norwegian Migration to America: The American Transition* (Northfield, Minn., 1940); Rowland Berthoff, *British Immigrants in Industrial America, 1790–1950* (Cambridge, Mass., 1953); and Moses Rischin, *The Promised City: New York's Jews, 1870–1914* (Cambridge, Mass., 1962). (The theme was introduced much earlier by William I. Thomas and Florian Znaniecki, *The Polish Peasant in Europe and America: Monograph of an Immigrant Group* (5 volumes; Boston, 1918–1920), the seminal sociological work in this field.) The parallel theme of gradual self-definition among old-stock Americans has been broached by Wesley Frank Craven, *The Legend of the Founding Fathers* (New York, 1956).

Negroes have usually been regarded as an adjunct of—and problem for—white society. In this regard it has been immaterial what the historian's basic premise was: that Negroes were naturally inferior, as in Ulrich B. Phillips, *American Negro Slavery: A Survey of the Supply, Employment, and Control of Negro Labor as Determined by the Plantation Regime* (New York, 1918); that they were "white men with black skins," the theme of Kenneth M. Stampp, *The Peculiar Institution: Slavery in the Ante-Bellum South* (New York, 1956); or that they constituted a class in a Marxian feudal order, an interpretation best developed by Eugene D. Genovese, *The Political Economy of Slavery: Studies in the Economy and Society of the Slave South* (New York, 1965). Recently historians have begun to consider the distinctive quality of Negro experience in both Africa and America, for its intrinsic interest as well as for its integral part in the society in which white Americans lived. The origins of American Negroes in Africa are sympathetically described by Basil Davidson, *Black Mother: The Years of the African Slave Trade* (Boston, 1961). The brief essays by Stanley Elkins, *Slavery: A Problem in American Institutional and Intellectual Life* (Chicago, 1959), have set historians working in several new directions, including the psychology of the slaves and a comparison of North American slavery with Negro slavery elsewhere.

Local politics and government in the nineteenth century have recently begun to be reinterpreted in social terms, particularly in terms of relations among ethno-religious groups. Lee Benson, *The Concept of Jacksonian Democracy: New York as a Test Case* (Princeton, 1961), finds party divisions to have been based largely on the voters' differing social identities, and Seymour Mandelbaum, *Boss Tweed's New York* (New York, 1965), blames the notorious failings of the late nineteenth-century city on lack of "communication" among these sociopolitical groups. Similar social and political discontinuities are graphically illustrated by two studies of the haphazard expansion of cities: John W. Reps, *The Making of Urban America: A History of City Planning in the United States* (Princeton, 1965); and Sam B. Warner, Jr., *Streetcar Suburbs: The Process of Growth in Boston, 1870–1900* (Cambridge, Mass., 1962). Even the slow-moving country towns of Lewis Atherton, *Main Street on the Middle Border* (Bloomington, 1954), were afflicted in much the same way.

For the twentieth century, study of local societies remains almost entirely the province of an early and highly prolific branch of sociology. The contemporary data thus unearthed is a prime source for historians; crude as some of the earlier studies were, their analysis is still instructive: Robert A. Woods, ed., *Americans in Process: A Settlement Study* (Boston, 1902); Robert A. Woods and Albert J. Kennedy, *The Zone of Emergence*, ed. Sam B. Warner, Jr. (Cambridge, Mass., 1962); Louis Wirth, *The Ghetto* (Chicago, 1928); Harvey Warren Zorbaugh, *The Gold Coast and the Slum: A Sociological Study of Chicago's Near North Side* (Chicago, 1929); Caroline F. Ware, *Greenwich Village, 1920–1930: A Comment on American Civilization in the Post-War Years* (Boston, 1935); E. Digby Baltzell, *Philadelphia Gentlemen: The Making of a National Upper Class* (Glencoe, Ill., 1958); and Arthur J. Vidich and Joseph Bensman, *Small Town in Mass Society: Class, Power, and Religion in a Rural Community* (Princeton, 1958). A useful survey of the

whole field is Maurice R. Stein, *The Eclipse of Community: An Inter-pretation of American Studies* (Princeton, 1960). The current racial crisis has made historians too impatient to wait for sociologists to work their way through the black ghettos; the most effective social history so far is Gilbert Osofsky, *Harlem, The Making of a Ghetto: Negro New York, 1890–1930* (New York, 1966).

Historians have only recently discovered that other great sociological domain, the family. The groundbreaking and now classic effort by Edmund S. Morgan, *The Puritan Family: Essays on Religious and Domestic Relations in Seventeenth-Century New England* (Boston, 1944), still stands virtually alone. For forty years it was generally supposed that the almost formless compendium by a sociologist, Arthur W. Calhoun, *A Social History of the American Family* (3 vols.; New York, 1917–1919), had adequately blanketed the subject. In fact Calhoun, having supplied historians with a great storehouse of quotations from the sources, was virtually issuing a challenge to interpret them in their own way. Historians have usually been concerned with the family only as it impinged on other matters: Richard B. Morris, *Studies in the History of American Law* (New York, 1930); Bernard Bailyn, *Education in the Forming of American Society: Needs and Opportunities for Study* (Chapel Hill, 1960); Christopher Lasch, *The New Radicalism in America, 1889–1963: The Intellectual as a Social Type* (New York, 1965). Like Calhoun, they have tacitly accepted the conventional notion that the modern family is the product of a centuries-old process of institutional disintegration. Sociologists have generally shared the same assumption, as is indicated by the convenient summary by John Sirjamaki, *The American Family in the Twentieth Century* (Cambridge, Mass., 1953).

The appearance of Philippe Ariès, *L'Enfant et la vie familiale sous l'ancien régime* (Paris, 1960)—translated by Robert Baldick as *Centuries of Childhood* (London, 1962)—has gained acceptance for the contrary view that only in modern times has the family become an institution well adapted to prepare children to enter the larger society. Both William E. Bridges, "Family Patterns and Social Values in America, 1825–1875," *American Quarterly*, XVII (1965), pp. 3–11, and William L. O'Neill, *Divorce in the Progressive Era* (New Haven, 1967), adjudge the modern family to be fully validated by that social function. Like Ariès, however, they stop short of asking how well adapted to human needs modern society itself may be. Certain French and English demographers, citing broader evidence than the art and literature upon which Ariès relies, have suggested that the seventeenth-century family, like other social institutions of that time, struck a better balance between medieval communal stability and modern individual mobility. Historians of colonial America have begun to follow that lead, so far with fragmentary but very promising results, especially Philip J. Greven, Jr., "Family Structure in Seventeenth-Century Andover, Massachusetts," *William and Mary Quarterly*, 3rd Ser., XXIII (1966), pp. 234–256, and John Demos, "Notes on Life in Plymouth Colony," *ibid.*, XXII (1965), pp. 264–286. (Greven's *Four Generations: Population, Land, and Family in Colonial Andover, Massachusetts* (Ithaca, 1969), and Demos's *A*

Little Commonwealth: Family Life in Plymouth Colony (New York, 1970), have also appeared since this book was written.) Doubts of the adequacy of nineteenth-century society pervade Bernard Wishy, *The Child and the Republic: The Dawn of Modern American Child Nurture* (Philadelphia, 1968).

Histories of religion in America, although vastly more numerous, have seldom presented the church as an explicitly social institution. At the same time, however, that the most influential recent historian of the subject, Perry Miller, was mainly concerned with theology as an intellectual development, he was fascinated—especially in *The New England Mind: From Colony to Province* (Cambridge, Mass., 1953)—with "the relation of thought or ideas to communal experience" (p. x). Since both social community and articulate thought were most highly developed in seventeenth-century New England, they have been most explicitly integrated by Miller and other historians of the region before and after him: Samuel Eliot Morison, *Builders of the Bay Colony* (Boston, 1930); Edmund S. Morgan, *Visible Saints: The History of a Puritan Idea* (New York, 1963), and *The Puritan Dilemma* (cited above, p. 507); and Richard L. Bushman, *From Puritan to Yankee* (cited above, p. 502).

In New England in later years and in other regions from the beginning, the progressive degeneration of social community and theology alike has left something of a historiographical vacuum as well, now partly filled, however, by Perry Miller, *The Life of the Mind in America: From the Revolution to the Civil War* (New York, 1965). Historians of immigrant groups looked into the phenomenon somewhat earlier, since immigration in the eighteenth and nineteenth centuries not only introduced foreign churches but also impelled them to take on a variety of communal functions and to accept their new role as specifically social institutions. The theme has been explored in detail among the Scotch-Irish by Leonard J. Trinterud, *The Forming of an American Tradition: A Re-examination of Colonial Presbyterianism* (Philadelphia, 1949), and by a number of postcolonial studies: George M. Stephenson, *The Religious Aspects of Swedish Immigration* (Minneapolis, 1932); Colman J. Barry, *The Catholic Church and German Americans* (Milwaukee, 1953); Charles Liebman, "Orthodoxy in American Jewish Life," *American Jewish Yearbook*, LXVI (1965), pp. 21–98; and Rudolph J. Vecoli, "Prelates and Peasants: Italian Immigrants and the Catholic Church," *Journal of Social History*, II (1969), pp. 217–268.

The accommodation of disestablished, denominational churches to American social circumstances is a major theme of Sidney E. Mead, *The Lively Experiment: The Shaping of Christianity in America* (New York, 1963). Social analysis is exceptionally well employed by Barbara M. Cross, *Horace Bushnell: Minister to a Changing America* (Chicago, 1958), and Robert D. Cross, *The Emergence of Liberal Catholicism in America* (Cambridge, Mass., 1958). The reaction against social accommodation, in the name of spiritual revival, has been explored much more extensively: Wesley M. Gewehr, *The Great Awakening in Virginia, 1740–1790* (Durham, N.C., 1930); C. C. Goen, *Revivalism and Separatism in New England, 1740–1800: Congregationalists and Separate Baptists in the Great Awakening* (New Haven, 1962); Catherine C.

Cleveland, *The Great Revival in the West* (Chicago, 1916); Fawn M. Brodie, *No Man Knows My History: The Life of Joseph Smith the Mormon Prophet* (New York, 1946); and Whitney R. Cross, *The Burned-Over District* (cited above, p. 502). In comparison, the later but rather less influential social-reform "gospel" has received disproportionate attention: Charles Howard Hopkins, *The Rise of the Social Gospel in American Protestantism, 1865–1915* (New Haven, 1940); Aaron Ignatius Abell, *The Urban Impact on American Protestantism* (Cambridge, Mass., 1943); Henry F. May, *Protestant Churches and Industrial America* (New York, 1949); Paul A. Carter, *The Decline and Revival of the Social Gospel: Social and Political Liberalism in American Protestant Churches, 1920–1940* (Ithaca, 1956); and Robert Moats Miller, *American Protestantism and Social Issues, 1919–1939* (Chapel Hill, 1958). That the contemporary opposition to the social gospel and to liberal theology had a reactionary character has always been more evident, and of less interest, to historians; recent works, however, include William G. McLoughlin, *Modern Revivalism: Charles Grandison Finney to Billy Graham* (New York, 1959), and Norman F. Furniss, *The Fundamentalist Controversy, 1918–1931* (New Haven, 1954).

Social reform, though idealistic in spirit, has generally followed secular leadership; the contrary cases presented by Timothy L. Smith, *Revivalism and Social Reform in Mid-Nineteenth Century America* (Nashville, 1957), seem exceptional. It has been through study of secular reformers, indeed, that the writing of American social history has recently acquired a rigor previously lacking. The dominant theme, of social anxiety as a prime cause of political reform movements, was sounded in the 1950s at several widely separated points: Richard Hofstadter, *The Age of Reform: From Bryan to F.D.R.* (New York, 1955); John Higham, *Strangers in the Land: Patterns of American Nativism, 1860–1925* (New Brunswick, 1955); David Donald, "Toward a Reconsideration of Abolitionists," in *Lincoln Reconsidered* (New York, 1956); and Marvin Meyers, *The Jacksonian Persuasion: Politics and Belief* (Stanford, 1957).

In the 1960s social psychology led historians to reinterpret many of the classic American reform movements as largely irrational, misguided, and therefore ineffectual. Previously reform had seemed to divide, left and right, into two quite different categories, one as reasoned and reasonable as most of the movements in Alice Felt Tyler, *Freedom's Ferment: Phases of American Social History to 1860* (Minneapolis, 1944), the other simply bigoted, like those in John Allen Krout, *The Origins of Prohibition* (New York, 1925); Ray Allen Billington, *The Protestant Crusade, 1800–1860: A Study of the Origins of American Nativism* (New York, 1938); and Heywood Broun and Margaret Leech, *Anthony Comstock: Roundsman of the Lord* (New York, 1927). The introduction of social psychology fortunately has not overly tempted historians simply to brush aside the earlier political, economic, intellectual, and moral interpretations. Avoiding the usual overemphasis of a new thesis, they have instead opened a direct route toward a balanced, more convincing resolution of a number of old historical problems.

From several directions a discernible advance has been made toward satisfactorily explaining what any basic interpretation of American history will have to account for, the coming of the Civil War: William R. Taylor, *Cavalier and Yankee: The Old South and American National Character* (New York, 1961); William W. Freehling, *Prelude to Civil War: The Nullification Controversy in South Carolina, 1816–1836* (New York, 1966); and Leon F. Litwack, *North of Slavery: The Negro in the Free States, 1790–1860* (Chicago, 1961). The underlying liberal-conservative tension among early twentieth-century progressives has also been revealed: Robert H. Wiebe, *Businessmen and Reform: A Study of the Progressive Movement* (Cambridge, Mass., 1962), and *The Search for Order* (cited above, p. 501); James H. Timberlake, *Prohibition and the Progressive Movement, 1900–1920* (Cambridge, Mass., 1963); Samuel P. Hays, "The Politics of Reform in Municipal Government in the Progressive Era," *Pacific Northwest Quarterly*, LV (1964), pp. 157–169; and Alan P. Grimes, *The Puritan Ethic and Woman Suffrage* (New York, 1967). A similar analysis of school reformers was at least implied by Merle Curti, *The Social Ideas of American Educators* (New York, 1935), and has been made explicit by Lawrence A. Cremin, *The Transformation of the School: Progressivism in American Education, 1876–1957* (New York, 1961).

Although voluntary association has been recognized at least since Tocqueville as the typical American social pattern, the voluntaristic organizations that have attracted the attention of historians, mainly for other reasons than their place in the social structure, have been the churches, the political parties, and the many self-constituted groups of reformers. The only general assessments of the equally ubiquitous fraternal orders of the nineteenth century are the work of a journalist, Charles W. Ferguson, *Fifty Million Brothers: A Panorama of American Lodges and Clubs* (New York, 1937), and a sociologist, Noel P. Gist, *Secret Societies: A Cultural Study of Fraternalism in the United States* (Columbia, Mo., 1940). The early years of one significant subtype are traced by Wallace Evan Davies, *Patriotism on Parade: The Story of Veterans' and Hereditary Organizations in America, 1783–1900* (Cambridge, Mass., 1955). The older work of Solon Justus Buck, *The Granger Movement: A Study of Agricultural Organization and Its Political, Economic, and Social Manifestations, 1870–1880* (Cambridge, Mass., 1913), is remarkable for having recognized the importance of the social as well as the obvious economic and political functions of that association. Organizations of professional men have now begun to receive the serious attention of historians: Daniel H. Calhoun, *Professional Lives in America: Structure and Aspiration, 1750–1850* (Cambridge, Mass., 1965), and Corinne Lathrop Gilb, *Hidden Hierarchies: The Professions and Government* (New York, 1966).

A word of caution may be in order for anyone who may be inspired to rush in to fill the enormous gaps in the historiography of American society. Since those gaps correspond to gaps in the social structure itself, the historian will often have to rely on inferences from negative evidence—on data conspicuous mainly by its absence. The result of years of research on a large subject may turn out to be as slim as a recent brief article of mine, "The Social Order of the Anthracite Region,

1825–1902," *Pennsylvania Magazine of History and Biography*, LXXXIX (1965), pp. 261–291. But history is not to be measured by the page or weighed by the pound. Conceivably the history that manages to deal with the organic elements present in most societies in the past but so conspicuously lacking in the American social structure will improve our understanding both of the common circumstances of all Americans and the conflicts that have arisen in spite, or because, of that common "consensus."

Index